A History of Film

SIXTH EDITION

Virginia Wright Wexman

University of Illinois at Chicago

PEARSON

Boston • New York • San Francisco
Mexico City • Montreal • Toronto • London • Madrid • Munich • Paris
Hong Kong • Singapore • Tokyo • Cape Town • Sydney

Series Editor: Molly Taylor
Series Editorial Assistant: Suzanne Stradley
Senior Marketing Manager: Mandee Eckersley
Editorial-Production Services: Omegatype Typography, Inc.
Electronic Composition: Omegatype Typography, Inc.
Composition Buyer: Linda Cox
Manufacturing Buyer: JoAnne Sweeney
Cover Designer: Kristina Mose-Libon

For related titles and support materials, visit our online catalog at www.ablongman.com.

Library of Congress Cataloging-in-Publication Data

Wexman, Virginia Wright.
    A history of film / Virginia Wright Wexman.— 6th ed.
        p.   cm.
    Rev. ed. of: A history of film / Jack C. Ellis, Virginia Wright Wexman, 5th ed. 2002.
    Includes bibliographical references and index.
    ISBN 0-205-44976-X
    1. Motion pictures—History.   I. Ellis, Jack C., History of film.   II. Title.

    PN1993.5.A1E4   2006
    791.43'09—dc22

                                                              2005047645

Printed in the United States of America

10   9   8   7   6   5   4   3   2   1   10   09   08   07   06   05

Contents

Preface

A History of Film is the creation of Jack Ellis, who crafted the first four editions and worked with me on the fifth. For this, the sixth edition, Jack has passed the torch to me to revise as I see fit. As an enthusiastic admirer of Jack's work, I have looked on the task of updating *A History of Film* as both an honor and a responsibility. Jack's aim was to give students a book that told a story and to engage them in the art as well as the business of film making. In revising the text, I have tried to build on these strengths even as I have incorporated new films, new filmmaking traditions, and new understandings of what film history is all about.

This new sixth edition of *A History of Film* incorporates some major changes. These alterations have been made with two complementary principles in mind: focus and coverage. To address the first of these principles, I have included more extended analyses of individual films. Such in-depth attention to particular cinematic works is intended to help students grasp large historical questions by presenting these in terms of specific cases rather than relying on abstract generalities. To further enhance this focus on individual films, I have replaced most of the movie stills that formerly served as the book's illustrations with frame enlargements. Although not as sharply focused as production stills, which are shot with a still camera on a film's set, frame enlargements represent shots taken from the films themselves and are thus more accurate. I have also keyed all illustrations specifically to discussions in the text. Chapters have also been given tighter focus. Two chapters each are devoted to Post–World War II developments in England (Chapters 9 and 18), France (Chapters 12 and 19), and Italy (Chapters 8 and 16).

Other changes in this new edition have been made to provide more balanced coverage. More female film makers are discussed, and a new section on Asian American film makers has been added in Chapter 20. Despite the growing prevalence of multinational productions, I have continued to stress, as far as possible, the specific cultural contexts in which movies are made. Discussions of popular genres in various national cinemas have been added: sections on Japanese animated films (*animés*), Italian horror films (*giallos*), and Hollywood "B" movies. In response to the lively film scene in Asia, the Indian and Chinese cinemas are now treated in separate chapters. *A History of Film,* Sixth Edition, now takes stock of recent developments in American cinema as well, including a new final chapter (Chapter 23) focusing on the effects of the digital revolution. To aid students in their understanding of all of these developments, a glossary now appears at the end of the text.

The strategy that guides this edition is the same as it has been from the beginning: to spotlight key national movements that have shaped the story of film history. This principle means that many film makers of note are necessarily omitted: the Greek Theo Angelopoulos, the Portuguese Manoel de Oliveira, and the Turk Yilmaz Güney, for example.

Though talented directors like these have produced powerful and influential work, their careers have not flourished within national film movements comparable to those covered here. *A History of Film,* Sixth Edition, is designed to highlight large patterns of influential moments. It is not an encyclopedia in which every fact of movie history is exhaustively chronicled, but rather a series of snapshots intended to help students come to terms with crucial issues and events of the past that have made cinema what it is today.

This revision would not have been possible were it not for the invaluable help of Kevin Smith, who supplied the illustrations, and JoAnne Ruvoli Gruba, who prepared the manuscript. I owe them both an enormous debt of gratitude. John Rohsenow generously proofread the chapter on China to verify spellings, facts, and usage. Thanks are also owed the reviewers of the sixth edition, including Ann Alter, Humboldt State University; Stephen Ambra, New Hampshire Technical Institute; Zareh Arevshatian, University of California, Los Angeles; Robert F. Edmunds, Marshall University; and Mark Gallagher, University of Missouri. The editors at Allyn & Bacon, too, have provided support and guidance every step of the way; thanks to Molly Taylor, Karen Mason, and my patient, careful copyeditor Simon Appleford. Finally, I want to acknowledge my husband's contribution to this project; his editorial judgment has saved me from numerous stylistic and structural infelicities.

Books on General Film History

Cook, David A. *A History of Narrative Film,* 4th ed. New York: W. W. Norton, 2004.

Mast, Gerald, and Bruce F. Kawin. *A Short History of the Movies,* 8th ed. Boston: Allyn and & Bacon, 2003.

Nowell-Smith, Geoffrey, ed. *The Oxford History of World Cinema.* New York: Oxford, 1996.

Petro, Patrice. *Aftershocks of the New: Feminism and Film History.* New Brunswick, NJ: Rutgers University Press, 2002.

Sklar, Robert. *Film: An International History of the Medium.* Englewood Cliffs, NJ: Prentice-Hall, 2001.

Thompson, Kristin, and David Bordwell. *Film History: An Introduction,* 2nd ed. New York: McGraw-Hill, 2003.

Usai, Paolo Cherchi. *Silent Cinema: An Introduction.* London: British Film Institute, 2000.

1

Birth and Childhood of a New Art

★ ★ ★ ★

1895–1914

The most important reason motion pictures came into being had nothing to do with their artistic potential. The theory underlying the motion picture was demonstrated in a succession of optical toys. Its tools and materials were invented out of a desire to make visual records of life and to study the movements of animals, including humans. Its capacity to provide peep-show entertainment attracted impresarios and paying customers to what scientists and inventors had made available. Later, as the novelty of lifelike movement began to pale, the technicians and entrepreneurs who had discovered how to project moving images onto screens stumbled onto an old interest latent in audiences—the story. They began to offer simple narratives in a new form.

When still pictures began to move, they acquired duration, and the photographer was challenged to deal with that fourth dimension. Temporal organization was demanded in addition to spatial composition. As in the novel, the play, music, or dance, an ordering of events into a beginning, middle, and end was required in even the simplest motion picture, whether it took the form of a documentary, an avant-garde work, or, most commonly, a fictional story.

Brief Motion-Picture Records of Actuality and of Performances

Initially the moving picture was scarcely more than still photographs extended into motion. The brief duration of the short strips of film demanded little beyond the still photographer's concern that there be an interesting subject appropriately lit and composed. The early motion-picture camera operator sought something that moved, but otherwise the concept was the same. The first films, made in the United States in the 1890s by the motion picture company founded by Thomas Alva Edison, the great inventor, were of vaudeville and circus acts. In France the **Lumière brothers, Louis and Auguste,** took their lighter-weight camera, developed from the Kinetoscope **peep-show** viewing machine manufactured by Edison from 1894 on, out into the everyday world. In one of their early films, *Feeding the Baby* (France, 1895, Louis Lumière), rather than a fixed instant of Mama and Papa Lumière at breakfast with baby, we see the infant being fed successive spoonfuls of cereal. In a short from the Edison Company (United States, c. 1894) we see two trained cats with tiny boxing gloves patting away at each other in a miniature ring, rather than standing in static pose. The novelty of captured motion was intriguing enough at first.

It was not self-evident from the outset that the motion-picture image would be projected onto a large screen. Peep-show machines for individual viewing were a viable possibility, not unlike present-day video monitors (Figure 1.1). It was the Lumière brothers who thought to project the image (onto a sheet) and began paid public performances of their films in a basement café in Paris in December 1895. In April 1896 the first commercial projection in a theater took place at Koster and Bial's Music Hall in New York City. The films shown were those made by the Edison Company.

As they chose the actions they would record, film makers soon discovered what painters and still photographers had already known: that some subjects have more intrin-

FIGURE 1.1 Kinetoscopes in the Peter Bacigalupi Parlour ★ San Francisco, c. 1894.

FIGURE 1.2   Early film taken at the Edison laboratory ★ United States, 1890–1891, W. K. Laurie Dickson; Edward Sandow.

sic (or in another sense extrinsic) interest than others do. Although the motions of knocking down a wall or of a woman feeding chickens satisfied the earliest audiences, such everyday scenes were shortly supplemented by scenes of ships being launched and heads of state addressing large crowds. A strong man flexing his muscles (Edward Sandow in Figure 1.2) or a sharpshooter rapidly breaking targets thrown into the air ("Little Sure Shot," Annie Oakley) was soon followed by a somewhat more eventful vaudeville skit, *Fun in a Chinese Laundry* (1894), and then by a piece of a popular stage success, *Rip van Winkle* (1896) with its star, Joseph Jefferson. Film historian Tom Gunning has labeled this early fascination with what moving images could show the **cinema of attractions.**

Even with more interesting subjects, however, the film makers' further choices were limited to two: where they placed the camera and when they started cranking. They usually chose the ideal position of a human observer—straight in front, at eye level, and far enough back to take in all the significant action. The amount of time was fixed at half a minute or less by the length of the short film strips.

In offering perfect reproductions of unmanipulated reality, Edison and Lumière succeeded (given the limitations of silence, black and white, and two dimensions) as well as anyone has since. The rowboat rounding the pier in early Lumière, or Fatima dancing for the Edison camera, is appealingly fresh, revealing the delight the first film makers and audiences must have felt when looking at natural movement in a new way. "It is life itself," one Frenchman is supposed to have exclaimed at a premiere screening; Lumière's train pulling into the station definitively established the way to record such an event—the camera low, stationary, and at an oblique angle.

As stripped to essentials as these primitive films seem, there were seminal differences between the programs of the Grand Café in Paris and those at Koster and Bial's in New York City. These differences suggest, in fact, the two main and divergent aesthetic impulses that have continued to today, impulses that began in still photography—as Siegfried Kracauer emphasized in his *Theory of Film: The Redemption of Physical Reality*. One tendency, what Kracauer called the *formative,* was to strive for the "artistic," to use materials and models from the older arts. Even before the motion picture, certain photographers had begun to pose their subjects, arrange their decor and lights, and manipulate the photographic emulsion in various ways intended to make their photos look more like paintings and less like mere mechanical recordings. The other tendency, the *realistic,* was to take pride in the verisimilitude of photographic reproduction and in its ability to capture and preserve unadulterated actuality of events and views.

Perhaps largely because of the cumbersomeness of his camera, Edison started along the "artistic" way, in that he recorded performances that had originated on stage or in the circus ring. The pleasure afforded by a film of this sort depended almost entirely on the quality of the performance. Film merely preserved and made widely available what had been created and offered to the camera. In essence, this is the theatrical tradition, characteristic of fiction films in which actors perform roles with scripts that follow the time-honored rules of the earlier forms of storytelling.

The "realistic" tradition, the documentary impulse, was the more vigorous at first. Louis Lumière, with a portable camera, had no need for a studio or prepared material. He could wander the streets and set up his camera in front of any aspect of observed reality that took his fancy. The large projected image supported the illusion that the viewer was looking out a window (rather than into a room with one wall missing, as on the stage). Another key factor sustaining the illusion was that in Lumière's work the people, animals, and vehicles frequently moved toward and away from the camera, not just laterally in relation to it—as in many Edison films that duplicated stage-bound movement (Figure 1.3a and b). As a result of his subjects and method, Lumière and his followers left us a fascinating surface view of what the people and the world they lived in were like at the turn of the twentieth century.

FIGURE 1.3a and b   *Arrival of Train at La Ciocat Station* ★ France, 1895, Louis Lumière.

Although film as record may not be film as art, these early topical and scenic views pointed to the capacity of film to find or to set its drama within real life. Lumière himself made a kind of fusion of the conceived and the actual, which seems to look way beyond Edison to the nonstudio fiction films of today. In the 1895 *L'Arroseur arrosé* (which means something like "the squirter is squirted") he set a concocted, vaudevillelike gag outdoors in an actual garden (Figure 1.4). A gardener is watering the lawn. When a boy steps on the hose, the water stops. The gardener peers into the nozzle to see what the trouble is. The boy takes his foot off the hose and the gardener is doused. In *A Game of Cards* (1896) Lumière made a somewhat similar attempt at a visual gag.

What *L'Arroseur* and *A Game of Cards* suggest, however, regarding an acted story in real settings would not be returned to for almost a decade. Instead, screens were filled alternately with Lumière-type *actualités* and Edison-like stage attractions, and before the end of the decade both firms were producing both types of films. The films continued to be brief, with single shots from one camera position, and were shown characteristically as part of vaudeville programs. At first they were featured attractions; then, as the novelty began to wear off, they were reduced to the function of "chasers"—shown while one audience was leaving and another was entering the theater.

It is entirely possible that the art of the motion picture might have been stillborn, along with its capacity for entertainment, if the story ingredient hadn't been added. It is not possible, however, to establish when the first film to incorporate a story was made or

FIGURE 1.4   Poster advertising early Lumière showings ⋆ *L'Arroseur arrosé* (France, 1895) is the film being shown.

who was responsible for it. Many of the early films have disappeared, so the "firsts" in film technique are subject to endless argument. National pride and individual partisanship further affect the writing of film history in this regard. But no one would deny the importance of Georges Méliès's contribution to the development of narrative full-length film.

Telling Stories through Staged and Filmed Pantomime

Unlike other of the earliest film makers, **Méliès** had a background in the arts, which led him to think of the motion picture in a different way. At the time of the first Lumière showings he operated the Théâtre Robert-Houdin (named in honor of a renowned French magician, who also received homage from an American who called himself Houdini). In Méliès's tiny theater, fantastic sketches and magical acts were performed with the aid of trap doors, mirrors, invisible wires, and other trappings of stage illusion. As a magician it was only natural that Méliès would be fascinated by the unprecedented apparitions offered with such seeming ease by the motion picture. Immediately after seeing the first Lumière program in the small café near his theater, he asked the brothers Lumière to sell him one of their cameras. They refused, adding that Méliès would eventually thank them for saving him from a folly certain to be ruinous once the public lost interest in the novelty. Undeterred, Méliès obtained apparatus from the English pioneer Robert Paul, assembled a machine, and soon was, like the Lumières, out on the streets photographing.

In April 1896 (the month the Edison Vitascope opened in New York) Méliès began showing movies at the Théâtre Robert-Houdin. His brief skits and slices of life on the street were evidently quite indistinguishable from those of others. But according to Méliès's later account, it was during that first year as a film maker that he discovered quite by accident what would make his contribution most distinctive: the capacity of the motion picture to move beyond the real into the fantastic. One day, while photographing in the Place de l'Opéra, the film jammed. When he succeeded in getting the camera functioning again, he indifferently cranked the film on through. Fortunately, he developed it to see if any of the footage would be usable. When projected, the film offered a succession of images that brought instant joy to the heart of the conjurer: a horse-drawn tram on the street suddenly metamorphosed into a hearse. What had happened, of course, was that the tram was passing in front of the camera when Méliès had first started cranking; by the time the film had gotten stuck and unstuck the tram had passed on and been followed by a funeral cortege.

Méliès took deliberate advantage of this accidental discovery in *The Vanishing Lady* and *The Haunted Castle* (both 1896), starting an early genre of "trick films." Within the next few years he mastered most of the technical means for what today are called "special effects." Using fades and dissolves, superimpositions and mattes, fast and slow motion, animation and miniatures, and even hand coloring of each frame, he created a delightful phantasmagoric world. Although he had many imitators, it was years later before film makers were able to figure out how some of his remarkable results had been achieved.

In addition to introducing trickery, Méliès also made the most important beginning steps in screen narrative techniques and helped increase the standard running time from less than a minute to ten to fifteen minutes—one reel. In 1897 he built France's first permanent film studio and founded Star Film Company, the first French firm devoted exclusively to making movies. By 1912 he had produced more than five hundred films of various types, but is best remembered for his fairy tales (beginning with *Cinderella* in 1900) and for a kind of fantastical science fiction (such as *An Impossible Voyage,* 1904; *The Conquest of the Pole,* 1912). Of the latter genre *A Trip to the Moon* (1902) is generally regarded as the master work; its enduring charm of conception and ingenuity of execution are easily appreciated today (Figure 1.5). It is one of the few early fiction films that modern audiences laugh with rather than at. This man of the theater brought to film an innate taste for eccentric humor and a developed sophistication of visual embellishment.

A *Trip to the Moon* is vaguely based on, but also parodies, a Jules Verne story; it lampoons scientific presumptions of the day as well. In making the film, an unprecedented thirty separate scenes were acted out by a sizable professional cast (including Méliès himself as the chief scientist) on the stage of his specially constructed glass-enclosed studio. Each scene is taken with an unbroken run of a stationary camera placed in an ideal position for viewing the whole—twelfth row center, as it were. The performers fully, not to say exaggeratedly, pantomime the action (intertitles were not yet in use), move laterally across the stage, make entrances and exits (for who was to know they didn't have to in this new medium?), and occasionally bow and gesticulate directly toward the audience (that is, the camera). The decor consists of painted canvas backdrops and highly stylized constructions and props; the robes and conical hats of the scientists, the shorts of the chorus-line guard of honor, and the devil suits of the moon men are all out of theater rather than life. Some of the trick effects are created by cinematic means; for example, scenes are joined by dissolves in place of opening

FIGURE 1.5 *A Trip to the Moon* ★ France, 1902, Georges Méliès.

and closing curtains. Other effects are achieved by such stage devices as scenery flats that are raised and lowered, trap doors, pulleys, and the like. What appears to be a dolly shot as the rocket ship approaches the moon (and lands right in the eye of its papier-mâché face) was achieved by moving the moon toward the camera rather than the camera toward the moon. In another shot, a matted drawing of the rocket enters an incongruously real ocean, proceeds down into an animated rendering of undersea life, then surfaces.

Méliès's marvelous contributions and ultimate limitations, in terms of film, are all clearly evident in *A Trip to the Moon.* He did manage to tell a complete story of many incidents in a coherent fashion; script, staging, and performances are carefully controlled to achieve a satisfying whole. The advance of what Méliès himself proudly called "artificially arranged scenes" over the single, undirected, and casually planned fragments that preceded him can only be admired. Where he stopped short, however, was in confining his camera to an uninterrupted view, making the photographic frame equivalent to the proscenium arch. Granting his intention "to push the cinema toward the theatrical way," we can say he succeeded too well. Although he achieved a theatrical sophistication of content and style, he failed to discover the capabilities of the unique tools of the motion picture—the camera and cutting shears. No one would want to be without those creations of his that remain (hundreds of them no longer exist). But once Méliès had established larger ambitions for storytelling in film, it remained for others to make further contributions by using methods unique to the new medium.

One other aspect of Méliès's importance should be acknowledged before we move on. With his trick films he established the basis for what would become the **avant-garde** tradition, which began in France in the 1920s and has continued to today in the experimental/underground/independent film.

It is possible to say, then, that the three main artistic modes of film were present in embryo form almost from the outset: **narrative fiction, documentary,** and **experimental.** The first represented a desire to tell stories with the new and increasingly rich effectiveness of moving pictures. The second had as its intention capturing the real world in a way that would help us to know and understand it more fully. The third creative impulse would lead beyond physical reality to humorous imaginings or frightful hallucinations, to the terrain of dream and the unconscious. The documentary and experimental possibilities were scarcely explored in the first decades of screen history; they did not evolve into mature forms until the early 1920s, when they did so with curious simultaneity. Though given their proper value by the cognoscenti, the documentary and experimental modes have never been as widely popular as the fiction film. It was storytelling that first attracted a loyal audience and built an economic base.

Telling Stories through Filmic Means

Edwin S. Porter, an American who began film work in 1896, was much less well equipped in artistic background or sensibility than Méliès. In the history of the motion picture, a lack of experience with the traditional arts has frequently proved an advantage, artistically as well as commercially. In a medium seeking its own way, vigor and vulgarity have often stimulated rather than inhibited valuable innovation. A film maker without preconceptions about the nature of artistic function and form is free to try anything. By his own admission

Porter was more mechanic than artist. In choosing a career he had considered both the horseless carriage and the "flickers," coincidental new engineering fields carrying unknown potential—of industrial expansion and cultural influence. (Henry Ford built his first car in Detroit in 1896; the last Model T was manufactured in 1927, the year the silent film ended.)

At the time Porter was hired by Edison, in 1900, film makers were first of all camera operators, valued more for their technical ingenuity in keeping the camera operating properly than for their creative imagination. Unconscious genius though he may have been, Porter appears to be the one to have made the next and crucial step—through primitive and tentative editing—that set film on its main road of advance.

One of the favorite subjects for the early actuality film makers was a horse-drawn fire engine rushing to a fire. It may have been commercial expediency that led Porter to use this available and conventional material in a new way, to "re-tread" what we would now call stock footage by adding some specially staged bits of action. At any rate, in late 1902 and early 1903 Porter made *Life of an American Fireman,* which raised the possibility of connecting different parts of a total action, all seeming to be happening at the same time but in various places.

The opening scene of *Life of an American Fireman* is of a fire chief who has fallen asleep in his office and is dreaming (in superimposition) of a mother and baby trapped by fire in a bedroom (Figure 1.6a). The next scene, very brief, is a closeup (perhaps the first, and what would later be called an insert) of a fire alarm box. A hand (and part of a body) enters the frame to send an alarm (Figure 1.6b). The third scene (which begins the stock footage) is of the firemen asleep in their fire station. They leap from their beds, presumably as the alarm is sounded (Figure 1.6c). Note the narrative linkage that Porter has managed to imply with these three separate shots. The fire chief dreaming of a woman and child in danger foreshadows what we will see, economically evoking the tension and responsibility of his job. The hand pulling the alarm tells us that at that very moment someone has observed such a fire. The alarm, turned on, goes to the firehouse and awakens the firemen.

This apparently interconnected and simultaneous action is followed by more stock footage: interiors of the firemen sliding down the pole, hitching up their apparatus, and starting off; the exterior of an engine house as fire wagons rush out; and finally, a splendid shot (from a moving vehicle) of horses, pulling firemen and equipment, galloping down a wide street (Figure 1.6d). Now there appears what must have been a specially taken shot: A fire engine enters the frame, and the camera pans with it to reveal the house that is on fire (Figure 1.6e). This is followed by a studio interior of the bedroom with mother and child amidst (rather unconvincing) wisps of smoke. At this point, Porter presents all the interior action—with mother and child and firemen entering the room to rescue them (Figure 1.6f)—and then presents the simultaneous exterior scene of the firemen (Figure 1.6g and 1.6h), covering the same action and the same time *without cross-cutting.*

Porter followed *Life of an American Fireman* with a radically abridged adaptation of a popular stage melodrama of the day, *Uncle Tom's Cabin.* Although this production consists of little more than a series of tableaus played out against patently artificial backdrops, the intertitles that introduce each scene are the first known in an American film.

Representing a considerable advance over *Life of an American Fireman* and everything else that had gone before was Porter's next film, *The Great Train Robbery* (1903). It is a remarkable achievement, containing virtually all of the elements that might be needed for a superwestern released tomorrow, and it warrants repeated study. Unlike *Life of an*

FIGURE 1.6a–h   *Life of an American Fireman*   ★   United States, 1903, Edwin S. Porter.

American Fireman, all of *The Great Train Robbery* was specially shot for the film, exteriors "on location," interiors in the studio. Although using "artificially arranged scenes," Porter dealt with a topical subject much in the headlines and built from realistic materials. In this respect his work was very different from Méliès's stylized theatricality; Méliès offered the first filmed fantasies, but realism became the main artistic style of the fiction film.

The plot of *The Great Train Robbery* progresses along three lines with three principal sets of characters. The first scene is in a railway telegraph office. Bandits enter and force the telegrapher to order the approaching train to stop for water. After binding and gagging him, the bandits leave. In scene two the desperadoes hide behind the water tank, then sneak aboard the train as it departs. Scene three takes place in the interior of the express car, which the bandits enter and rob. Scene four shows them commandeering the locomotive and forcing the engineer to stop the train. In scene five the engineer is made to uncouple the locomotive, pull ahead, and stop again. Scene six furthers the course of the robbery as the passengers empty out of the train, line up while the bandits collect all their valuables, and then depart. The robbers board the locomotive in scene seven, and it moves off. In scene eight the locomotive comes to a halt and the bandits run off into the countryside. Scene nine shows them moving down a hill and across a stream to mount their waiting horses. Back in the telegraph office, scene ten, the telegrapher's daughter enters and frees her father, who then rushes out (Figure 1.7a). In a dance hall, scene eleven, we see a number of couples square dancing; the telegraph operator staggers in (Figure 1.7b); the men grab their rifles and leave. In scene twelve the robbers, and then the posse in pursuit, gallop by the camera. In the thirteenth and final scene the bandits, thinking they have escaped their pursuers, are inspecting their loot; the posse surrounds them, and shoots them all down. The famous epilogue, a medium closeup of one of the bandits firing directly at the camera, had no narrative function (as did the alarm box closeup in *Life of an American Fireman*); it was added simply to startle. In fact, the Edison catalog of 1904 suggests that this scene "can be used to begin or end the picture."

Notice how neatly the thirteen scenes dovetail. The bandits enter the telegrapher's life, and then we follow them for the robbery and escape, which constitute the bulk of the picture. The dance hall is introduced without explanation, Porter evidently counting on our

FIGURE 1.7a and b *The Great Train Robbery* ★ United States, 1903, Edwin S. Porter.

being patient for a moment until the telegrapher arrives—thus bringing the dance hall men into the story and leading to the final dramatic action, the gunning down of the bandits.

The film's structure and characterization are so basically sound that one can easily imagine how its twelve minutes might be further expanded to ninety. The telegrapher would be a widower, let's say, whose daughter badly wants him to marry the local school-teacher so she can have a new mother and so her father won't be so lonely. The Eastern dude who has his heels shot at in the dance hall is really a fearless secret service agent whose job is to track down train robbers. There is also the possibility of adding preceding events that explain how the gang's leader entered into a life of crime. The sturdy bones are all there; only flesh would be needed to give that first western large and full life today.

Note also how time and space are dealt with. Between most scenes brief or longer ellipses are suggested, and the order is straight succession, as in *A Trip to the Moon*. When the film cuts from the mounted bandits back to the telegraph office, however, a reversal in time seems implied—since the bandits are still in the vicinity for the posse to catch them. There are instances of implicit simultaneity as well: In the beginning of scene three, in the express car, the bandits are evidently approaching as we watch the expressman's actions; or, at the start of scene eleven, in the dance hall, the telegraph operator is presumably on the way from his office as we see the dancing.

Each scene is still one continuous take—scene equals shot. Porter does not cut to varying distances or angles within scenes: The camera remains resolutely at eye level in long shot. But there are some interesting beginnings of camera variety, most likely forced on Porter by the exigencies of location shooting. First of all, in photographing the action of the robbers on the topside of a train in motion, a sort of moving camera results: The camera itself is stationary but the scenery passes by. Second, given the substantial number of "extras" lined up alongside the train, Porter probably couldn't get straight back far enough to include them all in the frame; and the side of the roadbed no doubt sloped down to a ditch. So he may have been required to move up the track for that effective oblique angle emphasized by the man who runs toward the camera to do a little dance of death at closer range. Finally, if horsemen are going to ride down a bluff and then turn left in front of the camera, the choice is to either pan and tilt with them or let them leave the frame. Though Porter's camera moves most hesitantly, the hesitation would be caused partly by a tripod head not constructed to accommodate such movement properly. It is possible also that he thought the odd angle and movement regrettable deviations from prevailing pro-priety rather than positive assets.

To us, if not to Porter, the conventionally painted canvas interiors mix poorly with the fine outdoor settings; they seem part of another and less innovative film. Looking back over the history of cinema we can find many valuable additions to technique forced on film mak-ers by the requirements of nonstudio shooting. In the studio everything can be constructed and adjusted for the convenience of the camera; outside, the film maker must adapt to the world as is. With *The Great Train Robbery* it is the exteriors that are inventive in composi-tion, depth, and movement; the interiors are conventionally horizontal and unimaginative. Learning comes from the kind of improvisation demanded by the unanticipated.

This simplified account of the evolution of narrative film technique of necessity ex-cludes other Porter films as well as hundreds of film makers and thousands of films that contained some of the same accidents and discoveries. These early films seem to evince a conscious pursuit of what would become standard narrative technique, but the motivation of the film makers at the time and what audiences were responding to may have been something quite different. Film historians are going back to the evidence of the films that still exist to try to understand better those original purposes. It seems evident, however, that Porter did not carry his remarkable discoveries much further than in the two seminal films previously discussed; in fact, he seems not to have been altogether clear about what it was he had achieved. In the time between them he made a most uninspired bit of recorded theater in *Uncle Tom's Cabin.* After *The Great Train Robbery* he frequently lapsed into earlier and less interesting modes, and never surpassed that 1903 achievement. Even the seductively entitled and brilliantly ingenious *The Dream of a Rarebit Fiend* (1906) appears to be a frank imitation of Méliès.

Porter's innovations were anticipated and developed by film makers in other countries whose work is now beginning to receive more scholarly attention. In the mid-1890s the British inventor R. W. Paul developed a camera and projection system that was widely used to create and show films all over the world. Subsequently a group based around the English resort town of Brighton, including George Albert Smith and James Williamson, produced films such as *Fire!* (1901) and *The Robbery of the Mail Coach* (1903), which bear striking similarities to Porter's later successes, *Life of an American Fireman* and *The Great Train Robbery.* The productions of another English entrepreneur, Cecil Hepworth, also met with great acclaim during these early years. Hepworth's best-known work, *Rescued by Rover,* which tells the tale of a baby kidnapped by gypsies and retrieved by the family pet, is distinguished by such innovations as smooth panning and a low angle shot (Figure 1.8).

In France, **Alice Guy** made what was perhaps the first fiction film, *The Cabbage Fairy,* in 1896. Guy, who had begun her career as a secretary in the French production company Gaumont, benefited—as did countless other women—from the anarchic structure of the industry in its earliest days, when willing workers were grabbed from wherever they could be found to feed the ever-increasing demand for movies. After serving for several years as head of film production at Gaumont, where she directed over 400 one-reelers, Guy emigrated to America, where, with her husband Herbert Blaché, she founded the Solax film company in 1909. "There is nothing connected with the staging of a motion picture that a woman cannot do as easily as a man," she once said.

The man who most effectively took over leadership from Porter, and whom Porter himself regarded with deference, was another American, **David Wark Griffith.** Griffith's introduction to film was in Porter's *Rescued from an Eagle's Nest* (1907); he played the father hero, calling himself Lawrence Griffith to keep his real name unsullied for anticipated fame as a playwright. Lack of success in the theater (as a dramatist he had only one play produced, and that unsuccessfully) kept Griffith tied to the movies. While acting in them for five dollars a day he learned that he could earn an additional ten to fifteen dollars apiece for story ideas. In 1908 he directed his first film, *The Adventures of Dollie.*

In a remarkably short time Griffith mastered what there was to know about the new medium and progressed beyond his contemporaries. Working with characteristically prodigious energy, his output of short films, the prevailing form, advanced virtually all aspects of technique. The one- and two-reelers contained experiments or refinements that carried forward the rudiments established by Porter; and by the time of Griffith's monumental feature *The Birth of a Nation* in 1915, the whole syntax of silent film had been laid out for use. The extent to which Porter, the Brighton School, and others were able to develop the narrative aspects of cinematic expression was severely limited. According to that most

FIGURE 1.8   *Rescued by Rover* ★ United Kingdom, 1905, Cecil Hepworth.

modern of film makers, Jean-Luc Godard, every development since Griffith had its origins in him. Whether Godard's statement is hyperbolic or not, it is unquestionable that Griffith contributed more to the evolution of film as an art form than any other individual in its history to date.

The Language of Film

Perhaps Griffith's single-most important insight was that the **shot** rather than the **scene** should be the basic unit of film language. With this discovery came the possibility of varying the standard, stationary, head-on long shot. Gradually Griffith moved his camera to setups closer to the action or farther away, altered its angle for the most effective view, let it follow a moving subject when appropriate or traverse a stationary scene for certain kinds of kinetic emphasis. These varied shots were then edited together to create the appearance of a continuous scene selectively viewed. Once understood, these options gave the film maker immeasurably greater control over the audience's emotional response, adding powerful connotations to the action itself. Méliès's framing, in unvaried long shots, had been emotionally neutral. Although Porter had begun to break away from fixed convention, the exceptions did not upset established rules even in his own films (and the deliberateness of his intentions is less than certain).

It was Griffith more than anyone who came to understand the separate psychological-aesthetic functions of the long shot, the medium shot, and the closeup, and who used this awareness consistently. In Griffith's work, and in that of his successors, the **long shot** usually begins a scene, establishing the action and its setting (Figure 1.9a). It might be used to "reestablish," after closer and partial views, so that the parts could be kept related to the whole. Full of information—one could go on and on describing all the things seen in it—it is emotionally cool: We are literally distanced from the action. As the camera is placed closer, or a longer lens is used to achieve much the same effect, there are fewer things included within the frame, but we tend to be more interested in them, feeling closer to them emotionally as well as perceptually. The **medium shot** rather than the long shot became the standard framing from which the director departs for special purposes, just as we usually deal with life around us from middle distance (Figure 1.9b). In it we are close enough to see and comprehend what is happening and what it means. Generally the stress of the medium shot is on relationships, on interaction: a person in conversation with another, or petting an animal, or cooking at a stove. When the camera is moved closer still, to a **closeup,** the visual information becomes quite limited—perhaps to one face, a hand stroking fur, a pot boiling over—but the emotional weight becomes very heavy (Figure 1.9d). Our attention is directed to what we might not have noticed otherwise or might not have been able to discern at a distance. The closeup can also be used to draw us into strong identification with a character, and to suggest through facial expression what is being

FIGURE 1.9a–d a, b, c. *The Battle at Elderbush Gulch* ★ United States, 1914, D. W. Griffith. d. *The Musketeers of Pig Ally* ★ United States, 1912, D. W. Griffith; Elmer Booth (closeup).

thought and felt. It is a freed visual statement that permits directors to show us exactly—and only—what they want us to see in the way they want us to perceive it.

Griffith called closeups "inserts," and he shot them after the scene had been filmed in long and medium shots. This frequently shifting point of view, especially to the closeup, offered a means of expression comparable to the use of spoken words in the theater. Although the stage director can block and light action in a way designed to lead our eye, we are still free to regard the whole proscenium—no more, no less—from one fixed position. Broad gestures and conspicuous props and symbolic settings may be employed, but most of what we learn comes from what the characters say to each other. Lacking the power of spoken words, Griffith substituted a kind of visual language with its own conventions and limitations. Though never as intellectually precise as words, the affective use of images can cause us to feel directly and deeply in a manner both unique and compelling.

Alternation of tempo through the **editing** of detached shots is something that Griffith came to understand from intuition and experiment, and that Porter understood not at all. Although Porter shifted from one scene to another, he did not break up the run of the camera within scenes. The pursuit of the bandits by the posse in *The Great Train Robbery* remains one of the slowest chases in memory as the first party of horsemen, and then the second, enters and passes through the frame. Griffith might extend screen time beyond actual time by means of **cross-cutting.** He would cut back and forth from shots of bandits to shots of a posse, building to a rhythmic climax, but his chases (honored as "the Griffith last-minute rescue") seem incredibly more tense—and even faster (Figure 1.10a and b). What he discovered, other film makers have learned and used since: Rapid cutting, or a succession of short shots, can create excitement; slow cutting, or shots held longer on the screen, will aid calm contemplation. Both the shifting spatial framing and the temporal alternation of shots give the film maker artistic resources extending well beyond the bare meaning of the action being recorded.

For transitions between shots Griffith used a larger range of optical effects than is generally employed today. The **cut** is basic within scenes; virtually unnoticed in itself, it is necessary for the variable ordering and pacing of the action. The **dissolve** is a more noticeable

FIGURE 1.10a and b   *A Girl and Her Trust* ★ United States, 1912, D. W. Griffith.

transition in which one image is gradually superimposed over, and then replaces, the other. As in early Méliès, it is usually used between scenes rather than within them and signals a change of place and/or time. When one image **fades out** to darkness and a new image **fades in** to full exposure, a different place and lapse in time are usually being signaled also. (Griffith tended to favor fades over dissolves.) As the heaviest screen "punctuation," the only one in which we are given nothing to look at for a few seconds, fade-outs frequently indicate a larger break in the dramatic action as well, marking off groups of scenes that are called **sequences** by some critics. (Other writers and many film makers use **shot** and **scene** synonymously and **sequence** for what is here being called **scene,** leaving no term for a larger dramatic/narrative unit [comparable to an act or a chapter] short of the entire film.)

Griffith also liked **irises** as connective devices (Figure 1.9c). An iris begins with a black screen containing only a small circle (or square or other shaped portion) of the total image: a girl's bowed head, for example. Then as the iris opens up it reveals the whole action and setting: a family standing over the girl at the dinner table in a farm kitchen. When the scene has run its course, with the girl explaining (in intertitles) how she has been orphaned and has come in desperation to these old friends of her parents, the final shot might iris out; within the contracting circle of black we see the girl's smiling, upturned face as she learns that the family will let her stay.

Griffith employed **masking** in several ways: the sides of the frame darkened to emphasize the height of a tower in the center; tops and bottoms darkened to form a CinemaScope-proportioned strip across the middle, stressing the horizontal movement and length of a column of galloping cavalry; or a cameo masking of the corners, to enhance the oval loveliness of Lillian Gish's face. He also experimented with **superimposition** and **split screen** for special effects—for the longing daydream in *Enoch Arden* (1911) or to make the awareness of burning Atlanta hang over the foreground of people fleeing in *The Birth of a Nation* (1915).

Griffith did not by any means limit his attention to the "grammatical" elements of screen language. Although of the theater, as Porter was not, Griffith soon began to sense that performance in film required a style quite different from that in fashion on the stage. If spoken words were lacking, the eloquence of body movement and gesture was magnified; in the new medium the camera registered and the projector projected. Actors on the screen appeared large, their every movement easily discernible from the back rows; as the camera came closer to them, its photographic authenticity rendered as false the prevailing theatrical histrionics. Griffith began to confine movement, dress, and makeup to an approximation of life; any exaggeration was kept small in scale and justified by character. Pantomime became more and more expressly tailored for the camera—the sad smile with only the face visible, the upper part of a body with hands plucking and fluttering in nervous excitement, the eyes revealing remorse or anger or frustrated passion. Richer and subtler characterizations began to replace the broad and simple performances of the first dramatic films. Faces and bodies, cut up and reassembled in edited sequence, were made to achieve a new precision of expression. Griffith commanded a thoughtfulness and invention from the actors in his developing stock company; with camera and cutting shears he shaped their performances into a dramatic entity that had existed initially only in his mind.

As for physical background to the action, Griffith's exterior locales were always carefully selected for their appropriateness to the events depicted and for their capacity to reinforce the mood of the story. Constructed sets in his films strike us as the real thing even when they're not; the style is invariably naturalistic in solidity and detail. What he couldn't find on location he had carefully and fully re-created on the back lot or in the studio. Griffith was able to achieve a scale that had no theatrical precedents: real trains rushing across a wide prairie, enemy hordes encircling a besieged city. His lighting initially advanced along existing stage lines and then, as brighter lights and more sensitive emulsions became available, finally surpassed theatrical possibility. At first he and cameraman G. W. "Billy" Bitzer were content to light scenes with sharp, even clarity, using controlled sunlight for interiors (with no ceiling or roof) as well as exteriors—standard practice at the time; but photographically the earliest Griffith/Bitzer films stand out from those of most of their peers, as they somehow manage to look fresh and sharp even today. In addition to exact exposure and focus, this quality must have something to do with choice of emulsion and care in processing. In later work Griffith began to experiment with the effective possibilities of modulated and directional artificial light, breaking some taboos in the process. An interior night scene might be lit as if suffused by the flickering softness of the firelight, underexposed by standards then current, or what is called **low-key lighting** today. In another scene the heroine's head might be lit from behind by simulated morning light streaming in through a window so that it bounced off her blonde hair to form a halo of overexposure, **halation** in photographic terms. Some of these experiments would be expanded and refined by the Germans in the 1920s, just as the Russians would further develop Griffith's editing.

Finally, Griffith was one of the leaders in the movement against the short length of films imposed by the American industry of the day. With few exceptions, the dominant companies were conservative in their adherence to established practice and their unwillingness to risk the capital that longer films would have required. At first Griffith was confined to the one-reel (ten to fifteen minutes) standard that Méliès and Porter had achieved. As film makers became more aware of the potential of the medium, they became increasingly ambitious in terms of subject matter. Larger subjects demanded more running time. In 1910 Griffith made a two-reeler entitled *His Trust,* which the studio released as two separate one-reel films. The same thing happened to his next two-reeler, *Enoch Arden,* but Griffith and others persisted until two reels became accepted as standard length. He continued to strive for more time and larger scale, and by the end of this first period of film history, he had reached a length of four reels, with *Judith of Bethulia* (1914). It was his last important film before *The Birth of a Nation,* and in narrative structure and historical spectacle it foreshadowed his even larger feature, *Intolerance.*

Increasing Films to Feature Length

In the early days movie makers experimented with a wide array of film forms, including **serial films,** which featured continuing story lines played out over many individual episodes, and **series films,** which featured a continuing set of characters engaged in various adventures, much like the *Star Wars* series of today. The best-known practitioner of these forms was the French director **Louis Feuillade,** whose masterful compositions created a striking visual style that has come to be known as fantastic realism. Utilizing elaborate, implausible plot lines built around the exploits of sinister criminal gangs who adopted multiple disguises, Feuillade crafted popular series such as *Fantômas* (1913); *Les*

Vampires (1915–1916), featuring the master criminal Irma Vep; and *Judex* (1917), which was later remade by Georges Franju as a tribute to Feuillade. Olivier Assayas's 1996 *Irma Vep,* which chronicles the attempt of a modern film company to remake *Les Vampires,* similarly honors Feuillade. Series and serials were screened everywhere, including Argentina, which produced the widely shown *Gaucho Nobility,* directed by Humberto Cairo and Ernesto Gunche, in 1915, and Mexico, where the twelve-part *The Grey Car,* directed by Joaquin Coss and Juan de Homs, was released in 1919. Serials were also popular in the United States. The most famous, *The Perils of Pauline* (Louis Gassner and Donald MacKenzie, 1914), starring Pearl White, featured individual episodes finished off with so-called cliffhanger endings designed so that audiences would feel compelled to return for the next episode.

Another popular form during these years was the short **animated film,** in which still images are drawn or photographed on single frames and then joined in such a way as to suggest movement. Emile Cohl developed this technique, creating nonnarrative films such as *Brains Repaired* (1911) by combining drawings, photographs, and live action. Other animators active in this period created popular cartoon characters such as Gertie the Dinosaur (Windsor McCay), Felix the Cat (Otto Messmer), and Koko the Clown (Max and Dave Fleischer).

In reaching feature length, Griffith had been passed by the French and the Italians. Free from the stringent limitation on running time imposed by the U.S. industry, the Europeans had begun to exploit subjects that led naturally to films of an hour and more. Available to French film makers was a long and uniquely distinguished theatrical tradition. From as early as 1908, with *The Assassination of the Duc de Guise,* directed by Charles de Bargy, they began to turn out film versions of successful plays starring well-known players. A company called Film d'Art was the first in the field, bestowing its name on the entire shortlived subgenre. In most respects the idea was retrogressive, extending back to Méliès, who had wanted to "push the cinema toward the theatrical way," and even to Edison, who had earlier recorded bits of popular theater. The principal difference of the **films d'art** was that the extreme deference paid to the older medium, however perverse, meant that whole plays rather than fragments were recorded exactly as performed. Intertitles were abridged substitutions for the unheard dialogue the actors mouthed. Except for the new length required, it was back to the camera in twelfth row center, the scene recorded in one shot, and using theatrical sets and gestures. These films did attract a certain following, however, especially among the middle class who knew or thought they ought to know the theater; and the somewhat snobbish appeal and contemporary prestige helped to drag films as a whole toward greater length.

The most consequential of the series was *Queen Elizabeth* (1912), directed by Louis Mercanton and Henri Desfontaines, and starring Sarah Bernhardt and Lou Tellegen (her leading man offstage as well as on). The divine Sarah, although sixty-eight years old at the time, still commanded an international audience (Figure 1.11). Unlike many theatrical artists, she seemed to have been extremely interested in film. "I rely on these films to make me immortal," she is supposed to have said. Alas, for Bernhardt and for us, much of her divinity must have resided in her reputedly remarkable voice and oral interpretation. What remains in *Queen Elizabeth* now seems more nearly a cruel travesty of a great talent and an exhumation of dead theatrical convention. Such problems only vaguely troubled contemporary observers, however. The film was acquired for distribution in the United States

FIGURE 1.11   *Queen Elizabeth* ☆ France, 1912, Louis Mercanton and Henri Desfontaines; Sarah Bernhardt.

by the young Adolph Zukor and played with substantial and prophetic success in converted "legitimate" theaters at the unheard of price of one dollar a ticket. It provided the first capital as well as the precedent for Famous Players Film Company, which eventually became Paramount Pictures.

Although *Queen Elizabeth* opened up the possibility for successful American distribution and exhibition of feature-length films, it was the Italians who contributed more importantly to the form that features would take—along lines close to those Griffith had begun to explore in miniature. The inclination of the Italians was toward historical and religious spectacle set in their own glorious past. The first of these, *The Last Days of Pompeii,* was produced in 1908, the same year as the first of the films d'art. *The Fall of Troy* (1910) and *Dante's Inferno* (1911), at five reels in length, continued the trend. A static and dully literal illustration of the epic poem, the *Inferno* was followed by *Quo Vadis?* (1912), at nine reels. Both were road-shown in the United States, the latter even more successfully than *Queen Elizabeth.* Noteworthy among similar films were another *Last Days of Pompeii* (1913) and *Cabiria* (1914). Of the early Italian spectacles perhaps only *Cabiria* (twelve reels), a worldwide success at the time, is of more than historical interest today. From a script credited to Gabriele D'Annunzio and directed by Giovanni Pastrone, it is placed in the Punic Wars. The plot centers on Hannibal's crossing of the Alps and the siege of Syracuse. Vast sets were employed as well as plaster models. The action is directed and shot with an unusual amount of energy and movement, and an appropriate symphonic score was specially composed. Like its predecessor *Quo Vadis?*, *Cabiria* had a definite influence on American production.

Massive in all respects, these extravaganzas not only established feature length but also demonstrated film's superior claim over the theater to this kind of spectacle. Patterns laid down in them would be followed by Griffith, Cecil B. DeMille, and all those who have subsequently worked in the genre. They also moved the movies out of the nickelodeons and converted stores into large theaters and auditoriums, where they were often accompanied by full orchestra. The Italian lead was lost only with the outbreak of World War I.

During its first two decades the motion picture advanced from vaudeville turns and brief cinematographic records of life on the street to short film narratives using the rudimentary grammar of the medium. By the end of this period the length of films had increased until precedent had been established for the feature running over an hour, which would become the staple form around which the art and the industry further developed. The subsequent consolidation of these early advances and the move toward an expanded future initially occurred mainly in the United States.

Films of the Period

1894
Fun in a Chinese Laundry (U.S., Edison Company)

1895
The Arrival of a Train at the Station (L'Arrivée d'un train à la Ciotat) (France, Louis Lumière)
L'Arroseur arrosé (France, Louis Lumière)
The Execution of Mary, Queen of Scots (U.S., Edison Company)
Feeding the Baby (Repas de bébé) (France, Louis Lumière)
Workers Leaving the Factory (La Sortie des usines Lumière) (France, Louis Lumière)

1896
The Cabbage Fairy (La Fée aux choux) (France, Alice Guy)
The Kiss (U.S., Edison Company, starring May Irwin and John C. Rice)
The Vanishing Lady (Escamotage d'une dame au théâtre Robert Houdin) (France, Georges Méliès)

1899
The Dreyfus Affair (L'Affaire Dreyfus) (France, Georges Méliès)

1900
Attack on a China Mission (U.K., James A. Williamson)
Cinderella (Cendrillons) (France, Georges Méliès)
Grandma's Reading Glass (U.K., George Albert Smith)

1901
Story of a Crime (Histoire d'un crime) (France, Ferdinand Zecca)

1902
A Trip to the Moon (Le Voyage dans la lune) (France, Georges Méliès)

1903
The Great Train Robbery (U.S., Edwin S. Porter)
Life of an American Fireman (U.S., Edwin S. Porter)

1904
An Impossible Voyage (Le Voyage à travers l'impossible) (France, Georges Méliès)

1905
Rescued by Rover (U.K., Cecil Hepworth)

1906

The Dream of a Rarebit Fiend (U.S., Edwin S. Porter)

1907

Ben-Hur (U.S., Sidney Olcott)
Rescued from an Eagle's Nest (U.S., Edwin S. Porter)

1908

The Adventures of Dollie (U.S., David Wark Griffith)
The Assassination of the Duc de Guise (L'Assassinat du duc de Guise) (France, Charles de Bargy)
The Last Days of Pompeii (Gli Ultime giorni di Pompeii) (Italy, Luigi Maggi)

1909

The Lonely Villa (U.S., David Wark Griffith)

1911

Brains Repaired (La Retapeur de cervelles) (France, Émile Cohl)
The Lonedale Operator (U.S., David Wark Griffith)

1912

The Conquest of the Pole (La Conquête du pôle) (France, Georges Méliès)
The Musketeers of Pig Alley (U.S., David Wark Griffith)
The New York Hat (U.S., David Wark Griffith)
Queen Elizabeth (Les Amours de la reine Élisabeth) (France, Louis Mercanton and Henri Desfontaines)
Quo Vadis? (Italy, Enrico Guazzoni)

1913

The Battle at Elderbush Gulch (U.S., David Wark Griffith)
Fantômas (France, Louis Feuillade)
A House Divided (U.S., Alice Guy)

1914

Anthony and Cleopatra (Marcantonio e Cleopatra) (Italy, Enrico Guazzoni)
Cabiria (Italy, Giovanni Pastrone)
The Perils of Pauline (U.S., Louis Gassner and Donald MacKenzie)
Les Vampires (France, Louis Feuillade)

Books on the Period

Abel, Richard. *The Red Rooster Scare: Making Cinema American 1900–1910.* Berkeley: University of California Press, 1999.

Bean, Jennifer M., and Diane Negra, eds. *A Feminist Reader in Early Cinema.* Durham, NC: Duke University Press, 2003.

Bean, Jennifer M., and Diane Negra, eds. *Early Woman Stars.* Durham, NC: Duke University Press, 2001.

Bowser, Eileen. *The Transformation of Cinema 1907–1915.* Berkeley: University of California Press, 1994.

Grieveson, Lee, and Peter Kramer, eds. *The Silent Cinema Reader.* New York: Routledge, 2004.

Kiel, Charlie. *Early American Cinema in Transition: Story, Style and Filmmaking, 1907–1913.* Madison: University of Wisconsin Press, 2002.

Lant, Antonia, and Ingrid Perez. *The Red Velvet Seat: Women's Writings on the Cinema: The First Fifty Years.* New York: Verso, 1999.

Musser, Charles. *The Emergence of Cinema: The American Screen to 1907.* Berkeley: University of California Press, 1994.

Robinson, David. *From Peep Show to Palace: The Birth of the American Film.* New York: Columbia University Press, 1996.

Stokes, Melvyn, and Richard Maltby. *American Movie Audiences: From the Turn of the Century to the Early Sound Era.* London: British Film Institute, 1999.

2

Rise of the American Film

★ ★ ★ ★

1914–1919

Except for the United States, the major film-producing countries—France, Germany, Great Britain, and Italy—were involved in World War I from its outbreak. The United States did not enter the war until 1917, and then our participation was far less than total. Because some of the materials required for the manufacture of high explosives are the same as those for photographic film (cotton, and nitric and sulfuric acids), film stock was in short supply abroad. A much more serious effect of war on European film producers was the curtailment of international distribution of completed films. Nations were separated from each other by battle lines; transportation was unavailable for many nonmilitary purposes; and the large American audience lay three thousand miles across a submarine-infested ocean.

Although the French and the Italians had been first to arrive at feature-length films, and although the French motion-picture industry had achieved unquestioned world dominance by 1910, the United States was now in a position to pursue that development as no other country could. With its sizable moviegoing public, an economy stimulated rather than drained by war, a tradition of business expertise, and film makers of considerable inventiveness and occasional genius, the United States had a crucial advantage at this important stage. The Americans made full use of their resources, and that is to their credit. If there had not been that four-year lead at exactly that historical moment, however, the subsequent domination of the world's screens by the United States might never have occurred, at least not to the extent that it has.

As it happened, during the second half of the 1910s, the Americans were the ones who expanded the art to a fuller expression, discovered the sorts of ingredients that would make the entertainment universally popular, and devised systems of manufacture, wholesaling, and retailing that could support the new expense of feature production. In the United States during those years, three parallel developments occurred that deserve particular attention. First was the culmination of Griffith's earlier experimentation in film form, his first features. Second, a very special tradition of American screen comedy began in the output of Mack Sennett and his co-workers, most notably Charles Chaplin. Finally, the new and prototypical systems of mass production, distribution, and exhibition evolved—with Thomas H. Ince among the leaders in organizing production—laying the groundwork for subsequent economic expansion.

The First American Epics

Griffith worked in both large and small scale. Many of his films that have aged well, or his scenes remembered with great pleasure, are close, intimate studies of character and feeling (for example, *Broken Blossoms* [1919]) or selective and heightened observations of everyday life in small-town America (*True Heart Susie* [1919]). Still, what was needed to shake film completely free from the stage, in a way so conspicuous that no one could fail to understand, was probably the kind of spectacular grandeur represented by Griffith's *The Birth of a Nation* (1915) and *Intolerance* (1916). Except for their length and expense, any other single element of these two films could no doubt be found in one or more of the over four hundred shorter Griffith films preceding them, especially in those produced from 1912 on. To bring together all these contributions, however, under complete control and on such a gigantic scale, was a truly staggering accomplishment. Nothing like these two films—in their size and intricacy of conception and in their mingling of history with passionate argument—had appeared before them.

The Birth of a Nation is the paradigm for the successful "big" Hollywood movie, through *Gone With the Wind* (1939) to *Titanic* (1997) and beyond. It also established the technique and style of film making that has come to be called classic Hollywood cinema. Today if *The Birth of a Nation* is not quite the fresh revelation of the breathtaking power of the screen that it was for its first audiences, it can still be an overwhelming experience, particularly when properly presented at silent rather than sound speed with a good print and the original music. It can come alive for those who free themselves from unjustified feelings of superiority to any film not in a current idiom, those who can accept Griffith's artistic postulates and understand that his racial attitudes are embedded in the myths and memories that formed such a dominant part of his life.

After completing *Judith of Bethulia* in 1913 (four reels, twice as long as any film he had previously made), Griffith left his first employer, the Biograph Company. Apparently he was restive under commercial restraints that had prevented him from proceeding to even larger projects. It is not clear to what extent Griffith was influenced by the Italian features; internal evidence suggests that *Intolerance* may owe more to them than does *Birth*. Griffith claimed not to have been influenced, and associates such as Lillian Gish have testified that he was so busy making films he rarely took time to see any. He was working along lines similar to the Italians, however, and their successes must have acted as competitive stimuli, if not models, demonstrating that the kind of thing he was trying to do could be done. In any case, after joining the small independent firm called Mutual, where he directed some routine productions to meet the payroll, he began to plan the huge film on the Civil War and Reconstruction that became *The Birth of a Nation*. Most of the latter part of the film was based on Thomas Dixon's novel *The Clansman* and the successful play made from it; there are lesser borrowings from Dixon's *The Leopard's Spots* and other sources.

The Birth of a Nation broke all sorts of precedents. Even in production, its cost, approximately $110,000, was said to be five times greater than the next largest sum spent on an American film up to that time. (*Judith of Bethulia* had cost $23,000—the most spent on a film prior to *Birth,* according to Seymour Stern, one of Griffith's biographers.) Having run through his backers' money, Griffith invested what he could raise and borrow on his own to finish it. There were six weeks of rehearsal; shooting extended from July into October of 1914; editing took another three months. This overall production time contrasted with the average in those days of six weeks or less. When completed, *Birth*'s length was an unprecedented three hours. It was accompanied throughout by a symphonic score specially composed by Joseph Carl Briel and was the first American film to be so treated.

In 1915 the film opened as *The Clansman* in Los Angeles and then as *The Birth of a Nation* in New York (Figure 2.1a and b). This title change was suggested by Dixon, the author of the novel, who felt something was needed to suggest the epic scope of Griffith's achievement. The new title referred to the end of the sovereignty of the states, achieved by the victory over secession. Although it played in "legitimate" theaters for as much as two dollars per ticket, it has been estimated that the first six months of its national run drew more people than had attended all the performances of all the stage plays in the United States during any given five-year period. More than merely a motion picture, it was a cultural phenomenon that everyone felt obliged to witness. Because of its evident racial biases, it created enormous controversy, even riots, and the notoriety attracted still more customers.

Because it was distributed on a "states' rights" basis, with flat fees paid for regional distribution franchises, there are no accurate figures of what *Birth* earned at the box office.

FIGURE 2.1a and b Two posters for the initial showing of *The Birth of a Nation* ☆ United States, 1915, D. W. Griffith.

Variety estimated that it had grossed as much as $50 million, and until recent years it was acknowledged as the top moneymaker of all time. It continues in active circulation among film societies and in nontheatrical series and academic courses, and receives occasional theatrical revivals. No doubt it is playing somewhere on the globe at this moment, and it is still capable of provoking picketing and threats of worse by civil rights groups who want to protect audiences from its depiction of African Americans.

Aside from the racial content (to be dealt with later), what may strike one most strongly about the film is the sheer massiveness of its subject. Part I deals with the North and South in the days before the War Between the States (as Griffith would have called it) and with the war itself; Part II covers the Reconstruction period in the South. The whole is much more than an "epic" in the vulgarized entertainment sense of a film loaded with extras; instead, it is a genuine effort to treat a national epoch in the fullest possible way.

Griffith's strategy included the portrayal of imaginary persons who touch on salient aspects of national events. Partly through the social positions and vocations of the characters—who help shape the historical forces at work as well as representing those persons affected by the forces—a structural pattern was created that allowed the large canvas to be colored and infused with personal drama. Historical tableaux frame and punctuate the fictional plot: the first slaves landing in Virginia, Lincoln brooding at night in the White House, Grant and Lee at Appomattox. (Griffith would use this sort of organization again in *Intolerance, Orphans of the Storm* [1921], and other historical works.) The fusing of fiction with history dates at least from Homer and was standard practice with Sir Walter Scott and other historical novelists; Griffith drew more or less consciously on nineteenth-century literary precedents for the shaping of his stories.

The dramatic parallels Griffith employed among his characters do not seem excessively schematic, given the full and lifelike detail of the incidents surrounding them. There are the two families, one northern and one southern, whose children become acquainted at a northern school—as they might well have done, given the southern aristocracy's practice of educating its sons in the North. The northern father, the Honorable Austin Stoneman, Leader of the House, is a powerful abolitionist politician (clearly modeled on Thaddeus Stevens, a prime factor in the passing of Reconstruction legislation). He is a widower whose dead wife has been succeeded by a scheming mulatto housekeeper. The southern father, Dr. Cameron, is an aging, wealthy planter with a gentle wife, thoroughly part of a chivalric tradition. Each family thus represents one of the strong causative elements in the impending conflict.

Because of their acquaintanceship, the invented characters can cross back and forth into each other's lives and surroundings: a friendly visit before the war, a fatal meeting on the battlefield, an encounter in a prisoner-of-war hospital, and the final merging through the postwar northern "occupation" of the South. They come in contact with actual personages at historical moments: when the Confederate mother approaches the Union president to plead for clemency for her captured son, when a brother and sister attend the play at the Ford Theatre on the night the president is assassinated (Figure 2.2), and so on. The fictional characters' lives are lived within the re-created events and conditions of those times. Griffith's structuring is also strangely persuasive, drawing us into an understanding and sympathy, if we allow it. President Woodrow Wilson, historian and southerner, is said to have exclaimed after seeing the film that it was "like writing history in lightning." After controversy arose over the film the White House disavowed any approval on the part of the president.

It is its passionate certainty that made *The Birth of a Nation* not only a *succès d'estime* but a *succès de scandale*. Although based in part on Dixon's novel, Griffith re-

FIGURE 2.2 *The Birth of a Nation,* Lincoln Assassination ★ United States, 1915, D. W. Griffith.

created the narrative world according to his own viewpoint. Born in Kentucky in 1875, he absorbed an understanding of the war and Reconstruction from his father—Colonel "Roaring Jake" Griffith of the Confederate Cavalry. The attitudes about black people in *Birth* are so much part of the total view of life the film encompasses that Griffith was evidently shocked when he was accused of racism.

Thoroughly embodied in the film, however, is an assumption of innate inferiority of black people. The bad, usually those of mixed blood, are led by evil or misguided white men, are vicious and greedy for power, and line up with the northerners. The good are dependent and childlike, and support the white South. Bad or good, these African Americans are given few individual attributes apart from caste role and function, and are mostly played by white actors in black face. Viewers today feel more uneasy with Griffith's approving patronization of "the faithful souls" than with his treatment of the villains.

Whatever documentation and evidence he might offer, it is the very unconsciousness of his assumption of black inferiority, that "that was how it was," that is most disturbing. The way in which this strand becomes an integral part of a credible whole makes it particularly effective "propaganda." The conviction of the film carries viewers along, and it is impossible to put aside one aspect of it as an aberration. Because the biases are so uncalculated and rawly emotional in their appeal, they may even get past our intellectual defenses. Given the film's enormous popularity, Griffith's assumptions must have been shared by a substantial number of his white contemporaries.

The nastiest aspect of Griffith's representation of black–white relationships is also the one closest to the national nerve—his preoccupation with possible sexual intermingling of the races. Would you want your sister to be molested by or married to a Negro? Griffith asks. For him the two possible fates exert an equally morbid fascination: Marriage to a black man is presented as unthinkable except as equivalent to rape. The much more prevalent forced submission of black women to white men is dealt with only through the congressman's weakness for his housekeeper. This is presented as close to a pathological failing on his part, with the woman exercising what is clearly a sexually based power over him. Stoneman's horrified reaction to his black political protégé's asking for his daughter's hand is of a piece with the rest. Perhaps more than any other white character in the film, the congressman seems to exist solely for rhetorical purposes.

There are many who cannot accept the content of Griffith's films—not only the racial bias in *Birth* but also the sentimentality and melodramatics that color so much of his presentation and possibly his view of life. Even in his own time, his conception—rooted in nineteenth-century Victorianism—apparently came to seem increasingly old-fashioned and irrelevant to his audiences. Some critics—unwilling to allow for what others see as a style, a set of conventions, a way of thinking about people and events—have tended to deplore the content while praising the form. But all agree that in *Birth of a Nation* Griffith's formal control over the medium achieved an unprecedented power.

Take, for instance, the extraordinarily moving scene of Ben Cameron's return from the war. After an intertitle, "The homecoming" (less than 1 second), there is a long shot of the street and the Cameron front yard: Everything is in need of repair; the columns are scorched, the fence is falling apart, the street and sidewalks are littered. Ben enters left background, shattered and weary; he pauses, leans against the fence, and looks about at the marks of war (Figure 2.3a). Limping, he walks slowly and weakly forward along the fence (34.5 seconds). In medium closeup in the living room, his younger sister, Flora, is by a mirror admiring the effect of "southern ermine" (strips of raw cotton daubed with soot) decorating her dress (Figure 2.3b). Ben's older sister, Margaret, and his mother hurry in, indicating that they have seen Ben coming; Margaret runs to the door and back; all run out of the room (18 seconds). Medium shot of the hall: The three rush forward, excited, joined by the father (6 seconds). Medium long shot of Ben pausing by the gate, opening it, supporting himself against it a moment and then going in (11 seconds) (Figure 2.3c). Medium long shot of the family, waiting in the hall breathlessly, smiling at Flora's excitement (3.5 seconds) (Figure 2.3d). Medium long shot of the front yard as Ben comes to the porch (7.5 seconds) (Figure 2.3e). Medium long shot of the family in the hall; Flora rushes forward (4.5 seconds) (Figure 2.3f). Medium shot of the porch as Ben climbs the steps; Flora comes out the door and meets him, smiling. They gaze at each other; she points to his worn and dirty uniform; he pulls off a piece of her "ermine" (Figure 2.3g). She explains, giggles, and points to a hole in his hat. They both pause and gaze off into space, thinking of all that has happened. Suddenly they stop pretending. Flora starts to cry and embraces Ben; he looks into the distance, kisses her hair, and pats her. They start into the house, arm in arm (57 seconds). Medium shot from side angle of the front door: Ben and Flora start in; a woman's arm comes from inside and encircles Ben's shoulders, gently drawing him and Flora in (17.5 seconds) (Figure 2.3h). Fade-out.[1]

---

[1] This shot list is taken from Theodore Huff, *A Shot Analysis of D. W. Griffith's* The Birth of a Nation (New York: The Museum of Modern Art, 1961).

FIGURE 2.3a–h   *The Birth of a Nation,* Ben's Homecoming ★ United States, 1915, D. W. Griffith.

The shots in this example have a much longer average duration than those in most other scenes in the film. Here much more emotional content is conveyed by each shot, especially by the first two and last two. Only against Griffith's usual practice of presenting a scene from varying points of view in a rapid succession of shots did the tension of Ben's slow movement within that static frame (and the arm of the unseen mother appearing to encircle him) achieve the kind of eloquence it possesses. In the pre-Griffith years such a shot was the invariable standard in which an action took place, and thus it was not useful for special emphasis. An analogy might be made to silence, which had no dramatic meaning until the coming of sound: There had to be sound, and the cessation of it, before silence had significance. Not until the camera was freed to interrupt the action, which would then be synthesized through editing, could a long-running wide-angle shot be used for contrasting emphasis.

Performances in *The Birth of a Nation* are advanced well beyond the larger-than-life conventions of stage pantomime, growing out of a more subtle sense of persons moving through the surroundings and incidents of everyday life. Actors register emotions by means of small changes in their facial expressions (captured in closeups) or meaningul interactions with objects. Although simplified and heightened for dramatic communication without spoken words, the gestures and expressions are generally toned down in comparison with other contemporary films and Griffith's own earlier work. For example, the contrast with *The Battle* (1911—a sort of sketch for *Birth*) is quite marked. There is some exaggeration in the young people's high jinks, which Griffith associates with youthful good spirits; Mae Marsh is fluttery—painfully so if projected at twenty-four frames per second; and the villainies or buffooneries of the blacks appear caricatured to modern eyes. But by and large the acting style seems quite consciously created for the silent camera, rather than being a theatrical performance recorded by it. Henry B. Walthall and Lillian Gish rise considerably above minimum expectations to create characterizations unrivaled on the screen up to that point, comparable to the best the mature silent film would offer. Their intense, nuanced performances do much to imbue the whole with its sense of loss and sadness, of feelings warped and impoverished by the cruel demands of the historic time.

The care in selection and design of interiors and exteriors surpasses historical recreation to achieve a semblance of documentary veracity that makes the past seem present. So vividly particularized are the interior settings that the rooms look lived in. The huge, period tableaux come alive: the ball on the eve of battle, the gigantic battlefield scenes, the gathering and ride of the Klan, the rioting and fighting in the streets.

Before *The Birth of a Nation* was released Griffith had completed a feature to be called *The Mother and the Law,* its opening sequences based on an actual incident of conflict and violence in a contemporary labor dispute. After the grandeur of *Birth,* however, particularly after its enormous success on the one hand and the angry criticism it provoked on the other, *The Mother and the Law* must have seemed an inadequate successor. As part of the *Birth* controversy, Griffith had published a pamphlet entitled *The Rise and Fall of Free Speech in America.* Then, apparently wanting to align himself clearly on the side of unquestionable social and moral rectitude to show his detractors how they had misunderstood him, and perhaps to castigate those he felt had been intolerant toward him, he conceived an even more elaborate narrative structure than that of *Birth.* Added to *The Mother and the Law* were three other stories, set in widely disparate historical periods and cultures. These four stories, according to a title prefacing the multilayered whole, would show "how hatred and intolerance, through the ages, have battled against love and charity." This undertaking, which perhaps remains the most ambitious in conception and largest in size of any film ever produced in the United States, became *Intolerance,* released in 1916.

The three stories added to the modern story were a re-creation of the fall of Babylon to the Persians (539 B.C.); vignettes from the life of Christ (A.D. 27), culminating in the crucifixion; and an account of the massacre of Protestant Huguenots in France on St. Bartholomew's Eve (1572). If the stories had been told consecutively, the task would have been difficult enough. But Griffith's design went even further, using intercutting so that narratives and characters became subservient to the overriding theme. He began with the modern story up to a certain point of development (Figure 2.4); then he moved to Jerusalem and an episode from the life of Christ; then to the introduction of the plotting at court in sixteenth-century France; back to the modern story; on to the beginning of the Babylonian sequences; then to the modern story again; and so on.

These parts are announced, separated, and connected with an image of "The Woman Who Rocks the Cradle" (Lillian Gish) accompanied by Whitmanesque intertitles: "Endlessly rocks the cradle—Uniter of Here and Hereafter—Chanter of Sorrows," or "Out of the cradle endlessly rocking. . . . " Later, as the tension in each of the stories increases, Griffith cuts ever more rapidly from one to another without interruption.

FIGURE 2.4 *Intolerance,* The Modern Story ★ United States, 1916, D. W. Griffith.

In order to finance this colossal spectacle, Griffith used all his profits from *The Birth of a Nation,* finally buying out the other backers when they lost their nerve. The total cost of the picture is said to have been $1.9 million; it has been estimated that it would cost much, much more to achieve the same results today. The sets of French streets, houses, and castles are all full scale, solid, and practicable. Babylon, constructed on a 254-acre site along Sunset Boulevard, is the most overwhelming: Its towers rise 200 feet; its walls are wide enough at their tops to allow two chariots to pass; and it took hundreds of extras to fill the courtyard and balconies in the film's victory celebration (Figure 2.5). *Intolerance* originally ran close to four hours, longer than *Birth,* and again a special score was composed by Joseph Carl Briel according to Griffith's specifications.

Although some critics praised the film lavishly, the public seemed to find the disjunctive organization and unprecedented length confusing and exhausting. The final climactic passages become almost an assault on the optical nerves as well as on the emotions, as the cutting tempo increases to many shots no longer than five frames. Also, the thematic material was out of keeping with the national mood by the time the film was released. Brotherly love was going out of fashion. President Wilson, who had been reelected on an isolationist peace platform, asserting that the United States was too proud to fight, was soon moving with the country itself toward entry into World War I. The sentimental idealism of *Intolerance* carries nothing of the direct conviction of *The Birth of a Nation* and was as dismal a financial failure as the preceding film had been an unrivaled success.

FIGURE 2.5 *Intolerance,* The Babylon Set ★ United States, 1916, D. W. Griffith.

Griffith's career was deflected and probably permanently damaged by the necessity of paying the debts incurred with *Intolerance*. In a desperate effort to recoup some of the losses, he cut into the original negative—without printing a copy—to make versions of *The Mother and the Law* and *The Fall of Babylon,* which were subsequently released separately. As a result of these mutilations, the copies of *Intolerance* that exist today are reduced approximations of the original. Even so, the overall effect is undeniably impressive. In many ways, it is an advance on *The Birth of a Nation.* What it lacks in coherence and genuine passion it makes up in its sweeping imaginativeness of conception and increased perfection of technique.

Intolerance* was to have an influence on film history quite disproportionate to its lack of popular appeal. After the war, Lenin arranged for it to tour the new Soviet Union, where it ran continuously for ten years. Very likely Lenin was most interested in the portrayal of exploitative and repressive managerial classes in the modern story—Griffith's viewpoint being strongly anticapital and prolabor. But two future giants of Soviet cinema, Sergei Eisenstein and V. I. Pudovkin, saw much more in it than that. Griffith had shown them how argument (education and propaganda) could be conveyed through dramatic incident, and how its effectiveness could be heightened by the dynamics of editing. (Indeed, the strike in Pudovkin's *Mother* [1926] has some direct borrowings from *Intolerance.*) Most of what the Soviet masters formalized and articulated in theories of montage Griffith had understood intuitively. In *Intolerance* the evolving unity rests on generalized idea and emotion—rather than solely on characters' decisions that forward a plot—and depends on the unique resources of the film medium. Through skillful juxtaposition of images, disjunctive in physical place-time but related by each phase of the developing theme, the effect of the whole becomes greater than the sum of its parts.

In other respects *Intolerance* represents Griffith's growing mastery over the medium. The alternation between large vista and small human detail (the page boy sleeping in the throne room of Charles V, or the fat woman throttling her dance partner when he steps on her toes) is even more assured. Performances are completely nonstagelike and are carefully broken into shots, with especially forceful use of closeups (for example, the often cited shot of Mae Marsh's twisting hands in the courtroom, or Little Brown Eyes' face, enormous and haunting in the St. Bartholomew's Eve massacre [Figure 2.6]). Griffith and Bitzer carried their experimentation with framing and lighting further than ever. Considerable camera movement was introduced: the long, cranelike dolly into Belshazzar's palace courtyard; the pan across the seated women in the marriage market, not to follow action but to compel our close attention to the women. There is some exterior night shooting in the Babylonian battle scenes, which seems almost impossible at that time. The full range of irises, fades, superimpositions, and masking (a CinemaScope shape to present the sun court of Cyrus) are employed throughout—all done in the camera. In total, *Intolerance* is felt by many to represent Griffith's fullest achievement; for all it must stand as one of the great landmarks in the history of film.

A Tradition of Screen Comedy Is Established

At about the time Griffith was contributing a new flexibility and power to screen language, a distinctive line of American film comedy began that would produce its own geniuses and masterworks. Although contrasting strongly with Griffith's high seriousness and Victorian

FIGURE 2.6   *Intolerance,* The St. Bartholomew's Eve Massacre   ★   United States, 1916, D. W. Griffith.

sentimentality (in fact, sometimes subjecting those qualities to parody), the early film comics nonetheless contributed importantly to solving some basic problems of the art form that concerned Griffith. Given funny-looking people behaving oddly in situations filled with humor, the amount of laughter obtained could still vary considerably depending on how it was presented. The requirements of pictorial narrative, the selection and arrangement of shots, were as important to the effectiveness of the comedians as they were to Griffith. One of Griffith's former co-workers and informal students, **Mack Sennett,** came to understand this newly evolved technique and put it into practice for comic purposes. Like Griffith, Sennett didn't invent so much as he applied insights gained from his own and others' experiments. His essential contribution was to fashion a kind of systematic, though unarticulated, comic aesthetic that would become a standard basis from which others would continue to develop.

As with most film genres, screen comedy was present in embryonic form from the very beginning—in fact, before the screen (for instance, *Fred Ott's Sneeze,* 1893, one of Edison's peep-show Kinetoscope fragments). Other early Edisons included visual records of comic vaudeville skits: *Fun in a Chinese Laundry* (1894) involved a chase, a policeman, and a thrown prop (not yet a pie), foreshadowing the later Sennett Keystone comedies—as did, even more clearly, the brief but fully developed *A Wringing Good Joke* (1896). Then there were the French "trick films" begun by Méliès and added to, most notably, by

Ferdinand Zecca and Emile Cohl. In these the "trickery" was usually designed for humorous as well as fantastic effect; for example, pumpkins roll off a wagon and bounce around town creating all sorts of havoc (*The Pumpkin Race,* Cohl, 1907). Méliès's *An Adventurous Automobile Trip* (1905) in many ways foreshadows Sennett's later fun with Model Ts.

It was another Frenchman, Max Linder, who from 1905 on established most clearly a pattern for the kinds of visual incongruities and surprises that were to screen comedy what verbal gags were to stage burlesque and vaudeville. The comic figure he created was a dapper, upper-class man-about-town involved with a hard-hearted lady love. Sennett admitted to having studied Linder closely, and Sennett's most brilliant discovery, Charles Chaplin, was even more obviously in Linder's debt. In Chaplin's first films for Sennett, before he developed his tramp persona, his costume and mannerisms not only suggest his own English music-hall background but also bear a resemblance to the smoothly maladroit and somewhat effete dandy that Linder had created. Sennett's work, however, which started a main line of film comedy lasting from 1912 (the year the Keystone Company was founded) through the 1920s and into the first years of sound, was vigorously and indigenously American. It was he who earned the broad popularity for the style known as *slapstick,* upon which Chaplin was to ring his own, subtler changes.

Whatever other influences there were, the precedents offered by Porter and Griffith would serve Sennett as a way of structuring his films. The chase, characteristic of the filmed action-melodramas, could be used for comedy as well as for pure suspense (Figure 2.7). With exciting action situations as backbone, comic muscle and flesh were added. Perhaps the essentials of the method can best be demonstrated by suggesting a composite Keystone

FIGURE 2.7   Keystone Kops in an unidentified comedy ★ United States, c. 1914–1919, Mack Sennett.

comedy made up of remembered scenes from several of the actual comedies. It opens in a bungalow bedroom, with two seedy-looking robbers climbing through the window. They waken the rotund homeowner at gunpoint, gag him, and tie him to a conveniently available hot water heater, which they set at HOT (insert of gauge). They then rifle his bureau, scoop up valuables, and leave. A freckle-faced, gap-toothed urchin peers in the window, sees the trouble, and sets off, presumably to summon help. (Note the similarity so far to Porter and Griffith.)

Cut to the interior of a police station, where an outsized sergeant sporting a large brush of mustache (Mack Swain) is snoozing at the desk. He bounces awake, answers the phone, then shouts off screen. A gaggle of policemen stumble over each other through a door and line up in front of the desk. An odder collection of physical types would be hard to imagine. There's a tall skinny one (Slim Summerville), a fat one (Roscoe "Fatty" Arbuckle), a wildly cross-eyed one (Chester Conklin), and so on. A number of them are decorated with bizarre mustaches, beards, and sideburns. Uniforms are too large or too small, and parts are as apt to be on backward as not. They twitch and weave in an irregular line as the sergeant shouts at them, then rush toward a door leading outside. Emerging onto the sidewalk, they jump into a couple of open jalopies at the curb. The floor on the rear car gives way under the impact. Its occupants then leap in with the others in the front car, though one can scarcely believe it is holding them all. Starting up rapidly in reverse, they crash into the rear car, which then totally collapses. Roaring out into the street, they barely slip in front of an oncoming truck; zigzagging from one side to the other, they obliviously scatter pedestrians and opposing traffic in their wake. An **undercranked** camera speeds up the movement to a surreal tempo.

Back in the bedroom, the nightgowned captive is still spread-eagled on a now swelling boiler. The needle of the gauge moves from HOT to BOILING and toward DANGER and EXPLOSION. Return to the police car, now careening along a highway at an improbable speed; the cops are all standing, overflowing the sides, peering ahead, gesticulating frenetically with their elbows in each other's faces.

Cut to a single file of laborers walking along a country road; the shovel on the shoulder of the last man catches a detour sign and turns it to point to a road other than the one it had been indicating. The police arrive in the patrol car, pause, zip backward and forward, then drive off on the route we know is not the detour. Coming down a hill at breakneck speed, they fail to stop as the road dead-ends into a lake; instead, they go straight off the end of a pier and submerge. On the other side of the lake, they emerge unfazed, still going full tilt toward their destination; and so on, with other impediments, other cross-cuts to the bulging boiler distending the fat man's stomach, until the final rescue.

Several things are noteworthy about this kind of comic invention. For instance, it is clear that the same Porter/Griffith excitement and suspense of crime, chase, and rescue or capture are here turned into comedy by visual and emotional exaggeration. Also, a recognizably real world (unlike that of Méliès) is madly distorted as if certain physical laws (of gravity, acceleration, solidity of objects, and the like) operated eccentrically or not at all. The incongruity between what is expected in the real world and what happens in Sennett's universe extends throughout the films. The pleasure we get from this sportive tampering with the expected is the same as would later be offered in animated cartoons. We know that floorboards usually remain in cars, that boilers have no rubbery elasticity, that humans and machines move at predictable speeds, and that no one can drive along the bottom of a lake and come up on the other side; still, it's fun to have the unlikely made manifest. As for the people in Sennett's films, they are incredibly incompetent; also, it is highly improbable that a random sample of beings would include the widely variant physical types and appearances of his cast. Further, they are always inhumanly unflappable: They cope with the irregularities of nature with a maniacal seriousness, only dimly aware that anything is amiss.

These funny-looking, oddball characters could be expected to send a less sophisticated, or perhaps only less inhibited, audience into gales of laughter merely by their cross-eyedness or fatness. This suggests that a certain sadistic pleasure in others' misfortunes underlies the jokes of physical discomfort that are such an integral part of silent screen comedy, including pratfalls and pies in the face. We enjoy the robbery victim being grilled and splayed on the water heater; the car going off the end of the pier looks like a multiple drowning, and we howl with glee. An emotional catharsis of some sort is provided by this controlled display of aggression and violence. The magical power of the characters to survive annihilation is probably also an important cathartic element. There is no death; Sennett's people are invulnerable, and we are free to indulge in comic-hysterical relief and reaction to normally destructive actions. Our laughter no doubt arises from a feeling of comfortable superiority—we are not the ones afflicted.

In Sennett's films the powerful and socially exalted characters are comic butts, helpless in the face of an onslaught by nature or one of its minions. The choice of policemen is significant in this respect. Although he would turn in his grave at any suggestion of Freudian notions about authority figures as resented parental surrogates, Sennett evidently did realize that the incongruous and the uncomfortable were a lot more humorous when inflicted on types of people who were taken seriously by society and themselves. The indignities to which the grotesque and ineffectual policemen are subjected are funnier because they *are* policemen. And if soup spilled down a back is amusing, it is at least twice as comical if the back belongs to a plump dowager in an evening gown at a formal function.

By puncturing pomposity and pretension, by making the leaders and guardians his victims, Sennett heightened our enjoyment. To this extent there is a social edge to his comedy. It is usually on the side of the little guy in the audience and directed against institutions and conventions outside his sympathies. This general satirical intention was even more pointed in the Sennett parodies of certain popular films he felt suffered from pretentiousness. *Barney Oldfield's Race for Life* (1913), for example, was an early kidding of the Griffith last-minute rescue. In the 1920s the first of the epic westerns, *The Covered Wagon,* became Sennett's *The Uncovered Wagon;* Erich von Stroheim's *Foolish Wives* was lampooned in *Three Foolish Weeks;* and there was nothing quite like Ben Turpin playing a Rudolph Valentino in *The Shriek of Araby* to put passion and heroics in proper perspective.

Slapstick was as natural to the silent screen as were the action-melodramas and spectacles, and for the same reasons: It utilized those aspects of the world best communicated through the moving image, those not requiring the supplement of language. Most of us who didn't grow up in the tradition of silent comedy have trouble getting back to its essence except through the works of the later, greater clowns—Buster Keaton, Harold Lloyd, Harry Langdon, Stan Laurel and Oliver Hardy, and post-Keystone Charlie Chaplin. One difficulty in our appreciation of early silent comedies is that we too frequently see them in excerpted and anthologized snippets, projected at a speed faster than intended (which undercuts Sennett's use of fast motion for precise effect). Exaggerated music and sound effects, and perhaps a commentator's condescending asides, act as further distractions.

The essential point to be understood is that the best of Sennett had a disciplined lunacy. His work is not merely a succession of unrelated inanities; although not intellectual, it is not mindless either. When properly constructed and executed, the rules of silent comic geometry are consistent, and a coherence is built from gag to gag to entire film. Sennett's special genius lay in understanding the construction and timing of sight gags. Careful manipulation of the standard ingredients, plus a sure feeling for what each shot includes, at what point it appears, and how long it is held on the screen, make all the difference. Start with the basic comic situation of a man falling down; make that man a ridiculously pompous, rotund, middle-aged suitor on the way to his lady love's, carrying a dainty corsage, dressed in top hat, cutaway, and striped trousers; then select, quite properly, a small boy to deflate this dignity by placing a banana peel in the man's path. The comic effectiveness of character and incident may still be profoundly altered by whether we first see the man walking and falling in long shot, then the banana peel in closeup, then the boy peering around the fence in medium shot, or whether the order of these shots is reversed so we can share the boy's anticipation and sense of achievement. Of course, the film maker must judge when the audience will have gotten the full impact of a shot, and thus cut on the rising laugh—not before, not after.

In silent comedy the gag construction could advance unimpeded: No pause was needed for lines to be heard and laughs registered. The silent film maker could build steadily, milking the visual joke for all of the variations it offered. Roars of laughter crescendoed until the comic climax was reached; only then was there a slowing of pace, a transition, and a hooking into the beginning of the next gag—which started building all over again. Ideally, the audience was left weak and helpless, weeping with laughter. It was this kind of robust creation, one uniquely suited to silent film, that Sennett mastered. His work is directly related to the cinematic technique that engaged Griffith's attention.

The early generation of American film makers that did not get its training from Griffith got it from Sennett. His transcendently brilliant protégé was, of course, **Charles Chaplin,** whom George Bernard Shaw called the only genius at work in motion pictures (as he thought himself the only genius at work in theater). Sennett and his partner Adam Kessel had seen Chaplin in the Fred Karno English music-hall company, which had been touring the United States extensively between 1910 and 1913. Though Kessel didn't get the name quite right, he wired off for "Charlie Chapman" at a time when Keystone's then reigning star, Ford Sterling, was being difficult about salary. Charlie's first film—entitled *Making a Living* (1914), with prophetic understatement—was pure Sennett. *Tillie's Punctured Romance,* directed by Sennett in the same year, and featuring Chaplin, Marie Dressler, Mabel Normand, Mack Swain, and Charles Bennett, is generally considered the first feature-length comedy (six reels). It too represents Sennett's slapstick humor rather than the tragicomic elaboration of Chaplin's finest work.

From later accounts by Chaplin, and from the evidence of his early films compared to his subsequent successes, it is clear that he was not altogether comfortable in Sennett's broad, knockabout style. Gradually, especially after leaving Keystone, Chaplin would develop a comedy character rich and subtle beyond anything Sennett had conceived. Chaplin made that character into one of the great comic figures (along with Falstaff, Til Eulenspiegel, Don Quixote and Sancho Panza, and the creatures of the **commedia dell'arte**). The personality and costume of the little tramp, assembled through dozens of one- and two-reelers, evolved full-blown by the end of the 1910s. The little fellow, ingenuously and ingeniously triumphant while maintaining his cheerfulness and dignity in an adverse world, was quickly taken to the hearts of audiences everywhere.

In addition to the creation of this persona, rounded and complex enough to encompass strains of pathos, from *The Tramp* (1915) on, Chaplin developed his unique pantomimic grace, evident early in *The Rink* (1916) (Figure 2.8a and b) and *The Cure* (1917). He handled his body as a dancer would, and there is an exuberant joy in merely watching him skip through the world, pirouetting to offer himself to the blondly beautiful Edna Purviance, bounding into and out of an open utility hole without apparent hurt, or running and gliding around a table, just out of reach of the giant Eric Campbell. From large movements to small (the dissection of a clock in *The Pawnshop,* 1916), there was a constant flow of invention. Chaplin turned what could be done with arms, hands, legs, feet, and stiff backbones into unexpected and sometimes unimaginable physical potential, a playful and precise bodily commentary on the human condition. And this is not to mention his uses of a Murphy bed (*One A.M.,* 1916), a lamp shade (*The Adventurer,* 1917), and other props.

The social dimension implicit in Sennett was expanded by Chaplin and tended to preoccupy him increasingly as his career progressed. Even in this early period his films generally included some pointed observations about people in relation to society. *Easy Street* (1917) is a veritable catalog: The main theme of law and order includes a delightful reversal of police brutality; revivalist religion, slums, poverty, welfare, anarchists, and drug addiction are all touched upon along the way. *The Immigrant* (1917) is frequently quite sardonic as well as broadly amusing in its depiction of the experiences of new arrivals in the "Land of the Free." For example, as the ship passes the Statue of Liberty, the

FIGURE 2.8a and b   *The Rink* ★ United States, 1916, Charles Chaplin; a. Chaplin; b. Chaplin and Eric Campbell.

FIGURE 2.9a and b   *The Immigrant* ★ United States, 1917, Charles Chaplin; b. Chaplin and Edna Purviance on left.

passengers are shoved and roped in like cattle (Figure 2.9a and b); Chaplin takes a quizzical second look at the statue. In *Shoulder Arms* the satirical treatment of military life and basic antiwar stance are all the more remarkable when you realize it was released before the armistice of 1918.

Chaplin's enormous popular success and shrewd handling of the income he earned from it allowed him, throughout his career, freedom for social-political comment and a degree of artistic autonomy (which Griffith lost after the failure of *Intolerance*). Chaplin's control over his films would become unique within the art industry. From the early 1920s he was his own producer; his artistic virtuosity permitted him to write the scripts for, direct, star in, compose the music for, and supervise all the other creative functions of his films. To make fully certain his works would reach the screen exactly as he intended, in 1919 he joined Griffith, Mary Pickford, and Douglas Fairbanks to form a distribution company called United Artists. Thus not only did Chaplin succeed in preserving his independence, but he was also able to proceed in a way quite opposite to the centrifugal, collective forces generally at work in the industry.

The feature length of *Tillie's Punctured Romance* proved something of an exception as far as comedies were concerned. Chaplin continued at two reels until 1918, when he left Mutual and joined First National. He then began a Griffith-like extension of running time (to three reels in 1918–1919) that would lead him to intermingle features and shorts in the early twenties. Although the short comedies held their own against features in popularity, the standard program by the late 1910s was organized around the feature attraction, with the preceding shorts adding variety.

Emerging Patterns of Industry

It was the independent producers who introduced and rose with the features. The Motion Picture Patents Company, the fixedly conservative combine that had included all of the principal early producers—most notably Edison, Biograph, and Vitagraph—finally failed in its efforts to exert a monopoly through its patent claims and its attempts to control the manufacture of equipment and film stock. Founded in 1908, the Trust, as it came to be known, consistently resisted longer films and stuck to the outright sale of prints—through its distribution arm, General Film Company, established in 1910. With the increasing acceptance of the more expensive features, a rental system evolved whereby after they had made the rounds of the theaters, the prints would return to the producers. By 1914–1915 the Trust was clearly being beaten by the amount and quality of its competition: The independents were too numerous, aggressive, and ingenious; there simply was no way to keep them from producing and distributing films. By 1917, through court decisions in a series of antitrust suits, the Motion Picture Patents Company was declared legally dead.

During those same years, partly as a result of the attempt by the independents to escape the legal harassment and goon squads of the Trust, the center of production shifted from New York to southern California. (From about 1907 to 1917 Chicago was also a production center, with three large Trust firms—Essanay, Selig, and Kalem—located there.) With the feature film as the staple commodity, with the former independents becoming the newly dominant powers as the old Trust companies faded away or were absorbed, with Hollywood the production center, and with distribution controlled out of New York, the model was established for industrial expansion for the next decade and beyond.

The general lines followed were already standard in the manufacturing, wholesaling, and retailing of other products. The movie industry had the same requirements as any industry in which the annual costs of production were enormous—as its close contemporary, the automobile industry, for example. As far as manufacturing was concerned, the motion-picture and automobile industries were both geographically centered near raw materials and sources of power, with specialized labor pools developed around them (the workers often being imported from abroad). Detroit was within reach of coal, oil, iron ore, and the steel mills. Hollywood's distance from New York and proximity to asylum across the Mexican border were initially among its chief attractions to the independents who settled there. Later Hollywood proved to have attributes similar to the raw materials and sources of power sought in other industries. The extraordinary variety of California's scenery meant that virtually any sort of locale—mountain, desert, ocean, forest, rolling fields—could be duplicated within a few hundred miles of Los Angeles. In those days when sunshine was still the principal source of illumination for movie making—even for interior scenes—southern California had more of it than did the eastern centers.

Gigantic Hollywood studios became the equivalents of Detroit's River Rouge plant; enormously expensive facilities and equipment were constructed and assembled in both. Motion-picture projection was standardized throughout the world. Any change that required retooling involved vast sums, and only economic crisis would induce it. The assembly-line method devised by Henry Ford eventually would have its analogue in the Hollywood production process; tendencies in that direction were already manifest in the late 1910s (Figure 2.10).

It was Thomas H. Ince who first functioned as a studio head/production supervisor, planning and overseeing an entire production program. He supervised the making of hundreds of films, developing especially the western genre (and its early star, William S. Hart) into a popularity that rivaled the melodramas of Griffith and the comedies of Sennett. In 1915 Ince joined Griffith and Sennett in the newly formed Triangle Film Corporation,

FIGURE 2.10   The Edison Company film studio in Menlo Park, New Jersey, 1915.

named in honor of the three of them. When Ince left Triangle to form his own company, he built a big new studio at Culver City, which later became the M-G-M Studios.

The production methods that began with Ince would become standard Hollywood practice in the 1920s. This piecemeal assembly—especially the practice of shooting out of sequence—however efficient and economical, tended to make the creative process disjointed and strained. The notion of separate specialists in charge of each of the many aspects of production seemed a bitter paradox to those who thought a work of art demanded, by definition, the absolute domination of a single personality. But there just wasn't enough individual genius around to supply the theaters with a steady and frequent change of bill. What generally resulted from this "art by committee"—as with American automobile manufacturing—was a high level of standardized technical excellence.

The mass-produced films inevitably came to look pretty much alike, especially to the critical eye. A crucial problem for the motion-picture industry thus became how to create the illusion of variety without fundamental differences involving wasteful experimentation and expense. One of the solutions was not unlike the development of automobile types— the sport roadster, the family sedan—and the offering of (slightly) different models each year. There evolved types of formula pictures (the "woman's picture," the comedy, the action-adventure) and cycles within each type (the vamp, the rural comedy, the war drama). Technicians could become expert at a particular kind of film making; one western, for example, could effortlessly follow the pattern of another. Audiences always had the choice of going to one of the popular genres one week and to another the next, keeping their entertainment sufficiently varied to obscure the similarities within the limited spectrum. Then, too, the familiar had its own attractions. Repetition with variation is pleasurable: Nobody wanted a western so different as to seem unlike a western.

Another device that kept audiences coming back for more was the cultivation of the star personality. People would go again and again to see Mary Pickford or Mabel Normand, Charlie Chaplin or Doug Fairbanks, just to be in their screen presence for an hour and a half on a Friday night. In this case, too, the fans didn't want radical innovation any more than did the producers; they enjoyed their favorites in vehicles carefully tailored to exploit their appeal. The stars commanded an automatic audience. As long as the range extended from femme fatale Theda Bara to melodramatic heroine Pauline Frederick, from robust comic John Bunny to matinee idol Francis X. Bushman, what more could be asked? Aspiring performers patterned themselves, or were patterned, along the lines of the already established, so that even the individuality of personality could be fitted into existing grooves.

Finally, the whole enterprise was enveloped in an unprecedented amount of promotion and advertising designed to whip up audience expectations. Each film, even if essentially indistinguishable from others preceding it, was presented as the most spectacular, the most action-packed, the funniest, the most heartwarming—in short, as something not to be missed. Press agentry soon encompassed the stars' lives off screen as well as on, and made them into demigods whose mythological existence commanded constant attendance and unswerving devotion. That was how the system came to work.

By the end of the first quarter century, film production—which had begun in a tar-paper shack or out on the street—had moved into large, permanent studios, clustered for the most part around Los Angeles. Distribution initially was a simple and direct affair: The producers sold prints of films outright to those showing them—at so much per foot, like cordwood; ten cents per foot, or one hundred dollars per reel, was common, regardless of the quality of the entertainment. As audiences tired of seeing the same films over again, it occurred to someone to set up an "exchange" whereby exhibitors could trade in their prints and—for a small fee for the service—obtain used prints of different films from other exhibitors. With increased competition among producers and discrimination on the part of the public, the practice of rental instead of sale gradually evolved; producers then received a share of the actual box-office drawing power of their films, greater for the more attractive and expensive, less for the others. This practice made for one of the singularities of the industry: The product is not bought or sold; customers merely pay to spend some time looking at it. The retailers (exhibitors) return a share of that income to the wholesalers (distributors), who in turn subtract their expenses and profits and pass the remainder on to the manufacturers (producers).

Exhibition, which had started as part of vaudeville programs, began to take place in nickelodeons in 1905, when films became longer and more of them narrative. Named for the price of admission, these first movie houses characteristically were converted store fronts, perhaps with chairs rented from a local funeral parlor. The nickelodeons showed continuous programs of assorted short films; the enormously successful *The Great Train Robbery* opened many of them. With the arrival of features and the increasing popularity of film, former stage theaters were converted for motion-picture exhibition. The big era of showing movies in the town's "opera house" and competing with stage road shows dates from 1913 to 1916. At that time, there were perhaps as many as 28,000 movie theaters of all types in the United States. A new and more pretentious type of screen theater was initiated in 1914 with the opening of the Strand on Broadway, soon to be followed by others with equal ambitions. Widespread construction of theaters designed especially for movies did not occur, however, until the 1920s.

By the time World War I ended, in late 1918, the American film had achieved all the essentials necessary to ensure its success as an art industry: a steady flow of features accompanied by shorts, especially by popular comedies; a national distribution in which prints circulated out of regional exchanges within a rental system that permitted the income to flow back through exhibitors and distributors to producers; and theaters gradually being formed into chains by enterprising exhibitors, accommodating larger and more demanding audiences paying higher prices. These fundamentals extended to an international scale gave the United States its lead in the conquest of the world's screens. Once the war was over, growth of the medium could resume unimpeded by national boundaries.

Films of the Period

1914
A Fool There Was (Frank Powell)
Judith of Bethulia (David Wark Griffith)
Making a Living (Charlie Chaplin)
The Squaw Man (Cecil B. DeMille)
Tillie's Punctured Romance (Mack Sennett)

1915
The Birth of a Nation (David Wark Griffith)
Carmen (Cecil B. DeMille)
The Cheat (Cecil B. DeMille)
The Tramp (Charlie Chaplin)

1916
Civilization (Thomas H. Ince)
Intolerance (David Wark Griffith)

The Pawnshop (Charlie Chaplin)
The Rink (Charlie Chaplin)

1917
Easy Street (Charlie Chaplin)
The Immigrant (Charlie Chaplin)
Teddy at the Throttle (Mack Sennett)

1919
Back to God's Country (Nell Shipman)
Blind Husbands (Erich von Stroheim)
Broken Blossoms (David Wark Griffith)
Male and Female (Cecil B. DeMille)

Books on the Period

Abel, Richard, and Rick Altman, eds. *The Sounds of Early Cinema.* Bloomington: Indiana University Press, 2001.

Brewster, Ben, and Lea Jacobs. *Theatre to Cinema: Stage Pictorialism and the Early Feature Film.* New York: Oxford University Press, 1998.

Cooper, Mark Garrett. *Love Rules: Silent Hollywood and the Rise of the Managerial Class.* Minneapolis: University of Minnesota Press, 2003.

De Bauche, Leslie Midkiff. *Reel Patriotism: The Movies and World War I.* Madison: University of Wisconsin Press, 1997.

Everett, Anna. *Returning the Gaze: A Genealogy of Black Film Criticism, 1909–1949.* Durham, NC: Duke University Press, 2001.

Koszarski, Richard. *An Evening's Entertainment: The Age of the Silent Feature Picture 1915–1928.* Berkeley: University of California Press, 1994.

Morey, Anne. *Hollywood Outsiders: The Adaptation of the Film Industry, 1913–1934.* Minneapolis: University of Minnesota Press, 2004.

Rollins, Peter C., ed. *The Columbia Companion to American History on Film.* New York: Columbia University Press, 2004.

Stokes, Melvyn, and Richard Maltby. *American Movie Audiences: From the Turn of the Century to the Early Sound Era.* London: British Film Institute, 1999.

3

Great German Silents

★ ★ ★ ★

1919–1928

Following the end of World War I, while the United States moved toward domination of the world motion-picture industry, Germany led the art into newly urbane subject matter and refinement of technique. This brief period of cinematic ascendancy occurred at a time when the country itself was desperately unstable in its political, economic, and social life. Loss of the war and the humiliation of the Versailles Treaty peace terms were damaging to national pride. The shaky and directionless Weimar Republic faced rioting and anarchy. Inflation, unemployment, and food shortages crippled the economy and inflicted great hardship on the German people. Morale was lower than it had ever been during the war. The highest point of German silent film (1922–1924) was precisely the lowest point for the nation. French troops occupied the Ruhr industrial heartland; the Deutschmark was utterly worthless; revolt was incipient in Bavaria.

With the stabilization of the mark in 1924 and the election of war hero Field Marshal Paul von Hindenburg to the presidency in 1925, a kind of order was restored. Within German society, however, the amorality and decadence portrayed in the American musical *Cabaret,* in Rainer Werner Fassbinder's *Berlin Alexanderplatz* (1980) television series, and in Bertolt Brecht and Kurt Weill's *The Threepenny Opera* (first produced in Germany in the late 1920s) succeeded the immediate postwar years and formed the setting for the triumph of Naziism. At the same time, the German film began to lose its particular excellence, a loss caused in considerable measure by American infiltration and dominance within the German film industry.

During the first half of the 1920s, however, there was a vitality in all the German arts, as if the nation's ill health had caused a feverish counteractivity. Literature and, especially, drama and the visual arts were released from the rigidities of a Hohenzollern monarchy and Prussian militarism. Prompted by the disillusionment of the war and the radically changed values that followed its end, newly expressive forms and styles were sought. At this time the plays of Bertolt Brecht, Ernst Toller, and Georg Kaiser were first produced; Max Reinhardt, in his more conventional historical-romantic stagings, added elements of lighting and handling of crowds that would be translated directly into film. Lyonel Feininger, Vasily Kandinsky, and Paul Klee were among the many active painters. Others affiliated with the Berlin *Sturm* group became stage and then film designers. The general aesthetic impulses would feed into film and in some ways find their ultimate expression in that collective and composite art.

In the United States, the West Coast center of film production was separated geographically (some would say culturally and spiritually as well) from the East Coast center of the other arts and communications media. In Germany, Berlin was not only the national capital but also the center for all the arts, including film. Those working in the traditional arts were free from feelings of condescension toward the movies like those of many Americans; on the contrary, German artists expressed a lively curiosity about the new art form and demonstrated their interest by trying their hands at it. It was possible for them to do so without changing their place of residence or lifestyle, and German films owed much of their sophistication to those trained in the older arts.

Whereas American films had been populated by good guys, bad guys, funny guys, and pretty women, the Germans started probing complex and frequently disturbed characters along loosely Freudian lines, which stimulated the additions to technique noteworthy in their work. While the Americans had concentrated on action and melodrama, the Germans explored the psychological and pictorial. In their quest for means to objectify inner consciousness, they created a world on film that represented not so much a physical reality, as most of us perceive it, as a state of mind: the universe distorted and stylized to express what we might feel about it. Expressionism, as opposed to American realism and naturalism, was the prevalent style. First appearing in extreme and sustained form in *The Cabinet of Dr. Caligari* (1920), it is also manifest in subtle ways in much of the German production of the 1920s, as will be noted.

Predominant Types and Themes

Looking at the German films of 1919–1925 as a body, film historians have identified three prominent types with concomitant themes that make evident most of the major German contributions. First were the historical/mythological films in which architectural settings, careful costuming, and romantic lighting, as well as the handling of massed crowds, reflect Max Reinhardt's theories and experiments in stage production. In these films, history is treated psychologically and spectacularly, rather than realistically; they might be called historical fantasies. **Ernst Lubitsch,** who had acted in Reinhardt's stage company, was one master of this genre. His accounts of the Bourbons (*Passion/Madame du Barry,* 1919) (Figure 3.1) and the Tudors (*Deception/Anna Boleyn,* 1920) center on a bedroom-keyhole view of the past, which suggests that great historical events can be seen as extensions of sexual intrigue. Someone once observed that Cecil B. DeMille, much indebted to Lubitsch, presented the Crusades as if they were fought for the sole benefit of Loretta Young; the same might be said about Lubitsch, the French Revolution, and Pola Negri. Onto gossipy biographies Lubitsch overlaid massive spectacles of the Bastille and the Tower of London, using hundreds of extras.

FIGURE 3.1   *Madame Du Barry/Passion*   ☆   Germany, 1919, Ernst Lubitsch; Pola Negri, kneeling.

Allied to the Lubitsch pageants were **Fritz Lang**'s less popular but more innovative and significant mythological/historical evocations. *Destiny* (1921), part legend, part fairy tale, includes three episodes placed in earlier times: one in a Moslem city, another in Venice during the Renaissance, and the final one in a charmingly fantastic China. Much of the pleasure in Lang's film is derived from the stylized settings. The dominant image is the enormous blank wall—in the connecting story—that fills the whole screen and dwarfs the humans. Trained as an architect, Lang went on to even fuller expression of his themes in gigantic re-creations of the German saga *Die Nibelungen* (1924)—a film that became so vast it had to be released in two parts: *Siegfried* (Figure 3.2) and *Kriemhild's Revenge.* (His *Metropolis,* 1927, though set in the future, is like the films about the past in that it re-creates another time and place through predominantly architectural means.) Much more serious in intent than Lubitsch's, Lang's spectacles are nonetheless offered as feasts for the eyes. The careful visual patterns and breathtaking scale are designed to be enjoyed in their own right as well as to be the expression of what seems an especially Germanic imagination about a prehistoric or fantasied past. Static they may be, but monumental too.

Also set in the past, though frequently even less specific as to time, were the second group of themes: the sinister, fantastic, macabre films in which expressionistic decor plays an important part and the subjects are often derived from old legends and ballads.

FIGURE 3.2 *Siegfried* ★ Germany, 1924, Fritz Lang.

The Cabinet of Dr. Caligari is the most famous of these. It could also be considered a precedent for the avant-garde film, predating the movement that would start in Berlin with Hans Richter's *Rhythmus 21* (1921) and Viking Eggeling's *Diagonal Symphony* (1925) and would then headquarter in Paris, while continuing to flourish in Germany with productions such as Walther Ruttmann's poetic documentary *Berlin: Symphony of a Great City.*

Originally Fritz Lang was to direct *Caligari.* When he withdrew to complete another film, Robert Wiene was appointed in his place. It was not the direction, however, so much as the eerily frightening story (by Carl Mayer and Hans Janowitz) and, particularly, the expressionistic settings, that made this film both seminal and enduring in its fascination. The names of the three painters who designed its sets—Hermann Warm, Walter Röhrig, and Walter Reimann—appear in various collaborations on the credits of many of the finest of the German films of this period. *Caligari* remains the purest and fullest use of the expressionist credo in film: "Films must be drawings brought to life," said Warm. The "exteriors" as well as the interiors were all constructed from wood, plaster, and canvas. The world created is that of a madman, a paranoid whose fears derive not only from the people and events around him but also from the shapes of nature, the town, a fairground, and an insane asylum. Jagged irregularity dominates: trees like barbed spears; pools of black shadow cast by no discernible light (shadows and light were in fact painted in order to better control them); a maze of crooked streets (Figure 3.3a); ramps and stairways foreshortened; and houses like clusters of strange geometrical blocks balanced precariously (Figure 3.3b).

Scarcely the sort of film to inspire popular imitation (it was moderately successful), there was nonetheless a small group of films that reflected its influence. Perhaps best remembered are Paul Wegener's *The Golem* (1920) and F. W. Murnau's *Nosferatu* (1922). *The Golem* is based on a Jewish legend about a practitioner of black magic—a rabbi of great erudition—who brings to life a clay monster to aid the Jews against their governing Christian oppressors in Prague in the sixteenth century. As Doctor Frankenstein also discovered, such monsters often attack those who create them, punishing us for our presumption. The abstractly fashioned medieval town, with its skyline of sharply angled roofs and tilted chimney pots, looks like twisted gingerbread; not a straight line is visible. A gigantic gate into the walled ghetto dwarfs the human beings. Irregular arches and inverted Vs predominate. The camera frequently shoots through the archways, imposing their strange shapes on the frame itself. The citizens—the males in tall conical hats and pointed beards—are again part of a nightmarish world like that of *Caligari.*

In Murnau's *Nosferatu,* the themes of somnambulism, a man under another's diabolical power, mass murder, and madness all recur, and the agent of death is destroyed while attacking the young female loved one in her bedroom. Count Orlock, who is Nosferatu-the-Vampire by night, strongly suggests Cesare of *Caligari* in appearance, bodily movement, and facial contortions. Tall, thin, grotesquely made up and costumed, he moves in a trance (not unlike Cesare) when under the curse of his vampirism (Figure 3.4). From real exteriors Murnau selected the sorts of buildings (the deserted castle, the town with its steep pointed roofs, the narrow twisting streets) and landscapes (rocky roads with abrupt inclines and turns, a deformed tree) that look as if they could have served as models for the abstractions created in the studio for *Caligari.* Going beyond the prototype, the expressionistic influence appears in specifically cinematic devices—fast motion, negative images, superimposition, and stop motion—which permits a tarpaulin to remove itself and a ship hatch to open of its own accord. The huge black shadow of Nosferatu, now created by light, moves horrifyingly toward and over his victims, unlike the painted theatrical shad-

FIGURE 3.3a and b   *The Cabinet of Dr. Caligari* ★ Germany 1919, Robert Weine.

FIGURE 3.4 *Nosferatu* ★ Germany, 1922, F. W. Murnau; Max Schreck.

ows in *Caligari*. Unreal, irrational, and hauntingly disturbing, these expressionist works offered a totally new kind of film.

The third group of German films from this period, marked least obviously by expressionistic tendencies, and most important in advancing film technique, began with the **Kammerspielfilm** (literally "chamber play film"), which derived from Reinhardt theater. This style was marked by unity of time, place, and action, with virtually no intertitles; few characters, usually lower middle class; sparse decor, with objects given extraordinary importance; and intimate psychological content. Its characteristics are further described, lovingly and sensitively, by Lotte Eisner in *The Haunted Screen: Expressionism in the German Cinema and the Influence of Max Reinhardt*. Key films were Paul Leni's *Backstairs* (1921), Lupu Pick's *Shattered* (1921), and Murnau's *The Last Laugh* (1924). Scripts for all three were written by Carl Mayer.

Finest of the Kammerspielfilms, and arguably of all German silent cinema, is *The Last Laugh*. It chronicles the pathos of a proud and majestic doorman at an elegant hotel, who, having become too old to handle heavy baggage and perform his other functions adequately, is demoted to washroom attendant. Seemingly loved and respected by his family and neighbors in his earlier status, he is reviled and ridiculed when they learn of his demotion. In the epilogue an eccentric American millionaire dies in the men's room, with a will in his wallet leaving his fortune to whomever is with him at his death. This whimsical conclusion, while lifting us out of the despair of the poor old man (played by Emil Jannings), by its very improbability reinforces the sense that real life is unhappy and that only stories have happy endings.

A genre related to the Kammerspielfilm is the **street film,** a term used by Siegfried Kracauer in his *From Caligari to Hitler: A Psychological History of the German Film.* Beginning with Karl Grune's prototypal *The Street* (1923), street films include G. W. Pabst's *The Joyless Street* (1925) and Bruno Rahn's *Tragedy of a Street* (1927). In these films, most typically, the male protagonists are drawn away from home, family, and bourgeois life by the lure of the city—the seductive promise of excitement and sensual pleasures. These were individualized studies of lower-middle-class life, often set within or alongside entertainment, and sometimes vaguely underworld, milieus. If extracted from the frequently superb skill of their realizations, the plot themes might appear melodramatic or morbidly sentimental. Though rooted in contemporary reality, these films were concerned primarily with character study—frequently with the personality disintegration of an individual or group of individuals.

The Joyless Street, featuring Scandinavians Asta Nielsen, Greta Garbo, and Einar Hanson, deals more directly with economic and political problems in postwar Vienna (inflation, black market, stock manipulation, ineffectuality of government) than do other street films. Its realistic visual style is also quite different from the other street films; it was said at the time to be an example of the ***Neue Sachlichkeit*** (new objectivity). Showing how these national problems lead to general corruption and dislocation of moral and spiritual values, Pabst concentrated on the pressures exerted on a bourgeois father: The man faces old age and poverty, and his beautiful daughter is about to be forced into prostitution; they are saved by a *deus ex machina* in the form of a U.S. aid commission.

Variety (1925), directed by E. A. Dupont, though not exactly a Kammerspielfilm or a street film, embodies some of the characteristics of both. It concerns trapeze artists involved in a romantic triangle; the husband (played by Emil Jannings) murders the partner who has cuckolded him. The film proper is presented as a long flashback within the framework of Jannings in prison, telling his story to the warden. It was a great international success, especially popular in the United States.

Principal Technical and Stylistic Advances

An underlying psychological function of all three major types of the German silent film is posited by Siegfried Kracauer in *From Caligari to Hitler.* According to him, they offered escape from contemporary social reality—into the past (historical or mythological), into fantasy (expressionist), or into the recesses of individual psyches (Kammerspiel and street films). Certainly it is true that German film makers were preoccupied with the psychological rather than the sociological, and that their new intentions brought innovations of technique to camera, lighting, set design, acting, and script construction.

To some extent the Germans, like the Soviets who would follow in the international spotlight, organized their industry as a vehicle of state. In 1917, when Germany's last great offensive in the West had failed, the giant firm Universum Film A. G. (Ufa) was founded by General Erich Ludendorff; over a third of its initial capital was supplied by the Reich. Mergers and affiliations with other large production firms and control of the biggest chain of first-run theaters led to its dominance. Unlike the Soviets, who used film directly for purposes of education and propaganda, the postwar German cinema was designed primarily to add to Germany's prestige through artistic accomplishment and to project Germany's image before the eyes of the world.

For these purposes the huge Ufa studios at Neubabelsberg were erected. Its facilities were unrivaled, and the craftspeople working there were the finest known. Many of their names later appeared on screen credits outside Germany, especially in the United States, decades after this original brilliant period of experiment and training.

Probably the single most striking contribution by the Germans was their fuller use of the **moving camera.** The Kammerspiel and street films in particular developed this possibility in order to probe character, to follow and bore into protagonists, and to let the world be seen from subjective points of view. In this latter respect the moving camera became part of the general expressionist tendency.

As far back as Porter's *The Great Train Robbery,* the camera had **panned** and **tilted;** Griffith had used **trucking** and **dollying** as well; but moving the camera while shooting was relatively rare and usually (not always) confined to the simple function of keeping a moving subject within frame. The standard Griffith method was to rehearse performances with actors, shoot them from the most effective angles and distances on a stationary tripod, then select and arrange the images, adjust the tempo of the action, and heighten the conflict through editing. Griffith thus transcended the spatial and temporal limitations of the stage, offering the varied filmic view rather than the fixed and continuous one available to the playgoer; but the viewpoint remained essentially objective, a recording of dramatic action.

The Germans made their camera part of the story in a more profound way. It became a narrative tool in addition to being a means of recording dramatic action. This potential was employed in two ways, both appearing together in many of the German silent films. First, the camera could become a narrator, like Joseph Conrad's Marlow, leading viewers into and through the story. *The Last Laugh,* for example, opens with the camera descending on an elevator, peering out through its wrought-iron grillwork at the passing floors of the hotel (Figure 3.5a). In one continuous take it moves down to the lobby and across to the revolving door, where it offers a view of the street and of the doorman whistling up cabs, greeting guests, and unloading luggage. It is for all the world like a novelist writing, "Evening was approaching at the fashionable Hotel Atlantic. On the upper floors maids scurried back and forth with fresh linen while guests moved toward the elevator and down into the lobby. There a string ensemble played to seated guests sipping aperitifs. If one crossed the lobby to the tall revolving door awhirl . . . ," and so on. Later, the camera follows at the shoulder of the little night watchman as he makes his rounds, permitting us to see what the light from his electric torch reveals as it bounces along the walls and floors of the corridors.

In the earlier sequences the doorman is viewed from a **low camera angle,** which exaggerates his size and importance in his splendid uniform and flowing mustache (Figure 3.5b). When he is reduced to washroom attendant he not only moves lower in social status (and physically below the street level), but also the camera is frequently placed at a **high angle,** further emphasizing the crushed spirit that makes the now stooped body seem small and pitifully vulnerable. Again, this kind of film making seems more analogous to a novelist's descriptive capabilities than to anything that can be achieved on a stage.

FIGURE 3.5a–d   *The Last Laugh* ★ Germany, 1924, F. W. Murnau; b, c. Emil Jannings.

Another special use of the moving camera fully exploited by the Germans was the possibility of its taking on a character's point of view and even state of mind—what is called **subjective camera.** In *The Last Laugh,* after a wedding party at his flat, the door-man is sitting alone amidst postparty debris, amiably bemused by drink (Figure 3.5c). First he is seen to spin in the room as the camera moves around him (the "narrator's" viewpoint); then the room itself revolves as the camera takes on his own tipsy vision. In *Variety,* the camera is mounted on a swinging trapeze to let us experience the vertigo of the disturbed catcher as the audience below seems to approach and then recede. In the same Wintergarten scenes, specially constructed **lenses** fragment and distort images to suggest psychological states, those of the excited members of the audience as well as those of the principals.

Karl Freund was cinematographer for both *The Last Laugh* and *Variety,* and it was the German camera work that most strongly impressed Hollywood. Freed entirely from a fixed base on a tripod and from a strictly objective view, the camera now ran or stumbled, got dizzy or suffered from hallucinations, and "saw" the sounds of a reveler's horn blown at midnight or of a woman's footsteps going down a corridor. In the less important films this use of narrative/subjective camera placement and movement was a mere trapping, a "special effect." In the best work this subtly profound innovation opened a whole new range of screen technique, not only affecting the way subjects could be dealt with but also making accessible themes and kinds of characters never before treated.

The other vital component of the cinematographer's craft, **lighting,** was important to all three major types of German silent film. In the historical-costume films it followed rather closely the stage lighting developed earlier by Reinhardt. The **tableaux** were bathed in pools of light and shadow, which enhanced the mood and fitted into the total composition of set design, massed extras, and featured players. In the expressionist films the lighting was one of the most evocative means of conveying the bizarre and the threatening as seen and felt by the characters. In the Kammerspiel and street films, often expressionistic in their subtler ways, lighting augmented camera movement to direct the viewer's eye where the film maker wanted it. Frequently the lighting was what most strongly evoked the feelings desired. Modeled lighting exposed a character's face (and soul) for examination. The essential significance of places and objects was rendered through the way they were lit. In these silent films things often seem to take on a life of their own, surrounding and commenting on the lives being led by the protagonists.

In all three types of German films the lighting was conceived and arranged specially to set the overall mood, and in the latter two types, to reflect the emotional states of the characters as well. Often eerie or sombre, at the same time romantic (softening) and decorative, it was vastly different from the consistent brightness and clarity of most American films. At its basic level, of course, film, the medium, is simply film, the material: the response to illumination by a coating of light-sensitive emulsion on a cellulose base. The title of cameraman John Alton's book, *Painting with Light,* suggests the way the Germans learned to conceive of and use this primary factor.

Two specific lighting contributions can be noted as well. First was the new prevalence of low-key lighting. Suddenly the screen went dark, with candlelit rooms, gloomy stairways, streets at night, cabarets, and all the other environments that would be habitual to the many "night people" of the German films. Sufficiently sensitive emulsions and expertness in laboratory processing had not been available before; nor, more important, had an understanding of the precise control that might be exercised over the cinematographic process. Second was the Germans' use of **key light** (not to be confused with low key, but often occurring in conjunction with it). The key light is the brightest light on the set, usually appearing to come from a source within the scene—a light fixture, a window, a street lamp. Griffith experimented with this possibility (notably in *Broken Blossoms*), but usually he led the eye and created emotional overtones by limiting the amount of area within the frame—cutting from long shot, to medium, to closeup—with the scene generally well and evenly lit.

The Germans came to realize that within a shot, if there is one brighter area amidst less brightly lit surroundings, it becomes the center of attention. They also sensed that it is much more satisfying aesthetically to have a variety of lighting intensities balanced around the frame—a monochromatic equivalent to the painter's placement of pigments. In short, they learned to lead the eye over the screen and to gratify it with the illumination, part of a total, ordered composition in which the main elements stand out and are reinforced by the lesser.

The importance of **set design** to the special effectiveness and unique qualities of the German silent film has already been noted, but can scarcely be exaggerated. Virtually all of the films were shot completely inside the studio, the "exteriors" frequently constructed painstakingly on a mammoth scale. In *The Last Laugh,* for example, the huge Hotel Atlantic and the busy intersection in front of it, with autos, buses, and pedestrians passing by, are studio creations (Figure 3.5d). Even an exception like Arthur von Gerlach's *The Chronicle of the Gray House* (1923), shot in part out-of-doors, uses the East Prussian moors as Thomas Hardy used those of Dorsetshire. Nature is bent to human purposes and given an anthropomorphic coding to reinforce human conflicts. Most of the crucial action, however, takes place within large, ornate, and calculatedly oppressive sets of baroque rooms and castle courtyards.

Two prevalent impulses in German set design were rarely separate from each other. The pictorial beauty and grandeur of the historical films had psychological dimensions as well, especially in the work of Fritz Lang. The expressionist tendency offered visual design that was striking in its own right (*The Cabinet of Dr. Caligari*) and large in scale (*The Golem*) as well as being expressive of overall moods and subjective states. Even in the Kammerspiel and street films, which embodied a modified expressionism, the pictorial and psychological functions of the sets were commingled. The Wintergarten scenes in *Variety* dazzle us by their size and opulence, besides serving as the public setting for the private tensions of star performers.

In Lang's *Nibelungen* the huge re-creation of a forest is breathtaking, with its Klieglight sunshine streaming through the branches of trees as big as sequoias (Figure 3.6a). The blond Siegfried riding slowly into frame on a white horse approaches a sizable, and palpably real, waterfall. Even the smoke-breathing dragon carries a rare conviction (Figure 3.6b). In a wide-angle long shot of a huge castle courtyard, human figures are placed on the checkerboard tiles to form part of a total visual pattern; Lang evidently intended that we study its vastness and ingenuity as the shot holds on the screen (Figure 3.6c). The costumes, too, are geometrically patterned. This sense of persons being segments of a decorative whole is confirmed by a scene in a treasure cave: A large round table piled with ornaments and jewelry is supported by carved dwarfs in chains (Figure 3.6d); when one of them moves slightly, we have an ultimate statement about person being interchangeable with object in a screen world remarkable for its nonhuman use of human beings. Lang seemed to like the idea of humans as statuary; he used it again in *Metropolis,* even more pointedly and ingeniously (Figure 3.7). The futuristic city of the latter film may have been Ufa's magnum opus as far as set construction was concerned. It also marks the last great burst of expressionism.

Obviously there was no **performance style** except the theatrical when film came into being, and the evolution of screen acting included breaking away from stage tradition—a progress to which Griffith and contemporary Scandinavian film makers had contributed substantially. Griffith's intentions were to make his actors perform with greater subtlety, and the Scandinavians continued and advanced that approach. The more intimate style of film acting would in turn influence the theater.

In trying to delineate internal states without the help of dialogue, the Germans went beyond realism to a deliberate expressiveness. Actors began working out their characterizations by "becoming" as completely as possible the persons they were playing. Immersing themselves sufficiently in the roles, they would inevitably reveal the characters' feelings through small gestures, the slope of a back, the movement of a head, the eyes—especially the eyes. But to these intuitive physical responses was added an intellectual refinement to make fullest use of silent film limitations (in this sense its strengths). Through closely observed facial expression and bodily movement the camera can capture what is

FIGURE 3.6a–d   *Die Nibelungen* ☆ Germany, 1924, Fritz Lang.

eloquent and seems true in the actors' understanding of the characters. This understanding is then "projected" effortlessly, to every seat in the house, by the projector shining a large likeness onto the screen. Gestures and expressions formed and shaped for the screen can reveal more than can actors on a relatively distant stage, or even people across a room.

The great actors in German silent film—Emil Jannings, Werner Krauss, Conrad Veidt, Lil Dagover, Asta Nielsen, Pola Negri, Greta Garbo—learned to retard and simplify their gestures to make precise psychological points. In *The Joyless Street* the neurotic energy of Asta Nielsen and the radiant inward beauty of Greta Garbo are conveyed without any of the stagelike busyness of Mae Marsh or Lillian Gish (fine as she was) in the earlier Griffith films. Nielsen, who appeared in Danish films (beginning with *The Abyss,* 1910) before moving to Germany after the war, remains one of the great artists of the silent screen. Perhaps she was the first to suggest a dimension and complexity of feeling beneath the surface of the screen presence. Her style of passionate intensity would be developed to even greater expressiveness by Garbo, who began in Sweden and worked in Germany before coming to the United States. Jannings created remarkable portrayals through a kind of stylization that called for an absolute comprehension of the psychological makeup of

FIGURE 3.7   *Metropolis*   ★   Germany, 1926, Fritz Lang.

his characters and an abstraction and heightening of the physical expression of feeling—
an artfulness that did not so much conceal art as transcend life. Jannings lived a great number of screen lives in the studio world, all of them consistent with the stylistic level of the
carefully designed sets and lighting.

   Given the complex interaction of the various elements of technique, the Germans
needed more-detailed **scripts** than did the simpler, more open-air and improvised American films. (Neither Sennett nor Griffith used scripts at all.) If the camera were going to
move in a sustained take down a studio street, lights had to be arranged along a predetermined path, sets built to accommodate the full range of its shifting angle and distance, and
actors directed and rehearsed to move in relationship to it. Thus scriptwriting, and the production planning growing out of it, achieved new importance. The German scriptwriters
could blueprint a film on paper, and the best of them, like Carl Mayer, could go beyond
the mechanics to communicate a complete sense of a film. Through written descriptions of
images, Mayer defined the kinds of emotional values required and suggested how to
achieve them. He also understood clearly what sorts of themes, characters, and emotions
lent themselves best to visual expression. The action in his scripts was invariably sparse
and simple; the plots, tight in construction, required few intertitles—and ultimately almost
none at all (for example, *Shattered,* 1921; *New Year's Eve,* 1923; and *The Last Laugh*). It
seems paradoxical that Griffith, without scripts, tended toward the literary, and required
screen words to connect and explain his action. Mayer, working with words, used them to

evoke self-explanatory images that were given physical form by directors, set designers, cinematographers, and performers—the extraordinary collective of German talent in the 1920s.

Influence on Hollywood

As the old Hollywood saw advises, "If you can't beat 'em, join 'em." In Hollywood terms this has often meant, "If you can't beat 'em, buy 'em up." There began in the 1920s an emigration of German film makers to the United States that would impoverish their native industry and further enrich the dominant American one.

Murnau, who had achieved worldwide prominence with German expressionist productions such as *Nosferatu* (1922) and *The Last Laugh* (1924), enjoyed a successful American career until his untimely death in 1931. *Sunrise,* a domestic melodrama he directed for Fox Studios in 1927, is sometimes cited as the greatest film ever made. The tale of a young husband's seduction by a *femme fatale* from the city, it boasts a **mise-en-scène** filled with stunning expressionistic effects. The city becomes a place of dazzling beauty and daunting complexity in scenes featuring reflective glass surfaces and deep space compositions, including a sequence in a restaurant that used a slanted floor, out-of-scale furniture, and midgets in the background to achieve a feeling of endless space and activity. William Fox gave Murnau complete control and an unlimited budget to make *Sunrise* in the belief that the film would enhance the studio's prestige. However, despite the critical acclaim that greeted its release, *Sunrise* lost money, and Murnau was never granted similar freedom again.

Germanic influence on American films was persistent, lasting decades after the first invasion. The imitation of German successes and the presence of German creative personnel combined to alter prevailing American style in regard to moving camera, lighting, and the use of visual narrative transitions rather than titles. Often this "Germanization" was somewhat arbitrary, being applied to native plots and themes without the aesthetic logic that had made form and content so interdependent in the best of the German silent films. Certain film types that developed later in the United States had their roots in the earlier Ufa and became sturdy hybrids. The horror series of Universal Studios, which began with *Dracula* and *Frankenstein* (both 1931), is one example, relying on sinister and fantastic subjects; expressionistic lighting, makeup, and costuming; and special-effects cinematography. A later instance is the cluster of *film noir,* as the French called them. Reminiscent of the street films, these dark crime melodramas of the mid-1940s also involve the probing of disordered psyches in a predominantly nighttime studio world.

In addition to the loss of talented creators, technicians, and performers, a kind of "internationalization" of German films, which began after the middle of the 1920s, vitiated the very distinctiveness that had made them popular as well as significant. This marked the appearance of a recurring problem of commerce affecting art. Once a country earns an international prominence through a special national contribution, it attempts to compete with Hollywood on its terms; that is to say, ingredients that are thought to make American films so successful are employed in an effort to obtain an even larger piece of the global box office (which includes the huge American audience). At the same time, American studios set about to coproduce within countries that demonstrated a successful competitiveness, contributing further to a blurring of national distinctions. In 1925 both Paramount and Metro-Goldwyn-Mayer negotiated with Ufa regarding joint production on the continent, using American-German casts and technicians. What Kracauer calls a "synthesis of Hollywood and Neubabelsberg" resulted in a further dilution of German themes and styles.

This is not to say that the German industry suddenly ceased to produce films of enduring value: With the arrival of sound there was a flurry of innovative and valuable work. American Josef von Sternberg made what many regard his masterpiece—*The Blue Angel* (1930)—and Fritz Lang, a German about to become an American, made what could be argued to be his—*M* (1931). G. W. Pabst, another of the great German film makers about to emigrate, did some of his best work during the early 1930s: *Westfront* (1930), *The Threepenny Opera* (1931), and *Kameradschaft* (1931). Among other German film makers of the early sound era, it may be Leni Riefenstahl who remains the most discussed—and the most controversial. After making a successful example of the mountain film genre, *The Blue Light*, in 1932, she worked with Hilter's government to craft a spectacular documentary celebrating Nazi power—*Triumph of the Will* (1935)—which chronicles the mass political rally at Nuremberg (Figure 3.8). She followed this with another masterful documentary, *Olympia,* made in 1938, which showcased the German-hosted Olympic Games.

But the exceptions to a general decline have to be weighed against the dozens of uniquely fascinating films of the first half of the 1920s. From about 1925 onward the eyes of the film world shifted from Germany to a star rising in the east, a red star. Made for the new government in Russia, another remarkable body of work began to appear that could scarcely be more different from the German films in form, content, and purpose.

FIGURE 3.8   *Triumph of the Will* ★ Germany, 1935, Leni Riefenstahl.

Films of the Period

1919
Passion/Madame du Barry (Ernst Lubitsch)

1920
The Cabinet of Dr. Caligari (Das Kabinett des Doktor Caligari) (Robert Wiene)
Deception/Anna Boleyn (Ernst Lubitsch)
The Golem (Der Golem) (Paul Wegener)

1921
Destiny (Der müde Tod) (Fritz Lang)

1922
Dr. Mabuse, the Gambler (Dr. Mabuse, der Spieler) (Fritz Lang)
Nosferatu (F. W. Murnau)

1923
The Street (Die Strasse) (Karl Grune)

1924
The Last Laugh (Der letzte Mann) (F. W. Murnau)
Die Nibelungen (Fritz Lang)

1925
The Joyless Street (Die freudlose Gasse) (G. W. Pabst)
Variety (Varieté) (E. A. Dupont)

1927
Berlin: Symphony of a Great City (Berlin: die Symphonie einer Grosstadt) (Walther Ruttmann)
Metropolis (Fritz Lang)

1928
Pandora's Box (Büchse der Pandora) (G. W. Pabst)

Books on the Period

Ascheid, Antje. *Hitler's Heroines: Stardom and Womanhood in Nazi Cinema.* Philadelphia: Temple University Press, 2003.

Cooke, Paul. *German Expressionist Films.* London: Trafalgar, 2002.

Eisener Lotte. *The Haunted Screen: Expressionism in the German Cinema.* Berkeley: University of California Press, 1969.

Elsaesser, Thomas. *Weimar Cinema and After: Germany's Historical Imagination.* New York: Routledge, 2000.

Elsaesser, Thomas, with Martin Wedel, eds. *The BFI Companion to German Cinema.* London: British Film Institute, 1999.

Fox, Jo. *Filming Women in the Third Reich.* Oxford, UK: Berg Publishers, 2000.

Hake, Sabine. *Popular Cinema of the Third Reich.* Austin: University of Texas Press, 2002.

Hake, Sabine. *German National Cinema.* New York: Routledge, 2001.

Kracauer, Siegfried. *From Caligari to Hitler,* 2nd rev. and ex. ed. Princeton, NJ: Princeton University Press, 2004.

Kreimeier, Klaus. *The UFA Story: A History of Germany's Greatest Film Company, 1918–1945* (trans. Robert and Rita Kimbar). Berkeley: University of California Press, 1999.

Kuzniar, Alice A. *The Queer German Cinema.* Stanford: Stanford University Press, 2000.

McCormick, Richard W. *Gender and Sexuality in Weimar Modernity: Film, Literature and "New Objectivity."* New York: Palgrave-McMillan, 2002.

Rentschler, Eric. *The Ministry of Illusion: Nazi Cinema and Its Afterlife.* Cambridge: Harvard University Press, 1996.

Scheunemann, Dietrich, ed. *Expressionist Films: New Perspectives.* Rochester, NY: Camden House, 2003.

Schulte-Sasse, Linda. *Entertaining the Third Reich: Illusions of Wholeness in Nazi Cinema.* Durham, NC: Duke University Press, 1996.

Taylor, Richard. *Film Propaganda: Soviet Russia and Nazi Germany,* 2nd rev. ed. London: I. B. Tauris, 1998.

Wager, Jans. *Dangerous Dames: Women and Representation in the Wiemar Street Film and Film Noir.* Athens: Ohio University Press, 1999.

Ward, Janet. *Weimar Surfaces: Urban Visual Culture in 1920s Germany.* Berkeley: University of California Press, 2001.

Welch, David. Germany. *Propaganda and Total War, 1914–1918.* New Brunswick, NJ: Rutgers University Press, 2000.

4

Art and Dialectic in the Soviet Film

★ ★ ★ ★

1925–1929

The Russians were even more profoundly affected by World War I than were the Germans. While there had been no fighting within the borders of Germany, Russia had been a vast battlefield. It had suffered defeat at the hands of the Central Powers and the peace treaty signed at Brest-Litovsk was even more vindictive than that of Versailles. While in Germany an abortive rebellion in 1919 was quickly suppressed, the Bolshevik Revolution of 1917 succeeded. At least five years elapsed, however, before it was clear that the new government of Russia, a communist government, could survive, and that a beginning stability would be achieved.

Not until 1925 did the Soviets fully launch into the final, and some would say most brilliant, phase of the silent film before the introduction of sound. The contrast between Soviet and German silent film, in both subject matter and technique, was even greater than that between the German film of the early 1920s and American film preceding it. Though the German effort had been state supported in part, it was directed toward the prestige of art. It can be valued precisely because of its extreme artificiality, but a prevailing aestheticism cannot be denied. There was an anarchic indifference to the social-political implications of content, which Kracauer interpreted as reflecting a kind of national neurosis. The introspection and morbidity of the major themes led to a slowness of tempo. As the veteran British director Anthony Asquith observed of German contributions, "While the film was gaining in its ability to convey mood, emotion and character, it was gradually losing touch with its life-source—movement."

Soviet film, completely state supported, was socially purposeful above all else: intended primarily to educate and indoctrinate the Soviet people in the events and causes of the Revolution. Vigorous and optimistic, the films came out of the East like a blast of cold Siberian air, blowing away the hothouse atmosphere of the German studios. Objective in approach (as opposed to German subjectivism) and epic in form (as opposed to the personal dramas of the Germans), they brought rapid pace and physical action back to the moving picture and resumed the line that emphasized editing inaugurated by Porter and advanced by Griffith.

The German film makers' intellectual sources included Sigmund Freud. Their concern with the psychological led to expressionism and the subjective camera as means of portraying internal states. As used by the Germans the moving camera became a kind of visual equivalent to the psychoanalyst's probing of the patient's psyche; the expressionistic design conveyed dreams, nightmares, and hallucinations.

In the Soviet Union the ideological basis was provided by Karl Marx and V. I. Lenin, and the film makers' concerns were social, political, and economic. The predominant aesthetic mode was futurism, which attempted to depict vividly the energetic and dynamic quality of contemporary life influenced by the motion and force of modern machinery. In film, pictorial realism rather than expressionism was the visual style required to portray the actual, external world. Cutting—paralleling the conflict and resolution of opposites in Hegelian/Marxian dialectic—was the principal formative method. A neat symbolic point is made by G. W. Pabst having directed *Secrets of a Soul,* a popularization of Freudian psychology, in the same year, 1926, that V. I. Pudovkin made *Mechanics of the Brain,* explaining the Pavlovian scientific dialectic of stimulus–response. Even a comparison of the titles of the German and Soviet films is revealing: *secrets* versus *mechanics, a* versus *the, soul* versus *brain.*

Historical Setting

In czarist Russia movies were not a popular art as they were elsewhere. There were few theaters, tickets were expensive, and the working classes couldn't afford to attend regularly. The high illiteracy rate made printed intertitles a general burden, and the literary-theatrical bent of the Russian silent films further helped confine their patronage to the educated middle classes. After the Bolshevik Revolution most of the film producers and actors emigrated, taking with them whatever equipment and film they could carry.

Those producers who chose to remain were at first allowed to continue along lines of private enterprise. Though they lacked revolutionary understanding, let alone zeal, not much attention was given to their output by a government preoccupied with more pressing matters. A Cinema Committee was set up, however, under playwright A. V. Lunacharsky, Minister of Education. With truly remarkable foresight, given the uses of film generally up to that time and the negligible Russian production, Lenin had said, "Of all the arts, the cinema is the most important for us." His statement contrasts as strongly as could be expected with one from the deposed Nicholas II, who had written: "I consider cinematography an empty, useless, and even pernicious diversion. Only an abnormal person could place this sideshow business on a level with art. It is all nonsense and no importance should be lent to such trash."

The national conditions that prevented Lenin and the other communist leaders from promptly turning film into the voice for the Revolution that it eventually became were not unlike those of postwar Germany, and considerably more severe. In the first year of the new government famine was widespread. During one of the cruelest Russian winters on record there was no fuel. Typhus raged in epidemic proportions. After participation in the war dragged to a halt, the Soviets faced Allied armies within their borders and continuing civil warfare with the counterrevolutionaries. One instance of the general instability was an episode in which some 50,000 escaped Czech prisoners of war ravaged the countryside unresisted along the route of the Trans-Siberian railway.

It took five years (1918–1922) to fully establish the new political regime and two more years before the film industry was functioning with anything approaching productivity. (Even by the end of 1923 only 13 percent of the films shown in the country were Soviet.) In 1919 the industry had been completely nationalized when it became clear that the old capitalist economics and mentality would not serve the needs of a socialist state. In the same year the State Institute of Cinematography (VGIK) was established in Moscow to train new Soviet film makers; it was thus the oldest, as well as one of the largest and best, film school in the world. In 1925 the Sovkino Trust was formed to try to bring some order into all aspects of the domestic industry and to reestablish distribution abroad.

Beginnings

The new Soviet cinema, which began its formative period about 1919, was thought of at the time as being divided into two creative camps. Although called the right and left wings, the labels weren't essentially political. At first the right wing carried on in the old theatrical tradition, using conventional methods and styles but substituting commissars, peasants, and Red Army soldiers for the upper-class characters of traditional theater. Romance, humor, and heroics persisted. The concerns of the new state motivated the action initially and appeared as background, but scarcely replaced standard dramaturgical elements: boy–girl, comic sidekicks, obstacles to be overcome, obstructive villains, and so on. *Kombrig Ivanov* (1923) is an example of this creative tendency; it was retitled *The Beauty and the Bolshevik* in the United States. Subsequently the work of the right wing achieved greater sophistication and addressed sociological problems. Abram Room's *Bed and Sofa* (1927), for example, deals with a romantic triangle, but the shifting allegiance of the woman toward the two men involves the housing shortage and her attitude and theirs toward the role of women in the new society. The general methods of the right wing became the only officially sanctioned approach after **socialist realism** was imposed in the 1930s, and continued to dominate Soviet cinema. *The Cranes Are Flying* (1957) and *Ballad of a Soldier* (1959) are later popular examples.

The left wing was much more radical in its innovation, which involved form as well as subject. When we think of the Soviet silent cinema, it is usually of the films growing out of the theories and experiments of two left-wing pioneers. One of these was **Dziga Vertov,** who followed Lenin's advice that the first work of Soviet film makers should be with newsreels and documentaries. This seemed advisable partly because of the drain on resources feature film production would have represented, but especially because of the urgency of communicating the history and spirit of the Revolution to the still largely apathetic and uninformed Russian public. In 1919 Vertov founded his **Kino-Eye Group** and began publishing manifestos.[1] "Life caught unawares" was Vertov's credo. What he meant by this was not

[1] Vertov's theories of film are available in *Kino-Eye: The Writings of Dziga Vertov,* edited and with an introduction by Annette Michelson, translated by Kevin O'Brien (Berkeley: University of California Press, 1984).

FIGURE 4.1 Kino-Pravda series ⋆ Soviet Union, 1922–1925, Dziga Vertov.

exactly candid camera (because the subjects usually knew they were being filmed) but that nothing be staged or directed. Life in front of the camera was permitted to run its natural course; the only creative control the film maker exerted was through choosing what and how to shoot, and the placement of one shot in relation to another during the editing. In 1922 Vertov began to produce **Kino-Pravda,** a series of monthly newsfilms that lasted for twenty-three issues (Figure 4.1). The title, incidentally, is synonymous with *cinéma vérité* (film truth), a term French anthropologist–film maker Jean Rouch coined in 1961 to apply to a new kind of documentary. What *cinéma vérité* added to *kino pravda* was essentially the lightweight, **synchronous sound** equipment that permitted the film maker to shoot and record virtually anything without interrupting or altering it for the benefit of camera or microphone.

Because Vertov had no control over the action he was filming, unlike a director of fiction films, editing took on a peculiarly central role in his work. Moreover, the shortage of raw stock in the Soviet Union in the early 1920s (before the Soviets began to manufacture their own) meant that Vertov had to use pieces of film as he found them, frequently short ends left over from other projects. In an impulse not unlike Porter's in *Life of an American Fireman,* Vertov learned that by juxtaposing shots from old czarist newsreels with newly shot materials he could create new meanings. Russian tanks crossing a no-man's land in the war could be followed by Soviet tractors breaking ground for cultivation. Juxtaposing a shot of the formal and elegant Nicholas stiffly reviewing his palace guard with a shot of a shirt-sleeved Lenin energetically addressing the workers added significance not inherent in either shot alone. In embryonic form this was precisely the kind of editing Sergei Eisenstein would develop into montage; the title of his film *Old and New* (1929) concisely sums up a principal propaganda device of Vertov's. Beyond that, one can say of Kino-Pravda that all the subjects were socially purposeful: There are no beauty parades, no animals in the zoo. Inspirational in tone, the films seem to be urging that there's a job to be done. In general they show one region or aspect of national life to the rest of the country (a major mission of the documentary film later to be picked up in Britain, with proper credit always given to the Soviets). Vertov's reports are not all sweetness and light by any means; hard-hitting exposés are included. "Save the starving children," one title proclaims, as we see pitiful young victims of famine. The directness of communication with the people is further revealed in end titles that encourage the audience to mail its "inquiries regarding traveling film shows" and "all film and photo work" to Kino-Pravda.

Another left-wing pioneer was **Lev Kuleshov,** film director, theorist, lecturer (from 1920 on), and later head of the State Institute of Cinematography.[2] As Sergei Eisenstein came out of the Vertov line, another great Soviet film maker, V. I. Pudovkin, was Kuleshov's star pupil. Eisenstein's impressively talented cameraman, Eduard Tisse, had worked for Vertov, as Pudovkin's cameraman, Anatoli Golovnya, had for Kuleshov. Kuleshov coped with the shortage of raw stock by conducting acting experiments performed for an empty camera. Also, he and his students spent much time analyzing and recutting existing motion pictures to learn filmic construction. When Kuleshov gained access to film stock he came to emphasize editing as heavily as did Vertov, but for different purposes. He discovered how, through cutting, to make nonactors appear to give skillful performances and how to give the acting of professionals meanings of which they were unaware at the time of performance. Following Vertov and Kuleshov, Eisenstein and Pudovkin made editing for the Soviet silent film makers virtually synonymous with the creative process itself.

A third early creative and theoretical group contributed to the scope of Soviet cinema. In 1922 a youthful Grigori Kozintsev (age 17) joined Leonid Trauberg (17), and Sergei Yutkevitch (18) to form the Factory of the Eccentric Actor: FEX. The virtually unlimited freedom for experimentation in the arts during the hectic years of revolution and civil war unleashed the progressive spirit among the young. (In 1922 Vertov was age 26, Kuleshov 23, Eisenstein 24, and Pudovkin 29.) This generation of Soviet artists, seeking new methods of expression, turned toward minor genres, "the kind of popular art which the aristocracy and bourgeoisie had scorned. To be precise: the music hall, the circus and the cinema." Eisenstein's first film, *Strike* (1925), is very closely related to these aesthetic impulses. After seeing it, Kozintsev told the FEX group, "All that we're doing is childish nonsense, we must all see *Strike* again and again, until we can understand it and adopt its power for our own."

Three Silent Masters

Ranked alongside Eisenstein and Pudovkin among the great Soviet silent film makers would be **Alexander Dovzhenko.** Because he stands somewhat apart from the principal

[2] His theories are available in *Kuleshov on Film: Writings by Lev Kuleshov,* selected, translated, and edited by Ronald Levaco (Berkeley: University of California Press, 1974).

thrust of Soviet film making, his work will be discussed first. A Ukrainian from a family of uneducated farmers, Dovzhenko includes in his films strange ethnic and mystical elements that color his Marxism and make his silent work quite distinct from that of the other Soviet film makers. He was a painter before he became a film maker, and montage was not as important for him as it was for the others; at least his use of it is quite different.

In Dovzhenko's three major silent films—*Zvenigora* (1928), *Arsenal* (1929), and *Earth* (1930)—the larger sequences seem separate from each other, circular in construction, and strangely complete in themselves. He emphasizes the relationships of scenes to scenes, within the sequences, rather than of shots to each other within the scenes. The numerous and varied scenes tend to be brief, but the shots (or even a single shot) that they comprise are often sustained. Contrasting and elliptical combinations involve quite extraordinary shifts of mood and statement. The connections of the parts to each other are often unclear or ambiguous on first viewing. In *Earth,* in a scene of the kulaks weeping and wailing, which follows the scene of the peasant grandfather dying, we assume initially that they are mourning his death (Figure 4.2a and b). When we learn that it is a threatened loss of possessions that has provoked their grief, the comment about them becomes a negative one. Ambiguity of this sort is rarely allowed to occur in the more didactic main body of Soviet work. It is as if Dovzhenko were serenely indifferent to conventional continuity in his pursuit of evocative, many-layered imagery.

Marking Dovzhenko's visual style are extremely wide-angled long shots in which a complexity of action and composition builds up within a single frame like an evolving painting. Also, there are the painterly "still" shots—the striking silhouettes of *Arsenal,* the trees heavy-laden with fruit in *Earth*—which convey a sense of timelessness, of fixity. In thinking of Dovzhenko's work we remember its many images of the Ukrainian countryside composed of low horizons and small human figures moving under an enormous open sky. The shocking and beautiful balletic death of Vasily in *Earth,* as he moves down a curving moonlit road toward the camera, to be cut down almost casually by a murderer's bullet, is not likely to be forgotten. Throughout his early films Dovzhenko's intentions are clearly more poetic than narrative (as with Pudovkin) or dramatic (as with Eisenstein).

FIGURE 4.2a and b   *Earth* ★ Soviet Union, 1930, Alexander Dovzhenko.

His symbols and metaphors are not forced or belletristic, however; they grow out of a conception of the closeness of the people to the soil. They also contain dialectical contradictions that advance the revolutionary argument; but because Dovzhenko sees life whole, there is nothing of the agitprop about his work. In *Earth* he is saying it is right for an old man to die (at peace) but wrong (against nature) for a young man to die (by violence). Yet death is followed by life in both instances. As the old man munches one apple, a child munches another, completing the cycle of generations. A woman gives birth during Vasily's funeral, and his comrades are clearly fulfilling the potential of his abbreviated life in building for the future. The autumn rain in the epilogue appears at first to be like tears, but it is also life-giving as it falls on the fullness of harvest. The tractor is regarded by the elderly as a replacement of themselves and their animals, and by the young as an extension of the people's productivity.

Though working in the service of the state, Dovzhenko's humanism causes him to extend sympathy to the old as well as the new. One can imagine that a Joseph Stalin might have regarded the ambivalence uneasily and ultimately as subversive. To a modern American viewer *Earth*'s unmistakably optimistic tone presents a remarkable argument for revolutionary change. But when it premiered in Moscow, it was attacked at length in *Izvestia* for being "defeatist" and "counterrevolutionary." Given its slowness of pace, ambiguities, obscurities, and dependence on the pictorial, it seems unlikely that it could have had the requisite popularity in the Soviet Union to do the indoctrinational job required of it by the sponsoring government. At any rate, after the brilliant experimental period of the 1920s, the hard line of socialist realism appeared; Dovzhenko never again achieved anything equal to the unique visual lyricism of his silent films. Even in the earlier time he seemed out of step with his colleagues. What attracted him most strongly was clearly the human and natural beauty that could be captured by the camera, rather than the arguments that could be fashioned by an editor's shears.

V. I. Pudovkin was educated as a physicist and chemist. (Dovzhenko's education, too, had been scientific and technological.) He became interested in acting for films, he said, as a result of seeing *Intolerance,* which had finally arrived in the Soviet Union in 1919. Although Pudovkin would appear as an actor in many of his own films as well as those of others, while studying under Kuleshov he came to see that the real creative fulfillment in motion pictures was for the director rather than the actor. Kuleshov, for his part, fully understood that Griffith had been working out of some of the same concepts that had begun to preoccupy him. A prominent concern of Kuleshov's was the difference between the actor's contributions to stage and to screen.

On stage, once the curtain rises the performer is in complete control of his or her performance. Direction and rehearsal are merely preparation to be used, or ignored for that matter, in interpreting a character in the presence of an audience. In film, the director is the principal "audience" of the live performance. The screen performance is constructed after the actor has finished his or her work, out of the selection made available by the camera: a long shot of the actor in a room full of people, a closeup of just the actor's profile, a reaction shot of someone else's face, and so on. It is no longer the actor's total performance that finally appears, no longer his or her rhythm or even whole body, but bits and pieces integrated into a synthetic whole. With systematic thoroughness Kuleshov began to test the possibilities of this basic cinematic technique.

His influence on Pudovkin was profound, and the latter claimed to have participated in a series of Kuleshov's experiments that explored the potential of editing to create a time

FIGURE 4.3   *Mother*   ☆   Soviet Union, 1920, V. I. Pudovkin: Nikolai Batalov, left, and Vera Baranovskaya, right.

and space existing (or seeming to exist) only on film. For one of these experiments Kuleshov assembled five shots. In the first a young man walks from left to right. In the second a young woman walks from right to left. In a third they meet and shake hands, and the young man points to something off screen. The fourth shot shows a large white building with a broad flight of steps. In the fifth the couple ascends steps. A viewer would accept this scene as one uninterrupted action, but in actuality the five pieces had been shot in completely different times and places—the man and woman (shots one and two) in separate parts of Moscow, and the handshake (shot three) in yet another. The white building (four) was in fact the White House, snipped from an American film, and the steps (five) were those of a cathedral.[3] Rudimentary and obvious as such experiments may seem, they nonetheless isolated and held up for examination the most basic aesthetic underpinning of the medium.

Returning from their practical experiments to a further study of *Intolerance,* Kuleshov and Pudovkin began to see how to apply their discoveries to the requirements of a new Soviet cinema. Although as far from being a Marxist as is conceivable, Griffith, in *Intolerance,* had carried on a moral and ethical argument through his separate historical

---

[3] V. I. Pudovkin, *Film Technique,* translated by Ivor Montagu (New York: Lear Publishers, 1949), pp. 60–61.

episodes, and in the modern story economic and social ones as well. (Not only the strike in Pudovkin's *Mother,* 1926, but also Eisenstein's *Strike,* 1925, contain unmistakable borrowings from the Griffith film.) In a succession of masterworks paralleling those of Eisenstein—warmer and more moving, if not as breathtakingly experimental and brilliant—Pudovkin gave full form to his learning. Unlike the highly intellectual appeal of Eisenstein's work, Pudovkin's films reach the emotions directly. They received instant acclaim and their power seems undiminished by the years. As with Dovzhenko, Pudovkin's major silent films—*Mother* (Figure 4.3)*, The End of St. Petersburg* (1927), and *Storm over Asia* (1928)—stand as his finest and most personal achievements, but he too continued to work for several decades in the sound film. Although he became a greater director than Kuleshov, Pudovkin also wrote theoretical essays—*Film Technique* and *Film Acting*—that explain and show the applications of his former teacher's insights. They remain among the best texts for beginning directors, especially for those interested in documentary film and work with nonactors.

Sergei Eisenstein, like Dovzhenko and Pudovkin, had a technical education (as a civil engineer) prior to defecting to the arts—first to theater in his case. Before beginning stage work, however, Eisenstein had developed an intense interest in Japanese language and culture, which would feed into his later profound and erudite theorizing about film. He was fascinated by the Japanese hieroglyphic writing, in which the word *weeping* is formed by combining the pictograph for *eye* with that for *water; singing* by combining that for *mouth* and *bird; listening,* by *ear* plus *door;* and so on. He came to believe that the two drawn symbols combined like film shots to provide a third meaning. Also, he noted a Japanese technique for teaching drawing, which limited the student to the composition of segments of a cherry tree branch within a frame. This attention to frame area and composition within it became useful preparation for Eisenstein's own painstaking composing of images. Finally, Kabuki theater seemed to him to bring various artistic elements together in a balance not unlike that of film. In Kabuki, and in the Nō plays, spoken language is not the almost exclusive carrier of content that it is in Western drama. Japanese theater is visual as much as verbal. Words are part of an ensemble in which formalized gesture, choreographed body movement, music, and even costumes carry equal weight and add nuances and qualifications to a complex whole.

Eisenstein's theatrical beginning was as a scene designer for the Proletkult Theatre. From childhood he had been a prodigious sketcher and painter; the Proletkult, dedicated to the development of proletarian artists and the education of the working class, accommodated his sympathies for the revolution. From the Proletkult he learned to distrust the character-centered theater of the nineteenth century and to seek ways to make the masses the hero and to present social problems in place of bourgeois romantic triangles. Moving on to work with Vsevolod Meyerhold, a radically innovative theatrical producer and director, Eisenstein completed the theoretical education and practical experience that would propel him into film.

Meyerhold's theories of acting were in polar opposition to those of Konstantin Stanislavsky, the other great contemporary force in Soviet theater. Whereas Stanislavsky started from within, in a psychological approach, instructing his actors to search out the emotions of their characters, Meyerhold began from without, in a theory he called biomechanics. Related to Pavlov's experiments in conditioned reflexes and consistent with the scientific spirit of the new Russia, Meyerhold's method was based on the idea that emotions could be stimulated in the actor (and conveyed to the spectator) through analysis of the emotive connotations of movement and by developing the actor's body into a precise machine capable of producing the exact effects desired. This approach pulled the Meyerhold theater closer to the *commedia dell'arte* tradition and even to the technique of circus performers. It may have helped lay the groundwork for German revolutionary Bertolt Brecht's aesthetic stance; certainly it had a profound effect on Eisenstein.

Returning to the Proletkult, Eisenstein arrived at his own eclectic fusion of all he had come to understand up to that point. What he sought was a **montage of attractions**—a series of sensory experiences that would involve the spectators and carry them along a predetermined path of emotional response. His most successful realization of these theories on the stage seems to have been a parody production of Alexander Ostrovsky's *The Wise Man.* In it he combined acrobats, a tightrope walker, and satirical asides directed at foreign political figures with a caricatured religious procession bearing candles, chanting litany, and carrying placards inscribed "Religion is the opium of the people." A short comic film was specially produced for incorporation into the performance.

Eisenstein's final attempt to transform theatrical art and get closer to the emotional needs of contemporary audiences led him in a direction opposite from the circus and music hall toward the reality outside the theater. His production of *Gas Masks,* a play by Sergei Tretyakov, was performed by workers and staged in the actual Moscow Gas Factory. Eisenstein regarded this experiment as a failure. Rather than eliminating "art" and replacing it with "life," as he had intended by using real setting and nonactors, he had succeeded only in exposing the artificiality of conventions that would have seemed perfectly at home in the theater. Seeking a means of capturing the reality of factory and workers that so fascinated him, he arrived at film as the medium that could make art out of materials much closer to life than could theatrical drama. As he put it, "The cart fell to pieces and the driver dropped into the cinema."

Strike (1925), his first film, also used a factory setting, with the workers as the collective protagonists (Figure 4.4). The **montage of attractions** now became the rapid and rhythmic cutting together of shots, startling in their visual contrasts, physical in their impact. Although all of the elements of Eisenstein's mature silent work are present, traces of the kind of theater in which he had been working account for some excesses and discordances. The "circus" elements—caricatures, gross symbolism, and exaggerated action—although striking in themselves, fit rather strangely into the prevailing naturalism. On the other hand, there is a documentary-like looseness of structure that makes the film more successful within its sequences than it is as a whole. *Battleship Potemkin* (1925) advanced on the first work by stripping away some of the flamboyance and disciplining the fertility of imagination. Built on a tight and firm dramatic line, its five sequences proceed with the cumulative power of the acts of classical tragedy.

Both films make essentially the same ideological points. Although *Potemkin* deals with the mutiny of the crew of an armored cruiser in the abortive 1905 Revolution, its officers are equivalent to the capitalists of *Strike;* its White Guards and Cossacks, who cut down the populace on the Odessa Steps, are like the army and police of the preceding film. In both films, the actions of the ruling class are arrogant and deceitful and lead to slaughter. The sailors and workers are simple and loyal to each other; except for their proletarian leaders, they are naive in the ways of the world. Incapable of evil unless duped into it by the authorities, they resort to violence only to counter unendurable oppression. The working classes are portrayed as the most productive resource of the nation and its only

FIGURE 4.4   *Strike* ★ Soviet Union, 1925, Sergei Eisenstein.

democratic force. A version of the desired dictatorship of the proletariat is offered in these two films. A recurrent image shows the revolutionary leaders haranguing the sailors or workers who then move together in a single group decision: "All for one, one for all!" the *Potemkin* titles shout.

The "hero" of both films is the masses—played by people who would have lived through situations much like those portrayed. In both cases, an epic scale of action is based on real or composite events. The viewpoint is broadly social-political and there is little de-lineation of characters except as types. Both films were shot on location rather than in stu-dios; in the case of *Potemkin,* Odessa was the actual place of some of the incidents portrayed. Eisenstein seized on and made full use of the accidents of setting—in *Strike,* the stairway tier of the workers' tenements; in *Potemkin,* the architectural characteristics of Odessa, a morning mist on the water, the stone lions, and the like. His play with mass, line, and movement is that of a dynamic painter; his handling of crowds is quite without peer. Always Eisenstein works through the kinetic. But, given the amount of movement within the frame and the rapidity of cutting, there is little moving camera. Instead there are an ex-traordinary number and variety of camera setups, as would be required by his kind of edit-ing. At moments of climactic action some of the shots are as short as two frames, and their content is frequently horrifying: a Cossack's saber slashing downward (Figure 4.5a), a woman's spectacles broken and her face bloodied (Figure 4.5b). Through an intended physiological response, Eisenstein aimed to bring his viewers to a political attitude. Close-

FIGURE 4.5a–d   *Battleship Potemkin* ★ Soviet Union, 1925, Sergei Eisenstein.

ups abound and there is a prominent use of what in literature would be called synecdoche, the parts representing a larger whole. In *Potemkin,* the maggoty meat, the doctor's pince-nez, which eventually dangles in the ropes (Figure 4.5c), the pounding pistons of the ship's engines (Figure 4.5d), and the final magnificent shot from below of its hull slicing through the water (Figure 4.6) all serve this function.

October (or *Ten Days That Shook the World,* 1928) marks the height of Eisenstein's "intellectual montage," but it lacks the passion and coherence of *Battleship Potemkin*—at least the versions of it that appear in the West. Like Griffith's *Intolerance,* in comparison to *The Birth of a Nation, October,* although in some respects Eisenstein's ultimate achievement, is on a canvas so large that the monumental conception remains only partially realized. *Old and New* (also known as *The General Line,* 1929) was his final silent film. In it, though his aesthetic sensibility and intelligence are as evident as ever, they seem essentially of the wrong kind for this account of Soviet farm life and collectivization.

Dovzhenko and Pudovkin adjusted to the conventions of socialist realism and continued a steady if scarcely distinguished output into the first decades of sound. Eisenstein could not adjust and was frequently the target of criticism from bureaucrats, critics, and other film makers. The problem was not that he was unwilling to serve the state in ways deemed

FIGURE 4.6 *Battleship Potemkin* ★ Soviet Union, 1925, Sergei Eisenstein.

socially useful, but that he was innately and supremely what he was accused of being—a formalist. His released sound films—*Alexander Nevsky* (1938) and *Ivan the Terrible,* Part I (1944), Part II (1958)—great though they are, are few. He spent much of the last fifteen years of his life teaching and writing. It may be that his theoretical writings, like George Bernard Shaw's prefaces to his plays, will retain a value beyond some of the creative work that grew out of them. In any event, Eisenstein's films and theories marked an enormous advance in a conscious and articulated understanding of how the cinema works as a means of communication—as a kind of language and as a form of art. Montage was the key concept.

Montage: Theory and Practice

The word **montage** was borrowed from the French; *monter* simply means to mount or assemble. For the Soviet film makers, however, this assembling and mounting through editing became the ultimate creative act. Although they had learned from Griffith and were nudged into the most economic use of the shot by the shortage of raw stock, their practical experiments, published theories, and finally the great works of Soviet silent film led them to a kind and level of accomplishment that has served to instruct film creators and critics ever since. Eisenstein and Pudovkin, friendly rivals as film makers, were also principal spokesmen in a running debate about the proper uses of montage. They agreed on the fundamental importance of editing, but for Pudovkin the cut was linkage, a joining of shots for the gradual accumulation of narrative meaning—the unfolding of a story. For Eisenstein its function was to achieve shock, the banging together of contrasting shots in a way that would force the audience into an understanding greater than the sum and different from any one of its parts. Eisenstein took particular satisfaction in what he regarded as the similarity of this process to the thesis-antithesis-synthesis of Hegelian dialectic. The argument is important as well as interesting, and worth pursuing through the words of the adversaries.

In *Film Technique,* Pudovkin, after acknowledging his indebtedness to Kuleshov and the importance of the concept of montage to Soviet film makers, writes:

> Kuleshov maintained that the material in film-work consists of pieces of film, and that the composition method is their joining together in a particular, creatively discovered order. He maintained that film-art does not begin when the artists act and the various scenes are shot— this is only the preparation of the material. Film-art begins from the moment when the director begins to combine and join together the various pieces of film. By joining them in various combinations, in different orders, he obtains differing results.[4]

Pudovkin continues by describing two more of the practical experiments (like the one with the couple, the steps, and the White House) that Kuleshov and his students supposedly carried out to test their theories.

The first involves three short strips of film. On one is the image of a smiling face, on another a hand pointing a revolver, on the third a frightened face. Pudovkin observes that if the shots are assembled in that order the impression we get is that the second man is facing the revolver and that he is a coward. If the order is reversed—frightened face, revolver, smiling face—the impression we get is that the man facing the revolver is very brave. Thus the meaning of precisely the same images is altered, even reversed, by changing their order.

In the second experiment recalled by Pudovkin he and Kuleshov selected some close-ups of the Russian actor Ivan Mozhukhin. They were static, neutral shots of Mozhukhin's face expressing no particular emotion. Those shots were then intercut with closeups of other material. First was a bowl of soup on a table; it seemed quite obvious that Mozhukhin was looking at the soup. Then the actor's face was followed by shots showing a coffin in which lay a dead woman. In the third instance the face was followed by a shot of a little girl playing with a funny toy bear. When the three combinations were shown without explanation to an audience, they raved about Mozhukhin's acting! They pointed out the heavy pensiveness of the mood created as he regarded the forgotten bowl of soup, the deep grief expressed as he looked at the dead woman, and the light, happy smile that played across his features as he gazed at the little girl. In all three cases, according to Pudovkin, Mozhukhin's facial expression had been virtually the same, and expressing very little at that.

Pudovkin concludes his recounting of these experiments with an additional observation:

> The combination of various pieces in one or another order is not sufficient. It is necessary to be able to control and manipulate the length of these pieces, because the combination of pieces of varying length is effective in the same way as the combination of sounds of various length in music, by creating the rhythm of the film and by means of their varying effect on the audience. Quick, short pieces rouse excitement, while long pieces have a soothing effect.[5]

[4] Pudovkin, *Film Technique,* pp. 138–139.

[5] Pudovkin, *Film Technique,* pp. 139–141.

In other words Pudovkin offers a sort of formula: Film creation equals (1) what is in the shots, (2) the order in which they appear, and (3) how long each is held on the screen. "To be able to find the requisite order of shots or pieces and the rhythm necessary for their combination," he summarizes, "that is the chief task of the director's art. This art we call *montage*—or constructive editing. It is only with the help of *montage* that I am able to solve problems of such complexity as the work on the artists' acting."[6]

Note the final emphasis given to performance. Unlike Eisenstein's silent films Pudovkin's make heavy use of professional actors and contain some superb characterizations. He portrays the awakening of revolutionary consciousness through the microcosm of individual experience more than through the action of the masses—for example, Vera Baranovskaya as the title character in *Mother* and Ivan Chuvelyov as the peasant lad in *The End of St. Petersburg.* Still, Pudovkin regards actors as "plastic material" not unlike any objects that might be photographed. They move and gesture, stare and weep, but for Pudovkin the film "performance" is created by the director cutting together strips of celluloid registering these actions. As might be expected, this is a position that horrifies and infuriates actors.

Pudovkin began the "Introduction to the German Edition" of *Film Technique* with: "The foundation of film art is *editing.*" Eisenstein, in an essay in *Film Form,* echoes Pudovkin: "To determine the nature of montage is to solve the specific problem of cinema." He goes on to explain:

> The earliest conscious film makers, and our first film theoreticians, regarded montage as a means of description by placing single shots one after the other like building-blocks. The movement within these building-block shots, and the consequent length of the component pieces, was then considered as rhythm.[7]

That was precisely what Pudovkin had written, as Eisenstein acknowledges with what is perhaps a feigned superiority of disbelief and an implied distinction between the theorist and the artist: "According to this definition, shared even by Pudovkin as a theoretician, montage is the means of *unrolling* an idea with the help of single shots: the 'epic' principle." (*Epic* is here used in the classical sense—narrative as opposed to dramatic.) In Eisenstein's opinion, however, "montage is an idea that arises from the collision of independent shots—shots even opposite to one another: the 'dramatic' principle."[8]

Elsewhere, in an essay in the companion volume, *The Film Sense,* Eisenstein continues the argument and expands on his own position. As he sees the Soviet films, they are "faced with the task of presenting not only a narrative that is *logically connected* but also one that contains a *maximum of emotion and stimulating power.* Montage is a mighty aid to the resolution of this task," he asserts. Eisenstein goes on to ask rhetorically, "Why do we use montage at all?"

> Even the most fanatical opponent of montage will agree that it is not merely because the film strip at our disposal is not of infinite length, and consequently, being condemned to working with pieces of restricted lengths, we have to stick one piece of it on to another occasionally.
>   The 'leftists' of montage saw it from the opposite extreme. While playing with pieces of film, they discovered a certain property in the toy which kept them astonished for a number

---

[6] Pudovkin, *Film Technique,* p. 141.

[7] Sergei M. Eisenstein, *Film Form,* edited and translated by Jay Leyda (New York: Harcourt Brace, 1949), p. 48.

[8] Eisenstein, *Film Form,* p. 49.

of years. This property consisted in the fact *that two film pieces of any kind, placed together, inevitably combine into a new concept, a new quality, arising out of that juxtaposition.*

This is not in the least a circumstance peculiar to the cinema, but is a phenomenon invariably met with in all cases where we have to deal with juxtaposition of two facts, two phenomena, two objects. We are accustomed to make, almost automatically, a definite and obvious deductive generalization when any separate objects are placed before us side by side. For example, take a grave, juxtaposed with a woman in mourning weeping beside it, and scarcely anybody will fail to jump to the conclusion: a widow. It is precisely on this feature of our perception that the following miniature story by Ambrose Bierce bases its effect. It is from his Fantastic Fables and is entitled "The Inconsolable Widow":

"A woman in widow's weeds was weeping upon a grave.

'Console yourself, madame,' said a Sympathetic Stranger. 'Heaven's mercies are infinite. There is another man somewhere, besides your husband, with whom you can still be happy.'

'There was,' she sobbed—'there was, but this is his grave.' "[9]

It is neatly coincidental that Pudovkin referred to a coffin in the experiment with the actor Mozhukhin. Both Eisenstein and Pudovkin are suggesting how the meaning of an action can be changed into something other than the actual or original through associative montage. But Pudovkin's addition of a coffin merely makes the actor's face seem sad when it was not necessarily. The attraction of Bierce's anecdote for Eisenstein is clearly that the normal additive principle is replaced by a combination of the unexpected, opposites in a sense, and the "widow" becomes an adulteress.

Eisenstein's reference to an obscure piece of American literature to illustrate his conception, rather than a practical experiment with several pieces of film, represents fairly the difference between his critical method and that of Pudovkin. Eisenstein explored the arts of other cultures to show that montage as he understood it existed quite separately from film and had existed long before film appeared. His analyses of the shooting-script-like ordering of images found in passages from the poems of Pushkin and the novels of Dickens offer a contribution to literary criticism as well as provocative analogues for those studying film. For Eisenstein the form and sense of film aesthetic extended into a total philosophical view of the world. For Pudovkin the insights montage provided were carefully restricted to film technique and film acting.

In practice the argument between the two is happily muddled by some of the best examples of Eisensteinian shock montage appearing in films of Pudovkin and by Eisenstein necessarily having to resort to Pudovkinian narrative to hold together the brief pyrotechnical bursts of collision. Whether as linkage or juxtaposition, one result of this extreme fragmentation of the scene was that both film makers could use nonactors to a degree that more sustained takes would not allow. Any embarrassed self-consciousness could be stripped away and the usable moments selected and combined with other visual materials—like the actor Mozhukhin with soup, coffin, and child—to give the illusion of a performance that in fact never occurred. This new possibility led to theories of **typage,** of choosing people who looked the part regardless of their thespian skills.

Another characteristic of Soviet film technique was that the naturalistic materials of "real people" (as opposed to actors) and "actual locations" (in contrast to studio interiors or back lots) were subjected to an extreme degree of highly conscious manipulation

[9] Sergei M. Eisenstein, *The Film Sense,* edited and translated by Jay Leyda (New York: Harcourt Brace, 1942), pp. 4–5.

through editing. Although the style is radically different from that of the Germans, in their own ways the Soviet films are just as stylized. Finally, in order to construct their intricate mosaics from small pieces of the total action, the Soviets—like the Germans and unlike Griffith—relied on highly detailed scripts and preplanning. Eisenstein sketched virtually all of his shots in advance; a substantial portion of Pudovkin's *Film Technique* is devoted to a method of precise script construction.

Unlike the films of any nation that had preceded them, however, all the Soviet films had social-political purposes and government sponsorship. Most of them interpreted the revolution in ways designed to improve the understanding and win the loyalty of the Soviet people. When *Battleship Potemkin* first went out into the world as a revolutionary emissary—feared and hated by reactionaries and philistines, elaborately praised by liberals and aesthetes—its success was as much a surprise to the Soviets as to anyone. That many of the Soviet silent films are universal and enduring works of art as well as being indoctrinational is a tribute to the sincere enthusiasm the film makers felt for the gigantic social experiment of which they were part.

Although the significance of this body of work in the history of film is enormous, giving the name **Russian formalism** to a style built on the principle of montage editing, specific applications of its themes and techniques, unlike those of the Germans, were limited in the capitalist countries. Soon the formal concerns and innovations of the left wing would become unacceptable in the Soviet Union itself. Perhaps the one clear and direct link between Soviet silent films and films elsewhere is with the British social documentaries of the 1930s, which were state supported for purposes of broad citizenship education and which indulged in their own experimentation with form—especially the joining of sound and image.

In the fictional film the arrival of sound largely reduced the use of montage to brief transitional sequences—of spinning locomotive wheels superimposed over a succession of billboards as the young opera star progresses toward fame and heartbreak, or of crowded beaches, golfers, and children eating watermelon to signal summer. To be sure, and for better or worse, every television commercial builds on the kinds of persuasiveness the Soviets discovered lay in the combination of short strips of film. But the body of Soviet silent cinema stands as a statement of the loftier purposes a theory of montage may serve.

Films of the Period

1925
Battleship Potemkin (Bronenosets Potyomkin) (Sergei Eisenstein)
Chess Fever (Shakhmatnaya Goryachka) (Boris Barnet)
Strike (Stachka) (Sergei Eisenstein)

1926
The Cloak (Shinel) (Grigori Kozintsev and Leonid Trauberg)
Mother (Mat) (V. I. Pudovkin)

1927
Bed and Sofa (Tretya meshchanskaya) (Abram Room)

The End of St. Petersburg (Konets Sankt-Peterburga) (V. I. Pudovkin)
The Fall of the Romanov Dynasty (Padeniye dinastij Romanovykh) (Esfir Shub)
Girl with the Hatbox (Derushka Kozobkoj) Boris Barnet)

1928
The Man with a Movie Camera (Chelovek s kinoapparatom) (Dziga Vertov)
October/Ten Days That Shook the World (Oktyabr) (Sergei Eisenstein)
Storm over Asia (Potomok Chingis-Khana) (V. I. Pudovkin)
Zvenigora (Alexander Dovzhenko)

1929
Arsenal (Alexander Dovzhenko)
Fragment of an Empire (Oblomok imperij)
  (Friedrich Ermler)
The New Babylon (Novyj Vavilon) (Grigori
  Kozintsev and Leonid Trauberg)

Old and New/The General Line (Staroye inovoye)
  (Sergei Eisenstein)
Turksib (Victor Turin)

1930
Earth (Zemlya) (Alexandra Dovzhenko)

Books on the Period

Attwood, Lynne, ed. *Red Women on the Silver Screen: Soviet Women and Cinema from the Beginning to the End of the Communist Era.* San Francisco: Pandora Press, 1993.

Gillespie, David. *Russian Cinema.* Essex: Pearson, 2002.

Gillespie, David. *Early Soviet Cinema: Innovation, Ideology and Propaganda.* London: Wallflower Press, 2001.

Kenez, Peter. *Cinema and Soviet Society: From the Revolution to the Death of Stalin.* London: I. B. Tauris, 2001.

Leyda, Jay. *Kino: A History of the Russian and Soviet Film.* Princeton, NJ: Princeton University Press, 1983.

McReynolds, Louise, and Joan Neuberger, eds. *Imitations of Life: Two Centuries of Melodrama in Russia.* Durham, NC: Duke University Press, 2002.

Shlapentokh, Dmitri, and Vladimir Shlapentokh. *Soviet Cinematography, 1918–1991: Ideological Conflict and Social Reality.* New York: Aldine de Gruyter, 1993.

Taylor, Richard. *Film Propaganda: Soviet Russia and Nazi Germany.* London: I. B. Tauris, 1998.

Taylor, Richard, ed. *The BFI Companion to Eastern European and Russian Cinema.* London: British Film Institute, 2001.

Tsivian, Yuri, and Richard Taylor, eds. *Early Cinema in Russia and Its Cultural Reception.* New York: Routledge, 1994.

Tsivian, Yuri, and Paolo Cherchi Usai. *Silent Witnesses: Russian Films, 1908–1919.* London: British Film Institute, 1990.

Youngblood, Denise J. *The Magic Mirror: Moviemaking in Russia, 1908–1918.* Madison: University of Wisconsin Press, 1999. CD-Rom

Tsivian, Yuri, and Barry Schneider. *Immaterial Bodies: A Cultural Analysis of Early Russian Films.* Annenberg Communications Institute, 2001.

CD-Rom

Tsivian, Yuri, and Barry Schneider. *Immaterial Bodies: A Cultural Analysis of Early Russian Films.* Annenberg Communications Institute, 2001.

5

Hollywood
in the Twenties

★ ★ ★ ★

1919–1929

Movies Become Big Business

The 1920s were characterized by intense competition among former independent companies that had become the new major studios. Old firms merged and disappeared; not one member of the Motion Picture Patents Company, with which the independents had competed between 1908 and 1915, survived.

In 1924 Metro-Goldwyn-Mayer was put together by Marcus Loew—president of Loew's, Inc., which had large theater holdings. Added to Metro Pictures Corporation (Loew's small production company) were the Goldwyn Picture Corporation and the Louis B. Mayer Pictures Corporation. Samuel Goldwyn had already left the Goldwyn Picture Corporation to become an independent producer; Mayer joined the newly created firm as studio head, beginning a reign that would last nearly thirty years. Also prominent were Universal (Carl Laemmle's outfit), Warner Brothers (Harry, Jack, Sam, and Albert), Paramount (which Adolph Zukor had brought along out of Famous Players-[Jesse] Lasky), Columbia (Jack and Harry Cohn), United Artists (Chaplin, Fairbanks, Pickford, Griffith), and the (William) Fox Film Corporation. The competition among these firms led to the need for increased capital, which was used to sign up stars, expand distribution and exhibition outlets, and buy out rivals. Public stock was issued, giving Wall Street a voice that would grow louder over the years.

The earlier economic battles had been fought largely in the field of production as the Motion Picture Patents Company trust attempted to stem the competition of the independents. During the first years after World War I, control of distribution was the major goal. National distribution became increasingly centralized and dominated by the major producing companies. The old "states' rights" franchise system, under which *The Birth of a Nation* and many of the first features had been distributed, faded away. For ultimate dom-

ination of the screen and long-term revenues, the struggle extended inevitably to ownership of the theaters themselves. There finally developed a pattern known as "vertical control," which lasted until it was outlawed by the federal courts in 1948. Under vertical
control a few huge firms (eventually the roster became fixed at eight) produced, distributed, and exhibited their own films.

By the mid-1920s the fight for control of exhibition was being waged by three giants, which looked as though they might divide the whole pie, either forcing the other companies out or making them sit at the table according to strict rules of etiquette. In 1919
Paramount had floated a $10 million issue of preferred stock, marking the beginning of the
new phase. By 1921 that company was in virtual control of five hundred key theaters in
the United States and first-run theaters in major cities around the world (Figure 5.1). By
the end of the 1920s Adolph Zukor had built up the most formidable combination in the

FIGURE 5.1   Advertisement for the
opening of the Paramount Theatre, New
York City, in 1926.

industry: Paramount had the stars, the production outfit, the distribution channels, and control of two thousand theaters.

First National, the next largest production-distribution firm, had been formed by a group of theater chains to get access to the product on their own terms. The third contestant was Loew's, Inc., the vast firm of which Metro-Goldwyn-Mayer, the production-distribution arm, was only one part. Within a few years nearly all the major and first-run houses in the United States and Canada had been acquired by Paramount, Loew's, or the large circuits affiliated with the First National group. Fox and Universal also had theater outlets, but on a lesser scale.

By 1927 some four hundred to five hundred feature films a year were being produced. Ideally, each of the large companies would release no fewer than fifty-two a year, permitting a weekly change of program for its own theaters. Distribution involved close to six hundred exchanges (that is, regional offices handling prints of the films) in forty-six key American cities. Approximately twenty thousand theaters in the country were attended by some eighty million customers a week. The center of return on investment and of ultimate control was where distribution and exhibition were headquartered: New York City, not Hollywood. Any would-be new independents were effectively kept out of this closed system. If they wanted to produce, the screens weren't available to them; if they wanted to exhibit, they couldn't get access to films.

The emphasis on exhibition made the 1920s the great decade of motion-picture theater construction. The "movie palaces"—most of which have been torn down, divided into smaller theaters, or converted to other uses—stem from that era (Figure 5.2). The Capitol Theatre in New York City, for example, was built in 1919 and seated 5,300. *Photoplay* magazine wrote of it: "The mezzanine floor looks as if it had been designed for eight-day bicycle races." Grauman's Egyptian and Chinese Theatres in Hollywood along with large and ornate New York City theaters, including the fabled Roxy, were all part of this extraordinary architectural tradition.

If the appeal of the films didn't always measure up to their surroundings, at least the increasing expensiveness of production kept pace with the new lavishness of presentation. Extravagance reigned, and the notion of spending money to make money was unquestioningly accepted. Salaries soared for directors, writers, and especially stars. The epic *Birth of a Nation* had cost around $100,000 in 1915; *Ben-Hur* cost $6 million a decade later. By the end of the 1920s the average production expenditure on features was up to $200,000. The studios' steady incomes, however, came from the "program" or **"B" movies**—unlike today, when television has taken over that kind of production, and theatrical features must offer something that seems special in order to attract an audience.

Ascendancy of the Director

With such expenditures, and attendant financial concern, by the mid-1920s the director had been replaced by the production supervisor as the person in charge of film making. The production supervisor made many of the artistic decisions as well as all of the business ones. Developing out of the pattern first established by Thomas Ince, this function was most brilliantly exercised by the legendary boy wonder at M-G-M: Irving Thalberg, model for the hero of F. Scott Fitzgerald's uncompleted novel *The Last Tycoon.* Sometimes called

FIGURE 5.2 Rialto Theatre, Joliet, Illinois.

production chief, head of studio, or vice-president in charge of production, this executive oversaw a whole program of pictures, deciding which ideas or literary and dramatic "properties" were to be developed into scripts, then casting players and assigning directors. With the cost and complexity of sound, added at the end of the 1920s, the power of this position would become even more complete than in silent days. Film makers such as D. W. Griffith and Erich von Stroheim were temperamentally incapable of working within this system and eventually were discarded by it. Griffith directed two sound films; von Stroheim directed one. Directors mostly became "glorified foremen" and, with assembly-line specialization, were as much typecast as were the players. There were directors of westerns, comedies, romances, and so on, with second-rank directors hired to imitate the work of first-rank ones. Nonetheless, certain directors stand out as having battled for control over their work and their image. Griffith played a pivotal role in this struggle. Through a variety of strategies—from placing his initials on all of the intertitles of his films, to taking advertisements in newspapers that trumpeted his achievements, to creating his own studio—Griffith devoted himself to the tasks of imposing his vision on his movies and his name on the lips of the moviegoing public.

   Another dominating figure, **Cecil B. DeMille,** has often been disregarded or disapproved of by critics and historians on grounds that his films are generally superficial and frequently meretricious, that they add nothing to film art. In recent years, a reevaluation has occurred in some quarters, based on the visual (as opposed to intellectual) merits of his films. In either case, no one can deny their enormous success. Unparalleled as a show-man, publicist, and businessman, DeMille also had a unique ability to move with the times. Although the artist in him may have been uncertain, the social psychologist was uncannily accurate in his intuitions. By examining DeMille's invariably successful pictures, today's social historians can infer much about the cultural climate of the American 1920s. To some extent those films may have affected that climate.

DeMille's father and mother were of the theater; his brother was the playwright William C. DeMille. Cecil himself had been associated with David Belasco, the "Dean of the American Stage." DeMille's initial film effort, *The Squaw Man* (1914), was one of the earliest features and among the first films to be made in Hollywood; it established at the outset his ability to anticipate trends in the industry. From 1915 to 1924 he turned out a rapid succession of widely popular films aimed at middle-class audiences and reflecting postwar changes in manners and morals, the best of which is probably *The Cheat.* Released in 1915, *The Cheat* tells the story of society matron Edith Hardy and her relationship with an Asian man named Tori (a role subtly performed by the acclaimed Japanese actor Sessue Hayakawa). Despite Hayakawa's nuanced and underplayed performance, however, the movie's unsympathetic portrayal of his character led to protests by the Japanese American community; as a result, Tori's nationality was changed to Burmese.

In addition to its controversial treatment of ethnicity, *The Cheat* is notable for its influential technical innovations in editing and lighting. DeMille pioneered a subjective editing style in a scene between Edith and her husband, Richard, by cross-cutting between Edith and Tori, who, although miles away, dominates her thoughts as she converses with her husband. In addition, working with his talented art director, Wilfred Buckland, DeMille employed a distinctive lighting style in *The Cheat,* which is also featured in other films he directed in these early years. Widely known at the time as *Rembrandt lighting* or *Lasky lighting* (after the name of DeMille's studio), this technique, like Rembrandt's paintings, features large areas of shadow punctuated by brightly illuminated points of dramatic interest. In scenes that feature this style, most of the frame remains dark while intense spotlights highlight the main actors and their immediate surroundings (Figure 5.3). A striking example of this lighting technique occurs in the scene in *The Cheat* in which Edith shoots her lover. As Tori collapses against a vividly lit Japanese screen, we watch from the other side as his blood smears the screen; meanwhile the rest of the frame is shrouded in darkness.

As the titles of some of DeMille's other productions suggest, this was indeed the roaring twenties: *Old Wives for New* (1918); *Don't Change Your Husband, For Better or Worse, Male and Female* (all 1919); *Why Change Your Wife? Something to Think About* (both 1920); *Forbidden Fruit, The Affairs of Anatol, Fool's Paradise* (all 1921); *Saturday Night, Manslaughter* (both 1922); and *Adam's Rib* (1923). These were promoted as "typical DeMille productions—audacious, glittering, intriguing, superlatively elegant and quite without heart." Following these essays on contemporary mores (they were called the "divorce comedies"), a shift began to occur in DeMille's preoccupations. *The Ten Commandments* (1923) had a long biblical prologue to a modern story, and *The King of Kings* (1927) was the first full work of the kind with which his name would subsequently become associated: religiosity along with sex and spectacle (Figure 5.4).

If DeMille's films of the 1920s were largely trivial in content, they had considerable influence on the craft of motion-picture making and on the popular culture of the United States at large. Although he made movies that were "production-conscious" (he was painstaking with details—clothes, makeup, lighting, properties, and sets), he also offered styles of in-

FIGURE 5.3 *The Cheat* ★ United States, 1915, Cecil B. DeMille; Sessue Hayakawa and Fannie Ward.

terior decoration and clothing fashions for imitation. He is often given credit for inaugurating the tendency of American bathrooms to aspire to the sumptuousness of throne rooms. Theatrical in his direction, he rarely used camera or cutting obtrusively, except for **special effects**—the parting of the Red Sea, for example. His historical spectacles are like a series of separate illustrations brought to life. The performances tend to be stiff, broad, and simple.

It must be conceded, however, that DeMille is one of a very few directors who have gotten their names onto marquees. People went to see a "DeMille picture." He achieved this star status partly from the size and dazzle of his productions, but also from a vigorous publicizing of his own personality. It is to DeMille that we owe the assumption that you could tell a motion picture director by his open-neck shirt, jodphurs, boots, and megaphone. Also, people went partly out of curiosity to see what all the other people were seeing. The consistency of DeMille's box-office record remains remarkable: Not one of his films lost money. When DeMille died, the prop Ten Commandments tablet used in his second film of that title was placed on a kind of altar under his lighted portrait in the Paramount commissary. The color of the tablet was gold.

Erich von Stroheim resembled DeMille in flamboyance, meticulousness with details, and extravagance. But von Stroheim could not put those qualities to consistent commercial use. The iron will, artistic integrity, and rebelliousness for which he is respected by those who admire his films kept him from seeking out what the public wanted. Instead,

FIGURE 5.4   *The King of Kings*   ★   United States, 1927, Cecil B. DeMille; H. B. Warner as Christ.

he gave audiences the world as he saw it—in a style notable for scathing naturalism laced with irony—in place of the usual coating of reality covering a sentimental center.

Of the eight films von Stroheim made between 1918 and the end of his directorial career in 1928, *Greed* (1925) is unquestionably the masterpiece (Figure 5.5). It remains one of the most impressive films in the total history of the screen. The legend surrounding it contains omens pointing toward the end of his career as a director and his subsequent canonization: its staggering cost; its length of forty-five reels (over seven hours) cut to a conventional ten; von Stroheim's disavowal of the released version; and the power that remains in spite of the mutilation. Controversy about the film can still be heard, and there are still unshakable hopes and occasional rumors that a copy of the complete version may somehow have survived.

Today most would agree that a handful of his films (*Foolish Wives*, 1922; *The Merry Widow*, 1925; *The Wedding March*, 1928; and *Greed*) are original and extraordinary, powerful in a way and to a degree unlike anyone else's work. His camera-editing style rested on the long take/long shot not much in vogue during the ascendancy of montage, with its stress on fast cutting and closeups. The sort of spatial-temporal coherence and realism represented by von Stroheim's style would later become a dominant aesthetic tendency.

FIGURE 5.5 *Greed* ★ United States, 1925, Erich von Stroheim; Zasu Pitts and Gibson Gowland, center.

The mirror von Stroheim held up to nature not only reflected warts and all but also emphasized the warts—the venality, selfishness, and perversity present in most of us. Sexuality is usually interwoven with money, station, or power in an uncompromisingly unpalatable view of life. Decadence and depravity are ubiquitous. In *Foolish Wives,* "Count" Wladislas Karamzin, played by Stroheim—"the man you love to hate"—evidently makes his way in the world through sexual enterprises based on seduction, blackmail, and the like. Although he seems to be involved with five women, there is no suggestion of love in any of these relationships. This character, whom von Stroheim had created in his first film, *Blind Husbands* (1919), appears in intermittent variation throughout his work—including his last released film, *Queen Kelly* (1928). Although he doesn't appear in *Greed,* the consistent point is made most explicit as a romantic attachment gradually deteriorates into a single-minded pursuit of gold.

For the audacity of his themes, as well as for his arrogance and financial disinterest, von Stroheim was denied access to the tools of his art. His directorial career ended about the same time as that of D. W. Griffith, for whom he had first worked in film. The last decades of von Stroheim's life, like Griffith's, were spent in semiretirement outside the film industry.

Unlike Griffith and von Stroheim, **Ernst Lubitsch,** whose German films were discussed in Chapter Three, adapted well to the changing realities of the Hollywood industry, becoming at one point head of production at the mammoth Paramount Studio. Lubitsch succeeded, in part, by attaching himself to tried-and-true genres. His German films made within the romantic-historical tradition (*Passion/Madame du Barry* and *Deception/Anna Boleyn*) were discussed in Chapter 3. They were very popular in the United States and Lubitsch followed them here in 1922. But neither those films nor his earlier training as an actor in Max Reinhardt's company foreshadowed the kind of film Lubitsch would turn to and make peculiarly his own. After studying contemporary American production, Lubitsch moved into comedy and light drama of the sort DeMille was making so successfully. Before the end of the decade he had outstripped DeMille, in quality at least, while DeMille had moved to spectacles not unlike those Lubitsch had made earlier. But he is most amazing for his command of the medium: the subtlety and flexibility with which he was able to use silent film to communicate nuances of a situation, and later his experimental leadership in sound.

Though differences of style and outlook mask the similarities, the films of Lubitsch are like those of von Stroheim in one important respect: They are about sex and money. To increase his freedom for comment, and to add a bit of glamor and suavity, Lubitsch, like von Stroheim, tended to set his plots against European backgrounds. But in Lubitsch's films, sexual intrigue is merely frivolity engaged in by the wealthy to occupy their leisure time. With few exceptions his American pictures are comedies of manners, peopled entirely with the well-bred, urbane upper classes. He delineates their fads and foibles with a Viennese charm and worldliness that made them seem novel, fascinating, and a bit naughty to American audiences. His sophisticated humor came to be well known as "the Lubitsch touch." Of his American silent films, *The Marriage Circle* (Figure 5.6a), *Forbidden Paradise* (both 1924), and *Lady Windermere's Fan* (1925) (Figure 5.6b) have best retained their charm.

Wall Street's growing influence in Hollywood, along with other factors, gradually shut down opportunities for women in the movie business. But during the 1920s, the feminine presence was still pervasive—especially in the scriptwriting arena. The writer Frances Marion partnered with the much-beloved star Mary Pickford to create a series of box-office smashes. June Mathis, who discovered Rudolph Valentino, briefly served as head of the M-G-M script department and headed up one of its production units as well.

FIGURE 5.6a and b   a. *The Marriage Circle* ★ United States, 1924, Ernst Lubitsch; Adolph Menjou and Marie Prevost; b. *Lady Windermere's Fan* ★ United States, 1925, Ernst Lubisch; May McAvoy.

Another screenwriter, Elinor Glyn, wrote and coproduced *It* (1927), which popularized the term *it* as a euphemism for "sex appeal."

Popular Genres

Perhaps more than the business acumen of the moguls or the technical resources of the big studios, more than the attractiveness of the stars and the skills of the directors and screenwriters, it is the popular genres that have most typified American film and given it its greatest strength and vitality. Until fairly recently, critics tended to discount or ignore the importance of genres. A case could be made, however, that the conventions of genre—fixed yet capable of infinite variation—have supported and given strength to the work of many of the finest American scriptwriters and directors (as Shakespeare, in Elizabethan England, had built on the conventional revenge tragedy introduced by Thomas Kyd). At the same time it must be acknowledged that genres bear a complex relation to the society that produces them, expressing the dreams, anxieties, and ambivalences of a given era.

During the 1920s all the major types of American film were present except, of course, the musical, which required sound. The **western** embodied some of the United States's most resonant national myths: the conception of land as private property and the rationalization of the conquest of indigenous peoples by the European settlers. The genre started at least with *The Great Train Robbery* (1903) and matured most notably in the films produced by Thomas Ince and starring William S. Hart (for example, *The Gun Fighter* and *The Aryan,* both 1916). In the 1920s the epic western was added to the line: *The Last of the Mohicans* (1920), directed by Maurice Tourneur; *The Covered Wagon* (1923), directed by James Cruze; *The Iron Horse* (1924), directed by John Ford; and *The Vanishing American* (1925), directed by George B. Seitz. Hart continued to work until 1925 (*Tumbleweeds* was his last and probably finest film) (Figure 5.7) and was succeeded in popularity by Tom Mix, Buck Jones, Tim McCoy, Hoot Gibson, Ken Maynard, and some lesser stars.

When the **comedy** genre moved from one- and two-reelers to include features, the 1920s became "Comedy's Greatest Era," as James Agee called it in a famous essay on the subject. The wonderful clowns—Charles Chaplin, Buster Keaton, Harold Lloyd, and Harry Langdon—created their masterworks during that decade. They confirmed and advanced the early discoveries and pioneering insights of Mack Sennett, making silent film comedy an art form offering timeless and universal pleasure.

The features included Chaplin's *The Kid* (1921) and *The Gold Rush* (1925) (Figure 5.8a); Keaton's *The Navigator* (1924) and *The General* (1927) (Figure 5.8b); Lloyd's *Grandma's Boy* (1922) (Figure 5.8c) and *Safety Last* (1923); and Langdon's *The Strong Man* (Figure 5.8d) and *Tramp, Tramp, Tramp* (both 1926). Along with the continuing shorts of Stan Laurel and Oliver Hardy, and others, these films gave American screen comedy an impetus that carried it through the 1940s and perhaps beyond.

If we include the work of Jerry Lewis, Woody Allen, and Mel Brooks within that tradition, and maybe of Bill Murray and Jim Carrey as well, the influence of the comedies of the 1920s has extended to the present. Although the introduction of sound required extreme modifications of style and introduced a new group of comics, the comedy, along with the western, the gangster film, and the musical, remains among the most distinctive, indigenous, and important American contributions to film forms.

FIGURE 5.7   *Tumbleweeds* ★ United States, 1925, King Baggot; William S. Hart.

The **problem picture,** dealing with social and moral concerns, had appeared among the first story films shortly after the turn of the twentieth century (for example, *The Ex-Convict,* 1905, and *The Eviction,* 1907). This has always been a significant genre and includes some of this nation's most substantial work. Often the problem pictures look at society from the vantage point of a new generation and deal with the alarms and discomforts caused by social change. A number of films attacked Bolshevism at home and abroad, revealing American uneasiness over the successful Soviet revolution. Other films dealt with strikes, usually portraying them as resulting from misunderstanding between management and labor, rarely acknowledging real economic causes. Director **Lois Weber,** working in collaboration with her scriptwriter husband, Phillips Smalley, created a number of noteworthy problem pictures during the 1910s and early 1920s, including *Where Are My Children* (1916), which deals with birth control; *The People vs. John Doe* (1916), on capital punishment; *The Blot* (1921) (Figure 5.9a), about the genteel poverty of college professors; and *A Chapter in Her Life* (1923), on Christian Scientism.

The overwhelming preponderance of "problems" considered in films of this genre had to do with morals and mores: the changing conception of marriage (*Too Wise Wives,* 1921 (Figure 5.9b); *Wine of Youth,* 1924; *Trial Marriage,* 1929); women's increased independence (*Daring Youth, For Ladies Only,* both 1927); youthful rebellion (*Flaming Youth,* 1923; *Our Dancing Daughters,* 1928); promiscuity (*Husbands for Rent,* 1927; *Breakfast at Sunrise,* 1927); bootleg debauchery (*The House of Youth,* 1924; *The Mad Whirl,* 1925),

FIGURE 5.8a–d a. *The Gold Rush,* The Oceana Roll ★ United States, 1925, Charlie Chaplin; Chaplin. b. *The General* ★ United States, 1927, Buster Keaton; Keaton. c. *Grandma's Boy* ★ United States, 1922, Fred C. Newmeyer; Harold Lloyd. d. *The Strong Man* ★ United States, 1926, Frank Capra; Harry Langdon.

FIGURE 5.9a and b a. *The Blot* ★ United States, 1921, Lois Weber; Philip Hubbard. b. *Too Wise Wives* ★ United States, 1921, Lois Weber; Louis Calhern and Claire Windsor.

and similar subjects. From the attempts of DeMille and others to treat the "jazz age," post-war morality, and the "modern generation" of the 1920s, there runs a more or less straight line to the Depression films of the 1930s.

In spite of a remark attributed to Samuel Goldwyn—"If you got a message, send it by Western Union"—the problem picture has been remarkably persistent in an industry presumably devoted to "escapist entertainment." This means, of course, that the problem picture has been good box office. Self-criticism and exposé form a strong thread that extends through American history beginning before Tom Paine and continuing past the "yellow journalism" of the 1920s to Sunday night's *60 Minutes* on CBS. Films in this tradition—even if frequently exploiting as well as examining problems—have remained significant in reflecting and changing an awareness of our culture.

War dramas were common before the 1920s but had only the old-fashioned wars for subjects and treated those from a historical perspective. Moviegoers of the 1920s had recently been through a world war, and the experience was influential to most of them. Although films about the war had been made during it, the "war is hell" prototypes were first offered in King Vidor's *The Big Parade* (1925) and Raoul Walsh's *What Price Glory?* (1926). A subspecies of the war dramas of the 1920s was the air-war cycle, including *The Lone Eagle* and *Wings* (both 1927); *The Legion of the Condemned* (1928); and *Lilac Time* (1928). The latter group suggests the impossibility of making an *anti*war film—at least along standard lines. The ultimate drama of war cannot be denied: life and death, bravery and fear, selflessness and leadership, comradeship and love; they are present even within the impersonal slaughter of modern warfare. War may be hell; but on film, war has always been highly dramatic.

Action and adventure—a category, if not exactly a genre—takes various forms, most of which appeared in the 1920s. Often the action-adventure films deal with a chase and pursuit, or with survival in some distant and colorful locale. There are adventures on the sea, under water, in the jungle (*Tarzan of the Apes* began the Tarzan series in 1918), in the mountains, in the desert, and in polar regions. Documentaries and semidocumentaries of the period appealed more factually to the same sort of interest—*Nanook of the North* (1922), *Grass* (1925), *Moana* (1926), and *Chang* (1927). Another kind of action-adventure of the 1920s (and 1930s) was the animal picture, with animal stars; Rin-Tin-Tin and Rex, "King of the Wild Horses," were successful enough to have their imitators. The actress Nell Shipman also produced, directed, and starred in a number of animal pictures during this era, including *Baree, Son of Kazan* (1917) and *Back to God's Country* (1919) (Figure 5.10). The scripts for Shipman's films frequently replaced the stalwart male rescuers of traditional melodrama with resourceful heroines who, when they don't rescue themselves, are saved by animals they have befriended.

If you think of action-adventure films of the 1920s, you might think first of the kind in which Douglas Fairbanks excelled. A star of considerable magnitude, his obvious attractions were a marvelous body, dazzling smile, acrobatic grace, and an ingeniously intricate way of moving about the world by scaling walls, sliding down draperies, leaping from roof to balcony and balcony to roof, and swinging on chandeliers. Those qualities and abilities, together with his enormous good cheer and easy superiority to the normal nagging concerns of the modern world, guaranteed the popular success of his films—*The Mark of Zorro* (1920), *The Three Musketeers* (1921), *Robin Hood* (1922) (Figure 5.11), *The Thief of Bagdad* (1924), *The Black Pirate* (1926), and others. As the titles of the Fairbanks films suggest, their action and adventure were usually set in a past time as well as a distant place; the improbable could be given freest reign in exotic settings.

FIGURE 5.10   *Back to God's Country* ⋆ United States, 1919, David M. Hartford; Nell Shipman and friend.

Another kind of historical film featured more **spectacle** than derring-do. *The Execution of Mary Queen of Scots* (1895) was the first of these, and it was Griffith who reached a level of spectacle—in *Intolerance* (1916)—that in some respects has never been equaled. DeMille, admitting his indebtedness to Griffith, took over the historical/biblical extravaganza with *The Ten Commandments* (1923) and *The King of Kings* (1927), and intermittently pursued his own special form of it until his last film, the second *Ten Commandments* (1956). Other especially noteworthy historical/religious spectacles of the 1920s were Griffith's *Orphans of the Storm* (1921), about the French Revolution, and Fred Niblo's *Ben-Hur* (1926) (Figure 5.12). *Variety*'s annual listing of all-time box-office champions has a preponderance of the spectacular in its upper echelons.

Finally, the period saw the flourishing of what have come to be known as **race movies.** Galvanized by their outrage at the depiction of black characters in *The Birth of a Nation,* African American entrepreneurs and film makers set out to create an alternative cinematic tradition, producing *Birth of a Race* in 1919 in response to Griffith's controversial epic. At the same time companies such as the Colored Players in Philadelphia and the Lincoln Motion Picture Company in Chicago released a series of films for African American audiences, including *The Trouper of Troup K* (1916) and *Scar of Shame* (1926) (Figure 5.13a). The most notable creator of these movies was **Oscar Micheaux,** who often worked as his own distributor and exhibitor as well as functioning as a writer, producer, and director, driving

FIGURE 5.11   *Robin Hood* ★ United States, 1922, Alan Dwan; Douglas Fairbanks, second from left.

prints of his films from town to town to show them in local venues. Two of his most widely admired productions are *Within Our Gates* (1920) (Figure 5.13b), a shocking story of incest, miscegenation, and attempted rape, featuring a climactic lynching sequence, and *Body and Soul* (1925), in which the distinguished actor Paul Robeson stars as an ex-convict posing as a clergyman.

Sound Arrives

The phrase *silent cinema* implies an absence of sound, but this was not the way in which movies were experienced by most audiences in the early days. Live lecturers often spoke to those who attended showings of actuality films and travelogues as the visuals unrolled. In Japan, commentators called ***benshi,*** who narrated the action and spoke the dialogue, were an integral part of the pleasure of moviegoing; and in Brazil, a popular form known as ***fitas cantatas*** involved filmed stage musicals lip-synched in theaters. In other cases, sound effects were created during projection. In addition, most early films were screened as music played. Such music took many forms, from pianola rolls to elaborate symphonic scores performed by full orchestras and choirs. In certain cases well-known composers created movie scores—for example, Saint-Saëns for *L'Assassinat du Duc de Guise* in 1908 and Shostakovich for *New Babylon* in 1929. The most common practice, however, was to have a pianist or organist draw on stock melodies and leitmotifs from standard cue sheets to improvise moods in keeping with the movie being screened. However, musicians using this method could not always be relied on to create an appropriate background for a given film, either because they lacked the requisite skill or because they were unacquainted with the movie until after the first showing. In some instances musicians simply chose to disregard the film entirely in favor of their own conception of what would make a suitable

FIGURE 5.12 *Ben-Hur* ★ United States, 1926, Fred Niblo.

FIGURE 5.13a and b a. *Scar of Shame* ★ United States, 1926, Frank Peregini; Evelyn Preer.
b. *Within Our Gates* ★ United States, 1920, Oscar Micheaux; Lucia Lynn Moses.

evening's entertainment. For example, an early reviewer writing in *The Chicago Defender* complained that a jazz band accompanying a movie presentation on the city's near south side played "Here Comes Charlie!" an up-tempo blues number, as a funeral scene was unfolding on the screen.

Sound accompaniments like these added a vital dimension to the moviegoing experience, but sound created in the theater rather than in the studio remained fundamentally separate from the film itself. From 1910 onward studios exercised increasing control over the sound accompaniments theater owners could add to their productions. However, the challenge of marrying sound and image in a permanent, predictable way remained unfulfilled for many years.

As with most technological innovations in film, synchronized sound was experimented with from the beginning. In fact, Edison seems initially to have conceived of the motion picture as illustration to go with his highly successful cylindrical phonograph—so that those purchasing the sound machines would have something to look at while they listened. W. K. L. Dickson, Edison's talented assistant (and the man most responsible for the development of motion-picture equipment at the West Orange, New Jersey, laboratory), had joined sound to image prior to the first Lumière showings. A film made by Dickson shows a pair of Edison technicians dancing in eerie slow motion to a violinist, supposedly Dickson himself, playing into a huge phonograph horn. The further problem of amplifying sound sufficiently to fill a theater had been solved by 1914, primarily by Lee de Forest's invention of the silenium, or vacuum, tube which allowed for a "loud speaker" (audio amplifier).

Like the later additions of color, wide screen, and 3-D, it took strong economic motivation to bring on sound. In 1924 and 1925 the comparatively small production firm of Warner Bros., which owned no theater chains, was competing against the large companies that controlled distribution and exhibition. According to the Warners' account, accepted by earlier film historians, they decided in desperation to try the novelty of sound to see if it would help them out of their financial difficulties. Another, more credible and thoroughly documented explanation is offered in Robert C. Allen and Douglas Gomery, *Film History: Theory and Practice* (New York: Alfred A. Knopf, 1985, pp. 115–124). According to this version, Wall Street interests looking for a favorable opportunity for investment in the motion picture industry chose Warner Bros. Although a small firm, it was tightly managed and well run financially. The infusion of new capital permitted competitive expansion along a number of lines, one of them being experimentation with sound.

For whatever reason, Warner Bros. added a sound track to a silent feature entitled *Don Juan,* starring John Barrymore, and released it in August 1926. Its Vitaphone system, as it was called, having acquired the Vitagraph company in 1925, used disc recordings mechanically synchronized with the projector. In the case of *Don Juan* the track consisted of a symphonic score plus some sound effects—especially the clanging of swords in the dueling scenes. To the feature Warner Bros. attached a few shorts of distinguished musicians in performance, including violinist Mischa Elman and Metropolitan Opera stars Giovanni Martinelli and Marion Talley.

Leading off this program was a short in which Will Hays appeared. Former Postmaster General and national chairman of the Republican Party, Hays had become president of the Motion Picture Producers and Distributors of America. This trade organization of the major studios (today called the Motion Picture Association of America) had come into being mainly as an attempt by the industry to protect itself—through public relations—from threats of censorship being provoked by the new frankness of the postwar films. Mr.

Hays welcomed the public to the epochal event presented by the Warner brothers and predicted a glorious future for the motion picture accompanied by recorded sound.

Although the opening night audience was enthusiastic enough, the success of Vitaphone was limited because of the few theaters equipped for it. It was not altogether clear that *Don Juan* with Vitaphone was making more money than it would have without recorded sound. Two other programs of shorts and features with synchronized musical scores released in the following year met with only moderate success. The Warners had gambled so much on the innovation, however, that they couldn't consider abandoning it.

With the exception of William Fox, who had begun experimenting with his own sound system, the rest of the producers were annoyed with the Warners for rocking the industrial boat. Box office was down slightly and competition from the new sound entertainment of radio seemed one possible cause, but it was by no means certain that the addition of recorded sound to movies would bring larger audiences into the theaters.

The other studios held back because of general uncertainty and for several specific reasons. First, the expense of changing equipment and facilities for production and, especially, for exhibition (in the eighty thousand theaters throughout the world) loomed as ominous as the national debt. Second, the studios didn't relish paying royalties to Warner Bros. or Fox for use of its patented sound system, and losing face to a competitor. Third, it was possible that sound might change production technique radically, and no one was yet trained to make sound features. Fourth, there was the backlog of silent films and others in production that might have to be written off as complete losses if they didn't conform to the new technology. Fifth, if the movies ever began to talk (a prospect only vaguely foreseen), the long-term contracts with silent stars, foreign stars, and directors might prove frozen assets if those individuals couldn't adapt themselves to the altered medium or to the English language. Finally, if the marvelous esperanto of the silent film were sacrificed, audiences abroad would be curtailed: Whereas titles could easily and inexpensively be translated and reshot, what could the Hungarians, for example, make out of conversations in English? The industry continued to watch and wait.

For their fourth Vitaphone feature the Warners chose a popular musical play, *The Jazz Singer*, which had starred George Jessel on the Broadway stage. When they approached Jessel to repeat his performance for the film, negotiations broke down over the amount of money he asked. As it turned out, the enormously popular Al Jolson was hired for twice as much and insisted that his salary be in cash. Although the film's sound was thought of principally in terms of Jolson's six numbers (concluding with his theme song, "Mammy"), two of his four sound scenes contain a little dialogue that seems scarcely to have been planned. In one scene, after finishing a song in a nightclub, Jolson utters the words that had become his trademark on Broadway: "Wait a minute! Wait a minute! You ain't heard nothin' yet." In this context the expression became unexpectedly prophetic. In the second scene, a bit of dialogue leading up to and intervening between two renditions of "Blue Skies" is certainly unscripted. It consists of Jolson joshing his little old screen mother, who is obviously embarrassed and can't think of a thing to say (Figure 5.14). It's almost as though the conversation had been recorded accidentally, or as a kind of test, and only afterward did the Warners decide to include it. Whatever the intent, the response of the moviegoing public was emphatic.

There are something like 354 words of dialogue in *The Jazz Singer*, but it was clearly those spoken words more than the songs that had audiences queuing up four-deep around the block of the Warner Theatre. The comparative indifference to the sound in *Don Juan*

FIGURE 5.14   *The Jazz Singer* ⋆ United States, 1927, Alan Crosland; Al Jolson and Eugenie Besserer.

had apparently occurred because it consisted solely of recorded music plus a few sound ef-fects in place of the usual live orchestra, organ, or piano to which audiences were accus-tomed. With the ensuing success of *The Jazz Singer,* the "talkie" was born, and a new dramatic dimension in the spoken word was suggested. Except for songs and fragments of dialogue, however, *The Jazz Singer* looks and sounds like the standard silent film of the time, with a recorded orchestral score (making heavy use of Tschaikowsky's *Romeo and Juliet* overture) and with printed intertitles carrying the bulk of the verbal communication.

On the basis of *The Jazz Singer*'s success, the Warners extended what looks as though it had been intended as a two-reel short into a seven-reel feature. Entitled *The Lights of New York* and released in July 1928, it became the first "100 percent talkie." It begins with a pro-logue, which transports the young hero from "Main Street" to "Broadway." There he and his sidekick get mixed up with a couple of con men and with a gang of bootleggers who use their barbershop as a front. The film contains what is surely the longest exposition in his-tory; in fact, it is all exposition. The characters talk about what has happened, will happen, should happen, and might happen; very little except conversation does happen on the screen.

We can feel a kind of morbid fascination in watching the limitations sound imposed at first on the brilliance of the best silent films. Everything is static, all is talk. The flexible fluency of the mature silent film is reduced to a jabbering infancy. (The M-G-M musical *Singin' in the Rain,* 1952, provides a marvelously enjoyable account of the pains of this transition; it is funny because it is so true.) Although we can relish *The Lights of New York*'s authentic "roaring twenties" flavor, it is impossible not to notice how much more dated it seems than many of its silent contemporaries (such as *The Crowd, The Wind,* or *The Last Command,* also released in 1928). Speech is more firmly rooted in the particularities of time and place than is image.

At first, some observers thought sound merely a fad, one that would pass away once audiences got over their fascination with lips moving and voices seeming to come from them. Others felt that the talkies might coexist with the silents, the one appealing to the rubes who liked the yackety novelty, the other for the more sensitive and intelligent. Whatever view was taken, the lines at the box office dictated that the rest of the industry could no longer afford to ignore the Warners' unsettling contribution.

By the close of the 1920s there was no doubt that the synchronous sound film would be the universal form of the future. At the end of 1928 Hollywood had only 16 recording machines in use; by the end of 1929 there were 116, and almost half the more than twenty thousand theaters in the United States were equipped for sound reproduction. The consensus was that a sound system using optical patterns along the edge of the film (Fox Movietone), rather than discs (Warner Vitaphone), would provide more reliable synchronization. In 1931, in order to achieve standardization, the patents on the various sound systems held by most of the major studios and others were pooled and divided between Western Electric and Radio Corporation of America (RCA). The sound systems of those two firms became the only ones in use.

As the industry borrowed money to retool, the financial center of gravity, which had gradually moved eastward with the expansion of exhibition and the mergers, now rested firmly in the big banks of New York City and Boston. Among the major studios, there were shifts in power (Warner up, having absorbed First National; Paramount down) and new alignments (RKO and Twentieth Century-Fox). Incidentally, the *R* in *RKO* stands for Radio Corporation of America, which had become involved in motion pictures because of sound; the *K* and *O,* for the Keith-Orpheum theater circuit, which stemmed from the days when vaudeville was still competing with film for popular audiences. As for the Fox (William) in Twentieth Century-Fox, he was forced out of his firm by the new large financial interests. He then commissioned a socialist author to expose the evils of capitalism, as he had experienced them, in the book *Upton Sinclair Presents William Fox.*

In general, Hollywood turned to Broadway for people who had had experience with spoken words. For a while, the Twentieth-Century Limited pulling out of New York City headed west with a load of actors, writers, and voice coaches. The silent directors were joined by a new crop who would carve their careers out of the possibilities opened up by sound; George Cukor, Leo McCarey, Rouben Mamoulian, Busby Berkeley, John Cromwell, and Tay Garnett all began to direct films in the first years of sound.

Three technical problems were solved during the early 1930s, allowing the sound film to return to the movement of the silent film, reducing the dependence on dialogue, and regaining the visual richness. The first of these problems was to find a means of removing the camera from its soundproof booth. For that purpose a "blimp" was constructed: a metal cover filled with acoustic insulation that encased the camera. As heavy and large as the blimped cameras were, they still could be moved about quite freely on dolly and crane.

The second problem was to free the actors so they could move about without regard to the stationary microphones. Lionel Barrymore, who directed as well as acted in those days, claimed credit for solving this difficulty. As an actor he no doubt felt the performer's frustration in being rooted to one spot; he insisted, against technicians' protests, that a mike be swung overhead from a fishpole and moved around to follow the actors. The directional boom microphone, able to capture sounds from overhead while remaining out of frame, completely replaced the nondirectional fixed microphones that had been hidden about the set.

The blimped camera and boom microphone permitted more dynamic studio shooting, but they did not help the camera get outside the sound stages into the world of unwanted noises, bad acoustic conditions, and wind roaring in the microphone. *In Old Arizona* (1929), codirected by Raoul Walsh and Irving Cummings, was the first sound feature known to be recorded principally out-of-doors. **Location shooting** was made fully possible when sound technology advanced sufficiently so that sight and sound did not have to be recorded at the same time: Footage could be shot silent; sound could be recorded separately, then added to the images. Noteworthy early experiments included King Vidor's *Hallelujah!* (1929). In a frightening chase scene at night in a swamp, snapping twigs, splashing water, and the heavy breathing of the actors are the principal sounds. The battle scenes of Lewis Milestone's *All Quiet on the Western Front* (1930) were shot with the sort of tracking camera movement and rapid cutting that marked the best silent work. The addition of rattling machine gun fire, the detonation of high explosives, and the screams of dying men made the images even more horrifying.

Because it was to the United States that sound first came, the Americans were the first and the most prolific (given their output of four to five hundred feature films per year) in their successes and mistakes. Their work will be surveyed in a subsequent chapter on Hollywood in the 1930s and early 1940s. By the mid-1930s the "100 percent all talking," "canned theater" had been largely transcended and the mature sound film achieved.

Films of the Period

1920
The Last of the Mohicans (Maurice Tourneur and
   Clarence Brown)
The Mark of Zorro (Fred Niblo)
Way Down East (David Wark Griffith)
Within Our Gates (Oscar Micheaux)

1921
The Blot (Lois Weber)
The Four Horsemen of the Apocalypse (Rex
   Ingram)
The Kid (Charles Chaplin)
Orphans of the Storm (David Wark Griffith)
Tol'able David (Henry King)

1922
Foolish Wives (Erich von Stroheim)
Nanook of the North (Robert Flaherty)
Robin Hood (Allan Dwan)

1923
The Covered Wagon (James Cruze)
Safety Last (Harold Lloyd)
The Ten Commandments (Cecil B. DeMille)
A Woman of Paris (Charles Chaplin)

1924
The Iron Horse (John Ford)
The Marriage Circle (Ernst Lubitsch)
The Navigator (Buster Keaton)
Sherlock Junior (Buster Keaton)
The Thief of Bagdad (Raoul Walsh)

1925
The Big Parade (King Vidor)
Body and Soul (Oscar Micheaux)
The Freshman (Harold Lloyd)
The Gold Rush (Charles Chaplin)
Greed (Erich von Stroheim)

Lady Windermere's Fan (Ernst Lubitsch)
The Phantom of the Opera (Rupert Julian)

1926
Ben-Hur (Fred Niblo)
Moana (Robert Flaherty)
The Scarlet Letter (Victor Sjöström/Seastrom)
What Price Glory? (Raoul Walsh)

1927
The General (Buster Keaton)
Hotel Imperial (Mauritz Stiller)
The Jazz Singer (Alan Crosland)
The King of Kings (Cecil B. DeMille)
Seventh Heaven (Frank Borzage)
Sunrise (F. W. Murnau)

Underworld (Josef von Sternberg)
Wings (William Wellman)

1928
The Crowd (King Vidor)
The Docks of New York (Josef von Sternberg)
The Last Command (Josef von Sternberg)
The Lights of New York (Bryan Foy)
Steamboat Willie (Walt Disney)
The Wind (Victor Sjöström/Seastrom)

1929
Applause (Rouben Mamoulian)
Hallelujah! (King Vidor)
The Love Parade (Ernst Lubitsch)

Books on the Period

Abel, Richard, ed. *Silent Film.* New Brunswick, NJ: Rutgers University Press, 1996.

Abel, Richard, and Rick Altman, eds. *The Sounds of Early Cinema.* Bloomington: Indiana University Press, 2001.

Bowser, Pearl, and Louise Spence. *Writing Himself into History: Oscar Micheaux, His Silent Films, and His Audience.* New Brunswick, NJ: Rutgers University Press, 2000.

Brewster, Ben, and Lea Jacobs. *Theatre to Cinema: Stage Pictorialism and the Early Feature Film.* New York: Oxford University Press, 1998.

Butters, Gerald R., Jr. *Black Manhood on the Silent Screen.* Lawrence: University Press of Kansas, 2002.

Crafton, Donald. *The Talkies: American Cinema's Transition to Sound, 1926–1931 (Vol. 4 of History of the American Cinema).* Berkeley: University of California Press, 1999.

Cripps, Thomas. *Slow Fade to Black: The Negro in American Film. 1900–1942.* New York: Oxford University Press, 1993.

Dale, Alan. *Comedy Is a Man in Trouble: Slapstick in American Movies.* Minneapolis: University of Minnesota Press, 2000.

De Bauche, Leslie Midkiff. *Reel Patriotism: The Movies and World War I.* Madison: University of Wisconsin Press, 1997.

Everett, Anna. *Returning the Gaze: A Genealogy of Black Film Criticism, 1909–1949.* Durham, NC: Duke University Press, 2001.

Eyman, Scott. *The Speed of Sound: Hollywood and the Talkie Revolution, 1926–1930.* New York: Simon & Schuster, 1997.

Gaines, Jane M. *Fire and Desire: Mixed-Race Movies in the Silent Era.* Chicago: University of Chicago Press, 2001.

Grieveson, Lee, and Peter Kramer, eds. *The Silent Cinema Reader.* New York: Routledge, 2004.

Haskell, Barbara. *The American Century: Art and Culture, 1900–1950.* New York: W. W. Norton, 1999.

Higston, Andrew, and Richard Maltby, eds. *"Film Europe" and "Film America": Cinema, Commerce, and Cultural Exchange, 1920–1939.* Exeter, UK: Exeter University Press, 1999.

Koszarski, Richard. *An Evening's Entertainment: The Age of the Silent Feature Picture 1915–1928.* Berkeley: University of California Press, 1994.

Marks, Martin Miller. *Music and the Silent Film: Contexts and Case Studies 1895–1924.* New York: Oxford University Press, 1997.

Morey, Anne. *Hollywood Outsiders: The Adaptation of the Film Industry, 1913–1934.* Minneapolis: University of Minnesota Press, 2004.

Morton, David. *Off the Record: The Technology and Culture of Sound Recording in America.* New Brunswick, NJ: Rutgers University Press, 2000.

Schaefer, Eric. *"Bold! Daring! Shocking! True!": A History of Exploitation Films, 1919–1959.* Durham, NC: Duke University Press, 1999.

Williams, Linda. *Playing the Race Card: Melodramas of Black and White from Uncle Tom to O. J. Simpson.* Princeton, NJ: Princeton University Press, 2002.

6

France in the Twenties and Thirties

★ ★ ★ ★

1919–1939

The economy of the French film has so persistently tended toward anarchy and chaos that it is easy to imagine its trade press keeping headline type standing to prophesize and then report "TOTAL COLLAPSE OF INDUSTRY." Made up of numerous small firms and individual impresarios, rather than a few huge studios, production companies have been born and laid to rest with single films. Individual successes and fitful bursts of popularity have been supplemented by various forms of government protection and subsidy in efforts to achieve sustained good health. The French have released only between one hundred and one hundred thirty films each year; as is the case in most countries, American movies have consistently dominated as popular entertainment. Nonetheless, the French film industry has produced a high proportion of carefully crafted works that are the equal of any in terms of artistic quality.

The contribution of France to the maturing art of the silent cinema was much more limited in appeal than that of either Germany or the Soviet Union, yet it followed some of the same lines and in particular instances even antedated achievements in the other two countries. Its strengths, like its limitations, came from the fact that it was rooted firmly in the aesthetic ferment that marked Paris in the 1920s and made it the artistic capital of the world. The outpouring of creation in many arts was accompanied by ongoing argument and polemic about the nature of art itself. Theory fed into practice, and practice back into theory—from the ateliers and garrets to the cafés and salons. A premium was placed on the new and the experimental, the daring and the shocking, in the search for artistic styles—for forms and functions—that would speak for and to the modern age.

The First Avant-Garde:
Impressionism

Louis Delluc—theorist, practitioner, crusader—set out not only to link film with the other arts and aesthetic movements of the time but also to find in what ways it was special and how it could be superior to the traditional modes of music, literature, and theater. He and other French intellectuals and artists had a particular appreciation for the popular American film genres. As they had earlier done with the mystery stories of Edgar Allan Poe, the French pointed out the formal and aesthetic beauties encased in the Hollywood western, for example, and insisted that those responsible for them were genuine artistic talents.

While editing a succession of film journals, Delluc wrote prolific criticism applauding the work of the Americans—especially Ince, Griffith, and Chaplin—as well as the Swedes. He also attacked the French tendency to revert to the theatrical tradition of films d'art or to blandly imitate the commercial successes of other nations. Around Delluc there gathered a group of film makers who have been labeled the **impressionists:** Marcel L'Herbier, Jean Epstein, Abel Gance, and Germaine Dulac, for whom Delluc wrote his first scenario, *La Fête espanole* (1919).

What Delluc and his followers wanted was a cinema that was distinctively filmic, with emphasis on the rhythmical and lyrical possibilities of the medium, and one that was distinctively French, with indigenous themes and images. In his early theoretical writings and in his films, Delluc championed what he termed **photogenie,** which could be defined as the camera's transformation of the actual world through lighting, framing, and the like. Movement was the most prized quality. Delluc's emphasis on the natural world as a precondition for cinematic art meant that he disapproved of films such as those produced by the German expressionists, which featured artificial sets and performances. Of the movies directed by Dullac, *Fièvre* (1921) and *La Femme de Nulle Part* (1922) are most often cited as those that best exemplify his theories. But he made his greatest impact through his intellectual leadership, his influence on other film makers, and his organization of the **ciné club** movement to build support for the kinds of films he valued.

The films of the impressionists contained elements of stylization and experimentation that set them apart from the bulk of French commercial production of the time. Eventually they embraced the term **cinématographie** to signal their growing interest in using film to render interior states rather than the external world. Germaine Dulac's *The Smiling Madame Beudet* (1923) exemplifies this new principle perfectly (Figure 6.1). Focusing on the fantasy life of a Madame Bovary–like young matron living in the French provinces, *Madame Beudet* makes little distinction between what happens without and within the young protagonist's mind. When quotidian reality takes over after the woman's scheme to murder her husband fails, the world appears bleak and meaningless.

Of those associated with the impressionists, **Abel Gance** is the most special case—too large and long-lasting a creator to be contained within a single school. As the one gigantic figure of the French silent film, he not only rivaled Griffith during the silent years but also continued to be ahead of his time up to the 1970s. Although his work was enormously influential, the vastness of Gance's conceptions and the originality of his technique were what made him unique in the history of film. The subjectivity and distortion in his *La Folie*

FIGURE 6.1   *The Smiling Madame Beudet* ★ France, 1923, Germaine Dulac; Germaine Dermoz.

du Docteur Tube (1915), achieved through the camera, preceded the later experiments of the impressionists, but its innovations so alarmed the producer that the film wasn't released at the time. The impressionistic technique and complex rapid cutting of his *La Roue* (1922) antedated the Soviet films and strongly influenced the French avant-garde just then developing.

In his enormous *Napoléon* (1927), Gance first employed a triptych screen process called **Polyvision,** which preceded **Cinerama** (the U.S. version of a wrap-around film experience) by a quarter century (Figure 6.2). Unlike the film makers of Cinerama, Gance used his separate panels to carry contrasting and complementary images as well as to extend one image to panoramic proportions. The film's force, however, did not depend solely on the novelty of those scenes projected in multiscreen (only four out of the whole). The eighty-minute single-screen version released originally in the United States by M-G-M is, as a historical-dramatic work, as powerful as the best of Griffith or Eisenstein. Numerous subsequent efforts have been made to reconstruct the film as close to the six-hour definitive version as possible. The most popular of these was sponsored by Francis Ford Coppola. Shown initially at New York's Radio City Music Hall in 1981 (the year Gance died), this four-hour version, with original live orchestral score composed by Coppola's father Carmine, then toured the United States. Many people who had never seen silent films, or even thought about them, were overwhelmed by this one. Its amazing power remains intact.

FIGURE 6.2 *Napoléon* ★ France, 1927, Abel Gance.

The Second Avant-Garde:
Pure Cinema

Working alongside the impressionists in the 1920s, carrying their technical and stylistic experimentation even further, were another group of French avant-garde film makers. The production of impressionist films was virtually ended by 1924; the second avant-garde waxed most strongly from about 1925 to the end of the decade. It emerged, however, quite directly from a nonfilmic historic line—one that began with the impressionist painters of the late nineteenth century and departed from the film impressionists' reliance on literary material. These avant-garde films, usually short, are like visual poems, jokes, or dreams— more akin to abstract or surrealist painting than to novels, plays, or feature films. The film makers who produced these kinds of films advocated a concept called **pure cinema** *(cinéma pur),* a cinema without plots.

Avant-garde film making was practiced in France more than elsewhere primarily because the right kind of personnel were there. French intellectuals and artists were among the most enthusiastic admirers of the **seventh art,** as critic Ricciotto Canudo called film at the time. Even more than the Germans, many French artists were demonstrating an eagerness to try their hands at more than one medium. Jack-of-all-arts Jean Cocteau—poet, novelist, playwright, painter, film maker—was one extreme case. Cocteau, along with other notable figures from the world of painting who made forays into film, gravitated toward animation. In 1930 he produced *The Blood of a Poet,* which mixed animation with live action. Similar experiments with animation were carried out by the cubist painter Fernand Léger (*Ballet mécanique,* 1924), the dadaist painter and photographer Man Ray (*The Starfish,* 1927), and the futurist artist Marcel Duchamp (*Anemic Cinema,* 1928).

The avant-garde movement in France was bolstered by the comparatively easy access to the tools and materials of the medium and by an audience receptive to experiment. In this period the French film industry was so loosely organized and lightly financed as to be almost amateurish by standards prevailing elsewhere. Rather than an oligopoly of a few large studios, there were many small companies and individual entrepreneurs. Given the relative inexpensiveness of the silent film, it was quite possible for a painter to raise a little money from the owner of an art gallery (to pay for raw stock and processing), borrow a camera from the studio where a friend worked, arrange for the use of an aristocratic art lover's château, invite friends (other artists) there, and then shoot a short, improvised experimental film in which they appeared. When completed it could be shown in one of the small cinemas on the left bank and among the ciné clubs founded by Delluc and Canudo that were beginning to show specialized programs. If the painter's reputation was sufficient, general public interest in the arts, including film, could assure enough of an audience to pay back the modest costs. Man Ray's *Les Mystères du Château de Dés (The Mysteries of the Chateau de Dés)* (1929), for instance, was produced and exhibited that way. With their new creative impulses, young poets and especially painters simply wrote themselves off their pages and painted beyond their canvases onto the cinema.

Another strand of the second avant-garde, **surrealism,** came out of the new psychological sciences pioneered by Sigmund Freud, whose equivalence in literature can be found in Proust (in his obsession with early memories) and Joyce (in his stream of consciousness and dream episodes). In painting, the surrealists informed their canvases with Freudian symbols and insights. Some thought the motion picture might be the art best able to capture and reveal the dream state so significant for Freud. Cinema's capacity for representing the fantasy world of dreams was as great as its ability to record the objective reality of the physical world; and so several surrealist artists turned to the film medium. A number of significant films were produced during this period under the surrealist banner. In 1924 René Clair made *Entr'acte,* a short movie consisting of logically unrelated images intended to be shown as a prologue and intermission entertainment at a ballet composed by fellow avant-garde artist Eric Satie. In 1928 Germaine Dulac made a surrealist-influenced short entitled *The Seashell and the Clergyman* with the participation of the theatrical innovator Antonin Artaud.

The best known of the surrealist films is *Un Chien andalou,* made in 1927 by the surrealist painter Salvador Dali working with his fellow Spaniard Luis Buñuel (Figure 6.3). *Un Chien andalou* might best be called an antinarrative film rather than a nonnarrative film insofar as it repeatedly violates one's expectations about spatial, temporal, and logical continuities. Characters open doors and find themselves on a beach. Intertitles contain phrases, such as "eight days later," that have no discernible relation to the action being shown. Characters behave erratically, with no rational motivations for their actions. Insofar as *Un Chien andalou* can be said to be "about" something, it deals with three people, a woman and two men, who participate in fantastical episodes, many of which focus on elemental sexual drives and hostility toward everyday civilized values. An especially shocking sequence near the beginning of the film shows a man (played by Buñuel) slitting a woman's eyeball. Buñuel and Dali went on to make another surrealist short film, *L'Age d'or,* in 1930, which continued to exploit surrealist shock tactics. Its most famous image features a woman sucking on the toe of a statue.

The expense of sound production and the inaccessibility and complexity of sound equipment and technique effectively ended the avant-garde film movements at the end of the 1920s. In the new technology, there was no place for the inspired amateur. However, several of the avant-garde film artists—including Clair, Buñuel, and Cocteau—later managed to establish careers for themselves in feature film making.

A second cause for the demise of the avant-garde spirit was the changing attitudes of the 1930s. Art for the sake of art seemed worthy of artists' full attention in the 1920s, but the 1930s became the years of art for society's sake. The Depression and rising fascism prompted new artistic intentions. The avant-garde film was replaced by the documentary as the artistic form most attractive to the artists and intellectuals of the 1930s. It is no

FIGURE 6.3   *Un Chien andalou* ★ France, 1927, Luis Buñuel and Salvador Dali.

coincidence that several of the avant-garde film makers of the 1920s became socially committed documentary film makers in the decade following their avant-garde successes.

The Golden Age of the 1930s

During certain periods of rapid change the lack of economic ballast, which has otherwise been a liability, has given the French a peculiar advantage. This was the case at the time sound was introduced at the end of the 1920s. At first the greatly increased expense meant that only the two largest firms, Gaumont and Pathé, were capable of exploiting the new medium. When both collapsed from overextension of their resources, the situation changed. In part because they didn't have the heavy investments the American industry did, the French moved more readily into the experimental stage with sound, and hence exerted considerable leadership in the development of the altered art. In France the individual film maker frequently enjoyed a freedom of and control over expression seldom granted in Hollywood's major studios, or, for that matter, in the Ufa of Germany or the state-financed cinema of the Soviet Union. A French film maker who could find a backer—wealthy lover, moribund aunt, reckless stockbroker—could hope to make a film. With sound, French production returned to an international prominence it had relinquished with the outbreak of World War I.

First there was a series of **René Clair** successes—*Sous les toits de Paris* (1930), *À nous la liberté* (1931), and *Le Million* (1931). Clair used music and noises fantastically (a flower in the field bursting into song, a crowd scrambling for a lottery ticket as an off-screen announcer delivers a play-by-play description of a soccer game) (Figure 6.4a) or satirically (assembly-line work performed to the same music and monotonous sounds in the factory as in the prison). Although dialogue had little place in his first sound works, Clair vastly expanded the range of cinematic effects sound could create.

In those same early sound years Marcel Pagnol began his memorable trilogy of *Marius* (1931), *Fanny* (1932), and *César* (1936). In these a warmly human story about simple people is enacted in definitive performances against a Marseilles setting. For Pagnol dialogue was perhaps too important and the overall style remained "theatrical."

Only a little later, Jean Vigo, the supreme poet of French cinema, made his two enduring and influential features before his tragically premature death. *Zero for Conduct* (1933), also concerning children, deals with life in a strangely surreal boys' school—a film to which Lindsay Anderson paid obvious and respectful homage in his own film *If . . .* (1968). *L'Atalante* (1934) is the tender and somewhat haunted, as well as haunting, love story of young newlyweds and a bizarre, elderly Caliban—set in a barge on the Seine (Figure 6.4b). Both films are models for sparse and assured use of sound in support of images. The poetry is primarily visual rather than verbal, and the words, noises, and music coming from the loudspeakers add reverberations to what is already clear and rich on the screen.

In 1934, however, the year of *L'Atalante,* it looked to many observers as though the French industry finally had reached that state of total collapse frequently predicted. The major cause of the catastrophe was the worldwide Depression that had by then hit France. Now no investment money was available for production, no films were being made, and film artists and technicians joined the millions of unemployed. Not unlike 1919 in Germany, 1934 was a year of grave political unrest in France. Demonstrations and riots preceded the formation of the Popular Front, a short-lived effort by the parties of the left to keep France from succumbing to fascism, as had Italy and Germany, and as Spain soon would. Perhaps this is yet another instance of periods of great national film expression growing out of troubled times. In any case, out of the ashes of 1934—and for reasons that aren't altogether clear in the general quirkiness of French film economics—a phoenix arose, becoming what is still referred to as the Golden Age of French Cinema.

FIGURE 6.4a and b   a. *Le Million* ⋆ France, 1931, René Clair. b. *L'Atalante* ⋆ France, 1934, Jean Vigo; Dita Parlo and Jean Dasté.

One of the causes of revival seems more evident to the historian of today than it would have been to investors at the time. France was specially blessed with a cultural tradition that, though not fully accessible to the silent film, offered the stuff of which the best sound films are made. Whereas action-melodrama, spectacle, and slapstick comedy were ideal forms for the strictly visual requirements of the silent medium, the addition of dialogue demanded a new thoughtfulness, subtlety, and refinement of dramatic values. From 1935 until the end of the decade French film makers utilized the resources of the new technology to emphasize intellectual content, to explore philosophical and psychological themes. Intelligent screenplays and superior screen acting were France's chief additions to the maturation of the sound film, contributed by some of its distinguished literary and theatrical talents. Those qualities, all of prime importance in the new medium, were often achieved without loss of visual brilliance—owing in no small measure to the well-known French affinity for the graphic arts. As tangible evidence of their excellence, it can be noted that French films of the late 1930s became the first substantial body of foreign-language pictures to interest American audiences. In major U.S. cities a few little "art theaters" sprang up to show them, somewhat as *The Great Train Robbery* had opened the nickelodeons in the earlier days. The first five annual New York Film Critics' Awards for the Best Foreign Film, which began in 1936, went to France.

In general, because of the avant-garde inheritance, the best of French cinema of the 1930s was saved from the "staginess" that often marred Hollywood studio output. The avant-garde's attention to *cinéma pur,* and the fact that some of France's major directors came out of that informal school, kept the French aware that *motion* and *picture* was still the best two-word aesthetic of the motion picture, even when accompanied by sound.

But the French sound feature film, although showing the influence of a painterly tradition and of silent avant-garde film making, drew even more heavily on literary and theatrical sources available to it. Historically, the French novel has been noteworthy for a kind of realism closely akin to the dominant style of the sound film. The works of Stendhal, Balzac, Flaubert, Zola, and de Maupassant comprise a main line in French literature; much of French cinema of the latter half of the 1930s can be seen as an extension of that inheritance. Often the films are set firmly within the provinces (*Carnet de bal,* 1937; *The Baker's Wife,* 1938) or amongst the urban working classes (*La Belle Équipe,* 1936; *Daybreak,* 1939). Violence and crime frequently occur but, in French fashion, more out of passion than hatred or greed. Robust, sexually based humor alternates with worldly *tristesse.* The earthiness and honesty strike the viewer at once. Small important details of a scene are searched out; nearly tangible contact between characters and audience is established. Principal script writers were Jacques Prévert, Charles Spaak, and Henri Jeanson—all of whom had literary as well as filmic reputations—and they can claim a substantial share of the creative credit for films bearing their names. Most of the finest work of the period had scripts by one or another of them.

Excelling in psychological depth and intimate characterization, these films also depended to considerable extent on the skill of French acting. Sound film was obviously more attractive than silent film to actors trained in the theater. France had its great heritage of private and state-supported theatrical companies that for decades, even centuries, had provided one of the finest cadres of performers in the world. French cinema owes much of its luster and subtlety to the contributions of such actors as Arletty, Jean Gabin, Louis Jouvet, Michèle Morgan, Raimu, and Michel Simon. They approached the new medium with enthusiasm and quickly learned to adapt their talents and techniques to its special requirements.

One of the most distinctive trends to emerge during this period was **poetic realism.** Concerned primarily with working-class protagonists trapped in a dark universe, these films featured low-key lighting and fatalistic themes. Jean Gabin became the personification of the tragic proletarian hero in many of these films. In this guise Gabin came to stand for the French proletarian leader, called by the critic André Bazin "Oedipus in a cloth cap." Among Gabin's many poetic-realist films were *Pépé le Moko* (Julien Duvivier, 1936), *Port of Shadows* (Marcel Carné, 1938), and *Daybreak* (Carné, 1939). In each of these productions he plays a doomed criminal ennobled by love.

Marcel Carné, director of some of the most accomplished poetic-realist films, was a superb craftsman who did his best work in collaboration with the poet/screenwriter Jacques Prévert; in fact, it seems quite possible that Prévert was the *auteur* (author) in the filmic as well as the literary sense. Their attention to tight dramatic structures, themes of doomed love, and evocative, studio reconstructions of the real world give their work a distinctive aura of serene melancholy. Their two greatest films of the period, *Port of Shadows* (1938) and *Daybreak* (1939), are also remarkably consistent in the dark and despairing view they present of society. In them Carné and Prévert follow the ubiquitous Jean Gabin through urban lowlife on the fringes of the criminal world. Forced and led into a crime of passion that causes his own destruction, Gabin meets his end with the special sort of stoicism that he carried with him from film to film. Even individual scenes seem almost interchangeable: The lighting and wallpaper in the forlorn hotel rooms look alike (Figure 6.5a); a woman (Michèle Morgan or Arletty), with a kind of tired sensuousness, peels off a silk stocking; the same little bistro reappears (Figure 6.5b), as do the same unadorned and cheerless flights of stairs. It's as if a bleak vision of the society had been frozen on the screen and Carné-Prévert insist that we see it over and over again with them.

The best-loved collaboration between Carné and Prévert took place under the German occupation in the 1940s. *Children of Paradise,* which was released immediately after World War II ended in 1945, creates a tapestry of plot lines set in the world of the nineteenth-century French theater. Prévert's witty script focuses on Debureau, the greatest pantomimist France had ever known, masterfully played by Jean-Louis Barrault (Figure

FIGURE 6.5a and b *Port of Shadows* ★ France, 1938, Marcel Carné; a. Jean Gabin and Michèle Morgan; b. Michèle Morgan.

6.6a). The film's most prominent female character is Garance, a free-spirited actress, played by the charismatic Arletty (Figure 6.6b). With its spectacular sets and large crowd scenes (Figure 6.6c), *Children of Paradise* is epic in scope, but it also offers intimate and nuanced views of individual characters (Figure 6.6d).

Out of the eclectic mix of film makers active in France during this time, one figure emerged whose work transcended all conventions and formulas: **Jean Renoir.** Renoir's total corpus places him among the foremost film makers in the history of cinema to date; he is protean, experimenting in many forms and styles, yet usually saying essentially the same things. For Renoir, life is fundamentally good—the life of the heart and of the senses. Sexual love and natural countrysides are to be celebrated along with food and wine. In Renoir's world there are no bores and few villains. (In *The Rules of the Game* one of his characters, played by Renoir himself, remarks, "Everyone has his own good reasons.") His people may cause themselves and others difficulties, but they are never less than human.

Renoir's worldview had already been formed in his sound films preceding the high years of French cinema. *La Chienne* (1931), *Boudu Saved from Drowning* (1932), *Madame*

FIGURE 6.6a–d *Children of Paradise* ★ France, 1945, Marcel Carné; a. Jean-Louis Barrault; b. Arletty; c. The Boulevard of Crime; d. Pierre Brasseur and Jane Marken.

Bovary (1934), and *Toni* (1934) can stand alongside his later work without apology. This is particularly true of *Boudu.* In it Renoir developed the notion of the social group, with the "outsider" (in one sense or another) serving as catalyst. This protagonist stirs up the group, unhinges it a bit; when he or she leaves, the group re-forms, changed by the experience. But the cohesiveness of the social unit, the need of people for each other, is one of the *idées fixés* in Renoir's universe of discourse.

In *The Crime of Monsieur Lange,* made in the landmark year 1935, Renoir restates these thematic materials in even fuller detail and more controlled form. He depicts the cooperative workplace established by the employees of a publishing firm, contrasting this utopian world with the oppression and exploitation they had suffered in the past under their corrupt capitalist boss Batala. One of Renoir's few unredeemed villains (played by Jules Berry in a tour-de-force performance), Batala asserts explicitly fascist sentiments near the end of the film. *The Crime of Monsieur Lange* was widely viewed at the time of its release as an endorsement of France's antifascist Popular Front movement. Yet with Renoir, these social themes never seem schematic: They are made manifest through close observation of particular, idiosyncratic human beings rather than through reliance on types.

Renoir's use of the camera is designed to capture what is happening to his characters without intruding on them. He favors wide-angle moving shots of considerable duration, composed in depth. At the climactic moment in *The Crime of Monsieur Lange,* for example, as the eponymous protagonist resolves to commit his "crime," the camera executes an elaborate panning movement around the courtyard as if to honor the wholeness of the idealized world the workers have created within this space, a world that Lange has come to feel he must protect at any cost.

Renoir's framing typically has a casual air. By allowing characters to enter and leave the cinematic stage freely, he creates an impression of a series of snapshots rather than posed portraits. He has referred to this style as one that fosters "the feeling of a frame too narrow for the content." The performances he elicits from his actors are so fresh and spontaneous they surpass an impression of improvisation to convey a sense of authenticity, of real persons at their core. At the same time, Renoir often alludes to the artificial quality of his creations by including amateur theatricals in many of his films. These performances within the films suggest the pleasure people take in make-believe and, by extension, refer to the activities of the film maker himself.

The Grand Illusion is unquestionably one of Renoir's masterworks (Figure 6.7). The script, which he wrote with Charles Spaak, is based on his own experiences during World War I and those recounted to him by others. He has said that the film is about "how to belong, how to meet." The tale is that of French prisoners of war in German prison camps, of two of the prisoners who have escaped, and of a German woman and her child with whom they stay for a while. According to the film, it is an illusion that war can solve national problems; instead, it merely frustrates human needs. For the two aristocratic professional soldiers, one French the other German, modern warfare doesn't even grant the traditional satisfactions of chivalry and male comradeship. (The latter character is played by Eric von Stroheim, popularly known as "the man you love to hate," in one of his few sympathetic roles.) For the remaining soldier-prisoners, war represents other kinds of deprivation—of freedom, primarily, but also of women's love. In one memorable scene the French prisoners try on costumes as they rehearse for an amateur show. When one emerges in a woman's dress and wig, the others stand transfixed. The camera lingers on their awestruck stares as it slowly

FIGURE 6.7   *The Grand Illusion*   ★   France, 1937, Jean Renoir; Jean Gabin, Fierre Fresnay, and Marcel Dalio, front row.

tracks among them. At this moment, the soundtrack lapses into silence, and the audience is invited to share the force of the emotional starvation these men feel as a result of the absence of women in their lives.

Renoir said that he was a pacifist, but *The Grand Illusion* is not a conventionally pacifist film. It contains no bloodshed, no atrocities, not even unbearable cruelties. (Punishment by solitary confinement comes closest; how like Renoir to regard being deprived of human companionship the cruelist of tortures.) If this is an antiwar film, it is even more profoundly a prohuman film, against all those restrictions placed on the human potential—nationality, class, military rank, religious prejudice—that keep us from solidarity.

After *La Marseillaise* and *The Human Beast* (both 1938) there came the final masterpiece of the 1930s: *The Rules of the Game* (1939). It was completed just before French liberty was extinguished by the nation's collapse in the face of German onslaught. The "game" refers to the behavior of the upper-class hosts and guests during a house party. We see much of the servants of the estate as well. Their jobs are to serve the masters; the masters' jobs are to entertain themselves. The chief entertainment (game) is sexual intrigue, in which all the principal players indulge. In addition there are the host's collection of mechanical toys (Figure 6.8a), a costume party (Figure 6.8b), a rabbit hunt (Figure 6.8c), and a variety show (Figure 6.8d) (another of Renior's characteristic set pieces built around a performance within the film).

FIGURE 6.8a–d   *The Rules of the Game*   ★   France, 1939, Jean Renoir; a. Marcel Dalio.

The "rules" in general require that things be done properly, style taking precedence over feeling. (The feelings of the characters seem atrophied, or, at most, light and variable.) Passion is not permitted, sexual infidelity is accepted; embarrassment is avoided; decorum is preserved; and the appearance of friendship, frankness, and generosity is maintained. It is not just that the rules don't relate to human wishes and desires; they are in opposition to them (similar to the illusions of *The Grand Illusion*). Although essentially a comedy, the diagnosis of social illness is disturbing enough that the film was banned by the French during the Occupation. One of Renoir's few dark films, *The Rules of the Game* became a requiem marking the end of an era.

If Renoir stands apart from all others in this period of diverse activities and movements, he is also emblematic of the high quality that has consistently marked French film culture. The era of the 1920s and 1930s in France ended as it had begun, with renewed efforts to understand and document the development of motion-picture artistry. A new generation of what the French call *cinéphiles,* or lovers of film, took up the work begun by Louis Delluc but in a more disciplined way. Henri Langlois, Georges Franju, and Jean Mitry began the Cinémathèque Française, an institution dedicated to archiving and screening the films of the past.

At the same time Jean Mitry, Georges Sadoul, and others began projects to create authoritative film histories and to theorize this new aesthetic phenomenon. Through such projects the French consolidated their position as leaders not only in the creation of film art but also in the production of film scholarship—a position they have maintained to the present day.

Films of the Period

1919
J'accuse (Abel Gance)

1922
La Roue (Abel Gance)

1923
L'Inhumaine (Marcel L'Herbier)
The Smiling Madame Beudet (Le Souriante Madame Beudet) (Germaine Dulac)

1924
Ballet Mécanique (Fernand Léger)
Entr'acte (René Clair)

1927
Napoléon (Abel Gance)
The Starfish (L'Etoile de mer) (Man Ray)
Un Chien andalou (Salvador Dali and Luis Buñuel)

1928
The Fall of the House of Usher (La Chute de la maison Usher) (Jean Epstein)
The Little Match Girl (La Petite Marchande d'allumettes) (Jean Renoir)
The Seashell and the Clergyman (La Coquille et le clergyman) (Germaine Dulac)

1930
L'Age d'or (Luis Buñuel and Salvador Dali)
The Blood of a Poet (Le Sang d'un poet) (Jean Cocteau)
Sous les toits de Paris (René Clair)

1931
À nous la liberté (René Clair)
La Chienne (Jean Renoir)
Marius (Marcel Pagnol)
Le Million (René Clair)

1932
Boudu Saved from Drowning (Boudu sauvé des eaux) (Jean Renoir)
Fanny (Marcel Pagnol)

1933
Zero for Conduct (Zéro de conduite) (Jean Vigo)

1934
L'Atalante (Jean Vigo)
Madame Bovary (Jean Renoir)
Toni (Jean Renoir)

1935
Carnival in Flanders (La Kermesse héroïque) (Jacques Feyder)
The Crime of Monsieur Lange (La Crime de Monsieur Lange) (Jean Renoir)

1936
César (Marcel Pagnol)
A Day in the Country (Un Jour du campagne) (Jean Renoir) (released 1946)
Pepé le Moko (Julien Duvivier)

1937
Carnet de bal (Julien Duvivier)
The Grand Illusion (La Grande Illusion) (Jean Renoir)

1938
The Baker's Wife (La Femme du boulanger) (Marcel Pagnol)
The Human Beast (Le Bête humaine) (Jean Renoir)
La Marseillaise (Jean Renoir)
Port of Shadows (Quai des brumes) (Marcel Carné)

1939
Daybreak (Le Jour se lève) (Marcel Carné)
The Rules of the Game (La Règle de jeu) (Renoir)

Books on the Period

Andrew, Dudley. *Mists of Regret: Culture and Sensibility in Classic French Film*. Princeton, NJ: Princeton University Press, 1995.

Crisp, Colin. *Genre, Myth, and Convention in the French Cinema, 1929–1939*. Bloomington: Indiana University Press, 2002.

Crisp, Colin. *The Classic French Cinema, 1930–1960*. Bloomington: Indiana University Press, 1997.

Dixon, Wheeler Winston, and Gwendolyn Audrey Foster, eds. *Experimental Cinema: The Film Reader*. New York: Routledge, 2003.

Hayward, Susan, and Ginette Vincendeau. *French Film: Texts and Contexts*. New York: Routledge, 1999.

Higston, Andrew, and Richard Maltby, eds. *"Film Europe" and "Film America": Cinema, Commerce, and Cultural Exchange, 1920–1939*. Exeter, UK: Exeter University Press, 1999.

Hughes, Alex, and James S. Williams, eds. *Gender and French Cinema*. New York: Berg, 2002.

Lanzani, Remi Fournier. *French Cinema: From Its Beginnings to the Present*. New York: Continuum, 2004.

O'Pray, Michael. *Avant-Garde Film: Forms, Themes, and Passions*. London: Wallflower Press, 2003.

Powrie, Philip, and Keith Reader. *French Cinema: A Student's Guide*. New York: Oxford University Press, 2003.

Rees, A. L. *A History of Experimental Film and Video*. London: British Film Institute, 1999.

Temple, Michale, and Michael Witt, eds. *The French Cinema Book*. London: BFI Publishing, 2003.

7

Hollywood in the Thirties and Early Forties

★ ★ ★ ★

1929–1945

The 1930s in the United States were the years of the Depression and of the New Deal—of business collapse and bank failure, of unemployment and poverty, and of the WPA, the CCC, and the NRA (Works Progress Administration, Civilian Conservation Corps, and National Recovery Administration). They were years of economic stagnancy, industrial strife, and individual frustration. At the same time, they were years of rediscovery of American tradition, of affirmation of an American character, of unearthing and preserving folklore and folk music, and of attempts at restoring and conserving our land and water through federal government efforts after decades of neglect and despoilation.

During these years the movies continued as a vital form of popular culture. Usually they seemed to avoid direct confrontation with the problems of the time, but inevitably they carried along its themes and concerns—even into seemingly escapist entertainment. Sometimes social stance was implicit in what was omitted or disguised. In other instances the movies spoke more or less directly to national fears and aspirations. The populist rhetoric and symbols of the first government documentaries, Pare Lorentz's *The Plow That Broke the Plains* (1936) and *The River* (1937), had their analogues in the fiction films of Frank Capra, *Mr. Deeds Goes to Town* (1936) and *Mr. Smith Goes to Washington* (1939).

American entertainment films of the 1930s were designed to function in a way quite different from theatrical feature films of today, at which attendance becomes something of a special occasion. Those earlier movies were more like current television series, and with similar audience expectations. Admission prices were much lower then; theaters were more easily accessible; and they were attended with greater casualness, more frequently—by eighty million customers a week. The men and women who created films for that mass audience conceived of themselves as making entertainment. They didn't think of their work as art.

117

A standard technique for screen narrative became fixed—what is now sometimes called the **continuity editing** system. It involves a **master long shot** covering the whole scene, which introduces it and is returned to from time to time to reestablish spatial orientation. Within it are inserted medium shots and closeups in **shot/reverse shot** order, back and forth between action and reaction to speaker and listener(s). Screen direction and screen action are matched perfectly from shot to shot, following a principle of **matching on action** (Figure 7.1a and b), and sight lines are carefully observed: When an actor looks, we see what he or she is looking at from approximately the same angle and distance (a principle called an **eyeline match**) (Figure 7.1c and d). American film makers working within that style aspired to the well-made film, and the best of them had very high standards for their craft. But to regard the motion picture as a means for personal expression would generally have been considered a somewhat peculiar idea. Art existed in the movies of course, but in comparison to other more self-conscious artistic endeavors it was arrived at surreptitiously, sometimes unconsciously. We can tell this from the evidence of the five thousand or so features produced during the decade, and from an understanding of the industrial system within which they were made and marketed.

FIGURE 7.1a–d *Only Angels Have Wings* ★ United States, 1939, Howard Hawks; a. Cary Grant about to go through door; b. Cary Grant on right, having just come through door; c. Jean Arthur looking at dancers; d. the dancers she is watching.

The 1930s were the years of the giant studios having nearly complete control over the careers of their employees, more absolute than that of today's professional football teams over their players. The studios assembled their rosters of creators, performers, and technicians who, as they worked together over the years, became expert indeed. Because of this continuity of personnel, which extended from top management to lowliest grip, each studio had its own "look." In some ways we can deal with the American films of the 1930s more adequately by identifying them with their studios rather than with individual film makers.

As much as we have come in recent years to think of the director as principal creator of a film, we must remember that in Hollywood in the 1930s producers and stars would generally have been considered the major factors in each production. Producers, with a stable of scriptwriters at their disposal, put together vehicles for stars. Producers such as Irving Thalberg, Hal Wallis, and Darryl F. Zanuck left strong imprints on films they produced. Actors such as Katharine Hepburn, Clark Gable, Marlene Dietrich, and James Stewart had their wishes carefully attended to. The director was sometimes merely a supervisor who oversaw the recording of images and sounds. It makes sense, then, to look first at the industrial system before considering its product and the work of a few powerful creative figures who emerged.

The Industry

After seismic upheavals and shifts during the transition from silence to sound, the Hollywood economic terrain hardened into a pattern that would remain virtually unchanged for two decades. In fact, vestiges of the modus operandi of the 1930s still characterize what is left of the once mighty feature film industry.

The system was built around eight major companies—five more major than the other three—and around the **vertical control** exerted by those firms over distribution and exhibition as well as production. Chains of theaters were owned by the five largest studios: Metro-Goldwyn-Mayer (M-G-M, the production arm of Loew's, Inc.), Twentieth Century-Fox, Paramount Pictures, Warner Bros., Radio-Keith-Orpheum (RKO). Each studio produced upward of fifty features a year for its theaters and for those of the others. Program or "B" pictures might play only within their producing company's chain as weekly or semi-weekly filler between hits. The more popular films were sought by all the exhibitors regardless of which studios produced them. Whatever part of the country you are from, chances are that names of local theaters still pay tribute to their former owners: the RKO Grand, the Paramount, Loew's, and so on. The three smaller studios—Universal, Columbia Pictures, United Artists—produced and distributed, but to survive had to have their films shown in the theaters owned and controlled by the big five. Besides the eight major studios there were also those producers called independents. Some of them were reasonably large and well established (Samuel Goldwyn Productions, Walt Disney Studio, Republic, Monogram); others were individual entrepreneurs working out of one of the major studios (David Selznick at M-G-M, Walter Wanger at Paramount).

In 1939 the eight majors were responsible for 76 percent of feature films released, and took in 86 percent of total rental income. These studios were the members of the Motion Picture Producers and Distributors of America (MPPDA)—the trade organization that self-censored the content of the films produced, bargained with foreign governments regarding export abroad, and performed other functions on behalf of the industry as a whole.

Through the MPPDA (now the **MPAA**—Motion Picture Association of America) the majors dominated the industry. If control of exhibition was crucial to their power, they also controlled distribution.

The distribution branches of the majors undertook to "sell" the films to exhibitors and to physically handle and circulate prints to theaters. Selling involved advertising and promotion, which took two forms. First, each film was presented through advertisements and reviews in the trade press, and by sales representatives and advance screenings at regional offices. Second, the distributor developed a promotional campaign to attract general public attention to the new release—through the national press, radio, billboards, sky writing, and any other means available or thinkable. The budget allocated for promotion of each film was a key factor in determining the rental the exhibitor would pay for it. The more important the studio thought the picture, the more money it spent on the campaign, and the more the exhibitor might expect to take in at the box office.

The distributor worked out the kinds of appeals thought to be best suited and most effective for selling each picture. Its staff designed the graphics, wrote advertising copy, even prepared canned "reviews" for those newspapers that didn't choose to hire their own reviewers. Often the approaches to the public and to the trade were strikingly different. We are all aware that sex and violence are not only staples of popular entertainment but of the advertising for it. It may be less obvious that novelty is stressed almost as often: "For the first time on the screen . . . ," "At last it can be told . . . ," "Never before in the history of the motion picture . . . ." Usually pains were taken to disguise the probability that the film would be rather like the ones shown last week and a month ago, and to promise a unique experience no one could conceivably miss. To the exhibitor, however, the exact opposite (and a bit more honest) appeal was more often used: "The studio, the director, and the star who gave you *Dark Victory,*" "Judy and Mickey together again in the kind of story that made *Babes in Arms* a smash." The exhibitor sought known quantities in relation to audience tastes as demonstrated by their purchase of tickets in the past.

Some two hundred to four hundred prints of each film, costing around $250 apiece, were shipped from the laboratories to the regional film "exchanges." There were roughly thirty distribution centers in the country—Chicago, Dallas, Seattle, Atlanta, and so on—the same cities used as wholesale outlets by the garment manufacturers, meatpackers, and other industries. Each distributor had an exchange along "film row." Prints were delivered from the exchanges to the theaters in time to open; prints of the closing program were returned for inspection and repair, then made available to other theaters in the region. In the eighteen to twenty thousand theaters across the country (estimates vary), nine thousand bookings were considered a good average for individual pictures. The first thirty-five hundred to four thousand bookings were scrutinized carefully to determine likelihood of success. If the projected income looked hopeful, more money might be spent on promotion. If not, the film was allowed to die quietly; prints would be kept in the exchanges, but no more money would be spent on promotion. Many fine films, particularly some small ones with quiet tone and subtle appeal, met this fate without being given a chance to reach the audience that might have existed for them.

The flow of money that started at the box office moved from the exhibitor to the distributor and finally back to the producer. Each took a cut to cover costs and make a profit, if any. With a looseness of accounting that flabbergasted people in other businesses, the distributor had to trust the exhibitor's report, and the producer the distributor's. Everyone cheated, it was said, and yet there was usually enough income to go around.

Helping to ensure the profits of distribution and production were certain character-istic trade practices. **Block booking,** for example, meant the exhibitor had to rent films in packages that included the "dogs" along with the "hits." This assured some return on even the weakest items in a studio's annual program. **Blind buying** occurred when an exhibitor was forced to book films unseen—sometimes even before they were made—to guarantee an advance market that would cover at least some of the considerable production and dis-tribution costs. Block booking and blind buying led to **overbuying.** In those days of sur-plus product, the exhibitor might have to book more films than could be shown in order to get those that would attract the largest audiences. In return for what might be regarded as economic harassment (in 1940 the federal courts ruled the practices illegal), the exhibitor got **clearance** or **zoning.** If the theater were a downtown first-run "house" in a city, the ex-hibitor was assured that the film booked would not be shown in any other theater down-town or in the neighborhoods or suburbs until a certain time had elapsed—six months, say; or, if the theater was in a small town, the exhibitor knew that the film would not be shown in a town closer than perhaps twenty miles away.

In the days of vertical control this set of ungentlemanly agreements successfully kept out independents in any of the three phases—production, distribution, exhibition—except by tolerance of the major studios. Because profits could be made at any of the three lev-els, competition was largely internal within a single company: among its production, dis-tribution, and exhibition branches. As for competition among the eight firms, because the members of the MPPDA parceled out their spheres of influence (kinds of production, re-gions in which theaters were owned), they competed with one another only in somewhat the manner of the several divisions of General Motors Corporation—Buick with Oldsmo-bile with Pontiac. Vertical control also meant that the industry could thoroughly police it-self in terms of kinds of screen content it felt would be acceptable to the public. By self-censoring it was able to forestall outcries of moral indignation that might hurt the box office and invite government intervention.

Censorship, Self-Regulation, and Pressure Groups

To some creators, the system of self-regulation that developed was an even more onerous fea-ture of the industrial organization than was the single-minded pursuit of profits by front of-fice and stockholders. Certainly it had substantial effect on what would appear on the screen or, more accurately, what would not. This "production code" remained in operation with only minor revisions until 1968, when the industry adopted the practice, common abroad, of reg-ulating attendance (the G/PG/R/X ratings) rather than content. The United States is almost unique among nations in never having had federal censorship of motion pictures.

As noted earlier, the move toward self-regulation began in the years immediately fol-lowing World War I. It came in response to public criticism and the industry's fear of in-creased state and municipal censorship, and perhaps even federal government involvement. Eight states and a number of cities had passed film censorship laws by the early 1920s. Public indignation had been provoked by films reflecting (exacerbating, some argued) a new, freer morality that featured hip flasks, knee-length skirts, and petting in the rumble seats of roadsters. Rocked by scandals surrounding the death of a starlet after an orgy (comedian Roscoe "Fatty" Arbuckle was accused of having caused her death), and by the unsolved murder of director William Desmond Taylor, Hollywood became the subject of particularly strident criticism.

In 1922 the Motion Picture Producers and Distributors of America hired Will H. Hays, Postmaster General and former national chairman of the Republican Party, to become its head. The response of the "Hays Office" to new threats of economic boycott and government intervention was the **Motion Picture Production Code.** Like the Ten Commandments, the Code's language was largely negative. Restrictions on what could be dealt with and how appeared under twelve main headings: crimes against the law, sex, vulgarity, obscenity, profanity, costume, dances, religion, locations (that is, bedrooms), national feelings, titles ("salacious, indecent, or obscene"), and repellent subjects (actual hangings or electrocutions, third degree, brutality, branding of people or animals, apparent cruelty to children or animals, the sale of women, surgical operations). Totally forbidden were presentations of drug traffic or the use of drugs, sexual perversion, "white slavery," sexual relationships between the white and black races, and nudity.

In 1934 Catholic forces, particularly unhappy about Hollywood flouting the Code drafted by two of their own, formed the Legion of Decency. Because the Legion's program rested on boycotting films that violated the Code (their titles to be announced from pulpits across the country), the industry finally became sufficiently alarmed to institute a mechanism to enforce adherence: the Code seal, to be applied by the Production Code Administration. Joseph I. Breen, a young Catholic newspaperman, was appointed director. The members of the MPPDA agreed not to release or distribute films unless they carried the seal. A $25,000 penalty was instituted for producing, distributing, or exhibiting any picture that had not received it. Given vertical and nearly complete control of the industry by the major studio members of the association, not a single important feature was released without the seal in the next two decades.

Naturally film makers working within the Code tried to suggest what they could not show; the leer replaced a frank look at many of life's realities. Because restrictions were greatest on sexual matters, sexuality was replaced by violence (regarded with more equanimity by the society as well as by the Production Code Administration). Hollywood's adherence to the Code ensured that reality was not so much excluded (as was argued by the social critics of the 1930s) as dealt with obliquely and within the fixed rubrics of the popular forms. In *Trouble in Paradise* (1932), for example, after Gaston and Lily embrace passionately on a couch, the culmination of that embrace is expressed by a dissolve to the same couch, now empty, followed by a cut to Gaston's hand hanging a "Do Not Disturb" sign on the bedroom door. The indirection of content, like the stylization of technique, frequently adds to rather than detracts from the charm and resonant effectiveness of the best films of the 1930s.

Color

Like sound, color was part of the experience of going to the movies from the earliest days. In the silent era color was used for decorative effect and to convey information. **Tinting and toning** were popular processes whereby particular scenes were washed with a single color to convey a special mood or signal the time of day (blue for night, yellow for day). Another popular procedure was hand coloring, a painstaking undertaking in which parts of each frame were painted in by hand. Explosions and fires were frequently given this treatment.

Experiments with techniques to develop full-color film culminated in the invention of **Technicolor** in the 1930s. Technicolor enabled not only color but also brilliant, highly saturated color. Initially the studios limited color to short sequences within films such as musical numbers or fashion shows. But the lure of color soon led them to use it throughout the story as well. Spectacles, westerns, animated films, and musicals were the genres most frequently given the color treatment. The famous moment in *The Wizard of Oz* in which Dorothy steps out of her house to enter the land of Oz showcased the vibrant Technicolor palette to full effect. In subsequent years, as color became more ubiquitous and other color processes replaced the cumbersome Technicolor method, most film makers came to prefer darker tones to the "Christmas present" colors identified with Technicolor. But the radiant glow of the old Technicolor movies—which, unlike the colors of newer processes, never fades—still gives the films of this era a unique vitality and charm.

Notable Directors of the 1930s

In part as a result of the efforts of the Directors Guild of America, which was formed in 1935 to advance the power and image of its members, directors as a group gained more control over the film-making process during the late 1930s than they had enjoyed in the early part of the decade. A few of the directors who did important work in the 1930s and early 1940s stand as emblems of how respect and recognition accorded to directors were beginning to grow. Josef von Sternberg, Howard Hawks, Frank Capra, and John Ford would appear on the lists of many historians as preeminent. Often with the help of valuable collaborators, each of these film makers managed to cultivate an identifiable personal style by ingeniously navigating a path through the headwinds, storms, and shoals that were part and parcel of the studios that employed them. Although all started in silent film in the 1920s and some continued to work fruitfully for decades after the 1930s, they all reached creative maturity during this time.

Josef von Sternberg is the supreme visual stylist. With him the shadow is the substance. In a series of films starring Marlene Dietrich—*Morocco,* 1930; *Dishonored,* 1931; *Shanghai Express,* 1932; *The Scarlet Empress,* 1934 (Figure 7.2); and *The Devil Is a Woman,* 1935—he fashioned and perfected his own unique, exotic screen world. Von Sternberg believed that a film should be capable of offering an aesthetic experience when projected upside down and backward. He had a thorough background as an editor and cameraman, and there is evidence suggesting he did much of the cinematography on the films he directed. Certainly he understood lighting and used it for extraordinarily intricate and consistent effect. It may be a mixed compliment to observe that a still from a von Sternberg film gives a fuller sense of its essence than would a still from any other director's work.

Howard Hawks is a quite different sort of artist. His is the art that conceals art. Working within genre conventions he nonetheless manages to state and restate what evidently were for him persistent preoccupations having to do with professionalism, individual courage (and cowardice, its complement), loyalty to the group, friendship among men, and the battle between the sexes. He began and ended the 1930s with films dealing with flying (*The Dawn Patrol,* 1930; *Only Angels Have Wings,* 1939), and he himself had been a flyer in World War I. In both films Hawks is obviously admiring in his treatment of the aviators. Dangerous flying can be senseless and frightening, but the camaraderie, pride, and bravery

FIGURE 7.2   *The Scarlet Empress* ★ United States, 1934, Josef von Sternberg; Sam Jaffe and Marlene Dietrich.

it allows for are to be honored. In *Dawn Patrol* there are no women (not even a mention of them except for the mothers of dead aviators), and their absence is filled by a "female" tenderness among the flyers toward each other. *Only Angels Have Wings* sets Jean Arthur off in pursuit of Cary Grant; but, because she is a woman, she can't really understand why the men behave as they do, and she represents a tacit threat to the group. These are some of the consistent thematic materials of Hawks the action director, the director of men's pictures.

Peter Wollen acknowledged the dynamism and stress prevalent in all of Hawks's work. Wollen also sees what he calls the crazy comedies (including *Twentieth Century,* 1934, and *Bringing Up Baby,* 1938) as the inverse of the adventure dramas. "They are the agonized exposure of the underlying tensions of the heroic dramas," he writes. "Whereas the dramas show the mastery of man over nature, over woman, over the animal and childish; the comedies show his humiliation, his regression. The heroes become victims; society instead of being excluded and despised, breaks in with irruptions of monstrous farce."[1] The two strata must be taken together, Wollen argues, if we are to get a full sense of the meanings Hawks offers in the recurrent motifs of his films.

Frank Capra's comedies are essentially social. They present an explicit view of American society, its economy and its politics—a view traditionally seen as uniquely Capraesque—though Joseph McBride's 1992 biography of the director called attention to the important

---

[1] Peter Wollen, *Signs and Meaning in the Cinema* (London: Secker & Warburg, 1972), p. 91.

contributions of Capra's longtime screenwriter Robert Riskin in establishing Capra's distinctive themes. *Mr. Deeds Goes to Town* (1936) and *Mr. Smith Goes to Washington* (1939) (Figure 7.3) celebrate the "little guy" (played by Gary Cooper or James Stewart)—not as dumb as he seems and, once aroused, able to defeat the city slickers and the power figures. His victories are achieved through pluck, persistence, Jean Arthur, and his overwhelming decency, which is matched by the decency of the American people when they see the true situation. Frequently even the villains are redeemed in Capra's films, because at heart they too are usually well intentioned. This rosy portrait of America was typically depicted in crisp, glowing images contributed by Joseph Walker, who photographed many of Capra's best films.

Capra country is essentially an idealized small-town America (no matter that *Mr. Deeds* ostensibly takes place in New York City and *Mr. Smith* is set in Washington, DC). His films celebrate lovable eccentricities and homely virtues. Even in the 1930s this view was clearly nostalgic. Richard Griffith, in *The Film Till Now*, labels Capra's conception the "fantasy of goodwill." The huge popular success of his pictures attests to the appeal his vision had in those troubled times. If Capra's sensibility was uniquely tuned to the prevailing mood of the 1930s, his post-1930s films suggest a man who has lost his popular

FIGURE 7.3 *Mr. Smith Goes to Washington* ☆ United States, 1939, Frank Capra; James Stewart.

touch. In 1941 Capra and Riskin fashioned a darker variation on the theme of the little guy making good in *Meet John Doe*. In this tale, a cynical newspaper columnist played by Barbara Stanwyck invents a character (John Doe) who is threatening to commit suicide because of the corruption rampant in American society. A good-looking hobo (Gary Cooper) is subsequently hired to play the character Stanwyck has created. The logical conclusion of this story would have Cooper's character kill himself. But Capra could not live with such a tragic finish. "In desperation—setting some kind of pointless record," he recalled in his autobiography, "I was to photograph five different endings, and then try them out on theater audiences; all collapsed like punctured balloons." Ultimately, he settled on a conclusion that conveyed a cautious optimism. Retreating from the confusion that *John Doe* created, Capra returned to the ingredients that had fueled his early successes with *It's a Wonderful Life* (1946). Although it is as finely crafted as any of his films (it's Capra's favorite and has become a television tradition at Christmastime), it flopped at the box office. Its failure suggests that the country in the mid-1940s was a radically different place after the experience of World War II. In spite of his own contribution to the war effort in the *Why We Fight* series of documentaries made for the armed forces, Capra's own thinking and feeling seem to have remained in the earlier time.

John Ford, who, like Hawks and unlike Sternberg and Capra, continued to do some of his finest work after the 1930s, nevertheless established his reputation during those years. The cycle that began with *Steamboat 'Round the Bend* (1935) and continued with *The Prisoner of Shark Island* (1936), *Stagecoach* (1939) (Figure 7.4), and *Young Mr. Lincoln* (1939) showed Ford as the chronicler of American history and the reworker of American folklore, especially of its frontier West.

Stagecoach set a standard for westerns that were to follow, with a script by Ford's frequent collaborator Dudley Nichols and a career-making performance by another Ford stalwart, John Wayne (who is introduced in a striking short tracking shot). The film is an ensemble piece, chronicling the adventures of a group of people thrown together in the confined interior of a moving vehicle. The plot follows a classic journey structure as the stagecoach traverses the arid landscape of Utah's Monument Valley. The spectacular setting was ever afterward identified as an archetype of the western genre, as were many of the film's characters: Wayne's good badman on the run from the law, Claire Trevor's warm-hearted dance-hall girl, Thomas Mitchell's alcoholic doctor, and Berton Churchill's corrupt banker. Even gravel-voiced western icon Andy Devine was on board as the stagecoach driver.

In his westerns that followed *Stagecoach,* including *My Darling Clementine* (1946) and *The Searchers* (1956), Ford continued to explore the forces set in motion by the European expansion in the New World. The savagery of the wilderness was frequently symbolized in these films by the figure of the Native American, bands of whom are often shown rampaging over the plains in wild disorder in contrast to the neat columns of cavalry troops led by widely admired stars such as John Wayne, Henry Fonda, and James Stewart. For Ford, as for other directors of westerns, the indigenous peoples of America represented what stood in the way of the advance of a civilizing order. In later years, Ford rethought his attitude toward the Native Americans; his elegiac 1962 western *Cheyenne Autumn* focuses on their plight of being displaced from their ancestral homelands by the policies instituted by an Anglo government.

Almost all of Ford's films of whatever genre reveal a profound reverence for nature. Ford favors outdoor scenes, often featuring expansive skyscapes that contrast with cramped,

FIGURE 7.4   *Stagecoach*   ★   United States, 1939, John Ford.

overcrowded interior spaces. To achieve an effect of oppressive closeness in his interiors, he frequently took the unusual step of putting ceilings on his sets; in many scenes these ceilings can be seen looming just above the characters' heads. Ford's traditional outlook also embraced the values of the family and the past: Graveside scenes, old-fashioned folk music, and the need to avenge wrongs done to relatives are recurring motifs in his films.

Emergent Genres in the 1930s

Although genres came about because of the requirements of mass production and popular appeal, they have nonetheless been consistently developed by American film makers. Of the popular genres that had formed into recognizable patterns during the 1920s, silent comedy was affected most radically by the introduction of sound. While lamenting the loss of comic pantomime and the great clowns who made it the universal and timeless form it is, we would still want to welcome the new kinds of comedies and the creators who entered with sound. Westerns, of course, could only be hampered by the sound stages; during the the first half of the 1930s they were relegated largely to "B" and "C" production budgets and comparable prestige. They became the "oaters" beloved by rural adult populations and small boys everywhere on Saturday afternoons, but had little to do with the advance of the motion picture generally. Of the narrative forms emerging with the new sound medium, most vigorous and characteristic of the 1930s were the musical, the gangster film, the horror film, the sound comedy, and the animated cartoon.

The **musical** was dependent on sound for its existence. In such harbingers as *The Merry Widow* of 1925, von Stroheim's most popular film, audiences had to be content with a live pit orchestra or organist providing a potpourri of Franz Lehar melodies to accompany the pantomimed action and printed titles. Fittingly, the film that caused the revolution, *The Jazz Singer* (1927), foreshadowed the backstage musical, an important early subgenre. What it lacked most essentially was dancing, for the appeal of the musical often came to depend as much on choreography as on music. From *The Hollywood Revue of 1929* through *Saturday Night Fever* (1977), *All That Jazz* (1979), *Flashdance* (1982), and *Chicago* (2002), the creators of musicals frequently have been men and women of dance as well as song.

The Hollywood Revue of 1929 was a prototype for one line of musical, the revue, which flourished in the 1930s and first half of the 1940s. It disappeared after World War II, with only a few exceptions (*Ziegfeld Follies,* 1946; *New Faces,* 1952). Consisting of separate "acts" unconnected by narrative linkage, like its stage counterpart, the screen revue let audiences throughout the world see the great entertainers whose performances had formerly been confined to Broadway and infrequent tours. Generally presented very much as they might have been on a superstage (by impresario Florenz Ziegfeld, for example), the film revues substituted the possibility of perfection—ideal performers in their best performances—for the special excitements of live theater.

Another early film musical form deriving from theater was the filmed operetta. It began with the romantic musical comedies of Ernst Lubitsch (starting with *The Love Parade,* 1929) and Rouben Mamoulian (*Love Me Tonight,* 1932). These operetta-like screen originals were made at Paramount and starred Maurice Chevalier and/or Jeanette MacDonald. Moving to M-G-M, in 1934 Lubitsch directed the same stars in his version of *The Merry Widow.* It was at M-G-M that the operetta continued, in a series of standard stage favorites beginning with *Naughty Marietta* in 1935. In them Chevalier was replaced by Nelson Eddy; he and Mac-Donald helped make a great deal of money for everyone concerned.

The first backstage musical may have been *Broadway Melody* (M-G-M, 1929), which was also the first Academy Award winner, but it was at Warner Bros. that the cycle was launched. In 1930 Warners imported Broadway veteran Busby Berkeley, who became master of the production number. His ranks and clusters of chorines moving with military precision through elaborate patterns are understandably the subject of "camp" appreciation today. Those extravagant creations nonetheless contain an exotic charm. Early in the period Berkeley's spectacular staging and bravura use of camera, cutting, and special effects were brought together in the narrative musical.

In the 1933 *42nd Street* Berkeley started full scale on that special kind of creation we associate with his name (Figure 7.5). The massed chorines are viewed by the camera from almost any position except a stationary one in front of a theater stage. They are seen from overhead as they form floral patterns or strange concentric rings suggesting interconnecting gears. Or the camera gets down on the floor and moves through their spread legs in a slyly elegant bit of erotica. Costumes and settings are designed to support and underscore the extravagant fantasy of the total choreographic conception; or, to put it the other way around, the dances grow out of and take full advantage of every suggestion pro-

FIGURE 7.5   *42nd Street* ★ United States, 1933, Lloyd Bacon/Busby Berkeley; Ruby Keeler.

vided by the visual decor. The chorus line performs a jerky, syncopated march up the stairs, they turn toward the camera and raise cardboard profiles of skyscrapers, covering themselves and becoming a miniature Manhattan. Berkeley would later sustain and elaborate on delights of this sort at their most breathtaking (and bizarre) in the *Gold Diggers* series (*of 1933, 1935, 1937*).

A series of films starring Fred Astaire and Ginger Rogers were the first to drop the theatrical setting as an excuse for music and dancing. Although they play professional dancers, thus making their terpsichorean skill plausible, they move from the theater out into the world, breaking into song and dance whenever the emotional charge is sufficient. Astaire and Rogers, whose films together extend from 1933 to 1949, served to link the backstage musical inaugurated by *42nd Street* (same year as *Flying Down to Rio,* the first Rogers/Astaire) and the vintage cluster of M-G-M musicals beginning with *On the Town* (same year as the last Astaire/Rogers, *The Barkleys of Broadway*), which offered song and dance as the normal response to life. The M-G-M cycle, overseen by producer Arthur Freed, included some of the films many historians feel mark the high point of the genre: *Meet Me in St. Louis* (Vincente Minnelli, 1944), *Singin' in the Rain* (Gene Kelly and Stanley Donen, 1952), and *The Band Wagon* (Minnelli, 1952). In more recent times the traditional musical has been eclipsed by mutant forms: "rock docs" such as *Woodstock* (Michael Wadleigh, 1970), dance contest pictures such as *Saturday Night Fever* (John Badham, 1977), fantasy films such as *Moulin Rouge* (Baz Luhrmann, 2001), and music videos.

Although there were many films about gangsters in the 1920s (von Sternberg's *Under-world,* 1927, is one example), the **gangster film** is indissolubly linked with the 1930s. It thrived on the growling of limousines in low gear, the squealing of tires and screeching of brakes, the ratchet noise of tommy guns, and the explosions and tinkling of glass. It was born and brought up within that decade. *Little Caesar* (1930) (Figure 7.6) began the cycle; *The Public Enemy* (1931) and *Scarface* (1932) confirmed its power. Later decades would retool the genre's "success at any price" theme to speak to social dilemmas differ-ent from the economic desperation that characterized the United States in the 1930s: the psychic dislocation occasioned by World War II (*White Heat,* 1940); post-Watergate cyn-icism about political corruption (*The Godfather* cycle, 1972, 1974, and 1990); and the amoral accumulation of wealth (*Goodfellas,* 1990).

As the prototype, *Little Caesar,* directed by Mervyn LeRoy, contains the essential thesis of the classic gangster film in its simplest and clearest form. Rico (Edward G. Robin-son), the hero, or perhaps the antihero, begins as a gun-toting thug with ambition—the toughest, most ruthless of the lot. What motivates him is the exercise of power. The film makers don't feel obliged to justify their dramatic premise: It is presented as a given. Those on top are enviable because they are rich and powerful. But as one climbs upward there's a danger of becoming soft. Refinement and sentiment make people vulnerable and lead to destruction through "loss of nerve." The film begins with Rico murdering a robbery vic-tim and ends with Rico being gunned down by the police after he fails to shoot his friend, Joe Massara (Douglas Fairbanks, Jr.), who becomes indirectly responsible for his death.

FIGURE 7.6 *Little Caesar* ★ United States, 1930, Mervyn LeRoy; Edward G. Robinson, center right.

While the musical and gangster genres flourished at Warner's, **horror films** were the specialty of Universal. The appearance of these successors to *The Golem* and *Nosferatu* seems to have had less to do with the advent of sound technology than with American mastery of the lighting techniques originated earlier in Germany. Chiaroscuro lighting was crucial to the evocation of terror, and the names of German emigrés dot the technical credits of this series. Also, as in Germany, it may be that audiences respond especially to horror on the screen during times of national instability. At any rate, as with the gangster films, the two prototypical American horror films set forth fully the traits of their progeny. *Frankenstein* and *Dracula,* both released in 1931, are still in active circulation on video and in college series and courses.

The opening graveyard scene of *Frankenstein*—with its low-angled shots among the tombstones, an iconic cross, and a figure of death (Figure 7.7a)—establishes the mood. The desolate landscapes, the remote ancestral castle, the forbidding stone tower in which Dr. Frankenstein conducts his experiments, the laboratory interior with its flashing electrodes—all would become familiar images of the gothic horror movie. A sense of impending doom hangs over the film like a pall. Stylized Ruritanian settings and the bleak black-and-white cinematography create the visual atmosphere of shadowy gloom that dominates successive films of the genre.

As an outcast of society, the monster prompts an empathic response drawn from our own feelings of loneliness and alienation (Figure 7.7b). Perhaps a Depression-ridden society, economically and culturally deprived, was particularly attuned to this appeal—and also to the suggestion that there is madness in high places, which can set loose a monstrous, impersonal, uncontrollable, destructive force.

The archetypical horror film, like the gangster film, waxed in the 1930s and waned after that decade, degenerating into more simplistic tales of horror and finally even to self-parody (the series of *Abbott and Costello Meet* films; *Frankenstein,* 1948; the *Invisible Man,* 1951; and others). Though ailing, the genre didn't die with the 1930s. Instead, the horror films produced by Val Lewton in the 1940s—such as *Cat People* (1942), *I Walked with a Zombie* (1943), and *The Body Snatcher* (1945)—mark a sharp departure from the broad effects of the earlier cycle and are noteworthy for their subtlety. Later the horror film

FIGURE 7.7a and b *Frankenstein* ★ United States, 1931, James Whale.

was restored to something like full health by Roger Corman in his series of Edgar Allan Poe adaptations (such as *The Fall of the House of Usher,* 1960; *The Masque of the Red Death,* 1964) made in England. Though not as distinctively American as the musical or gangster film, like the other genres, the horror film has been worked at consistently by American film makers including Corman, Brian De Palma, George Romero, John Carpenter, and Wes Craven. It is another lasting contribution of the American 1930s.

Comedy, which had flourished from the earliest days of film making, found new modes of expression in the sound era. One line took advantage of the new possibilities for repartee and double entendre. Although like drawing room comedies of the theater, in the best film examples (Lubitsch's *Trouble in Paradise,* 1932) visual interest was retained and sight and sound were worked into counterpoint. A second line, out of vaudeville and stage, and replacing the silent clowns, featured talking comic stars in vehicles tailored to their special talents and the verbal styles associated with them. The Marx Brothers, for example, merely transferred to film their theatrical hits *The Cocoanuts* and *Animal Crackers,* in 1929 and 1930. W. C. Fields had been a popular vaudeville performer whose most memorable film bits (for instance, the crooked cue-stick routine) had frequently been worked out before on stage. Mae West, long before she appeared in movies, had played her particular version of herself on stage (Figure 7.8). The point is that the great comic movie stars of the 1930s were experienced with sound, especially with their own distinctive voices, as supplement to pantomime. In fact, they required sound for full comic effect.

FIGURE 7.8   *My Little Chickadee*   ★   United States, 1940, Edward Cline; W. C. Fields and Mae West.

A third kind of comedy developed in the 1930s was called the "screwball" comedy. This style combined intellectual sophistication with slapstick behavior. It depended on fast, witty dialogue and a battle of the sexes in which male and female roles were often reversed (in terms of traditional expectations of male strength and dominance). The performers most frequently inhabiting the screwball world were Claudette Colbert, Gary Cooper, Irene Dunne, Cary Grant, Jean Harlow, Katharine Hepburn, Carole Lombard, Rosalind Russell, Barbara Stanwyck, and James Stewart.

Frank Capra's enormously successful *It Happened One Night* (1934) may have been the first of the screwball comedies. Howard Hawks also directed effectively in this subgenre (*Twentieth Century,* 1934; *Bringing Up Baby,* 1938; *His Girl Friday,* 1940; *Ball of Fire,* 1941). Other directors who did memorable work in this style were Gregory La Cava (*My Man Godfrey,* 1936), William Wellman (*Nothing Sacred,* 1937), and Leo McCarey (*The Awful Truth,* 1937). The distinctive series of comedies written as well as directed by Preston Sturges are also of this type (*The Lady Eve,* 1941; *The Palm Beach Story,* 1942; *The Miracle of Morgan's Creek,* 1944; *Hail the Conquering Hero,* 1944 [Figure 7.9]; and others).

Scripts, even more than direction or performance, seem to provide the basis for the screwball cycle; the writers (especially Ben Hecht, Robert Riskin, Charles Brackett, Billy Wilder, and Preston Sturges) worked out the typical patterns of theme, plot, and dialogue. Ludicrously improbable situations were devised and then dealt with as if they were everyday occurrences. In *Bringing Up Baby,* screenplay by Dudley Nichols and Hagar Wilde, the plot is furthered as Katharine Hepburn, playing an heiress, has her dress torn off while

FIGURE 7.9 *Hail the Conquering Hero* ★ United States, 1944, Preston Sturges; Ella Raines, Eddie Bracken, and Franklin Pangborn.

in an elegant dining room—much to the embarrassment of Cary Grant, a paleontologist. Subsequently (1) they collide with a truck full of chickens; (2) Grant chases her aunt's dog around a country estate, to find a brontosaurus bone; and (3) a wild leopard is mistaken for a tame one (Baby of the title). The dialogue is filled with unmistakably American exuberance. These films all evidence a close and sensitive attention to the native idiom— wisecracks, slang, and wrenched clichés are rapped out with uproarious effect.

What the trade called the **woman's picture,** aimed at the female customers who comprised most of the matinee audience, consisted mainly of love stories and domestic melodramas. The genre originated in the 1920s, when women attending entertainments on their own became socially acceptable; it came into full flower during the 1930s. As vehicles for glamorous stars, love stories fed the enormous fan appeal of actors such as Rudoph Valentino and Greta Garbo. The incandescent Garbo was set off to advantage in vehicles such as *Flesh and the Devil* (Clarence Brown, 1927), *Queen Christina* (Rouben Mamoulian, 1933), and *Camille* (George Cukor, 1937), whereas Valentino had earlier made millions swoon when he commanded Agnes Ayres, "Lie down, you little fool!" in *The Sheik* (1921). A series of memorable love stories directed by Josef von Sternberg during the 1930s showcased screen goddess Marlene Dietrich (*Morocco,* 1930, and *Blonde Venus,* 1932).

In *Queen Christina,* Garbo plays a sexually ambiguous Swedish monarch whose aborted love affair with a foreign envoy leads her to abdicate her throne. In the film's famous final shot, Christina stands at the prow of the ship that will take her away from Sweden and into the unknown. She gazes at the sea with an inscrutable expression. Mamoulian reportedly told Garbo to clear her mind of all thoughts for this shot so that viewers could read into it their own desires about what Christina's future might be like. Recent films, such as *The English Patient* (1997) and *Titanic* (1998), have attempted to revive the genre of the tragic love story, but in a certain sense *Queen Christina* and other films like it are irreproducible today. For whatever reasons, Hollywood is no longer able to manufacture the kind of love goddesses and matinee idols who could carry off such grandiose fantasies.

Domestic melodramas, which chronicle the travails and rewards of family life, came to the fore during this time as well, with stars Barbara Stanwyck, Bette Davis, and Joan Crawford delivering tour-de-force performances in productions such as *Stella Dallas* (King Vidor, 1937), *Now, Voyager* (Irving Rapper, 1942), and *Mildred Pierce* (Michael Curtiz, 1945). In these films, all problems become family problems as issues such as illegitimacy, adultery, and parent–child relationships are explored.

Stella Dallas, a moving tribute to mother love, marks a high point in the cycle. Stanwyck won an Oscar for her role as a mother whose lower-class background drives a wedge between her and her upwardly mobile daughter Laurel. As Laurel becomes more refined, Stella becomes more frowzy and vulgar. She is ultimately reduced to watching Laurel's wedding through a picture window, where the spectacle created by her garish clothes and loud manner is placed at a safe distance from the elegant society marriage into which her daughter is entering.

Bette Davis undergoes another kind of transformation in *Now, Voyager,* this one from dowdy old maid to glamorous foster mother. Under the care of an avuncular psychiatrist played by Claude Rains, Davis's Charlotte Vale rebels against her dominating mother (Figure 7.10a) and meets her soul mate Jerry Durrance (Paul Henreid) on an ocean voyage (Figure 7.10b). Although the two are prevented from marrying, Charlotte takes Jerry's troubled daughter Tina under her wing (Figure 7.10c). The film's final scene, in which Jerry lights

Charlotte's cigarette as the two stand together on a balcony gazing into the night sky, concludes with a famous statement of womanly renunciation. "Oh, Jerry, don't let's ask for the moon!" Charlotte exclaims, "We have the stars!" (Figure 7.10d).

Mother–daughter relationships again take center stage in *Mildred Pierce* (1945), starring Joan Crawford as a self-made restaurateur who uses her hard-earned wealth to spoil her daughter Veda. The story was given a dark edge by a climax that featured murderous passions and romantic betrayals. The film's director Michael Curtiz used two styles for this domestic melodrama–whodunit: an evenly lit balanced look for the early scenes and a dramatic deeply shadowed style for the later ones.

Dorothy Arzner, the only major female director working in Hollywood during this era, made a specialty of women's pictures, turning out a series of films celebrating women's lives and women's relationships. Her work with actresses—especially Clara Bow in *The Wild Party* (1927), Katharine Hepburn in *Christopher Strong* (1933), and Rosalind Russell in *Craig's Wife* (1936)—showcased their talents to great effect and played a significant role in furthering their careers. Arzner's best-known film, the 1940 *Dance, Girl, Dance,* juxtaposes Judy, an aspiring ballerina (Maureen O'Hara) with Bubbles, a burlesque queen (Lucille Ball), in a story about female rivalry and female friendship (Figure 7.11).

FIGURE 7.10a–d *Now, Voyager* ★ United States, 1942; Irving Rapper.

FIGURE 7.11   *Dance, Girl, Dance*   ★   United States, 1940, Dorothy Arzner; Maureen O'Hara and Lucille Ball.

The film's climactic scene depicts Judy performing before a jeering audience at a burlesque house where her desperate financial situation has forced her to accept employment. Suddenly turning her gaze back on the crowd, she stops the show to challenge the audience's complacent assumption that the position they occupy as spectators makes them invulnerable to criticism. "Go ahead and stare!" she exclaims. "I'm not ashamed. Go on. Laugh! Get your money's worth. Nobody's going to hurt you. I know you want me to tear my clothes off so's you can look your fifty cents worth." At this point in the film, the spectators in the movie house who are watching O'Hara pirouette may begin to feel that the comfortable, passive role they enjoy is also being impugned.

In the 1930s and early 1940s, what weren't genres and originally conceived for the screen were **adaptations** from literature, drama, history, or a combination of those sources, and included the most expensive and prestigious productions of the decade. In 1935 alone there were the spectacular *Mutiny on the Bounty* (Figure 7.12); Max Reinhardt's production of Shakespeare's *A Midsummer Night's Dream; Becky Sharp,* the first feature in three-color Technicolor; *Captain Blood,* with some marvelously conceived and executed sea battles; *David Copperfield;* and *Lives of a Bengal Lancer.* All manifested the scale and skill associated with the big-studio Hollywood film of the 1930s. They cost a lot and made a lot. Created by experts at that special sort of opulent illusion, they were enjoyed by audiences who responded to it unself-consciously and in large numbers.

FIGURE 7.12 *Mutiny on the Bounty* ★ United States, 1935, Frank Lloyd; Clark Gable and Charles Laughton, white shirts, center.

Foremost among the Hollywood professionals who created these prestigious products was William Wyler, who won Academy Awards for *Mrs. Miniver* (1942) and *The Best Years of Our Lives* (1946), both based on well-known literary sources. Also nominated for Oscars were Wyler adaptations of Sinclair Lewis's *Dodsworth* (1936), Sidney Kingsley's *Dead End* (1937), Emily Brontë's *Wuthering Heights* (1939), Somerset Maugham's *The Letter* (1940), and Lillian Hellman's *The Little Foxes* (1941). The complex character interactions that characterized these literary works found eloquent cinematic expression in Wyler's celebrated compositions in depth, which enabled audiences to focus on more than one dramatic center in a given scene. One memorable example occurs in *The Best Years of Our Lives,* when several characters gather at a bar. A group at the piano, including two of the protagonists, is in the right foreground; several persons at the bar are in left middle ground, reacting to the piano playing; the third protagonist is telephoning in center background.

The live-action comedies and other feature films of the 1930s were often preceded on the program by the enormously popular cartoon shorts. **Animated cartoons,** which had appeared intermittently from the early days, were given a boost by sound, color, and **Walt Disney.** Disney's first big hit, *Steamboat Willie* (1928) (Figure 7.13), was also one of the first animated films with synchronized sound. Soon cartoon shorts, provided by Disney and his imitators, became almost obligatory in theater programs, and Disney's ambitions carried him on to animated features. Among twentieth-century comic figures only Charlie's Tramp could rival the universal affection in which Walt's Mickey Mouse was held.

FIGURE 7.13   *Steamboat Willie* ★ United States, 1928, Walt Disney; Mickey Mouse.

What Disney started, others continued. Ub Iwerks seems to have become the princi-pal creative force at the Disney Studio as Walt concerned himself more and more with administration. The Fleischer Studios followed up their Koko the Clown character with the sexy Betty Boop and later Popeye, and M-G-M produced a mischievous cat and mouse named Tom and Jerry. In 1938 Chuck Jones, who had worked with Iwerks and Disney, moved to Warner Bros. and created a rival menagerie in Bugs Bunny, Tweetie Pie, Daffy Duck, Speedy Gonzalez, Road Runner, and Wile E. Coyote. Others who left Disney about the same time later established United Productions of America (UPA). It was UPA that offered the first radical departure from Disney in the extreme simplification and stylization of its drawings, much in the manner of modern French painting, and in the use of the human characters Mr. Magoo and Gerald McBoing Boing.

Poorly paid animation workers staged a series of strikes at various studios during the early 1940s. The strikes, along with the labor shortages occasioned by World War II, con-tributed to the waning enthusiasm for the animation genre among the studios that were its main producers. The disappearance of short subjects from movie programs was also a factor in the commercial decline of the form. Creative leadership passed from the Disney Studio to UPA and to government film making like that of the National Film Board of Canada, with Norman McLaren, and especially to animation units in Poland, Czechoslo-vakia, Yugoslavia, and Japan.

Who Framed Roger Rabbit? produced by the Disney Studio in 1988, was a technically extraordinary fusion of live action (directed by Robert Zemeckis) with animation (by Richard Williams). It featured cartoon characters created by animators at Disney, Warner Bros., M-G-M, and other studios in the 1940s. With new animated features such as *Beauty and the Beast* (1991), *The Prince of Egypt* (1998), and the Japanese animé film *The Princess Mononoke* (1999), as well as the new forms of computer animation on display in *Toy Story* (1997) and *Shrek* (2002), the enthusiastic critical as well as popular response that had greeted earlier Disneys was repeated, perhaps even exceeded.

Wartime

Along with other social and economic abrasions, the 1930s contained the beginnings of World War II in military conquest and imperialist expansion. Japan gobbled up chunks of a China weakened by internal factionalism. Italy overran a defenseless Ethiopia. Germany joined Italy in testing weapons and tactics and helping to defeat the Republicans in Spain. The Germans continued to bluff their way through a series of territorial acquisitions culminating in the notorious Munich agreement concluded between Reichskanzler Adolph Hitler and Prime Minister Neville Chamberlain. On September 1, 1939, German dive bombers took to the skies, and tanks and trucks rolled across the Polish border, causing England and France to declare war on Germany. By some ten months later, not only Poland but also France (along with Denmark, Norway, the Netherlands, and Belgium) had been ignominiously defeated. Germany's occupation of virtually all of western Europe was complete and Britain was left to fight on alone against that massed power.

The preceding decade ended with the outbreak of World War II in Europe, but for the United States 1940 and 1941 were pretty much a continuation of the 1930s. The United States had been backing into the war, pushed by the commitment President Roosevelt and other opinion leaders felt to Great Britian and its struggle against Nazi Germany. But the majority of the American public remained isolationist, preoccupied with ongoing domestic dificulties. When the Depression finally ended, it didn't die of natural causes; it was merely replaced by the artificial boom of a wartime economy after the Japanese attack on Pearl Harbor pulled the nation into the conflict in December 1941.

The United States would continue to provide the Allied and neutral countries with the bulk of their screen entertainment. The Hollywood films of wartime, for the most part, were more an extension of those of the 1930s—appropriately trimmed with references to the war—than a prelude to those of the second half of the 1940s. The memorable *Casablanca* (1943) (Figure 7.14) is one prominent example, its bittersweet romance tinged with antifascist idealism. Aljean Harmetz's book on the making of this consummate Hollywood product attributes the film's initial popularity to the timeliness of its release, just after Roosevelt and Churchill were finishing a crucial meeting in Casablanca. But the production was marketed on the basis of its human drama rather than its historical importance. A voice-over narrator for the trailer stated, "Against this fascinating background is woven the story of an imperishable love and the enthralling saga of six desperate people, each in Casablanca to keep an appointment with destiny." The story features a romance between Rick (Humphrey Bogart) and Ilsa (Ingrid Bergman) as Dooley Wilson plays and sings, "As Time Goes By."

Some of the films dealing directly with the war, derived from popular genres and toughened by wartime realities, antedated a postwar tendency toward realism. Among the

FIGURE 7.14   *Casablanca* ★ United States, 1943, Michael Curtiz; Claude Rains (in dark uniform), Paul Henreid, Humphrey Bogart, and Ingrid Bergman.

most popular were *Wake Island* (1942); *Air Force, Bataan, The Moon Is Down* (all 1943); *Lifeboat, Thirty Seconds Over Tokyo* (both 1944); and *The Story of G. I. Joe* (1945). But it has been estimated that less than a third of the wartime films dealt with the war. More characteristic was the continuation, with home-front themes or military ruffles and flourishes added, of the comedies, the light romantic or family dramas, and the musicals, now increased in number and vitality. Still, the bulk of American films of World War II undoubtedly contributed to the war effort. When not inspirational and hortatory, they were wholesomely entertaining and supportive of the culture the war was being fought to preserve.

A 1940s Genre: Film Noir

During the first half of the 1940s a body of films began that represented a sort of substratum amidst wartime patriotism and wholesomeness. This subgenre or style subsequently identified by French critics as ***film noir*** was referred to in the close of Chapter 3. These dark melodramas of crime and corruption, of psychological dislocation and aberration, reveal a Germanic influence in their intricate and artificial visual style and their preoccupation with disordered psyches. *Noir* is an attitude as well as a style, however, and is descended not only from German expressionism of the 1920s but also from French poetic realism of the 1930s, especially the films of Marcel Carné and Jacques Prévert.

Some would say that the success of *The Maltese Falcon* (1941), John Huston's first directorial effort, established not only a private-eye formula but also the beginning of *film noir. Noir,* however, was subsequently developed especially in the work of a few German and Austrian expatriates. Austrian-born Billy Wilder was one of the masters of the black film; his *Double Indemnity* (1944), coscripted by Raymond Chandler, is a prime example. Along with Wilder there were Robert Siodmak (*Phantom Lady,* 1944; *The Spiral Staircase,* 1945; *The Killers,* 1946), Otto Preminger (*Laura,* 1944; *Fallen Angel,* 1945), and Fritz Lang (*The Woman in the Window,* 1944; *Scarlet Street,* 1945). The style spread to include films of a number of other distinguished Hollywood professionals, among them Edward Dmytryk (*Murder, My Sweet,* 1944) and Howard Hawks (*The Big Sleep,* 1946). Prominent among later examples are *Gilda* (Charles Vidor, 1946), *Kiss of Death* (Henry Hathaway, 1947), *Out of the Past* (Jacques Tourneur, 1947), and *Kiss Me Deadly* (Robert Aldrich, 1955).

The fantasies the *noir* films offered were nightmare hallucinations full of indecipherable complications, a pervasive sense of fear and helplessness in the face of enigmatic human malevolence. The protagonists are typically trapped, seeking to find a way out of a tortuous labyrinth of violence and evil. The antagonists are frequently seductive women, career criminals, worldly foreigners, or members of a decadent and sexually permissive upper class. As opposed to the idealism of a society fighting together to combat the political evil of fascism, *film noir* dealt with individuals conspicuously antisocial in their greed and selfishness, driven to crime out of an incurable sickness. Their malaise was presented as endemic to the human species, and the world they inhabited was a dark one literally as well as morally. The films take place mostly at night, in seedy furnished apartments and on rain-washed streets of big cities. Studio sets were fashioned into urban jungles with predators stalking prey and danger lurking in the shadows, intermittently revealed by flashing electric signs. Perhaps even more than most other cinematic styles, *film noir* depends for its impact on nonverbal, essentially visual effects, whereby form far outstrips content. The scene in *Phantom Lady* featuring a hopped-up jazz drummer (Elisha Cook, Jr.) surrounded by swirling cigarette smoke, glaring lights, and harsh shadows and photographed from low, oblique angles is characteristic of *noir.*

The most accomplished director of *noir* films was **Fritz Lang.** As the film maker responsible for such German masterpieces as *Metropolis* and *M,* Lang came to the United States with a distinguished pedigree that was ideally suited to the *noir* style. He continued his exploration of dark themes, typically expressed through hard lighting and occasional overhead shots that pinned characters to the ground like ants. His two *noir* films with Edward G. Robinson, Joan Bennett, and Dan Duryea, *The Woman in the Window* (1944) (Figure 7.15) and *Scarlet Street* (1945), stand as classics of the cycle. In *The Woman in the Window,* Robinson, playing a timid professor called Richard Wanley, becomes enmeshed in a tangled web of intrigue with Alice Reed (Joan Bennett), an alluring stranger whose portrait he greatly admires. In Alice's apartment, Richard repeatedly confronts his image reflected in mirrors as he begins to confront new facets of his personality. In a coldly analytical style, the film examines the way in which illicit behavior and criminality emerge from hidden parts of people's personalities.

Another influential director whose career is closely identified with the *noir* style was **John Huston.** Following the *noir* tradition of dark passions, criminality, and pessimism,

FIGURE 7.15   *The Woman in the Window* ★ United States, 1944, Fritz Lang; Joan Bennett and Edward G. Robinson.

Huston's films often feature groups of people undertaking dangerous enterprises at great risk; most of these endeavors end in failure. In Huston's world of male adventurers, women are typically seen as weak, manipulative, and not to be trusted; his films rarely end with the traditional Hollywood romantic clinch. *The Maltese Falcon,* which Huston adapted from a novel by hard-boiled writer Dashiell Hammett, features Mary Astor as the worldly temptress Brigid O'Shaugnessey (Figure 7.16) and *noir* icon Humphrey Bogart as detective Sam Spade. Like many *noir* films, *The Maltese Falcon* features a cast of villains obliquely identified as homosexuals and associated with the cosmopolitan cultures of Europe and Asia. Bogart stands in contrast as unambiguously heterosexual and American. The film's many tightly composed three-shots make palpable the threat represented by the villains' otherness. Later in the decade Huston followed *The Maltese Falcon* with other downbeat *noir*-inspired dramas, including *Key Largo* (1948) and *The Asphalt Jungle* (1950).

Because *noir* films typically told stories of weak men ensnared by manipulative *femme fatales,* critics have sometimes viewed them as a response to the anxiety caused by women taking jobs that men had vacated to go to war. Perhaps they also appealed to something in audiences that distrusted the official rhetoric and optimism espoused by the dominant political forces. If not among the big hits, for the most part, the *noir* films have continued as a steady stream to the present day, including such productions as *Chinatown* (1973), *Body Heat* (1982), and *L. A. Confidential* (1998).

FIGURE 7.16 *The Maltese Falcon* ★ United States, 1941, John Huston; Mary Astor.

Orson Welles: Boy Genius

Orson Welles came to Hollywood following a phenomenal burst of creative leadership and experimentation in theater and radio. He was twenty-six years old when his first film, *Citizen Kane,* was released in 1941. It became a landmark like *The Birth of a Nation* and *Battleship Potemkin* before it. Although influenced by the emerging *noir* style, it went far beyond genre conventions. *Citizen Kane* moved American film into the modernism present in the other arts. With its unconventional approach to theme, character, and narrative, as well as its range of cinematic technique, it became a sourcebook for future film makers. If modernist narrative is usually associated with the foregrounding of filmic language, multiple levels of narration, and estrangement of the spectator, *Citizen Kane* might be said to be fully if not overly qualified for modernity.

The fictional Charles Foster Kane, played by Welles, was modeled closely enough on the real William Randolph Hearst to make Hearst furious and vengeful. After trying unsuccesfully to suppress the film, he ordered the reviewers in his newspaper chain to trash it. As a result, *Citizen Kane* had little success at the box office and was largely passed over for Academy Award consideration.

Like Hearst, Kane is a newspaper tycoon, a lonely and egocentric man of vast wealth and failed political ambition. We learn the facts of his life as a reporter questions people close to him for a filmed obituary. Using investigative journalism as a device, scriptwriters Herman J. Mankiewicz and Orson Welles track back through Kane's life with interview and flashback recollection from his banker-guardian, his business manager, his best friend, his second wife (Figure 7.17a), and his butler. From their divergent points of view, we are presented with different Kanes. Although we learn about the complexity of his activities, neither we nor the reporter get at Kane's essence. We do find out what *rosebud,* his final word, referred to, as the reporter does not; rather, we are left standing at a distance from him—the sort of distancing or estrangement of the spectator employed by Bertold Brecht.

To complement its kaleidoscopic narrative, *Citizen Kane* pushes filmic language into the foreground. Low angles and chiaroscuro lighting abound. The great depth of field of the images was provided by cinematographer Gregg Toland and made possible by improvements in film stock, light sources, and optics. It introduces a new intricacy in the relationship of characters to setting and to each other as well as demands a fuller "reading" than was necessary to interpret the selective emphasis that had become the standard technique for creating filmed narratives by this time. For example, in an early scene that focuses on Kane's childhood, his mother, having unexpectedly come into a fortune, relinquishes her son to be raised in privileged surroundings by Thatcher, a heartless banker. As the transaction is finalized, we see Mrs. Kane and Thatcher in the foreground, Kane's skeptical father in the middle background, and, through a window in the far background, the oblivious young boy playing outside in the snow (Figure 7.17b). This single shot thus contains three distinct centers of dramatic interest.

FIGURE 7.17a–d   *Citizen Kane* ★ United States, 1941, Orson Welles; a. Dorothy Comingole; b. Harry Shannon, George Coulouris, and Agnes Moorhead; c and d. Welles and Ruth Warrick.

The sound track takes on the acoustical character of the surroundings. Sound montage, growing out of Welles's radio work, includes sequences in which a character begins a sentence in one scene and completes it in another. For example, at one point, we see Thatcher wishing a nine-year-old Kane "Merry Christmas," but in the following shot, as the stuffy banker completes his thought by adding "and a Happy New Year," his young charge reappears as a twenty-one-year-old.

One of the most famous scenes in *Kane* combines sound and image montage by splicing together numerous shots of Kane and his first wife, Emily, as they breakfast together over a period of years (Figure 7.17c and d). In less than a minute of screen time, the film signals the disintegration of the marriage by juxtaposing brief snippets from a series of increasingly acrimonious conversational exchanges between the two.

Welles's career continued until his death in 1987, but he was never again to enjoy the freedom and financial support that made *Citizen Kane* possible. Nonetheless, he made a number of other *noir*-influenced films such as *The Lady from Shanghai* (1948) and *Touch of Evil* (1959) as well as several adaptations of Shakespearan plays and other literary works, among them *The Magnificent Ambersons* (1942) and *Macbeth* (1948). In his later years he made several films in Europe, including *The Trial* (1962) and *Chimes at Midnight* (1966), a conflation of Shakespeare's *Henry IV, Part 2* and *The Merry Wives of Windsor* with Welles as Falstaff. As a film maker, Welles had some inspired flashes and some partially realized creations, but it is for *Citizen Kane* that he is most remembered.

In addition to the pleasures they may offer individually, the American films of the 1930s and early 1940s are studies in paradox. The studio system with its big bosses and front office, mass production and distribution, allowed and even encouraged the scattering of masterpieces among the thousands of films made within its purview. The system's prodigious resources and the opportunities for ongoing team activity enabled by the studio structure set the stage for a fuller panoply of creative opportunities than may ever have existed in human history. At the same time, the studio system fostered a repressive self-regulation that attempted to bleach art into the palest imitation of life. In the face of this kind of censorship, Hollywood craftspeople managed to abide only by the letter of the law, often playing with the prim conventions in inventive ways. The genres, cycles, and formula pictures with their fixed patterns, which the studios loved for their predictability and easy marketability, could also be manipulated in ingenious ways, enabling inventive directors to create some of their best work.

Films of the Period

1929
The Cocoanuts (Joseph Stanley and Robert Florey)

1930
Little Caesar (Mervyn LeRoy)
Morocco (Josef von Sternberg)

1931
City Lights (Charles Chaplin)
Dracula (Tod Browning)

Frankenstein (James Whale)
The Public Enemy (William Wellman)
Tabu (F. W. Murnau and Robert Flaherty)

1932
I Am a Fugitive from a Chain Gang (Mervyn LeRoy)
Scarface (Howard Hawks)
Shanghai Express (Josef von Sternberg)
Trouble in Paradise (Ernst Lubitsch)

1933
Christopher Strong (Dorothy Arzner)
Duck Soup (Leo McCarey)
42nd Street (Lloyd Bacon)
Gold Diggers of 1933 (Mervyn LeRoy)
King Kong (Merian C. Cooper and Ernest B.
   Schoedsack)

1934
It Happened One Night (Frank Capra)
Queen Christina (Rouben Mamoulian)
The Scarlet Empress (Josef von Sternberg)
Twentieth Century (Howard Hawks)

1935
A Night at the Opera (Sam Wood)

1936
Fury (Fritz Lang)
The Great Ziegfeld (Robert Z. Leonard)
Mr. Deeds Goes to Town (Frank Capra)
Modern Times (Charlie Chaplin)
The Story of Louis Pasteur (William Dieterle)
Swing Time (George Stevens)

1937
The Awful Truth (Leo McCarey)
Camille (George Cukor)
The Life of Emile Zola (William Dieterle)
Snow White and the Seven Dwarfs (Walt Disney)
A Star Is Born (William Wellman)
Stella Dallas (King Vidor)
You Only Live Once (Fritz Lang)

1938
Angels with Dirty Faces (Michael Curtiz)
Bringing Up Baby (Howard Hawks)

1939
Gone with the Wind (Victor Fleming)
Mr. Smith Goes to Washington (Frank Capra)
Ninotchka (Ernst Lubitsch)
Only Angels Have Wings (Howard Hawks)
Stagecoach (John Ford)
Young Mr. Lincoln (John Ford)

1940
Dance, Girl, Dance (Dorothy Arzner)

Fantasia (Walt Disney)
Foreign Correspondent (Alfred Hitchcock)
The Grapes of Wrath (John Ford)
The Great Dictator (Charlie Chaplin)
The Great McGinty (Preston Sturges)
His Girl Friday (Howard Hawks)
The Letter (William Wyler)
The Philadelphia Story (George Cukor)
Rebecca (Alfred Hitchcock)

1941
Citizen Kane (Orson Welles)
High Sierra (Raoul Walsh)
How Green Was My Valley (John Ford)
The Lady Eve (Preston Sturges)
The Little Foxes (William Wyler)
The Maltese Falcon (John Huston)
Sergeant York (Howard Hawks)
Sullivan's Travels (Preston Sturges)
Suspicion (Alfred Hitchcock)

1942
The Magnificent Ambersons (Orson Welles)
Mrs. Miniver (William Wyler)
Now, Voyager (Irving Rapper)
The Palm Beach Story (Preston Sturges)
To Be or Not to Be (Ernst Lubitsch)
Yankee Doodle Dandy (Michael Curtiz)

1943
Air Force (Howard Hawks)
Casablanca (Michael Curtiz)
Meshes of the Afternoon (Maya Deren)
Ox-Bow Incident (William Wellman)
Shadow of a Doubt (Alfred Hitchcock)

1944
Double Indemnity (Billy Wilder)
Gaslight (George Cukor)
Hail the Conquering Hero (Preston Sturges)
Laura (Otto Preminger)
Meet Me in St. Louis (Vincente Minnelli)
The Miracle of Morgan's Creek (Preston Sturges)
The Woman in the Window (Fritz Lang)

1945
The House on 92nd Street (Henry Hathaway)
The Lost Weekend (Billy Wilder)

Mildred Pierce (Michael Curtiz)
Scarlet Street (Fritz Lang)

The Southerner (Jean Renoir)
Spellbound (Alfred Hitchcock)

Books on the Period

Altman, Rick. *Film/Genre.* London: British Film Institute, 1999.

Balio, Tino T. *Grand Design: Hollywood as a Modern Business Enterprise, 1930–1939* (Vol. 5 of *History of the American Cinema*). Berkeley: University of California Press, 1933.

Barrier, Michael. *Hollywood Cartoons: American Animation in Its Golden Age.* New York: Oxford University Press, 1999.

Basinger, Jeanine. *The World War II Combat Film: Anatomy of a Genre.* Middletown, CT: Wesleyan University Press, 2003.

Bernstein, Matthew, ed. *Controlling Hollywood: Censorship and Regulation in the Studio Era.* New Brunswick, NJ: Rutgers University Press, 2000.

Berry, Sarah. *Screen Style: Fashion and Femininity in 1930s Hollywood.* Minneapolis: University of Minnesota Press, 2000.

Cohan, Steve, ed. *Hollywood Musicals, The Film Reader.* New York: Routledge, 2002.

Dickos, Andrew. *Street with No Name: A History of the Classic American Film Noir.* Lexington: University Press of Kentucky, 2002.

Doherty, Thomas. *Pre-Code Hollywood: Sex, Immorality, and Insurrection in American Cinema, 1930–1934.* New York: Columbia University Press, 1999.

Girgus, Sam B. *Hollywood Renaissance: The Cinema of Democracy in the Era of Ford, Capra, and Kazan.* New York: Cambridge University Press, 1998.

Glassy, Mark C. *The Biology of Science Fiction Cinema.* Jefferson, NC: McFarland, 2001.

Haskell, Barbara. *The American Century: Art and Culture, 1900–1950.* New York: W. W. Norton, 1999.

Horne, Gerald. *Class Struggle in Hollywood, 1930–1950: Moguls, Mobsters, Stars, Reds, and Trade Unionists.* Austin: University of Texas Press, 2000.

Keyishian, Harry. *Screening Politics: The Politician in American Movies, 1931–2001.* New York: Continuum, 2003.

Knight, Arthur. *Disintegrating the Musical: Black Performances and American Musical Film.* Durham, NC: Duke University Press, 2002.

Loy, R. Phillip. *Westerns and American Culture, 1930–1955.* Jefferson, NC: McFarland, 2001.

Lyons, Arthur. *Death on the Cheap: The Lost B Movies of Film Noir.* Cambridge, MA: Da Capo Press, 2000.

Mason, Fran. *American Gangster Cinema: From "Little Caesar" to "Pulp Fiction."* London: Palgrave, 2003.

Miller, Toby. *Spyscreen: Espionage on Film and TV from the 1930s to the 1960s.* New York: Oxford University Press, 2003.

Mizejewski, Linda. *Hard Boiled and High Heeled: The Woman Detective in Popular Culture.* New York: Routledge, 2004.

Morey, Anne. *Hollywood Outsiders: The Adaptation of the Film Industry, 1913–1934.* Minneapolis: University of Minnesota Press, 2004.

Naremore, James. *More than Night: Film Noir in Its Contexts.* Berkeley: University of California Press, 1998.

Paris, Michael, ed. *The First World War and Popular Cinema: 1941 to the Present.* New Brunswick, NJ: Rutgers University Press, 2000.

Prats, Armando Jose. *Invisible Nations: Myth and Identity in the American Western.* Ithaca, NY: Cornell University Press, 2002.

Prince, Stephen. *Classical Film Violence: Designing and Regulating Brutality in Hollywood Cinema, 1930–1968.* New Brunswick, NJ: Rutgers University Press, 2003.

Saunders, John. *The Western Genre: From Lordsburg to Big Whiskey.* London: Wallflower Press, 2001.

Schaefer, Eric. *"Bold! Daring! Shocking! True!": A History of Exploitation Films, 1919–1959.* Durham, NC: Duke University Press, 1999.

Schatz, Thomas. *Boom and Bust: The American Cinema of the 1940s* (Vol. 6 of *History of the American Cinema*). Berkeley and Los Angeles: University of California Press, 1999.

Shull, Michael S., and David E. Wilt. *Doing Their Bit: Wartime American Animated Short Films, 1939–1945,* 2nd ed. Jefferson, NC: McFarland, 2004.

Silver, Alain, and James Ursini. *The Noir Style.* London: Aurum Press, 2000.

Silver, Alain, and James Ursini, eds. *Film Noir Reader 2.* New York: Limelight Editions, 1999.

Simmon, Scott. *The Invention of the Western Film: A Cultural History of the Genre's First Half Century.* New York: Cambridge University Press, 2003.

Stanfield, Peter. *Horse Opera: The Strange History of the 1930s Singing Cowboy.* Champaign: University of Illinois Press, 2002.

Stanfield, Peter. *Hollywood, Westerns and the 1930s: The Lost Trail.* Exeter: University of Exeter Press, 2001.

Stokes, Melvyn, and Richard Maltby. *American Movie Audiences: From the Turn of the Century to the Early Sound Era.* London: British Film Institute, 1999.

Studlar, Gaylyn, and Matthew Bernstein, eds. *John Ford Made Westerns: Filming the Legend in the Sound Era.* Bloomington: Indiana University Press, 2001.

Trumpbour, John. *Selling Hollywood to the World: U.S. and European Struggles of Mastery of the Global Film Industry, 1920–1950.* New York: Cambridge University Press, 2002.

Viera, Mark A. *Sin in Soft Focus: Pre-Code Hollywood.* New York: Harry N. Abrams, 1999.

Wager, Jans. *Dangerous Dames: Women and Representation in the Wiemar Street Film and Film Noir.* Athens: Ohio University Press, 1999.

Wells, Paul. *The Horror Genre: From Beelzebub to Blair Witch.* London: Wallflower Press, 2001.

8

Italian Neorealism

★ ★ ★ ★

1945–1959

The eruption of a brilliant cluster of Italian films that began with Roberto Rossellini's *Open City* (1945) was stimulated by the removal of fascist power after nearly a quarter century and the release of bottled-up feelings of frustration and humiliation generated by Italy's ambiguous and shifting position in World War II. Beginning as a nominal equal to the other two Axis powers, Germany and Japan, Italy subsequently was reduced to a subservient role. When Mussolini was overthrown, a separate peace was signed with the Allies. The Germans in Italy then turned into an occupying force, retreating slowly as the Allies advanced up the peninsula to replace Germany as the new occupier. It is against this background that *Open City* is set, at the point when Allied forces were approaching Rome and had already begun bombing its outskirts. An agreement was then reached whereby the Germans did not attempt to hold the Eternal City, thus averting its destruction.

In *Open City* Rossellini chronicles in cross-sectional form the activities of the partisans, the raids and reprisals of the German military and the Italian police, the painful tensions among collaborators, resisters, and the great majority of people who simply wanted enough bread and wine, and an end to the killing and misery of war. The film begins with German soldiers arriving outside the building lived in by Manfredi (Marcello Pagliero), a partisan activist (Figure 8.1a). After he flees, his former lover (Maria Michi), now dependent on the Gestapo to supply her with drugs, tries to reach him by phone (Figure 8.1b). Manfredi goes to the apartment of a friend and fellow partisan, whose fiancée (Anna Magnani) takes him in (Figure 8.1c) and sends for a Catholic priest who is aiding the resistance. The friend returns from work and the action proceeds with the Gestapo net closing in on Manfredi and the priest (Figure 8.1d). But equal attention is given to the daily lives of the Roman people under the stress of a foreign presence, from child resistance-fighters to an irritable old man who scarcely comprehends what is happening but attempts to supply his needs nonetheless.

Scriptwriters Sergio Amidei and Federico Fellini, and director Rossellini, make as good a case as they can for the instances of courage, heroism, and martyrdom that occurred

149

FIGURE 8.1a–d *Open City* ✳ Italy, 1945, Roberto Rossellini; b. Maria Michi; c. Anna Magnani and Marcello Pagliero; d. Aldo Fabrizi on right.

in a generally demoralized Italy. *Open City* seems in part an attempt to ease the national conscience in regard to the immediate past and, for the grim postwar problems yet to be solved, to provide models of behavior. The Catholic priest and the professional communist revolutionary unite in their efforts and sacrifice their lives in the fight to free their country from fascist rule. The film is a passionate requiem, like Verdi's for his novelist friend Alessandro Manzoni, and its rough beauty and emotional intensity carry all before it.

The Italian industry had become heavily controlled and subsidized by the fascist government, and dictator Benito Mussolini used it as a relatively harmless field in which to place some of his less able relatives. After a few unsuccessful attempts to use the fiction film for direct propaganda—invoking the glories of ancient Rome and associating them with the contemporary Italy of the black shirts, for example—the fascists had to accept the evidence that audiences would simply stay away. Instead, the authorities became content to keep films from making any significant statement about modern reality; the filmed opera, costume melodrama, and romance built around a box-office idol became ubiquitous. The latter type were known as the "white telephone films," because an ultimate in luxurious dalliance was frequently portrayed as a langorous heroine lounging in negligee on an elaborate bed cooing to her lover on the phone.

At the same time, the fascist regime managed to put into place an infrastructure that was to serve the industry well in the decades to come. A national film school, inaugurated in 1935, trained future star directors such as Roberto Rossellini, Pietro Germi, and Michelangelo Antonioni, as well as other production personnel. In 1937, the mammoth Cinecettà Studios, subsequently known as "Hollywood on the Tiber," was built. Cinecettà later housed the production of American blockbusters such as *Cleopatra* (Joseph Mankiewicz, 1963) along with distinguished home-grown features mounted by film makers Luchino Visconti, Federico Fellini, and others. Although the neorealist directors of the immediate postwar era turned away from the artificiality implied by the studio style, they benefited from these initiatives insofar as they created a cadre of trained production workers, provided material resources, and gave momentum to the ideal of a national film culture.

That *Open City* was made at all is something of a marvel. Rossellini filmed secretly between 1943 and 1945, scraping together funds from various sources. The money kept running out and at one point Rossellini and Magnani, who plays her first great screen role in the film, sold all their clothes to obtain enough lire to carry on for a few more days. Production conditions were incredibly primitive. Shooting was done on odds and ends of raw stock of various manufacturers. Studios weren't available to them, and nearly all the scenes were enacted on the actual locations they represent in the film. Even the electrical power in wartime was so erratic that maintaining consistent exposure was a constant problem. In spite of the technical and financial difficulties (dead broke, Rossellini is said to have sold the rights for $28,000; *Open City* grossed $5 million in the United States alone), the film emerged as a towering achievement that would inspire other Italian film makers to emulate its concepts and its method of dealing with contemporary reality.

Theory and Practice of Neorealism

The working principles of the neorealist films that Rossellini had first improvised partly by necessity and accident, partly out of conviction, became loosely codified into a theory of cinema. The premises underpinning neorealism were most forcefully articulated by scriptwriter **Cesare Zavattini,** who became spokesman for, as well as one of the principal creators in, the movement. Perhaps the only other screenwriter to have achieved a comparable intellectual-aesthetic dominance in a period of national excellence is Carl Mayer, in relation to the German expressionist films of the 1920s.

In a famous interview, Zavattini had the following things to say about the content and purposes of neorealism:

> The most important characteristic, and the most important innovation, of what is called neorealism, it seems to me, is to have realized that the necessity of the "story" was only an unconscious way of disguising a human defeat, and that the kind of imagination it involved was simply a technique of superimposing dead formulas over living social facts. Now it has been perceived that reality is hugely rich, that to be able to look directly at it is enough; and that the artist's task is not to make people moved or indignant at metaphorical situations, but to make them reflect (and, if you like, to be moved and indignant too) on what they and others are doing, on the real things, exactly as they are.

FIGURE 8.2   *Umberto D* ★ Italy, 1952, Vittorio de Sica; Maria-Pia Casilio and Carlo Battisti.

Asking himself what effects on narrative structure the neorealist style had, Zavattini answered:

> To begin with, while the cinema used to make one situation produce another situation, and another, and another, again and again, and each scene was thought out and immediately related to the next (the natural result of a mistrust of reality), today, when we have thought out a scene, we feel the need to "remain" in it, because the single scene itself can contain so many echoes and reverberations, can even contain all the situations we may need. Today, in fact, we can quietly say: Give us whatever "fact" you like [a stolen bicycle, for example], and we will disembowel it, make it something worth watching.[1]

The newly realistic Italian films were based on a real incident or a composite of several events; they had factual rather than fictional bases. For example, a film might be based on an actual situation of a staircase collapsing under the weight of hundreds of unemployed young women applying for jobs as typists (*Rome, Eleven O'Clock,* 1952) or on a typical one such as that of an old man finding it difficult to live on his pension (*Umberto D,* 1952) (Figure 8.2). The problems treated by these films had some degree of immediacy and broad concern. Their themes were not necessarily universal and timeless, as those of the arts tend to be; they were more tied to the here and now, like documentary: sociological as much as psychological in their approach. Among the prevalent concerns were poverty (*Miracle in*

---

[1] Cesare Zavattini, "Some Ideas on the Cinema," *Sight and Sound,* 23 (October–December 1953): 64, 65.

Milan, 1951; *Two Cents Worth of Hope,* 1952), prostitution (*Without Pity,* 1948), collaboration with and resistance to occupying military forces (*Outcry* and *To Live in Peace,* both 1947), exploitative agricultural conditions (*The Tragic Hunt,* 1947, and *Bitter Rice,* 1949), and continuing tensions between the industrial north and the agrarian south that had simmered since the time of Italian unification in the late nineteenth century.

In these semidocumentary-like films there *is* a plot and there *are* characters, but they are less fully developed than in pure fiction and are used quite directly to embody the theme and ideas. The conflict and resolution are apt to be drawn out of the larger situation rather than out of interpersonal relations. A poor fishing family is in contention with the boat owners; when the owners win, the fishermen are forced to work the boats on the owners' terms. The family that had been resisting is broken (*La Terra Trema,* 1948) (Figure 8.3). In other words, in films of this sort the characters and their lives (plot incidents) are used deliberately to express an ideology.

Finally, in these films the film-making methods are drawn from both fiction and documentary. They tend to depend less on performance and dialogue than do conventional fiction films. Actors may appear in principal roles, but frequently nonactors are used in lesser roles and as extras (*Open City,* 1945; *The Tragic Hunt,* 1947) and even as leads (*Shoeshine,* 1946; *The Bicycle Thief,* 1948; *Umberto D,* 1952). In any event there is usually an avoidance of stars. Considerable location shooting (exteriors) is combined with studio

FIGURE 8.3 *La Terra Trema* ★ Italy, 1948, Luchino Visconti.

(interiors). Sometimes candid or newsreel footage is interpolated. Frequently commentary, montage, and even maps suggest a broader scope and help bridge a less-tight plot. Lighting, costumes, makeup, and sets are actual, or naturalistic in style. The editing is less "smooth" than in the usual story picture, being dictated by the subject-matter requirements. The cutting pace is frequently more rapid, too, as it tends to be when ideas more than emotions are being dealt with, and when film makers (as in documentary) are working with persons (nonactors) who cannot sustain performances. There tends to be emphasis on source sounds and avoidance of heavy musical scoring.

Three Major Directors of the Neorealist Era

Many of the basic strategies of neorealism had been put into practice during the early days of cinema by Neapolitan director Elvira Notari. Notari's widely distributed productions of the 1910s and 1920s featured location shooting, amateur actors, and a focus on the poor. Her films had, in turn, been influenced by the *sceneggiata,* a popular Italian theatrical form that mixed melodrama with songs and was performed by nonprofessionals. After World War II, these time-honored conventions gained new relevance by virtue of Italy's political and economic woes. At the same time, the theoretical writings of Zavattini and others provided such traditions with deeper meanings. In the cultural context thus created, the careers of two major directors peaked during this period: Roberto Rossellini and Vittorio de Sica. The films of both represent the characteristics of the neorealist movement as a whole. A third director, Luchino Visconti, played a crucial role in the development of neorealism, but subsequently evolved into a stylist of a more modernist stripe.

Rossellini quickly followed *Open City* with his other major film fully within the general terms of neorealist style and intention, *Paisan* (1946) (Figure 8.4). In six separate episodes it traces the Allied campaign up the long boot of Italy, exploring the contacts between the conquerors (principally American) and the conquered. Maps and newsreel footage connect the parts, suggesting that the dramatic vignettes are incidents happening within the larger historical context. Each episode sketches one aspect of the complex and changing American–Italian relationships, which move from an initial distrust to a growing closeness.

Rossellini worked the stories out as he went along, with the aid of a group of writers that included Federico Fellini. Each incident is particularly representative of that phase of the campaign. Taken together they treat, with extraordinary comprehensiveness as well as precision, the significance of the American presence in Italy. The camera and editing techniques are as sparse and unprettified as the stories. Of *Paisan*'s large cast only four members had had previous acting experience (the GI and the prostitute in Rome, the nurse in Florence, the Catholic chaplain in Bologna); the others were picked up by Rossellini as he found them on location. The whole achieves a directness and power through its spontaneity. Rossellini's style is in perfect keeping with the material and his attitude toward it.

De Sica and his scriptwriter, Cesare Zavattini, continued this national saga with an examination of the immediate postwar years. Before directing, de Sica had been a well-known screen actor in the 1930s. His first important film as director, *The Children Are Watching Us* (1943), was also his first collaboration with Zavattini. Roughly contemporary with Visconti's *Ossessione,* it was somewhat comparable in its realistic tendencies. In the

FIGURE 8.4   *Paisan* ★ Italy, 1946, Roberto Rossellini.

main line of postwar neorealism, de Sica's *Shoeshine* (1946) is concerned with the Roman *ragazzi* who eked out a living shining GIs' shoes, pimping, and dealing in black market American cigarettes, candy bars, and, in this instance, blankets. Two boys are apprehended, tried, convicted, and sent to a reformatory, where their affection for each other is turned into hatred, resulting in the death of one of the boys. There are no villains, however, but simply a bad system. We are not sure why there aren't enough staff and money to run this institution properly, except that there never are in institutions of this sort. Nor are we told what steps might be taken to obtain adequate resources. Although the neorealist films dealt with social problems, they tended to hold them up for examination in terms of their effects on individual lives rather than explain causes or propose solutions.

Zavattini and de Sica's most successful collaboration, and among those films closest to the neorealist ideal, was *The Bicycle Thief* (1948). It deals with the simplest possible situation. An unemployed laborer with his first chance to work for some time has the bicycle stolen that he must have in order to keep his job (Figure 8.5a). The events leading up to the theft and the attempt to recover the bicycle provide sufficient "plot" for a complete and significant work of art, even including implied social and political criticism. In following the man's and his young son's search for the bicycle, various aspects of Italian society are sketched, with apparent casualness it may seem at first; on reflection the highest degree of economy and skill become evident. *The Bicycle Thief* was shot almost entirely outside the studio, in the streets and apartments and offices of Rome. The father in the film

FIGURE 8.5a and b   *The Bicycle Thief* ★ Italy, 1948, Vittorio de Sica; a. Lamberto
Maggiorani; b. Enzo Staiola and Lamberto Maggiorani.

was in real life a machinist in the big Breda steelworks. The boy who plays his son was a
Roman newsboy (Figure 8.5b). The performances elicited from the pair can only be described as miraculous. De Sica's work with nonactors, especially children, is always sensitive and sure; here he surpassed himself. Although methods formerly found only in
documentary are basic to its conception, the emotional richness of *The Bicycle Thief* depends to considerable extent on the portrayals of its Everyman and his small son.

    Luchino Visconti, along with Rossellini and de Sica, could lay claim to being one of
the founders and principal practitioners of the neorealist movement. His *Ossessione* (1942)
was clearly a precurser, with its harshly naturalistic approach to character, theme, and setting at a time when Italian films were either patriotic or escaping the realities of wartime
Italy—optimistic or cheery in either case. Adapted from a hard-boiled crime novel by the
American writer James M. Cain, it was set in the bleak, flat Po Valley (Figure 8.6a and b).
A charmless trattoria (Figure 8.6c) forms the backdrop for a steamy love affair between an
aimless drifter and a disaffected young wife (Figure 8.6d). Made six years later, Visconti's
La Terra Trema (1948) is among the great neorealist films, although its overlay of highly
stylized studiolike cinematography and staged groupings onto actual fishermen and Sicilian
village make us think of Eisenstein of *Old and New* rather than of the other neorealists.

Period of Transition: 1952–1959

It must be admitted that cosmic meaning arising from the ordinary was not always, and
seldom completely, attained in neorealist films. Melodrama superimposed on reality was
still the rule. But films of the neorealist style attracted Italy's most talented directors,
writers, and performers; received the widest foreign distribution; and exerted the strongest
influence on the film production of other countries during the immediate postwar years.
The neorealist films began in a defeated and occupied country, with a badly disorganized
economy and political life, widespread poverty and unemployment, and uncontrolled
inflation—another instance of a film movement growing out of troubled times, like the
post–World War I German and Soviet cinemas.

FIGURE 8.6a–d *Ossessione* ★ Italy, 1942, Luchino Visconti; b. Massimo Girotti; d. Massimo Girotti and Carla Calamai.

Problems of national identity, political turmoil, economic misery, and social dislocation continued, but by 1949 neorealism had begun to wane as the predominant force in Italian film making. Pressure from the Roman Catholic Church and the Italian government in the early 1950s resulted in a decline of the export of "social problem" films to the United States, the chief source of economic support for neorealism. A realization by the film makers themselves that the neorealist conception of reality, with its externalized nonpsychological approach, was limiting, led to an enlargement or alteration of their scope of concern. An often quoted comment by Michelangelo Antonioni about *The Bicycle Thief* is revealing. He said that if he had directed the film, he would have told more about the people and less about the bicycle.

If neorealism began with Rossellini's *Open City* in 1945, it ceased, or changed direction anyway, after the de Sica–Zavattini *Umberto D* of 1952. The latter is about an old man whose fixed income had become insufficient to support life with any dignity, let alone pleasure. After that last great neorealist film, Italian film makers began shifting their attention from the lower classes and poverty to the upper classes and the unsatisfying and corrosive values of much of modern life that are most evident among them. Some of Rossellini's films of the middle and late 1950s look ahead to a later kind of cinema, exerting great influence on the upcoming generation of French as well as Italian film makers. His *Voyage to Italy* (1953) is startlingly predictive; Antonioni's *L'Avventura* (1960) seems to grow directly out of it—though on its initial release, the Italian critics panned it as a betrayal of neorealist ideals. (One wrote, "*Viaggio in Italia* does nothing but confirm the absolute, progressive, and irredemable decadence of Rossellini.")

Fellini also can be considered a transitional figure who moved from the essentially materialistic concerns of the neorealist films to the (for want of a better word) spiritual concerns of the next generation of Italian film makers. "For me," he said, "neorealism means looking at reality with an honest eye—but at any kind of reality; not just social reality, but also spiritual reality, metaphysical reality, anything man has inside of him." His *La Strada* (1954) might in many ways be regarded as a pivotal film. Although set among the lower classes, it is not concerned with poverty but with inadequacies in human relationships. With a haunting musical score by Nino Rota and a delicately stylized performance by Fellini's wife, Giulietta Masina, which was modeled on the ancient *commedia dell'arte* tradition, *La Strada* came across more as a fable than as a study in quotidian reality. When the film was attacked by the Italian critics as a betrayal of neorealist traditions, Fellini replied, "Reality needs poetry."

De Sica attempted to return to neorealism with *The Roof* (1955), but this tale of a young couple trying to obtain their own place to live seemed strangely old-fashioned and inessential in the newly prosperous Italy. Rossellini's *General della Rover* (1959) and de Sica's *Two Women* (1960) are also efforts to recapture some of the themes of the immediate postwar films. In spite of the professional polish, in part because of it of course, and some excellent things in each, both seem anachronistic. It may be fitting that in the former film Rossellini is directing de Sica, playing the lead as the General's impersonator who dies a hero. Those two films were a kind of final reprise, not so much for the two directors—because by then even those stalwarts of neorealism were making other kinds of films—but for the original movement.

The practice and the theory of neorealism did not cease to exist, however, and its influence has been discernible ever since the initial period. In Italy the films of Ermanno Olmi (*Il Posto*, 1961; *The Fiancés*, 1962) embodied it most directly. Also the works of Vittorio de Seta (*The Bandits of Orgosolo*, 1961) and Pier Paolo Pasolini (*Accatone*, 1961), in their methods and explicitly Marxist ideologies, recalled the earlier films, as did the films of Francesco Rosi (*Salvatore Giuliano*, 1962; *Hands Over the City*, 1963). The French New Wave, eastern European cinema, and the British social-realist features, all to be dealt with later, owed something to the kind of film making practiced in Italy between 1945 and 1952.

Films of the Period

1942
Ossessione (Luchino Visconti)

1945
Open City (Roma, Città Apperta) (Roberto Rossellini)

1946
Paisan (Paisà) (Roberto Rossellini)
Shoeshine (Sciusià) (Vittorio de Sica)

1947
Germany, Year Zero (Germana anno zero) (Roberto Rossellini)

1948
The Bicycle Thief (Ladri di biciclette) (Vittorio de Sica)
La Terra Trema (Luchino Visconti)

1949
Bitter Rice (Riso amero) (Giuseppe de Santis)
Stromboli (Stromboli, terra de dio) (Roberto Rossellini)

1950
Chronicle of a Love Affair (Cronaca di un amore)
  (Michelangelo Antonioni)

1951
Miracle in Milan (Miracolo a Milano) (Vittorio
  de Sica)

1952
Umberto D (Vittorio de Sica)
The White Sheik (Lo sceicco bianco) (Federico Fellini)

1953
I Vitelloni (Federico Felllini)
Voyage to Italy (Viaggio in Italia) (Roberto Rossellini)

1954
Senso (Luchino Visconti)

1956
The Nights of Cabiria (La notti di Cabiria)
  (Federico Fellini)

1957
Il Grido (Michelangelo Antonioni)

1959
General Della Rover (Il Generale della Rover)
  (Roberto Rossellini)

Books on the Period

Landy, Marcia. *Italian Film.* New York: Cambridge University Press, 2000.

Reich, Jacqueline, and Piero Garofalo, eds. *Re-Viewing Fascism: Italian Cinema, 1922–1943.* Bloomington: Indiana University Press, 2002.

Rocchio, Vincent F. *Cinema of Anxiety: A Psychoanalysis of Italian Neorealism.* Austin: University of Texas Press, 2000.

Sorlin, Pierre. *Italian National Cinema, 1896–1996.* New York: Routledge, 1996.

9

The Documentary Impulse: British Film after the War

★ ★ ★ ★

1945–1963

American money and personnel are so inextricably interwoven with British production and distribution that it is difficult to determine where one industry leaves off and the other begins. If in the days of gunboat diplomacy commerce followed the flag, in modern economic imperialism culture follows the dollar. American films had so overwhelmed the British market during the 1920s that the British government passed the Quota Act in 1927, which restricted the distribution of Hollywood films in Britain and required U.S. distributors to finance a set number of British films every year. Through the years, a large number of British actors, directors, and production personnel have been quick to move across the Atlantic, and many of these are rewarded for their change of allegiance by being honored in Hollywood on Academy Awards night. The trend reached a crescendo of sorts at the end of the twentieth century when the British productions *The English Patient* and *Shakespeare in Love* swept the Oscars in 1997 and 1999, respectively.

To be sure, Britain has a cache of subject matter all its own. British films about World War II, for example, dealt with British wartime experiences: *The Cruel Sea* (1953, Charles Frend), *The Dam Busters* (1953, Michael Anderson), and *The Battle of the River Plate* (1956, Michael Powell and Emeric Pressburger). Also, many individual British films followed a sort of **academic** tradition—significant subjects treated with self-effacing expertise—but prestigious ventures of this sort have become increasingly multinational in conception, financial backing, and creative personnel. John Huston's *The African Queen* (1952), *Moulin Rouge* (1953), and *Moby Dick* (1956) as well as David Lean's *Summertime* (1955) and *The Bridge on the River Kwai* (1957) are prominent examples.

The problem that British films present, then, is one of national identity, not of artistic quality. However, the British have made certain kinds of films with a particular excellence, such as films drawn from their literary, dramatic, or historical heritage, or a type of sophisticated crime or espionage thriller. Prominent British heritage films include the David Lean versions of literary works by Noël Coward and Charles Dickens (*Blithe Spirit,* 1945; *Brief Encounter,* 1945; *Great Expectations,* 1946; and *Oliver Twist,* 1948), adaptations of William Shakespeare by Laurence Olivier (*Henry V,* 1944; *Hamlet,* 1948; and *Richard III,* 1955) and later Kenneth Branaugh (*Henry V,* 1989; and *Hamlet,* 1996), the Carol Reed collaborations with Graham Greene (*The Fallen Idol,* 1948, and *The Third Man,* 1949), Michael Powell and Emeric Pressburger's *The Red Shoes* (1949), and in the 1980s and 1990s, the productions of director James Ivory and producer Ismael Merchant (*A Room with a View,* 1986 and *The Remains of the Day,* 1993). In the realm of thrillers, Alfred Hitchcock's work is preeminent, although his British films were all produced before the war (most notably, *The Thirty-Nine Steps* in 1935 and *The Lady Vanishes* in 1938). After the war, Michael Powell's psychologically acute *Peeping Tom* (1960) became a critical favorite, although its interest in perverse sexuality made it atypical of the British thriller mode. More conventionally British were *The Ipcress File* (Sidney J. Furie, 1965), starring Cockney actor Michael Caine, and the wildly popular, over-the-top James Bond cycle initially featuring the urbane, ironic Edinburgh native Sean Connery.

Distinctive cultural strengths have nurtured British cinema over the years. At its most characteristic, British film making draws on indigenous traditions of comedy and progressive politics as well as a less pronounced vein of **gothic fantasy** and horror. From Chaucer to Hogarth to Dickens, British humor has long been an honored form. The British have a keen eye for identifying the foibles of a rich assortment of social types, and the large cohort of highly skilled British actors are adept at bringing such portraits to life. An equally fruitful tradition has been that of progressive politics. An impulse toward reformist agendas has historically distinguished the British social and political scene. A less prominent element in the British cultural character is a gothic mode of horror and fantasy, historically represented in literary works such as *Frankenstein* and *Dracula.* These three traditions, singly and in combination, have informed every significant British film-making movement since the war: the comedies of the 1950s and later those of Bill Forsyth and Mike Leigh; the socially progressive films of directors such as Tony Richardson and Ken Loach; and the gothic fantasy and horror tales of the Archers during the 1950s and the Hammer Studios during the 1960s. Even American directors who have worked in Britain—for instance, Joseph Losey, Richard Lester, Stanley Kubrick, and Terry Gilliam—have been decisively influenced by the fertile cultural traditions of their adopted country.

Underlying all of these developments was a series of prewar documentaries that created a distinctive identity for British cinema on which later film makers could build. This documentary movement was initiated by John Grierson. More than any other person, Grierson is responsible for the documentary film as it has developed in English-speaking countries. The three hundred or more British documentaries made during the 1930s and the system that spawned them became models for other countries, including New Zealand, Australia, South Africa, and most significantly Canada, where Grierson established the National Film Board in 1939. The documentary film culture Grierson nurtured among associates Basil Wright, Humphrey Jennings, and Paul Rotha cast a long shadow over subsequent feature film production in Great Britain, inspiring generations of film makers who came of age following the Second World War: documentarians such as Peter Watkins, whose 1965 production *The War Game* presented a searing portrait of life after a nuclear holocaust, and an array of fiction film makers both at home and abroad.

Postwar Comedies

If the British documentary became as rare soon after the war as it had been prevalent before and during wartime, it might be argued that it didn't so much cease as go underground and come up looking and sounding like the **Ealing comedy.** Michael Balcon, head of Ealing Studios, had always been a friend of the documentary movement and favored fiction films that were distinctively British rather than imitatively American. When the documentarians began to cross over into feature film making it was to Ealing they came. Alberto Cavalcanti, former production head of the government Crown Film Unit, as well as Harry Watt, one of its star directors, were among these. Three of the principal directors of the Ealing comedies—Charles Crichton, Charles Frend, and Alexander Mackendrick—had had considerable documentary experience. The result of these biases and this personnel, plus the fine writing talents Balcon acquired, especially T. E. B. Clarke, gave the string of comedies their distinctive flavor.

The first of the series was *Hue and Cry,* directed by Crichton in 1947. The lower- and middle-class milieu, location shooting, bumbling crooks and police, and fast pace all typify the Ealing manner. There followed, in fairly rapid succession, *Whiskey Galore* (1949, Mackendrick; *Tight Little Island* in the United States), *Passport to Pimlico* (1949, Henry Cornelius), *A Run for Your Money* (1949, Frend), *Kind Hearts and Coronets* (1949, Robert Hamer), *The Lavender Hill Mob* (1951, Crichton), *The Man in the White Suit* (1951, Mackendrick), *Genevieve* (1953, Cornelius), *The Titfield Thunderbolt* (1953, Crichton), *The Maggie* (1954, Mackendrick; *High and Dry* in the United States), and *The Ladykillers* (1955, Mackendrick). In 1952 financial problems caused Ealing to sell its studios to BBC-TV; in 1955 the company itself was dissolved. Between 1951 and 1955 similar kinds of comedies were being made at Group 3, a government-financed experiment in feature production headed by Grierson.

These British comedies turn documentary seriousness on its ear. *The Ladykillers,* for example, features a daring robbery that occurs in London's well-known St. Pancreas Station (Figure 9.1a). The house in which the crime is planned is situated in the midst of an industrial London area next to the railway yards (Figure 9.1b). But these documentary-like elements are undercut by the gallery of cartoon crooks that plan the heist and the stereotypical sweet little old lady that foils their every scheme (Figure 9.1c and d). The themes of the Ealing films are notably social, economic, political, or at least cultural (in the anthropologist's sense), designed to bring out a particular facet of national life. They deal with the Scots' fondness for a wee drop, strict Calvinism, dislike of the English (*Tight Little Island*), the bureaucratic entanglements in which the British found themselves after the war (*Passport to Pimlico*), the expected honesty and trustworthiness of the English middle class (*The Lavender Hill Mob*), the collusion among management and labor, and government and opposition within the English system (*The Man in the White Suit*). Laughter is provoked only through the incongruities and exaggerations with which these subjects are treated; even so, the comic style is noteworthy for its deadpan seriousness, underplaying, and throwaway delivery of lines.

Casting called on nonglamorous, quintessentially British actors (rather than stars)—Alistair Sim (*Hue and Cry*), Stanley Holloway (*Passport to Pimlico*), and Alec Guinness (*The Lavender Hill Mob, The Man in the White Suit, The Ladykillers*)—and used local citizens as extras. Their performances were built around mimickery of a wide array of social types rather than on subtle renditions of the interior lives of complex individuals, as is the custom among American method performers. In a performance *tour de force* Alec Guinness created a gallery of these broadly satiric portrayals in *Kind Hearts and*

FIGURE 9.1a–d *The Ladykillers* ⋆ United Kingdom, 1955, Alexander Mackendrick; c. Herbert Lom, Alec Guinness, Danny Green, Cecil Parker, and Peter Sellers; d. Katie Johnson.

Coronets, in which he played eight different characters, from a doddering old lady to an urbane country squire (Figure 9.2a–h).

In *Tight Little Island* the documentary influence is especially pervasive. The novel on which it is based—by Compton Mackenzie, who appears in the film in a small part as Captain Bucher—was drawn from an actual disaster to a whiskey-laden ship during World War I. Mackenzie (assisted on the screenplay by Angus MacPhail) elaborated a hilarious plot about the reactions of the citizens of a small Scottish village to having such a ship wrecked off their coast with its cargo intact. The cast is a blend of well-trained actors, many of them Scottish by birth, and local inhabitants. Alexander Mackendrick, who directed, was trained in wartime documentary; this was his first feature. The story is indigenous to the people it is about. It seems to stem from a series of questions. What if Scottish islanders during World War II rationing ran out of whiskey? How would they be affected? What if they had a chance to steal as much of 50,000 cases as they could carry away? What if this chance occurred late on a Saturday night among people whose respect for the Sabbath vies with their love of good whiskey? How would government officials—home guard, regular army, customs inspectors—react to all this? And so on, with acute insights and hilarious comedy being drawn from seeming ordinary people in conceivably real situations.

Tight Little Island was shot almost entirely on location, interiors as well as exteriors (Figure 9.3). A kind of mobile studio unit was established on the Hebridean island so that no time would be lost waiting for good weather. Mackendrick even set up processing equipment so he could look at the rushes without undue delay, just as Robert Flaherty had done for his famous documentary feature *Man of Aran,* shot on an island off the coast of Ireland some fifteen years earlier. Though its indebtedness is apparent, *Tight Little Island*

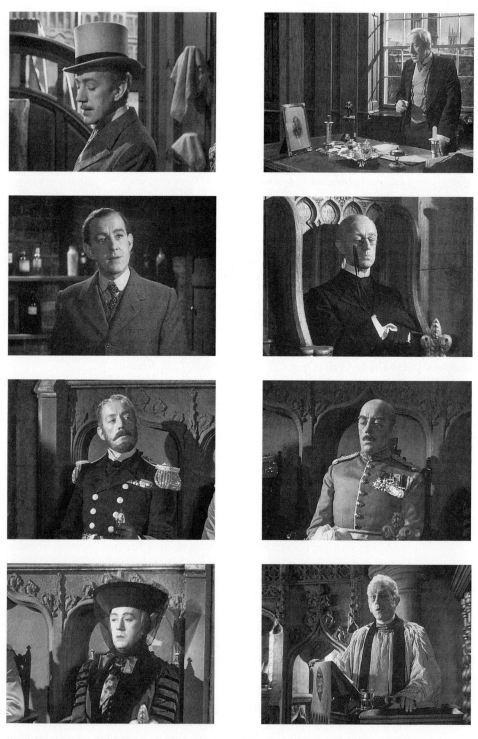

FIGURE 9.2a–h *Kind Hearts and Coronets* ★ United Kingdom, 1949, Robert Hamer; Alec Guinness.

FIGURE 9.3 *Whiskey Galore/Tight Little Island* ★ United Kingdom, 1949, Alexander Mackendrick.

pointedly kids the style of British documentary in its opening postcard shots of the Hebrides (almost identical with those of the General Post Office Film Unit's *The Islanders*) and voice-over commentary. This gentle kind of spoofing is well within an old and honorable British tradition, enjoyed abroad as well as at home. If we would not expect the British to kill the thing they love, their famous sense of humor could be aimed at it. From their documentary of the 1930s has come a lot that is finest and most British in British cinema, and the rest of the world has shared in their achievement.

Free Cinema and Social-Realist Features

The year 1956 was a crucial one in the political and cultural life of Britain. It was the year of a last gasp of imperial arrogance in the foolish and failed invasion of Suez. As a result of that debacle the whole governmental system was discredited. To many on the Left, the Labour Party, which worked within the system, seemed as culpable as the ruling Conservatives. It was also in 1956 that Khrushchev ordered the Soviet invasion of Hungary, which caused many Marxist intellectuals finally to become disillusioned with Stalinist communism. Partially in reaction to those events, a politically sophisticated younger generation of dissidents arose around the universities—particularly at Oxford, which most of the Free Cinema group had attended. The label "New Left" was attached to them, and their publication was entitled *New Left Review* (originally *Universities and Left Review*). The New

Left wanted to go beyond the old-line socialists, with their basis in dialectical materialism, trade unionism, nationalization of industry, and social welfare. They were concerned more with theory and a fundamental reorganization of society that would affect the total quality of people's lives. As an intellectual movement that also encompassed the arts, the New Left in Britain was more like the continental Left.

The artists in various media who arose out of the spirit of the time, many of them from the working classes, were dubbed the Angry Young Men for their attacks on the establishment and the rigidities and inequities of the class system. In 1956 John Osborne's play *Look Back in Anger,* directed by Tony Richardson, opened at the Royal Court Theatre. At about the same time Joan Littlewood's Theatre Workshop was started. Playwrights such as Arnold Wesker and Shelagh Delaney soon joined Osborne to create an outpouring of plays set among the lower classes that were articulate and sometimes strident in their social criticism. A new crop of actors—Albert Finney, Rita Tushingham, Rachel Roberts, Tom Courtenay, Richard Harris, and Ronald Fraser—also came out of that sort of theater and later worked in film. Novels of a similar tone began to appear as well, with John Braine's *Room at the Top* in 1957 followed by Alan Sillitoe's *Saturday Night and Sunday Morning,* Stan Barstow's *A Kind of Loving,* and David Storey's *This Sporting Life,* among others.

In this dynamic atmosphere, the British documentary tradition was again revived in a movement called Free Cinema. Early in 1956 a program of three short films was shown at the National Film Theatre under the Free Cinema banner. *O Dreamland* (1954), by Lindsay Anderson, castigated the dull and synthetic pleasures being offered the bemused masses at a seaside amusement park. *Momma Don't Allow* (1955), by Karel Reisz and Tony Richardson, celebrated a lively London jazz club patronized by working-class teenagers. *Together* (1955), by Lorenza Mazetti and Denis Horne, described the emotionally impoverished lives led by two deaf-mute dock workers in the East End. The films' makers stated in their program notes for the occasion that Free Cinema was free from serving the sponsor's purpose (as in documentaries) and free from pandering to the demands of the box office (as in fiction features). It was to be an "entirely personal cinema," socially committed but also poetic. "Implicit in our attitude," they wrote, "is a belief in freedom, in the importance of people and in the significance of the everyday." The Free Cinema trio of Anderson, Reisz, and Richardson were later joined by John Schlesinger, an Oxford classmate of Richardson's. Together they constituted the main directorial talent of the social-realist features of the early 1960s. All of their films were based on the writings of the so-called Angry Young Men (or Women, as the case might be).

Although Free Cinema had in fact appeared slightly before the explosions that were to occur in the other arts, it wasn't until it connected with the new drama and literature that its kind of expression moved over into the feature film and became economically viable. Following *Nice Time* (Claude Goretta and Alain Tanner) and *Every Day Except Christmas* (Anderson) in 1957, the Free Cinema movement as such virtually ceased with *We Are the Lambeth Boys* (Reisz) in 1959. Nonetheless, the attitudes and some of the rough-hewn style of Free Cinema were carried into the new social-realist features that began as the Free Cinema shorts ended. Although much more conventional than Free Cinema in both content and form, the 1959 production *Room at the Top,* directed by Jack Clayton, who had come up through the commercial industry, launched the new phase (Figure 9.4a). Set in an industrial northern town, the plot deals with the compulsions and confusions of a cynical young arriviste determined to climb up out of his slum origins. Its romantic conflict is class based—to marry the daughter of a local industrialist in order to get ahead, or to stay with the mistress he loves but who would impede his chances for success.

Look Back in Anger, released in the same year and directed by Free Cinema stalwart Tony Richardson, put some of the same matters, and others, in a clearer and less ambiguous way (Figure 9.4b). Through the Jimmy Porter character's brilliant and paranoiac monologues, we could begin to understand what the anger was all about. At least it was clear what he was trying to tear down (the Establishment, personified by his wife's parents) and what he was trying to preserve (the working-class virtues represented by his friend Ma Tanner). It was not so clear what the replacement society would be like, and certainly not how it might come about. Class frustration was what was at issue, not social policy making.

In any case, these two films, double-billed in the United States, began the social-realist cycle that dealt with various aspects of working-class character and problems. The cycle continued with such notable titles as *Saturday Night and Sunday Morning* (Reisz, 1960) and *The Loneliness of the Long Distance Runner* (Richardson, 1962). As a body the films tended to be set in the industrial regions north of London. Thus they contrasted with British entertainment films up to that time that, according to the Free Cinema group at least, had reflected almost exclusively the outlook of metropolitan southern English culture and the middle and upper classes. Here were efforts to include "the rich diversity of tradition and personality which is the whole of Britain" called for in one of Free Cinema's manifestoes.

Lindsay Anderson, although acknowledged as leader and spokesman of the Free Cinema group, was the last to arrive at features. Curiously, his first, *This Sporting Life* (1963), if it marked a high point in the social-realist cycle, also indicated a turning away from the sources that had given that demimovement its character and strength. From a novel and script adaptation by David Storey, it has the requisite general characteristics of a northern industrial town and working-class background. Where it departs from the other films is in its concentration on the tortured love affair between the miner–turned–football player and his widowed landlady, and in its flashback sequences of surrealist exaggeration. At the time of its release Anderson was complimented by British reviewers for having broken out of the confines of the social-realist films, with their air of objectivity and use of broadly drawn social character types to make their criticism stick, into a more complex focus on individual feeling. Perhaps what was by then being referred to as the "kitchen sink" school of film making was limited in certain important ways and had run its course. Whatever the reasons, *This Sporting Life* along with *Billy Liar* (directed by John Schlesinger in 1963) proved to be the last films directly connected with the line that had begun with *Room at the Top.* Of

FIGURE 9.4a and b   a. *Room at the Top* ☆ United Kingdom, 1959, Jack Clayton; Laurence Harvey and Simone Signoret. b. *Look Back in Anger* ☆ United Kingdom, 1959, Tony Richardson; Claire Bloom and Richard Burton.

the directors who worked in it, Anderson stuck closest to the earlier commitments (and made the fewest features). *If . . .* (1969), *O Lucky Man!* (1973), and *Britannia Hospital* (1982), although different in subjects and settings, grew out of the same impulses of social criticism as the earlier films—even though their fantastical style had little in common with the documentary mode that had initially given birth to the Free Cinema movement.

The Gothic Strain

After World War II the British gothic tradition, with its emphasis on horror and magic, found its most viable outlet in film, an art form uniquely well suited to showcase the atmospheric effects that were the genre's stock-in-trade. British movies took the gothic form in new directions, adding unconventional sexuality to the mix of terror, suspense, and eerie locales for which such stories have long been known. Hammer Studios turned out a series of stylishly lurid horror movies of this type during the 1950s and 1960s, most of the best directed by Terence Fisher. The Hammer films featured a new stable of British acting talent including Peter Cushing and Christopher Lee, the latter of whom became a popular postwar reincarnation of Bela Lugosi's famous movie vampire. Notable among the Hammer productions are *The Curse of Frankenstein* (1957) and *Dracula* (1958), both directed by Fisher.

Michael Powell, another director drawn to fantasy and horror, has produced some especially beautiful images, carefully photographed and lushly colored. The series of romantic fantasies he created in collaboration with Emeric Pressbuger after the war include *The Red Shoes* (1948) and *Tales of Hoffman* (1951). Powell and Pressburger called their production company The Archers and took joint credit for writing, directing, and producing all the films they made together. Despite its fairy-tale atmosphere, *The Red Shoes* provides a realistic inside look at the world of ballet and also functions as a meditation on the meaning of art. The Archers' 1947 release, *Black Narcissus,* is set in a convent deep in the Himalayas. The film's exotic locale (reproduced in a gloriously artificial manner in London's Pinewood Studios) becomes a backdrop for a study of repressed sexuality. These two themes, art and sexuality, come together in the 1960 release, *Peeping Tom,* which Powell made following a break with Pressburger. In this strikingly self-reflexive film, often regarded as Powell's masterpiece, an emotionally twisted photographer combines his penchant for voyeurism and sadism by taking pictures of women as he murders them (Figure 9.5a and b). A Hitchcockian meditation on the perverse pleasures inherent in the act of looking at images, *Peeping Tom* makes its criminal protagonist sympathetic so as to implicate its audience in the cruelties we, like him, may enjoy watching.

In a sense gothic exercises such as those of Powell and Hammer Studios can be seen as the shadowy underside of the British documentary impulse. In response to the rationally based political agenda that underlay the documentary model—the real social settings and real social problems that animated the films produced by Ealing and the Free Cinema group—the gothic strain represented an eruption of unconscious fantasies, a return of the repressed as it were. In future years, Britain would build on both of these strains, producing a long series of movies for English-speaking adults who were averse to reading subtitles but turned off by the nonstop violence that had come to dominate many Hollywood productions. Though designed for entertainment, these movies frequently featured socially progressive messages as well. Thus Grierson's legacy, though altered and updated to suit a changing cultural climate, lived on.

FIGURE 9.5a and b   *Peeping Tom* ★ United Kingdom, 1960, Michael Powell, Karlheinz Böhm and Moira Shearer.

Films of the Period

1946
Great Expectations (David Lean)

Hue and Cry (Charles Crichton)
Odd Man Out (Carol Reed)

1947
Black Narcissus (The Archers [Michael Powell and
    Emeric Pressburger])

1948
Hamlet (Laurence Olivier)
Oliver Twist (David Lean)

The Red Shoes (The Archers)

1949
Kind Hearts and Coronets (Robert Hamer)
Passport to Pimlico (Henry Cornelius)
The Third Man (Carol Reed)
Whiskey Galore (Tight Little Island) (Alexander
   Mackendrick)

1951
The Lavender Hill Mob (Charles Crichton)
The Man in the White Suit (Alexander
   Mackendrick)

1954
The Maggie (High and Dry) (Alexander
   Mackendrick)

1955
The Ladykillers (Alexander Mackendrick)

1957
The Curse of Frankenstein (Terence Fisher)

1958
Dracula (Terence Fisher)

1959
Look Back in Anger (Tony Richardson)
Room at the Top (Jack Clayton)

1960
The Entertainer (Tony Richardson)
Saturday Night and Sunday Morning
   (Karel Reisz)

1961
A Taste of Honey (Tony Richardson)

1962
A Kind of Loving (John Schlesinger)
Lawrence of Arabia (David Lean)
The Loneliness of the Long Distance Runner
   (Tony Richardson)

1963
Billy Liar (John Schlesinger)
This Sporting Life (Lindsay Anderson)

Books on the Period

Barton, Ruth. *Irish National Cinema.* New York: Routledge, 2004.

Chibnall, Steve, and Robert Murphy. *British Crime Cinema.* New York: Routledge, 1999.

Gillett, Philip. *The British Working Class in Postwar Film.* London: Palgrave, 2003.

Gledhill, Christine. *Reframing British Cinema, 1918–1928: Between Restraint and Passion.* London: BFI Publishing, 2004.

Harper, Sue, and Vincent Porter. *British Cinema of the 1950s.* New York: Oxford University Press, 2003.

Hewing, Wendy. *British Cinema in the 1960s: An Educational Resource.* London, BFI Publishing, 2003.

Higson, Andrew. *English Heritage, English Cinema.* New York: Oxford University Press, 2003.

Hogenkamp, Bert. *Film, Television, and the Left in Britain: 1950 to 1970.* London: Laurence and Wishart, 2000.

Hunter, I. Q., ed. *British Science Fiction Cinema.* New York: Routledge, 1999.

MacKillop, Ian, and Neil Sinyard, eds. *British Cinema in the 1950s: An Art in Peacetime.* London: Palgrave, 2003.

McIlroy, Brian. *Shooting to Kill: Filmmaking and the "Troubles" in Northern Ireland.* Richmond, BC: Steveston Press, 2001.

Murphy, Robert. *British Cinema and the Second World War.* New York: Continuum, 2001.

Petrie, Duncan. *Screening Scotland.* London: BFI Publishing, 2000.

Rowbotham, Shelia, and Huw Beynon, eds. *Looking at Class: Film, Television, and the Working Class in Britain.* New York: New York University Press, 2001.

Street, Sarah. *Transatlantic Crossings: British Feature Films in the USA.* New York: Continuum, 2002.

Sutton, David. *A Chorus of Raspberries: British Film Comedy 1929–1939.* Exeter, UK: Exeter University Press, 2000.

Williams, Tony. *Structure of Desire: British Cinema, 1939–1955.* Albany: State University of New York Press, 2000.

10

Hollywood in Transition

1945–1962

After World War II ended in 1945, the United States lost no time in returning to a settled state. In 1952, General Dwight Eisenhower, hero of World War II, was elected President of the United States; he was reelected in 1956. These were the Cold War years in which the United States defined itself largely through its ideological differences with the Soviet Union. The struggle between these two superpowers for global dominance led to a war in Korea, which ended in 1953. Apart from this conflict, the Eisenhower years were prosperous, placid, and very "American." Undercurrents of disaffection that hindsight has revealed didn't come to the fore until the 1960s.

Much the same might be said of most Hollywood films of the 1950s in terms of placidity and Americanism—at least on the surface. The postwar years marked the beginning of a transition that would lead the American film industry from the hardened confines of a production-distribution-exhibition pattern that had lasted for over two decades into uncertainty and changing forms and functions. In film, what affects the industry affects the art; what happens in the United States influences the world.

A central factor accounting for and accompanying the changes that occurred during this era was the decline in theater attendance from the booming war and postwar years (from 90 million weekly in 1948 to 51 million in 1952). The former "family audience" was now a minority audience, administered to mainly by Walt Disney Productions. Going to the movies, once the staple form of entertainment, became more of a special occasion somewhere between staying home to watch TV and attending live theater or a concert. With increased public affluence, motion pictures were now competing for leisure time with spectator sports, bowling, motorboating, hi-fi sets, and a whole range of new activities. Whereas in 1946, as *Variety* noted, almost $1.7 billion (or almost 20 percent of all U.S. expenditures for recreation) were paid in movie admissions; by 1962 that figure had plummeted to $930 million (or about 4.5 percent)—in spite of inflating ticket prices.

172 Chapter 10   www.ablongman.com/wexman6e

By 1952 the major studios had had to divest themselves of their theater holdings. After a decade of litigation, from 1938 to 1948, the Supreme Court finally ruled, in *U.S. v. Paramount Pictures et al.,* that the practice of vertical control was in restraint of trade and tended toward monopoly. The majors might continue to produce and distribute but not exhibit. In the mid-1940s about 400 features were produced annually—300 by the major studios, 100 by independents. Every week between 80 million and 100 million persons had paid admission to see the movies in 18,719 "hard-top" theaters and 300 drive-ins. By 1960 the average weekly attendance—in 13,200 indoor and 4,600 outdoor theaters—had dropped to an estimated 46 million. Of the 136 features produced that year, only 70 came from the major studios, whereas 66 were from the independents. Those trends—fewer pictures, more of which were by independents; smaller audiences; and a decrease in the number of theaters, with the proportion of drive-in theaters increasing—would continue throughout the 1960s and into the 1970s.

During the 1950s, Hollywood gradually abandoned its earlier practice of presenting its wares as a program in which a cartoon, a newsreel, a short subject, and two features were provided for the price of a single admission. The "B" productions that were churned out at breakneck speed to fill the second half of these double bills enjoyed their last hurrah during this era. Many of these "poverty row" pictures were later rediscovered by critics who found artistry amid the schlock. Edgar G. Ulmer's *Detour* (1950) was one of the rediscoveries; Joseph H. Lewis's *Gun Crazy* (1950) was another. **Ida Lupino,** the so-called "Queen of the Bs," was the only woman working as a director in Hollywood during this period. She made several well-regarded movies of this type, including *The Bigamist* (1953) and *Hard, Fast and Beautiful* (1951), the latter of which casts a jaundiced eye on women's amateur tennis. Lupino's 1953 production of *The Hitchhiker* is one of her best. Set amid the desert scrub of the Baja peninsula, it tells the tale of two suburban husbands out on a fishing trip who pick up a serial killer. Alternating between claustrophobic three-shots of the men in their car (Figure 10.1a) and wide-angle panoramas of the parched desert surrounding them (Figure 10.1b), the film offers a glimpse of the strains and fissures that lay beneath the accepted standards of masculinity during this outwardly tranquil time. If the male community always contains the threat of treachery and violence, the film suggests, what lies outside of this uncomfortable circle appears bleak and unreceptive.

FIGURE 10.1a and b *The Hitchhiker* ★ United States, 1953, Ida Lupino; a. Frank Lovejoy, William Tallman, and Edmund O'Brian.

Television

It was TV, of course, that occupied most of the leisure time of the public who formerly would have gone to the movies. The shifting relationship between motion pictures and broadcasting is one of the main chapters in the history of those two industries during the 1950s and 1960s. Television had begun on an experimental basis just before World War II, but wartime priorities and shortages had frozen its development until the postwar years. From five stations and a few hundred sets in 1946 it expanded rapidly to the first year of big-time television in 1948, when Milton Berle and Ed Sullivan were seen and heard in the large urban centers. Between 1948 and 1952 approximately 17 million TV sets were sold. In 1951 coaxial cable and microwave relay had connected the nation coast to coast. In that year major TV production began its move from New York to Hollywood. From the early 1950s the audience continued to expand. Today there are more television sets than persons in the country. The most popular television series (*CSI*, for example) average between 25 million and 30 million viewers a week. A special occasion (such as the last episode of *Seinfeld* in 1998) may attract more than 60 million; even greater numbers worldwide watch some big sporting events.

Until 1948 the motion-picture industry's reaction to the TV threat was ostrichlike. At one studio it was reported to be forbidden even to use the word *television* in executive conversation. Then the stance shifted to passive resistance through deliberate withholding of the enormous resources of talent and reservoir of product. No actors, writers, or directors under contract were permitted to work for television. No feature films produced by the major studios were offered for airing. Films playing in theaters were not advertised on television. Revenues from the box office continued to decline, and complaints from stockholders about dwindling dividends steadily increased.

The critical problem was finding access to an audience. Because the production companies no longer owned the theaters, which anyway were being converted into supermarkets or razed to make way for parking lots, their loyalty to the theater owners and resolve to try to protect them from even greater television competition was weakened. When the pressures finally became too great, the studios followed the old industry saw about if you can't beat 'em, join 'em. They began by making available to TV the vast libraries of feature films that had accumulated during the past decades. By the early 1970s not only had the backlog of old features been used up, but the supply of recent theatrical film releases was also far below the television demand.

The ultimate response of Hollywood to television was to undertake production directly for the tube. It began in 1952 when Columbia Pictures formed the first of the television subsidiaries among the major studios—Screen Gems. This television film making started with the half-hour entertainment series, which became hour-long and, in some instances, even ninety minutes in length, resembling more and more the old "B" pictures that were no longer a profitable kind of production for the more choosy audiences who went out to the theaters. In 1957 Desilu, the company formed by Desi Arnaz and Lucille Ball out of the extraordinary success of their *I Love Lucy* series, shot more film than all the major studios together. By the mid-1960s Hollywood began to make feature films directly for TV rather than for initial theatrical showing.

The production for television exerted a gravitational pull toward the West Coast. Soon virtually all nighttime television entertainment was being produced in the Los Angeles area. Only news, documentary and public affairs, and some daytime game shows and soap operas continued to come out of New York. As television became established,

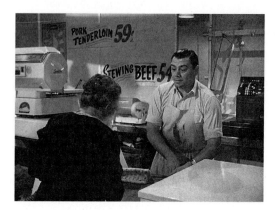

FIGURE 10.2a and b *Marty* ☆ United States, 1955, Delbert Mann; a. Ernest Borgnine and Betsy Blair; b. Borgnine.

people and product began to flow from it into film. Out of the so-called Golden Age of live TV drama in the late 1940s and early 1950s, theatrical feature films were created from the writings of Paddy Chayefsky, Rod Serling, and others. *Marty* (1955), *Twelve Angry Men* (1957), and *Requiem for a Heavyweight* (1962) had all appeared live on the tube. Befitting their origins on the small screen, these productions leaned toward a style that emphasized closeups of actors (Figure 10.2a) and simple, homey settings (Figure 10.2b).

Directors as well as writers came to features from television: John Frankenheimer, Sam Peckinpah, and Norman Jewison among them. Some of the new stars (male only, it seems)—Steve McQueen, James Garner, Clint Eastwood—also got their start in television. Financial control, studio facilities, story material, production personnel, and performers have continued to move back and forth between film and television.

New Screen Processes

All three major technological additions to the silent black-and-white film—sound, color, and wide screen—were around from the very beginning. Their introduction was in every case dependent more on economic considerations than on technical feasibility. Whenever the industry is in trouble somebody will say, "There's nothing wrong with the movies that a few good pictures can't cure." But if producers knew how to make consistently profitable films, there wouldn't have been any trouble in the first place. Although popular success can't be guaranteed, technical novelty can be tried. Sound came in 1927 because of the competition radio then offered for the audiences of silent films, and because Warner Bros. was attempting corporate expansion. Technicolor was added to feature film production in 1935 in an attempt to remedy the continuing Depression slump. In 1952 the failing box office and television competition once again goaded the industry into introducing a number of "new screen processes." All were designed to offer sights and sounds that the competitive medium could not duplicate and to give the screen a greater illusion of depth.

Stereoscopic, or 3-D, feature films first appeared in the fall of 1952. (In the 1930s there had been a series of M-G-M black-and-white 3-D shorts; polaroid lenses now permitted the addition of color.) With *Bwana Devil* it seemed to the audience that a lion was charging them (promotion promised "A lion in your lap") or a spear was being thrown over their heads.

At first, the **3-D films** were extremely successful, but their attraction wore off within less than a year. It was said that audiences didn't like the special glasses required. By the time any substantial work was undertaken in 3-D (such as Alfred Hitchcock's *Dial M for Murder,* released in 1954), the audience had lost interest. 3-D came and went while the wide screen has lasted in one form or another ever since. It was the grandeur the wide screens added that caught public fancy. The first of the new wide-screen processes was the biggest and best of them in terms of spatial illusion. *This Is Cinerama* opened in New York City in September 1952 (Figure 10.3). Developed by Fred Waller in 1939, it had been used in an earlier version by the Armed Forces during World War II for aircraft identification and mock gunnery practice. The screen, with a 2.85 to 1 **aspect ratio** of width to height, was deeply curved and vast. A necessarily small audience sitting well forward had virtually everyone's whole field of vision filled by the image. Viewers felt they really were on that roller coaster or on that plane coming in over the Chicago skyline. Accompanying the visual format of great width and depth was a hi-fidelity, stereophonic, magnetic sound system. Its enormously increased range of frequencies brought sound reproduction much closer to life than the woefully inadequate optical recording in standard use.

The development of Cinerama had been backed by people outside the Hollywood industry—Mike Todd, Louis de Rochemont, Lowell Thomas, and others—but the studio heads could scarcely be blind to its huge financial success. *This Is Cinerama* was soon numbered among the great moneymakers of all time, and the several features that followed it, playing in only a few specially equipped and converted "legitimate" theaters at live theater prices, consistently appeared high on *Variety*'s box-office tallies. But Cinerama's cumbersome technology and the small audiences that could be accommodated at each

FIGURE 10.3 Artist's representation of an audience watching *This Is Cinerama* ★ United States, 1952, Merian C. Cooper.

showing presented too severe a wrench to existing production and exhibition practices to be contemplated without alarm. Furthermore, the Cinerama films were essentially a group of travelogue shorts anthologized to feature length. The kinds of stories that might fill that monstrous screen seemed extremely limited. An appropriate size and shape for parades down Fifth Avenue, a train speeding across the Mojave Desert, or two boa constrictors copulating, as someone observed, it offered no clear advantage in dealing with individual human beings (who happen to stand upright), unless they were in quantities of thousands. Even more basically, the use of closeups and editing, essential to screen narrative technique as practiced, would be greatly reduced if not prohibited by what seemed acres of image. What was needed was a sort of poor man's Cinerama—one that spiced up but didn't depart too much from the existing standard.

It was Spyros Skouras, head of Twentieth Century-Fox, who performed the trick. The rabbit he pulled out of the hat was called **CinemaScope** (and better not forget to capitalize the middle *S* if you were a Fox employee). It was based on a principle worked out in the 1920s by a French inventor, Henri Chrétien. Its wide screen was less wide than Cinerama's and curved only enough to accommodate focus. Though wider than standard (2.55 to 1 aspect ratio rather than 1.33 to 1), CinemaScope did not approximate peripheral vision. It was accompanied in its premiere by hi-fidelity four-track stereophonic sound.

Unlike the inauguration of the earlier 3-D, CinemaScope was launched with a feature that probably would have made money no matter what size and shape the screen. As it was, *The Robe,* which opened in September 1953, proved a tremendous success with its DeMille-like blend of spectacle and religiosity. It was followed by a series of expensive and well-made features, musicals and comedies especially, equally designed to show off the attractions of the new screen process—for example, *Gentlemen Prefer Blondes* (1953), *A Star Is Born* (1954), and *Seven Brides for Seven Brothers* (1954). Frequently featured trios of stars called attention to the expansiveness of the visual field, such as Marilyn Monroe, Lauren Bacall, and Betty Grable in *How to Marry a Millionaire* (1953) and Dorothy McGuire, Jean Peters, and Maggie McNamara in *Three Coins in the Fountain* (1954).

Fox was to wide screen what Warner had been to sound, and again the rest of the industry soon followed along. CinemaScope proved the almost ideal compromise between Cinerama and the conventional screen ratio. It required no major change in production technology or even technique, and it was simple and inexpensive to install in existing movie houses. Although it favored certain film types—historical spectacles, musicals, and westerns—and was awkward for others—intimate romances and social dramas—stories could be told in it, with fewer camera setups and less editing required. Some of the purists complained that the image it offered was like looking at the world through a postal slot, and Jean Cocteau is credited with remarking that he recognized progress when he saw it and henceforward would put paper in the typewriter sideways when he wrote his poems. But who cared about the purists?—the box office was registering public response in large figures. As with sound, directors learned to work with CinemaScope, many reluctantly at first. The new technology was incorporated into the medium, with resultant aesthetic shifts and even some gains—like all of the earlier technological additions. In *East of Eden* (1955), for example, director Elia Kazan and cinematographer Ted McCord made stunning and highly dramatic use of the new proportions for what was essentially an intimate story of family strife. Other wide-screen systems soon appeared. VistaVision, from Paramount, was a good alternative, providing a sharper image than CinemaScope. Todd A-0 was the first to use 70 mm film, a gauge still employed for a few prestige productions. Today **Panavision** is

Hollywood's widescreen process of choice. But the extremely wide screens didn't become the exclusive shape, as some feared they might when CinemaScope first appeared. Rather, they eventually became reserved for the extravaganza—the big musical (*My Fair Lady,* 1964, and *The Sound of Music,* 1965), the blockbusting war picture (*The Guns of Navarone,* 1961, and *The Longest Day,* 1962), and the historical spectacular (*Lawrence of Arabia,* 1962 (Figure 10.4), and *Doctor Zhivago,* 1965). For more conventional pictures what is called the "standard wide screen"—1.85 to 1 its most common ratio—has replaced the former 1.33 to 1 "Academy ratio" that has remained standard for television sets.

Fall of the Studios, Rise of the Independents

Another result of the pressures and changes experienced by the industry in the early 1950s was a shakeup in production-distribution practices, which also affected the content and form of the films being made. Among the producing companies it was the former giants, now stripped of theaters, that were hit hardest by the dwindling and erratic earnings of their films. The enormous overhead in real estate, sound stages, expensive equipment, and high-salaried technical and creative personnel under long-term contracts could no longer be supported by the fewer, costlier films that current audience response dictated. Whereas M-G-M had once boasted as its greatest asset "More Stars Than There Are in Heaven," expensive nonworking actors, along with the writers and directors, had become a liability. All of the major studios except one were keeping their books in red ink.

That exception was United Artists (UA), which had never owned theaters and didn't even have a studio. Instead, it had acquired films from independent producers and distributed them to theaters owned by others. It would choose from among the projects presented to it, perhaps supervise the scripts, put up some money, and go to the bank for more. What

FIGURE 10.4 *Lawrence of Arabia* ☆ United Kingdom, 1962, David Lean; Peter O'Toole in Arab dress.

it could guarantee to its producers was major distribution, for which it took a healthy cut. Its production overhead consisted mostly of offices, secretaries, and smart lawyers good at contracts and finance. Billy Wilder, one of United Artists' top producer-directors, observed ruefully, "We used to make pictures; now we make deals." A weak competitor in the old days, when the larger studios controlled exhibition, under the new conditions UA prospered and became the model others would imitate.

The rest of the studios freed themselves from employees under long-term contracts, except for skeleton technical crews. The actors, directors, and former staff producers went into production for themselves or worked for other independents, with corporate profits and shares in the income from a picture replacing salaries. The studios rented out production space and facilities to the independents, financed their productions wholly or in part, and distributed the completed films. Rather than reading simply "Produced by" Paramount or Warner Bros., opening credits now read "A Judd Bernard–Irwin Winkler Production for Metro-Goldwyn-Mayer" or "A Horizon Picture, Released through Columbia Pictures Corporation," and the like.

The independent companies were by no means totally independent, however, and the kinds of films they produced departed very little from those that had preceded them. The domination once exercised by the heads of five studios (Metro-Goldwyn-Mayer, Paramount, Warner Bros., Twentieth Century-Fox, and RKO) was steadily being reduced. But the independents still had to play ball with the majors, whose remaining strongholds were their worldwide distribution organizations. This gave them power to exercise substantial control over the choice of subject matter and its presentation.

Another reason there was less change than might have been expected in the kinds of films being made with this new independence was that the smaller companies were subjected to exactly the same necessity for popular appeal as the large ones had been. In fact, in the case of the independents, the pressure was even greater. With only one picture produced at a time on borrowed money, rather than an annual production program of forty or fifty features financed out of studio reserves, each film had to be a success. Hits couldn't pay for flops. In some respects there seemed less room for experiment and risk than there had been under the old system. Many of the former studio personnel who formed their own companies stuck even closer to tested ingredients than the studios had done. Those who had cried for freedom from the repeated formulas of studio production and expressed the desire to strike out into bold new areas, to do something "really worthwhile," settled for the tried and true. To paraphrase G. B. Shaw, there's nothing as timid as several million dollars.

It is more than coincidental that in those years of the 1950s in which the studios were declining, directors were gaining a new status. When M-G-M, once biggest and proudest of the studios, virtually went out of the motion-picture business altogether in the 1970s, the film makers who would have worked for M-G-M still found their way to film making if they were smart enough and tough enough—constant prerequisites to creation in motion-picture art. If film artists spent a lot of their time making deals, as Wilder quipped, they were free from the power and overzealous supervision of production chiefs such as Irving Thalberg, and from conceptions of God, country, and motherhood, as revealed to Louis B. Mayer.

Internationalization

Along with all the other sweeping changes there even seemed some danger that Los Angeles might cease to be the film capital of the world and fall into ruins like Carthage or ancient Rome. American films were in increasing competition with foreign ones—especially with those of Britain, Italy, and France—for audiences abroad and even in this country. Co-national productions and multinational crews and casts became commonplace. And "American" films themselves were as likely to be shot anywhere in the world as within proximity of Hollywood Boulevard and Vine Street.

The first consideration to prompt this increased internationalization may have been in part an artistic one. Wide screens encouraged special emphasis on authentic and exotic locales. For conventional sorts of love stories that formerly would have been shot on sound stages and back lots, film makers now journeyed to Rome (*Three Coins in the Fountain,* 1954), Hong Kong (*Love Is a Many-Splendored Thing,* 1955), or Tokyo (*Sayonara,* 1957). Audiences of the 1950s began to get moving-picture postcards along with stars and stories. Some of the spectacles made for the wide screen were very much about the places and terrain where the stories took place—such as the Southeast Asian jungle for *The Bridge on the River Kwai* (1957) and the Middle Eastern desert for *Lawrence of Arabia* (1962).

The secondary considerations were exclusively financial. First, by shooting abroad, American producers could more easily assemble a cast drawn from a number of countries to better ensure warm reception of their films in various parts of the globe. Then, too, there was the advantage, for the Americans involved, of delayed payment of U.S. corporate and income taxes on work done outside the country. Also, it was thought to be, and in many cases actually was, cheaper to make films abroad. Generally costs were less in Mexico, Spain, and Italy, for example—especially for labor. (A counterargument was that the apparent saving was often canceled out in working with less efficient crews who used unfamiliar methods and languages.) There was no doubt that the various schemes of subsidy offered by most foreign governments to encourage national production were a real incentive. Many essentially American films were disguised as British—for instance, their production set up in a way that met minimum requirements for assistance from Britain's National Film Finance Corporation. In addition, where a quota system existed for proportionate release of foreign to domestic films, as in Britain and elsewhere, a film flying the local flag would be assured immediate exhibition there rather than having to wait among the films of other nations. In some cases—India, for example—American profits had become "frozen currency" and couldn't be taken out of the country. One way to make use of that money was to spend it on a production that could then be distributed worldwide and earn revenue elsewhere.

Distribution along with production became increasingly internationalized. American companies began to seek income from the distribution of foreign films in the United States as well as elsewhere. Also, as their own production expenses increased and the size of the domestic audience decreased, they attempted to earn back more and more of their costs from abroad. In former years the huge American market could return a profit on a film, and what was earned elsewhere was gravy. Now over 50 percent of the income from American films came from overseas. More than ever, Hollywood courted the world audience.

Finally, the motion-picture industry developed its own equivalent to the plants set up abroad and the multinational corporations that had become common practice among other industries. Not only was there a British M-G-M, as there was an English Ford, but the United States dominated and to some extent controlled foreign financing of production and international distribution. In terms of financial backing and distribution, Antonioni's *Blow-Up* (1966), made in England, was as much an American film as his *Zabriskie Point* (1970), made in the United States. American influence began to reach even into films that appeared to be totally French. Jean-Luc Godard's *A Married Woman* and *Band of Outsiders* (both

1964) were financed by Columbia Pictures. Four of François Truffaut's films were financed by United Artists. Although the European Economic Community tried to set up an alternative financing-distribution pattern to counter American domination, little came of the effort.

Loosened Controls on Content

In the United States, social controls placed on the content of motion pictures began to be eased in the 1950s. This encouraged, if not always a greater maturity, at least a new freedom and frankness in the presentation of sexual behavior, states of undress, and kinds of language. During those years, the United States Supreme Court rendered a series of decisions that curtailed the activities of state and local censoring bodies. The Motion Picture Association of America liberalized its code of self-regulation and then started to classify rather than regulate screen content. Organized pressure groups—religious, ethnic, and political—turned their attention away from what was showing in the theaters to what was appearing ever more widely on the tube. Producers eagerly, some desperately, took advantage of the new freedom to try to attract audiences away from television and to compete with the forthrightness of European films.

In 1952, in *The Miracle* case, the Supreme Court delivered what became a historic decision. The Rossellini short (which had been packaged with Pagnol's *Joffroy* and Renoir's *A Day in the Country* to be shown as *The Ways of Love*) had incensed Catholics in the New York City area, especially a Catholic veterans' organization. A modern parable of Christ's birth, *The Miracle* stars Anna Magnani as a feeble-minded peasant "Mary" (Figure 10.5); a bearded Federico Fellini appears as an itinerant "Joseph". After a round of contretemps, including picketing and bomb threats, the New York State Board of Regents, the censoring agency, revoked the film's license on grounds that it was "sacrilegious." When the case eventually reached the Supreme Court, the Court seemed to reverse its own precedent. In 1915, in *Mutual Film Corporation* v. *Ohio,* it had been held that motion pictures were "business pure and simple . . . not to be regarded as part of the press of the country or as organs of public opinion," and hence not subject to the freedom from censorship guaranteed by the First Amendment to the Constitution. The 1952 Court did not rule on the constitutionality of film censorship as such, however. It simply stated that "sacrilege," particularly one faith's conception of it, was not sufficient grounds for the Board of Regents' action. Nonetheless, the decision suggested some sympathy toward affording the motion picture the same freedom from restraint prior to release as that enjoyed by the other media of communication and art. There followed a succession of cases in which the decisions seemed to support that interpretation of the Court's position.

With a later shift in Court membership toward the conservative, however, a 1973 decision regarding obscenity cases was rendered that many, not just those within the motion-picture industry, regarded with consternation. It altered and clarified the former criteria for determining what constituted obscenity. Specifically the Court mandated that the affront need be only to local—as opposed to national—community standards, and that local standards were employable in determining appeal to prurient interest. Additionally the Court withdrew the "utterly without redeeming social value" test and substituted for it a mere lack of "serious literary, artistic, political, or scientific value."

The way now seemed open for every interested local body to impose conflicting sets of requirements on every film released within conceivably thousands of areas of jurisdiction. That

FIGURE 10.5 *The Miracle* ★ Italy, 1948, Roberto Rossellini; Anna Magnani, center foreground.

this was not an imaginary danger was made clear when, less than a month after the Supreme Court ruling, the Georgia Supreme Court confirmed a ban on *Carnal Knowledge* and the conviction of a theater owner for showing it. While the citizens of Albany, Georgia, were prevented from seeing Mike Nichols's serious dark comedy about sex, the exploitive and frankly pornographic *Deep Throat* was playing to packed houses in other communities across the land. (The U.S. Supreme Court subsequently reversed the Georgia decision on *Carnal Knowledge,* holding that no jury could legally find that film obscene, and indeed it looks tame today.)

During the same years the Motion Picture Association of America was making its own efforts, on the one hand to allow producers greater freedom of subject and treatment, and on the other to fend off attacks from those who protested that what had resulted was license rather than freedom. Since 1934 no important picture had been distributed without the seal of the MPAA's Production Code Administration. In the 1950s, when two "A" features of United Artists were denied a Code seal, UA released them anyway, without it. The MPAA, now that the theaters were no longer owned or controlled by the studios, was unable to prevent the films from playing to large audiences. The first, *The Moon Is Blue* (1953), was from a popular stage comedy and would appear today patently moral. It was in fact about Maggie McNamara's successfully resisting the charms of David Niven. But it did contain considerable talk about sex and the words *virgin* and *pregnant* were used. The Code office subsequently conceded that it had been unwise in refusing that film a seal. No such option existed for the second one, *The Man with the Golden Arm* (1955) (Figure 10.6). Taken from the Nelson Algren novel, it dealt directly with narcotic addiction, a subject expressly forbidden by the Code.

Both films were produced and directed by Otto Preminger, who made much of the publicity and set himself up as a champion of free speech. In a show of self-righteous indignation United Artists withdrew from the MPAA; however, it rejoined after it had collected all its profits from the two offending films. This defiance of the Production Code Administration clearly threatened the whole system of self-regulation, and other production companies, especially the independents, were becoming restive. In 1956 the Code was revised, the main change being to permit the treatment of narcotics.

A decade later Jack Valenti succeeded Eric Johnston as president of the MPAA. Since pressures from producers for increased freedom from restraint had continued to mount, and an ever-increasing number of films were being released without the Code seal (distributors of foreign films rarely bothered to apply), one of Valenti's first acts was to further liberalize the Code. Among the concessions in the 1966 revisions were permitting the use of common profanity (*Gone With the Wind*'s famous final line, "Frankly, my dear, I don't give a damn," had required a special ruling in 1939), the treatment of abortion, and justifiable suicide. In general the Code language was softened, with phrases such as "good taste" and "dramatic necessity" replacing the strict prohibitions of the earlier Code.

Still, the onrush of new explicitness continued. Inasmuch as the trend seemed irreversible and the outcries provoked were largely on behalf of impressionable children, the MPAA decided that rather than attempt to control screen content, it would regulate audience attendance. The shocking language and sexual intensity of *Who's Afraid of Virginia Woolf?* (1966) were allowed when its advertising carried the statement "Suggested for Mature Audiences." In 1968 the MPAA adopted, not without protest from members of the industry who objected to potential earnings being limited in any way, a system of age classification like those already operating in many countries, such as the United Kingdom. The rating "G," for

FIGURE 10.6   *The Man with the Golden Arm* ★ United States, 1955, Otto Preminger; Frank Sinatra, right.

"general," meant suitable for all. "M" advised parents that the content was "mature" (subsequently this became "GP" and then "PG"—"parental guidance suggested"). "R" stood for "restricted": Those under age seventeen had to be accompanied by a parent or adult guardian. "X" indicated that only those age eighteen and older would be admitted.

By 1990 the X rating had come to imply the frankly pornographic; it drastically limited distribution, advertising, and hence box-office returns. To avoid the stigma of the X rating and acknowledge films with adult themes and serious intentions, a new classification was devised: NC-17 (no one under age seventeen admitted). *Henry and June,* about writers Anaïs Nin and Henry Miller in Paris of the 1930s, was first to receive it.

What had been the Production Code Administration became the Classification and Rating Administration. Enforcement was left to the theaters. Much dissatisfaction about classification was expressed. Producers complained when they felt their films had been given a too-restrictive rating. Theater owners resented the encroachment on their domains and the nuisance involved. Organized pressure groups, notably the National Catholic Office of Motion Pictures (which replaced the Legion of Decency), protested that the ratings were too laxly administered. All pointed to the inevitable inconsistencies in the labeling of particular films. Even so, in the face of the continuing threat of legal censorship, most of the industry accepted the MPAA classification system as the least of possible evils.

By the turn of the twenty-first century a new tempest had erupted as politicians called for further clarification and better enforcement of the **ratings.** Films now were required to carry descriptive language indicating why they had received the rating they had (for example, " 'R' for language and sexual content"). The big studios were further enjoined not to flaunt their disregard for the spirit of the Code by testing "R"-rated movies on teenage audiences. Although Hollywood paid lip service to the sentiment that prompted these reforms, little was actually altered. *Plus ça change, plus ça même chose* (i.e., "The more things change, the more they stay the same") appeared to be the film industry's response, as had been the case so often in the past.

Liberalism, Communism, and Anti-Communism: The House Un-American Activities Committee and Blacklisting

Although in some ways World War II was a cataclysmic event in the history of the United States, in other ways it proved to be only an interruption of some of the tensions of the 1930s, especially the political ones. In the decade before the war left-wing activities in the United States had achieved an unprecedented vigor and popularity. Whereas the forces of conservatism and reaction feared the "communist influence" at home and abroad, and attempted to check it through the power of capitalist business and government, they were ultimately ineffectual in halting a leftward swing. Some felt the New Deal itself represented a kind of totalitarian communism, with its powerful presidential leader and its sweeping program of social change. Even more unsettling, during the war the preeminent communist state, the Soviet Union, became a U.S. ally in the fight against fascism.

In the United States following the war, after a brief period of optimism about the recently established United Nations and attempts to ameliorate racial and ethnic discrimination and class and partisan differences, a new climate, or a return to an older climate, developed.

By the late 1940s, the United States was locked into a fierce struggle with the U.S.S.R. and international communism, and had become prey to fears of communist subversion. Now the reactionaries, supported by great numbers of conservatives and some frightened liberals, led to a period of military belligerence and political repression that would climax in the early 1950s in the Korean War and in congressional investigating committees.

Films of the time reflected the prevailing shift in political sentiment. When the Soviet Union had been our ally during World War II, Hollywood had made some pro-Soviet films, most notably *Mission to Moscow* (1943), *The North Star* (1943), and *Song of Russia* (1944). By 1951 one of the increasing number of anti-communist films, *I Was a Communist for the FBI,* was nominated by the Academy of Motion Picture Arts and Sciences as best feature-length documentary. In 1952 another anti-communist film, *The Hoaxters* (more recognizably a documentary), received a nomination for the same award, and the anti-communist fiction feature *My Son John* was named by the National Board of Review among its ten best for the year. The rest of the films receiving major awards in 1952 were noticeably removed from contemporary domestic reality and its problems.

The appearance of the first anti-communist films after the war occurred following an investigation in 1947 by the House Un-American Activities Committee (HUAC) into alleged communist influence in Hollywood. Initially the industry united to oppose such an inquiry as unnecessary, punitive, and itself un-American in infringing civil liberties. In Hollywood a Committee for the First Amendment (which guarantees freedom of speech and opinion) was organized by film directors William Wyler and John Huston, and screenwriter Philip Dunne. A sizable delegation from the industry, headed by Eric Johnston, president of the Motion Picture Association of America, and including such celebrities as Lauren Bacall, Humphrey Bogart, Gene Kelly, Danny Kaye, and Jane Wyatt, appeared before HUAC in Washington to protest its activities.

They weren't called on immediately, however. Instead the committee called on a series of witnesses whose ties or sympathies with the Communist Party had been suggested by its earlier investigations. John Howard Lawson, screenwriter and leader in Hollywood guild and union organizing, was first to be heard. He angrily denounced the committee and refused to answer its questions. His prepared statement, which he was not allowed to read, began: "For a week this committee has conducted an illegal and indecent trial of American citizens, whom the committee has selected to be publicly pilloried and smeared." Lawson was followed by nine other "unfriendly" witnesses, who also refused to answer the committee's questions about their political beliefs and associations and invoked the First Amendment to the Constitution. The "Hollywood Ten," as they came to be known, comprised, in addition to Lawson, screenwriters Alvah Bessie, Lester Cole, Ring Lardner, Jr., Albert Maltz, Samuel Ornitz, and Dalton Trumbo; directors Herbert Biberman and Edward Dmytryk; and producer Adrian Scott. All were cited for contempt of Congress.

In the face of the unfavorable publicity occasioned by the truculent defiance of these ten witnesses and the allegations of communist infiltration made by "friendly" ones (including actors Adolphe Menjou, Robert Taylor, Robert Montgomery, George Murphy, Ronald Reagan, and Gary Cooper; producer-directors Sam Wood, Leo McCarey, and Walt Disney; and executives Jack Warner and Louis B. Mayer), the Committee for the First Amendment collapsed. The studio heads and principal independent producers hastily met at the Waldorf-Astoria Hotel in New York City. The resultant Waldorf statement deplored the action of the ten men who had refused to testify. Its key concession, a complete reversal from the producers' earlier opposition to the intentions and procedures of HUAC, read as follows: "We will not knowingly employ a Communist or a member of any party or group which advocates the overthrow of the Government of the United States by force or by any illegal or unconstitutional methods" (aims alleged to be those of the Communist Party U.S.A.).

The Hollywood Ten were sent to prison, and the industry moved into the era of blacklisting, in which people who were suspected of opinions and activities on the political left were denied employment. Failing to establish the presence of communist propaganda in the Hollywood film, HUAC sought to remove from the industry those who might have been able to support communism through their incomes and prestige. The studio heads were not concerned primarily either with possible communistic subversion or with violation of democratic principles. What rendered them compliant with the committee's wishes was the fear of boycott and picketing of theaters by indignant citizens. Such picketing did actually occur and numerous pressure groups joined HUAC in attacking the industry. The largest, most energetic, and most powerful of these was the American Legion, which insistently demanded that Hollywood "clean house."

In 1951 and following, in the Hollywood "mass hearings," more than two hundred motion-picture workers were named by HUAC as suspected communists or communist supporters. These congressional investigations into communism, in fact, became trials of the witnesses called. Those appearing before the committee who claimed protection under the Fifth Amendment to the Constitution (designed to protect witnesses from incriminating themselves) were automatically assumed to be guilty. A bizarre extralegal system of "clearances" was set up by the industry and representatives of the pressure groups to "rehabilitate" those accused individuals who were willing to meet the requirements made of them. Public confession and recantation, including the naming of former political associates, was required from the admitted communists. Noncommunists with suspicious liberal tendencies had to repudiate their past political attitudes and behavior and promise to sin no more in a letter to the studio executive employing them. Those named by HUAC or one of the anti-communist organizations who were unwilling to take such steps could no longer find employment in the Hollywood industry. Some screenwriters were able to sell their work under assumed names, at greatly reduced rates; some directors worked under pseudonyms on low-budget productions abroad. The blacklisted actors and actresses, whose presence on the screen could not be concealed, had no recourse. Blacklisting continued even after HUAC's final Hollywood hearing in 1954. The economic damage suffered by hundreds of individuals and their families—with accompanying anger, fear, bitterness, and humiliation—was matched by the corrosive effect on the morale of the industry as a whole.

A director whose work was deeply marked by his experiences with HUAC was **Elia Kazan.** An almost mythic presence on the New York theater scene, he was famed primarily through his work with actors. But Kazan's career is also notable because of its connection with the communist scare. In 1952, he was called before the House Un-American Activities Committee, confessed to his own Communist Party membership between 1934 and 1936, and named those he had known as Party members. He placed an ad in the *New York Times,* justifying his change of political attitude and calling on others to join him in confessing past error and denouncing communism and communists.

Elements of self-justification repeatedly cropped up in Kazan's subsequent films. *On the Waterfront* (1954), the most powerful and empathic of these social-political statements, is from a script by Budd Schulberg, who also had confessed past Party membership to the House of Un-American Activities Committee and named people he had known as communists. The film deals with the matter of informing to a government crime commission.

Longshoreman Terry Malloy (Marlon Brando) comes to realize that in order to stand upright as a moral being he must expose the gangster forces controlling the waterfront labor
unions and inform on his former associates (Figure 10.7a). (Lee J. Cobb, who plays the
union boss, and Leif Ericson, who plays one of the Waterfront Crime Commission investi-
gators, were others involved in the production who had confessed and named names to
HUAC.) The symbolism built around Terry's care and training of his flock of pigeons (Figure 10.7b) takes on a special significance when we remember that screenwriter John Howard
Lawson, one of the "unfriendly witnesses," had charged that HUAC's "so-called 'evidence'" had come from a parade of "stool pigeons, neurotics, publicity-seeking clowns,
Gestapo agents, paid informers and a few ignorant and frightened Hollywood artists."

Major Genres

The film industry's desire to overwhelm audiences with awesome visual spectacles in vivid
color mounted in generous wide-screen formats led movie makers to return with renewed
energy to the most visually enticing formulas of earlier eras. Three genres that flourished
most prominently during this decade—westerns, musicals, and biblical epics—answered
this need. Some of the greatest films of the decade grew out of these tried-and-true generic
patterns. By contrast, a new genre, the juvenile delinquency film, looked to the future,
defining a new audience of teenagers that Hollywood began to court during this decade and
continued to woo ever more assiduously as the century progressed.

In an era when many people were moving into homes of their own on sizable plots
of land in suburbias all over the nation, Hollywood produced a series of westerns that provided glorious vistas of the American landscape (frequently seen in sweeping wide-screen
compositions), taking advantage of location shooting to show filmgoers unfamiliar views
of their country's terrain. Many of the most enduring examples of the genre were produced
during this decade, including films by directors Howard Hawks (*Red River,* 1948), Anthony
Mann (*The Man from Laramie,* 1955), Budd Boetticher (*The Tall T,* 1957), and John Ford
(*The Searchers,* 1956).

FIGURE 10.7a and b   *On the Waterfront* ★ United States, 1954, Elia Kazan; a. Marlon
Brando on left; b. Marlon Brando

One of the most famous westerns ever made was *High Noon,* released in 1952 (Figure 10.8). Produced by Stanley Kramer, directed by Fred Zinnemann, and photographed by Floyd Crosby, whose credits include most of the major documentaries of Pare Lorentz, it is tightly scripted along generic lines. In allegorical fashion it deals with the political paranoia called McCarthyism. Only the sheriff (Gary Cooper) will stand up against the vengeful outlaw and his gang as other members of the community think of reasons they cannot act. The sheriff finds his most sympathetic ally in a Mexican woman who owns most of the property in the town, but whose minority status prevents her from aiding him and ultimately forces her to leave the community altogether. Carl Foreman, the scriptwriter of *High Noon,* was one of the Hollywood professionals who, because of being blacklisted following his testimony before the House Un-American Activities Committee, exiled himself in England.

Another classic western, *Shane* (1953), was filmed mostly on location in Wyoming under the direction of George Stevens. Its setting is a lovely valley enclosed by snow-capped mountains seen in expansive panoramic shots (VistaVision and Technicolor). A drab clapboard settlement squats along a muddy street in the middle of the valley. The farmers settling the valley look real enough and seem to have real problems—with the land and with the ranchers who don't want them on it. Into this community rides the mysterious title character (played by Alan Ladd in white buckskin) at the time the homesteaders need someone to face up to the cattle baron's hired gun, the black-garbed Wilson (Jack Palance). The simple story is seen through the eyes of a boy (Brandon de Wilde) who idolizes Shane. Shane almost becomes part of the community, almost acknowledges the attraction he and the wife (Jean Arthur) of the farmer (Van Heflin) feel for each other. But

FIGURE 10.8 *High Noon* ★ United States, 1952, Fred Zinnemann; Lon Chaney, Jr., and Gary Cooper.

the gunfight with Wilson (Jack Palance) is what he has to do. After Wilson's death, Shane rides off into a mountain sunset.

A less troubled view of the world is offered in the musicals made during the 1950s. Film scholar Richard Dyer has argued that these films present a utopian vision that sets forth a world filled with abundance and pleasure. The slender plot lines of such productions were designed to maximize the opportunities for major stars of the decade—such as Fred Astaire, Vera Ellen, Doris Day, and Gene Kelly—to display their considerable singing and dancing skills. The unabashedly romantic view of life offered in these delicious confections was set off by cinematography based on smooth tracks and crane shots that picked up the lyrical rhythms and cadences of music composed by some of the masters of the classical pop style, such as Cole Porter, Richard Rogers, and George Gershwin. The most accomplished examples of the form were produced at M-G-M by a tightly knit group of craftspeople under the supervision of producer Arthur Freed. The glossy M-G-M house style and the studio's generous production budgets created an atmosphere in which this team could function at top form.

An American in Paris was one of a number of memorable musicals the Freed unit turned out during these years. Released in 1951, it featured the work of seasoned talent in every department: music and lyrics of George and Ira Gershwin, choreography and dancing by Gene Kelly, with Leslie Caron as his partner in her first screen appearance. The film's director, Vincente Minnelli, is responsible for its expressive use of color and lighting. In the elaborate twenty-minute daydream ballet sequence, set to the Gershwin music of the title, the changing settings mimic the styles of various painters—Renoir, Rousseau, Toulouse-Lautrec, Dufy, Van Gogh, and Manet (Figure 10.9). Within those artistic worlds, the dancers interpret the feeling evoked by each painter with American energy and grace. It is a dazzling, breathtaking climax.

The following year the Freed unit produced another classic of the genre, *Singin' in the Rain,* this one codirected by Gene Kelly, its star, and Stanley Donen. A lighthearted spoof of the difficulties created in Hollywood by the coming of sound in the late 1920s, *Singin'* features memorable numbers such as "You Are My Lucky Star," "Make 'em Laugh," and, of course, the inimitable title tune. In addition, the film boasts a deliciously over-the-top performance by Jean Hagen as a spoiled movie star with a voice like chalk on a blackboard. Its script, by Betty Comden and Adoph Green, is surely one of the cleverest ever to come out of the Hollywood dream factory.

Scores of other musicals were released during the 1950s, including Howard Hawks's and Anita Loos's arch *Gentlemen Prefer Blondes* with Marilyn Monroe in 1953 and a series of Doris Day vehicles produced at Warner Bros. Like the westerns of the period, these were regarded at the time as highly professional but undistinguished undertakings aimed at pleasing the mass audience—not as Oscar material. However, time has proved kind to them. When the British film journal *Sight and Sound* conducted a poll of critics from around the world in 1992, a 1950s western, *The Searchers,* was named the tenth-best film of all time. And the 1950s musical, *Singin' in the Rain,* placed tenth on the American Film Institute's 1999 list of the greatest American movies ever. The other major cycle of film spectacles that flourished during the 1950s, biblical epics, fared less well in the eyes of latter-day scholars. Although productions with biblical themes—such as *Quo Vadis* (Mervyn LeRoy, 1951), *The Robe, The Ten Commandments* (Cecil B. DeMille, 1956), and *Ben-Hur* (William Wyler, 1959)—won a fair share of Academy Awards when they were released, they have subsequently lapsed into critical obscurity.

FIGURE 10.9   *An American in Paris*   ★   United States, 1951, Vincente Minnelli; Leslie Caron and Gene Kelly, foreground.

In search of new, more specialized audiences, Hollywood also developed a new movie formula during the 1950s, this one aimed at youth: the juvenile delinquency film. The label *juvenile delinquent* was coined during this era to refer to a rebellious young person. The increasingly widespread idea that adolescence should be viewed as a special stage of life that carried with it unique psychological challenges formed the background of this new interest in troubled youth. Hollywood's juvenile delinquent movies responded in kind by foregrounding tormented teenage heroes. Productions such as the 1955 *The Blackboard Jungle* also drew on the emerging musical style of rock music to appeal to youthful audiences.

The juvenile delinquent genre gained momentum from the excitement generated by a new crop of young male actors, including Marlon Brando and James Dean, who were dubbed "rebel heroes." Both Brando and Dean were trained in the performance style known as "the Method," which had originated in the Russian theater of Konstantin Stanislavsky. As interpreted in 1950s America, the Method emphasizes the fusion of performer and role through what is termed affective memory. Method actors are trained to relate their own experiences to those of the characters they play. To maximize this identification, improvisatory techniques are used. Method acting is particularly effective when employed in emotionally charged melodramas set in the present that call for the depiction of extreme anguish or rage—the kind of stories actors can readily relate to their own deepest frustrations and traumas. The juvenile delinquent films, which put adolescent passions and angst at center stage, were perfectly suited to showcase this approach to performance. Both Brando and Dean developed some of the tics of the Method style along with its other techniques; they slouched, mumbled, and glowered through their parts in a provocative manner that made an almost visceral connection with teenage audiences.

The young Brando first defined the rebel hero type in the 1953 production *The Wild One,* in which he played a reckless, hostile leader of a motorcycle gang. When asked what he was rebelling against, Brando responded, "What've you got?" But it was James Dean who made the most lasting impression as a juvenile delinquent type. As a result of his early death, he was forevermore identified as a tragic symbol of troubled youth. Dean's 1955 release *Rebel Without a Cause,* directed by Nicholas Ray, marked the high point of the genre (Figure 10.10). As Jim Stark, the confused son of a dysfunctional suburban family, Dean created an arresting portrait of an alienated teenager. Although Dean's character in this film is depicted as unambiguously heterosexual, his sympathetic response to the homosexual advances of Sal Mineo's Plato (though, in keeping with the times, only obliquely hinted at) set a newly accepting tone for the representation of gay interactions on screen. Directed by Nicholas Ray in his customary overheated manner, the film's style was perfectly adapted to its melodramatic story about tortured youth. The look is marked by strong colors and odd camera angles. (In one scene, Jim watches as his mother comes down the stairs of his house upside down.) Wide-screen compositions alternate empty, alienating outdoor scenes with claustrophobic interiors.

Rebel was loosely based on a book written by clinical psychologist Robert M. Lindner, in which he described one of his cases. Though the staid *New York Times* described it as "a picture to make the hair stand on end," the film was a tremendous hit, especially with its target teenage audience. The red cotton windbreaker Dean wore in most of his scenes began a fad for such jackets in high schools all over the nation. Having thus discovered a lucrative new audience for whom filmgoing represented an opportunity to escape from parental control and to enjoy the company of peers, Hollywood never looked back. Youth movies, in endless variations, were here to stay.

FIGURE 10.10   *Rebel Without a Cause* ★ United States, 1955, Nicholas Ray; Ann Doran, James Dean, and Jim Backus.

American Directors of the 1950s

Among the most illustrious film makers of the postwar era were Vincente Minnelli, George Cukor, Billy Wilder, Douglas Sirk, and Alfred Hitchcock. Although all worked before and afterward, their work at this time fairly represents the qualities of American film most valued by those within the Hollywood industry, by the major critics, and by the domestic audience. The success of each was founded on his ability to remain safely within the conventional boundaries that defined industry practice at the time while creating bodies of work that were identifiably unique.

Hollywood's foremost director of musicals, **Vincente Minnelli,** arrived in Hollywood in 1940 after a substantial career as a stage designer and director. Following an apprenticeship at M-G-M, his first film direction was a version of the all-black Broadway musical *Cabin in the Sky* (1943). Minnelli proceeded to produce a series of distinctive musicals during the 1940s, including *Meet Me in St. Louis* (1944) and *The Pirate* (1948), but he directed noteworthy films in other genres as well, such as *The Clock* in 1945 (a romantic drama) and *Father of the Bride* in 1950 (a domestic comedy, remade in 1991 by Charles Shyer with Steve Martin in the Spencer Tracy role). During the 1950s Minnelli continued to alternate between musicals, such as *An American in Paris, The Band Wagon, Brigadoon* (1954), and *Gigi* (1958), and melodramas, such as *The Bad and the Beautiful* (1952), *Lust for Life* (1956), *Some Came Running* (1958), *Home from the Hill* (1960), and *Two Weeks in Another Town* (1962).

Much of Minnelli's best work brings art and life together. Some of his productions *(The Bad and the Beautiful* and *Two Weeks in Another Town)* are about the film-making process itself; others *(An American in Paris, The Band Wagon, Lust for Life,* and *Some Came Running)* feature artists, theater people, or writers. Minnelli's penchant for letting his audience in on the spirit of creation adds a playfulness to his musicals; in the serious dramas it provides an irony that amplifies and intensifies the strong emotionality.

Like Minnelli, **George Cukor** came to Hollywood after a successful stage career. A warm, hospitable man whose gay lifestyle was widely accepted by the Hollywood community, Cukor staged innumerable gatherings at his Beverly Hills home, including film industry workers of all stripes. He was the consummate professional, his direction stylish and impeccable. He began in theater in 1919 as stage manager and then director, and his films always had qualities traceable to theater. Invariably his productions were praised for their performances, especially those of women: Katharine Hepburn, Norma Shearer, Greta Garbo, Joan Crawford, Judy Holliday, Judy Garland, and Marilyn Monroe among them. Cukor frequently captured the interactions between various pairs of such charismatic stars in extended two-shots.

Cukor specialized in literary adaptations, sophisticated comedies, musicals, and period pictures. With *A Double Life* (1947), he began a collaboration with Garson Kanin and Ruth Gordon, the husband–wife screenwriting team, which lasted through six more of their original scripts. *Adam's Rib* (1949), starring Spencer Tracy and Katharine Hepburn, with Judy Holliday in a supporting role, was the first of a series of intelligent, witty, and urbane battle-of-the-sexes comedies. It was followed by *Born Yesterday* (1950), starring Judy Holliday. These performers—Tracy, Hepburn, and Holliday—continued working with Cukor in breezy vignettes of middle-class American life, many of them shot on the East Coast. With *A Star Is Born* (1954) Cukor was back to Hollywood full scale, and then some. This CinemaScope Technicolor extravaganza musical-melodrama was not only shot on the sound stages and back lots of Hollywood but it was also about Hollywood. Although it was passed over at Academy Award time, Cukor eventually received his first and only Oscar for directing another musical, the lavish *My Fair Lady,* in 1964.

Billy Wilder, a film maker with a more sardonic turn of mind, began his Hollywood career as a scriptwriter during the 1930s, coauthoring a series of sophisticated comedies for directors such as Ernst Lubitsch (*Ninotchka,* 1939), Mitchell Leisen (*Midnight,* 1939), and Howard Hawks (*Ball of Fire,* 1941). Wilder, the consummate creator of well-made plots and witty dialogue, frequently claimed that he had turned to direction only "to protect my scripts." After a series of atmospheric *film noir* projects during the 1940s, including *Double Indemnity* (1945) and *Sunset Boulevard* (1950), he turned back to comedies during the 1950s. *Ace in the Hole,* released in 1950, was Wilder's first film after the breakup of his fruitful scriptwriting collaboration with Charles Brackett, which had begun in 1938. A darkly cynical satire on the exploitative nature of the modern media, it tells the tale of an ambitious reporter (played by Kirk Douglas) who puts a man's life at risk to get a scoop. The film's overall tone is conveyed in an offhand remark delivered by Jan Sterling, who plays the wife of the victimized man. "I never go to church," she confesses, "because kneeling bags my nylons."

Wilder next turned to another cynical tale, *Stalag 17* (1953). Based on a Broadway hit about American prisoners of war held by the Germans during World War II, it starred William Holden. Although it was popular with audiences, some reviewers complained of the story's nihilism and tastelessness (jokes made about the Nazis and the like). Wilder followed *Stalag 17* with three frothier productions: *Sabrina* (1954), *The Seven Year Itch* (1955), and *Love in the Afternoon* (1957). All are very Lubitsch-like, a comparison Wilder readily acknowledged. The last was Wilder's first film with the screenwriter who would become his second long-lasting collaborator, I. A. L. Diamond. The next three comedies produced by the team— *Some Like It Hot* (1959), *The Apartment* (1960), and *One, Two, Three* (1961)—succeeded in creating a fusion of the acidic *film noir* with the *joie de vivre* of the Lubitsch comedies.

Some Like It Hot, which some critics have called the funniest film ever made, combines elements of the gangster film, knockabout farce, fast-paced witty dialogue *à la* screwball comedy, and transvestism. To escape mobster Spats Colombo, played by George Raft, stars Tony Curtis and Jack Lemmon become "girls" in an all-female band that includes Marilyn Monroe (Figure 10.11a and b). Confused identities and sexual mismatches escalate to incredible limits. The film's inimitable closing line is delivered by lustful millionaire Osgood Fielding III (Joe E. Brown). When his fiancée (Jack Lemmon in drag) confesses she's a man, he scarcely skips a beat before responding, "Nobody's perfect."

Another German emigré who achieved considerable Hollywood success during the 1950s is **Douglas Sirk,** whose most memorable work includes a number of highly profitable women's pictures produced by Ross Hunter for Universal, many starring Sirk's favorite leading man, Rock Hudson. The term *Sirkian irony* was later coined to describe his distinctive style, which never condescended to his tearjerker plots but overlaid them with a layer of self-consciousness and distance.

Sirk was a master at employing *mise-en-scène* to comment on character. Mirrors and glass surfaces abound in his films, repeatedly suggesting the complicated relationship between identity and role. An especially admired instance of this technique occurs in his 1956 production *All That Heaven Allows* when the film's main character (played by Jane Wyman) gazes at her likeness reflected in a television set her children have purchased for her and foresees herself as being trapped within its confines for the remainder of her days (Figure

FIGURE 10.11a and b   *Some Like It Hot*   ★   United States, 1959, Billy Wilder; a. Tony Curtis and Jack Lemmon; b. Marilyn Monroe.

10.12a). The conclusion of the film finds her, similarly disillusioned, next to a picture window that reveals a fawn grazing in the winter landscape outside (Figure 10.12b): The glass separating her from this vision seems an impassible barrier between her "natural" desires and her position in an endlessly constricting culture.

FIGURE 10.12a and b   *All That Heaven Allows* ★ United States, 1956, Douglas Sirk; a. Jane Wyman; b. Rock Hudson and Jane Wyman.

Sirk's typically wide-angle compositions frequently juxtapose characters and their surroundings in revealing ways. In his 1957 *Written on the Wind,* for instance, Dorothy Malone, playing the spoiled daughter of a powerful oil baron, is shown at one point against a background of oil derricks, suggesting the devastation wreaked by her father's industrial prowess and, by implication, the devastation she herself seeks to impose on others through sexual manipulation. Sirk also employed costuming to comment on his characters and their world. In his last major production, *Imitation of Life,* released in 1959, Lana Turner's gowns become ever more artificial and affected as she increasingly loses sight of what truly matters to her in life.

Yet another emigré, this one from England, **Alfred Hitchcock** hit the peak of his Hollywood career during the late 1940s and 1950s. "Cinema is not a slice of life," he once said, "it's a piece of cake." In this spirit, he produced a series of hugely entertaining thrillers that often explored the dark recesses of his audience's fascination with the cinematic image. His motto, "Always make the audience suffer as much as possible," was fulfilled with particular relish in tense mysteries such as *Notorious* (1946), *Strangers on a Train* (1951), *Rear Window* (1954), *The Man Who Knew Too Much* (1956), *Vertigo* (1957), and *Psycho* (1960). Such disturbing exercises in murder and espionage (the last capitalizing on America's fearful Cold War mentality) were alternated with more purely enjoyable roller-coaster rides on similar topics, such as *To Catch a Thief, The Trouble with Harry* (both 1955) and *North by Northwest* (1959). Many of these productions were filmed in such colorful tourist locales as Monaco (*To Catch a Thief*), Marrakesh (*The Man Who Knew Too Much*), and Mount Rushmore (*North by Northwest*).

Hitchcock's distinctive visual style is based on the strict control of the audience's point of view, often isolating people and objects ominously in the frame (such as in the repeated shots of stuffed birds of prey in *Psycho*). Heavy editing, most famously in *Psycho*'s terrifying shower scene, created bravura set pieces filled with terror and suspense (Figure 10.13a–h). The dizzying tracking shots that circle around embracing couples in *Notorious, Vertigo,* and *North by Northwest* evoke the sensation of sexual euphoria. In *Vertigo* Hitchcock also introduced an even more perceptually disorienting track in–zoom out technique that reproduces the unsettling emotional state referred to in the film's title. Supporting these displays of visual pyrotechnics in most of Hitchcock's productions of this era were tense, modernist-inflected scores by the great Hollywood composer Bernard Herrmann.

Hitchcock's films often feature coolly glamorous blonde heroines—for instance, Grace Kelly, Kim Novak, Eva Marie Saint, and Tippi Hedren—whose sexual allure becomes a trap for the male protagonists, typically played by familiar stars such as James Stewart and Cary Grant. The eroticism that hovers over most Hitchcock productions is countered by stern references to the punishing power of the police as well as by frequent allusions to his characters' own guilty consciences. The films also examine the perverse pleasures offered by the spectacle of cinema and the complicity of audiences who partake in this kind of pleasure. In a tacit acknowledgment of this motif, Hitchcock scholar William Rothman subtitled his book on the director, "The Murderous Gaze."

Hitchcock's films have been extraordinarily attractive to both pit and gallery. Huge audiences have gone to see each release because it carries his name. More serious critical writing has been published about Hitchcock films than about any other film maker. His films represent the fusion of the popular and the critically acclaimed. Like many of the most honored artists of other eras, such as Shakespeare and Dickens, Hitchcock, along with the other Hollywood directors of the postwar era discussed here, developed a style that managed to combine popular appeal with profundity.

The changes that followed in the wake of television's impact on the American motion picture were pervasive—technological, economic, and sociological. It took the industry time to absorb the changes and to adjust to the newly reduced and more specialized sorts of production, distribution, and exhibition that emerged. Changes in the actual content and form of American films during this period—except for those caused by the wide screen,

FIGURE 10.13a–h   *Psycho* ★ United States, 1960, Alfred Hitchcock; Janet Leigh.

stereophonic sound, and increased use of color—were not nearly so evident. As distinguished as was the work of the directors discussed in this chapter, and of other American
film makers in the 1950s, it came out of firmly established tradition. Not until the middle
and late 1960s did American films begin to take on some of the characteristics identified

with trends of modern cinema that had begun germinating in Europe from the mid-1950s on. Moreover, the distinctive youth culture that emerged during the 1950s and was addressed in the juvenile delinquency films of that era was destined to develop into a far more radical force in the decade ahead.

Films of the Period

1946
The Best Years of Our Lives (William Wyler)
The Big Sleep (Howard Hawks)
It's a Wonderful Life (Frank Capra)
My Darling Clementine (John Ford)
Notorious (Alfred Hitchcock)
Ritual in Transfigured Time (Maya Deren)

1947
A Double Life (George Cukor)
Fort Apache (John Ford)
The Lady from Shanghai (Orson Welles)
Monsieur Verdoux (Charlie Chaplin)
Red River (Howard Hawks)
They Live by Night (Nicholas Ray)
The Treasure of the Sierra Madre (John Huston)

1949
Adam's Rib (George Cukor)
On the Town (Gene Kelly and Stanley Donen)
White Heat (Raoul Walsh)

1950
All About Eve (Joseph L. Mankiewicz)
The Asphalt Jungle (John Huston)
Born Yesterday (George Cukor)
In a Lonely Place (Nicholas Ray)
Sunset Boulevard (Billy Wilder)

1951
Ace in the Hole (Billy Wilder)
An American in Paris (Vincente Minnelli)
A Place in the Sun (George Stevens)
Strangers on a Train (Alfred Hitchcock)
A Streetcar Named Desire (Elia Kazan)

1952
The African Queen (John Huston)
The Bad and the Beautiful (Vincente Minnelli)
High Noon (Fred Zinnemann)
Limelight (Charlie Chaplin)
Singin' in the Rain (Gene Kelly and Stanley Donen)

This Is Cinerama (Merian C. Cooper)
Viva Zapata! (Elia Kazan)

1953
The Big Heat (Fritz Lang)
From Here to Eternity (Fred Zinnemann)
Gentlemen Prefer Blondes (Howard Hawks)
The Robe (Henry Koster)
Shane (George Stevens)
The Wild One (Laslo Benedek)

1954
Dial M for Murder (Alfred Hitchcock)
On the Waterfront (Elia Kazan)
Rear Window (Alfred Hitchcock)
Sabrina (Billy Wilder)
A Star Is Born (George Cukor)

1955
The Blackboard Jungle (Richard Brooks)
East of Eden (Elia Kazan)
Kiss Me Deadly (Robert Aldrich)
The Man from Laramie (Anthony Mann)
The Man with the Golden Arm (Otto Preminger)
Marty (Delbert Mann)
The Night of the Hunter (Charles Laughton)
Rebel Without a Cause (Nicholas Ray)
Written on the Wind (Douglas Sirk)

1956
All That Heaven Allows (Douglas Sirk)
Around the World in Eighty Days (Michael Anderson)
The Man Who Knew Too Much (Alfred Hitchcock)
The Searchers (John Ford)
The Ten Commandments (Cecil B. DeMille)

1957
The Bridge on the River Kwai (David Lean)
Funny Face (Stanley Donen)
Paths of Glory (Stanley Kubrick)
Shadows (John Cassavetes)

The Sweet Smell of Success (Alexander Mackendrick)
The Tall T (Budd Boetticher)
Twelve Angry Men (Sidney Lumet)
Vertigo (Alfred Hitchcock)

1958
Anticipation of the Night (Stan Brakhage)
Gigi (Vincente Minnelli)
A Movie (Bruce Conner)

1959
Anatomy of a Murder (Otto Preminger)
Ben-Hur (William Wyler)
Imitation of Life (Douglas Sirk)
North by Northwest (Alfred Hitchcock)
Some Like It Hot (Billy Wilder)
Touch of Evil (Orson Welles)

1960
The Apartment (Billy Wilder)
Primary (Richard Leacock, Albert and David
    Maysles, Terence McCartney-Filgate)
Psycho (Alfred Hitchcock)

1961
The Birds (Alfred Hitchcock)
Breakfast at Tiffany's (Blake Edwards)
Lolita (Stanley Kubrick)

1962
The Cool World (Shirley Clarke)
Lawrence of Arabia (David Lean)
The Manchurian Candidate (John Frankenheimer)
The Man Who Shot Liberty Valance (John Ford)

Books on the Period

American Film Institute Staff. *The American Film Institute Catalog of Motion Pictures Produced in the United States: Feature Films, 1941–1950,* 3 vols. Berkeley: University of California Press, 1999.

Bernard, Gordon. *Hollywood Exile, or How I Learned to Love the Blacklist.* Austin: University of Texas Press, 2000.

Bernstein, Matthew, ed. *Controlling Hollywood: Censorship and Regulation in the Studio Era.* New Brunswick, NJ: Rutgers University Press, 2000.

Buhle, Paul, and David Wagner. *Hide in Plain Sight: The Hollywood Blacklistees in Film and Television, 1950–2002.* London: Palgrave, 2003.

Kashner, Sam, and Jennifer MacNair. *The Bad and the Beautiful: Hollywood in the Fifties.* New York: W. W. Norton, 2003.

Prince, Stephen. *Classical Film Violence: Designing and Regulating Brutality in Hollywood Cinema, 1930–1968.* New Brunswick, NJ: Rutgers University Press, 2003.

Schatz, Thomas. *Boom and Bust: The American Cinema of the 1940s* (Vol. 6 of *History of the American Cinema*). Berkeley and Los Angeles: University of California Press, 1999.

Smoodin, Eric, and Ann Martin, eds. *Hollywood Quarterly: Film Culture in Postwar America, 1945–1957.* Berkeley: University of California Press, 2002.

Studlar, Gaylyn, and Matthew Bernstein, eds. *John Ford Made Westerns: Filming the Legend in the Sound Era.* Bloomington: Indiana University Press, 2001.

11

Japanese Film: A Pictorial Tradition and a Modernist Edge

★ ★ ★ ★

1951–

The Japanese film industry has been strong from the earliest days, leading the world in the number of films it produces for most of the century. The first Japanese studios were established in 1904–1905; they continued to expand until the devastating Tokyo earthquake in 1923 forced them to regroup. Because of the popularity of the *benshi,* live performers whose spoken narration accompanied silent films, sound was slow in coming to Japanese cinema, arriving finally in the mid-1930s. The Second World War brought about another hiatus, and the subsequent American occupation, from 1945 to 1952, carried with it a policy of censorship that cramped the style of many major Japanese film makers. Nonetheless, Japanese cinema has remained notable not only for the quantity of films produced but also for the high quality many attained. Despite its rich tradition, however, Japanese movies remained largely unknown abroad until after World War II. Few Japanese films made before 1940 are available to Western audiences because over 95 percent of them have been lost or destroyed.

The structure of the Japanese industry was curiously like the "classic" American one of the 1930s and 1940s (which was breaking up in the 1950s): Six major production companies controlled distribution and the theater circuits as well. Japanese film also had popular genres, some with close American counterparts. In a general way Japanese films were divided into two main categories: *jidai-geki,* or historical films, and *gendai-geki,* or contemporary films. The division between "historical" and "contemporary" times was marked by the year 1868, when the Emperor Meiji acceded to the throne and first opened Japan to commercial and cultural exchange with the West. It was during his reign that the country passed from feudalism to a modern way of life. Because the change was both sudden and radical, Japanese society in the contemporary period offered a striking contrast to that of the historical period. The two categories of films were also in sharp contrast to each other because each faithfully depicted the mores, thought, and feeling of the two periods. Each category had its own conventions, not only in regard to sets and costumes, but also production style and even acting. Studios, directors, and actors tended to specialize in one or the other of the two modes. The *jidai-geki* (historical) accounted for only 40 percent of Japanese production, but it enjoyed constant popularity with the domestic audience and achieved the first successes abroad.

Japanese film became internationally celebrated in 1951 when *Rashomon,* directed by Akira Kurosawa, won the grand prize at the Venice Film Festival (Figure 11.1). After its victory at Venice, *Rashomon* was distributed worldwide. Daiei Motion Picture Company, which had produced it, was Japan's most prestigious studio, like an earlier M-G-M. Daiei followed *Rashomon* with other films sent out for (and possibly in part produced for) world distribution. Masaichi Nagata, the Irving Thalberg of Daiei, to pursue the analogy, was producer of many of these. *Ugetsu* (1953) came next, directed by the veteran Kenji Mizoguchi. *Gate of Hell* (1953), the first Japanese film in the new Eastman Color, was directed by Teinosuke Kinugasa. Kurosawa's *Seven Samurai* (1954) reached the United States in a truncated version: two-and-a-half rather than three-and-a-half hours long. His *Ikiru,* though pro-

FIGURE 11.1   *Rashomon* ★ 1950, Akira Kurosawa; Toshiro Mifune, Masayuki Mori, and Machiko Kyo.

duced earlier (1952), followed. The latter was the first of the *gendai-geki* (contemporary films) to be seen here. The lovely Machiko Kyo, who appeared in the first three Japanese films to be imported, was much appreciated abroad, and Toshiro Mifune, whose finest work has been done with Kurosawa, established an international reputation with *Rashomon* and *Seven Samurai.*

The Japanese Style

Although the world hadn't seen Japanese films until the early 1950s, the Japanese had been seeing the world's films since the late 1890s, and their use of the medium had developed along lines parallel to those of other countries. Whereas American film makers most frequently concerned themselves with action and Europeans with the psychology of character, the Japanese often seemed to be more interested in overall mood and atmosphere. Even when the themes are universal, they embody unfamiliar assumptions and artistic conventions. In treatment there often seems to American audiences a sentimentality different in kind from their own. A didactic quality is also common in Japanese cinema, as is slower pacing. Shots and scenes are allowed to extend beyond the requirements of the narrative point being made to let audiences savor the feelings just expressed.

Other, more precise formal characteristics were equally noteworthy, especially in contrast to the immediately preceding Italian neorealism. Many of the Japanese films are beautiful and visually elegant. If one of them were stopped at random during projection, any frame held on the screen would probably be perfect in terms of composition and lighting. Long passages without dialogue give emphasis to the image. Coming from a cultural tradition that places great importance on the visual arts, Japanese directors and cinematographers thought as painters. Their frame lines always serve as organizational matrices for graphic design as well as for enclosing chunks of content.

These visual qualities are especially striking in *Ugetsu* (and in Mizoguchi's work generally). In it images are designed not only to create feelings of unease or of calm security but also to offer aesthetic pleasure in the very arrangement and balance of the blacks, whites, and grays. The full-color palette of *Gate of Hell* allows for the most dynamic and dramatic use of color film anyone had seen up to that point—especially in its first glowing orange-red scenes of violent action in a civil war. Camera movements, too—for these films are full of kinetic energy along with their careful pictorial patterns—have a calculation and control in relation to subject movement that frequently results in a kind of cinematic dance. In *Rashomon* the shots of the woodsman moving through the forest, the camera tracking with him and tilting up into the sunlight glinting down through the tall trees, are a breathtaking example. *Rashomon* suggested what would be confirmed by *Seven Samurai:* Kurosawa was a special master of camera movement. Another even more extraordinary instance in *Rashomon* occurs when Machiko Kyo weaves about after yielding to the bandit, confronting her husband's accusing stare as the camera swoops, backs, and glides with her. Reviewers resorted to phrases such as "painting in motion" to describe the visual riches the Japanese films offered.

In terms of performance, the Japanese films drew on another ancient artistic tradition—that of the theater. Classical Nō plays, which go back for centuries, and the popular Kabuki have both reflected and influenced Japanese culture generally. They express national sentiments and beliefs, at least of the older Japan, which gave way more slowly and less fundamentally than appeared on the surface. There is something very different from Western performance styles in the Japanese historical (not the contemporary) films. A composite outline of the conventional samurai films (of which *Gate of Hell* is one example; another is *Samurai,* 1954, directed by Hiroshi Inagaki) may suggest some of the differences.

A young warrior is in love with his lord's wife. Out of loyalty to his master he does not show that love. The acting in the first two-thirds of the picture would be not only restrained but also extremely formalized. We can infer that each gesture and every movement (as well as costumes, makeup, and hairdos) have some sort of fixed and known meaning. An enormous tension is built up through this constraint of powerful feeling expressed in behavior limited by rigid, social/aesthetic convention. Then, when the young warrior can bear it no longer and his passion overleaps those self- and society-imposed bounds, he pursues the lady, fights the lord, and gives vent to his charged-up store of emotion. These scenes feature full-blown representations of lust and anger, complete with lunging and sweating, crawling and panting. *Rashomon* first showed us these two extremes of performance—theatrical stylization in the trial scene, earthy naturalism in the bandit's behavior—within a single film.

Assessing the implications of such exotic charm is part of the problem in evaluating these films, which come out of a culture and tradition vastly different from the Greco-Judeo-Christian one. The historical films usually are based on ancient legends well known to the Japanese audience. The stories about the Forty-Seven Ronin (masterless samurai), for example, have been the source for a good many films, those of Inagaki among the most popular. These period films reveal that the Japanese historical experience has had certain similarities to that of western nations, feudalism for instance, as well as certain differences, such as religion. It is the differences that fascinate most.

Three Japanese Masters

That initial cluster of five films opening the world's screens to Japanese cinema introduced two of Japan's greatest film makers: Akira Kurosawa and Kenji Mizoguchi. Both carry their personal concerns from film to film, whether the setting is modern or feudal. The work of the third, Yasujiro Ozu, is even more resolutely fixed on certain themes and is always set in contemporary Japan. Of the three, in terms of content and style, **Akira Kurosawa** is the most easily appreciated by Westerners. A number of his films are adaptations of European literary classics: Dostoyevsky's *The Idiot* (1951) and Gogol's *The Lower Depths* (1957) as well as Shakespeare's *Macbeth* (*The Throne of Blood,* 1957) and *King Lear* (*Ran,* 1985). He also filmed an adaptation of a novel by the popular American mystery writer Ed McBain (*High and Low,* 1963). In turn, some of Kurosawa's productions have inspired Hollywood remakes, notably *Rashomon* (*The Outrage,* Martin Ritt, 1964) and *Seven Samurai* (*The Magnificent Seven,* John Sturges, 1960). *Rashomon* is based on two stories by the popular author Ryunosuke Akutagawa, who was much influenced by Western culture. Although set in the Heian period (794 to 1184), its four-times-told tale of a rape (or seduction), murder (or suicide), and robbery (or disappearance) is indebted to Robert Browning's novel-length poem *The Ring and the Book,* while the musical score is a close imitation of Maurice Ravel's *Bolero;* thus it makes use of a cinematic *lingua franca* available to all. With its fragmented narrative and pointed ambiguities, *Rashomon* was received by many Occidental critics as a continuation of the tradition of European modernism.

Kurosawa's action-filled samurai films, such as *Yojimbo* (1961) and *Sanjuro* (1962), share many features with American westerns. Substitute swords for six-guns and samurai warriors for professional gunslingers and much else remains the same. *Seven Samurai,* the best of these, is set in the sixteenth century at a transitional time when the ancient and honorable profession of the samurai was coming to an end as gunpowder and new military tactics appeared. The samurai we see have fallen on hard times, and in their unemployment a group of them accept a proposal by a committee of peasants to protect their village from bandit raids. The film combines discerning psychological observation with stunningly choreographed action and violence. Each of the seven warriors is carefully delineated. The leader and eldest (played by Takashi Shimura, who also plays the woodcutter in *Rashomon* and the lead in *Ikiru*) is a compelling personality. He eschews wasteful bloodshed, advocates strategy over force, and is wise, calm, and compassionate, with a sad acceptance of his destiny for leadership. Of the others, one samurai is tired of fighting, another is cool and skillful, a third bloodthirsty, a fourth a frightened youth, and so on. Crammed with action, the larger scenes of the bandits attacking the village are shot and cut with immense dynamism. Kurosawa's *The Throne of Blood* (1957), a Japanese version of *Macbeth,* offers more of the same.

In *Seven Samurai* the action of the smaller, more intimate scenes carries with it fuller emotional meaning. But even then Kurosawa works through physical movement, and orchestrates emotion in relation to it. For example, there is the scene in which the preeminent swordsman is introduced. He is challenged by another samurai to a test of skill, using staffs in place of swords. The result is contested: The challenger says that their blows landed at the same time; the master says the other would be dead. The former foolishly insists they fight again, with swords. When the great swordsman cuts his adversary down, he shows little emotion, simply having proved what he already knew (Figure 11.2a). His interest is solely in further perfecting his awesome skill. The two seduction scenes between the youngest samurai and a peasant girl—one on a sunny flower-covered hillside (Figure 11.2b), the other in the dark interior of a hut dappled by light (Figure 11.2c)—are also played largely with their bodies. His intense shyness and uneasy attraction and her almost wild abandonment to awakened sensuality are portrayed wordlessly. A final instance of Kurosawa's exceptional ability to transmute the physical into the emotional occurs in the scene of the raid on the bandits' fort. In the eerie early-morning light amidst a surrealist, Dantesque inferno of fire, torn bodies, and steaming pool, there is a haunting exchange between a husband and wife. She has come out of the burning fort after having been kept there as a concubine since the last raid. As she stands at the door, he runs to her; they look at each other for a full minute; nothing is said; then she turns and runs back into the flames (Figure 11.2d).

In Kurosawa's films set in contemporary times he tends to subdue this kind of direct sensory appeal. Instead he keeps us focused on the subtler, more complex characters and on the sorts of social problems that more clearly show his dimension as a humanist. *Ikiru,* made in the same year as de Sica's and Zavattini's *Umberto D,* bears some resemblance to the Italian film. It concerns an inconsequential petty official who, after learning he has terminal cancer, tries to instill some meaning into his life as he faces death. His final positive

FIGURE 11.2a–d   *The Seven Samurai* ★ Japan, 1954, Akira Kurosawa.

act of helping create a children's playground in a poor section allows him to die satisfied, but it sets off social and political reverberations that are reviewed and discussed in a crazy drunken Joycian wake. In *Red Beard* (1965) we must look through and beyond its sentimental surface to get at the greatness of the film. The title character (played by Toshiro Mifune) is a crotchety, selfless, driven physician who devotes his whole life to treating the poor. The kind of spiritual journey and discovery at the core of these two contemporary films appear frequently in Kurosawa's work. Even in his historical pieces he is always commenting on contemporary life, and the concerns are profoundly social and moral.

Kurosawa died in 1998. In his later years he produced some notable *jidai-geki,* some set during the period of change in the last quarter of the sixteenth century, when Japan was beset by ceaseless internal wars. Featuring militaristic spectacle and themes of charismatic authority, these films were well received internationally. In *Kagemusha (The Shadow Warrior,* 1981) a poor thief is chosen for his resemblance to the dying leader of the Takeda clan to take the latter's place, to become a "shadow warrior." At first frightened, the thief gradually falls under the spell of the visionary leader he is impersonating. The most accomplished of Kurosawa's late films, *Ran* (1985), balances the pageantry of its elaborately staged battle sequences with the mental agonies suffered by its protagonist, Hidetora. Unlike Shakespeare's *King Lear,* on which it was based, *Ran* (which means "chaos") shows a hero driven mad not simply by the ingratitude of his children but also as a consequence of the guilt he has incurred in the course of a long reign marked by conquest and aggression. Numerous virtuoso battle sequences punctuate the action of the film, including one in which the massacre of Hidetora's army is viewed in slow motion with no audible sound save for somber and foreboding music. In both *Ran* and *Kagemusha,* Kurosawa exploits color to create magnificent pictorial effects in battle sequences by outfitting the soldiers with brightly hued flags, which are strapped to their backs. The flags provide a dramatic means of distinguishing among the clashing forces. In *Ran* the flags correspond to the colors of the king's three sons: red, yellow, and blue.

The second of Japan's triumverate of top-ranked directors, **Kenji Mizoguchi,** favored the *jidai-geki* genre to an even greater degree than Kurosawa. Because Mizoguchi's attitudes, subjects, and style are more traditionally Japanese than those of Kurosawa, his films have been less widely appreciated in the United States and Europe. Mizoguchi had a long career, beginning in 1923, but only with the international success of *The Life of O'Haru,* which won the grand prize at Venice in 1952, was he able to achieve a meaningful stability and independence, working at the prestigious Daiei Motion Picture Company to create a series of masterpieces during the 1950s. He died in 1957.

Following in the footsteps of earlier Japanese directors such as Mikio Naruse, Mizoguchi frequently focused on the plight of women. Scripted by his long-standing scenarist Yoshikata Yoda, many of his films make a case for women's rights. This concern, which built on Mizoguchi's early experience as a director of "tendency" films that dealt with social problems, is especially apparent in such productions as *Sisters of the Gion* (1936), *Women of the Night* (1957), and *Street of Shame* (1956), which treat prostitution; *The Life of O'Haru* and *Princess Yang Kwei Fei* (1955), which focus on society's obsession with women's appearance; and *Osaka Elegy* (1936), which highlights the powerlessness of women within the Japanese family structure.

The varied visual environments Mizoguchi creates as a background for his stories invariably contain thematic overtones. He often presents leisurely tracking shots that move across a scene before the characters enter the frame as a way of emphasizing that human behavior is inevitably conditioned by and reflected in the context (both physical and, by extension, social) in which it occurs. *Crucified Lovers* (1954), for example, contrasts the obstructions of its interior spaces, where the lovers are constrained by a repressive social system, with later scenes in which the delicate play of light in a leafy forest and the gentle rocking of a small boat in the water suggest the fragility of their happiness together after they elope. *Princess Yang Kwei Fei* employs an exquisite palette of pastel hues to chronicle the fate of an innocent young woman who is no match for the palace intrigue that surrounds her. In this film deep space compositions give visual expression to the rigid formality of the emperor's court, a world based on a set of intricate rules that mask political power plays. *The Story of the Last Chrysanthemum* (1939) contains many images in which the top and/or bottom of the screen is shrouded in darkness, creating a wide-screen look. In one pivotal scene the protagonist, a young actor, receives some crucial advice from the woman who later gives her life to help him succeed. The scene is photographed with long tracking shots taken from a conspicuously low angle below the boardwalk on which the two characters are walking; the camera looks up at them in such a way as to emphasize the precariousness of their situation.

FIGURE 11.3   *Ugetsu* ★ Japan, 1953, Kenji Mizoguchi; Kinuyo Tanaka and Masayuki Mori.

Ugetsu, Mizoguchi's best-known film, deals with war and peace in relation to work and love—or perhaps, even more simply and broadly, war as it affects the total human condition. Set in the sixteenth century, the story centers on two brothers, a potter and a farmer, and their wives (Figure 11.3). The profiteering that wartime makes possible goads both men into an inordinate desire for gain. The potter wants money to buy extravagant presents for his wife and child, the farmer to equip himself as a samurai in order to impress his wife. While in the city selling his pots, the potter is seduced (partly through flattery about the aesthetic qualities of his pottery) by a mysterious and finally sinister Lady Wakasa. She causes him to abandon his wife for the carnal pleasures and luxury she seems to offer. During the same time the farmer comes to be regarded as a military commander through a faked heroic exploit. But the potter is no more an artist (nor should be) than the farmer is a warrior, Mizoguchi seems to be saying. Work ought to be for its own sake, not for money (or false praise for creativity) or glory (based on feigned valor). Also, it should be part of the family, not done away from home with the results brought back. The end of the film marks a return to the original state: work in peace, and conjugal and parental love.

Stylistically *Ugetsu* is even more "painterly" than Kurosawa's films. Mizoguchi's shaping of the visual-dramatic content takes place within the shot more than through juxtaposition of shots. Composition is always conceived in depth, often with objects at the side of the frame in the foreground to accentuate the perspective. Also, he uses the long shot quite deliberately to frame action at a distance—for example, there are the repeated views across the courtyard of Lady Wakasa's house, the scenes of the soldiers pillaging the village, and the shot of the farmer shopping for armor seen at a distance and from behind the armorer. Mizoguchi's frequent pans, too, are used pointedly as a compositional device rather than merely to follow action. One particularly memorable usage of the sort is the high-angled pan across the refugees from the village as they are camping for the night. In constructing his scenes he typically allows the camera to pick up action and then follow it remorselessly to its conclusion. But unlike the films of the German silent film makers who worked this way, there is an enormous amount of action within Mizoguchi's shots, and sharp contrasts—calm to frenetic, lyrical to horrifying—from scene to scene. He likes to have action explode into the frame. Looting soldiers move around a corner and emerge in the middle of the frame, the potter's wife rushes directly toward the camera (shot from low angle with short-focal-length lens) and scoops up her child right under our noses. Entrances are frequently from behind the camera—from right or left and sometimes from below—which creates a startling, disruptive effect.

In *Ugetsu* the music is extremely important. More of it is Oriental than Western, the opposite of Kurosawa's usual practice, and it is fully integrated with the visuals. It complements and frequently takes precedence over the dialogue. In part it is used in place of natural sounds; elsewhere it is used as *leit motif,* evocative and symbolic. The bright piercing bell of Lady Wakasa's theme is matched by a gently melodic ensemble of bells in the return of the potter's wife. On the other hand, cries in the background sometimes supply an almost musical accompaniment to the action. When the two men and the farmer's wife leave the potter's wife and child on the shore of the lake, the farewells become a melancholy round. The ghost of Lady Wakasa's father groans in eerie and wordless recitative accompanied by strange and discordant instrumentation.

In contrast not only to the work of Mizoguchi and Kurosawa but also to that of almost any other film maker of any country one might think of, the style of **Yasujiro Ozu** is marked by the most rigorous austerity. In later films he rarely moved the camera, and then slightly and slowly solely to accommodate the action. Interiors predominate in his films and the action consists almost entirely of conversation among a few people. He worked exclusively in the formerly standard three-by-four screen ratio; although he used color when it became available to him for his last pictures, it was always muted and unemphatic, as if he were trying to keep the full palette from distracting. Characteristically, his camera sits at seated eye level, as if taking part in a formal tea ceremony, unblinkingly observing two of his characters reacting to each other. Very often the pair is made up of one old person and one young adult—an old man and a young woman perhaps most frequently in the final films. Above all Ozu, who began his career in 1922 and died in 1963, was concerned with the relationships between the traditional ways and the newer ones in a changing Japan. Implicit in all his films is an awareness of the extraordinary cultural dislocations that began to occur when Japan was opened to the West in the late nineteenth century. Ozu observed these changes and tensions not on a broad social scale but within the intimacy of the family unit—parents and children, husband and wife—where they finally have their deepest effect. Of the three giants of Japanese cinema, Ozu is unquestionably the most "Japanese." His view is a calm and balanced one. Although sad to see the old go, he has to acknowledge its passing, with sympathy but without complaint.

A philosophical stance growing out of the Japanese historical experience appears in the modern as well as the period films. It is distinctively and characteristically Japanese and is identified by one of those terms for which translators offer a sensible-enough English explanation but add that the concept remains essentially untranslatable. The phrase in this case is *mono no aware.* According to Richie, in *Japanese Cinema,* it means something like "that awareness of the transience of all earthly things; the knowledge that it is, perhaps fortunately, impossible to do anything about it; and celebration of resignation in the face of things as they are." Ozu's films have this attitude in abundance. Many of them are names to reflect the changing seasons: *Late Spring* (1949), *Early Summer* (1951), *Late Autumn* (1960), and *An Autumn Afternoon* (1962). Such titles suggest the cyclical movement of nature in which change takes place within a larger pattern of order and stability. Frequently the films include tranquil montages of cityscapes that create a comforting, solid background within which human behavior and customs can find a meaningful context. Sometimes called "pillow shots," these transitional moments function as serene oases that punctuate the dramatic action surrounding them. In *Tokyo Story* (1953), often considered Ozu's masterpiece, an old woman dies. Immediately afterward we see a fishing boat slowly leaving the harbor and hear the gentle putt-putt of its engine. We subsequently witness the grief and loneliness of the woman's husband (Figure 11.4a). In the final shot of the film we watch as a similar fishing boat again crosses the harbor (Figure 11.4b). The image overlays the widower's sorrow with a feeling of serenity: Death is part of life; the world goes on. The lives and events we have just witnessed are part of a universal and timeless human condition.

The Japanese New Wave

In the postwar years, the Japanese cinema developed new formulas, including the youth film and the action film. Gradually individual studios began to specialize exclusively in specific popular genres: Toho made monster movies and science-fiction spectacles, including the international blockbuster *Godzilla* (Ishiro Honda, 1954), whereas Toei produced **yakuza** or gangster films. During the 1970s Daiei went bankrupt, and Nikkatsu Studios began to specialize in soft-core pornography, or **pink films** (also called *roman poruno*). Increasingly, quality film making suffered as a result of these developments.

FIGURE 11.4a and b   *Tokyo Story* ★ Japan, 1953, Yasujiro Ozu; a. Nobuo Nakamura.

Nonetheless a group of innovative directors emerged during the 1960s and 1970s, supported in part by the Arts Theater Guild, which had begun to finance and exhibit more adventuresome fare than the big studios were willing to risk. These directors—including Shohei Imamura and Nagisa Oshima—produced films with an iconolastic modernist bent. They were soon labeled the New Wave in recognition of their kinship with the contemporaneous New Wave directors in France. Often the films they made reworked the popular genres of the day, such as the pink film (Oshima's *In the Realm of the Senses,* 1976) and the yakuza film (Imamura's *Vengeance Is Mine,* 1975).

Shohei Imamura's films might best be described as ethnographic, a quality announced in the title of his 1966 production, *The Pornographers: An Introduction to Anthropology.* Imamura's films describe groups and individuals whose habits and traditions are unfamiliar and frequently repellent. For example, his 1983 *The Ballad of Narayama* tells a tale about the nineteenth-century inhabitants of a mountain village in Japan who practice infanticide, bestiality, and ritual suicide, and who bury wrongdoers alive. Dispite their monstrous practices, however, Imamura's characters typically inspire sympathy as well as repugnance. His stories are often punctuated with shots of insects or reptillian life; like the characters themselves, these creatures inspire disgust but are also possessed of compelling beauty and grace. Even the titles of some of Imamura's films (for example, *The Insect Woman,* 1963, and *The Eel,* 1997) make the connection between human beings and lower forms of life. *The Eel,* which, like *The Ballad of Narayama,* took the Palme d'Or at Cannes, contains numerous shots of a pet eel belonging to the film's protagonist, a murderer who is trying to begin his life anew as a barber. Similarly one of the main characters in *The Pornographers* feels a strong affinity to her pet carp, which she believes contains the soul of her dead husband. A closeup of this creature appears early in the film (Figure 11.5a). Eventually, another character takes up residence on a ramshackle boat, as if to make himself more fish-like (Figure 11.5b). "We all want to be animals," one of the other characters comments at one point. "We want to be free." Imamura takes a similarly ethnographic approach to a horrific event in modern world history in his 1988 production *Black Rain,* which depicts the bombing of Hiroshima and its aftereffects on the people who lived there.

Of the Japanese film makers discussed in this chapter, **Nagisa Oshima** is the most "modern." Using narrative structures and techniques comparable to those of the French Jean-Luc Godard, Oshima is yet profoundly Japanese in his sensibility. He challenges the moral assumptions underpinning Japanese society as well as its institutions. The values of the older generation are seen as neither valid nor relevant to the problems faced by youth, with whom he identifies.

Death by Hanging (1968) not only attacks capital punishment but also goes further to suggest that the very concept of crime (and punishment) is a conception of the police, at considerable variance with actual human conduct and the motives behind it. It is the police rather than the criminal who are obsessed with crime. *Diary of a Shinjuku Thief* was made in the same year. Within an extremely fragmented structure and a mixture of modes, from the actuality of student riots to the artificiality of a ghost play, it links themes of sex as performance with theft as a revolutionary act. The film is dense and difficult; the actions of its individuals are intended to be read as symbolic statements about Japan. *Boy* (1969), based on a real incident, as was *Death by Hanging,* is about a child trained by his parents to run in front of moving autos to be hit and injured slightly so they can collect damages. It is about that particular situation, but the indictment, as Oshima has said, is not of the parents, but of

FIGURE 11.5a and b   *The Pornographers: An Introduction to Anthropology* ★ Japan, 1966, Shohei Imamura.

a society that makes it necessary for them to live in that manner. In *The Ceremony* (1971), often regarded as Oshima's masterpiece, the plot revolves around a family for a period of twenty-five years since the end of the war. As they come together for weddings and funerals their traditional attitudes become increasingly divorced from the realities of modern life, their behavior ever more ritualistic, abstract, and finally strange.

Disjunctive narrative, diverse styles within a given film, reality mingled with surrealist fantasy, formalized patterns achieving the effect of ritual—all are present in Oshima's work. As a Japanese film maker Oshima also offers images of exquisite beauty, especially unnerving when they are of events horrifying in their human meanings. He received his greatest international attention, not to say notoriety, with *In the Realm of the Senses* (1976) (Figure 11.6). It centers exclusively on a couple obsessed with each other and with sensual experience; sexual activity is its content, death and madness its conclusion. *Empire of Passion* (1979), dealing with a pair of rural lovers, is a companion piece, though more restrained emotionally, less explicit sexually, and more social in its content.

FIGURE 11.6 *In the Realm of the Senses* ⋆ Japan, 1976, Nagisa Oshima; Tatsuya Fuji and Eiko Matsuda.

At the end of the 1970s Oshima increasingly turned away from movie making and became active as a political commentator—a more direct form of social protest. Nonetheless, his films have remained influential. Like other modern political film makers, he has fashioned new forms to express new ideas. Disjunctive narrative, diverse styles within a given film, reality mingled with surrealist fantasy, and formalized patterns achieving the effect of ritual are present in his work.

The golden age of Japanese cinema of the 1950s and 1960s came to an end by the mid-1970s. The situation in Japan paralleled developments in the United States, which were dealt with in Chapter 10. Television broadcasting began in 1954; by the early 1980s, 99 percent of Japanese homes had color television sets. The old studio system broke down in the 1960s as the major companies faced declining audiences. Significant films from established directors were few in number and exceptions to the general scramble to match popular taste.

By the turn of the millennium it was clear that Japanese popular taste had given rise to a new kind of film export: animation—or, as the Japanese called it, **animé.** Inspired by comic books called manga, which were in turn inspired by the Japanese woodblock prints of the nineteenth century, animé films such as *Ghost in the Shell* (1996) and *Princess Mononoke* (1997) feature surprisingly Western-looking characters with huge round eyes. Typically, these hand-drawn figures are set against computer-generated backgrounds and move in a slightly jerky manner. Compared to recent Hollywood 3-D animation, the overall effect of the Japanese animés is flat and rough, but the visual design of these films and the imaginative force of their conception are indisputable. In these productions, the Japanese talent for pictorial artistry is given free reign, frequently to breathtaking effect. *Ghost in the Shell,* created by animé master Mamoru Oshii, shows what the form is capable of. The story follows a female cybercop through a Byzantine futuristic world, creating a delirious confection for adults who still crave the kind of fantasies that transported them as children into strange and wonderful realms (Figure 11.7a and 11.7b).

An increasing number of new Japanese movies are being released commercially in the United States. In addition, film festivals around the world, especially those in Pordenone,

FIGURE 11.7a and b   *Ghost in the Shell* ★ Japan, 1996, Mamoru Oshii.

Italy, and Kyoto, Japan, have unearthed many older Japanese productions that had been believed lost, helping us fill in the huge gaps in our knowledge about Japanese film tradition. New English-language studies of Japanese cinema are also adding to our knowledge of Japanese film history. As America develops closer ties to its neighbor across the Pacific, Japanese cinema, with its pictorial riches and modernist leanings, is becoming more familiar to us, prized not only for its aesthetic qualities but also for what it reveals about the values and sensibilities of an ancient and fascinating culture.

Films of the Period

1950
Rashomon (Akira Kurosawa)

1952
Ikiru (Akira Kurosawa)
The Life of O'Haru (Saikaku ichidai onna)
   (Kenji Mizoguchi)

1953
Gate of Hell (Jigokumon) (Teinosuke
   Kinugasa)
Tokyo Story (Tokyo monogatari) (Yasujiro
   Ozu)
Ugetsu (Kenji Mizoguchi)

1954
Crucified Lovers (Chikamatsu Monogatari) (Kenji
   Mizoguchi)
Sansho Dayu/The Bailiff (Kenji Mizoguchi)
Seven Samurai (Akira Kurosawa)

1955
Princess Yang Kwei Fei (Yôkihi) (Kenji Mizoguchi)

1956
The Burmese Harp (Biruma no tategoto) (Kon
   Ichikawa)

1957
The Lower Depths (Donzoko) (Akira Kurosawa)
The Throne of Blood (Kumonosu jo) (Akira
   Kurosawa)

1958
Enjo (Kon Ichikawa)

1959
Fires on the Plain (Nobi) (Kon Ichikawa)

Floating Weeds (Ukigusa) (Yasujiro Ozu)
Odd Obsession (Kagi) (Kon Ichikawa)

1961
An Autumn Afternoon (Sanma no aji) (Yasujiro Ozu)
The Human Condition (Ningen no joken)
   (1958–1961, Masaki Kobayashi)
The Island (Hadaka no shima) (Kaneto Shindô)

1962
An Actor's Revenge (Yukinojo henge) (Kon
   Ichikawa)
Harakiri (Masaki Kobayashi)

1964
Kwaidan (Masaki Kobayashi)
Onibaba (Kaneto Shindô)
Woman of the Dunes (Suna no onna) (Hiroshi
   Teshigahara)

1965
Red Beard (Akahige) (Akira Kurosawa)

1968
Death by Hanging (Koshikei) (Nagisa Oshima)
Diary of a Shinjuku Thief (Shinjuku dorobo nikki)
   (Nagisa Oshima)

1969
Boy (Shonen) (Nagisa Oshima)
Double Suicide (Shinju ten no amijima) (Masahiro
   Shinoda)

1970
Dodeska-den (Akira Kurosawa)

1971
The Ceremony (Gishiki) (Nagisa Oshima)

1975
Dersu uzala (Akira Kurosawa)
Kaseki (Masaki Kobayashi)

1976
In the Realm of the Senses (Ai no corrida) (Nagisa Oshima)

1979
In the Realm of Passion (a.k.a. *Empire of Passion*) *(Ai no borei)* (Nagisa Oshima)

1981
Kagemusha/The Shadow Warrior (Akira Kurosawa)

1983
The Ballad of Narayama (Narayama Bushiko) (Shohei Imamura)
Family Game (Kazoku geimu) (Yoshimitsu Morita)

1985
Ran (Akira Kurosawa)
Tampopo (Juzo Itami)

1986
A Taxing Woman (Marusa no onna) (Juzo Itami)

1987
Gonza the Spearman (Yari no gonza) (Masashiro Shinoda)

1990
Dreams (Yume) (Akira Kurosawa)

1991
Rhapsody in August (Hachigatsu no kyoshikyoku) (Akira Kurosawa)

1996
Ghost in the Shell (Kôkuku kidôtai) (Mamoru Oshii)
Maborosi (Hirokazu Kore-eda)

1997
Cure (Kyua) (Kiyoshi Kurosawa)
The Eel (Unagi) (Shohei Imamura)
Princess Mononoke (Momonoke-kime) (Hayao Miyazaki)

2001
Spirited Away (Sen to chihiro no kamekakushi) (Hayao Miyazaki)

2003
Zaitôichi (Takeshi Kitano)

2004
Nobody Knows (Dare mo shirani) (Hirokazu Kore-eda)

Books on the Period

Bernardi, Joanne. *Writing in Light: The Silent Scenario and the Japanese Film Movement.* Detroit, MI: Wayne State University Press, 2001.

Ehrlich, Linda C., and David Desser. *Cinematic Landscapes: Observations on the Visual Arts and Cinema of China and Japan.* Austin: University of Texas Press, 2000.

Napier, Susan J. *Animé from Akira to Princess Mononoke: Experiencing Contemporary Japanese Animation.* New York: Palgrave, 2001.

Nornes, Abe Mark. *Japanese Documentary Film: The Meiji Era through Hiroshima.* Minneapolis: University of Minnesota Press, 2003.

Richie, Donald, and Paul Schrader. *A Hundred Years of Japanese Film.* Tokyo, Japan: Kodansha International, 2002.

Yoshimoto, Mitsuhiro. *Kurosawa: Film Studies and Japanese Cinema.* Durham, NC: Duke University Press, 2000.

12

Films of the Auteurs: The French New Wave

★ ★ ★ ★

1954–1968

Auteurism

In January 1954 an article by a young critic named François Truffaut, published in *Cahiers du Cinéma,* established the designation and first premise for a critical position that would gain increasing strength in both France and elsewhere in the years to come. Quietly entitled "A Certain Tendency in the French Cinema," Truffaut's piece was against the writer's film—the well-wrought "literary" scenario executed by expert craftsmen. In place of the creations of scriptwriters, Truffaut called for films that would reflect as totally as possible the creative personalities of their directors. He argued that only in this way could French cinema overcome literary stasis and utilize the dynamic filmic potential available. A handful of French directors were capable of this sort of creation, he wrote, and they were the "authors" of their films—that is, in control of, or at least fully involved in, conception as well as execution. He cited Jean Renoir, Robert Bresson, Jean Cocteau, Jacques Becker, Abel Gance, Max Ophüls, Jacques Tati, and Roger Leenhardt as *auteurs* who often wrote their dialogue and some of whom invented the stories they directed. In asking for the elimination of the old psychological realism and dominance by scriptwriters, to be replaced by strongly original directors in creative control, Truffaut declared that he could not believe in the peaceful coexistence of the *tradition of quality* and a *cinema of auteurs.* What his criticism pointed toward was the French New Wave, which would break a few years later and carry him along with it.

The background for Truffaut's manifesto extends at least to Alexandre Astruc's call, as early as 1948, for *la caméra-stylo* (camera as pen)—that is, creating the film in its making rather than merely supplying images and sounds for a fully realized and prefixed conception. Also, by those early postwar years, the French national film archive and screening center, the Cinémathèque Française, had been thoroughly reestablished, making available a systematic viewing of great amounts of the international history of the motion picture. It became

215

possible to see that the moments of aesthetic excitement among the hours upon hours of films were provided by directoral vision, such as that of Griffith or Eisenstein, Murnau or Gance.

Perhaps of even greater consequence was the arrival of the backlog of American films that had been kept from France by the German Occupation. Seeing in rapid succession films produced over a period of years permitted comparisons that provoked new insights. Even among the popular generic entertainments turned out by the big Hollywood studios there were differences, not only of artistic quality but also, more importantly, of artistic personality attributable to certain directors. Both Howard Hawks and John Ford made excellent westerns, and yet a Ford western was subtly but nonetheless surely and consistently advancing different themes and offering a different visual style than one by Hawks. The same was true of the musicals of Vincente Minnelli compared to those of Stanley Donen and Gene Kelly. Further, directors who had been thought of only as having been involved with a few good pictures along with some less good ones could be seen to carry with them a certain special vision; among these were Orson Welles, Fritz Lang, and Alfred Hitchcock. For the young French critics, films by the latter kind of director were much more interesting and rewarding than those of others, however prestigious and expert, whose direction was impersonal. Especially was this so when they regarded all of a director's films together—that is, the director in relation to the total body of work. Even—sometimes especially—the humble action directors working on "B" budgets were able to maintain and articulate their own particular visions: Raoul Walsh in gangster films, Anthony Mann in westerns, Samuel Fuller in war pictures, and Edgar G. Ulmer in horror stories, for example.

It was the application of *la politique des auteurs* to the popular American movie that created the most excitement and controversy. Reevaluations of the total corpus of the American sound film were prompted by the young writers of *Cahiers,* who announced and defended newly discovered masters and masterpieces with enthusiastic rhetoric. The criterion was the consistency with which a uniquely personal point of view was expressed through recurring themes, characters, situations, imagery. Pushed to its extreme, the position was that any film directed by Otto Preminger, Nicholas Ray, or Douglas Sirk (among the auteurists' favorites) was of more value than any film directed by William Wellman, William Wyler, or Robert Wise. The former were auteurs, the latter merely interpreters, realizers of someone else's conception. What's more, auteurists seemed often to value most those auteur films in which the script was weakest or the content slightest precisely because they allowed the director's creative personality to be disclosed most nakedly, without the cloak of satisfying literary content.

Whatever the merits of the arguments, the French word *politique* translated badly as *theory;* what it means more nearly is *position* or *policy.* As with Truffaut initially, the auteur critics' positions were partisan and polemical. What they were insisting was simply that, after looking at hundreds of films in relation to who directed them, certain directors they valued and others they did not.

As the **auteur theory,** it moved westward to the United States in 1961, as evidenced by Andrew Sarris's writing in *Film Culture* and by the appearance of the *New York Film Bulletin.* The auteur theory appeared in Great Britain in 1962, upon the publication of *Movie* magazine. Auteurism was attacked by the more conventional critics for ignoring the collective nature of film making, especially Hollywood's, and for turning critical standards upside down by insisting that bad films were good merely because they were made by favored directors. Eventually, however, even the founts of English-language criticism that had been under attack by the auteurists—*The New York Times, The New Yorker,* and *Sight and Sound,* for example—gradually came to reflect their tastes. In 1968 Sarris consolidated the auteur position in his book *The American Cinema: Directors and Directions 1929–1968.*

Precursors to the New Wave

Among the directors Truffaut cited as important French auteurs of the past were Jacques Tati, Max Ophüls, and Robert Bresson. Although very different from one another, each cultivated a readily distinguishable style that set his films apart from those of others and allowed him to create distinctive *oeuvres.*

Jacques Tati preceded the New Wave with *Jour de fête* (1949), *Mr. Hulot's Holiday* (1953) (Figure 12.1), and *Mon Oncle* (1958). During its height he produced nothing, but in his last two films before his death in 1982, *Playtime* (1968) and *Traffic* (1971), he created intricate, oblique, amusing commentaries on contemporary life that have served as texts for postmodernist theorists. Tati's arresting experiments in sound design add to the increasingly abstract quality of his films. Anchoring these formal flourishes, the character he conceived and performed, Hulot, remains one of the enduring comic figures of the screen.

Max Ophüls, father of the documentary film maker Marcel Ophüls, began his career as a director in Germany but produced most of his most memorable films in France. An

FIGURE 12.1 *Mr. Hulot's Holiday* ★ France, 1953, Jacques Tati; Tati.

incurable romantic, he celebrated passionate commitments and the sensitivity of women in films such as *La Signora di tutti* (*Everybody's Woman*) (Italy, 1934), *Letter from an Unknown Woman* (USA, 1948), *La Ronde* (France, 1950), *The Earrings of Madame de . . .* (France/Italy, 1953), and *Lola Montèz* (France/Germany, 1955) (Figure 12.2). The stories of these films are frequently presented in flashback, accompanied by voice-over narrators. Ophüls favored period settings that could give free reign to his taste for opulent decorative effects. He also had a predilection for complicated **crane** and **dolly shots.** During one such shot in *Letter from an Unknown Woman* the narrator offered a self-reflexive commentary on the meticulous planning that went into the creation of such effects. "I know that nothing happens by chance," she states. "Every moment is measured; every step is counted."

    Lola Montèz is often regarded as Ophüls's masterpiece, though it was clumsily re-edited by its American distributor and only partially restored in 1968. A chronicle of the life of the most famous courtesan of the nineteenth century, the film begins in a circus where Lola (Martine Carol), at the end of her career as an *amoureuse*, has been hired to sell kisses. Part of the show is built around the scandalous events of her former life; the ringmaster (Peter Ustinov) recounts her past exploits, which appear on the screen as flashbacks.

    Ophüls once commented that *Lola Montèz* was about "the annihilation of the personality through the cruelty and indecency of spectacles based on scandal." The film's style supports this theme via a thoroughgoing critique of its own status as spectacle. Each episode of Lola's life is preceded by a clownish dumb-show created as part of the circus performance. She is displayed to the audience in a cage, like an animal; as the cage revolves to provide each member of the audience under the big top an unrestricted view, the camera tracks around it in the opposite direction, assertively calling attention to its presence even as it collaborates with the ringmaster's titillating narration by creating a sensation of dizzying romanticism. The film's sumptuous decor, lavishly displayed in wide-screen color images, also implicitly announces the constructed nature of what is depicted. Ophüls's overall strategy thus puts the film audience into a position not far removed from that of

FIGURE 12.2 *Lola Montèz* ⋆ France–Germany, 1955, Max Ophüls; Martine Carol.

the gawking, sensation-seeking spectators at the circus—but his technique presents this voyeuristic position in terms that are self-conscious rather than crudely exploitative.

A wholly antithetical approach to Ophüls's self-reflexive romanticism is represented in the restrained, straightforward style of **Robert Bresson.** Bresson's important films began shortly after those of the great French film makers of the 1930s and extend to the early 1990s. Throughout his career he remained an isolated figure, among the most personal of film makers. The austerity of his subject matter, concerned more with moral and theological questions than with psychological analysis, and his insistence on rigorous control over every aspect of production, have kept him removed from critical and creative fashion and have limited his output to thirteen films, which stand as monuments to his intellectual and aesthetic integrity. Although Bresson is part of the Catholic humanist tradition, his views take on a particular severity, which led to his being called the Jansenist of French cinema.

With *Diary of a Country Priest* (1950), adapted from a novel by Georges Bernanos, Bresson moved into the main themes and mature style of his subsequent work (Figure 12.3). Set firmly in the midst of French provincial Catholicism, it is concerned not so much with religion as with faith, with the preservation and sharing of belief in God. Shot on location in the Artois region in bleak fall and early winter weather, it is about the misunderstanding and misinterpretation of motives to which the truly saintly are subjected in a world of petty selfishness, rivalry, ambition, and smallness of spirit. Like all of Bresson's films,

FIGURE 12.3   *Diary of a Country Priest*   ✶   France, 1950, Robert Bresson; Claude Laydu, right.

Diary of a Country Priest creates an effect of stasis and contemplation, in large part because its characters invariably wear expressions of stoic calm. Bresson referred to his performers as "models," preferring untrained people who would behave in a subdued manner to professionals given to exaggerated histrionics.

Although his films have never been widely popular with audiences, Bresson has emerged as one of the rare examples of a consummate individual stylist. Like Tati and Ophüls, his films offer an inimitable aesthetic experience that provided a template from which a new generation of French film makers could build.

The New Wave Arrives

Having constructed a critical system exalting the director, it is little wonder the young *Cahiers* critics soon left criticism to become directors themselves. Most of them had from the outset considered criticism only a stepping-stone to creation. Still, the ensuing development of a creative movement out of a critical movement is unique in the history of film and seems, to Anglo-Saxons at least, particularly Gallic. In the United States to date only Peter Bogdanovich and Paul Schrader have come to film directing from writing about film. In France, however, many of the leading film makers of the New Wave, which began at the end of the 1950s, were *Cahiers* alumni and auteurists. Aside from Alexandre Astruc and Roger Leenhardt, already established directors at the time they were writing for *Cahiers,* there were among the younger generation of critics-turned-film-makers François Truffaut, Jean-Luc Godard, Claude Chabrol, Jacques Rivette, and Eric Rohmer.

While the critical context of auteurism was being constructed, conditions in the French film industry also came to favor a new kind of film maker. The glut of Hollywood film released during the late 1940s—a backlog from the Occupation years plus current releases—not only gave rise to its reevaluation by the *Cahiers* critics but also provoked an important series of responses from French producers and government attempting to meet the competition.

Immediately after the war, in 1946, a rather halfhearted quota system was established. Known as the Blum-Byrnes agreement (Léon Blum, President of France, and James F. Byrnes, U.S. Secretary of State), it required French cinemas to show French films at least sixteen weeks of the year. All this did was to establish modest limits on importation. It did not encourage French production, which dwindled in the years immediately following the agreement. In short, it scarcely checked the Americans and further contributed to the stagnation of French film about which Truffaut would complain.

In 1948 a new agreement was reached that stretched the period for exclusive showing of French films to twenty weeks and offered what was intended as temporary government subsidy to the French industry. The aid was financed through a tax on admissions. Money was refunded to the producers in proportion to the amount taken in at the box office. It was a system that favored the established and already successful: The rich got richer while the poor remained poor. Because producers were afraid to risk a share of future admissions, the norm became the repetition of tested ingredients. Kinds of films that had made money in the past were repeated; scriptwriters who had solid success to their credit were hired again; stars who were in public favor had vehicles created for them. But audiences became restive with the standard programming, and the industry soon had yet another crisis on its hands as it became more and more difficult to anticipate public reaction on the basis of the old formulas.

In 1953 André Malraux, Minister of Culture, put forth a new variation on the "temporary" assistance offered to producers. Feature films were given an *avance sur recettes,* a method of funding before the film was finished if the project looked worthwhile to the government advisers. Bresson's *A Man Escaped* (1956) was financed in that manner when he had difficulty finding private backing. Shorts as well as features were covered under the new system, being awarded money in relation to their artistic quality. These *primes de qualité* for the production of short films encouraged directors such as Georges Franju, Alain Resnais, and Chris Marker.

Taken together, the developments in France by the mid-1950s—an industry that began to support talented individual film makers, the critical climate created by the *Cahiers* group, the beginning rise of European auteurs such as Ingmar Bergman, plus new works by Max Ophüls, Jacques Becker, Jean-Pierre Melville, and Robert Bresson—prepared an audience to accept innovation and a more personal kind of film making. The dominating scriptwriter's cinema of standard dramaturgy based on psychological realism began to give way to the director's cinema of eccentric artistic vision and varied style.

At the same time what would prove to be the precursors of the New Wave began to appear: Alexandre Astruc's *Les Mauvaises rencontres* (1955), Jean-Pierre Melville's *Bob le flambeur* (1955), Agnès Varda's *La Pointe courte* (1955), and Roger Vadim's *And God Created Woman* (1956). The last, enormously successful and creating a new sex goddess in Brigitte Bardot, also bore—superficially at least—many of the thematic and stylistic marks of the supsequent body of New Wave work. Louis Malle's *The Lovers* and Claude Chabrol's *Le Beau Serge* were so close to the main upswing, both in their year of release (1958) and in their artistic character, as to be part of the larger whole. But 1959 was the decisive year and the Cannes Film Festival the appropriate occasion on which three French features signaled to the world the beginning of the first new period of heightened national creativity since Italian neorealism of the late 1940s and early 1950s.

Of the three the most popular was *Black Orpheus,* the second feature of Marcel Camus, who had worked for many years as an assistant director. Based on the Greek legend of Orpheus and Eurydice, shot on location in Rio de Janeiro among Brazilian blacks at carnival time, it became an international success, winning an Academy Award as best foreign picture of the year. However, with its exoticism on the one hand and derivative narrative technique on the other, it belongs to the New Wave only by virtue of its year of release. Camus, in his mid-forties at the time, was part of an earlier generation; he made no other important film after *Black Orpheus.*

Hiroshima, mon amour, directed by Alain Resnais, whose background was in editing and documentary film making, was a far less conventional work (Figure 12.4). The script for *Hiroshima,* by the eminent *nouveau roman* novelist Marguerite Duras, concerns a transient and strained love affair between a French actress and a Japanese architect. The personal relationship is embedded in painful memories of the German occupation of France and the atomic holocaust in Japan. Its innovative transcendence of temporal-spatial unities, Proustian emphasis on memory, and linkage of sexual love and global war were strange and absorbing—and typically Resnais, as it would turn out.

FIGURE 12.4   *Hiroshima, mon amour* ★ France, 1959, Alain Resnais; Eiji Okada and
Emmanuelle Riva.

The 400 Blows, by former critic François Truffaut, also heralded major changes
in French film making (Figure 12.5). An account of a young boy estranged from his parents, who is caught up in the juvenile judicial and penal system, *The 400 Blows* began Truffaut's semiautobiographical Antoine Doinel series, with the twelve-year-old Jean-Pierre
Léaud playing his first role. If the film's warmth and humanity owe something to Renoir,
one of Truffaut's heroes, it bears resemblances to Italian neorealism as well, specifically
to de Sica–Zavattini's *Shoeshine*. It was, however, a very personal project. In addition,
bravura flourishes—tracking shots in wide screen and the famous final freeze-frame
closeup of the young Léaud—announce the presence of an individualistic stylist and look
ahead to Truffaut's later work and to the work of other young French directors.

The year 1960 saw the release of Jean-Luc Godard's first feature, *Breathless,* an idiosyncratic tribute to the American gangster film (Figure 12.6). Filled with verve and originality in its fragmented storytelling and iconoclastic camera and editing style, Godard's
debut film showcased the radical experimentation that would characterize the director's
subsequent output. Deeply indebted to Jean-Pierre Melville's *noir*-ish existential crime
film *Bob le flambeur*, it told the story of the last days of a self-destructive small-time criminal, played by Jean-Paul Belmondo as a self-conscious tribute to Humphrey Bogart. Like
many of Godard's early films, *Breathless* conveyed a certain misogyny. Nonetheless, more
than any other film, it epitomized the salient aspects of the New Wave style with its
episodic plot, improvised dialogue, handheld camera work, jumpy editing, grainy images

FIGURE 12.5 *The 400 Blows* ★ France, 1959, François Truffaut; Jean-Pierre Léaud.

shot on location with available light, and ubiquitous references to American culture—especially Hollywood movies.

These first films marked the beginning of what was not so much a movement as an explosion. Approximately one hundred directors made their film debuts in France between 1959 and 1962. Naturally the majority of these young and new film makers were less than geniuses and the bulk of their films scarcely masterpieces. When the novelty and excitement began to wear off, self-indulgence and ineptitude became a kind of commercial undertow. Audiences grew increasingly resistant and producers wary. But before the New Wave receded an extraordinary number of valuable and/or interesting films were produced that left a permanent mark on the international history of film and established a whole new generation of French film makers.

The term *nouvelle vague* was said to have been coined by a journalist. Used for promotional purposes, it covered a diversity of film makers many of whom had little in common with each other. If the New Wave was not as cohesive a movement as, say, German expressionism in the 1920s or post–World War II Italian neorealism, still there are certain characteristics that either were shared or received a new and strong emphasis beginning about 1959 in France.

First was a base in the existentialist philosophy of Jean-Paul Sartre and Albert Camus, especially the latter. Camus's short novel *The Stranger* seems in many ways prototypical of the attitudes and approaches of the New Wave. There is, arguably, a direct line between

FIGURE 12.6   *Breathless* ⭑ France, 1960, Jean-Luc Godard; Jean-Paul Belmondo and Jean
Seberg.

it and *Breathless*. A distanced, antisentimental stance on the part of their creators typifies
both works and much of the New Wave (Truffaut being generally a notable exception).
Within those films it is as if no preexisting, external moral codes operate, even to be rebelled against. Events happen that are not prepared for or explained in the usual manner,
such as the seemingly gratuitous death of the heroine at the end of Godard's *My Life to
Live* (1962) and the suicide-murder of two of the three principals climaxing Truffaut's *Jules
and Jim* (1961). Characters make decisions that appear arbitrary or lacking in motivation,
of a conventional sort at least (Resnais's *Last Year at Marienbad,* 1961, is an encyclopedia
of such behavior). They conceive of themselves as responsible only to themselves (Charles
Aznavour in Truffaut's *Shoot the Piano Player* is one instance) in a world devoid of logic,
justice, or even order.

  Then there is the looseness and openness of narrative construction—the picaresque
quality that dominates so many of the films (Godard's *Pierrot le fou,* 1965, a prime example of the general tendency). At the least they are narrative rather than dramatic, more
allied to the New Novel than the well-made play. The ascending climaxes of traditional
dramaturgy were abandoned, even the ends of narrative threads were no longer neatly
tucked in. Randomness replaced the mechanisms of omnipresent fate at work in the French
films of the 1930s noted earlier. Audiences were left to put together the disjointed experience as they exited the theater. When asked by an exasperated interviewer if a film
shouldn't have a beginning, middle, and end, Godard thought a moment and replied, "Yes,
but not necessarily in that order."

Accompanying the freedom from strict narrative confines was a tendency to organize time and space according to the dictates of feeling (the film maker's and the characters') rather than the requirements of chronology or contiguity. The intricacies of memory are so dealt with in Resnais's work. *Last Year at Marienbad* seems to contain three tenses—past, present, and future conditional; the real and the imagined are jumbled as the protagonist tries to persuade the heroine and perhaps himself of what had happened between them during the previous summer. The jump cuts, abrupt transitions, and asides of Godard and Truffaut in *Breathless* and *Shoot the Piano Player* similarly defy orderly linear perception.

Finally, many of the New Wave films are about films and film making. Because these young film makers, many of them former critics, felt so at home in their medium, they played with it in uninhibited ways. These included encouraging improvisation by actors (Jeanne Moreau, Jean-Paul Belmondo, and Charles Aznavour rose to stardom in their films), taking advantage of the accidents of location shooting, and using new lightweight equipment to attach onto the unfolding action without making it conform to the restraints imposed by the studio method. (*Breathless* was shot in four weeks in indoor and outdoor locations, night as well as day, using "fast" still-photographic stock, a handheld camera, and postrecorded sound.) There are allusions to other film makers and films, a use of the full range of cinematic conventions, some of them stemming from the silent years (irises, intertitles, masking to change the size and shape of the images), and in-jokes (film friends appearing in apt and amusing bit parts, such as director Jean-Pierre Melville as a novelist in *Breathless* as well as two critics from *Cahiers* as blind men in *A Woman Is a Woman*, 1961). Truffaut's *Day for Night* (1973) is, of course, a summation of this tendency: Its subject is film making. Often the films were created as objects for contemplation in their own right rather than as commentaries on the world outside the darkened confines of the theater. These were "movie movies," dedicated to the proposition that if not more real than life, film is a good deal more interesting. In general the New Wave seems not so much art imitating life as life, at least as it is portrayed in those films, imitating art.

One way of thinking about these aesthetic and stylistic innovations is that the modernism percolating in the other arts since the turn of the century had at last seeped into narrative fiction film. The modernism of the French avant-garde films of the 1920s was allied to and mostly came out of painting and painters. The New Wave modernism was literary in origins, sometimes bearing striking resemblances to what James Joyce had explored in *Ulysses,* published in Paris in 1922. What we now generally think of, in relation to the feature film, as contemporary cinema or modern film can be said to have begun in France at the end of the 1950s.

New Wave Directors

As the New Wave began to roll in the 1960s it was Godard and Truffaut who first emerged as the major figures. Like Eisenstein, Pudovkin, and Dovzhenko in the Soviet 1920s, the French duo maintained their preeminence. Along with additional New Wave directors such as Chabrol, Rivette, Rohmer, and others, they created a filmic tradition that commanded critical attention worldwide throughout the 1960s.

Perhaps it is **Jean-Luc Godard** who represents better than any other single film maker the sort of experimental stretching of the medium the New Wave provided. In fact, it may be only Griffith and Eisenstein who have contributed as much formal innovation—additions to the "language" of the medium—as Godard. His early work included variations on the melodrama and chase conventions of popular American movies. It is not surprising that his first feature, *Breathless*, was dedicated to Monogram Pictures, a defunct Hollywood studio of "B" production. *Band of Outsiders* (1964), another "gangster film," has musical numbers as well, with Anna Karina singing on the Metro and dancing with two of the petty crooks; in *A Woman Is a Woman* (1961), Karina says she wants to be in a musical choreographed by Bob Fosse.

On the other hand, Godard employed the sort of "distancing" associated with avant-garde theater, or with Bertolt Brecht, whom Godard frequently invoked in interviews. To this end, he repeatedly disrupted the films' narratives with printed intertitles and interludes in which actors addressed the camera directly, often offering commentary that had little or nothing to do with the story being told. His visual rhetoric was similarly designed to disrupt the audience's suspension of disbelief through patently artificial devices that included the use of bold, primary colors that mimicked the style of advertising posters and ostentatious camera movements, such as the long tracking shot of a series of supermarket checkout counters in the 1972 *Tout va bien*. In the opening scene of *My Life to Live* (1962) the camera remains mostly on the backs of Nana and Paul, preventing us from seeing their facial expressions as they converse (Figure 12.7a and b). Its twelve episodes are punctuated by titles, pulling us further out of the narrative, which is already deliberately disjunctive, and suggesting a series of moral lessons (Montaigne furnishes the text for one of the tableaux). At one point Nana weeps as she watches a scene from Dreyer's *Passion of Joan of Arc* in which Renée Falconetti, who plays the heroine of the film within the film, weeps (Figure 12.7c and d). During this most emotionally transporting of movie moments, Godard tacitly reminds us that his heroine, too, is an actor in a make-believe world.

But a new kind of realism was also present in Godard's cinematic collages. In *Sympathy for the Devil* (1968) and elsewhere, cinéma vérité actuality mingles with fictive elements. Godard has said that there are two kinds of cinema, Flaherty and Eisenstein: There is documentary and there is theater; but that ultimately, at the highest level, they are one and the same. Through documentary realism we arrive at the structure of theater, and through theatrical imagination and fiction we arrive at the reality of life. Even when working with actors, as he generally did, Godard observed aspects of their actual personalities as much as the created roles they played. In *Breathless*, Belmondo's energy and toughness, coiled-spring tension and handsome-ugliness were first revealed. Jean Seberg, who had failed badly as Joan of Arc in Preminger's film, succeeded completely in playing a young American in Paris whom we suspect might be rather like herself. The series of films with Anna Karina, Godard's wife for a time, were, among other things, essays on the difficulties of understanding and communicating with her (*Le Petit Soldat*, 1960; *A Woman Is a Woman, My Life to Live, Band of Outsiders, Pierrot le fou*, and *Alphaville*, 1965). In *Contempt* (1963) Fritz Lang played himself as a renowned film director.

As Godard's work progressed his philosophical observations came increasingly to obtrude. Concomitant with this move toward philosophical abstraction, the dialogue became denser and was assigned a more significant share of the total communication. In *My Life to Live*, Brice Parain, a philosopher in real life, carried on a long dialectical near-monologue that was only tangentially related to the slight plot. Later in the same film

FIGURE 12.7a–d *My Life to Live* ★ France, 1962, Jean-Luc Godard; a. Anna Karina; b. André Labarthe; c. Renée Falconetti; d. Anna Karina.

Godard's voice on the sound track reads an Edgar Allan Poe story to the heroine. In *See You at Mao* (also called *British Sounds*, 1969) there is so much speech over the images that the words become incomprehensible. Despite this alienating tendency, however, Godard's films of the 1960s stand as models of how far film language can be stretched and what forms it can take.

After *The 400 Blows,* **François Truffaut** made *Shoot the Piano Player* (1960), *Jules and Jim* (1961) (Figure 12.8), and the other films (see Films of the Period) that earned for him the appellation of auteur that he first coined to apply to others. He has written or cowritten all of his films. Generally they are imbued with the sort of romantic realism we would expect from a spiritual godson of Bazin and Renoir. But they also, especially the earlier ones, contain amusing and astute references to the conventions of the medium within which he was working. Throughout there are signs of the well-informed former *cinéphile* and critic, and *hommages* to particular films and favorite film makers, most pointedly to Hitchcock in his thriller *The Bride Wore Black* (1967).

Among his later films the most effective and commercially successful was *The Last Metro* (1981). It deals with the theater in affectionate and knowledgeable detail (as *Day for*

FIGURE 12.8 *Jules and Jim* ★ France, 1961, François Truffaut; Henri Serre, Jeanne Moreau, and Oscar Werner.

Night does with film making) and as a means of getting at the strange, muted, complicated, unnerving human tensions in German-occupied Paris of 1942. A wife (Catherine Deneuve) continues to run the Théâtre Montmartre in place of her Jewish husband. But the husband did not flee the country, as was assumed; he hides in the cellar of the theater and observes its continuation, including the addition of a young actor (Gérard Depardieu) with whom his wife has an affair.

Aside from the undervalued *Shoot the Piano Player* and *Jules and Jim,* which many regard as his masterwork, the Antoine Doinel series (*The 400 Blows;* an episode in *Love at Twenty,* 1962; *Stolen Kisses,* 1968; *Bed and Board,* 1970) may be Truffaut's most distinctive contribution to the history of film. In addition to their worth as separate artworks, they represent the closest fictional feature films have come to sustained use of autobiographical material, except perhaps those of Fellini. In *Day for Night* (1973) Truffaut added his own performance to Léaud's to infuse his art with his life. This sort of creation is recognized as the basis for much of the world's great literature, from Cervantes to Faulkner. The idea of a director's life, at least his personal vision, being reflected in his films was inherent in *la politique des auteurs.* Truffaut brought his own experiences more directly to the screen through the evolving Doinel character than any other director has so far done. *L'Amour en fuite* (*Love on the Run,* 1979) was his farewell to Antoine Doinel. Truffaut died in 1984 at the age of 52.

Claude Chabrol has continued—with increasing strength and control in later years—a succession of cohesive works. Narrow in vision (usually they involve an ill-fated triangle and often end in death), they nonetheless gain power from their concentration. Overtaking Godard as the most prolific of the New Wave directors, Chabrol has consistently pictured a dark underside of bourgeois morality. He favors portraits of wealthy French families whose surroundings are both luxurious and tasteful. His dinner scenes are justly celebrated for their revelations of knives figuratively thrust into people's backs as they are literally thrust into expensive roasts. Chabrol's sharply etched images, clear and elegant compositions, and crisp, pointed editing place his work firmly in the category critic Leo Braudy has labeled "closed films"; that is, films that create a carefully controlled environment while keeping the messiness of the actual world at bay. Among the most carefully wrought, intense, and disturbing of his films are *Les Biches* (1968) (Figure 12.9), *La Femme infidèle* (1969), *Le Boucher* (1970), and *Just Before Nightfall* (1971). His work would seem to be the most conventional of the New Wave directors—frequently following lines laid out by Lang and Hitchcock, whose films Chabrol admires—steadily produced and commercially successful.

While Truffaut, Godard, and Chabrol were being prolific, **Jacques Rivette** made only two films in the 1960s following *Paris nous appartient*, released at the beginning of

FIGURE 12.9 *Les Biches* ★ France, 1968, Claude Chabrol; Jacqueline Sassard, Jean-Louis Trintignant, and Stephane Audran.

the decade: *La Religieuse* (1965) and *L'Amour fou* (1968). In 1971 he completed *Out One* (running twelve hours and forty minutes and never released), which became *Out One: Spectre* (1974), re-edited from the same footage. The most eccentric and obscure of the New Wave directors, he has nonetheless been influential. *Celine and Julie Go Boating* (1974) is his most "accessible" film, whimsical and amusing (Figure 12.10). All of his films maintain the enigmatic qualities of his first feature, either attacking or toying with the whole notion of illusionistic storytelling. In most of them the characters are in some ways involved in the production of plays from classical drama that are intricately interwoven with the modern stories. Rivette has said that his films "are about theater, about truth and lies."

Rivette's *La Belle Noiseuse* (1991, which means something like "The Beautiful Trouble Maker"), transfers the central setting from theater to a famous painter's studio; but it explores the process of creation even more intently, and the development of characters and their shifting interactions remain linked to drama as in his earlier works. (It is credited as being "Based on the story *Le Chef d'oeuvre inconnu*" by Honoré de Balzac [that is, "The Unknown Masterpiece."]) Also its length, at four hours, is characteristic. But, while being something of a personal statement, it became the first commercial hit of Rivette's career.

Eric Rohmer's passage has been much smoother, his films much more within the main lines of French production. *My Night at Maud's* (1969), the first feature of his *Six Moral Tales* to be released, achieved commercial success and established his international reputation. In Rohmer's work the "literary" is even more conspicuous than in Rivette's

FIGURE 12.10   *Celine and Julie Go Boating* ★ France, 1974, Jacques Rivette; Bulle Ogier, Marie-Fance Pisier, and Barbet Schroeder.

(whose films abound in references to books) and even in Resnais's. Whereas Resnais has collaborated with authors, Rohmer is one. His *Six Moral Tales* (published in translation under that title by Viking in 1979) were written as stories before he made them into films between 1962 and 1972. *The Marquise of O . . .* (1976) and *Perceval* (1978) are films of world literary classics. Consistent with this literary quality, the settings within which his characters are placed are observed with a particularity that suggests the term *described,* and his characters talk a lot. The way Rohmer thinks of his films is that they deal "less with what people do than with what is going on in their minds while they are doing it." (They have been referred to as "talking cure" films.) His intricate explorations of what are essentially conservative moral positions—supported by a perfection of performance, intelligent and witty dialogue, and subtle and exact psychological observation—continue to intrigue. *The Aviator's Wife* (1980) began a new series that Rohmer entitled "Comedies and Proverbs." Truffaut, interviewed twenty years after the New Wave began, when asked about "the new directors in France," said, "The one I like best is Eric Rohmer, but of course he is of my generation." Rohmer was sixty-eight years old at the time the last film of his *Comedies and Proverbs* series, *Boyfriends and Girlfriends* (1988), was released. *A Tale of Springtime* (1990) launched yet another new series, *Tales of the Four Seasons,* completed with *An Autumn Tale* in 1999.

Left Bank Directors and Others

Not all veteran French film makers currently at work were part of the New Wave. Another group of intellectuals, known as the Left Bank directors, included Alain Resnais, Agnès Varda, Chris Marker, Alain Robbe-Grillet, and Marguerite Duras. Chantal Akerman and Louis Malle were other directorial talents that emerged during this period. Together with New Wave films, the output of these movie makers created a critical mass of cinematic art that made France the unquestioned leader of international film culture and created a legacy that continues to reverberate around the world.

A skilled film maker, **Alain Resnais** makes movies that display a dazzling technical virtuosity and formal elegance, separating them from the films of the New Wave proper. Also, his concern with older characters and the past contrasts with the youthful protagonists and current attitudes dominant in the films of Truffaut and Godard. With noteworthy consistency Resnais has pursued his absorption with the processes of memory, his features—including *Hiroshima, mon amour; Last Year at Marienbad* (1963); *La Guerre est finie* (1966); *Stavisky* (1974); *Providence* (1977); and *Mélo* (1987)—all reveal and insist on the presence of times past in every present moment. This was true even of the earlier shorts, especially the greatest of them, *Night and Fog* (1955). This elegiac, mournful documentary examination of the Nazi concentration camps juxtaposes color footage showing the state of the camps a dozen years after the war with black-and-white archival images of the atrocities committed there in another era. Critic Jay Cantor has commented about this film, "Resnais makes the horrible ordinary so that we might believe it; and then he makes the ordinary horrible, so that we might fear it." In *Mon Oncle d'Amérique,* Resnais's 1981 part-documentary, part-fiction hybrid film, the real-life biologist Dr. Henri Laborit, on whose theories the film is based, says, "A living creature is a memory that acts." This might be a description of the protagonists of Resnais's films.

The problem Resnais presents in his candidacy for authorship is that on his features he has usually collaborated with strong literary figures such as Marguerite Duras and Alain Robbe-Grillet (who subsequently directed their own scripts) or Jean Cayrol. He has always been generous (perhaps more than) in acknowledging his indebtedness to others, and self-effacing in regard to his own contributions to the conceptions. According to published statements from some of those collaborators, Resnais is almost insistent that the scripts be conceived quite apart from his personal style as a film maker and without special deference to the medium of film. "Give me an original 'literary' work," he seemed to be saying, "and I will make it into cinema."

Resnais's English-language film *Providence* (1977) is about literary creation. The script was by playwright David Mercer. Its protagonist, a famous novelist, draws from his relationships with his children and dead wife to shape and reshape scenes intended for his final novel. His characters are at variance with what we are permitted to see of the "real" persons who exist outside his imagination, and the whole, of course, is presented to us in a filmic illusion that is, ultimately, Resnais's interpretation and creation.

His next three films, *Mon Oncle d'Amérique, La Vie est un roman,* and *L'Amour à mort* were scripted by Jean Gruault. The first two are complex three-part narratives: the former telling the stories of three quite different modern characters whose lives interact; the latter consisting of three stories set in different times and filmed in different styles, but yet connect thematically. Both are based on philosophical propositions: The first relates to the aggression innate in humans and human responses to it; the second relates to utopias, education and imagination, and adulthood and childhood. *L'Amour à mort* is also experimental in its narrative structure and stylized imagery—in this case the philosophical argument concerns the dictates of love.

Although the level of achievement may vary, it nonetheless seems clear that as a body of work Resnais's films remain notably coherent regardless of who is credited with the script. We can assume that, whatever the creative relationship between writer and director during production, Resnais is not altogether part of the tradition of writer's cinema about which Truffaut complained.

From the 1960s on **Agnès Varda** has had scattered successes. Following *Cleo from 5 to 7* (1961)—close enough to the New Wave to be part of it—there were *Le Bonheur* (1965), *Lion's Love* (1969), and *One Sings, the Other Doesn't* (1977). Generally regarded as a more solid achievement is *Vagabonde* (1985), a bleak and existential story of a lonely vagrant, Mona, wandering through the wintry landscapes of the South of France. It won the Golden Lion at Venice.

Another member of the Left Bank group, **Chris Marker**, developed a form of personal essay film within the documentary mode in films such as *Letter from Siberia* in 1958 and *Le Joli Mai* in 1963. Not only are his movies set in specific places, but they are allso about those places. He is especially interested in transitional societies, in "life in the process of becoming history," as he put it. His tone is frequently ironical and implicitly judgmental. In 1962 he directed a much admired short fiction film about time travel, *La Jetée,* composed almost wholly of still images. His 1982 production, *Sans Soleil,* which many critics consider his best work, grafts a similar time-travel story onto a documentary-like series of scenes shot in Tokyo and Guinea Bissou.

Marguerite Duras also belonged to the Left Bank group. After collaborating with Resnais on *Hiroshima, mon amour* she went on to direct a series of films on her own, in-

cluding *Drive, She Said* in 1969 and *India Song* in 1975. As one of the French New Novelists, Duras had a strong interest in formal experimentation; her films feature elliptical
narratives in which image and sound are only tangentially related. Their unorthodox style
represents, in part, the search for a distinctively female film language. Many of Duras's
later films, including *India Song* (perhaps her best), also took up colonial themes through
their use of stories set in 1930s Vietnam.

Duras's search for a cinematic discourse that would foreground a woman's sensibility was a project also taken up by **Chantal Akerman,** a Belgian film maker who did most
of her work in France. Influenced by French New Wave directors, Akerman was also
deeply impressed by the work of North American avant-garde film makers such as Stan
Brakhage and Michael Snow. Her most widely admired film, the four-hour *Jeanne Dielman, 23 Quai de Commerce, 1080 Bruxelles,* released in 1974, focuses on a Belgian housewife and part-time prostitute (Delphine Seyrig) who unexpectedly murders one of her
clients (Figure 12.11). But rather than building up suspense surrounding this shocking act,
the film directs most of its attention to Jeanne's daily routine, which includes activities such
as doing the dishes, making a meatloaf, taking a bath, and searching the local shops for a
button. These tasks are typically observed impassively, by a motionless camera that

FIGURE 12.11 *Jeanne Dielman, 23 Quai de Commerce, 1080 Bruxelles* ★ France, 1974,
Chantal Akerman; Delphine Seyrig.

watches her head-on, but from a distance. Although Akerman's approach has been labeled minimalist because so little of seeming consequence occurs, films such as *Jeanne Dielman* can nonetheless prove more absorbing than many more conventional productions.

A director more traditional in formal terms if not in his choice of content was **Louis Malle**, who died in 1999. Malle's output was varied and innovative, alternating documentary and fiction and later French and American. His most memorable documentary work was the series *Phantom India,* shown on French television in 1970. Malle won a Golden Lion at Venice with *Au revoir, les enfants* (1987), an autobiographical account of a boarding school for upper-class boys in German-occupied France that gave sanctuary to three Jewish youngsters in 1944 (Figure 12.12). Of his French work beginning in the 1960s, *Zazie dans le Metro* (1960) and *A Very Private Affair* (1962) are contemporary with the New Wave and somewhat related in spirit. The first explores the conventions of film making in a comedy centered on a young girl; the second caricatures the harried movie star (played by Brigitte Bardot).

Although the New Wave movement lasted only a few years, roughly from 1959 to 1962, its effects have extended down to the present. It completely revitalized French cinema and spawned most of the major directors subsequently at work. Together with the critical reevaluation of *la politique des auteurs* that preceded it, it gave more emphasis than had previously been the rule to a personal cinema under individual artistic control. Thinking of

FIGURE 12.12   *Au revoir, les enfants* ★ France, 1987, Louis Malle; Gaspard Manesse, second from left.

film as an art, and of the director as the controlling artist, became a predominant view in France and extended widely abroad.

Further, the influence of the New Wave extended not only to other countries but also into popular cinema. New Wave elements can be seen in Tony Richardson's *Tom Jones* (1963), Arthur Penn's *Mickey One* (1964, shot by one of the New Wave cameramen, Ghislain Cloquet), the Beatles films of Richard Lester (*A Hard Day's Night,* 1964, and *Help!* 1965) and his *American Petulia* (1968), John Schlesinger's *Darling* (1965), Stanley Donen's *Two for the Road* (1967, set appropriately in France), Nagisa Oshima's *Death by Hanging* (1968), and Wong Kar-Wai's *Chungking Express* (1994). These are only a few among the many films made subsequently elsewhere using styles and themes that first came to the fore during the New Wave.

Films of the Period

1955
Lola Montèz (Max Ophüls)
Night and Fog (Nuit et brouillard) (Alain Resnais)
La Pointe courte (Agnès Varda)

1956
And God Created Woman (Roger Vadim)
Bob le flambeur (Jean-Pierre Melville)
A Man Escaped (Un Condamé à mort s'est échappé) (Robert Bresson)

1958
Le Beau Serge (Claude Chabrol)
Black Orpheus (Marcel Camus)
Mon Oncle (Jacques Tati)

1959
The Cousins (Les Cousins) (Claude Chabrol)
The 400 Blows (Les Quatre cents coups) (François Truffaut)
Hiroshima, mon amour (Alain Resnais)
Pickpocket (Robert Bresson)

1960
Les Bonnes Femmes (Claude Chabrol)
Breathless (À Bout de souffle) (Jean-Luc Godard)
Paris nous appartient (Jacques Rivette)
Shoot the Piano Player (Tirez sur le pianiste) (François Truffaut)
Zazie dans le Metro (Louis Malle)

1961
Chronicle of a Summer (Chronique d'un été) (Jean Rouch)

Cleo from 5 to 7 (Agnès Varda)
Jules and Jim (François Truffaut)
Last Year at Marienbad (Alain Resnais)

1962
My Life to Live (Vivre sa vie) (Jean-Luc Godard)
The Trial of Joan of Arc (Robert Bresson)

1963
Contempt (Le Mépris) (Jean-Luc Godard)
Le Joli Mai (Chris Marker)

1964
Band of Outsiders (Bande à part) (Jean-Luc Godard)
La Jetée (Chris Marker)
A Married Woman (Une Femme mariée) (Jean-Luc Godard)
The Umbrellas of Cherbourg (Les Parpluies de Cherbourg) (Jacques Demy)

1965
Alphaville (Jean-Luc Godard)
Le Bonheur (Agnès Varda)
Pierrot le fou (Jean-Luc Godard)

1966
Au hasard, Balthasar (Robert Bresson)
Belle de jour (Luis Buñuel)
La Guerre est finie (Alain Resnais)
Masculine-Feminine (Jean-Luc Godard)
The Rise to Power of Louis XIV (La Prise de pouvoir par Louis XIV (Roberto Rossellini)

1967
Mouchette (Robert Bresson)
Playtime (Jacques Tati)
Le Samourai (Jean-Pierre Melville)
Weekend (Jean-Luc Godard)

1968
Les Biches (Claude Chabrol)
One Plus One (Sympathy for the Devil)
  (Jean-Luc Godard)

Books on the Period

Austin, Guy. *Stars in Modern French Film.* New York: Oxford University Press, 2003.

Hayward, Susan, and Ginette Vincendeau. *French Film: Texts and Contexts.* New York: Routledge, 1999.

Lanzani, Remi Fournier. *French Cinema: From Its Beginnings to the Present.* New York: Continuum, 2004.

Mazdon, Lucy. *France on Film: Reflections on Popular French Cinema.* London: Wallflower Press, 2001.

Mazdon, Lucy. *Encore Hollywood: Remaking French Cinema.* London: BFI Publishing, 2000.

Powrie, Phil. *French Cinema in the 1990s: Continuity and Difference.* New York: Oxford University Press, 2000.

Tarr, Carrie, with Brigitte Rollet. *Cinema and the Second Sex: Women's Filmmaking in France in the 1980s and 1990s.* New York: Continuum, 2001.

Temple, Michale, and Michael Witt, eds. *The French Cinema Book.* London: BFI Publishing, 2003.

Wilson, David, ed. *Cahiers du Cinéma: Volume 4, 1973–1978: History, Ideology, Cultural Struggle.* New York: Routledge, 2000.

13

Other Western European Cinemas: National Cinemas or Eurofilms?

★ ★ ★ ★

1945–

Like Italy, Britain, and France, other western European nations struggled after the Second World War to rebuild their film industries. All viewed their cinematic traditions as a source of pride at home and goodwill around the world. Unlike the United States, where narrative film making has mostly been privately financed and hugely profitable, European countries have felt the need to subsidize their motion-picture industries to ensure the viability of home-grown movies. Ironically this process has increasingly taken the form of international rather than national initiatives, sponsored in part by the European Community. MEDIA, set up by the European Community in 1987, provides production loans through a variation of the French *avance sur recettes* system, and the European Film Distribution Office has provided financial incentives to nationally based distributors for handling films from other European nations. An official EU communiqué of 1997 states, "Within the union, film and television productions are seen as extremely important instruments for the dissemination of culture and identity." The statement goes on to assert, "Carefully targeted support is intended to offset the effects of the fragmented market [and] to emphasize cultural variety within Europe."

Despite the EU's pledge to sustain cultural specificity, some commentators have seen the trend in Europe moving toward a new breed of culturally bland Eurofilms (sometimes disparagingly referred to as *Euro-puddings*), including an ever-larger group of so-called heritage productions that celebrate the histories and cultures of individual countries in an impersonal style that adds nothing new or distinctive to film language. The increasing role of television, both public and privately owned, in European movie financing has also fostered a large number of stylistically conservative productions. Many of the films produced under these new forms of financing, however, have also managed to incorporate the traditions of individual national film cultures and have at times carried those traditions in new directions. At the same time, although such productions may come to the fore at international festivals, they are rarely box-office hits in their countries of origin. Nonetheless, the patriotically motivated policies of support for local movie making that have increasingly held sway all over Europe since World War II have produced many undeniably significant films that could not otherwise have been made, and have given birth to a number of influential nationally based cinema movements as well. Three film industries that have developed under these conditions are Scandinavia, Germany, and Spain.

Scandinavia

The story of Scandinavian cinema begins during the early days of the medium. Like the Americans, whose initial noninvolvement and later brief participation in World War I had given them such an advantage at a crucial time in film history, the neutral Swedes and Danes were free to pursue movie-making activities during the war years. Denmark was in the best position to take advantage of the opportunity, having a well-established industry that had competed successfully throughout the world in the years before 1914. In certain ways, Denmark provided a transition from the forms and styles of the American film being developed by Griffith, Sennett, Ince, and others, to the distinctive Swedish cinema arising during the War, which in turn was succeeded by the high period of German silent film. As had the Americans, the Danes made important use of the outdoors; and Scandinavian films have continued to be marked by the beauty and moodiness of their landscapes.

The stories, however, began to take advantage of the darker and more mystical tradition of Scandinavian folklore and literature. Predominantly psychological rather than sociological in their concerns, the narratives are frequently subjective, seen from a character's point of view—more often than not from the perspective of a woman. The stories the Danes told tend to dwell on spiritual or, alternatively, sexual conflicts. In these latter respects they foreshadowed the Swedes as well as the Germans. Given their themes, the acting style was required to be more subtle and introspective than the broad, emphatic performances generally employed in the American historical spectacles, action-melodramas, and comedies.

Giant directorial figure **Carl-Theodor Dreyer** links the early contributions of the Danish cinema most directly to the near present. Dreyer began in film as a writer of titles for the Danish studio Nordisk in 1912. He then took on various jobs, including editing and scriptwriting, until directing his first film, *The President,* in 1920. His second film, *Leaves from Satan's Book,* in 1921, although based on a novel (by Marie Corelli), was clearly influenced by Griffith's *Intolerance.* It also had much in common with *Witchcraft through the Ages* (1922), the most well-known film of his pioneering countryman Benjamin Christiansen. Dreyer's career continued in Berlin, Copenhagen, and France with a steady succession of features during the first half of the 1920s. Beyond that period stand his scattered masterpieces: *The Passion of Joan of Arc* (1928), *Vampyr* (1932), *Day of Wrath* (1943), and *Gertrud* (1964).

It is this latter body of work—sparse because of Dreyer's rigid integrity, the difficulty of his themes, and the absolute control he demanded over every phase of production—

that has assured Dreyer of his place in film history. He moved increasingly away from dependence on editing as a primary means of creative control and toward lengthy wide-angle shots with almost imperceptible camera movement, framing a succession of painterly compositions (Figure 13.1a and b). His obsessive concern for the effects of organized religion in relation to individual belief—effects that he sees as usually repressive but capable of being transcended by the human spirit—characterizes *Joan of Arc, Day of Wrath,* and *Ordet.* The ambiguous malignity of what would have been a much more mechanical horror story in other hands gives *Vampyr* metaphysical dimensions; in *Gertrud* human love is expressed in terms of a creed. Only the Swedish Ingmar Bergman (who owes much to Dreyer), Robert Bresson in France, and the Spaniard Luis Buñuel have devoted themselves in such a consistent manner to themes that are religious in a broad sense and sometimes theological in their bases.

In the late 1910s and early 1920s Swedish film had achieved artistic heights and a unique national expression, primarily in the work of Victor Sjöström (*The Outlaw and his Wife,* 1917, and *The Phantom Carriage,* 1920) and Mauritz Stiller (*The Treasure of Arne,* 1919, and *The Story of Gösta Berling,* 1924). Following this period it descended to a kind of accomplishment appreciated mainly by Scandinavian audiences. The one major director at work in the years between Sjöström and Stiller and the rise of Ingmar Bergman was Alf Sjöberg. It was with Sjöberg that Bergman began his film career, as scriptwriter of *Torment,* the first postwar Swedish international success (produced in 1944). Coming out of theater, as playwright and director, Bergman continued his theatrical work alongside the cinematic, directing plays in winter and making films in summer. He has said that the theater is his wife, the cinema his mistress.

To date **Ingmar Bergman** stands unchallenged as Sweden's preeminent film maker. To a remarkable extent, his productions were responsible for inspiring the widespread serious intellectual consideration of film in the United States during the late 1950s. His great appeal to this new kind of audience was that his films dealt with matters of transcendent importance, and the manner in which he addressed those issues resonated powerfully in modern consciousness.

Stylistically Bergman is conservative and somewhat theatrical in manner. He emphasizes script and performance and makes heavy use of closeups. In addition to providing

FIGURE 13.1a and b *Day of Wrath* ✦ Denmark, 1943, Carl-Theodor Dreyer.

script and direction, he commanded a devoted stock company of some of the finest performers in film, including Ingrid Thulin, Bibi Andersson, Liv Ullmann, and Max von
Sydow. He also oversaw a crew of technicians who, after years of working together, had
grown accustomed to making tangible his every inclination; most notable among these was
the master cinematographer Sven Nykvist. "There's a sensual satisfaction in working in
close union with independent and creative people," Bergman wrote in his autobiography.

Bergman's debut film as director was *Crisis* (1945), from his own script, interesting
now chiefly as a harbinger of things to come. The first works of stature were *Three Strange
Loves* (1949), *Summer Interlude* (1951), *Secrets of Women,* and *Monika* (both 1952). All
were shown abroad. *The Naked Night* (1953, also called *Sawdust and Tinsel*) marked a
turning point; it is a small masterpiece. But it was *Smiles of a Summer Night* (1955), *The
Seventh Seal* (1957), and *Wild Strawberries* (1957) that confirmed the earlier promise and
set forth fully the thematic preoccupations we associate with the mature Bergman.

In *The Seventh Seal* we could see clearly what the director felt to be the essential
problems confronting humanity, or at least himself. Salvation, for Bergman, had to come
through faith rather than knowledge or good works—the young couple Jof and Mia, and
their baby, apparently have it and are saved; the Knight and his companions do not have it
and are not saved (although the Knight, in his one meaningful deed, does distract Death so
that Jof's family can escape). If in Bergman's world you can't learn or earn your way to
faith, it is occasionally granted to the elect, who are saved. Invariably the faith is simple
and unquestioning. On the other hand, we might see human love, although largely unattainable, as the key to salvation: the love of the young couple for each other and their child
in *The Seventh Seal,* and the beginning love of the old doctor for his daughter-in-law in
Wild Strawberries (Figure 13.2)*,* which brings him an almost paradisiacal dream. Through
love between human beings, faith may come, and from faith, salvation.

In *Persona* (1966) Bergman's preoccupation with the nature of personal identity takes
center stage. A nurse (Bibi Andersson) cares for a traumatized actress (Liv Ullmann) in an
isolated beach cottage (actually Bergman's own summer house) (Figure 13.3a). The actress
refuses to speak. As time goes on, the nurse grows more and more aggressive toward her
passive charge and eventually takes over her patient's character, even playing the role of
wife when the actress's husband pays a visit. At one point Bergman shows the two women,
who look very much alike, in a single split-screen image that merges their faces in closeup
view (Figure 13.3b). In this frightening study of the porous limits of the self, Bergman suggests that intruders may invade not only our outer dwellings but our inner space as well.

Sex in Bergman's films is frequently presented as a compulsive and destructive itch
(*The Silence,* 1963), the scratching of which can sometimes quite literally draw blood
(*Cries and Whispers,* 1972). Sex is the field of conflict rather than the source of fulfillment
between the sexes (*Smiles of a Summer Night,* 1955, and *The Passion of Anna,* 1970). Mar-
riages evidently contain their own heavens and hells, but we see much more of the latter
(*Scenes from a Marriage,* 1973).

Finally, Bergman is consistently absorbed with the role and function of the artist in
society, and even in the cosmos. Bergman sees the artist as a charlatan, a kind of fake who
may *almost* achieve understanding of the inscrutable mysteries of the universe and the mysterious ways of humankind. Artists may come closer to this understanding than other people, but thereby suffer more for their ultimate failure and the exposure of their pretensions

FIGURE 13.2 *Wild Strawberries* ★ Sweden, 1957, Ingmar Bergman; Victor Sjöström and Ingrid Thulin.

FIGURE 13.3a and b *Persona* ★ Sweden, 1968, Ingmar Bergman; a. Bibi Andersson and Liv Ullmann; b. Bibi Andersson (left half of frame) and Liv Ullmann (right half of frame).

and pretenses. The artist is invariably subjected to humiliation. *The Magician* (1958) is one of the serious films in which this concern is the center of attention; *Now About These Women* (1964) is one of the comedies. It is hard to say whether Bergman is sincere in this view or whether it is merely an engaging conceit. But in *Persona,* which many regard as the most profound statement of all of his recurrent philosophical/psychological probings, he takes pains to remind us that we are seeing a movie. A projector shines its beam directly at us, a break in the film is simulated, and so on. He has expressed his delight with the basic technology and perceptual illusion on which his medium is based: that about half the time while one is watching a film the screen is actually in darkness as successive frames are moved into place. In a figurative sense, it's "all done with mirrors," as is said scornfully about certain kinds of magic performances.

In some quarters Bergman is faulted for the narrow range and frequent morbidity of his themes. Increasingly he became vulnerable to this sort of criticism after he abandoned God altogether and concentrated on the ways in which human beings can torture each other out of impulses that may have started as (and may still contain something recognizable as) love. It is true that in his pictures there isn't room for the pleasures and positive aspects of human existence celebrated by, say, Jean Renoir. Although Bergman's people are mostly physically attractive, intelligent, successful in their vocations, well-to-do, and living in pleasant surroundings, they are generally miserable. Part of their suffering is caused by their inability to understand why they are miserable. In Bergman's films misery seems to come from a lack (an absence of meaning, significance, or fullness) rather than from an active cause.

Fanny and Alexander (1983), regarded by many critics as Bergman's most fully realized achievement, is like a huge old-fashioned novel. The well-worked themes are present, but this time Bergman's regard is mellow and valedictory. Beginning on Christmas Eve in 1907 in a Swedish town that might be Uppsala, where Bergman was born, it is about a large, influential family, almost a dynasty. There are many sharply differentiated characters and varied relationships among those living and visiting in the seemingly vast apartment presided over by the grandmother of twelve-year-old Alexander and his younger sister, Fanny. It has elements traceable to what we know of Bergman's own growing up, and Alexander serves as the observer. Although a lot of curious and awful things may happen in this world, life is colorful and full, rich in its stimulations, and tender and tranquil in old age—well worth living.

Bergman's towering achievement has tended to dwarf the contributions of his peers and successors, but other Scandinavian directors emerged during the last decades of the twentieth century to make distinctive contributions to world cinema. A number of these have participated in the growing European trend toward heritage productions that drew on the rich history of that part of the world and attracted international audiences. Bo Widerberg's lyrical *Elvira Madigan* (1967) was the first of these, followed by Jan Troell's eloquent portraits of Swedes struggling to make new homes in America, in *The Emigrants* (1970) and its sequel *The New Land* (1971), both starring two of Bergman's favorite actors: Max von Sydow and Liv Ullmann. Ullmann herself went on to a career in directing, most notably with another **heritage film,** *Kristin Lavanstdatter* (1995), this one set in the medieval era. Bille August also produced a notable heritage film with his 1987 Cannes prize-winner *Pelle the Conqueror,* again starring von Sydow, this time as a down-and-out nineteenth-century Swedish peasant who emigrates to Denmark with his young son in search of a better life.

Like most heritage films, these productions were all distinguished by elegant, straight-forward visuals designed to bring out the drama of the events chronicled. In a different vein, a Scandinavian comedy, Lasse Hallström's *My Life as a Dog* (1985), propelled its director into a hit-and-miss Hollywood career, the high point of which to date has been the 1993 *What's Eating Gilbert Grape?,* which offered a young Leonardo di Caprio the chance to shine in a plum role, and the 1999 Oscar-nominated production, *The Cider House Rules.*

In the 1990s Danish cinema regained center stage through the iconoclastic work of the audacious **Lars von Trier.** Although von Trier's irreverence and brash style place him at a distance from the austere, conservative Bergman, he too is interested in spiritual questions. His 1996 *Breaking the Waves,* made in England and winner of the Grand Jury Prize at Cannes, tells of a young married woman who achieves a kind of spiritual transcendence through sexual martyrdom. It was distinguished by a career-making role for British actor Emily Watson, who played the part with breathtakingly raw emotional bravado. The unflinching realism of the film's depiction of sexual desire was countered by artificial stylistic touches: sequences broken up into chapters separated by storybook images of Scotland, which were accompanied by bland pop music; church bells chiming as the heroine makes the final sacrifice of her body.

In 2000 von Trier's work took a new direction with the melodramatic musical, *Dancer in the Dark,* starring the Icelandic pop star Björk. Winner of the grand prize at Cannes, it features a story set in the United States during the 1960s. In an over-the-top plot typical of von Trier, *Dancer in the Dark* casts Björk as a saintly young single mother who is going blind; she must get money to save her son from a similar fate. Through it all, she sings and dances in lavish musical numbers captured by a hundred digital video cameras (Figure 13.4). The film's swooping handheld camerawork and looming closeups (orchestrated by cinematographer Robby Muller) make it almost unwatchable for those who suffer from motion sickness. But many loved the experience. "I've never, ever cried so much during a single movie," confessed one fan on an Internet website.

FIGURE 13.4 *Dancer in the Dark* ★ Denmark, 2000, Lars Von Trier.

For von Trier, every movie is a new experiment. "Every time he makes a film, it's a great shock to everyone," his protégé Thomas Vinterberg has said of him, "and therefore a great amusement to himself." Peter Aalbeck Jensen, von Trier's longtime producer, is equally sanguine about the helmer's penchant for forging into uncharted stylistic territories. Speaking of the films' distributors, he comments, "We've had the same buyers for ten years. They must be masochists. But they say, 'OK, we need to have something that's weird. Then we can have five stupid commercial films that will make us some money, but we can survive mentally on having a Lars von Trier film also and a couple of other lunatics.'"

Von Trier banded together with Vinterberg, Soren Kragh-Jacobsen, and Kristian Levring to form the Dogma 95 group. The "vow of chastity" the group presented at the 1998 Cannes Film Festival championed nongenre films shot in 35 mm on location with handheld cameras, available light, diegetic sound, and no special effects. Von Trier's 1998 *The Idiots* followed this formula to a certain degree (though it was shot on video), as did Vinterberg's 1998 *The Celebration.* Then came Kragh-Jacobsen's *Mifune* (2000). "I was losing spontaneity over the years," Kragh-Jacobsen commented on the release of this film. "Dogma taught me to play the game again." Although all of these productions attempted to simplify the filmmaking process and to make it more actor-friendly, none conformed in spirit to the most radical statement in the Dogma document, which forbade any directorial credit. The manifesto concluded with the pledge, "I swear as a director to refrain from personal taste! I am no longer an artist. . . . My supreme goal is to force the truth out of my characters and settings."

Meanwhile, the Scandinavian heritage film continues to thrive. A noteworthy addition to the genre was offered in 1997 by director Bille August. Originally produced as a television miniseries, *Jerusalem* tells the tale of a Swedish agrarian community torn apart by religious strife. The last part of the story is largely set in Palestine, where some of the group has resettled, joining an American colony that had established itself there. This plot turn provides an opportunity for exotic locations, English dialogue, and the addition of U.S. actor Olympia Dukakis, who plays the group's American leader—all features designed to appeal to the international market. However, the film is, at the same time, deeply Scandinavian. The story is adapted from a novel by Selma Lagerlöf, who had provided material for many of the earliest Swedish productions by Victor Sjöström and others. In keeping with its feeling for Scandinavian artistic traditions, its Swedish scenes are shot in subdued colors against the background of a harsh, unforgiving landscape, and its cast of characters are driven by moral and religious obsessions. As the work of a Swedish film maker who had, only a few years before, directed *Best Intentions* (1992), a production based on a Bergman script, could it be entirely coincidental that the patriarchal figure in *Jerusalem* is named Ingmar and that his young son—also named Ingmar—must struggle to make his own place in this world?

Germany

For Germany, the issue of the heritage film presents special problems, for modern German history is itself a problem for those who live there. After World War II Germany declared 1945 "Year Zero," the year of a new beginning. Until early 1989, when the wall dividing East and West Berlin came down, it was a divided country: East Germany, part of the Soviet Bloc, and West Germany, allied with Western powers. Much of West German postwar culture, including cinema, involved attempts to escape or, alternatively, to come to terms with the events of the recent past, a process seen by some historians as a form of cultural mourning. West German film making took a leading role in this political self-examination, achieving international stature in a movement known as New German Cinema.

Before the process of enlisting cinema to exorcize the demons of the past could be undertaken, however, West Germany had to patch together the remnants of its film industry, which had been dismantled by the occupying forces after the war. Unlike other European nations, Germany had no quota on the number of American films that could be shown in its theaters. The low cultural prestige of cinema among the German people and the advent of television made the situation worse; by the early 1960s the film audience had dwindled to one-quarter of its former size. Despite these unpropitious conditions, however, an internationally recognized cinema movement emerged in Germany during the late 1960s and early 1970s. Film historian Thomas Elsaesser singles out four factors that enabled this movement to thrive: (1) a system of public funding for feature film production (begun in 1966); (2) a legal framework for television coproductions; (3) the establishment of international reputations for a group of "star" directors; and (4) the appearance of a new audience culled from the group of media-oriented student radicals of the era.[1] Despite the support of this new domestic audience, however, New German Cinema remained more of an international than a national phenomenon, winning prizes at festivals and attracting fine arts audiences around the world while never achieving significant popularity at home.

At the Oberhausen Film Festival of 1962, a group of young film makers presented a manifesto denouncing "Papa's cinema" and offered to make better films at half the cost. The group soon came to be regarded by the world at large and eventually in Germany itself as the new *Wunderkinder.* Under the leadership of Alexander Kluge, the movement became known as the Young German Film during the 1960s and the New German Cinema during the 1970s. The energy and influence of the New German Cinema were at their height during the 1970s; after the death of Rainer Werner Fassbinder, its most innovative figure, in 1982, the movement offered little further in the way of significant innovations; its moment had passed.

The Oberhausen Manifesto represented an attempt to reject the past completely, espousing what it called "free cinema." "The old film is dead," the document declared. "We believe in the new film." The group's politics was Leftist: critical of Germany's Nazi heritage and the fascist movies it had produced. The films that emerged from this new vision were marked by unconventional narratives, new kinds of heroes, and novel ways of involving spectators. The directors were drawn to the politically potent images of documentary as well as to the portraits of society's victims found in melodrama. The conventions of Hollywood film making served as a model for some members of the group, as did images and motifs from American popular culture. A few of the new German directors, especially Werner Herzog and Wim Wenders, were inspired by these techniques and materials to create works designed to escape politics altogether in what was called a cinema of "pure being as pure seeing"; others, such as Alexander Kluge, Volker Schlöndorff, Margarethe von Trotta, and Rainer Werner Fassbinder, attempted a more engaged form of film making that could offer a revisionist view of modern German history.

Alexander Kluge's own film-making style combines fictional and documentary footage in collage structures in which fragmented story lines often center on female

---

[1] Thomas Elsaesser, *New German Cinema: A History* (New Brunswick, NJ: Rutgers University Press, 1989), p. 8.

protagonists. His features include *Yesterday Girl* (1966), *Artists at the Top of the Big Top: Disoriented* (1968), and *The Part-Time Work of a Domestic Slave* (1974). The last deals with a twenty-nine-year-old woman trying to achieve some order, meaning, and effectiveness in a life that includes roles as wife and mother, abortionist, and political militant. Kluge has also championed the production of collectively made films, the most famous of which is the 1978 *Germany in Autumn,* which lists no less than ten directorial credits, including some of the most illustrious names of the New German cinema. A prolific writer as well as a film maker, Kluge has been profoundly influenced by the ideas of the Frankfurt school, a group of German Marxist intellectuals that had come together before the Nazi era. Since the late 1980s, he has devoted his attention to television, in which realm he has been active in producing noncommercial programming. "You only need one percent of alternative television, of calmness within the television set," he has said. "If you have it, people will accept that this television world isn't the only one."

Volker Schlöndorff, the most commercially successful member of the New German Cinema, also made his first feature (*Young Törless*) in 1966 and has remained active since, both as a director and as a movie executive. He is probably the most internationally oriented of the group, having been trained at the Institut des Haute Études Cinématographique in Paris and apprenticed under Louis Malle, Jean-Pierre Melville, and Alain Resnais. He subsequently worked all over Europe and America. In 1973 Schlöndorff founded his own production company with two partners; in 1992 he was named Chief of Production at Studio Babelsberg Grots, a company that represented a merger between the old Ufa studios and the East German studio DEFA.

Schlöndorff's *The Lost Honor of Katharina Blum* (1975) was written and directed in collaboration with his wife, Margarethe von Trotta. It concerns a young woman who spends the night with a fugitive political activist and is, as a result, hounded and exposed to humiliation by the authorities and the tabloid press. *The Tin Drum* (1978), Schlöndorff's adaptation of Günter Grass's novel, is his most substantial international success to date, winning top honors at the prestigious Cannes Film Festival. Subsequently, he has become something of a specialist in literary adaptation and a leading creator of Eurofilms. His *Swann in Love* (1984) presents part of the first novel of Marcel Proust's multivolume *Remembrance of Things Past*. A French film, its cast and crew were multinational. In the United States he directed the film-for-television *Death of a Salesman* (1985), starring Dustin Hoffman. His features during the 1990s have been financed under the banners of many nations: *The Handmaid's Tale* (1990) by Germany and the United States; *The Voyager* (1992) by France, Germany, Greece, and the United Kingdom; *The Ogre* (1996) by France, Germany, and the United Kingdom; and *Palmetto* (1998) by Germany and the United States. In 1999 he returned to a more nationally oriented model with *Legends of Rita,* a film based on the life of a well-known German radical.

Following her initial collaboration with her husband, **Margarethe von Trotta** became active on her own, producing a body of work focused on issues concerning women that has won her a large international following. Throughout the 1970s and 1980s her productions were financed by Schlöndorff's production company; during the 1990s she had a more difficult time finding support and her production slowed. Many of her films explore aspects of modern women's lives: the symbiotic relationship between sisters (*Sisters, or the Balance of Happiness,* 1979, and *Three Sisters,* 1988) and the effect of politics on romantic attachments (*The Promise,* 1994). In another group of her films women are viewed in the context of historically significant radical movements, offering moving accounts of the lives of people on the far left, such as a female member of the terrorist Baader-Meinhoff group (*Marianne and Juliane,* 1981) (Figure 13.5) and a legendary Marxist political leader (*Rosa Luxemburg,* 1986). Throughout her career, von Trotta has favored conventional narrative forms, although her interest in psychological interiority leads her to include many dream and fantasy sequences. "The unconscious and subconscious behavior of the character is more important to me than what they do," she has said. To emphasize the complexity of her characters' inner lives she uses a large number of closeups, typically set off by dark, pared-down settings. Her films are elegant yet intense studies of women whose deepest fears and desires are shaped by large social forces.

A more radical group of German women film makers have clustered around the journal *Frauen und Film,* launched in 1974. This group has experimented with unconventional techniques to present their vision of female angst and anger, turning to such techniques as fragmented narratives, direct address to the camera, and mosaic-like forms that mix documentary and fictional footage. Foremost among these German feminist directors are Helke Sander *(Redupers, or the All-Around Reduced Personality,* 1977), Helma Sanders-Brahms (*Germany, Pale Mother,* 1979), Ulrike Ottinger (*Ticket of No Return,* 1979), Jutta Brückner (*One Glance—and Love Breaks Out,* 1986), and Monica Truet (*Warrior of Light,* 2001).

Another experimentalist, **Jean-Marie Straub,** an Alsatian, was in exile from France for political reasons from 1958 on. A committed Marxist, he is associated with the

FIGURE 13.5   *Marianne and Juliane* ☆ West Germany, 1981, Margarethe von Trotta; Jutta Lampe and Barbara Sukora.

development of what he has called a minimalist cinema. His later films have been made in collaboration with his wife, **Danièle Huillet.** *Not Reconciled* (1965) probed the ways in which the dominant Junkerism and Nazism of past generations carried over into contemporary German life, accompanied by lingering guilt and continuing need for explanations. *Chronicle of Anna Magdalena Bach* (1967) presents performances of Bach's music with reverence but also attempts to imply the feelings and social ambience that surrounded the life of the composer. *History Lessons* (1973), a freely adapted version of a novel by Bertolt Brecht, combines a Marxist interpretation of the economic motives underlying the usual rendering of the history of ancient Rome with a slow automobile drive through the crowded streets of the present-day city. *Moses and Aaron* (1975) is a faithful rendition of Arnold Schönberg's twelve-tone opera with added ideological emphasis and characteristic straining of the formal conventions of narrative cinema. *Class Relations* (1985), an adaptation of Franz Kafka's *Amerika,* is literary and minimalist, in black and white. Its thesis is that the nature of human relationships is determined by class and capital rather than by individual psychologies. Of the modern German film makers the Straubs are the most "difficult," the least "accessible" to general audiences. At the same time their work is valued by the few as the most innovative in their attempts to analyze and expose the medium itself, and to make it serve the purposes of truly radical, politically committed film making.

Three German film makers who speak to the pit as well as the gallery and who emerged as the major names of the New German Cinema movement were Rainer Werner Fassbinder, Werner Herzog, and Wim Wenders. **Rainer Werner Fassbinder**'s style is characterized by cold colors and harsh lighting. He usually worked with a loyal stock company of actors, including Hanna Schygulla, Briggitta Mira, and Irm Hermann. Often, too, he himself acted in his productions. Committed to an avant-garde approach, especially as articulated in the theories of Bertolt Brecht and Antonin Artaud, he frequently drew attention to the film-making process by framing his characters in doorways, windows, and mirrors, and by hyperbolically foregrounding their gazes at one another. His early films, including *Katzelmacher* (1969) and *Beware of a Holy Whore* (1970), are squarely in the avant-garde mode. Artaud's idea of a Theater of Cruelty appealed to Fassbinder, who often seemed to flaunt his exhibitionistic tendencies in the audience's faces, daring us to look away. In the 1978 compilation film *Germany in Autumn* he plays himself as a domineering lout who throws his long-suffering male companion out of their apartment on a whim. Later in the film, the pampered auteur is seen conducting a lengthy telephone conversation in the nude; his body is not the stuff of which pinups are made.

As his career progressed, Fassbinder was increasingly influenced by the audience-pleasing model represented by Hollywood melodrama. He was especially drawn to the films of Douglas Sirk, a German expatriot who made a number of popular women's pictures in Hollywood during the 1950s that subtly critiqued the social system that victimized his characters. Carrying Sirk's approach one step further, Fassbinder's melodramas infused the dilemmas of his characters (who were frequently women or homosexuals) with broad political meanings. *The Merchant of the Four Seasons* (1971), for example, about a *lumpen* fruit peddler hounded by the women in his life (mother, girlfriend, and wife) into drinking himself to death, is essentially a critique of bourgeois manners. In it wildly incongruous behavior becomes part of everyday reality. *The Bitter Tears of Petra von Kant* (1972), dealing with female homosexuality, explores various permutations of freedom and slavery evident in the women's relationship with each other. *Ali: Fear Eats the Soul* (1974), a remake of Sirk's

1955 *All That Heaven Allows,* is about a sixty-year-old German cleaning woman who falls in love with and marries a much younger immigrant Moroccan laborer and is ostracized by her family and the community because of racial prejudice and ageism. A subtitle suggests that "happiness is not always fun."

At the end of his career, Fassbinder began to produce more politically pointed studies of the German past. The first and best known of these is the *The Marriage of Maria Braun* (1979) (Figure 13.6). It stars Hanna Schygulla as a woman buffeted by and adapting to the changing social conditions in Germany, from the stressful end of World War II to later affluence. The material success she achieves does not free her, however, from the constraints of the patriarchal capitalist system of which she is a part. The devastated urban landscape that forms the backdrop to her struggles reflects and shapes her own psychic economy. History is presented here as a never-ending cycle: The film begins and ends with explosions, and the last words we hear are "Germany is master of the world!" (uttered in the 1970s by the announcer of a soccer game). *Maria Braun* is the first of a trilogy that includes *Lili Marleen* (1980) and *Veronika Voss* (1981). All three films mount harsh criticisms of German history as revealed in microcosm through the lives of the heroines of each story, creating a devastating triptych of capitalism in crisis. The picture of a lost society was rounded out with Fassbinder's masterful 1980 television miniseries, *Berlin Alexanderplatz,* which

FIGURE 13.6   *The Marriage of Maria Braun* ★ West Germany, 1979, Rainer Werner Fassbinder; Ivan Desny, Gisela Uhlen, Gottfried John, Anton Schirsner, Hanna Schygulla, and Elizabeth Trissenaar.

FIGURE 13.7a and b   *Aguirre, the Wrath of God* ★ West Germany, 1973, Werner Herzog; Klaus Kinski.

some consider his greatest achievement. Based on a classic novel, it chronicles the misadventures of a down-and-out petty criminal in 1930s Berlin. "I try to illustrate that we have been led astray by our upbringing and the society we live in," the director once commented. "When I show people on the screen the ways things can go wrong, my aim is to warn them that that is the way things *will* go if they don't change their lives."

A film maker who resists making films about his homeland as strenuously as Fassbinder embraced this project is **Werner Herzog.** Herzog's style is characterized by slow pacing, frequent repetitions, and a focus on aberrant characters. The performances in his films often betray an eerily unreal quality—for example, the actors in *Even Dwarfs Started Small* (1970) are all dwarfs, and in *Hearts of Glass* (1976) all are hypnotized. The leading role in *The Mystery of Kaspar Hauser* (1976) is played by a derelict. Herzog's settings—the Amazon jungle (*Aguirre, the Wrath of God,* 1973, and *Fitzcarraldo,* 1981), the Sahara Desert (*Fata Morgana,* 1970), and an island with a volcano that is about to erupt (*La Soufrière,* 1978)—range from exotic to bizarre. His most celebrated film, *Aguirre, the Wrath of God,* concludes with a delirious depiction of the story's megalomaniacal hero adrift on a raft populated by dead men and monkeys still, in his own mind, a godlike conquistador (Figure 13.7a and b). "There is no harmony in the universe," Herzog has said. "We have to get used to this idea."

Herzog's documentaries, including *Fata Morgana* and *La Soufrière,* make the real world appear more fantastical than fiction. In 1994 he made *The Transformation of the World into Music,* the title of which could stand as a symbol of his film-making project as a whole. Repeatedly drawn to the abstract, the mystical, and the sublime, he offers up a world of cosmic wonder and inchoate emotional resonance that is more closely related to musical themes than to ideological ones.

Like Herzog, **Wim Wenders** has been interested in creating a cinema of "pure being as pure seeing." Of his feelings about the German past, he has said, "Trying to remember how it was to grow up in post-war Germany seems so . . . there are so many other layers of experience over it that I can't even get back to the feeling of it." Wenders, too, is interested in the spiritual and the fantastic, a vision typically rendered in carefully composed images created by ace cinematographer Robby Müller. Slow rhythms add a dimension of other-worldliness to the stories he tells. Drawn to self-reflexive strategies and fragmented forms, he is the most clearly postmodern of the major New German directors.

Most of Wenders's best-known films, *The Goalie's Anxiety at the Penalty Kick* (1972), *Alice in the Cities* (1974), *False Movement* (1975), *Kings of the Road* (1976), and *The American Friend* (1977), all involve, to one degree or another, individual alienation from society, aimless wandering, cities, and a fascination with the United States. One of the characters in *Kings of the Road* says, "The Americans have colonized our subconscious." Two of his other films, *The American Friend* (1977) and *Lightning Over Water* (1980), feature the American director Nicholas Ray.

Wenders's fascination with America quite naturally took him there. *Paris, Texas* (1984) is the best film to have come out of his stay. Although shot in the United States with a script by two Americans, Sam Shepard and L. M. "Kit" Carson growing out of the former's *Motel Chronicles,* it was said by many to be a German picture made in America (as had been said of Murnau's *Sunrise* before it). In Wenders's typically slow-motion manner, it tells the tale of an amnesiac (played by vintage Western character actor Harry Dean Stanton) who wanders the Texas highways until he is rescued by his brother. If *Paris, Texas* is a continuation of Wenders's road pictures and of his personal preoccupations, within that body of work, it surely would have to be recognized as one of the finest. It won the Grand Prix at Cannes.

At that festival in 1987, Wenders was awarded the prize for best direction for *Wings of Desire,* his first German-language film in a decade (Figure 13.8). It is a homecoming in

FIGURE 13.8 *Wings of Desire* ★ West Germany, 1987, Wim Wenders; Solveig Dommartin and Bruno Ganz.

a profound sense, an effort to capture the feeling of Berlin in the years since the end of World War II to the present, including the wounds left by that war. The fanciful elements that distinguish it from anything Wenders had done before are both daring and effective. These include angels (males and females in black overcoats) who fly the heavens and also patrol the streets of Berlin, listening to the unspoken thoughts of its inhabitants. The angel protagonist (played by Bruno Ganz) falls in love with a trapeze artist (Solveig Dommartin) and has to choose whether to continue his spiritual existence or opt for mortality with its attendant pains and uncertainties. It was remade in Hollywood in 1998 by director Brad Silberling as *City of Angels,* with Nicholas Cage and Meg Ryan in the leading roles. In 1994 Wenders made a sequel to *Wings of Desire;* entitled *Faraway, So Close,* it tells the tale of another angel who becomes mortal.

The escape from the German past represented in the work of the Romantic visionaries Wenders and Herzog has been countered by the thematic thrust of several films that explicitly attempts a revisionist history of modern Germany through the lives of individuals—a variant of the heritage genre that sees it as a means of purging a national sense of guilt and loss. One of the most admired of these is Edgar Reitz's television miniseries of the early 1980s, *Heimat (Home),* which chronicles the sweep of twentieth-century German history as it affects the members of a single family. *Heimat* raises the issue of German nationalism by questioning what it means to be "home." A similar project is represented in Helma Sanders-Brahms's *Germany, Pale Mother,* which also explores the interaction of the personal and political in Germany, in this case through the experiences of a young mother who must fend for herself during the Second World War. In one dramatic instance of the interrelation between the personal and the historical, a scene of the heroine giving birth is intercut with images of bombs being dropped on Berlin. *Germany, Pale Mother* begins with a 1933 Brecht poem that, in a foresightful mode, raises the question of how Germany can mourn for its past. "What have your sons done to you," the poem concludes. "That you sit among the peoples a mockery or a threat!"

The close of the twentieth century saw Tom Tykwer's jazzy, ahistorical *Run, Lola, Run* become an international hit; at the same time, an increasing number of German films focused on the matter of the country's past, including Max Färberböck's *Aimée and Jaguar* and Roland Suso Richter's *After the Truth.* Other productions in a similar vein are planned. "The Second World War period still represents the most captivating and morally ambiguous challenge of the [twentieth] century," German producer Ortwin Freyermuth has said. "Ten years after reunification and with the government moving to Berlin again, Germany seems to have come around in a historical sense. German talent may feel even more encouraged to deal with this period in a historical way."

Spain

The most prominent director to emerge from Spain is more an international figure than a national one, though his iconoclastic films have little in common with the bland Eurofilm formula.

Luis Buñuel was not only a truly independent and therefore isolated artist, like Bresson and Bergman, but also his work stands outside a particular national culture. Perhaps one might better say that he carried his Spanish inheritance and later adoption of surrealism with him in films made in a number of countries, both in Europe and the New World, over a period of fifty-five years. His films can be divided into two types: the psychoanalytic, which explore the sexual proclivities of an individual, and the ethnographic, which examine the mores of an entire culture or social class.

Buñuel's first work in cinema was in France in the 1920s, as an assistant to Jean Epstein and other impressionist film makers, culminating in his turn to surrealism and collaboration with Salvador Dali on *Un Chien Andalou* (1928) and *L'Age d'or* (1930). After a long fallow period spent mostly in the United States—except for *Land Without Bread* (1932), a searing documentary about the impoverished Las Hurdes region of Spain—Buñuel settled in Mexico in 1946. There his production became steady and commercially successful, for the most part, within the popular Latin American genres of melodrama and comedy.

The most exceptional film in the Mexican period was *Los Olvidados* (1950), which won the international critics prize at Cannes. It extends out of the naturalism of *Land Without Bread,* examining the violence and squalor in a shantytown on the edge of Mexico City as experienced by a gang of juvenile delinquents. An introductory title asserts that the film is "entirely based on actual incidents and all characters are authentic." But, as with *Land Without Bread,* Buñuel's unsparing and unsentimental observation of the horrors created by poverty and the inadequacies or callousness of social institutions in the face of human need moves beyond the usual ways of presenting social problems. As in the earlier Spanish film, reality in *Los Olvidados* becomes *surreal* because we are not used to being forced to contemplate a situation as hopeless as this, or its implications about the structure of society and perhaps the nature of humankind. More conventionally surreal is the beautiful dream sequence in slow motion. Dreams and hallucinations appear throughout Buñuel's work as part of his efforts to capture the irrational drives and fears underlying human behavior.

In 1955 Buñuel returned to France and began a body of films, some of them cofinanced by Italian, Mexican, and Spanish sources and shot outside France, which constitute his latter-day career and confirm his position among the great auteurs of international cinema. Among these is *Viridiana* (1961), which, although made in Spain, was denounced and banned in that and other Catholic countries after its completion. *Viridiana* represents Buñuel's most unambiguous attack on what he views as the unhealthy sentimentality and restrictive and warped morality of institutionalized Christianity. The film climaxes as the filthy and deformed, cynical and misanthropic collection of beggars—whom Viridiana has assembled in order to save their souls through prayer—enter into a drunken orgy that includes an outrageous parody of da Vinci's *The Last Supper* (Figure 13.9). In his own way Buñuel was preoccupied with religion—"Thank God I am still an atheist," he would say.

Buñuel's last films satirized the social and sexual conceits of wealthy Europeans. Among the most admired of these is *The Exterminating Angel* (1962), which concerns a group of guests mysteriously (miraculously?) unable to leave a sumptuous dinner party for days, maybe even weeks, and the ways in which their enforced proximity to each other brings out the idiosyncrasies and destructiveness lurking beneath their conventionally elegant exteriors. In *Diary of a Chambermaid* (1964), based on the novel about the French upper classes by Octave Mirbeau (from which Renoir also made a film, in Hollywood, almost twenty years earlier), Buñuel examines the pervasive evil and moral decadence of an updated, crypto-fascist society. The heroine/protagonist of *Belle de jour* (1967), frigid and sexually unfulfilled with her husband, whom she nonetheless loves, attempts to bring alive her masochistic fantasies of sexual debasement by volunteering her services to a chic brothel. *The Discreet*

FIGURE 13.9 *Viridiana* ★ Spain, 1961, Luis Bunuel; Silvia Pinal, fifth from left.

Charm of the Bourgeoisie (1972) is a loosely structured, amusing, and anecdotal attack on the values of polite society. It reverses the situation of *The Exterminating Angel,* with six persons attempting to hold a dinner party that is constantly interrupted. *The Phantom of Liberty* (1974) is a darker companion piece to *The Discreet Charm.* It turns on a series of chance encounters by various individuals that expose the illogic at the core of modern society.

Throughout Buñuel's work his unflinching contemplation of human cruelty reminds us that he comes from the land of the Inquisition and the bullfight. Some of his films seem clearly to follow the tradition of Goya's horrifying documentation of the human capacity for inhumanity in his series of etchings entitled *The Disasters of War.* (A live reenactment of a Goya painting opens *The Phantom of Liberty.*) On the other hand, Buñuel's surrealism led him to explore the unconscious and powerful forces of sexuality, dangerous and destructive when suppressed, rendering any view of life incomplete and invalid when unacknowledged. His attacks on bourgeois institutions (religion and state, class distinctions, and conventional morality) carry the political charge of the surrealists' revolt. Closer to the anarchist's goal of individual freedom than to the Marxist's credo of cooperative endeavor, *The Phantom of Liberty* suggests that for Buñuel the concept of individual freedom remained a ghostly one.

An easing of censorship that began in the early 1970s has allowed a newly serious and critical examination of the national culture. Following the death of dictator Francisco Franco in 1975, a variety of topics that had long been off limits—church, army, sexual relations, and the Civil War, for example—have been treated with candor and humor. Spanish politics, from the turn of the twentieth century to the present, is the note that recurs most frequently. Three Spanish film makers who stand out clearly are Carlos Saura, Victor Erice, and more recently Pedro Almodóvar.

Carlos Saura's *The Hunt* (1966) (Figure 13.10) was one of the first Spanish films to return to the painful experience of the Civil War with an honesty designed to lay bare and perhaps to cauterize the old wounds. It proceeds obliquely, however, from a kind of allegory of a hunting expedition undertaken by a group of friends who had earlier fought together in that dreadful conflict under Franco. In *Cousin Angelica* (1974) Saura also looked back to the 1930s from a modern perspective, with a protagonist who revisits a town for the first time in thirty years and relives episodes of his childhood, especially those centering on his relationship with his cousin Angelica. Saura's distinctive narrative style, combining allusion and association with chronological disruption, the past falling into place alongside the present, grew out of his need to deal with subjects that would otherwise have been taboo. *Hurry, Hurry* (1980) seems to be the first film in which he confronted a present reality, probing the lives of four young delinquents rushing headlong into tragedy. He also directed a stylish "flamenco trilogy" of ballets based on well-known literary works: *Blood Wedding* (1981), *Carmen* (1983), and *El amor brujo* (*Love, the Magician,* 1985). In the 1990s he continued to explore the political and cultural traditions of his country in internationally popular films such as *¿Ay! Carmela* (1990), an account of a performance troup sympathetic to the Republican cause caught behind enemy lines during the Spanish Civil War; and *Tango* (1997), a self-reflexive fantasy about a director engaged in making a film about the tango.

FIGURE 13.10 *The Hunt* ★ Spain, 1966, Carlos Saura.

Updating the Spaniards' penchant for surreality is **Pedro Almodóvar**'s playful post-modernism. Almodóvar's widespread popularity is testimony to the vitality his films convey. Not only was *Women on the Verge of a Nervous Breakdown* the most successful Spanish film in Spain up to that point, but it was also the highest grossing foreign film in North America in 1989. At present, all the films he has made since 1982 are available on video and DVD in the United States, and all have made a profit here.

Critical reaction to Almodóvar's work has varied from critic to critic and film to film, probably because of the paradoxical nature of the films themselves. They grow out of a gay sensibility and yet have women at their centers, played most notably by the actress Carmen Maura. Dark and deviant sexual fantasy and violence (including death) abound. Though situations and characters may seem bizarre, they are treated with a seriousness and sensitivity that enable us to identify and empathize with them. Plot outlines more often than not are straight melodrama, which is then undercut with witty references to pop culture, citations of earlier films (*Duel in the Sun, Johnny Guitar*), and parodies of the styles of pantheon film makers (Buñuel and Bergman). Perhaps this eclectic mix is most satisfyingly achieved in Almodóvar's prize-winning 1999 release *All About My Mother,* thought by many to be his best effort. Almodóvar's style is so widely recognized and copied as to have become almost a cliché. "I became commonplace," the director has said. "They made me an adjective. 'This is Almodóvarian.'"

Almodóvar's films are sometimes thought of as representing a new Spain—democratic and permissive, sophisticated and irreverent—totally different from the Spain of the Franco years and reflecting the egalitarian ethos of the Socialist government of Felipe Gonzàlez, which came to power in 1982. Spanish film historian Marsha Kinder places Almodóvar at the forefront of a rethinking of Spanish national identity in terms of gender during the 1980s. "Almodóvar succeeded in establishing a mobile sexuality as the new cultural stereotype for a hyperliberated Socialist Spain," she writes.[2]

All About My Mother illustrates the notion of identity as a role a person plays rather than the core of one's being through the adventures of Manuela, a seemingly respectable nurse, played by Cecilia Roth. After the death of her son, Manuela goes to look for his father. In the course of her search we discover that in former times she lived in a community of prostitutes and transvestites. The tenuous nature of her bourgeois position as a mother and professional woman is revealed to us only after her son's death. But it is hinted at early in the film when acting and role-playing is emphasized. We first see Manuela and her son watching Bette Davis play an actress in *All About Eve* on television. In the next scene, mother and son attend a performance of *Streetcar Named Desire,* and Manuela appears outside the theater dwarfed by a huge, blurred image of a woman's face (Figure 13.11a). The image mimics the effect of a larger-than-life movie closeup, reminding us that we are looking not only at a character named Manuela but also at the celluloid representation of an actress named Cecelia Roth. And to further complicate matters, we soon learn that Manuela herself is an actress. After the play, she confesses to her son that she feels sad. "Sad for Blanche?" he asks, referring to the character in Williams's play. "No," she answers, "sad for me. I was in an amateur theater group once and played Blanche."

[2] Marsha Kinder, "Refiguring Socialist Spain: An Introduction." In *Refiguring Spain: Cinema/Media/Representation* (Durham, NC: Duke University Press, 1997), p. 3.

FIGURE 13.11a–d *All About My Mother* ★ Spain, 1999, Pedro Almodóvar; a. Cecelia Roth; b. Cecelia Roth on right; c. Cecelia Roth on left; d. Cecelia Roth and Penelope Cruz.

As the action unfolds, the idea that people possess an inner self that transcends the roles that play in society comes increasingly under fire. We are led to see Manuela's most private moments as performances. In the course of her job as a nurse, Manuela trains social workers at the hospital by acting in scenes in which doctors persuade newly bereaved people to donate the vital organs of their deceased loved ones to others. In this setting we witness her give a convincing performance as a woman whose husband has just died (Figure 13.11b). Then, shortly afterward, Manuela must "play the role" for real, as the same doctors confront her about donating her dead son's heart to another (Figure 13.11c). Through such strategies, the film poses the question: Where does performance end and identity begin?

In *All About My Mother,* as in his other films, Almodóvar stages his themes on a canvas of wildly clashing designs. Manuela's apartment in Barcelona, for example, features a couch upholstered in a red zigzag fabric set against boldly patterned art deco wallpaper in mustard and brown tones (Figure 13.11d). Here is a *mise-en-scène* that has been constructed with a vengeance! Ever the postmodernist, Almodóvar makes films not to reveal truths but to create effects. Like Cecelia Roth, who plays the role of a mother, Almodóvar continually reminds us that he himself is playing the role of an artist.

Thanks in part to Almodóvar's energy and popularity, a new generation of Spanish film makers has emerged on the international scene, including Bigas Luna (*Jamón Jamón,* 1992), Fernando Trueba (*La Belle Époque,* 1993), Julio Medem (*Sex and Lucia,* 2001), José Luis Cuerda (*Butterfly,* 2000) (Figure 13.12), and Alexandro Aménabar (*The Sea In-*

FIGURE 13.12   *Butterfly* ✦ Spain, 2000, José Luis Cuerda; Alexis de los Santos, Uxia Blanco, and Mañuel Lozano.

side, 2004), leading to talk of a New Spanish Cinema. Film attendance in Spain swelled; cutbacks on government subsidies in 1994 were compensated for by newly available funding from television. Production soared from forty-four features in 1994 to ninety-six in 1998. In 1995 the National Film School, which had been closed for twenty-five years, reopened.

The new directors have moved away from a reliance on heritage productions (over three hundred of which were released between 1976 and 1992); instead, Hollywood formulas such as the thriller and the screwball comedy became the norm—a trend that gave Spanish cinema tremendous appeal not only at home but also around the world. María Lozano, director of the Instituto Cervantes in New York, has commented on this trend. "Whether for good or bad, we've become more Euopean," she says.

The vitality of Spanish film making in the 1990s and beyond, and of Almodóvar in particular, is deceptive; even at its healthiest, the scale of European cinema is miniscule compared to that of Hollywood. At their peak in the heyday of Ingmar Bergman in the 1950s, foreign films represented 7 percent of American box-office revenue; at the turn of the twenty-first century, however, they accounted for less than 1 percent of the pie. Although a few productions from abroad, such as *Life Is Beautiful, Shine,* and *Shakespeare in Love,* generated considerable interest during the 1990s, few foreign films find American distributors. Cable stations, such as the Independent Film Channel and the Sundance Channel, have compensated for this lack to some degree by showing foreign titles on a regular basis, as has the availability of videos and DVDs, but there is no doubt that these forms offer a diminished experience of most films—even those made with television money. In September of 2000, *Variety,* the show business Bible, reported yet another cooperative European financing venture to produce English-language films for the international market, this one between England, Germany, and Spain. So the Eurofilm mentality continues to thrive. But despite this trend, European cinema continues to thrive. In eastern Europe, historically, the issue of the marketplace that has driven so much of the development of the cinemas of neighboring countries to the West has meant something quite different, as will be explored in the next chapter.

Films of the Period

SCANDINAVIA
1944
Torment (Alf Sjöberg)

1955
Smiles of a Summer Night (Sommarnattens leende) (Ingmar Bergman)

1957
The Seventh Seal (Det Sjunde inseglet) (Ingmar Bergman)
Wild Strawberries (Smultronstället) (Ingmar Bergman)

1958
The Magician (Ansiktet) (Ingmar Bergman)

1960
The Virgin Spring (Jungfrukällan) (Ingmar Bergman)

1961
Through a Glass Darkly (Säsom i en spegel) (Ingmar Bergman)

1963
The Silence (Tystnaden) (Ingmar Bergman)

1966
Persona (Ingmar Bergman)

1968
The Girls (Flickorna) (Mai Zetterling)
Hour of the Wolf (Vargtimmen) (Ingmar
   Bergman)

1969
The Passion of Anna (En Passion) (Ingmar
   Bergman)

1970
The Emigrants (Utvandrarna) (Jan Troell)

1971
The New Land (Nybyggarna) (Jan Troell)

1972
Cries and Whispers (Viskningar och rop) (Ingmar
   Bergman)

1973
Scenes from a Marriage (Scener ur ett äktenskap)
   (Ingmar Bergman)

1982
Fanny and Alexander (Fanny och Alexander)
   (Ingmar Bergman)

1985
My Life as a Dog (Lasse Hallström)

1986
The Sacrifice (Andrei Tarkovsky)

1987
Pelle, the Conqueror (Pelle erobreren) (Bille
   August)

1991
Zentropa (Europa) (Lars von Trier)

1994
The Kingdom (Riget) (TV miniseries) (Lars von
   Trier)

1996
Breaking the Waves (Lars von Trier)

1997
The Kingdom II (Riget II) (Lars von Trier)

1998
The Celebration (Festen) (Thomas Vinterberg)
The Idiots (Ideoterne) (Lars von Trier)

2000
Dancer in the Dark (Lars von Trier)

2002
Lilya 4-ever (Lilja 4-ever) (Lukas Moodysson)

2004
Dogville (Lars von Trier)

GERMANY
1966
Yesterday Girl (Abschied von Gestern) (Alexander
   Kluge)
Young Törless (Der junge Törless) (Volker Schlöndorff)

1967
*Chronicle of Anna Magdelena Bach (Chronik der
   Anna Magdalena Bach)* (Jean-Marie Straub and
   Danièle Huillet)

1971
*The Merchant of the Four Seasons (Der Händler der
   vier Jahreszeiten)* (Rainer Werner Fassbinder)

1972
*The Bitter Tears of Petra von Kant (Die bitteren
   Tränen der Petra von Kant)* (Rainer Werner
   Fassbinder)

1973
*Aguirre, the Wrath of God (Aguirre, der Zorn
   Göttes)* (Werner Herzog)

1974
Ali: Fear Eats the Soul (Angst essen Seele auf)
   (Rainer Werner Fassbinder)
*The Mystery of Kaspar Hauser (Every Man for
   Himself and God Against All) (Jeder für sich
   und Gott gegan alle)* (Werner Herzog)
*The Part-Time Work of a Domestic Slave (Gelegen-
   heitsarbeit einer Sklavin)* (Alexander Kluge)

1975

The Lost Honor of Katharina Blum (Die verlorene Ehre der Katharina Blum) (Volker Schlöndorff and Margarethe von Trotta)
Moses and Aaron (Moses und Aaron) (Jean-Marie Straub and Danièle Huillet)

1976

Kings of the Road (Im Lauf der Zeit) (Wim Wenders)

1977

The American Friend (Der amerikanische Freund) (Wim Wenders)
Our Hitler (Hitler—Ein Film aus Deutschland) (Hans-Jürgen Syberberg)

1978

Germany in Autumn (Deutschland im Herbst) (Alf Brustellin, Hans Peter Cloos, Rainer Werner Fassbinder, Alexander Kluge, Maximiliane Maintan, Edgar Reitz, Katja Ruppé, Volker Schlöndorff, Bernard Sinkel)
The Tin Drum (Die Blechtrommel) (Volker Schlöndorff)

1979

Germany, Pale Mother (Deutschland, bleiche Mutter) (Helma Sanders-Brahms)
The Marriage of Maria Braun (Die Ehe der Maria Braun) (Rainer Werner Fassbinder)
Nosferatu (Werner Herzog)
Sisters, or the Balance of Happiness (Schwestern oder die Balance des Glücks) (Margarethe von Trotta)
Ticket of No Return (Bildnis einer Trinkerin) (Ulricke Ottinger)

1980

Berlin Alexanderplatz (TV miniseries) (Rainer Werner Fassbinder)
Lili Marleen (Rainer Werner Fassbinder)

1981

Das Boot (The Boat) (Wolfgang Peterson)
Marianne and Juliane, or The German Sisters (Die Bleierne Zeit) (Margarethe von Trotta)
Veronika Voss (Rainer Werner Fassbinder)

1982

Fitzcarraldo (Werner Herzog)
Parsifal (Hans-Jürgen Syberberg)

1984

Heimat (Home) (television series) (Edgar Reitz) (begun in 1981)

1986

One Glance—and Love Breaks Out (Ein Blick—und die Liebe bricht aus) (Jutta Brückner)
Rosa Luxemburg (Margarethe von Trotta)
Sugarbaby (Zuckerbaby) (Percy Adlon)

1987

Cobra Verde (Werner Herzog)
Wings of Desire (Himmel über Berlin) (Wim Wenders)

1994

Faraway, So Close (In weiter Feine, so nah!) (Wim Wenders)
The Promise (Das versprechen) (Margarethe von Trotta)
The Transformation of the World into Music (Die Verwandlung der Welt in Musik) (Werner Herzog)

1999

Legends of Rita (Die Stille nach dem Schub) (Volker Schlöndorff)
Run, Lola, Run (Lola Rennt) (Tom Tykwer)

2001

Invincible (Werner Herzog)
Nowhere in Africa (Nirgendwo in Afrika) (Caroline Link)

2003

Goodbye Lenin (Wolfgang Becker)

2004

Head On (Gegen die wand) (Fatih Akin)

SPAIN

1952

Welcome, Mr. Marshall! (Bienvenido, Mr. Marshall!) (Luis García Berlanga)

1955
Death of a Cyclist (Muerte de un ciclista) (Juan
Antonio Bardem)

1961
Viridiana (Luis Buñuel)

1966
The Hunt (La caza) (Carlos Saura)

1970
Tristana (Luis Buñuel)

1973
*The Spirit of the Beehive (El Espiritu de la
colmena)* (Victor Erice)

1974
Cousin Angelica (La Prima Angelica)
(Carlos Saura)

1975
Poachers (Furtivos) (José Luis Boreau)

1976
Cria (Cria Cuervos) (Raise Ravens) (Carlos Saura)

1977
*That Obscure Object of Desire (Cet Obscur
objet du desir)* (Luis Buñuel)

1981
Blood Wedding (Bodas de sangre)
(Carlos Saura)

1983
Carmen (Carlos Saura)

1984
*What Have I Done to Deserve This? (Qué me
hecho yo para merecer esto?)* (Pedro
Almodóvar)

1987
*Women on the Verge of a Nervous Breakdown
(Mujeres al borde de un ataque de nervios)*
(Pedro Almodóvar)

1990
¿Ay! Carmela (Carlos Saura)

1991
High Heels (Tacones leganos) (Pedro Almodóvar)

1992
Jámon, Jámon (Bigas Luna)

1993
La Belle Époque (Fernando Trueba)

1995
The Flower of My Secret (Le Flor de mi secreto)
(Pedro Almodóvar)

1997
Open Your Eyes (Abre los ojos) (Alexandro
Aménabar)

1998
*Lovers of the Arctic Circle (Les Amantes del
Circulo Polar)* (Julio Medem)
Tango (Carlos Saura)

1999
All About My Mother (Pedro Almodóvar)

2000
Butterfly (La Lengua de las Mariposas) (Jorgé Luis
Cuerda)
Goya in Bordeaux (Goya en Burdeos) (Carlos Saura)

2001
Sex and Lucia (Lucía y el sexo) (Julio Medem)

2002
Salomé (Carlos Saura)
Talk to Her (Habla con ella) (Pedro Almodóvar)

2004
Bad Education (Mala education) (Pedro
Almodóvar)
The Sea Inside (Mar adentro) (Alexandro
Aménabar)

Books on the Period

Aitken, Ian. *European Film Theory and Cinema: A Critical Introduction.* Bloomington: Indiana Unversity Press, 2001.

Eleftheriotis, Dimitris. *Popular Cinemas of Europe: Texts, Contexts, and Frameworks.* New York: Continuum, 2001.

Holmes, Diana, and Alison Smith, eds. *100 Years of European Cinema: Entertainment or Ideology?* Manchester, UK: Manchester University Press, 2001.

Stollery, Martin. *Alternative Empires: European Modernist Cinemas and Cultures of Imperialism.* Exeter, UK: University of Exeter Press, 2000.

Totosy de Zepelnek, Steven, ed. *Comparative Central European Culture.* West Lafayette, IN: Purdue University Press, 2001.

Vinecendeau, Ginette, ed. *The Encyclopedia of European Cinema.* New York: Facts on File, 1995.

SCANDINAVIA

Bono, Francisco, and Maaret Koskinen, eds. *Film in Sweden.* Stockholm: Svenska Institutet, 1997.

Soila, Tytti, and Astrid Widding Soderbergh. *Nordic National Cinemas.* New York: Routledge, 1998.

GERMANY

Bergfelder, Tim, Erica Carter, and Deniz Gokturk, eds. *The German Cinema Book.* London: BFI Publishing, 2003.

Davidson, John E. *Deterritorializing the New German Cinema.* Minneapolis: University of Minnesota Press, 1999.

Flynn, Caryl. *The New German Cinema: Music, History and the Matter of Style.* Berkeley: University of California Press, 2003.

Hake, Sabine. *German National Cinema.* New York: Routledge, 2002.

Halle, Randall, and Margaret McCarthy, eds. *Light Motives: German Popular Cinema in Perspective.* Detroit: Wayne State University Press, 2003.

Kuzniar, Alice A. *The Queer German Cinema.* Stanford: Stanford University Press, 2000.

McCormick, Richard W., and Alison C. Gunether-Pal, eds. *The German Library, Vol. 81, German Essays on Film.* New York: Continuum, 2004.

Meurer, Hans Joachim. *Cinema and National Identity in a Divided Germany, 1979–1989: The Split Screen.* Lewiston, NY: Edwin Mellen Press, 2001.

SPAIN

Deveny, Tomas G. *Cain on Screen: Contemporary Spanish Cinema.* Metuchan, NY: Scarecrow Press, 1999.

Evans, Peter, ed. *Spanish Cinema: The Auteurist Tradition.* New York: Oxford University Press, 2000.

Kinder, Marsha, ed. *Refiguring Spain: Cinema/Media/Representation.* Durham, NC: Duke University Press, 1997.

Martin-Marquez, Susan. *Feminist Discourse and Spanish Cinema.* New York: Oxford University Press, 2000.

Perriam, Chris. *Stars and Masculinities in Spanish Cinema: From Banderes to Bardem.* New York: Oxford University Press, 2003.

Smith, Paul Julian. *Contemporary Spanish Culture: Television, Fashion, Art, and Film.* London: Blackwell, 2003.

Triana-Toribio, Nuria. *Spanish National Cinema.* New York: Routledge, 2003.

14

Eastern European Cinema: Film Making for the State

★ ★ ★ ★

1954–

Throughout the first years of the new revolutionary government in the Soviet Union, in the 1920s, considerable freedom and experimentation existed in the arts as well as in other aspects of life. With Stalin's consolidation of power, permissiveness and variety gave way to enormous monolithic control. By the early 1930s socialist realism was the official and only state aesthetic. Prescribed content was locked into straightforward unambiguous narrative form. The seductive artistry of the Soviet silent films was replaced by the positive, wholesome, uplifting, and bland portrayal of communist heroes whose lives might have some implication for the revolution, or by the presentation of ideologically "correct" modern peasants, workers, and professional people. Socialist-realist films were expected to feature groups rather than individuals. Their plots focused on collective endeavors that always ended triumphantly. *Chapayev* (1934) was the prototype.

With rare exceptions contemporary Soviet films aroused little interest in the West. Conversely, when Fellini's *8½* was shown at the first Moscow Film Festival, in 1963, it was subjected to violent criticism as a decadent bourgeois work full of "vagueness and morbidity." Only after considerable argument and insistence on the part of the invited Western judges was it awarded first prize. Neither it nor other of the new French and Italian films were shown generally in the Soviet Union.

In the communist countries the effect of a film on the audience's social and political attitudes was regarded as more important than the money it brought in. Given this concern, film content was carefully scrutinized and regulated to one degree or another by the state. Consequently film production in the Soviet bloc could be analyzed as a kind of barometer measuring political pressure operating within a society at any given time. A few months before the 1963 Moscow Festival, Communist Party Chairman Nikita Khrushchev delivered an important speech regarding his attitude toward the arts in the Soviet Union. He said, in part:

> We adhere to class positions in art and resolutely oppose peaceful coexistence between socialist and capitalist ideologies. Art belongs to the sphere of ideology. . . . Abstractionism and formalism, whose right to a place in socialist art is advocated by some of their champions, are forms of capitalist ideology.

Only near the end of the century did this position change. The breakup of the Soviet Union in 1989 occasioned a new challenge to film-industry practices to adapt to a market-driven economy.

In the eastern European countries within the Soviet sphere, the situation was not as consistently restrictive as within the Soviet Union itself. On the contrary, the idealistic aspects of communism melded with an apparently unquenchable nationalism, and exposure to new films from the West accounted for fertile periods of creativity in the cinema of Poland, Hungary, Czechoslovakia, and the former Yugoslavia.

Prior to World War II the film production of eastern European countries was negligible in quantity and quality. Few of their films found audiences beyond their own borders, and the small national populations could not be counted on to return the profits necessary to private enterprise. With the establishment of communist governments in those countries immediately after the war, there were new incentives for production, like those in the Soviet Union earlier, and a new base for economic support in the form of state funding. It took a few years for the ground to be prepared, but once the state film schools had begun turning out graduates, and film production, distribution, and exhibition had been stimulated and coordinated, the Eastern People's Republics were ready to take their places in the international spotlight.

These governments wanted films that would inform and indoctrinate, that would interpret events of the immediate past to give a sense of solidarity, and that would instill attitudes contributing to future progress. Replacing the subject of the Bolshevik Revolution, dealt with by the first Soviet film makers, was the resistance to Nazi Germany during World War II. The national traumas of the war were returned to again and again. Often the social and psychological insights they contained were clearly if indirectly applicable to the postwar societies. Communism was represented as the only force with the people's interest at heart capable of opposing fascism effectively and offering an alternative, more democratic way of life. At the same time, many of the young film-school graduates were critical of prevailing conditions. To avoid censorship, they often cloaked their views by adopting strategies of indirection and allegory. Some disaffected film makers went so far as to emigrate to the West; others drew on international financing to reach out to foreign audiences and gain leverage that would allow them to tackle unorthodox themes in their home countries.

As in Russia itself, the political situation under which eastern European directors worked changed radically after the fall of the communist regime. The 1990s saw a good deal of turmoil in the former eastern bloc countries, both politically and within the film industries themselves.

Poland

A Pole once remarked that his homeland was "a fine country, but badly located." Historically, Poland has been overrun by almost every nation in Europe; and during World War I, Poles were drafted into the Austrian, German, and Russian armies. Given their historical affinity with the West, Poles felt trapped and betrayed when, after the debacle of Naziism and World War II, the Western allies decided to barter Poland off to its traditional enemy, Russia.

In the realm of art, Poland has been deeply affected by western European traditions, especially those of France, a country with which the Poles feel a special bond. The nineteenth-century romantic movement in music found one of its foremost exponents in Polish composer Frédéric Chopin. Polish writers such as Adam Mickiewicz and Stanislaw Wyspiański created mystical, dreamlike works that have been seen as forerunners to the surrealist art of the twentieth century. In more recent times this tradition has merged with that of absurdism, most importantly in the work of Stanislaw Ignacy Witkiewicz (known as Witkacy) and Witold Gombrowicz. The most powerful force in the Polish contemporary theater is the director Jerzy Grotowsi, whose approach closely follows surealist and absurdist principles. Grotowski's minimalist or "poor" theater (as he calls it) draws on theories of myth and the unconscious, which were first sketched out by Witkacy but bear a close affinity with ideas espoused by the French surrealist Antonin Artaud.

Immediately following World War II the communist regime in Poland rigidly followed the Stalinist line, including tight controls on the arts. Polish productions of the time had in common as major or minor themes the inability of individuals to discover places for themselves in the national community. At the end of the 1940s the most famous and influential of the new national film schools of the eastern European republics was established at Łódź. As a result of its training and leadership a whole generation of young film makers emerged who would change the nature of Polish film and bring it to worldwide attention.

After Stalin died in 1953 a lessening of Soviet domination, a relaxation of internal controls, and a growing expression of national sentiment gradually began at the rate of two steps toward liberalization followed by one step back to repression. In September 1954, Jerzy Toeplitz, director of the Łódź Film Academy, publicly condemned the simplistic approach of socialist realism. Together with Jerzy Bossak, head of the school's documentary production unit, as well as others, Toeplitz produced a series of films that dealt with social and political problems in sober, naturalistic terms. Their efforts were enabled by a reorganization of the national film industry into independent production groups, which took place in the same year.

From the early days of cinema Poland has nurtured a tradition of documentary film making. The 1920s saw the formation of the Society of Devotees of the Artistic Film (START), which had much in common with the Italian neorealist movement. Carrying this tradition forward, Jerzy Bossak originated a "black series" of documentaries that were released from 1954 to 1956, presenting harsh political and social realities that undermined the sanguine optimism of socialist realism.

After the Poznan uprising of 1956, during which Poles protested Soviet control over their country, censorship loosened. Polish directors began to express their predilections more openly, although by so doing they largely cut themselves off from their colleagues in the eastern European bloc. In 1957, at a conference of eastern European film makers held in Prague, the main spokesman condemned the new Polish films as "hostile to the socialist system." Thereafter, the productions of the Polish school were rarely shown in other communist countries.

Andrzej Wajda led a sudden upsurge of Polish production that reached a peak between 1955 and 1958. Wajda's *A Generation* (1954) began an unplanned trilogy completed with *Kanal* (1956) and *Ashes and Diamonds* (1958) (Figure 14.1). Together the three films explored the conflicting loyalties, confused politics, bravery, and sacrifice that had characterized Poland's sad history during the years following German invasion and occupation to the first days of peace.

With their romantic attachment to the past, Poles have always encouraged historical films. Although Wajda's romanticism tends to soften and mythologize, his intellectual stance is often antiheroic, probing, and implicitly critical of the leadership and causes for which so many young men his age died. In *Ashes and Diamonds,* and in his and others' subsequent films, the actor Zbigniew Cybulski frequently portrayed a young man trying to sort out values and create a life amidst the shifting and unclear postwar conditions. He resembled an existentialist antihero more than a working-class hero of orthodox socialist realism. (He and his roles occasioned comparison with his contemporary, American actor James Dean.) Wajda's *Everything for Sale* (1968) was in part a tribute to Cybulski, who was killed accidentally in 1967 as he jumped from a train. It is also Wajda's reflection on his own relationship to life and art. With a film director protagonist and a film within a film, as in works of Fellini and Godard earlier and Truffaut later, it is one of the major

FIGURE 14.1 *Ashes and Diamonds* ★ Poland, 1958, Andrzej Wajda; Zbigniew Cybulski and Adam Pawlikowski.

examples of this reflexive tendency of modern cinema. In *Landscape After Battle* (1970) Wajda returned to the war, but now the underlying philosophy seemed truly existential and some of the action and imagery almost surreal.

Wajda's visual style is romantic, dramatic, and symbolic all at the same time. *Ashes and Diamonds,* for instance, contains a scene in which Cybulski lights glasses of vodka lined up along the bar in salute to dead comrades. In another scene, a discordant but still stately polonaise is danced in the early morning hours, a dreamlike souvenir of former patriotic sentiments now tired and faded. The film ends as the mortally wounded Cybulski staggers through sheets hanging on a clothesline to fall to his death on a garbage heap.

In 1980 the shipyard workers in Gdansk struck and wrested from the authorities concessions that created Solidarity, eastern Europe's first independent labor union. The national euphoria that followed was short-lived, but before and during it two of Wajda's films were released that expressed to Poland and the rest of the world the spirit of the times (and also the deeply embedded official distrust that might cause it to end). *Man of Marble* (1977) encompassed the events of 1970, when workers rebelling against food prices were shot down in Gdansk and elsewhere along the Baltic coast. Although it was temporarily suppressed and kept from export for several years, the film had such an impact it is said to have precipitated a government shake-up. *Man of Iron* (1981), its sequel, carried the story into the 1980 events. Its frankness about government control and manipulation of the media and its obvious commitment to Solidarity are breathtaking, particularly in light of subsequent developments. It was considered by many to be the most important and courageous film to have been made in eastern Europe up to that time. Both *Man of Marble* and *Man of Iron* were produced by the so-called X unit, which Wajda had formed in the early 1970s and subsequently used to nurture a new generation of Polish film makers, including Agnieszka Holland and Ryszard Bugajski.

In 1981 martial law was imposed, in part to counter the threat of Soviet invasion, and Solidarity was outlawed. Wajda left for France, where he made a number of films during the 1980s. Late in the decade, after Solidarity had been reinstated in 1986, he became a senator in the Polish parliament while continuing to pursue his film-making activies.

The abstract, oracular nature of absurdist and surrealist art makes it ideally suited to represent the humiliation and trauma the Poles have suffered in allegorical terms. Such a style can speak to the Polish experience in an acceptably apolitical manner while at the same time appealing to an international audience. Out of this aesthetic came introspective, expressionistic Polish films, the best known of which include Jerzy Kawalerowicz's *Mother Joan of the Angels* (1961), Walerian Borowszyk's *Story of Sin* (1974), Wojcieck Has's *The Saragossa Manuscript* (1965), and Jerzy Skolimowski's trilogy *Identification Marks: None* (1964), *Walkover* (1965), and *Barrier* (1966). Typical of this approach was the work of **Roman Polanski,** whose films show the influence of both absurdist theater and surrealist painting. After his first feature, *Knife in the Water* (1962), a tight triangle of latent sexuality and violence with an absurdist sense of psychological inertia (Figure 14.2a and b), Polanski moved on to England and the United States, where he directed a number of surrealist-influenced horror films, including *Repulsion* in 1965 and *Rosemary's Baby* in 1968. *Chinatown* (1974), a Hollywood production featuring Jack Nicholson and Faye Dunaway, has a warmer, more romantic edge than his other work and was generally regarded as his masterpiece until his 2002 triumph *The Pianist,* a searing portrait of Warsaw's World War II ghetto community, which drew raves wherever it played and swept the 2003 Oscars.

FIGURE 14.2a and b *Knife in the Water* ＊ Poland, 1962, Roman Polanski; Zygmunt Malanowixz, Jolanta Umecka, and Leon Niemczyk.

Following a scandal in his personal life in 1977, Polanski moved to Paris, where he continues to turn out the surrealist-tinged horror tales and thrillers for which he has become famous, including *Bitter Moon* (1992), *Death and the Maiden* (1995), and *The Ninth Gate* (1999). His frequent collaborator is French scriptwriter Gerard Brach.

The films of a younger generation of new Polish talents were labeled the "cinema of moral concern." Prominent among this group was **Agnieska Holland.** In addition to scripting for others she has directed her own scripts, including films made outside Poland. *Europa, Europa* (1991) (Figure 14.3), a French–German coproduction based on a true story of a German Jew who takes on the identity of a Nazi during World War II, was a considerable international success. *Olivier Olivier* (France, 1991), also said to be based on an actual person and events, deals with the disappearance of a son and his subsequent replacement by an impostor who causes incestual sexual tensions and confusions within the family. Subsequently, Holland moved her base of operations to Hollywood, where she continued to thrive, helming a series of distinguished children's films and literary adaptations.

The most important, original, and highly respected member of the younger Polish generation identified with the cinema of moral concern is **Krzysztof Kieślowski,** who has been called "the most truly European director." His fiction features at first continued the realist, aggressive approach of his documentary shorts. *The Calm Before the Storm* (1976) was about then current Polish working conditions; *Camera Buff* (1979) revealed a reportedly quite accurate picture of the way the film-making system functioned in Poland. Following the 1981 crackdown Kieślowski's *No End* (1984) was much admired. It deals with the private tragedies and public conflicts under martial law as seen through the eyes of a widow whose husband had been a defense lawyer for the accused. Eventually she decides to commit suicide, not able to bear her personal loss.

No End was Kieślowski's first film coscripted with Kryzysztof Piesiewicz. Subsequently the two created a series of ten films for Polish television based on the Ten Commandments (*Decalogue*). All are set in a bleak postwar Warsaw high-rise apartment complex. Featuring coldly lit, starkly simple compositions, the films ponder complicated ethical and spiritual dilemmas as we witness characters becoming entangled in unfamiliar, stressful situations. Two of these productions, *A Short Film about Killing* (Thou shalt

FIGURE 14.3   *Europa, Europa*   ★   France–Germany, 1991, Agnieska Holland; Marco Hofschneider.

not kill) (Figure 14.4) and *A Short Film about Love* (Thou shalt not commit adultery), were released as theatrical features in 1988. The former won a Special Jury Prize at Cannes and an Oscar for best foreign feature. Its story focuses on a young boy who murders someone for no apparent reason and the moral quandary this situation creates for the lawyer who must defend him.

After completing this magisterial work, Kieślowski moved his base of operations to France, as so many other Polish film makers have done. There he produced a series of stylish, metaphysically tinged character studies, including *The Double Life of Veronique* (1991) and a trilogy based on the colors of the French flag (*Three Colors: Blue,* 1993; *Three Colors: White,* 1994; and *Three Colors: Red,* 1994). In *The Double Life of Veronique,* he and cowriter Piesiewicz imagine two girls—one a Polish Veronika, the other a French Veronique—born on the same day, who are alike in all respects, including lovely singing voices and potentially fatal heart conditions. The film moves back and forth between them in their separate countries as one gives up her boyfriend to pursue her singing career and dies, while the other abandons singing, engages in a love affair, and lives.

Kieślowski died in 1996. The evolution of his preoccupations during the course of his relatively brief career evolved from a resolute social realism focused on political and societal issues to an increasing concern with moral choices being made by ordinary people well outside the public issues of their time, and finally to the more supernaturally inflected preoccupations evidenced in his last French productions. (Someone remarked that

FIGURE 14.4   *A Short Film about Killing* ★ Poland, 1988, Krzysztof Kieślowski; Miroslaw Baka, on the left.

Kieślowski's films of the past decade represent an "agnostic mysticism.") In 1998 his producer, Martin Karmitz, initiated the *Prix Kieślowski,* which is awarded annually to the winner of an international competition for young film makers.

In response to the forces of free enterprise prevailing in the 1990s, Polish cinema became more commercialized, with American movies dominating the marketplace. Native-born film makers scrambled to patch together financing packages from advertising, television, international funding entites, and a new Ministry of Film that granted monies on a matching basis. As the country's economy continued to struggle toward stability, the number of movie houses dropped, from twenty-five hundred in the 1970s to nine hundred in 1992. In the 1990s, however, Polish cinema received welcomed international recognition when Hollywood's Steven Spielberg chose to shoot his prestigious production *Schindler's List* in Poland in 1993, resulting in Academy Awards for the film's Polish cinematographer Janusz Kamiński and Polish art director Allan Starski. Local productions, too, prospered. By the turn of the century Polish films were receiving warm domestic support, and by 2004 over 40 percent of the Polish box-office take came from locally produced films.

Hungary

In 1956 there were uprisings in Poland and Hungary. Both occurred in populations who, having been given a small taste of increased liberty and independence, wanted more. In the case of Poland, concessions were made to "the Polish road to socialism." Soviet troops were withdrawn, a new era of greater freedom and nationalism began, and the Polish film flourished. As for Hungary, the Soviet army quashed the rebellion; hundreds were killed, nearly 200,000 fled the country, and the national film flowering just beginning was temporarily ended.

It wasn't until about 1963 or 1964 that a new era began with the reorganization of the film industry and of the Academy of Film and Dramatic Art. The first works of a younger generation appeared during those same years, including films by András Kovács (it was the later *Cold Days,* 1966, that gained him international attention), István Gaál (*The Falcons,* 1970, his fourth and best-known feature), and István Szabó (whose *25 Fireman's Street,* 1974, presented a brilliant kaleidoscope of the Hungarian historical experience).

Two major factors were evident among the twenty to twenty-five Hungarian films produced each year. One was their emphasis on life in the villages rather than life in the big city. The other was their strong ties to Hungarian literature. For example, Károly Makk's *Love* (1970), which won a batch of international prizes, was an adaptation of a famous novel by Tibor Déry. A second successful example from this period, *Sinbad* (1971), directed by Zoltán Husárik, was based on novels by Gyula Krúdny, one of the greatest Hungarian writers of the twentieth century.

A conspicuous exception to this literary connection was **Miklós Jancsó.** It was Jancsó who—beginning with his third feature, *My Way Home* (1964)—carried Hungary's banner most prominently out into the world. Dominated by an obsessive subjective vision and intricate formal design that make it unique within eastern European cinema, his work is coherent and consistent almost to a fault. The strange world of his films has no exact counterpart anywhere, for that matter; reviewers habitually referred to it as "Jancsó country." All of his works are part of a distinctively Hungarian subgenre that Jancsó initiated, the historical parable, which treats past events in symbolic form.

The Red and the White, seen most widely, is typical (Figure 14.5). Like so many of Jancsó's films, it takes place on a vast windswept plain. The historical setting is the civil war following the Russian Revolution. Armies battle, but the causes seem arbitrary and unavailing in relation to universal and casual inhumanity. Sides cannot be told apart once uniforms are removed; nationalities are not distinguishable except when characters speak. At one moment the Whites are winning, at the next the Reds. Everyone is subject to pursuit, capture, humiliation, and execution.

Applied to this disturbing narrative material, and informing and affecting its meaning profoundly, is an equally extraordinary visual style. Shot in wide-screen black and white, the takes are long in duration. Camera movement is almost continuous and exceptionally varied: pans, tilts, dollies, tracking, and helicopter shots all combined. In addition to the insistently moving camera, there is constantly shifting and complex movement within the frame—mainly of men and horses. The movement is unusually frantic, with much running and galloping, and its meaning tacitly ironic. These humans behave instinctively, like other animals; their capacity for reason and emotion merely causes unnatural self-destruction. All of the frenzied activity leads only to death in this land of the still. The highly stylized and decorative visual treatment applied to ugly human actions formalizes and distances them from us—they form part of a *danse macabre.* The choreographic quality plus the repetition of event, as each side achieves temporary victory or suffers more certain defeat, turns the action into arcane ritual.

The Hungarian director who has achieved the most prominence abroad is **István Szabó.** Beginning his career with a series of lyrical and abstract films made in his native

FIGURE 14.5   *The Red and the White*   ★   Hungary, 1967, Miklós Jancsó.

country, Szabó subsequently moved on to direct a series of sumptuously mounted international coproductions that investigated the nature of European identity, focusing on the ways in which periods of historical trauma such as the Second World War brought about personal crises centered on ethnic and national identity. *Mephisto* (1981) (Figure 14.6), starring Szabó favorite Klaus Maria Brandauer, is the best known of these. Brandauer here plays an opportunistic actor in Hitler's Germany who shifts his personal allegiances (including his wife and mistresses) and adjusts his principles to conform to the requirements placed on an artist in a totalitarian state. A huge critical and commercial hit, *Mephisto* won the Academy Award for best foreign-language film and the best screenplay award at Cannes.

    The films of **Márta Mészáros** deal resolutely with the problems of women in contemporary Hungary. The life presented is bleak; the view of it unsparing. Her first film, *The Girl* (Figure 14.7), in 1968, was followed by *Riddance* in 1973. Her most well-known production, *Adoption,* was released in 1975 and won the Golden Bear at the Berlin Film Festival. In the 1980s Mészáros turned to a trilogy of autobiographical works, *Diary for My Children* (1984), *Diary for My Loves* (1987), and *Diary for My Mother and Father* (1990), in which she chronicles the effect Stalinist repression has had on her personal relationships.

    Despite the economic confusion of the 1990s, Hungarian film making has remained relatively healthy. More than a dozen first films were made in the early 1990s, and directors such as Béla Tarr (*Satantango,* 1994) attracted a good deal of international attention. Among the socialist states, which generally demanded of their film makers positive and constructive service in the building of new societies, Hungary has consistently allowed surprisingly personal and critical examinations of the shared cultural experience. Under capitalism, it continues to do so.

FIGURE 14.6   *Mephisto*   ★   Hungary, 1981, István Szabó. Klaus Maria Brandauer.

Czechoslovakia

In Czechoslovakia the stirrings of 1956 were quietly quelled by the indigenous communist hierarchy so that the Czechs neither gained additional freedom and independence, as did the Poles, nor were subjected to Soviet invasion, as were the Hungarians. It wasn't really until the 1960s that the political and cultural climate warmed sufficiently for the Czechs to expand freely into their own equivalent to the New Wave. Unlike the melancholy Poles or the historically minded Hungarians, the Czechs created a cinema of sharply observed social comedy.

In 1963 a generation of graduates of the national film academy in Prague (FAMU), which included Miloš Forman and Věra Chytilová, made their feature debuts. But the big international success was *The Shop on Main Street* (1965), by two veterans, Ján Kadár and Elmar Klos. The first Czech film to win an Academy Award, it is made up of known ingredients skillfully and movingly blended. Set in a small town under German occupation it exposed the evils of fascist mentality and its most heinous manifestation in anti-Semitism and genocide. *The Shop on Main Street* treats these large themes on an intimate scale. The horrors inflicted on inconceivable millions are expressed through events occurring in the lives

FIGURE 14.7 *The Girl* ⋆ Hungary, 1968, Márta Mészáros; Teri Horvath and Zsuzsa Pálos.

of a simple carpenter, his greedy wife and fascist brother-in-law, and an ancient Jewish shop-keeper. Their paradoxical situation, as the carpenter tries to save the old lady from extermination, becomes credible through the fully rounded performances. Warmly and delicately observed detail and humor mingled with pathos characterize script and direction. Satisfying within its own terms, *The Shop on Main Street* was more conventional than the Czech films that would follow.

One of the leaders of a truly new Czech cinema was **Miloš Forman,** whose widely seen *Loves of a Blonde* (1965) and *The Fireman's Ball* (1967) might be compared to Italian Ermanno Olmi's early work. Like *Il Posto, Loves of a Blonde* is about a young person experiencing the impersonality and loneliness of the industrial world in a first job away from home. Forman uses a style similar to *cinéma vérité* and draws the same remarkable performances from casts surely composed largely of nonprofessionals. In *The Fireman's Ball,* Forman's observation of average people and everyday situations is more humorous and satiric than Olmi's (Figure 14.8a and b). The cross-purposes, confusions, and inarticulateness of the petit-bourgeois characters in their relationships with each other, the tensions and misunderstandings between generations, and the hopeless incompetence and self-inflated importance of bureaucracy are all wryly commented on in a totally disarming way. Despite its aura of unassuming charm, it was widely viewed in Czechoslovakia at the time of its release as a comment on the communist system and was banned there from 1973 to 1989.

Other Czech film makers with similarly comic sensibilities who came to prominence during this era were **Ivan Passer** and **Jiří Menzel.** Passer, who coscripted *The Fireman's Ball,* conceived and directed *Intimate Lighting* (1965) in much the same warmly humorous

FIGURE 14.8a and b   *The Fireman's Ball* ★ Czechoslovakia, 1967, Miloš Foreman.

manner. In it he observes the reunion in a provincial Czech town of two old musician friends, one with a wife and family, the other with a mistress. Of Jiří Menzel's films, the best known in the West is *Closely Watched Trains* (1966) (Figure 14.9). (It, too, won an Academy Award.) Like Forman and Passer, Menzel observes with careful attention and detached amusement the actions of "the little people." Although set in World War II and including partisan sabotage of the German-controlled railway, instead of epic events, *Closely Watched Trains* concentrates on the coming of age of a shy and ineffectual young station attendant and the peculiar sexual goings-on around him in the isolated post.

The Czech feel for comedy was given an avant-garde twist in the work of **Věra Chytilová,** whose best-known productions are *Daisies* (1966) and *The Apple Game* (1976). *Daisies,* which Chytilová characterized as "a philosophical documentary in the form of a farce," eschews conventional narrative in favor of a series of vignettes linked by repeated elements—more like a lyric poem than a story. The film focuses on two exuberant young women, both named Maria, cavorting amid a series of surreal landscapes. Their adventures center on food, which they both consume and destroy in an orgy of nihilistic provocation. "Everything's spoiled in this world," says one; to which the other responds, "Then we'll be spoiled, too." Widely understood as an allegory of political nihilism, the film concludes with a banquet scene in which the women demolish the feast that has been laid out. It concludes with the chandelier crashing down, an image photographed to suggest nuclear annihilation.

A Czech New Wave director of a different stripe was **Jan Němec.** Němec makes one think of the Poles, especially of Jerzy Skolimowski. *Report on the Party and the Guests* (1966) carries the surrealist impulses of Skolimowski's *Barrier* even further. In fact, it is a sort of political allegory clothed in trappings of the avant garde; at times it looks like Resnais's *Last Year at Marienbad* with overtones of Kafka. The party takes place at formally set tables beside a lake in a lonely wood. The characters move and behave as though they are part of some sort of game with arcane rules, frenetic endeavor being followed by somnambulistic languor. The threat of violence and punishment hangs over the whole. Promptly banned after completion, it was defiantly awarded the Czech Critics Prize a year later. Němec was forcibly exiled in 1974.

FIGURE 14.9   *Closely Watched Trains* ★ Czechoslavakia, 1966, Jiří Menzel; Václav Neckář and Jitka Bendová.

The Czechs have long fostered a proud tradition of world-class animation, the leading figures of which are Jiří Trnka (*The Emperor's Nightingale,* 1948, and *Old Czech Legends,* 1953), Karel Zeman (*A Journey to Primeval Times,* 1955, and *An Invention for Destruction,* 1958), and Jan Švankmajer (*Dimensions of Dialogue,* 1982, and *Alice,* 1987). The skills of these and other Czech animators were honed in one of the state-supported animation studios set up throughout eastern Europe after World War II. Profoundly influenced by surrealism, these artists produced short and feature-length fantasies intended for both adults and children. Like their colleagues in the animation industries of other eastern bloc nations, many Czech animators left the country during times of repression and found ready employment in Hollywood.

Even if unenthusiastic and vacillating, an official liberalization had clearly occurred within Czechoslovakia that permitted statements from film artists who were either openly or covertly critical of the society. The Czechs, like the Poles and Hungarians before them, responded by striving for still more freedom from Communist Party conformity and for self-identification as Czechoslovaks. The years 1966 to 1968 saw the greatest ferment. Then, in the summer of 1968, an uprising was crushed by Soviet tanks, and Czechoslovakia once again became an occupied country for a time. As with the Hungarians earlier, many who weren't killed, imprisoned, or forced underground fled. Some came to the

United States and continued to work here—for example, Ján Kadár (*Lies My Father Told Me,* 1975), Miloš Forman (*One Flew Over the Cuckoo's Nest,* 1975; *Hair,* 1979; *Ragtime,* 1981; *Amadeus,* 1984; *Valmont,* 1989; *The People Versus Larry Flynt,* 1996; and *The Man in the Moon,* 1999), and Ivan Passer (*Cutter's Way,* 1981).

In 1993, the country divided itself into its two ethnic components: Czech and Slovak. Despite the country's political and economic upheaval, however, Czech films again began attracting international acclaim during the latter part of the decade, with productions such as Jan Sverák's *Kolya* and Petr Zelenka's *Buttoners* in 1997, and Sasa Gedeon's *Return of the Idiot* in 1999. About twenty Czech and Slovak films were produced every year during the 1990s, and between 1993 and the turn of the century thirty first films by new Czech and Slovak directors were released, most of these produced by graduates of the famed FAMU film-making school. These productions build on the tradition of the Czech "Golden Age" cinema of the 1960s by focusing on intimate portraits of ordinary people, frequently leavened with gentle humor. Some critics have hailed these developments as heralding a new Czech New Wave, a claim that will be tested in the new century.

Yugoslavia

Among the eastern European countries Yugoslavia was special in that its communism was resolutely national and its economy was a compromise between socialist and capitalist. In 1948 it removed itself from the Soviet orbit and maintained its independence in spite of every effort short of invasion to make it return to the fold. Stalin took out his resentment on the other "satellite" nations in severe repressive measures designed to make certain they did not follow the Yugoslav example. After Stalin's death the new Soviet leaders journeyed to Belgrade to offer public apologies for past Soviet policies. From that time on, Yugoslavia's territorial integrity, as the phrase goes, was more assured.

Although the Yugoslavs, following earlier Czech example, developed an animation industry in Zagreb that remained among the most imaginative if not most prolific in the world, its live-action features plodded along the path of socialist realism as doggedly as if still being guided by the Soviets. It wasn't until the late 1960s that there appeared a new generation of feature film makers, including Dušan Makavejev, Aleksander Petrović, Živajin Pavlović, and a cluster of their innovative films (such as *Man Is Not a Bird,* 1965; *I Even Met Happy Gypsies,* 1967; and *When I Was Dead and White,* 1967). The group was labeled the Yugoslav Black Wave for the corrosive, iconoclastic satires they mounted against the communist system. Their films had no heroes; instead they used kaleidoscopic techniques to unmask bureaucratic corruption and hypocrisy.

Dušan Makavejev burst on the scene like some sort of Slavic bombshell. His early works—*Love Affair, or The Case of the Missing Switchboard Operator* (1967), *Innocence Unprotected* (1968), *WR: Mysteries of the Organism* (1971), and *Sweet Movie* (1974)— were seen widely abroad. Makavejev's work makes one think of the most stylistically mixed of Godard's features.

In subject matter *Innocence Unprotected* is quite different from Makavejev's other films; in technique it has aspects in common. An affectionate recall of the first Serbian talkie, made in 1942 during the German occupation, it is subtitled "A New Edition of a Good Old Film." Interspersed with the original are interviews with its surviving creators, who talk about its production, and newsreels of military and political events of that time. *Love Affair, WR,* and *Sweet Movie,* on the other hand, all elaborate on the relationship between sexuality and the social-political restraints and expectations faced by the individual. Wildly funny, bawdy (if not obscene), and irreverent, jumbled, and complex, they are finally impossible to describe, even thematically. Of the three, *Love Affair* is the most coherent, with two central characters and a slender thread of plot spun out in flashes forward as well as back, preceded by a lecture on sex and interrupted by another on murder. *WR* includes an informal television-style "profile" of psychologist Wilhelm Reich, replete with interviews of people who knew him, a fragmented account of two zany sexually preoccupied young women and their encounters with men, satirical political references, phallic jokes about Stalin, and other odds and ends including a demonstration by a markedly strange lady making a cast of a penis. Makavejev encapsulated the film's message in an interview published in *Film Quarterly:* "The main thing in sexual repression or sexual freedom is actually the political content of human personal freedom," he stated.

After this extraordinarily creative period, Makavejev's work began to fall off as he began to work abroad. *Sweet Movie,* made partly in the United States, is a dark mixture of diverse elements, scatology added to sexuality and politics. It threw haymaker punches at both the capitalist and communist mythologies, in about equal proportion, and provoked enraged responses from all sides. *Montenegro* (1981), shot in Sweden, was much more straightforward in narrative form. It can be viewed, in part, as a tract on animal rights in which wearing fur is implicitly deplored and the bestial behavior of human beings is ascribed to their animal nature (Figure 14.10a and b). The film begins with an intertitle that states, "A little girl questioned a monkey in a zoo: 'Why do you live here? Isn't it nicer where you came from?' "

A successor Yugoslavian star director is **Emir Kusturica,** whose first film, *Do You Remember Dolly Bell?* (1981), won a Golden Lion at Venice. His next project, *When Father Was Away on Business* (1985) (Figure 14.11), won the Palme d'Or at Cannes and has been seen widely abroad. It is a Bosnian comic drama set in Sarajevo in 1950. Father isn't really away on business but in a political prison camp during the period following the momentous break with the Soviet Union. He has been accused of "Stalinist tendencies." The film examines the family under the pressures that stem from the nation at a crossroads. The warmth and understated humor of its observation of individuals and society are in a manner reminiscent of the Czechs. And, in fact, Kusturica, and other Yugoslav directors and cinematographers of his generation, attended the FAMU school in Prague.

Kusterica is the formost exponent of what has come to be known as the gypsy genre of films. The gypsies (or Romanys) are found all over eastern Europe and are identified with a distinctive cultural style that is interpreted by these movies in terms of celebratory feasting, passionate love affairs, a streetwise mentality, and a colorful nomadic lifestyle. The protagonists of such stories are frequently worldly young people. Although the films sometimes exoticize and sentimentalize the Romany, they may also view the group's situation as a prototype of the region's political woes. As a universally oppressed ethnic minority, the gypsies provide a means of examining the phenomenon of ethnic hatred, which has inflamed such destructive passions throughout the eastern European world. Of all the European nations, Yugoslavia has taken up this genre most energetically, the foremost cinematic examples being Alexander Petrović's picaresque *I Even Met Happy Gypsies* (1967) and Slobodan Sijan's wildly popular *Who's Singing Over There?* (1980), which chronicles

FIGURE 14.10a and b *Montenegro* ★ Sweden–United Kingdom, 1981, Dušan Makavejev; b. Susan Anspach, Erland Josephson, and John Zacharias.

the adventures of two gypsy musicians during the Second World War. Kusterica's *Time of the Gypsies* (1990) is crafted as a folktale about a homely and unlucky gypsy lad who sets out to steal enough money to marry the girl he desires. Kusturica returned to the topic of the Romany in 1998 with *Black Cat, White Cat,* a high-spirited fantasy about a family of gypsy gangsters, featuring Fellini-esque imagery and earthy humor.

FIGURE 14.11   *When Father Was Away on Business* ★ Yugoslavia, 1985, Emir Kusterica.

The peaceful breakup of Czechoslovakia into two states was preceded by the dissolution of Yugoslavia into separate republics beginning in 1990, which devolved into a bloody civil war among the three main ethnic/religious factions: Serbs, Croats, and Muslims. In this politically charged atmosphere, Kusterica returned to the topic of Yugoslavian history in his 1995 film *Underground,* which spans the period from 1941 to the early 1990s. Despite being honored with the Palme d'Or at the Cannes Film Festival, this production proved controversial and was seen by some as Serbian propaganda. As a result of the criticism he received, Kusterica withdrew from movie making in 1996. However, his retirement proved to be short-lived and he was soon back at work, joining others in the newly constituted nations of his homeland in crafting a cultural agenda that could help to define them afresh.

The Soviet Union and After

In the dominant power of the eastern bloc, trends of reform began in 1985 at the 27th Congress of the Communist Party that eventually would lead to the breaking up of the Soviet Union. At that time Mikhail Gorbachev became First Secretary, and *glasnost* (openness) and *perestroika* (restructuring) became key terms in his program. By 1986, when Gorbachev announced his commitment to "frank debate," films that had been "shelved," going back as far as 1966, were reexamined and many of them released. One of the most shelved of contemporary Soviet film makers, **Elem Klimov,** became one of the major figures involved in bringing revision, reassessment, and new latitude into the cinema. Klimov's films include *Rasputin* (1975, released in the United States in 1986) and *Come and See* (1985, released in the United States in 1987). Following a tense and significant election, Klimov became First Secretary of the Union of Soviet Filmmakers in 1986.

Klimov's wife, **Larisa Shepitko,** who met an untimely death in an automobile accident in 1979, was also rediscovered after *glasnost. The Ascent* (1976), which won the Golden Bear at Berlin, chronicles the fate of a group of Soviets during the Second World War with strong spiritual overtones. Skepitko's next project, *Farewell* (1983, released in the United States in 1987), deals with a Siberian village that is destroyed by a flood and is based on a story by Valentin Rasputin. It was completed by Klimov after her death.

One of the most uniquely talented of contemporary Soviet film makers resumed his career after fifteen years of enforced idleness. **Sergei Paradjanov** is known abroad for his *Shadows of Our Forgotten Ancestors* (1964) and *The Color of Pomegranates* (1969). *Shadows* (Figure 14.12) is an extraordinary and unique epic blend of fact, fiction, and poetry in celebration of peasant life, lore, and mythology in a remote part of the Ukraine. Loose and elliptical in construction, "formalistic" and at the same time sensual, it is a film that would seem to stand quite outside the requirements of a modern socialist state, as did Dovzhenko's

FIGURE 14.12   *Shadows of Our Forgotten Ancestors* ★ Soviet Union, 1964, Sergei Paradjanov; Ivan Nikolaichuk, in tub.

Earth before it. *The Color of Pomegranates* is about Sayat Nova, an eighteenth-century Armenian poet monk who suffers in an alien society. It was shelved after completion and reedited by others, over the film maker's protest, before release in 1973. Paradjanov's subsequent projects were either not accepted for production or not permitted to be completed. In 1974 he was convicted of homosexuality (a criminal offense in the Soviet Union), illegal currency dealings, and "incitement to suicide," and sentenced to six years of hard labor. Although tried as a citizen and not as an artist, considerable suspicion was expressed that his real crime may have been his ebullient and rebellious spirit and the individualistic and iconoclastic nature of his finest and most important films.

By 1983 Paradjanov was out of prison and working on *The Legend of Suram Fortress* (1984). Based on Georgian sources, it apparently contains the sort of folk elements and pagan traditions mixed with Christianity and nationalism, heroism and sacrifice and breathtaking imagery, as did his earlier films. He died of cancer in 1990.

Another contemporary Soviet film maker, to whom Paradjanov's last film, *Ashik Kerib* (1988), was dedicated, managed to escape the dictates of socialist realism and express a strong personal vision through structures and styles more nearly resembling those of contemporary film makers in western Europe. **Andrei Tarkovsky**'s *Ivan's Childhood* (1962), *Andrei Rublev* (1966), and *Solaris* (1972) all won prizes at festivals abroad. *Ivan's Childhood,* with its strong and clear humanist message carrying along its unusual display of technical virtuosity, was extremely popular at home as well. *Andrei Rublev,* however, a more involuted and complex film about a monk icon painter who lived at the turn of the fifteenth century, was held up for several years and then released in a cut version. Evidently it was suspect because of its religious themes, unorthodox view of history, and scenes of brutality. *Solaris,* a science-fiction film, evoked comparisons with Stanley Kubrick's *2001,* although Tarkovsky eschewed spectacular technology and psychedelic fantasy in favor of the philosophical implications of his vision of the future and its effects on human lives. *The Mirror,* released in a very limited way in the Soviet Union in 1974 and not until nearly a decade later in the United States, is autobiographical as well as experimental, mingling dream and reality, childhood memories with an ongoing marriage.

Tarkovsky's next two films were made in Italy. In *Stalker* (1979) he returned to science fiction. It is a grim odyssey of two Russian intellectuals led by the title character into "the Zone," a devastated postapocalyptic wasteland sealed off by the authorities. *Nostalgia* (1983), a brooding account of a journey through Italy by a Russian scholar, was made for European television. Its main theme seems to be the impossibility of transcultural understanding.

In 1984 Tarkovsky sought political asylum in the West. His last film, *The Sacrifice* (1986) (Figure 14.13), was made in Sweden with a mostly Swedish crew, including Sven Nykvist, Bergman's cinematographer. Erland Josephson, from Bergman's repertory company, is the principal actor (as he is in *Nostalgia*). Like Bergman, Tarkovsky tends toward the poetic and the mystical, makes much use of philosophical dialogues, and creates his visual style by relying on prolonged takes with a slowly moving camera. He seems to be trying to transcend the limitations of plot, character, and dialogue to arrive at pure feeling states; images that don't advance narrative meaning but intensify the desperate dark despair are held relentlessly and returned to repeatedly. It is a strange and troubling metaphysical inquiry.

In *The Sacrifice* a woefully unhappy collection of humans on an isolated estate, most of them family members, torture themselves and each other psychologically. A nuclear war

FIGURE 14.13   *The Sacrifice*   ★   Soviet Union, 1986, Andrei Tarkovsky; Allan Edwall and
Erland Josephson, on right.

may break out or may be imagined; it may be countered by religious belief or by supernatural forces, if it ever happened. As the sacrifice promised to God for release from his fear
of dying, the father burns down the house and is taken away by medical attendants. Although
some aspects of the film parallel *Shame* and *The Seventh Seal,* it is slower than Bergman's
films, more attuned to the visual—remarkably so. The film's closing shot, a slow 360-
degree movement around the yard as various characters and vehicles weave in and out of
view, positions the burning house in the background. The first take of this complexly orchestrated tracking shot was spoiled when Nykvist's camera jammed. By that time, the
house had already burned to the ground. But Tarkovsky's loyal crew rebuilt the house so
the shot could be repeated.

   Tarkovsky died in Paris in 1986. His slender body of work may well be the most important and lasting by a Russian film maker since that of the Soviet artists of the 1920s. It
is markedly different from theirs and from the socialist realism that followed, in subject
matter and themes particularly—intensely personal and private rather than public and social. The individual preoccupied Tarkovsky more than the society; the society is seen only
through individuals. So it is not to Eisenstein, Pudovkin, or Dovzhenko that we would compare Tarkovsky; rather, the comparison is to Bergman and other western European auteurs,
and in many respects his creation seems unique.

   But the country from which Tarkovsky emigrated has itself changed more radically
than could have been imagined at the time of his death. Following an attempted coup in
1991 aimed at unseating Gorbachev and reversing the changes he had begun, the Soviet

Union itself has ceased to exist, being replaced by twelve autonomous republics, and the planned economy of communism has been succeeded by attempts toward achieving the market economy of capitalism.

Given the near anarchy that has characterized the political and economic life of the country during the 1990s, it is little short of miraculous that film making has continued in Russia. Although the number of motion pictures produced dropped from three hundred in 1990 to about one-tenth this number by the mid-1990s, that level of production has held steady since then. In the absence of the old state-controlled monolithic film industry, European coproduction arrangements have been sought, film festivals and prizes have been established, and television financing and exhibition have been welcomed. In 1996 a new state funding organization, Roskomkino, was founded. In 1997, Nikita Mikhalkov, the acclaimed director of films such as *Burnt by the Sun* (1994), was elected chair of the Union of Film Makers of the Russian Federation and initiated sweeping reforms in the movie industry, from the building and refurbishing of theaters to taxes on videos and sales to television to subsidize new production. By 2004 Mosfilm Studios with its thirteen sound stages was routinely booked to near capacity, half of its facilities used for television series, half for feature films.

All of this activity produced demonstrable results. Films such as Sergei Bodrov's *Prisoner of the Mountains* (1996) (Figure 14.14) and Andrei Zvagintsev's *The Return* (2003) garnered honors around the world. In 2002 Russian helmer Alexander Sokurov created

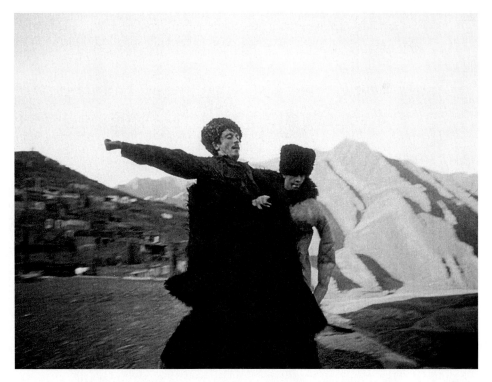

FIGURE 14.14 *Prisoner of the Mountains* ✶ Russia, 1996, Sergei Bodrov; Oleg Men'shikov, on left.

something of an international sensation with *Russian Ark,* a production filmed on location in St. Petersburg's Hermitage Museum. Shot on digital video using a steadycam apparatus, the entire ninety-six-minute movie is composed of a single shot. The camera travels from room to room in the palatial building to observe various activities that mark significant events and personages in Russian history (Figure 14.15). A legion of actors in historical costume participated in this awesome tour de force, reminding the world of the grandeur of Russia in both its past and its present.

Over the past four decades the films of Poland, Hungary, Czechoslovakia, Yugoslavia, and Russia have had intermittent periods in which critical self-examination, doubt, and even despair have appeared. Often the questioning, criticism, and satire seemed remarkably pointed and frank to Westerners whose biases and ignorances may have precluded an understanding of how these nations actually functioned socially and politically. Also, within the Soviet bloc there was an equally surprising amount of experimentation with form and the development of personal styles that include the ambiguous and the obscure. In these societies the French New Wave has affected film makers' creations and audiences' responsiveness.

Beginning in the late 1950s eastern European countries, joining France and Italy, achieved their own versions of a New Wave. Despite prominent differences, one thing common to all of these countries was a new emphasis on personal expression in film with the director as artist. Another was the use of new methods and techniques, defiance of former conventions, and the breaking up of traditional forms. In a general way the most interesting and important films from the countries on the continent, West and East, departed from the usual entertainment "package" as commercially conceived and from earnest Marxist

FIGURE 14.15   *Russian Ark*   ★   Russia, 2002, Alexander Sokurov.

exhortation. Instead they attempted to offer directly the kinds of moral, ethical, and aesthetic sustenance looked for in artworks. It is these qualities in total that roughly characterize the New Wave, or Contemporary Cinema, or Modern Film, as the terms have come to be understood.

Two films made in eastern Europe during the 1990s encapsulate the challenges these countries have been facing and the aesthetic forms in which these challenges may be cast. Milcho Mikhalov's *Before the Rain* (1994) and Sergei Bodrov's *Prisoner of the Mountains* (1996) both deal with religious strife between Christians and Muslims, the former in Macedonia, the latter in the Caucasian Mountains of Russia. Both show families driven to the extreme of slaughtering their own relatives. Both set their brutal tales in barren mountain landscapes that isolate warring factions in a world that offers little in the way of natural sustenance. The vast scale of these majestic backdrops make the characters' acts seem insignificant and unavailing in comparison to the mighty forces that surround them. Despite the fatalistic message conveyed by this harshly drawn *mise-en-scène* and by the action as a whole, both films dwell on romantic attachments formed between a pair of young people on opposing sides of the conflict that seem to offer them a kind of spiritual if not physical salvation. Just as devastation follows from divisiveness and the delineation of differences, the films seem to argue, so does connectedness imply hope for a better world. Such a belief, perhaps, is what sustains the film-making activities of the eastern European nations; for films, too, are a way of forging connections, in this case initiating a larger connection between countries in turmoil and the larger world of which they see themselves as part.

Films of the Period

POLAND

1954
A Generation (Pokolenie) (Andrzej Wajda)

1956
Kanal (Andrzej Wajda)
Man on the Tracks (Czlloiek na torze) (Andrzej Munk)

1958
Ashes and Diamonds (Popiól i diament) (Andrzej Wajda)
House (Dom) (Walerian Borowczyk)

1960
Bad Luck (Zezowta szczéscie) (Andrzej Munk)

1961
Mother Joan of the Angels (Matka Joanna od aniolp) (Jerzy Kawalerowicz)

1962
Knife in the Water (Nóź w wodzie) (Roman Polanski)

1963
Passenger (Pasaźerka) (Andrzej Munk)

1964
Identification Marks: None (Rysopis) (Jerzy Skolimowski)

1965
The Saragossa Manuscript (Rękopis znaleziong w Saragossie) (Wojcieck Has)
Walkover (Walkower) (Jerzy Skolimowski)

1968
Everything for Sale (Wszystko na sprzadaz) (Andrzej Wajda)

1969
The Structure of Crystal (Sturctura krysztalu) (Krzysztof Zanussi)

1970
Landscape After Battle (Krajobruz po bitwie) (Andrzej Wajda)

1973
Illumination (Illuminacja) (Krzysztof Zanussi)

1977
Man of Marble (Czlowisk z marmura) (Andrzej
    Wajda)

1980
The Contract (Kontract) (Krzysztof Zanussi)

1981
Blind Chance (Przpadek) (Krzysztof Kieślowski)
Man of Iron (Czlowisk z żelaza) (Andrzej
    Wajda)

1984
No End (Bez Końca) (Krzysztof Kieślowski)
The Year of the Quiet Sun (Rok spokojnego slonka)
    (Krzysztof Zanussi)

1988
*A Short Film about Killing (Krótki Film o zabi
    janiu)* (Krzysztof Kieślowski)
A Short Film about Love (Krótki Film o milósci)
    (Krzysztof Kieślowski)

1990
Korczak (Andrzej Wajda)
The Silent Touch (Dotknięci) (Krzysztof Zanussi)

1991
*The Double Life of Veronique (Podwójne życie
    Weroniki)* (Krzysztof Kieślowski)
30 Door Key (Ferdydurke) (Jerzy Skolimowski)

1993
Three Colors: Blue (Trzy Kolory: Niebieshy)
    (Krzysztof Kieślowski)

1994
Three Colors: Red (Trzy Kolory: Czerwory)
    (Krzysztof Kieślowski)
Three Colors: White (Trzy Kolory: Bialy)
    (Krzysztof Kieślowski)

1997
Love Stories (Historie milosne) (Jerzy Stuhr)

1999
Pan Tadusz (Andrzej Wajda)
With Fire and Sword (Ogniem i mieczem) (Jerzy
    Hoffman)

2002
The Piano (Pianista) (Roman Polanski)

HUNGARY

1963
Cantata (Miklós Jancsó)

1965
The Round-Up (Szegénylegények) (Miklós Jancsó)

1967
The Red and the White (Csillagosok, katonák)
    (Miklós Jancsó)

1968
The Girl (Eltánozott nap) (Márta Mészáros)

1970
Love (Szerelem) (Károly Makk)

1971
Agnus Dei (Égi bárány) (Miklós Jancsó)

1972
Red Psalm (Még ker a nép) (Miklós Jancsó)

1975
Adoption (Örökbefogadás) (Márta Mészáros)

1976
The Fifth Seal (Ciz Ötödik pecsét) (Zoltán Fábri)

1981
Mephisto (István Szabó)

1982
Prefabricated People (Panelkapscolat) (Béla Tarr)

1984
Diary for My Children (Napló gyermekcimnek)
    (Márta Mészáros)

1987
Diary for My Loves (Napló szerelmeimnek) (Márta Mészáros)

1988
Damnation (Kárhozat) (Béla Tarr)

1990
Diary for My Mother and Father (Napló apámnak, anyámnek) (Márta Mészáros)
My Twentieth Century (Az én xx. századom) (Ildykó Enyedi)

1992
Sweet Emma, Dear Böbe (Édes Emma, drága Böbe) (István Szabó)

1994
Satantango (Béla Tarr)

1999
Sunshine (A Napfény íze) (István Szabó)

2000
Werkmeister Harmonies (Werckmeister harmóniák) (Béla Tarr)

CZECHOSLOVAKIA

1964
Black Peter (Miloš Forman)
Diamonds of the Night (Jan Němec)

1965
Intimate Lighting (Intimitri osvĕteni) (Ivan Passer)
Loves of a Blonde (Lásky jedné plavovlásky) (Miloš Forman)
The Shop on Main Street (Obchod na korze) (Ján Kadár and Elmar Klos)

1966
Closely Watched Trains (Ostre sledované vlaky) (Jiří Menzel)
Daisies (Sedmirkrásky) (Vĕra Chytilová)
Report on the Party and the Guests (Oslavnosti a hostech) (Jan Němec)

1967
The Fireman's Ball (Horí má panenko) (Miloš Forman)

1976
The Apple Game (Ovoce strp, i rakslucj jíme) (Vĕra Chytilová)

1987
Alice (Nĕco z Alenky) (Jan Švankmajer)

1997
Buttoners (Knoflíkári) (Petr Zelenka)
Kolya (Kolja) (Jan Sverák)

1998
Traps (Pasti, pasti, pasticky) (Vĕra Chytilová)

1999
Return of the Idiot (Navrat idiota) (Sasa Gedeon)

2001
Ban from Paradise (Vyhnáni z ráji) (Vĕra Chytilová)

YUGOSLAVIA

1965
Man Is Not a Bird (Čovek nije tica) (Dušan Makavejev)

1967
I Even Met Happy Gypsies (Sakupljaci perja) (Alexandar Petrović)
Love Affair, or the Case of the Missing Switchboard Operator (Ljubavni slučaj ili tragedija službenice P.T.T.) (Dušan Makavejev)

1968
Innocence Unprotected (Nevinost bez zaštite) (Dušan Makavejev)
When I Was Dead and White (Kad budem mrtav i beo) (Živojin Pavlović)

1971
WR: Mysteries of the Organism (W. R.—misterije organizma) (Dušan Makavejev)

1980
Who's Singing Over There? (Ko to tamo peva?)
(Slobodan Sijan)

1981
Do You Remember Dolly Bell (Sječaš li se Dolly Bell) (Emir Kusturica)

1985
When Father Was Away on Business (Otac na službenom putu) (Emir Kusturica)

1990
Time of the Gypsies (Dom za vešanje) (Emir Kusturica)

1994
Before the Rain (Pred dozhdot) (Milcho Manćhevski)
Underground (Bila jednom jedna zemlja) (Emir Kusturica)

1998
Black Cat, White Cat (Crna macka, beli macor) (Emir Kusturica)

RUSSIA
1957
The Cranes Are Flying (Letyat Zhuravli) (Mikhail Kalatozov)

1959
Ballad of a Soldier (Ballada o soldate) (Grigoy Chukrai)

1962
Ivan's Childhood (Ivanovo detstvo) (Andrei Tarkovsky)

1964
Shadows of Our Forgotten Ancestors (Teni zabytykh predkov) (Sergei Paradjanov)

1966
Andrei Rublev (Andrei Tarkovsky)

1969
The Color of Pomegranates (Tsvet granata) (Sergei Paradjanov)

1972
Solaris (Solyaris) (Andrei Tarkovsky)

1974
The Mirror (Zerkalo) (Andrei Tarkovsky)

1976
The Ascent (Voskhozhdenie) (Larisa Shepitko)
A Slave of Love (Raba lubvi) (Nikita Mikhalkov)

1979
Moscow Does Not Believe in Tears (Moskva slezam ne verit) (Vladimir Menshov)

1983
Farewell (Proschchanie) (Larisa Shepitko and Elem Klimov)

1984
The Legend of Suram Fortress (Legenda o Suramskoi kreposti) (Sergei Paradjanov)

1988
Little Vera (Malen'kaya) (Vasili Pichul)

1991
The Inner Circle (Blizhnii krug) (Andron Mikhalkov-Konchalovsky)
Urga, Territory of Love (Urga, Territoriya lyubvi) (Nikita Mikhalkov)

1994
Burnt by the Sun (Utomlennye solntsem) (Nikita Mikhalkov)

1996
Prisoner of the Mountains (Kavkazskii plennik) (Sergei Bodrov)

1997
Mother and Son (mat' i syn) (Alexander Sokurov)

1998
The Land of the Deaf (Strana glukhikh) (Valeri Todorovsky)

1999
The Barber of Siberia (Sibirski tsiriul'nik) (Nikita Mikhalkov)

2001
Taurus (Alexander Sokurov)

2002
Russian Ark (Russkij kovcheg) (Alexander Sokurov)

2003
The Return (Vozvrashcheniye) (Andrei Zvagintsev)

Books on the Period

Beumers, Brigit, ed. *Russia on Reels: The Russian Idea in Post Soviet Cinema.* London and New York: Tauris, 1999.

Burns, B. *World Cinema: Hungary.* Cranbury, NJ: Farleigh Dickinson University Press, 1996.

Falkowska, Janina, and Marek Haltof, eds. *The New Polish Cinema.* London: Flick Books, 2003.

Goulding, Daniel J. *Liberated Cinema: The Yugoslav Experience,* rev. ed. Bloomington: Indiana University Press, 2003.

Iordanova, Dina. *Cinema of the Other Europe: The Industry and Artistry of East Central European Film.* London: Wallflower Press, 2003.

McReynolds, Louise, and Joan Neuberger, eds. *Imitations of Life: Two Centuries of Melodrama in Russia.* Durham, NC: Duke University Press, 2002.

Taylor, Richard, Nancy Wood, Julian Graffy, and Dina Iordanova, eds. *The BFI Companion to Eastern European and Russian Cinema.* London: British Film Institute, 2000.

Woll, Josephine. *Reel Images: Soviet Cinema and the Thaw.* London and New York: Tauris, 2000.

15

India: A People's Cinema

★ ★ ★ ★

1956–

The Indian industry gained Western consideration through a single entry in an international film festival. In 1956 at Cannes, *Pather Panchali* was voted the "best human document." It was the first film of a young director named Satyajit Ray. Appropriately, its screening followed right after a Kurosawa film, *I Live in Fear.* Unlike Kurosawa's works, however, Ray's film was created completely apart from his national film industry and was not representative of it. Whereas *Pather Panchali* recalled the Italian neorealist films in its deep social concern as well as in its use of nonactors and location shooting, the big studios in India were producing a very different kind of product.

The Indian film audience is huge—roughly twelve million a day. To meet this demand, the number of films produced is the largest in the world, currently in the range of eight hundred features a year, more than that of any other nation. The main center of production for the popular Hindi cinema is Bombay (now Mumbai), dubbed "Bollywood" because of its focus on big budget entertainments for the masses. These productions reach an audience of up to 3.6 billion, both at home and in places such as Egypt, South Africa, eastern Europe, and the Figi Islands. (By 2004 fifteen to twenty percent of Bollywood's profits came from overseas.) In contrast to the "all-India" orientation of Bollywood film making, smaller production centers in Calcutta, Madras, and other cities produce films to serve regional populations with movies in the sixteen officially recognized languages as well as in others. These regionally oriented productions sometimes turn into Bollywood-style blockbusters as well. Running times are long—typically three hours—to give as full an evening's entertainment as possible. Exhibition venues in rural areas are often primitive; Indian film producer Ismael Merchant writes, "Villagers gravitate to the makeshift cinemas, sometimes nothing more than wooden structures with a tin roof, to sit on the floor or on benches to be transported to another world."

India remains the only film industry to have developed under colonial rule: The British raj controlled the country until 1947. As a colonialist culture, many of the country's popular entertainments have traditionally been derived from Western models. But indigenous artforms also flourished, encouraged by the political philosophy of "swadeshi" espoused by the liberation forces led by Mohandas Gandhi and Jawaharlal Nehru, which called for support of locally made products over foreign imports. As a result, India is the only third-world country that has a larger audience for its own cinema than for foreign imports—this despite government policies in relation to the film industry that have historically included heavy taxation, burdensome censorship laws, and no subsidies.

In 1913 the nationalist impulse that was to define future Indian film making was made explicit. This was the year of *Raja Harishchandra,* directed by **D. G. Phalke,** often called "the father of Indian film." Phalke, whose writings declare his support of the swadeshi policy, was inspired to make a film about the Indian religious pantheon after viewing a Western religious epic. "Could we, the sons of India, ever be able to see Indian images on the screen?" he later recalled thinking at the time. A huge hit on its release, *Raja Harishchandra* became the first in a long line of Indian films that drew on Indian mythology for their subject matter. Other distinctively Indian genres developed soon afterward, including the devotional (*Sant Tukaram,* V. Shantaram, 1936), the social (*Two Acres of Land,* Bimal Roy, 1953), the epic melodrama (*Mother India,* Mehboob Khan, 1957), and the historical (*Mughal-e-Azam,* K. Arif, 1960).

Sometimes called "masala films" because of their polyglot makeup, popular Indian movies freely mix music, dance, comedy, romance, and family melodrama. All such films include musical numbers (called song sequences or song picturizations), a convention that undoubtedly plays a major role in their ability to reach a linguistically diverse audience across the country. Highly publicized stars, along with lavish sets and costumes, also add to the wide appeal of these productions, as do playback singers, whose distinctive and well-known voices routinely stand in for those of the stars in song sequences. In their history, *Indian Film,* Erik Barnouw and S. Krishnaswamy observe that every film requires "a star, six songs, three dances." Favorite themes include the plight of the rural poor, the position of women, and the caste system.

A representative production is *Awara (The Tramp),* directed by its star, **Raj Kapoor,** in 1951 from a script by the left-wing writer Ahmad Abbas (Figure 15.1). The film's theme about the determining role played by the social environment rather than genetic inheritance in shaping human personality is implicitly critical of the Indian caste system. Kapoor plays Raj, son of Judge Raghunath, who is played by Kapoor's own father, Prithviraj Kapoor. Disowned by the judge, Raj is cast into poverty and becomes a criminal. Later, on trial for murder in his father's courtroom, he is defended by the judge's adopted daughter, Rita, a lawyer, played by popular star Nargis. Raj and Rita fall in love. Ultimately, Judge Raghunath, who has advocated the belief that heredity is more important than environment in shaping character, recants his opinion and accepts his son. Although Raj is condemned to serve a three-year prison sentence for the crimes he has committed, Rita promises to wait for him. Symbolic overtones are created by the judge's name, which recalls the name of the Hindu god who is thought to watch over the Indian caste system.

This socially progressive fable is played out against a lavish background that counters its sombre message. The judge's house, where Rita resides, is like a palace, with vast,

FIGURE 15.1 *Awara* ★ India, 1951, Raj Kapoor; Nargis.

marble-floored rooms and sweeping staircases. Bathed in glowing, romantic lighting, the lovers sing many ballads of longing and fulfilment. An extravagant dream sequence uses expressionist techniques to render Raj's tortured state of mind, evoking visions of heaven and hell in the process. Using gestures and expressions reminiscent of a melodramatic Charlie Chaplin, Kapoor himself exudes a wholesome energy that belies the seriousness of his character's plight. Like many other Indian films, *Awara* resembles a sugar-coated pill, cloaking its message of social reform in a frothy package of engaging spectacle.

The Second World War and the move to independence that soon followed affected the Indian film industry in numerous ways. The economic turmoil of the war led to the breakup of the studios and the rise of independent production (a development that was also to occur in Hollywood). In addition, the new government headed by Nehru commissioned a report recommending more proactive policies to regulate India's film culture. Eventually, a film school was established at Poona and government financing was put in place to encourage what would become an alternative cinema. At the same time a radical grassroots organization, the Indian People's Theater Association (IPTA), sprang up. The IPTA's philosophy of mixing folk art with international avant-garde techniques was applied to film as well as to the stage. Its political platform emphasized rural activism and took the devastating 1943 famine as a rallying point. A number of India's most influential directors were associated with this movement, including Mehboob Khan, Guru Dutt, Mrinal Sen, Ritwik Ghatak, and Shyam Benegal. The first production sponsored by the IPTA, *Children of the Earth* (1946), directed by the group's general secretary, K. A. Abbas, told a tale of a Bengali immigrant family in the city. It was advertised with the IPTA slogan "People's Theater Stars the People."

A transitional figure in the move toward a progressive Indian art cinema was **Guru Dutt,** sometimes called the Douglas Sirk of India because the highly stylized melodramas he produced recall the woman's films Sirk helmed in America during the 1950s. Like Sirk, Dutt, who wrote and acted in his movies as well as directing them, was critical of the social mores of the day, especially the plight of women and the poor, and the colonialist mentality. His heroes are typically artist figures who suffer at the hands of society through no fault of their own. After his autobiographical *Paper Flowers* flopped at the box office in 1959, Dutt refused to take directorial credit for any of his future productions—though he is commonly understood as the creative force behind films such as *King, Queen, and Slave* (1962). The 1957 *Pyaasa* is generally regarded as his crowning achievement.

Dutt's style is romantic and elegiac. *Paper Flowers,* for example, begins and ends with the has-been director hero (played by Dutt) revisiting his old studio at night; the cavernous space, with its vast expanses and ghostly shadows, overwhelms him with longing and regret. Dutt's wife Geeta sings many of the haunting melodies that contribute mightily to the powerful emotions these films call forth.

Dutt's style can be viewed not only as an Indian variation on a Hollywood model of melodramatic excess but also as a uniquely Indian vernacular. In an essay on the conventions of Indian cinema, critic Ravi Vasudevan observed that the Hindu ritual known as *darsana* can be invoked to account for the treatment of gazes in many Indian films. Darsana refers to the way in which devotees are granted permission to look worshipfully at a god (or, by analogy, any other figure of authority) in anticipation of an answering gaze that acknowledges their devotion. In this way, relations of unequal status are affirmed. Cinema's point-of-view editing system, which relies on the looks of characters to motivate cuts, may be employed to symbolize a darsanic relationship. Using *Pyaasa* as an example, Vasudevan points out the way in which the darsanic gaze creates a suspenseful narrative conflict followed by a satisfying resolution. In a crucial scene, the film's prostitute-heroine Gulab (played by Dutt discovery Waheeda Rehmann) gazes raptly at Vijay (Dutt), the man she worships (Figure 15.2a), while he, heedless of her adoration, withholds his answering look (Figure 15.2b). It is only at the end of the film that Vijay is moved to look long and lovingly back at Gulab as the two achieve a meeting of minds and hearts (Figure 15.2c and d). The harmony that is thereby achieved keeps the man at the helm (treating him as a substitute for a god), but includes the woman within its scope as well. This distinctively Indian film grammar positions the man, not the woman, as the object of desire, and the woman, not the man, as the person who gazes. As we will see when we discuss the influential theory about the gaze put forward by British film scholar Laura Mulvey in Chapter 18, in Hollywood the way in which characters look at one another has quite another meaning.

Dutt, along with other members of the IPTA, helped to make the transition to a new way of thinking about Indian film. With these elements in place, the stage was set for a new Indian cinema. Ironically, however, the Indian filmmaker who first broke through to international prominence stood apart from all of these developments. From the outset **Satyajit Ray** was a maverick. A commercial artist by profession, he was one of the founders of the Calcutta Film Society and a passionate student of film. In his free time he saw as many movies as he could and paid particular attention to the work of such American directors as John Ford, William Wyler, Frank Capra, John Huston, and Billy Wilder. He was influenced

FIGURE 15.2a–d   *Pyaasa* ☆ India, 1957, Guru Dutt; a. Waheeda Rehman; b. Guru Dutt; c. Rehman; d. Dutt.

strongly, he has said, by Flaherty's *Nanook of the North,* Jean Renoir's *The Southerner,* and "of course, all the Chaplins."

In 1950 Ray met Renoir, who was in Calcutta shooting *The River.* Renoir encouraged him and permitted him to observe production. Later that year Ray was sent by his advertising agency employers to their headquarters in London for six months. While there he talked with leading British film critics and theorists and attended movies daily. He was especially inspired, he said, by Vittorio de Sica–Cesare Zavattini's *The Bicycle Thief.* The principles of neorealism this film represented shaped Ray's ideas about how movies should be made. "For the truly serious, socially conscious film maker, there can be no prolonged withdrawal into fantasy," he later wrote. "He must face the challenge of contemporary reality, examine the facts, prove them, sift them and select from them the material to be transformed into the stuff of cinema."

On the boat going home he wrote the first draft of the script for *Pather Panchali,* adapted from a popular novel (Figure 15.3). The film was almost an amateur production—in personnel as well as scale. Only two of the cast and only one of the crew of eight—the

FIGURE 15.3   *Pather Panchali*   ★   India, 1955, Satyajit Ray; Karuna Manerji, Uma Das Gupta, and Subir Banerji.

art director—were professionals. The cinematographer was an amateur still photographer. To show him what he wanted, Ray, who had never directed a film before, drew pen-and-ink sketches from the camera's viewpoint. Shot on weekends over a period of almost four years, production was frequently halted for lack of funds. Eventually the money ran out. Ray was about to give up when the West Bengal government agreed to back him in return for ownership of the film.

First of a trilogy (followed by *Aparajito,* 1956, and *The World of Apu,* 1958), *Pather Panchali* (1955) begins the account of a Bengali family of five, which extends from the time the boy Apu is about age twelve until he himself has a son about that age. When social, religious, and economic themes and problems appear, it is within the detailed texture of the family's daily life.

Ray's trilogy is made up solely of diverse incidents; the films have no story in the usual sense. *Pather Panchali* ends when Apu's father, who has been away trying to earn enough money to support the family, returns home. In his absence the aged aunt has died, and more recently and cruelly, his older child, a lovely adolescent girl, has died of pneumonia, caught while playing in the first of the rains. Father, mother, and Apu—their grim and intractable economic situation unresolved—load their few belongings onto an oxcart and depart for Benares. Early in *Aparajito* the father dies, and the remainder of the film, with its sustained note of moving sadness, concerns the gentle and loving tension created by Apu's ambition for an education (which also means Westernization) and his mother's conflicting need for his affection and the traditional ways. *The World of Apu* deals with Apu's early manhood—his life in Calcutta and his marriage—and concludes with his relationship to his young son after his wife dies in childbirth.

With dialogue in Bengali rather than the more widely spoken Hindi, Ray's films were accessible only to a relatively small audience in his homeland. Somewhat like the Italian film makers, he shifted from the poorer to the middle and upper-middle classes of which he was a member and away from material to spiritual and psychological themes. In *Devi* (*The Goddess,* 1960), a deeply religious feudal landlord becomes obsessed with the notion that his daughter-in-law is a goddess. *Kanchanjungha* (1962), his first film in color, *Charulata* (*The Lonely Wife*) (1964), *Days and Nights in the Forest* (1970), and *Home and the World* (1984) are all concerned with complicated and shifting family, marital, and sexual relationships among the well-to-do and well educated. Frequently, like Ozu in Japan, Ray treated the old in a changing India, and the peculiar and fascinating mixture of East and West left as a legacy of the British raj. *The Music Room* (1958), for example, deals with a vanishing feudal culture, the protagonist being the last in a line of landed aristocrats in British India. It contains a fine selection of traditional Indian music. *The Chess Players* (1977) is set amidst nineteenth-century expansion of British colonial power. Ray has also been consistently concerned with the role of females. *Mahanagar* (*The Big City,* 1963), addressing attitudes about women and work and independence from male-dominated households and traditional roles, is one example.

Although Ray stands as a somewhat isolated figure against the panoply of forces that define Indian cinema, his more elite style of film making found further expression in the work of other, more politically grounded, directors. Around 1969–1970 there developed what was called New Indian Cinema, or Parallel Cinema, financed in part by the government's National Film Development Corporation and more recently by the government-sponsored Doordarshan television network. Ritwik Ghatak and Mrinal Sen are considered the movement's founding fathers. Other notable directors associated with New Indian Cinema are Shyam Benegal, Mani Kaul (*Our Daily Bread,* 1969) and Kumar Shahani (*The Wave,* 1984).

Ritwik Ghatak, who died in 1976, directed only eight feature films, but he made a good many documentaries and wrote scripts for others' features. Practically all of his films are about the social stress and turmoil in Bengal after the country's partition. A Marxist activist, his life and work were deeply marked by the partition that divided India from Pakistan in 1947 and drove his family from their home. One of his finest films, *The Cloud-Capped Star* (1960), revisits the personal and social trauma the partition brought about. The film focuses on a group of Bengali refugees living in a shantytown on the edge of Calcutta. Once respectably middle class, they have been reduced to near destitution. Through close observation of the family's relentless exploitation of their eldest daughter Neeta (played by Bengali star Supriya Choudhury) (Figure 15.4), Ghatak mounts a devastating critique of the oppressive nature of family life. In the course of the film Neeta sacrifices everything for her parents and siblings only to find her own life in ruins by the end. Many allusions draw an implicit comparison between Neeta's plight and the myth of the Hindu goddess Durga. Ghatak also embellished the movie's audio track with symbolic allusions, most notably when the sound of a whip is at moments when Neeta's family exploits her in a particularly egregious manner.

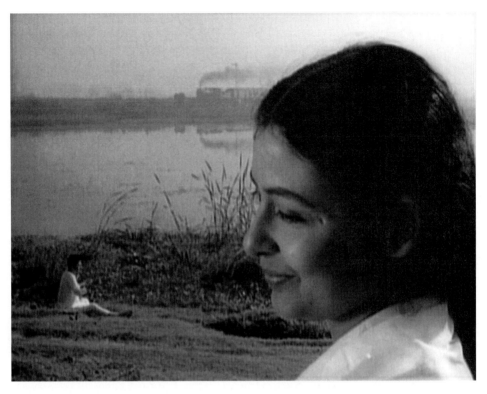

FIGURE 15.4   *The Cloud-Capped Star* ☆ India, 1960, Ritwik Ghatak; Supziya Choudhury.

    Mrinal Sen's features, some twenty-five or more in number, are quite different from those of either Ray or Ghatak, although all three men are Bengalis. Also a Marxist, Sen experimented for a while with form as well as content, in the manner of Frenchman Jean-Luc Godard, in an effort to create a revolutionary cinema. *Bhuvan Shome* (*Mister Shome*, 1969), Sen's biggest success, was the first low-budget feature financed by the Indian government (Figure 15.5). Its title character is a stuffy senior executive of the Indian railways. During a holiday in rural India he is transformed by his experience of country people and country ways, especially those of the cheeky young wife of a lowly railway clerk. It is both funny and lyrical. *In Search of Famine* (1980) is about film makers visiting a rural settlement in order to get the villagers to reenact the terrible famine of 1943 (also the subject of Ray's *Distant Thunder*, 1973). The interaction between the urban film crew and the rural subjects generates friction and ultimately forces the crew to abandon the actual and retreat to the security of the make-believe world of the studio. Biting irony is the prevailing tone. *The Ruins* (1983), less didactic than Sen's work generally, also concerns urban in relation to rural. A city-bred photographer spends a country weekend with some friends at a ruined estate where a lonely girl, forsaken by her betrothed, tries to keep her ailing mother alive with the hope that he will return. *Genesis* (1986), too, is set amidst ruins, but those of a town long deserted, which two men and a woman try but fail to bring back to life.

FIGURE 15.5   *Bhuvan Shome/Mister Shome* ★ India, 1983, Mrinal Sen; Suhasini Mulay.

Among the directors of New Indian Cinema proper, **Shyam Benegal,** who lives and works in Bombay, is perhaps the best known. *Ankur* (*The Seedling,* 1974), his first feature, was a considerable success. It is a strong, tragic protest against the feudal society that has persisted in rural India. *Manthan* (*The Churning,* 1976) was financed by individual contributions from the farmers of Gujarat State and deals with the attempts of an Indian government administrator to set up a milk cooperative in a little village. The official becomes ensnared in caste and hierarchical entanglements that arise to thwart his efforts. The film portrays the difficulties, misunderstandings, and cross-purposes that surely would face an outsider attempting to bring about change in a tradition-bound society. *Bhumika* (*The Role,* 1977), another considerable success, is based on the biography of Hansq Wadkar, a female star of theater and film in the 1940s, dubbed the "Joan Crawford of India." It reveals much about the world of popular entertainment and the constrictions placed on the life of even a successful woman in Indian culture. Benegal's concerns embody both feminism and Marxism; his style is more extravagant and sensuous than that of other directors of the New Indian Cinema.

While the New Indian Cinema was developing, popular film continued to thrive. In recent years Tamil productions have seized the Indian public's imagination. The Tamil star and political figure M. G. Ramachandran had produced a series of wildly popular quasi-historical films in the 1950s and 1960s, some of which were supported by the progressive DMK party and posed new interpretations of Tamil history. In the 1990s Tamil film maker **Mani Rathnam** came to the fore, especially with the controversial *Roja* (1992), which plays provocatively on Hindu–Muslim tensions within the country, and *Bombay* (1995), which focused on the 1993 Hindu–Muslim riots in that city in spectacular and grim detail (Figure 15.6). Influenced by the conventions of music video, Rathnam developed a hip, glamorized style that fearlessly mixed the most disparate elements: playful love stories, over-the-top melodrama, and sharp social criticism. In 1998 he tackled another hot political topic with *Dil Se,* a story about a Hindu journalist who falls in love with a Kashmiri terrorist.

Another recent trend is the film-making activity of Indians living abroad. Notable among this group are two women directors: Mira Nair and Deepa Mehta. **Mira Nair** enjoyed great international success with the 1988 *Salaam Bombay!,* which used actual slum children to portray the grim lives of many of India's orphans and castoffs. During most of the 1990s Nair worked in the United States on productions with ethnic themes, such as *Mississippi Masala* (1991), starring Denzel Washington and Sarita Choudbury. In 2001 she returned to her native land to make the colorful and exuberant *Monsoon Wedding,* which won the Golden Lion at the Venice Film Festival that year (Figure 15.7). **Deepa Mehta,** based in Toronto, Canada, has also made controversial productions about India. Her 1996 *Fire,* about a love affair between two women, mounted a scathing critique of the treatment of women in traditional Indian households (Figure 15.8). The film created a stir in India because of its implicit comparison of the lesbian couple with revered goddesses. Mehta followed up this *success de scandale* in 1998 with *Earth,* a compelling tale of a young girl in Lahore caught up in the religious and cultural strife that accompanied the India–Pakistan partition.

The arc of Indian film history as a whole suggests a growing tendency toward Balkanization. Ray and the New Indian Cinema movement have split popular and elite audiences, and regional and diasporic film-making traditions have appealed to disparate linguistic,

FIGURE 15.6 *Bombay* ★ India, 1995, Mani Rathnam; Arvind Swamy and Manisha Koirala.

FIGURE 15.7   *Monsoon Wedding* ★ India, 2001, Mira Nair.

FIGURE 15.8   *Fire* ★ India, 1996, Deepa Mehta; Nandita Das.

religious, and cultural traditions. But India is a country of unity as well as diversity. The Indian public's fascination with the songs, dances, stars, stories, and spectacle of its cinema transcends regional boundaries, creating bonds among Indian communities both at home and abroad as well as reaching out to audiences in other nations with a message of progress and good feeling in the face of adversity.

Films of the Period

1951
Awara (Raj Kapoor)

1952
Nagarit (Ritwik Ghatak)

1955
Pather Panchali (Satyajit Ray)

1956
Aparajito (Satyajit Ray)

1957
Mother India (Mehboob Khan)
Pyaasa (Guru Dutt)

1958
The Music Room (Jalsaghar) (Satyajit Ray)
Pathetic Fallacy (Ajantrik) (Ritwik Ghatak)
The World of Apu (Apu Sansar) (Satyajit Ray)

1959
Paper Flowers (Kaghaz ke Phool) (Guru Dutt)

1960
The Cloud-Capped Star (Megh Dhaka Tara) (Ritwik Ghatak)
The Goddess (Devi) (Satyajit Ray)

1962
King, Queen, and Slave (Sahib bibi aur Ghulam) (Guru Dutt)

1964
The Lonely Wife (Charulata) (Satyajit Ray)

1969
Mister Shome (Bhuvan Shome) (Mrinal Sen)

1970
Daily Bread (Uski Roti) (Mani Kaul)
Days and Nights in the Forest (Aranyer Din Ratri) (Satyajit Ray)

1973
Distant Thunder (Ashani Sanket) (Satyajit Ray)

1976
The Churning (Manthan) (Shyam Benegal)

1977
The Chess Players (Shatranj Ke Khiladi) (Satyajit Ray)
The Role (Bhumika) (Shyam Benegal)

1979
And Quiet Rolls the Dawn (Ekdin pratidin) (Mrinal Sen)

1980
In Search of Famine (Aakaler Sandhaney) (Mrinal Sen)

1983
The Ruins (Khandahar) (Mrinal Sen)

1984
Home and the World (Ghare-Baire) (Satyajit Ray)
The Wave (Tarang) (Kumar Shahani)

1986
Genesis (Mrinal Sen)
Trikal (Shyam Benegal)

1988
Salaam Bombay! (Mira Nair)

1991
Agantuk (Satyajit Ray)

1992
Roja (Mani Rathnam)

1994
The Bandit Queen (Shakhar Kapur)

1995
Bombay (Mani Rathnam)
The Brave Heart Will Take the Bride (Dilwale Dulhaniya le jayenge) (Aditya Chopra)

1996
Fire (Deepa Mahta)

1998
Dil Se (Mani Rathnam)
Earth (Deepa Mehta)

2001
Lagaan (Ashutosh Gowriker)
Monsoon Wedding (Mira Nair)

2002
Devdas (Sanjay Leela Bhansali)

Books on the Period

Borooah, Vidya. *Pather Panchali*. London: BFI Publishing, 2003

Chatterjee, Gayatri. *Mother India*. London: BFI Publishing, 2002.

Chowdry, Prem. *Colonial India and the Making of Empire Cinema: Image, Ideology and Identity*. Manchester, UK: Manchester University Press, 2000.

Cooper, Darius. *The Cinema of Satyajit Ray: Between Tradition and Modernity*. New York: Cambridge University Press, 2000.

Desai, Jigna. *Beyond Bollywood: The Cultural Politics of South Asian Diasporic Film*. New York: Routledge, 2004.

Dwyer, Rachel, and Divia Patel. *Cinema India: The Visual Culture of Hindi Film*. New Brunswick, NJ: Rutgers University Press, 2003.

Ganti, Tejaswini. *Bollywood: A Guidebook to Popular Hindi Cinema*. New York: Routledge, 2004.

Gopalan, Lalitha. *Cinema of Interruptions: Action Genres in Contemporary Indian Cinema*. London: British Film Institute, 2002.

Kabir, Nasreen Munni. *Talking Films: Conversations on Hindi Cinema with Javed Akhtar*. New York: Oxford University Press, 2000.

Mankekar, Purnima. *Screening Culture, Viewing Politics: An Ethnography of Television, Womanhood, and Nation in Postcolonial India*. Durham, NC: Duke University Press, 1999.

Mishra, Vijay. *Bollywood Cinema: Temples of Desire*. New York: Routledge, 2002.

Rajadhyaksha, Ashish, and Paul Willemen, eds. *Encyclopedia of Indian Cinema*, 2nd ed. Bloomington: Indiana University Press, 1999.

Vasudevan, Ravi S., ed. *Making Meaning in Indian Cinema*. New York: Oxford University Press, 2000.

Virdi, Jyotika. *The Cinematic Imagination: Indian Popular Films as Social History*. New Brunswick, NJ: Rutgers University Press, 2003.

16

Modernism and Metaphor: Italy

1960–

A new kind of Italian cinema emerged at the Venice International Film Festival in 1960. The films were by experienced directors whose landmark works of that year were set within careers that extended back into immediate postwar neorealism. The films also pointed ahead to the subsequent development of their directors and to a younger generation that would quickly grow up around them. The films were *Rocco and His Brothers, La Dolce Vita,* and *L'Avventura;* their directors were, respectively, Luchino Visconti, Federico Fellini, and Michelangelo Antonioni.

Emergence of a New Style: Three Directors of the 1960s

The Italian film makers were reacting against classical Hollywood narrative with a basic orientation that might be called modernist. Visconti was the exception; *Rocco and His Brothers* looked back to neorealism, although, like the bulk of Visconti's work, it departed from accepted neorealist tenets in its melodramatic emotionality and its heightening of character and incident. *La Dolce Vita* and *L'Avventura,* on the other hand, contained much identifiable as new in both subject and form.

The films had an existentialist base, derived from the novels of Cesare Pavese, whom Antonioni much admired, as well as the writings of Sartre and Camus: the sense that life was merely the sum of actions lived, the emphasis on alienation and the failure of communication. There was also a similarity with Ingmar Bergman, acknowledged by both Antonioni and Fellini, in picturing a world in which divine faith has been lost and human love seems unattainable.

The narrative structure of the new Italian films was loose. Both *L'Avventura* and *La Dolce Vita* are episodic, rather than tightly woven, and picaresque. The first is organized around a journey and search for a missing person; the second centers on a sort of spiritual quest for values amidst various physical settings and social groups in and near contemporary Rome. Much of Fellini's work gives us the sense of being on the road; *La Strada* (1954) is the extreme case, the emphasis acknowledged in the title. Antonioni's films, too, set people in motion through countrysides and across cities. He is resolutely narrative rather than dramatic, in a low key of slight action and sparse, inconclusive dialogue. Of all film makers perhaps he is closest to certain tendencies in the modern novel in his attempts to deal with the interior lives of his characters. Because little is accidental in an Antonioni film, significance can be attached to a copy of F. Scott Fitzgerald's *Tender Is the Night* lying open on a footstool in *La Notte* (1961). The characters and themes of his "trilogy" (*L'Avventura, La Notte, The Eclipse,* 1962) suggest Fitzgerald. Perhaps he is closer still to the French *nouveau roman* and a novel like Alain Robbe-Grillet's *Jalousie* in his efforts to convey feeling states through presentation of the particularities of physical surroundings. *The Eclipse* ends with a seven-minute montage of images devoid of people: Places and objects that had appeared earlier were stripped of anthropomorphic meaning.

Unlike the French film makers of the New Wave (dealt with in Chapter 19), new Italian film makers as a whole have shown little interest in manipulating time and space in extra-real, purely filmic ways. Fellini, of course, does make use of fantasy (in *8½,* 1963, and *Juliet of the Spirits,* 1965, for example), in which he plays with the physical laws of the universe as well as with subjective and hallucinatory emotional states, but he clearly sets the imagined and remembered apart from the ongoing present reality. In *La Dolce Vita* and elsewhere, in his approach to the "real world," time and space are dealt with in a perfectly straightforward manner—that is, within the conventions generally employed in realistic films. Antonioni, on the other hand, gets even closer than the conventional to the felt passage of time and experienced movement across space. After seeing Antonioni's long-held shots, with slow panning and trucking, in *L'Avventura,* the filmgoer could make out a complete itinerary, with a journal and a map. Fantasy scenes occur only rarely in Antonioni's work—for example, in *Zabriskie Point* (1969), in the ghostly desert love-in, and in the conclusion, in which the heroine imagines the destruction of her boss's modern mansion.

Fellini's films can be playful, but his fun and games are more likely to be drawn from the circus and music hall than from the characteristics of the film medium or the work of other film makers. Antonioni and Visconti, by contrast, are notably unplayful in every respect, though the former in later work undertaken abroad—*Blow-Up* (Britain, 1966), *Zabriskie Point* (United States), and *The Passenger* (Italy/United States, 1975, shot in Algeria, Spain, England, and Germany)—departed sharply from the austerity of his Italian films. *Blow-Up* offers a rich aesthetic, even ontological commentary on the very nature of the photographic image (upon which motion as well as still pictures depend) and its relationship to reality. *The Passenger* so emphasizes the shifting frame area and perspective of a moving camera that it too forces the viewer to consider the cinematic process that adds to the cryptic nature of the events observed.

What the new Italian cinema was moving away from and toward was consolidated at the Venice Festival of 1960. In an Italy that had recovered with astonishing rapidity from the social-political-economic upheaval and aftermath of World War II, the concerns were with the beliefs one might live by now that life itself and the living of it were more assured and comfortable. One indication of the change was that the new Italian film makers turned their attention from the lower to the upper classes. With their capacity to spend life more or less as they chose, the wealthy made most clearly evident the moral vacuum, the angst, the idle pursuit of meaningless pleasures that had accompanied the "economic miracle." In Italy of the 1960s, gone or seriously eroded were, on the one hand, the support of traditional Catholic morality and faith in God and His church, and on the other, the solidarity and militancy of the Left that had infused Italian society and political life in the immediate postwar years. Whatever the differences among their films, Visconti, Fellini, and Antonioni established a newly prominent moral, even spiritual, concern, and redirected attention to individual psyches, rather than collective conditions, in a contemporary Italy.

In *Rocco and His Brothers* **Luchino Visconti** in a sense returned to his southern Italians of *La Terra Trema,* but now they are immigrants in Milan (Figure 16.1). Although social and economic forces are shown as contributing to the destruction of the family, the drama grows out of the personal conflicts and psychological flaws of the characters. Subsequently Visconti used various sorts of historical and literary materials—initiated in *Senso* (1954) and *White Nights* (1957) and continued in *The Leopard* (1963) (Figure 16.2), *Sandra* (1965), *The Stranger* (1967), *The Damned* (1969), *Death in Venice* (1971), and *Ludwig* (1972). As a nobleman whose distinguished family had figured prominently for centuries in Italian history, Visconti had the deep concern for tradition (at odds with his Marxism) and the cultivated taste you would expect. His penultimate film before his death

FIGURE 16.1 *Rocco and His Brothers* ★ Italy, 1960, Luchino Visconti; Alain Delon, center, white T-shirt.

FIGURE 16.2   *The Leopard* ☆ Italy, 1963, Luchino Visconti; Claudia Cardinale, Burt Lancaster, and Alain Delon.

in 1976, *Conversation Piece,* offers an elegiac commentary on an aristocratic intellectual and art lover forced into uneasy but fascinated contact with the strident exigencies and vulgarities of modern political and social reality. We can imagine that the protagonist (played by Burt Lancaster, who also had played the prince in *The Leopard*) must have been seen by Visconti as some kind of equivalent to himself.

The Visconti who evolved out of neorealism traveled as far from it in style and subjects as could be imagined. If Marxism and the scenographic baroque combined in his earlier films, the creation of lush imagery and re-creation and examination of various forms of decadence, usually aristocratic, seem to carry the main weight in the total body of his work. An interest in homosexual motifs, overt or implied, also marks his *oeuvre.* His lyrical tracking and **crane shots** were most often orchestrated by his longtime collaborator, master cinematographer Giuseppe Rotunno. A film maker of international scope as well as stature, Visconti can be thought of as Italian primarily because of the "operatic" qualities of his films.

Federico Fellini had been the scriptwriter on *Open City, Paisan,* and *Europe 51* (for Rossellini), *Without Pity* and *Mill on the Po* (for Alberto Lattuada), and *In the Name of the Law* (for Pietro Germi), among other noteworthy neorealist films. The first works he directed as well as wrote—*Variety Lights* (1951, with Lattuada), *The White Sheik* (1952), and especially the autobiographical *I Vitelloni* (1953)—fell clearly within the neorealist tradition, even if they had already begun to reflect Fellini's predilection for the popular arts and his own personal experiences as source material. The enormously successful *La Strada*

(1954) represented a turning point. Although set amidst the poverty and drabness of small-town rural Italy, its protagonists are vagabonds (a traveling strong man and his female assistant) rather than workers or peasants. Fellini was onto new themes quite outside the persistently materialistic view of the earlier neorealism. What we care about in *La Strada* is not that times are hard and social institutions culpable, but that Zampanò fails to learn to receive the warmth and comfort of Gelsomina's love.

Fellini's films, more obviously Italian in attitude and subject than Visconti's, departed more gradually from the accepted limitations of neorealism. What attracted him, instead of the historical and literary, was the subjective and fantastic. The only films of his that have literary-historical bases are *Fellini Satyricon* (1969) and *Fellini's Casanova* (1976). In these, as their titles imply, Petronius's ancient Rome and Casanova's eighteenth-century Europe are converted into the director's fantasies of debauchery and sexuality, and into extravaganza. Fellini has remarked of his *Satyricon* that it may be even more autobiographical than his much more obviously autobiographical *8½* (1963). Even the two filmed essays, *The Clowns* (1970) and *Fellini's Roma* (1972), keep the film maker's own interests, experiences, tastes, and, yes, fantasies at their center: It is *his* fascination with clowns from young boyhood on, *his* Rome. *Amarcord* (1973) is a sort of compendium of his recollections filtered through the exaggeration and imagination of adolescent perception. *City of Women* (1980) brought together and made quite explicit (as dreams) the sexual fears and desires that appear throughout his work.

From the beginning of Fellini's directorial career the autobiographical elements are present in either foreground or background, and usually both. *Variety Lights* deals with the music-hall milieu that he had experienced firsthand. *The White Sheik* satirizes the comic book industry, and Fellini had been a cartoonist. *La Strada* is again about touring entertainers. *Il Bidone* (1955), although perhaps not drawn so directly from experience, contains many of the recurring themes and images, especially the religious ones. *The Nights of Cabiria* (1957) portrays the life of Roman prostitutes as Fellini had come to understand it. A special aspect of Fellini's "personalizing" of his work is that his wife, Giulietta Masina, played in all but one of those early films, as well as in many of the later ones.

Up through *Nights of Cabiria,* however, Fellini maintained that he was still working within the neorealist tradition, that he had simply shifted his concentration from external to internal reality. Certainly his films have much the look of the earlier neorealism. If shot more carefully and intimately, with emphasis on composition and the symbolic reverberations of the images, they are still objective in point of view. *I Vitelloni* is especially remarkable in the feeling it gives that the camera just happened to be there to capture bits of lives as they are being lived. Also, those early films make significant use of actual locations and nonactors and are set among the lower classes, the outcasts and dispossessed. But the poverty that concerned Fellini most was the impoverishment of the spirit. In his work, as in the original neorealist films, there are things to be sad about and no solutions are outlined; however, the hope that is offered for the human condition lies not in working-class solidarity but in the joy and love, in an almost religious sense, of which the individual soul is capable. The ending of *Nights of Cabiria,* with the little prostitute picking herself up after a near drowning and walking down a lane encircled by playing children, is very different in its implications from that of *The Bicycle Thief,* with father and son walking hand in hand off into the crowd, however similar the action. Both attest to human resiliency, but Antonio and his son, though comforted by their love for each other, merge into the masses to face another jobless day; Cabiria, through the children, recovers her own optimism and sense of self-worth.

With *La Dolce Vita* (Figure 16.3), Fellini took a long step farther away from neo-realism. It is concerned with the effete idle rich of Rome and the sensational press that reports their doings to a voracious public. The journalist-protagonist (played by Marcello Mastroianni, who would become "Fellini" in *8½*) is in search of meaning in life and values to live by. His passage through the sort of café society life well known to Fellini is like a descent into Dante's *Inferno*. The various pursuits to which he might devote himself—wife and family, business success, sexual excitement, religious fervour, philosophical contemplation—are successively shown to be corrupting or insufficient to support meaningful existence. By inference we learn that God is absent from this world. (The pointedly ironic opening scene of a gilded statue of Christ being hauled by helicopter over the rooftops of modern Rome, and the sequence of a highly publicized fake miracle flail at the hollow and superstitious religion subscribed to by the masses and tacitly approved by the Church.) Although it deals with the upper classes and matters of the spirit, *La Dolce Vita* is still in a completely realistic style. It is merely that the locations now include *palazzi* and the non-actors are actual members of Roman high society.

It wasn't until "The Temptation of Dr. Antonio" episode for *Boccacio 70* (1962) that Fellini turned to fantasy—one of his own, more than likely. Not until *8½* (Figure 16.4) did

FIGURE 16.3 *La Dolce Vita* ★ Italy, 1960, Federico Fellini.

FIGURE 16.4 *8½* ★ Italy, 1963, Federico Fellini; Marcello Mastrionni, center, arm outstretched.

he combine the autobiographical and the extravagant personal phantasmagoria that would depart from neorealism entirely and mark the remainder of his work. Certainly his most complex film, *8½* may also be his finest. It is a witty and revealing account of a director's harried life and the difficulties he has in conceiving his next film. (That was this film, hence the title. Fellini had directed eight films up to that point.) Just to make certain there would be no mistake, Mastroianni wore a wide-brimmed western hat like the one Fellini habitually wore on the set.

Fellini died in 1993. In his last films he moved away from the autobiographical, with indifferent results. *And the Ship Sails On* (1983), a slight tale unfolding during an Adriatic cruise in 1914, parodies the conventions of early cinema and the inflated emotions of the operatic world. In *Ginger & Fred* (1986) the object of satire is television. A 1930s dance team (played by Masina and Mastroianni, whose dancing is scarcely up to that of their namesakes, of course) are reunited for a superproduction variety show. *Frederico Fellini's Interview* (1987) returned more directly to his own past: to his early days at Cinecittà studios, in fact. It includes an homage to *La Dolce Vita*—Fellini coming full circle, you might say.

Michelangelo Antonioni served his apprenticeship as a critic and scriptwriter, including work on films in the neorealist tradition, such as Giuseppe de Santis's *Tragic Hunt* and Fellini's *White Sheik*. He also directed a number of documentary shorts. But his features, aside from *Il Grido* (1957), which is set amidst working-class surroundings in the Po Valley, treat personal values and interpersonal relationships of the middle and upper classes.

In extreme contrast to Fellini's ebullience is Antonioni's austerity. Although *La Dolce Vita* and *L'Avventura* deal with the same social strata (and both are organized around protagonists on the fringes rather than part of the aristocracy) and contain the same themes (loss of meaning and values replaced by promiscuity and debauchery), these two films and the subsequent work of their respective makers could scarcely be more different from each other. Whereas Fellini's films are informed with a Catholic humanist view of the world (evidently deep-rooted if informal and anticlerical), Antonioni's view is that of a postreligious Marxist and existentialist intellectual. While Fellini exposes the shoddiness of the moral values offered by "the sweet life," at the same time he is clucking moralistically he seems to be enjoying the naughtiness and the glamor.

Antonioni offers no such titillation or spectacle. In *L'Avventura* and his Italian films that follow it—*La Notte* (1961), *The Eclipse* (1962), *The Red Desert* (1964), *Identification of a Woman* (1982), and *Beyond the Clouds* (1995)—he dissected the values he saw operative in upper-class modern Italy with the disinterested precision and functional grace of a skilled surgeon, or perhaps of a weary but alert coroner conducting a postmortem. The "sweet life" in Antonioni's portrayal of it seems closer to death in that the souls have left the bodies. Not only is meaning lacking, but so is feeling, except for the instinctual sexual twitching as bodies refuse to acknowledge what minds know. Eroticism is prominent in the films of Antonioni, as it is in those of Fellini; Antonioni has described it as "a dominating factor in our civilization." The orgy at the end of *La Dolce Vita* has some prurient appeal (the striptease and the horsey-back ride on the bovine blonde actress), the sexual interludes in *L'Avventura* leave us cold and sad: the early scene with Anna in Sandro's apartment, Sandro with Claudia outside the deserted town and later in the hotel room after his encounter with the young architect, and Sandro with the high-class prostitute in the early morning. Never has "sin" looked less inviting. The sensuality, pleasure, guilt, and remorse felt by Fellini's characters are replaced by pervasive ennui and irritability, and a sense of the inability of any person to make contact with another even in the most intimate moments. Sex in Antonioni's world may stem from a desire to communicate, but it frequently takes the form of aggression or tired surrender to habit. Among his characters a life in which the sexual act has meaning or even offers enjoyment seems unavailable and perhaps unimaginable.

The extraordinary visual surface of *L'Avventura,* and of Antonioni's succeeding work, seems less radical now than it did when it first appeared precisely because it has been incorporated into the language of film as one of the prominent styles. Growing out of Antonioni's artistic intentions and statements, of course, it also takes peculiar advantage of the attributes of the wide screen, seems almost to require it. The camera is placed at a medium distance more often than close in, frequently moving slowly; the shots are permitted to extend uninterrupted by cutting. Thus each image is more complex, containing more information than it would in a style in which a smaller area is framed, and the shots are briefer in duration. In this respect he harks back to Murnau or Dovzhenko rather than Eisenstein. In Antonioni's work we must regard his images at length; he forces our full attention by continuing the shot after others would cut away.

Antonioni offers us a view in certain respects closer to life than is usual. He is an artist of superb control, which extends into and balances every aspect of his films. His method does not include the spontaneity and improvisation of Fellini, nor does it permit the rough edges that Visconti allows to go uncorrected in his impatience to outline a grand plan. Consider, for example, the much-noted island sequence in *L'Avventura*. In it the characters are continually being commented upon, linked, and separated by their positions in relation to each other and within the frame: Their movements and the camera's are choreographed with equal care. The growing awareness and desire of Sandro and Claudia for each other is initially signaled through such means. For instance, one shot begins with the camera looking down on Sandro (Figure 16.5a). Then it tilts up and, on another plane above him, frames Claudia in the distance as she walks toward the camera (and Sandro's position) (Figure 16.5b). In another shot, there is a slight, slow pan from left to right with Claudia in the background (Figure 16.5c). As the shot proceeds, Sandro enters frame left, midforeground (Figure 16.5d). Then there is the *pas de deux* in successive shots when Claudia is trying to avoid Sandro and he, somewhat unconsciously and helplessly, tries to attach himself to her. Sometimes the camera even becomes like a member of the group as it moves ahead of the actors until they catch up with it and walk into frame again.

But with Antonioni, that kind of visual calculation—the framing and movement of actors and camera, the settings (barren rocky island, eerie deserted town), the way the light falls (the cold gray of early morning in the halls of the palatial hotel)—is everywhere designed to enrich narrative. A director like Eisenstein, who planned and executed his films with equal attention to detail, for all of his visual and kinetic brilliance, was saying simple things. The complexity in his films resides almost entirely in their visual artistry. Antonioni, on the other hand, has provided the sorts of ambiguity considered proper to modernist art.

FIGURE 16.5a–d *L'Avventura* ★ Italy, 1960, Michelangelo Antonioni; Gabriele Ferzetti and Monica Vitti.

It is his kind of imagery and storytelling, rather than the more selective and directive method of Eisenstein, that has come to characterize the best of modern cinema and to represent a profound break with what had gone before.

Neo-Neorealism: Three Directors of the 1960s and 1970s

Following Visconti, Fellini, and Antonioni were a cluster of other talented Italian film makers whose careers came to fruition during the 1960s and 1970s and who, rather than paralleling the concerns of their celebrated contemporaries, returned to some of the earlier neorealist impulses. One had accumulated extensive documentary experience before turning to fiction; another began his film career as assistant director on a neorealist feature; and the third was committed to a Marxist philosophy that prompted him to follow a neorealist path.

    Ermanno Olmi's first features contain socially significant themes, were shot on location, and use nonactors as in the earlier tradition. But instead of unemployment and poverty, he deals with jobs that offer little satisfaction and the difficulties of achieving fulfilling lives and relationships within the conformist demands of an industrialized society. What Olmi provides is a subtle and absorbing attention to the individual among the working classes. *Il Posto* (1961) is about a teenage boy from a small village on his first job as messenger for a large firm in Milan (Figure 16.6). The tenderness and gentle humor with which

FIGURE 16.6 *Il Posto* ★ Italy, 1961, Ermanno Olmi; Sandro Panzeri, second from right.

the director regards the boy's tentative relationship with a girl, his loneliness at a dreary office party, and his feelings when he first sits at a clerk's desk are uniquely Olmi's own.

Francesco Rosi, little known in the United States, is much admired in Italy and in Europe generally. His first considerable achievement was *Salvatore Giuliano* (1961), shot entirely on location in Sicily with an almost exclusively nonprofessional cast. It concerns a Mafia leader whose murder becomes the occasion for tracing political machinations in Sicily. The enigma of power, the pervasiveness of political influence, and the factual source remain characteristic of Rosi's finest work. Of the neo-neorealist directors, perhaps it is Rosi who has made most fully manifest the ideology implicit in the original movement.

Piero Paolo Pasolini—a novelist, poet, linguist, and film theorist before he directed his first feature, *Accattone!* in 1961—consistently dealt with the "subproletariat"—beggars and outcasts. Even *The Gospel According to St. Matthew* (1964), his best-known film, conforms to that generalization. In it Christ is portrayed as a revolutionary orator-leader from the masses, of a sort common in the history of the Middle-Eastern peoples (Figure 16.7). Shot as if it were reportage rather than re-creation, handheld camera and nonactors give the biblical story a feeling of contemporary actuality and urgency. *The Hawks and the Sparrows* (1966), an allegorical comedy, reveals and examines the interdependency between Christianity and Marxism, between religion, ideology, and existence. *Teorema* (1968) and *Pigpen* (1969) include strange mythic evocations of transcendental states, perverse sexuality, and cannibalism in their attacks on capitalist society. Pasolini's ability as a writer and translator led him to attempt new interpretations of classic literary works. Following *Oedipus Rex*

FIGURE 16.7 *The Gospel According to St. Matthew* ☆ Italy, 1964, Piero Paolo Pasolini.

(1967) were *Medea* (1970), *The Decameron* (1971), *The Canterbury Tales* (1972), and *The Arabian Nights* (1974). His last film, *Salò—The 120 Days of Sodom,* suggested by a work of the Marquis de Sade and full of violence, was completed just before his own violent death in 1975. Brilliant and multitalented, at the same time idiosyncratic and unpredictable, Pasolini occupied a position of leadership among the new Italians.

Finally among the neorealist-inspired films of the newer Italian film makers especially popular in the United States have been those by the **Taviani brothers,** Paolo and Vittorio. Though *St. Michael Had a Rooster,* made in 1971, is considered by some to be their most fully realized work, they first became known in the United States chiefly for *Padre Padrone* (1977), an adaptation of a best-selling account of the progress of an ignorant Sardinian from shepherd to university professor. *The Night of the Shooting Stars* (1982), shot in their native Tuscany, was based on their own experiences as young boys and on oral accounts of fellow Tuscans (Figure 16.8). It concerns a group of villagers who in 1944 left their town in defiance of the retreating Germans and resident fascists to search for the advancing Americans.

Industry Travails

Following the extraordinary flowering of Italian film from 1945 through the 1960s, the end of the century brought hard times to the industry. As in all of the Western world, the late

FIGURE 16.8   *The Night of the Shooting Stars* ★ Italy, 1982, Paolo and Vittorio Taviani.

1960s was a time of political turbulence. In Europe, especially, Marxist readings of class warfare were taken up with renewed passion, especially by young people. Most movie industry workers and students then enrolled in Italian film schools were deeply affected by these developments. In 1968 there were widespread protests and turmoil in the institutions devoted to Italian cinema, including the Venice Film Festival, which was canceled for political reasons. With the 1970s, overt political activity largely ceased, although Italy saw a series of political assassinations mounted by terrorist groups beginning in 1972.

The film industry suffered during these years and has never managed to regain its vigor. Despite continued help from the government and additional sponsorship from television, production has fallen off: In 1965 Italy produced three hundred films; by 1999 the number had dropped to one hundred. Many of these films failed to find distributors; audiences for those that were released were typically siphoned off in short order by Hollywood blockbusters. Some industry analysts blamed the crisis on a lack of strong, hands-on producers, such as the late Franco Cristaldi, who could reign in the excesses of headstrong directors. Cristaldi helped shape many of the legendary productions of an earlier era, such as Germi's 1961 *Divorce, Italian Style,* Rosi's 1961 *Salvatore Giuliano,* Visconti's *Sandra,* and Fellini's *Amarcord.* He was credited with much of the international success enjoyed by Giuseppe Tornatore's 1988 *Cinema Paradiso,* cutting forty-seven minutes from the original version; the resulting version went on to win an Academy Award as best foreign film. Italy has no new generation of producers of this caliber. As the Italian critic Otello Angeli observed as early as 1979, "The rigidity of today's film market has resulted in the absorption of the figure of the producer and the transformation of his role into a managerial and bureaucratic function." In the late 1990s American independent distributor Miramax and its owners Bob and Harvey Weinstein stepped into the void. The Weinsteins ordered deep cuts in Roberto Benigni's 1997 *Life Is Beautiful,* enabling it, too, to garner an Oscar. Despite such rescue efforts by producers and distributors, however, Italian films were entirely shut out of the competition at Cannes in 2000, causing much consternation in the industry. A few film makers have continued to produce valuable work, however, most notably Bernardo Bertolucci, one of the preeminent directors now active anywhere in the world.

The 1970s and Beyond: A Metaphoric Cinema

Again, during the 1970s Roberto Rossellini showed the way for a younger generation. In the 1960s and 1970s he had shifted his own attention to what he called "informational" films made for television, the most admired of which is his 1966 production *The Rise to Power of Louis XIV.* A manifesto signed by Rossellini and other Italian film makers, including Bertolucci, during this time states, "We wish, again, to present man with the guidelines of his own history, and depict drama, comedy and satire, the struggles, the experiences and the psychology of the people who have made the world what it is today, making it a criterion to fuse together entertainment, information and culture."

This statement articulated a renewed interest among Italian directors in taking up political subjects—this time from a perspective informed by the radical movements of the 1960s, often combined with a sophisticated Freudian worldview. Film historian Mira Liehm has called the resulting movement "metaphoric" cinema, because in it the realities of Italian life are rendered obliquely. This move to a more allegorical representational mode, arising from a distrust of the tenets of realism, can be inferred from a statement made by director Marco Bellocchio in 1980 about the political movements of the 1960s of which he was a part: "At the time of the union of Marxist-Leninist communists," he observed, "the conjecture was that in order to change, the bourgeois intellectuals should serve the people, live among the people, for the people have the correct ideas, etc. But actually the people in question did not exist, were nowhere to be found. It was a myth, an abstraction, and all that came to nothing." Some of the most significant works by Italian film makers made during the 1970s, 1980s, and 1990s grew out of this politically sophisticated and metaphorical worldview, including Bertolucci's *The Conformist* (1970) and *1900* (1976), Gianni Amelio's *Lamerica* (1994), and Bellocchio's own *In the Name of the Father* (1971) and *The Nanny* (1999).

Bernardo Bertolucci, who served as assistant director on *Accattone!* achieved a prodigious international success with *Before the Revolution* (1964), which he completed at the age of twenty-four. His films resemble those of the later Visconti, in their concern with intertwined personal relationships and political attitudes, and in their bold painterly style—*The Conformist* and *The Spider's Stratagem,* both 1970, for example. In these two films he put together a talented production team consisting of cinematographer Vittorio Storraro, production designer Ferdinando Scarfiotti, and editor Kim Arcelli, all of whom helped craft the sinuous camera work, striking art deco *mise-en-scène,* and seductive rhythms of *The Conformist,* perhaps Bertolucci's most influential film.

Last Tango in Paris (1972) bears some resemblance to Antonioni thematically and aroused something of the same excitement as *L'Avventura* in suggesting a new sort of film language, or personal idiom at least. An international *success de scandal,* the production starred Marlon Brando as Paul, a down-on-his luck American in Paris whose wife has just committed suicide. Paul's clandestine affair with a young Parisian girl, conducted in an empty apartment, occasioned some of the most explicit sex scenes yet to appear in a commercially released film. For this role, Brando improvised some soliloquies that were deeply personal and patently autobiographical.

Last Tango in Paris was followed by the vast panorama of *1900* (1976), covering some seventy years of life and social conflict in the Emilia region of Italy, which the director later called "the nicest cinematic adventure of my life." The film treats class conflict and the rise of fascism through the story of two young men, one a peasant (Gerard Depardieu) and one an aristocrat (Robert De Niro), both born on the same estate on the same day at the turn of the century.

Bertolucci's *The Last Emperor* (1987) was a triumph on all counts. A huge multinational production, it tells the story of Pu Yi, the last emperor of China. The film can be seen in several ways. It is a sumptuous visual feast of elegance and display on a colossal scale (Figure 16.9). As cultural and political history it is less satisfactory; too much is crammed into too little time, with large events hinted at or dealt with obliquely. Perhaps it can best be understood as the story of a person whose emotional life becomes constricted and empty as a result of early traumas. He is torn from his mother and then from his wet nurse; ritual obeisance is substituted for love and nurturing. He is told he is the most powerful person in the world who can do anything he wants, when in fact he is someone who experiences one loss after another. In a sense he is a prisoner throughout his life. This aspect of the film is consistent with Bertolucci's persistent fascination with psychological tensions that lead to loneliness and aberrant behavior. He has suggested that his films and his method of film making are part of his own psychoanalysis. In any event, the gamble at high

FIGURE 16.9   *The Last Emperor* ☆ Italy, 1987, Bernardo Bertolucci.

stakes paid off handsomely. *The Last Emperor* attracted great critical attention, won eight Academy Awards, and became an international financial success.

The subjects of Bertolucci's films of the 1990s and beyond have moved away from overt politics and history to a more personalized concern with romantic obsession, often blended with a motif of cultural otherness rendered as an alluring exoticism. *The Sheltering Sky* (1990), *Stealing Beauty* (1996), and *Besieged* (1998) fall into this pattern. In these films the director's genius for rendering intense emotional states is given full play. *The Sheltering Sky* is perhaps the most effective of the three. Its long, complex traveling shots of North Africa, accompanied by Ryuikchi Sakamoto's haunting love theme, weave a spellbinding web of ineffable longing.

Similar to Bertolucci in his commitment to metaphoric renderings of Marxist and psychoanalytic theories, **Marco Bellocchio** began his career at about the same time as his more internationally celebrated colleague. With a style more coldly allegorical than Bertolucci's, he relies more heavily on the aberrant and grotesque. Bellocchio's first feature, *Fists in the Pocket,* released in 1965, drew a mordant portrait of a middle-class family in which epilepsy, matricide, fratricide, and incestuous longings form the basis of the plot. In 1971 he helmed another black comedy, *In the Name of the Father,* this one set in a boys' boarding school. By the late 1990s, the director had begun to couch his social criticism in more mellow, sympathetic terms. His 1999 film *The Nanny,* made for Italian television, is set in the early part of the century. Its story centers around a peasant girl who is hired by a psychiatrist to wet-nurse his new baby. With a style featuring Bellocchio's characteristic chiaroscuro photography and an elegantly designed *mise-en-scène,* the film, based on a story by Luigi Pirandello, showcases a broad range of issues, including parenthood, class difference, Italian nationalism, and literacy.

Two controversial Italian women directors who work in the metaphorical style also rose to international prominence during the 1970s but have since dropped from view on the international festival circuit. **Liliana Cavani** caused an international sensation with *The Night Porter,* her 1974 chamber piece on sadomasochistic relationships between former inhabitants of a Nazi concentration camp. **Lina Wertmüller** achieved a comparable notoriety with a series of broad social satires focused on gender relations and political follies, including *The Seduction of Mimi* (1972), *Love and Anarchy* (1973), and *Seven Beauties* (1976).

The most critically acclaimed Italian director to emerge in the 1990s, **Gianni Amelio,** also created a cinema of political metaphor. Best known in the United States for his prize-winning 1994 production *Lamerica,* he also directed *Stolen Children* (1992) and *The Way We Laughed* (1998), both of which received major international awards. *Lamerica* tells the tale of a pair of Italian capitalists who attempt to exploit the newly opened market in Albania after the fall of communism there. One, who becomes the story's protagonist, finds himself drawn into an increasingly fantasmagorical world of ambiguous identities and economic ruin. The gaunt faces of the Albanians and the arid, rocky devastation of the landscape gradually grind down his cocky self-assurance until he is reduced to the status of a nameless refugee, like the thousands of Albanians he had formerly treated with insouciant contempt (Figure 16.10a). *Lamerica* is replete with haunting images of droves of starving people, especially children, who descend like waves on anything that might present them with a means of escape from the intolerable world in which they are imprisoned (Figure 16.10b). In the tradition of neorealism, the film tackles a social problem affecting the poor and socially downtrodden, but its allegorical style has more in common with the metaphoric cinema of early Bertolucci and Bellocchio.

Popular Genres

Mainstream Italian film, like the movies of the United States, has always relied on the presold appeal of popular genres. In the postneorealist era, many of these Italian film formulas have found success abroad as cult classics or art-house favorites.

The first Italian genre to achieve cult status was the **spaghetti western,** including such titles as *The Good, the Bad, and the Ugly* (1966) and *Once Upon a Time in the West* (1967). As directed by Italian maestro **Sergio Leone,** these films exploit the iconic presences of then-second-tier American stars such as Clint Eastwood and Eli Wallach to create mythic studies of revenge and bloodshed. Leone set his stories in the wind-swept arid landscape of southern Spain, which substituted for the American West. Cinematographer Tonino Delli Colli's bravura camera work alternates extreme long shots with tight close-ups, each shot held for an inordinate length of time as Ennio Morricone's signature musical scores rise up on the sound track.

Once Upon a Time in America (1984), perhaps Leone's greatest film, is a variant on another American genre, the gangster story, and was produced with American money. Featuring a more naturalistic visual style than Leone's earlier spaghetti westerns, *Once Upon a Time in America* renders its setting in 1930s America in subdued tones of browns and grays. A riveting performance by Robert De Niro in the film's central role gives the tragic events of the plot an aching immediacy. Along with Coppola's 1972 *The Godfather,* Leone's gangster saga ranks as one of the most accomplished examples of the genre produced during the last half of the twentieth century.

FIGURE 16.10a and b *Lamerica* ☆ Italy, 1994, Gianni Amelio.

Another popular formula the Italians made their own in the 1970s was the horror film, in a variant known as the **giallo.** Though initiated by the films of Mario Bava, the genre reached its pinnacle (or, some would claim, its nadir) in the work of Italian helmer **Dario Argento.** Argento's exercises in horror, including *Deep Red* (1975), *Suspiria* (1977) (Figure 16.11), and *Opera* (1987), feature plots that turn on the predictable devices of ghosts and mad killers. But the inimitable style in which these stories are presented sets them apart from more workaday Hollywood fare. All are built around spectacular set pieces in which lurid art direction and stomach-churning gore combine to produce a fever pitch of overwrought emotion. One of Argento's favored strategies is to linger over closeups of the hands of killers; he invariably uses his own hands as substitutes for those of his villains in these shots.

One of the enduring pleasures of the Italian cinema has always been **comedy,** with a string of classic titles running from Pietro Germi's *Divorce, Italian Style* in 1961 to Franco Brusati's *Bread and Chocolate* in 1974 and beyond. In the 1990s, this tradition took on a new significance internationally as Italian comedies, often given a bittersweet edge, captured worldwide interest. The trend began in 1988 with Giusseppe Tornatore's *Cinema Paradiso,* a touching tale of a young provincial boy's love affair with the movies. *Il Postino* followed in 1994 (Figure 16.12). Although directed by British film maker Michael Radford, this story about the relationship between an idealistic mailman and a famous poet was spearheaded by its star, the venerable Italian comedy actor and director Massimo Troisi,

FIGURE 16.11   *Suspiria* ★ Italy, 1977, Dario Argento.

FIGURE 16.12   *Il Postino* ★ Italy, 1994, Michael Radford; Linda Moretti and Phillippe Noiret.

who died shortly after production was completed. Also in 1994, another comic talent, Nanni Moretti, directed and starred in *Dear Diary,* a humorous jaunt through his life, told in three chapters; it, too, became an international prize winner. And in 1997, yet another well-known Italian comic, Roberto Benigni, directed *Life Is Beautiful,* a moving fable about a winsome little man and his family caught up in the nightmare of World War II.

Seen as a whole, Italian film from 1945 onward represents a tradition of artistic innovation tempered by a continuing awareness of the role of film in society. From the neorealism of the late 1940s to the modernism of the 1960s to the metaphoric cinema of the 1970s, 1980s, and 1990s, a common sense of national identity among the film makers has strengthened individual efforts. In spite of obvious personal and generational differences, contemporary Italian directors share many aesthetic and political as well as cultural assumptions. That cohesiveness permitted artists of the stature of Visconti, Fellini, and Antonioni to have long productive careers. It has also provided a background from which newcomers such as Bertolucci, Bellocchio, and Amelio have emerged to command worldwide attention. Through it all, popular genres have continued to thrive. The story of postwar Italian cinema is one of an evolving sense of national purpose and of the ongoing search for a filmic style best suited to represent that purpose. A similar pattern appears in the history of film in Great Britain, the subject of Chapter 18.

Films of the Period

1960
L'Avventura (Michelangelo Antonioni)
La Dolce Vita (Federico Fellini)
Rocco and His Brothers (Rocco e i suoi fratelli)
  (Luchino Visconti)
Two Women (La ciociara) (Vittorio de Sica)

1961
Accattone! (Piero Paolo Pasolini)
The Bandits of Orgosolo (Banditi a Orgosolo)
  (Vittorio de Seta)
Divorce, Italian Style (Divorzio all'Italia)
  (Pietro Germi)
La Notte (Michelangelo Antonioni)
Il Posto (Ermanno Olmi)
Salvatore Giuliano (Francesco Rosi)

1962
The Eclipse (L'eclisse) (Michelangelo
  Antonioni)

1963
8½ (Federico Fellini)
The Fiancés (I fidanzati) (Ermanno Olmi)

The Leopard (Il Gattopardo) (Luchino Visconti)

1964
Before the Revolution (Prima della revoluzione)
  (Bernardo Bertolucci)
*The Gospel According to St. Matthew (Il vangelo
  secondo Matteo)* (Piero Paolo Pasolini)
The Red Desert (Il Deserto Rosso) (Michelangelo
  Antonioni)

1965
Fists in the Pocket (I pugni in tasca) (Marco
  Bellocchio)
Juliet of the Spirits (Giulietta degli spiriti)
  (Federico Fellini)
Sandra (Vaghe Stelle dell'orsu) (Luchino Visconti)

1966
The Battle of Algiers (La battaglia di Algeri)
  (Gillo Pontecorvo)
*The Good, the Bad, and the Ugly (Il buono, il
  bruto, il cattivo)* (Sergio Leone)
*The Hawks and the Sparrows (Uccellacci e
  Uccelllini)* (Piero Paolo Pasolini)

1967
China Is Near (La Cina è vicina) (Marco
   Bellocchio)
*Once Upon a Time in the West (C'era una volta
   il West)* (Sergio Leone)

1968
Dillinger Is Dead (Dillinger è morte) (Marco
   Ferreri)

1969
Burn! (Queimada!) (Gillo Pontecorvo)
The Damned (La caduta degli dei) (Luchino
   Visconti)
Fellini Satyricon (Federico Fellini)
Zabriskie Point (Michelangelo Antonioni)

1970
The Conformist (Il conformista) (Bernardo
   Bertolucci)
*The Garden of the Finzi-Continis (Il giarino dei
   Finzi-contini)* (Vittorio de Sica)
*Investigation of a Citizen above Suspicion
   (Indagene su un cittadino al di sopra di ogni
   sospetto)* (Elio Petri)
The Spider's Stratagem (Strategia del ragno)
   (Bernardo Bertolucci)

1971
Death in Venice (Morte a Venezia) (Luchino
   Visconti)
In the Name of the Father (Nel nome del padre)
   (Marco Bellocchio)
*St. Michael Had a Rooster (San Michele aveva un
   gallo)* (Vittorio and Paolo Taviani)

1972
Last Tango in Paris (L'ultimo tango à Parigi)
   (Bernardo Bertolucci)
The Mattei Affair (Il caso Mattai) (Francesco Rosi)
*The Seduction of Mimi (Mimì metallugico ferito
   nell'onore)* (Lina Wertmüller)

1973
Amarcord (Federico Fellini)
Diary of a Schoolteacher (Diario di un maestro)
   (Vittorio de Seta)

La Grande Bouffe (La grande abbouffatta) (Marco
   Ferreri)
*Love and Anarchy (Film d'amore e d'amore e
   d'anarchia)* (Lina Wertmüller)

1974
Bread and Chocolate (Pane e cioccolata) (Franco
   Brusati)
The Night Porter (Il potiere de notte) (Liliana
   Cavani)

1975
The Passenger (Professione: reporter)
   (Michelangelo Antonioni)

1976
Fellini's Casanova (Federico Fellini)
1900 (Novocento) (Bernardo Bertolucci)
Seven Beauties (Pasqualino Settebellezze)
   (Lina Wertmüller)

1977
Padre Padrone (Vittorio and Paolo Taviani)
Suspiria (Dario Argento)

1978
*The Tree of the Wooden Clogs (L'albero degli
   zoccoli)* (Ermanno Olmi)

1982
The Eyes, the Mouth (Gli occi, la bocca) (Marco
   Bellocchio)
*Identification of a Woman (Identicazione de
   una donna)* (Michelangelo Antonioni)
*The Night of the Shooting Stars (La Notte de San
   Lorenzo)* (Vittorio and Paolo Taviani)

1984
Carmen (Francesco Rosi)
Chaos (Kaos) (Vittorio and Paolo Taviani)
*Once Upon a Time in America (C'era una volta
   in America)* (Sergio Leone)

1987
The Last Emperor (Il ultimo imperatore)
   (Bernardo Bertolucci)

1988
Cinema Paradiso (Nuovo cinema paradiso)
    (Giuseppe Tornatore)

1990
The Sheltering Sky (Il tè nel deserto) (Bernardo
    Bertolucci)

1991
Mediterraneo (Gabriele Salvatores)

1992
Stolen Children (Il ladro di bambini) (Gianni Amelio)

1994
Dear Diary (Caro Diaria) (Nanni Moretti)
Lamerica (Gianni Amelio)
Il Postino (Michael Radford)

1997
Life Is Beautiful (La vita è bella) (Roberto Benigni)

1998
Besieged (L'Assedio) (Bernardo Bertolucci)
The Way We Laughed (Così ridevano) (Gianni Amelio)

1999
The Nanny (La Balia) (Marco Bellocchio)

2001
The Son's Room (La Stanza del Figlio) (Nanni Moretti)
The Profession of Arms (Il Mestiere delle armi)
    (Ermanno Olmi)

2002
*Religion Hour (My Mother's Smile) (L'Ora di reli-
    gione: Il sorriso di mia madre)* (Marco Bellochio)

2003
Good Morning, Night (Buongiornio, notte) (Marco
    Bellochio)
The Dreamers (Bernardo Bertolucci)

Books on the Period

Landy, Marcia. *Italian Film.* New York: Cambridge University Press, 2000.
Reich, Jacqueline. *Beyond the Latin Lover: Marcello Mastroianni, Masculinity and Italian Cinema.* Bloomington: Indiana University Press, 2003.
Restivo, Angelo. *The Cinema of Economic Miracles: Visuality and Modernization in the Italian Art Film.* Durham, NC: Duke University Press, 2002.
Sorlin, Pierre. *Italian National Cinema, 1896–1996.* New York: Routledge, 1996.

17

American Reemergence

★ ★ ★ ★

1963–1974

On November 22, 1963, President John F. Kennedy was shot and killed in Dallas. Almost everyone who was an adult during that period remembers where he or she was when this event occurred. Not only was it a national tragedy, but it also heralded major changes for the country. The young president's White House had been held up as a modern Camelot; he was succeeded by his vice-president, Lyndon Johnson, a less popular figure who pursued an even less popular war in Vietnam. The mood in the United States shifted from the optimism of the 1950s toward a more self-critical stance, spearheaded initially by the development of the civil rights movement, with its sit-ins, marches, and riots; then by the rebellious spirit of a growing youth culture that called into question both the war in Vietnam and the bourgeois complacency into which the country had lapsed. The median age in the United States fell to below age twenty-five in 1964; an increasing number of these young people were clustered together on college campuses. For the rest of the decade and well into the 1970s, a youthful sensibility ruled. Then, in 1972, burglars broke into the Democratic offices in Washington's Watergate apartment complex; by 1974, then-President Richard Nixon, who had been implicated in the cover-up of this political skulduggery, resigned. The United States entered a new era of cynicism about its government officials, and the idealism that had fueled the reformist agendas of the previous decade was set aside.

For Hollywood, the 1960s and early 1970s were dismal years. Theater attendance dropped to half of what it had been ten years before. In 1963 only 121 features were released, an all-time low. Prestige productions such as *Cleopatra* (1963) and *Paint Your Wagon* (1969) bombed at the box office. In the studios, chaos reigned. Devastated and demoralized by the advent of television, the divestiture of their theaters, and the challenge of European art films, management was at a loss about where to turn. The old-time movie moguls who had ruled their empires with iron fists for so many years had died, retired, or been forced out. A series of sell-offs to large conglomerates made the studios part of much larger corporate entities, answerable to financial wizards who had little background in the movie business. In 1969 Warner Bros. was purchased by Kinney National Services, a company that owned parking lots and funeral homes. The once great and powerful Metro-Goldwyn-Mayer was sold to financier Kirk Kerkorian, who wanted the studio's logo to put on his Las Vegas hotel. M-G-M went out of business entirely for almost a decade, beginning in 1973. This corporate instability led to many inefficiencies, not the least of which was a revolving-door system for top executives. Each new regime was, quite naturally, inclined to ignore the films made under the auspices of the last group in its quest to make its own mark; thus, many worthy productions got dumped or shelved.

The new, green studio chiefs had less confidence and authority than the old-timers did; popular stars who could promise an audience therefore gained more power, as did directors. As always, their interests were ably advanced by the Directors Guild of America, which negotiated ever-more directorial control over every aspect of the production process. In 1964 the Guild won the right for all its members to produce an initial director's cut on each of their films. But perhaps the biggest winners in the struggles following the breakup of the old-style studios were the agents, whose list of "bankable" clients and deal-making skills put them in the catbird seat in the new Balkanized climate of Hollywood. In fact, in 1962 a talent agency, MCA, gained control over one of the biggest studios: Universal.

Even though the Hollywood studios were floundering, film was far from dead. The youth movement had taken up movies in a serious way. Following the publication of Andrew Sarris's *auteurist* manifesto, *The American Cinema,* in 1963, a novel sort of creative vitality began to make itself felt, especially on college campuses—new kinds of films and new film makers. New genres emerged to capture the interests of a changed society. Among intellectuals, European art films by directors such as Ingmar Bergman, Federico Fellini, and Jean-Luc Godard became chic. In response, Hollywood began to hire younger, "hipper" directors whose movies had a European flavor. These new talents soon became known as the American New Wave. More radical kinds of films appeared as well—independent documentary and avant-garde productions that protested against prevailing conditions and affirmed the values of the youth culture.

Popular Genres

In response to the new mood of social unrest in the United States and the increasing visibility of groups with militant agendas, Hollywood scrambled to devise new genres that might appeal to these recently constituted specialized audiences. The juvenile deliquency films of the 1950s mutated into the youth films during the following decade; in the early 1970s a series of movies aimed at African American audiences, the so-called "blaxploitation" cycle, were released.

Made for the youthful audiences who were now the principal patrons of the theaters, **youth films** were about young people and new lifestyles. All of them explored social, and some of them political, problems in one way or another. A few sounded strong notes of dissent. They also combined forms—documentary and experimental styles and subject matter along with those of conventional fiction—in ways that some of the recent films coming from abroad were doing (those of Godard, for example). The trend started off indirectly in 1967 with two of the most popular releases of that year: Arthur Penn's *Bonnie and Clyde* and Mike Nichols's *The Graduate*. *Bonnie and Clyde* was a sort of gangster film set in rural America of the 1930s, but encoded within it were themes of current youthful protest: the individual against the system (Figure 17.1a); an unconventional and hedonistic lifestyle that put emphasis on "kicks" (Figure 17.1b); and the implicit justification of

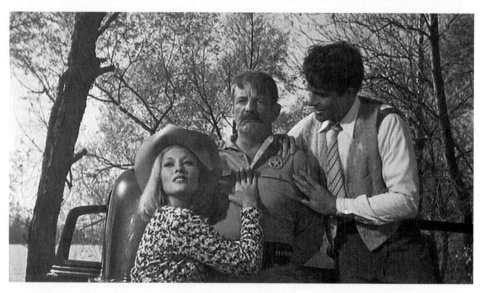

FIGURE 17.1a and b   *Bonnie and Clyde* ★ United States, 1967, Arthur Penn; a. Faye Dunaway and Warren Beatty on left; b. Faye Dunaway, Denver Pyle, and Warren Beatty.

violence directed against the impersonal institutions of society and against the conscientious, middle-aged, and humorless who served them. *The Graduate* more explicitly, if less boldly, expressed other manifestations of contemporary youthful tension and conflict.

It took Hollywood two years to contemplate those two films before producing more that incorporated some of the elements that seemed to have been responsible for their success. In 1969 the youth cycle proper began with *Easy Rider, Medium Cool, Zabriskie Point,* and *Alice's Restaurant. Easy Rider,* the seminal film, became an immediate favorite with the eighteen- to twenty-five-year-old audience. Directed by Dennis Hopper, who had learned about the potential of the youth genre when he was a supporting player in *Rebel Without a Cause* a decade before, *Easy Rider* starred Hopper and Peter Fonda, with support from a young Jack Nicholson. The episodic plot centered on two young men, Billy and Captain America, riding their motorcycles "in search of America," as pop-song lyrics of the time put it, and getting high on pot and LSD. Like Bonnie and Clyde, Billy and Captain America were quickly adopted as youth-cult heroes. *Easy Rider* spawned a profusion of features with related themes, some of them much more direct in their criticism of the dominant values of contemporary American society.

Two years later, in 1971, the **blaxploitation** genre was kicked off by the runaway success of Melvin Van Peebles's independent feature *Sweet Sweetback's Baadasssss Song.* Seeing a potentially lucrative and previously untapped market, Hollywood quickly jumped on the bandwagon with a series of action movies set in the urban ghetto featuring black heroes. Most of these played exclusively in inner-city theaters. The first of the cycle, *Shaft* (1971), directed by the award-winning African American photographer Gordon Parks, chronicled the adventures of a New York private eye played by Richard Roundtree. Shot on the gritty New York streets largely with telephoto lenses, *Shaft* depicts the in-your-face confusion of life in the big city with arresting *panache.* Its score, by Isaac Hayes, evoked a funky, with-it mood from the outset. Made for a paltry $1.2 million, *Shaft* was an enormous hit and was quckly followed by two inferior sequels: *Shaft's Big Score* (Parks, 1972) and *Shaft in Africa* (John Guillerman, 1973). (The original *Shaft* was remade in 2000 with Samuel L. Jackson in the title role.) Other black action films appeared in short order, including *Superfly* in 1972 and *Foxy Brown,* starring Pam Grier, in 1973. Though all were popular, they proved controversial; groups such as the NAACP protested their glorification of violence and criminality as well as their escapist mentality. A contemporary review in the *New York Times* by Clayton Riley voiced the concern. "Shaft Can Do Everything," the headline read. "I Can Do Nothing."

Around the same time, a series of more down-to-earth, sentimentalized, and comic productions aimed at black audiences was also released, including Parks's own *The Learning Tree* in 1969 (Figure 17.2), Ossie Davis's *Black Girl* in 1972, John Berry's *Claudine* in 1974, Michael Schultz's *Cooley High* in 1975, and a series of films directed by black actor Sidney Poitier (*Buck and the Preacher,* 1972, and *Uptown Saturday Night,* 1974).

The American New Wave

During those years of national turmoil and dissidence, a number of young film makers working within the Hollywood system established careers, touching off a movement variously known as the American New Wave or the American Renaissance. The New Wave di-

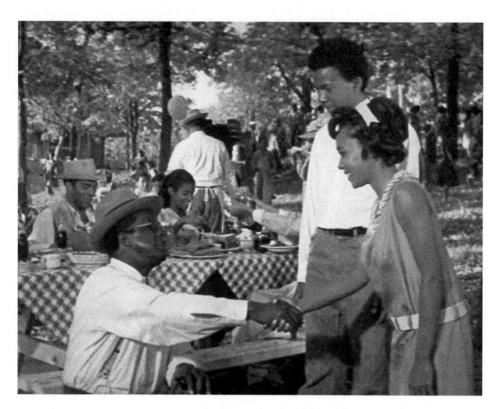

FIGURE 17.2   *The Learning Tree* ☆ United States, 1969, Gordon Parks; Joel Fluellen, Kyle Johnson, and Mira Waters.

rectors maintained a strong interest in critically examining aspects of American culture, including the violence so prevalent during the country's recent history. Some of these had established roots earlier; all continued their careers into the 1980s and most into the 1990s. The new interest in directorial styles manifested by the *auteur*-minded youth culture led Hollywood to give these new film makers unprecedented freedom—with the assurance that the movies they produced could be marketed as *auteurist* statements. Taking advantage of these new freedoms, the American New Wave directors developed stylistic signatures that were far more individualistic than the styles associated with the studio stalwarts of the 1950s. The European look cultivated by the New Wave group was characterized by loosely plotted story lines, ambiguous character motivations, low lighting levels, and jarring juxtapositions of tone (this last often achieved by the addition of already existing pop-music scores). These new Hollywood talents included Arthur Penn, Sam Peckinpah, Robert Altman, Francis Ford Coppola, Martin Scorsese, and John Cassavetes. Some of the group, such as Coppola and Scorsese, were trained in university film programs. Others—for example, Penn, Peckinpah, and Altman—got their start in television. Coppola and Scorsese also served apprenticeships under "B" movie entrepreneur Roger Corman.

Arthur Penn was the first of the New Wave directors to be widely recognized. Like others in the group, he was critical of prevailing mores. Every one of the films he directed explicitly examines a facet of American culture. The people who interest him most are the outcasts from this society—most typically, young ones. Some of his films, such as *Alice's Restaurant* (1969) and *Four Friends* (1981), explicity focus on youth cultures. Others enact stylish variations on traditional American genres: westerns (*The Left-Handed Gun,* 1958; *Little Big Man,* 1970; and *The Missouri Breaks,* 1976), gangster stories (*Mickey One,* 1965, and *Bonnie and Clyde,* 1967), and private-eye tales (*Night Moves,* 1975).

Although Penn's preoccupation with things American has remained a constant throughout his work, of all the American New Wave directors he had the strongest attraction to the kind of artistic modernism in film that had been emanating from Europe since the late 1950s. *Bonnie and Clyde* was originally conceived by its scriptwriters, David Newman and Robert Benton, for direction by Truffaut or Godard. *Mickey One* and *Night Moves* are the full-scale examples—what the trade would call art movies—experimental and philosophical within their genre trappings.

Almost all of Penn's productions take up violence as a major motif. *Mickey One* explores the fear and threat of violence omnipresent in American cities through the eyes of a paranoid and desperate nightclub comic pursued by the Mob. *The Chase* (1966) follows that same climate of violence into a small southern town and adds to it the general erosion of sexual morality. "I think that one of the functions of art is to purge or exorcise the crap that encrusts society," Penn once commented when asked about his repeated use of violence, "to blow out those undesirable capacities in all of us."

Penn's *Bonnie and Clyde,* surely among the most influential of American films, sets real-life bank robbers of the 1930s in the light of the myth they themselves had helped create. The film's star, Warren Beatty, who had earlier worked with Penn in *Mickey One,* acted as producer. As Bonnie, Faye Dunaway sported a stylish 1930s wardrobe that started a fad for such clothes. The film's bone-chilling violence was rendered even more shocking by its incongruous musical score, an upbeat banjo number, "Foggy Mountain Breakdown," by country-and-western composers Flatt and Scuggs. The narrative concluded with an innovative and stunning slow-motion sequence, superbly edited by Dede Allen, featuring an ultraviolent, yet strangely romanticized, ambush in which the title characters are killed.

Like Penn, **Sam Peckinpah** came to features from television. He had been a writer-director on several TV western series and remained mostly loyal, even when working in a form that was not outwardly a western, to that most American of film genres. To the basic elements of the formula he added his attraction to the grandeur of nature, which he celebrated in resplendent location photography, and his absorption with violence. Among the most memorable of his many variations on the western formula are *Deadly Companions* (1961), *Ride the High Country* (1962), *Major Dundee* (1964), *The Ballad of Cable Hogue* (1970), *Pat Garrett and Billy the Kid* (1973), and *Bring Me the Head of Alfredo Garcia* (1974). He died in 1984 at the age of fifty-nine. Best remembered for his uncompromising vision of the lost values of heroic individualism represented by the closing of the American West, Peckinpah celebrated traditional, larger-than-life masculinity. His stories focused on loners and losers who have outmoded responses to cultural change.

Often considered Peckinpah's greatest achievement and one of the greatest westerns ever made, *The Wild Bunch* (1969) brings violence to the fore—gross and gruesome, yet also poetic (Figure 17.3). Its opening sequence, in which a group of children torture a scorpion, has been widely lauded for the bitter, uncompromising statement it makes about the ingrained nature of human cruelty. At the same time, however, the film is deeply commit-

FIGURE 17.3   *The Wild Bunch* ☆ United States, 1969, Sam Peckinpah; Ben Johnson, Warren Oates, William Holden, and Ernest Borgnine.

ted to the values of heroism and honor. For example, a famous exchange between two of the members of the story's eponymous outlaw gang, Pike (William Holden) and Dutch (Ernest Borgnine), focuses on the ethics of promises. Discussing a former gang member, Thornton (Robert Ryan), who has made a deal with the law-enforcement establishment to hunt them down, Pike defends Thornton's disloyalty by declaring, "He gave his word." Dutch responds passionately, "It's not whether you give your word; it's who you give your word to." The film's final episode, an extended slow-motion sequence in which the heroes are brutally massacred by a degenerate Mexican general and his forces, was shot in elegiac slow motion that took the technique of the similar closing scene in *Bonnie and Clyde* several steps further.

Like Penn and Peckinpah, **Robert Altman** came to film out of directing for television. *M*A*S*H* (1970), his first substantial success (which spawned an even more successful long-running TV show), rode the crest of the youth cycle and launched Altman's subsequent career. An outrageous satire of both the military and medical professions, it simultaneously desecrated our memories of *All Quiet on the Western Front* and *Young Doctor Kildare.*

Of all the American New Wave directors, Altman is the most prolific, averaging over a film a year. Many of his productions—including *M*A*S*H* (1970), *Brewster McCloud* (1971), *McCabe and Mrs. Miller* (1972), *The Long Goodbye* (1973), and *Nashville* (1975)—dissect the traditional American movie genres, in the course of which he pokes fun at, questions, and attacks the values and shibboleths that their conventions support. Another group of Altman's films, more mysterious and dreamlike, explore the interior lives of women (*That Cold Day in the Park,* 1969; *Images,* 1972; and *3 Women,* 1977). Each of his productions has a unique look, ranging from the foggy, desolate air that hangs over the town of Presbyterian Church in *McCabe and Mrs. Miller* to the postcard brassiness of *Nashville* to the quaintly cartoonish ambience of *Popeye* (1981). Altman's 1992 production, *The Player,* catapulted him into a new prominence near the end of the century, after a period of obscurity during which he was unable to find commercial backing for his projects. It was followed by a number of diverse productions, the most notable of which are *Short Cuts* in 1993, *Kansas City* in 1996, *The Gingerbread Man* in 1997, and *Dr. T. and the Women* in 2000.

Altman's accomplishment has been aided by a group of actors who appear regularly in his work during the 1970s: Shelley Duvall, Keith Carradine, Sissy Spacek, Geraldine Chaplin, and Elliott Gould among the stalwarts. Like Ingmar Bergman, he invariably obtains distinctive and compelling performances. But Altman, the playful postmodernist, is an artist of a different order from the somber Swedish director. "This is just like Bergman," comments Geraldine Chaplin's Opal upon arriving at a garden party in *Nashville.* "Of course, the people are all wrong for Bergman." Altman's predilection for in-jokes like this one and the easygoing satirical jabs he takes at his characters have led some commentators to denounce him as glib and condescending; critic Robin Wood's essay about the director is entitled "Smart-Ass and Cutie-Pie."

Altman's style is perhaps best described as fragmented. He has claimed that he is interested in "splitting areas of reality—in other words, dealing with emotional reponses rather than intellectual responses." He frequently employs wide-screen compositions in which many interactions happen simultaneously, all rendered in overlapping dialogue. "Found" musical scores, such as the Leonard Cohen songs that run through *McCabe and Mrs. Miller,* often have a contrapuntal relation to the film's narratives rather than simply underlining story points. Altman is also fond of pausing to zoom in or shift focus in order to emphasize objects in the environment that hold particular fascination—for example, the stained glass in *That Cold Day in the Park* and the pool murals in *3 Women.*

Improvisation adds to the sense of fragmentation in Altman's work. It is no accident that *Kansas City* is about jazz. To give free rein to his actors, he favors loose-jointed narratives that will accommodate frequent digressions, like the riff about a parrot Elliott Gould delivers in the 1974 *California Split.* In a spirit of open-endedness, Altman shot so much footage of actors' improvisations in *Nashville* that at one point he spoke of making two films of it: "Nashville Red" and "Nashville Blue."

A big, ambitious film, some regard *Nashville* as its director's crowning achievement; Altman himself has referred to it as his "metaphor for America." Its twenty-four characters are caught up in the music industry and in the presidential campaign of a populist demagogue. The movie's plot advances by intercut episodes from the lives of each of the characters, all of whom become involved in putting on a show for the political rally that forms the story's grand finalé (Figure 17.4). The subjects of parody and satire here are popular music and popular politics, the sorts of performance and manipulation involved in both, and the audiences to which both appeal.

Another director who has given us indelible portraits of America is **Francis Ford Coppola,** the first major American director to have graduated from a university film program (UCLA). Given that academic training, with its emphasis on personal expression, it is interesting that during the first part of his career he largely withheld or concealed his own personality in his work, opting instead for a "professional" range of subjects and styles in productions such as *Dementia 13* (1963), a low-budget horror film; *You're a Big Boy Now* (1967), a charmingly light and unpretentious comedy; and *Finian's Rainbow* (1968), a semi-blockbuster musical. Beginning with *The Rain People* (1969), however, his work became more distinctive. Flawed in part, and oddly unresolved, *The Rain People* nonetheless gets at

FIGURE 17.4   *Nashville* ★ United States, 1975, Robert Altman.

the stresses felt by a particular American woman, which cause her to leave her husband, though she is several months pregnant, to try to find herself in a cross-country journey by car.

With *The Godfather* (1972), adapted from a popular novel by Mario Puzo, Coppola's career took off in a rocketlike trajectory. What quickly became one of the great financial successes in the history of cinema is also a work of enduring value. Expert in every respect, the great appeal of the film clearly comes from the warm glow of people and times remembered, when not only were men men and women women, but families were families, including especially the Mafia. The sentiments expressed were especially close to Coppola, who was himself from an Italian American background. The film portrayed the Mob as a more naked form of capitalist competition in which business rules and competition are literally cutthroat. "Basically, both the Mafia and America feel they are benevolent organizations," the director once said. "And both the Mafia and America have their hands stained with blood from what it is necessary to do to protect their power and interests."

With deeply saturated, chiaroscuro images contributed by cinematography's "dark prince," Gordon Willis, and an unfogettable score by Fellini's favorite composer, Nino Rota, *The Godfather* brought a new level of European-style artistry to mainstream American cinema. To play the role of godfather Don Corleone, Marlon Brando stuffed his cheeks with cotton and adopted the raspy tones of an aging potentate who speaks softly but carries a very big stick. As the Don's youngest son, Michael, Al Pacino undergoes a major transformation in the course of the story, from an innocent and protected family favorite to the next Mob chieftain. The turning point occurs when Michael is forced to commit murder to save the family business. At this moment, the movie's sound editor, Walter Murch, added the screech of an L-train to the film's mix; the grating noise subtly signals the mental agony Michael's bland exterior conceals.

The Godfather, Part II and *The Godfather, Part III* expanded on the cinematic fresco outlined in the first movie. But Coppola's subsequent work encompassed other subjects as well. *The Conversation,* which won the Palme d'Or at the Cannes Film Festival in 1974, is an intimate portrait of a single individual, Harry Caul, played by Gene Hackman. An electronic eavesdropper who applies his expertise impartially and amorally, Harry gains his only satisfactions from his considerable skill and from vicariously experiencing fragments of other lives. The searing Vietnam War chronicle *Apocalypse Now* (1979) won Coppola yet another Palme d'Or at Cannes. In 2001 he took a recut version featuring fifty-four minutes of added scenes and entitled *Apocalypse Now Redux* back to the French festival. In the 1980s and 1990s Coppola went on to numerous other projects, including the musicals *One From the Heart* in 1982 and *The Cotton Club* in 1984, and the biopic *Tucker* in 1988. In 1992 he directed a lush, romantic horror story, *Bram Stoker's Dracula,* which manages to be both a faithful adaptation of the classic novel and a self-reflexive study of the nature of the modern world.

Coppola's style has been justly described as operatic. He often focuses on the complexities of obsessive, larger-than-life heroes such as Preston Tucker or *The Godfather*'s Michael Corleone. At its worst, this approach leads to productions that feel bloated and overblown. "If he directs a little romance," critic Kenneth Tynan once remarked, "it has to be the biggest, most overdone little romance in history." On the other hand, Coppola has given us some of the most riveting set pieces in cinema, including the famous baptism scene that concludes *The Godfather,* in which a solemn organ piece plays over dynamic images of carnage taking place in numerous locations (Figure 17.5a–h), and the helicopter attack in *Apocalypse Now,* which is accompanied by an actual operatic score, Wagner's "Ride of the Valkyrie."

In addition to his career as a director, Coppola played a key role in the reorganization of Hollywood during these uneasy years through his role as an entrepreneur. He founded Zoetrope studios in San Francisco in 1969 following his experience working on *The Rain People.* In typically 1960s fashion, he used the studio not only to make his own films but also to produce and distribute movies by European *auteurs* Wim Wenders (*Hammett,* 1982), Hans-Jurgen Syberberg (*Our Hitler,* 1979), Jean-Luc Godard (*Sauve qui peut [La vie],* 1980), Agnieska Holland (*The Secret Garden,* 1993), and Kenneth Branaugh (*Mary Shelley's Frankenstein,* 1994). He also arranged, in 1981, for the American re-release of French director Abel Gance's classic *Napoleon* as an event movie that played in major cities with live orchestral accompaniment composed and conducted by his father, Carmine Coppola. The younger Coppola also functioned as producer on American projects such as George Lucas's *American Graffiti* in 1973, Paul Schrader's *Mishima* in 1985, and Gregory Nava's *My Family/Mia Familia* in 1995. In part as a result of these grand undertakings, Coppola's finances have been subject to more major roller-coaster rides than those of most Hollywood players. His desperate finanical straights forced him to sell Zoetrope in 1984. But he has never stayed down for long. His universally acknowledged talent has always assured him of prestigious directing assignments that return him, at least temporarily, to financial health.

Martin Scorsese, born in 1942, is the newest and youngest of the major mainstream directors who emerged in the early 1970s; Coppola, born in 1939, is next. The careers of these two Italian American film makers in some ways parallel one another. Both attended university film departments (New York University in Scorsese's case). But Coppola has ranged widely in terms of his subjects and forms, whereas Scorsese has stuck quite closely to what he learned while growing up in New York's Little Italy. When Coppola tried his hand at a musical, it was *Finian's Rainbow,* a bit of Irish whimsy replete with leprechaun and a pot of gold at the rainbow's end; Scorsese's musical was *New York, New York* (1977), about a self-absorbed tenor saxophone player obssessed with jazz.

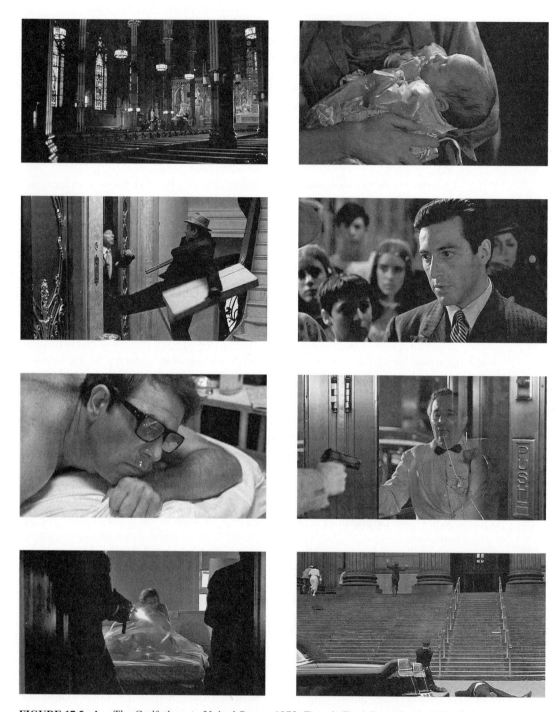

FIGURE 17.5a–h   *The Godfather* ★ United States, 1972, Francis Ford Coppola; d. Al Pacino;
e. Alex Rocco; f. Richard Conte.

After a few apprentice works, including *Who's That Knocking at My Door?* (1968) and *Boxcar Bertha* (1972), Scorsese made *Mean Streets* (1973), a fuller, tougher, more assured treatment of the same sorts of characters, themes, and milieu that had appeared in *Who's That Knocking?* In *Mean Streets* the protagonist (Harvey Keitel) attempts to reconcile his persistent sense of decency and concern for others with his ambition to succeed in the Mafia-imbued life around him. His maddeningly irresponsible buddy is played by Robert De Niro, who would subsequently become a fully participating collaborator in the expression of Scorsese's mythos. Since *Mean Streets,* Scorsese has managed his career with canny pragmatism, alternating the crime stories he is most famous for with chancier experiments involving an array of genres and subjects. The most notable examples of the former group include *Taxi Driver* (1976), *Goodfellas* (1990), and *Casino* (1995). Among the latter endeavors are *Alice Doesn't Live Here Anymore* (1975), *The Age of Innocence* (1993), and *Kundun* (1997).

Scorsese's visual style—edgy and kinetic—pegs him as a New Yorker. His crime films have a dark and often gritty appearance. The jerky, handheld camera work that characterized early efforts such as *Mean Streets* has given way in later productions to the smoother rhythms made possible by the development of the more stable, shoulder-mounted Steadicam (which was introduced in 1976). *Goodfella*'s long Steadicam shot of Ray Liotta and Lorraine Bracco entering the Copacabana nightclub through a back door and winding their way through the kitchen and back hallways before arriving at their front-row table is often held up as a textbook example of the bravura effects the Steadicam has made possible (Figure 17.6a–d). Scorsese's noncrime films have provided him with opportunities to

FIGURE 17.6a–d *Goodfellas* ☆ United States, 1990, Martin Scorsese; Ray Liotta and Lorraine Bracco.

experiment with other styles and effects, such as the shimmering glow of the sea behind Michelle Pfeiffer's silhouetted figure in *The Age of Innocence* and the lengthy montage of the Dalai Lama's vision of his devasted nation that ends *Kundun.*

Although he has become famous for his depictions of the seamy side of life, Scorsese's first ambition was to be a priest, and his interest in religion is directly expressed in films such as *The Last Temptation of Christ* (1988) and *Kundun* (which takes the Dalai Lama as its subject). Even when his subjects are not overtly relgious, symbolism often adds a spiritual dimension to Scorsese's stories, as when the image of a pool table takes on a sacramental character at a certain moment in *The Color of Money* (1986) or when Bach's "St. Matthew Passion" can be heard over a panorama of gambling tables in *Casino.* From this perspective, much of Scorsese's *oeuvre* can be viewed as an attempt to portray a fallen world filled with people desperately trying, by whatever perverse means, to find salvation.

Taxi Driver (1976) might be seen as an extreme variation on the failed saint figure who appears as protagonist in many of Scorsese's films. Here, the character, played by De Niro, is locked into near catatonia and becomes obsessed with cleansing the world's evil through a bath of blood. The isolation of the De Niro character is truly frightening and the homicidal violence unnerving. The film, which deals with attempted political assassination, was released just a few years after prominent U.S. leaders (Martin Luther King, Jr., John F. Kennedy, and Robert Kennedy) had been gunned down. *Taxi Driver* also featured Jodie Foster, the obsessive love object of the man who would wound Ronald Reagan.

Scorsese's *Raging Bull* (1980), which a poll of critics later ranked as the best film of the 1980s, has the New York City setting and Italian American context of many of the director's other works. What is different about this film is its tone. The life of fighter Jake La Motta, who rose to become middleweight champion and then descended into dissoluteness and a self-parodic nightclub act, is presented with what seems to be La Motta's own lack of understanding of his animal violence and self-indulgence. The film won Academy Awards for Robert De Niro, who gained fifty pounds to play La Motta, and Thelma Shoonmaker, Scorsese's long-standing editor. Also nominated for an Oscar was cinematographer Michael Chapman, whose silvery black-and-white photography overlaid the film's brutal story line with a patina of delicacy and elegance.

Of all the American New Wave directors, probably the most radical was **John Cassavetes.** Operating on the fringes of the Hollywood industry with a group of actor-collaborators, most notably his wife Gena Rowlands, Cassavetes created a series of films that he financed primarily through his work as an actor in mainstream productions such as *Rosemary's Baby* (1968). His own movies are built around performance, making extensive use of improvisation, loose story lines, and accommodating handheld camera work. "I've been concerned from the beginning with the problems confronting real people rather than emphasizing dramatic structure or bending characters to the plot," he once said. Deeply committed to the Method acting technique, he created a series of highly charged melodramas about characters at turning points in their lives, foregrounding the kind of emotional venting for which the Method style is famous. His first effort, *Shadows* (1960), developed out of a Method acting workshop he was teaching. Among the most well-regarded films he made subsequently are *Faces* (1968); *Minnie and Moskowitz* (1971); *A Woman Under the Influence* (1974) (Figure 17.7); *Gloria,* which won a Golden Lion at Venice in 1980; and *Love Streams,* which won at Berlin in 1986. Cassavetes died in 1989.

FIGURE 17.7 *A Woman Under the Influence* ✶ United States, 1974, John Cassavetes; Peter Falk and Gena Rowlands.

Though some commentators complained that his plots lack form, his technique is sloppy, and his scenes run far too long, Cassavetes stuck with his vision and produced a body of work that steadily gained ground with the critics. Fascinated by the intensity of people's inner lives, and the capacity of cinema to expose this intensity to view, he consistently focused on the problem of finding emotional stability and order in a world of self-indulgence and overprivilege.

Independent Voices

The counterculture mentality of the 1960s and early 1970s created a climate in which film makers whose ambitions went beyond creating entertainment for the masses were motivated to abandon Hollywood in favor of artisanal methods that could speak to larger social concerns or make more thoroughgoing individual statements. Many of those who had social or political agendas turned to documentary film making; others, wanting to express more personal or purely aesthetic visions, looked to the traditions of the avant-garde. Both groups were aided by the advent of cheaper 16 mm equipment as well as by avid audiences who congregated at museums, galleries, and college campuses, and responded enthusiastically to their efforts.

The documentary film movement that had begun in the 1920s with productions such as Robert Flaherty's *Nanook of the North* (1921) and had continued with New Deal–sponsored projects in the 1930s by directors such as Pare Lorentz was taken up by a group of left-leaning film makers in the 1960s who wanted to put the spotlight on social and political trends and events. Disdainful of the the heavy-handed educational tone and barely disguised ideological agendas of most television documentaries, they looked for fresher approaches to nonfiction movie making. Some—for instance, Emile de Antonio—made films that openly advocated political positions (*Year of the Pig,* 1969). Others developed a style of "direct cinema" in which the director(s) recorded contemporary events in a putatively neutral manner. This mandate was enabled by the development of relatively cheap portable cameras and lightweight sound-recording devices that could be taken to various locations so that events could be recorded as they occurred.

Prizing the principle of collective rather than individual authorship, the practitioners of direct cinema often worked in groups. The first major documentary to illustrate the method was *Primary,* an examination of John F. Kennedy's Wisconsin primary campaign for president. Released in 1960, it was produced by a team called Drew Associates. David and Albert Maysles, who customarily worked with Charlotte Zwerin, also practiced the direct cinema technique in documentaries such as *Salesman* (1968), a chronicle of the life of a Bible peddler, and *Grey Gardens* (1975) (Figure 17.8), a look at two eccentric cousins of

FIGURE 17.8   *Grey Gardens* ★ United States, 1975, Albert and David Maysles, Ellen Hovde, and Muffie Meyer; Little Edie and Big Edie Bouvier.

Jacqueline Kennedy Onassis. Shirley Clarke (*Portrait of Jason,* 1967) was another major figure in this movement. A popular series of "rock docs" used direct cinema methods to chronicle the massive gatherings of young people at the music festivals of the era, most notably *Monterey Pop* (D. A. Pennebaker, 1968) and *Woodstock* (Michael Wadleigh, 1970). *Gimme Shelter* (Albert and David Maysles), also released in 1970, marked something of an end point of the youth culture by inadvertently capturing an incident in which a member of the Hell's Angels motorcycle gang stabbed and killed a member of the audience at a Rolling Stones concert. The direct cinema style continued to be employed in later years, with major productions such as *Harlan County, USA* (Barbara Kopple, 1976), *Hoop Dreams* (Steve James and associates, 1994), and *The War Room* (D. A. Pennebaker and Chris Hegedus, 1998).

The most famous and prolific exponent of an approach that closely approximates the direct cinema mode was **Frederick Wiseman.** Wiseman's first film was an exposé of a Massachusetts mental hospital, *Titticut Follies* (1967). Since then, he has continued to produce increasingly lengthy film examinations of an array of social institutions, including the educational system (*High School,* 1968), the police (*Law and Order,* 1969), and public housing (*Public Housing,* 1997). Wiseman has claimed that he tries to give his films the greatest possible sense of immediacy "so there is no separation between the audience watching the film and the events in the film."

At the same time the documentarians were examining political and social phenomena, another group of independent movie makers focused on personal emotions, developing lyrical forms rather than essayistic ones. Calling themselves "underground film makers" to emphasize their antiestablishment orientation, they were inspired in large part by the pioneering work of Maya Deren in the 1940s. Deren's cinematic poems, including *Meshes of the Afternoon* (1943) (Figure 17.9) and *Ritual in Transfigured Time* (1946), had in turn been inspired by the European avant-garde movements of earlier eras. Following the pattern Deren and others had laid out, the underground film makers of the 1960s and 1970s worked either alone or in small, close-knit coteries, creating highly idiosyncratic, painterly works. The most prominent members of the group included Bruce Conner (*A Movie,* 1958), Jack Smith (*Flaming Creatures,* 1963), and Kenneth Anger (*Scorpio Rising,* 1964).

The father figure of 1960s underground film making was Jonas Mekas, whose magazine *Film Culture* and column in the *Village Voice* introduced and explained the work of these *cinéastes* to an ever-growing audience. Mekas also founded the Film-Makers Cooperative to distribute avant-garde and documentary works, and he cofounded the Anthology Film Archives to provide regular screenings and archive writings related to the movement's key figures. Mekas was himself a film maker, the creator of lengthy cinematic ruminations on his life, family, and friends (*Diaries, Notes, and Sketches,* 1964–1969, and *Lost Lost Lost,* 1976).

Foremost among the practitioners of avant-garde movie making during this era was the prolific **Stan Brakhage,** who produced approximately 250 films between 1952 and 1995. Early in his career, Brakhage received the imprimateur of Mekas, who declared in his *Village Voice* column in 1961, "Brakhage is one of the four or five most authentic film artists working in cinema anywhere, and perhaps the most original filmmaker in America today." Working alone, often with low-tech, 8 mm stock, Brakhage turned out a series of movies, almost all without sound, to correspond to his belief in the expressivity of what he called "pure film." Many of his productions are autobiographical (*Dog Star Man,*

FIGURE 17.9 *Meshes of the Afternoon* ★ United States, 1943, Maya Deren and Alexander Hamid; Maya Deren.

1961–1964); others are abstract (*Mothlight,* 1963). To express the nature of the cinematic medium itself in these works, Brakhage sometimes scratched the film or painted directly on it. Explaining his approach, he wrote in his 1963 book, *Metaphors of Vision,* "Imagine an eye unruled by man-made laws of perspective, an eye unprejudiced by compositional logic, an eye which does not respond to the name of everything but which must know each object encountered in life through an adventure of perception."

An almost polar opposite approach to movie making governed the work of the other major avant-garde film artist of the era, **Andy Warhol.** Warhol's cinematic technique could fairly be described as involving no technique at all. Having begun his career as a commercial artist, he had gone on to fame in the New York art world as one of the chief exponents of the Pop Art movement by making silkscreens of everyday objects such as soup cans and movie-star portraits. He began his film making work with a series of productions that enshrined his belief in boredom. (He was fond of asserting, "I love to be bored.") The six-hour *Sleep* (1963) showed a man sleeping; *Empire* (1964) went even further, consisting of a single, eight-hour view of the Empire State Building. Warhol's next group of films made good on another of his beliefs—"Everyone should be famous for fifteen minutes"— by allotting somewhat more than fifteen minutes to showcase the antics of the denizens of his New York studio (called "The Factory"). These productions, including *Chelsea Girls* (1966) and *Lonesome Cowboys* (1968) (Figure 17.10), were made in collaboration with Warhol's associate, Paul Morrissey. Iconoclastic in nature, they consisted of fragmentary narratives that pushed the limits of censorship with semipornographic representations of sexuality and displays of drug use. Warhol, who died in 1987, ultimately turned the directorial reigns over to Morrissey. Morrissey proceeded to make a number of more conventional films under the Warhol banner—including *Trash* (1970), *Andy Warhol's Frankenstein* (1974), and *Andy Warhol's Bad* (1975)—moving away from the ultrapassive filming technique favored by Warhol himself to introduce more traditional plots, camera work, and continuity editing. Despite these innovations, however, Morrissey's commitment to shocking audiences with explicit sexuality and bloody violence continued to tie his films to the Warholian aesthetic.

During the 1970s a new avant-garde movement came to the fore. Called *structuralist film making,* it highlighted the process of creating and viewing film in a highly abstract and self-reflexive manner. The name *structuralist* was suggested by critic P. Adams Sitney, a major interpreter of avant-garde cinema. "The film insists on its shape," he wrote, "and what content it has is minimal and subsidiary to its outline." The structuralist film movement's most famous exponent is Canadian artist Michael Snow, whose 1967 *Wavelength* consists of a forty-five-minute slow zoom in on a photograph of waves attached to the wall

FIGURE 17.10   *Lonesome Cowboys* ✳ United States, 1968, Andy Warhol; Joe Dallesandro on left.

of a loft apartment. Other structuralist film makers of note include George Landow (*Remedial Reading Comprehension,* 1970), Ernie Gehr (*Serene Velocity,* 1970), and Hollis Frampton (*Zorns Lemma,* 1970).

By the early 1970s feminism had produced a new crop of independent movie makers who were committed to women's issues. Some, interested in unearthing facets of women's history and the conditions of women's lives, made documentaries such as *Janie's Janie* (Geri Ashur, New York Newsreel, 1971), *Union Maids* (Jim Klein and Julia Reichert, 1976), and *The Life and Times of Rosie the Riveter* (Connie Field, 1976). Others, taking to heart the feminist adage "the personal is political," made confessional films; this group included Carolee Schneemann (*Fuses,* 1964), Joyce Chopra (*Joyce at 34,* 1972), and Barbara Hammer (*Sappho,* 1978). Still others worked with mixed forms, including the Canadian Joyce Wieland (*Reason Over Passion,* 1969), Michelle Citron (*Daughter Rite,* 1978), Sue Friedrich (*The Ties That Bind,* 1984), and Trinh Min-Ha (*Surname Viet, Given Name Nam,* 1989).

The most important avant-garde film maker to emerge from the feminist movement of the early 1970s was **Yvonne Rainer.** Like Deren before her, Rainer had started out as a dancer. Absorbing a range of influences, from the structuralism of Snow to the Brechtianism of Godard to the poststructuralism of contemporary film theory, she has produced a series of films that feature fragmented, self-reflexive narratives, printed texts, clips from films of the past, and documentary materials, all combined in collage-like structures. Feminist critic B. Ruby Rich has characterized the ultimate effect of these highly original and challenging works as "landmining emotional terrain." Rainer's first production, *Lives of Performers* (1971), grew out of the dance performance art in which she had previously been engaged, but she moved quickly beyond this beginning effort to create more abstract, theoretically informed works, most notably *Film About a Woman Who . . .* in 1974 and *The Man Who Envied Women* in 1985. In 1990, she made her most accessible film, *Privilege* (Figure 17.11), which focuses on a woman dealing with menopause.

By the mid-1970s the radical impulse that had powered the cinematic breakthroughs of Rainer and other film makers of the 1960s and early 1970s had run its course. Most of the directors who had launched their careers during this period continued to work on into the next decades, but the new film makers who appeared were of a different stripe. By this time, however, the United States had regained its place among the leading nations of film art. Hollywood used its preeminence to establish a new global film culture based on a new genre: the blockbuster.

*Films of the Period*_____

1963
The Birds (Alfred Hitchcock)
Flaming Creatures (Jack Smith)
Dr. Strangelove (Stanley Kubrick)

1964
Cheyenne Autumn (John Ford)

Dog Star Man (Stan Brakhage) (1961–1964)
Empire (Andy Warhol)
My Fair Lady (George Cukor)
Scorpio Rising (Kenneth Anger)

1965
The Sound of Music (Robert Wise)

FIGURE 17.11 *Privilege* ★ United States, 1990, Yvonne Rainer.

1966
Chelsea Girls (Andy Warhol)
Don't Look Back (D. A. Pennebaker)

1967
Bonnie and Clyde (Arthur Penn)
The Graduate (Mike Nichols)
Guess Who's Coming for Dinner (Stanley Kramer)
Portrait of Jason (Shirley Clarke)
Titticut Follies (Frederick Wiseman)
Wavelength (Michael Snow)

1968
Faces (John Cassavetes)
High School (Frederick Wiseman)
Lonesome Cowboys (Andy Warhol)
Rosemary's Baby (Roman Polanski)
Salesman (Albert and David Maysles)

1969
Butch Cassidy and the Sundance Kid
   (George Roy Hill)
Diaries, Notes, and Sketches (Jonas Mekas)
   (1964–1969)
Easy Rider (Dennis Hopper)
Law and Order (Frederick Wiseman)
The Learning Tree (Gordon Parks)
Medium Cool (Haskell Wexler)
Midnight Cowboy (John Schlesinger)
The Wild Bunch (Sam Peckinpah)
The Year of the Pig (Emile de Antonio)

1970
Gimme Shelter (Albert and David Maysles
   and Charlotte Zwerin)
Little Big Man (Arthur Penn)
*M*A*S*H* (Robert Altman)

Trash (Andy Warhol and Paul Morrissey)
Woodstock (Michael Wadleigh)

1971
The French Connection (William Friedkin)
The Last Picture Show (Peter Bogdanovich)
McCabe and Mrs. Miller (Robert Altman)
Minnie and Moskowitz (John Cassavetes)
Shaft (Gordon Parks)
Sweet Sweetback's Baadasssss Song
  (Melvin Van Peebles)

1972
Cabaret (Bob Fosse)
The Godfather (Francis Ford Coppola)

1973
American Graffiti (George Lucas)
Badlands (Terrence Malik)
The Exorcist (William Friedkin)
The Long Goodbye (Robert Altman)
Mean Streets (Martin Scorsese)

1974
Chinatown (Roman Polanski)
The Conversation (Francis Ford Coppola)
Film About a Woman Who . . . (Yvonne Rainer)
The Godfather II (Francis Ford Coppola)
A Woman Under the Influence (John Cassavetes)

Books on the Period

Biskind, Peter. *Easy Riders, Raging Bulls: The Generation That Transformed Hollywood.* New York: Simon and Schuster, 1998.

Cobley, Paul. *The American Thriller: Generic Innovation and Social Change in the 1970s.* New York: Palgrave, 2001.

Cook, David. *Lost Illusions: American Cinema in the Shadow of Watergate, 1970–1979* (Vol. 9 of *History of American Cinema*). Berkeley: University of California Press, 2002.

Curran, Daniel. *Guide to American Cinema, 1965–1995.* Westport, CT: Greenwood Press, 1998.

Elsaesser, Thomas, ed. *The Last Great American Picture Show: New Hollywood Cinema in the 1970s.* Amsterdam: Amsterdam University Press, 2004.

Gilbey, Ryan. *It Don't Worry Me: The Revolutionary American Films of the Seventies.* New York: Faber and Faber, 2003.

Hoberman, J. *The Dream Life: Movies, Media and the Mythology of the Sixties.* New York: New Press, 2003.

Kolker, Robert. *A Cinema of Loneliness: Penn, Stone, Kubrick, Scorsese, Spielberg, Altman.* New York: Oxford University Press, 2000.

Lev, Peter. *American Films of the 70s: Conflicting Visions.* Austin: University of Texas Press, 2000.

Lewis, Jon. *Hollywood v. Hard Core: How the Struggle over Censorship Created the Modern Film Industry.* New York: New York University Press, 2002.

Man, Glen. *Radical Visions: American Film Renaissance, 1967–1976.* Westport, CT: Greenwood Press, 1994.

Monaco, Paul. *The Sixties: 1960–1969* (Vol. 8 of *History of American Cinema*). Berkeley: University of California Press, 2003.

18

Art Cinema Lite: British Film

1963–

As American distributors have increasingly shied away from films with subtitles, the English-language British art film has become the dominant entry in the American art-house market. To audiences in the United States, contemporary British films offer the appeals of an unfamiliar culture and challenging subject matter. The international festival circuit, as well, has recognized the originality and thoughtfulness of modern British cinema. To be sure, some of the newer British releases fall into the predictable clichés of heritage productions. But others build on the socially progressive documentary model that John Grierson pioneered. The British reservoir of wit, acting prowess, and social insight also comes into play in many of these newer films. And the British gothic strain, too, is alive and well. In the 1960s and 1970s Britain also discovered its cultural diversity, and movies were made not only about the working classes but also about regional communities, Scots, Irish, immigrant Pakistanis and Turks, and members of gay subcultures, along with many other citizens of the British Isles—even, in some cases, displaced Americans. Members of such groups frequently helmed these productions as well.

State of the Industry

The ebb and flow of the British film industry is inextricably tied to the ebb and flow of American production dollars and American audiences. In the early 1980s there was talk of a British film renaissance. *Chariots of Fire,* directed by Hugh Hudson, had become the most successful British film ever released in the United States and won the Oscar for best picture of 1981. In the exhilaration of the moment the cry "The British are coming!" was uttered (by a Brit, admittedly).

Adding support to the British film renaissance was a television channel, Channel 4 of the quasi-governmental BBC, named in reference to the other two BBC channels, plus the commercial channel, ITV. Set up in 1980, Channel 4 went on the air in 1982. In that year it began to finance feature films in the manner of Italian (RAI) and West German (ZDF) state television. *The Draughtsman's Contract* (1982) and *Dance with a Stranger* (Mike Newell, 1984) were made because Channel 4 was prepared to supplement monies obtained elsewhere as required. In 1984 ten out of twenty-eight British features had financial investment from Channel 4; several of the others were presold to the network (*Insignificance,* for example). In 1985 *My Beautiful Laundrette* was fully financed by Channel 4, as was most of *Wetherby* (1985). The British Film Institute, another partly governmental agency, has also contributed to the financing and cofinancing of a number of British successes, as has a related organization, British Screen. After these sources had run short of funds in the late 1980s, the government stepped in again, dedicating some of the proceeds from the national lottery to the support of film production.

Supplementing these resources in the 1990s was a commercially oriented group of U.S. and multinationally financed British-based production companies such as Polygram (*Four Weddings and a Funeral,* Mike Newell, 1994; *Elizabeth,* Shakhar Kapur, 1998), Pathé (*Ratcatcher,* 1999), and HAL, an offshoot of the American independent powerhouse Miramax (*Mansfield Park,* 1998). By the late 1990s, as a result of these varied initiatives, the industry was again on a roll, though its scale remained modest in relation to the American behemoth. As one British producer commented, to compare the English movie industry to that of Hollywood is "like comparing the space program with people in the Hebrides knitting scarves."

British Comedy Flourishes

As the twentieth century turned into the twenty-first, British comedy stayed on course, expanding its horizons to focus more specifically on heretofore marginalized classes and groups. For the most part, the mood of the films created was bittersweet—funny, yes, but packing a social wallop. Gender stereotypes are spoofed in *The Full Monty* (Peter Cattaneo, 1997) (Figure 18.1), *Billy Elliott* (Stephen Daldry, 2000), and *Calendar Girls* (Nigel Cole, 2003). *Waking Ned Devine* (Kirk Jones, 1998) ridicules the finagling ways of the Irish. The difficulties faced by East Indians in Britain are gently mocked in Gurinder Chadha's 1993 *Bhaji on the Beach.*

A new generation of stellar comic talents emerged during this period. Julie Walters's no-nonsense beautician won hearts on both sides of the Atlantic in *Educating Rita* (Lewis Gilbert, 1983). John Cleese showed his mastery of expressions of frustrated ardor in *A Fish Called Wanda* (Charles Crichton, 1988). Hugh Grant stuttered and stumbled his way to international stardom in *Four Weddings and a Funeral* (Mike Newell, 1994).

New comic directorial talents have also flourished in the new British cinema. Gurinder Chadha, who has worked on both sides of the Atlantic, had an international hit in 2002 with *Bend It Like Beckham,* in which a young Pakistani-British girl rebels against her traditional parents in order to play competitive soccer (Figure 18.2). Sharon Maguire captured the women's market at home and abroad with *Bridget Jones's Diary* (2001) and *Bridget Jones: The Edge of Reason* (2004). Two of the directors who specialize in comedy, Bill Forsythe and Mike Leigh, have each created a substantial body of work that bears close examination.

FIGURE 18.1 *The Full Monty* ★ United Kingdom, 1997, Peter Cattaneo.

FIGURE 18.2 *Bend It Like Beckham* ★ United Kingdom, 2002, Gurinder Chadha.

FIGURE 18.3a and b *Local Hero* ★ United Kingdom, 1983, Bill Forsyth; b. Denis Lawson (middle), Peter Riegert (right).

Bill Forsyth, a Scot, has worked within what can be described as a revival of the Ealing comedy tradition. Forsyth-directed films—such as *That Sinking Feeling* (1979), *Gregory's Girl* (1981), and *Comfort and Joy* (1984)—have offered Scottish looks and Scottish ways with a knowing and affectionate humor that marks them as emanating from the British Isles. Like many of the earlier Ealing directors, Forsyth began film making with documentaries. His most widely seen feature, *Local Hero,* released in 1983, was shot on location in Fort William (Figure 18.3a). The plot concerns the oil strike in the North Sea and a visiting agent for a Houston oil company. It is reminiscent of the situation in *Tight Little Island* (1949), with an American intruder replacing the earlier English one. In this case, however, the foreigner succumbs to the charms of the villagers and longs to be one of them (Figure 18.3b).

In the 1980s and 1990s a new group of directors carried the tradition of British comedy forward. The most innovative of these was **Mike Leigh.** Leigh's films draw on the considerable resources represented by the large pool of talented British actors, making performers partners in the creative process by developing scripts from scenes they improvise together. In time-honored British fashion, Leigh's films, including *High Hopes* (1988) and *Life Is Sweet* (1991), focus on strongly defined social types, often from the lower classes. At times, however, his characters reveal depths of feeling not often seen in comedies. Leigh's most admired production, *Secrets and Lies,* which won the Palme d'Or at Cannes in 1996, features a scene in which a middle-aged matron is confronted by a young woman who unexpectedly reveals that she is the former's long-lost daughter. In the role of the mother, actor Brenda Blethyn improvised an in-character response to this news that is one of the greatest performances ever recorded on film. In 1999 Leigh made a more conventional costume drama, *Topsy Turvy,* about the collaboration of the popular nineteenth-century operetta composers, Gilbert and Sullivan (Figure 18.4). The emphasis on the collaborative nature of theater artistry in this production can be seen as a comment on Leigh's own philosophy of shared creative endeavor.

New Social Critiques

The advent of a conservative government led by Prime Minister Margaret Thatcher in 1979 gave renewed impetus to the British cinema of social criticism. In response to Thatcherism, artists in all media created works that protested the large-scale cutbacks in social programs

FIGURE 18.4   *Topsy Turvy* ☀ United Kingdom, 1999, Mike Leigh.

and hawkish foreign policies that were adopted. This attitude, which built on the long-standing British tradition of progressive politics and more particularly on the conventions of the documentary model of the 1930s and the kitchen sink school of the 1960s, gave new energy to Britain's cinema of social awareness. As befitting a new era in which local identities and ethnic pride increasingly held sway, the new cinema of social critique found its subjects among ethnic minorities and other marginalized subcultures. Prominent among those whose work fits this category are Ken Loach, Stephen Frears, Michael Winterbottom, and Lynn Ramsay.

Beginning with *Kes,* his first feature, in 1969, **Ken Loach**'s films all deal with the plight of the poor and those who have progressive political ideas. "I think it is very important to let people speak who are usually disqualified from speaking or who've become non-persons," he has said, "activists, militants, or people who really have any developed political ideas." Loach has made many incisive films about the English social scene, including *Family Life* in 1973, which deals with the efforts of a working-class family to deal with mental illness; *Raining Stones* in 1993, about the effects of chronic unemployment on a well-meaning husband and father; and *Ladybird, Ladybird* in 1994, about a lower-class woman whose children are taken away from her. He has also made films about international issues, including *Land and Freedom* in 1995, which deals with the British radicals who fought in the Spanish Civil War, and *Carla's Song* in 1996, which tells of an Edinburgh bus driver who follows his Nicaraguan girlfriend to her homeland and becomes involved in the conflict there (Figure 18.5). Loach's unprettified *mise-en-scènes* reflect the grungy lifestyles of his characters, and his loose narrative structures follow their adventures in a *laissez faire* manner. Many Loach films are highly comedic, but the humor is

FIGURE 18.5 *Carla's Song* ★ United Kingdom, 1996, Ken Loach; Oyanka Cabezas.

always carried off with a feeling of affection for the characters, who are seen as constrained more by social circumstances than by innate limitations. Although he uses skilled actors, they typically speak in the thick dialects characteristic of their characters' class and region, making Loach's films generally unattractive to American distributors.

Stephen Frears began his career as an assistant to Lindsay Anderson, but he has developed a much more eclectic body of work. His most memorable films, however, contain an undercurrent of social criticism that is identifiably British, often combined with an emphasis on ethnic and gender issues. The most radical of these, *My Beautiful Laundrette* (1985) (Figure 18.6) and *Sammy and Rosie Get Laid* (1987), were the results of a collaboration with scriptwriter Hanif Kureishi, whose screenplays reveal facets of English ethnic and homosexual subcultures never before committed to film. "Hanif took me to a different country and brought me out alive," Frears later commented. Frears has gone on to direct a number of beautifully crafted productions made on both sides of the Atlantic that have had a less clearly discernible social agenda, most notable among which are *Dangerous Liaisons* (1988), *The Grifters* (1990), *The Snapper* (1993), and *High Fidelity* (2000). In 2003 he again took up a hot political subject with *Dirty Pretty Things,* a thriller about third-world immigrants in London who are forced to sell their kidneys in order to raise money.

The troubles of immigrants, legal or otherwise, and the problems of regional minorities continue to fester in the face of Britain's increasing prosperity. To be sure, under the administration of Prime Minister Tony Blair, a liberal centrist who took power in the early 1990s, the motivation for a cinema of social protest has been somewhat blunted. New social programs were enacted under Blair, and the rising economic and political power of the European Union carried the United Kingdom with it. Nonetheless, the social sensitivities that are the heritage of British film makers have ensured that they will continue to be

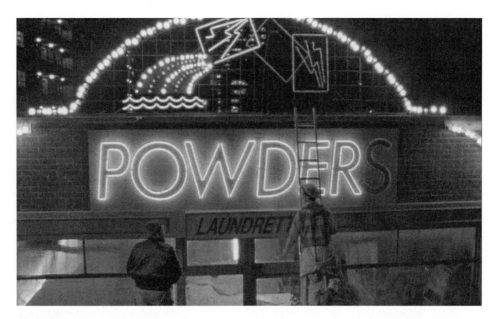

FIGURE 18.6   *My Beautiful Laundrette*   ★   United Kingdom, 1985, Stephen Frears; Daniel Day-Lewis on right.

drawn to issues of political injustice and cultural deprivation. The careers of two widely praised film makers of the new millennium, Michael Winterbottom and Lynn Ramsay, demonstrate this commitment.

Michael Winterbottom has produced an eclectic body of work, but many of his films focus on subcultural communities. His widely praised *In This World* (2002), which deals with Afghani refugees, is virtually a semidocumentary. To get an inside view of the refugee experience, Winterbottom and his producer took a small crew to the Pakistan-Afghanistan border, where they interviewed hundreds of Afghanis living in a refugee camp. They then accompanied two young men from the camp on a harrowing journey to London. Though much of the action of the film is staged, the harrowing experiences the two men undergo in their quest for a better life in the West are based on actual events. Winterbottom's next production, *24 Hour Party People,* portrays quite a different subculture. It explores Manchester's music scene during the 1970s and 1980s and features a hip British punk soundtrack along with a dizzying array of cinematic effects created by ace German photographer Robby Muller.

Scottish native **Lynn Ramsay** also makes films that demonstrate an acute observation of overlooked subcultures. Her 1999 *Ratcatcher* portrays the interior landscape of a melancholy young boy through images of the Glasgow slum in which he lives. A garbage strike has left piles of decaying trash dotting the streets, generating vermin and disease (Figure 18.7a). The fetid canal that runs through the neighborhood carries even more ominous overtones, acting as a treacherous lure to the children of the community (Figure 18.7b). Ramsay followed up this stunning debut with *Morvern Callar,* another portrait of an impoverished Scot, this one a young woman. "It's as if poor people were in a war that no one else was," Ramsay has said of her concern with the Scottish underclass.

FIGURE 18.7a and b   *Ratcatcher* ★ United Kingdom 1999, Lynn Ramsay; a. Lynn Ramsay Jr.

British Postmodernism

In the latter part of the twentieth century, British gothicism took a postmodern turn with films that combined the eerie, otherworldly qualities and shock tactics of the gothic mode with fractured plots, self-referential asides, and showy visuals. These productions found small but dedicated audiences who wanted to be provoked and challenged. Among the directors who gave expression to this new direction were Nicolas Roeg, Peter Greenaway, and Sally Potter.

Nicolas Roeg, who initially made his reputation as a topflight cinematographer (working, for example, on Truffaut's *Fahrenheit 451,* 1996), turned to directing with the surrealistic *Performance* (1970) (on which he shared credit with Donald Cammell). Featuring rock star Mick Jagger, *Performance* intermingled music, drugs, sex, and identity confusion. Roeg's subsequent solo work was distinguished, as one might expect, by handsome visuals, often representing exotic and alluring locales. In keeping with the spirit of postmodern gothicism, his films increasingly take the form of Byzantine mosaics in which logic is transcended, like the stories of Argentinian writer Jorge Luis Borges (who was, in fact, invoked in *Performance).* Roeg's most widely seen film, *Don't Look Now* (1973), with Julie Christie and Donald Sutherland, combines murder, illusion, and the supernatural in the manner of Hitchcock's *Vertigo.* It offers what is surely one of the most ravishing portraits of Venice ever committed to film (Figure 18.8).

Another director in the postmodern tradition, **Peter Greenaway,** began as a painter. Although not appealing to all tastes, Greenaway's work is stylish, inventive, and enigmatic, offered as a delightful game between film maker and audience. From 1966 he made experimental shorts; in 1980 he turned to features. The first of these to receive international attention was *The Draughtsman's Contract* (1982). An extremely clever, mannered evocation of the mores and morals of aristocratic seventeenth-century England, it revolves around seduction and murder in a stately country house. Eventually it becomes a metaphysical puzzle that proves insoluble, at least in terms of the evidence offered. *The Cook, the Thief, His Wife, and Her Lover* (1989), thought by some to be his best film, benefited at the box office from the notoriety earned by its scandalous content: adulterous copulation being carried on mostly in the washrooms of a posh London restaurant while the title characters are engaged in sumptuous dinners (Figure 18.9a and b). Its form includes sets and lighting palettes of red, blue, or dazzling white, and references to famous painters' paintings.

FIGURE 18.8 *Don't Look Now* ⋆ United Kingdom, 1973, Nicolas Roeg.

FIGURE 18.9a and b   *The Cook, the Thief, His Wife, and Her Lover* ★ United Kingdom, 1989, Peter Greenaway; a. Alan Howard and Helen Mirren

In the 1970s a British academic film journal, *Screen,* became the English-language voice for a new, more politically and theoretically engaged way of looking at cinema. Represented most infuentially by critic–film maker Laura Mulvey's seminal 1975 essay "Visual Pleasure and Narrative Cinema," *Screen* led film scholars on both sides of the Atlantic to turn their attention to the ways in which mainstream cinema portrays the female body as an object displayed for the benefit of what became known as "the male gaze." A British director whose style evolved in sympathy with this feminist perspective on the nature of film narratives was **Sally Potter.** Potter's first production, the thirty-minute *Thriller,* released in 1979, was conceived as a deconstruction of the gender politics of the opera *La Boheme.* Her most widely seen feature, the 1992 *Orlando* (Figure 18.10), takes as its guiding principle the proposition that gender roles are social constructions. Based on a Virginia

FIGURE 18.10 *Orlando* ★ United Kingdom–Russia–France–Netherlands, 1992, Sally Potter; Tilda Swinton and Charlotte Valandrey.

Woolf novella, *Orlando* traces the adventures of a Renaissance man who is reincarnated as a woman and lives many lives throughout the centuries that follow. The film's spectacular *mise-en-scène* features lavish costumes and sumptuous backgrounds of castles and estates in England and on the continent.

Americans Abroad

British cinema of the last half of the twentieth century was distinguished by a cluster of sometimes brilliant directors whose films, for the most part, had an international rather than a national identity. They worked on either side of the Atlantic and for American money in any case. Of the former social-realist directors, Reisz (*The French Lieutenant's Woman,* 1981) has worked in the United States and on U.S. projects; Richardson (*The Charge of the Light Brigade,* 1968) and Schlesinger (*Midnight Cowboy,* 1969) have alternated between the United Kingdom and the United States. Another group of British directors who work in Hollywood are hardly distinguishable from their U.S. colleagues, including Adrian Lyne (*Flashdance,* 1973, and *Fatal Attraction,* 1987), Alan Parker (*Mississippi Burning,* 1988, and *Evita,* 1996), Mike Figgis (*Leaving Las Vegas,* 1995), and Ridley Scott (*Blade Runner,* 1982; *Thelma and Louise,* 1991; and *Gladiator,* 2000). On the other hand, four Americans, long-time residents in England, clearly became English to the extent that Henry James and T. S. Eliot became English: Joseph Losey, Richard Lester, Stanley Kubrick, and Terry Gilliam. Each drew on aspects of the British cultural heritage to create works that built on the traditions of which they subsequently became part.

FIGURE 18.11   *The Servant* ✶ United Kingdom, 1963, Joseph Losey; Dirk Bogarde and James Fox.

After a modestly successful Hollywood career, **Joseph Losey** exiled himself in 1951 in order to escape the blacklisting of the McCarthy era. In Britain his reputation was first established with a succession of moderately budgeted pictures within conventional idioms that are packed with political meaning and psychological, even philosophical, complexities. With *The Servant* (1963) (Figure 18.11) Losey began his association with playwright Harold Pinter and moved from the partially covert investigation of British society to a clear emphasis on social observation less restricted by rigid and complex plotting. To be more exact, beginning with *The Servant* and continuing with *King and Country* (1964), *Accident* (1967), *The Go-Between* (1971), *The Romantic Englishwoman* (1979), and *Steaming,* completed just before he died in 1984, a group of Losey's films comment directly on a culture that he observed with the eye of an outsider who has experienced fresh what others had absorbed from birth. Implicit criticisms of British manners and the British class system abound in these films, which differ from earlier kitchen sink productions in their emphasis on middle- and upper-class characters and their stylish cinematography.

Richard Lester was attracted to a much different kind of England than was Losey— the rock, the mod, and the trendy. Lester drew lavishly on the tradition of British comedy, updating it with a hip 1960s spin. Moving to London in 1955 (at the age of twenty-three) Lester worked on television commercials during his first years there, developing the technical facility—including rapid cutting, freely moving camera, and improvisational performance style—that is associated with his earlier, and some of his later, work. *The Running, Jumping, and Standing-Still Film* (1959), a short for BBC-TV's *The Goon Show* (predecessor to the more famous *Monty Python's Flying Circus*), set forth his special talents in capsule form. It was followed by two features starring the Beatles: *A Hard Day's Night*

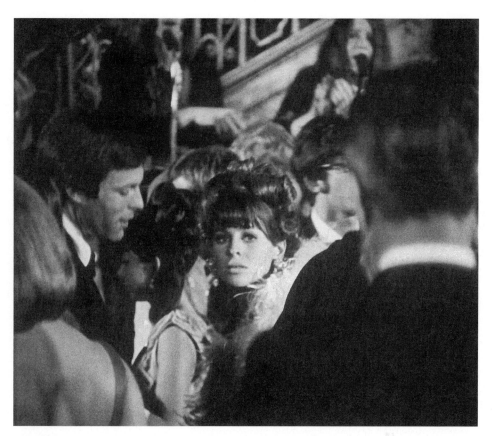

FIGURE 18.12 *Petulia* ✶ United Kingdom, 1968, Richard Lester; Richard Chamberlain and Julie Christie.

(1964) and *Help!* (1965). *Petulia* (1968), his first feature shot in the United States, may also be his best. Following the British tradition of acute social analysis, it appraises the American scene through the revealing exaggerations that California manners and mores offer (Figure 18.12). Featuring American Method actors George C. Scott and Shirley Knight along with British star Julie Christie, it also attempts a much more intense and sustained probing of character than any of Lester's other films.

Stanley Kubrick, who arrived in Britain ten years after Losey and six years after Lester, had an even more substantial career before leaving the United States. In his American films Kubrick seemed to be setting off in several directions at once, however: antiwar statement (the youthful outcry of *Fear and Desire,* 1953, and the mature condemnation of *Paths of Glory,* 1957); gangster film (the experimentally expressionistic *Killer's Kiss,* 1955, and the expertly professional *The Killing,* 1956); and even historical spectacle (*Spartacus,* 1960). Beginning with his first film made in Britain, *Lolita* (1962), he began gradually to settle into a consistently cynical, increasingly misanthropic view of humankind, a mordant variant on the British legacy of social criticism, which he combined with corrosive satire, his own version of English humor. Kubrick came to depend on strong literary

FIGURE 18.13   Stanley Kubrick shooting a scene from *A Clockwork Orange* ⋆ United Kingdom, 1971; Adrienne Corri and Malcolm McDowell.

figures for sources and/or collaboration: Vladimir Nabokov for *Lolita,* Terry Southern for *Dr. Strangelove, or, How I Learned to Stop Worrying and Love the Bomb* (1964), Arthur Clarke for *2001: A Space Odyssey* (1968), Anthony Burgess for *A Clockwork Orange* (1971) (Figure 18.13), William Thackery for *Barry Lyndon* (1975), Stephen King for *The Shining* (1980), and Arthur Schnitzler for *Eyes Wide Shut,* which he completed just before his death in 2000. Each of those films is laced with dark humor and enlivened by extraordinary set constructions. All feature the clean, hard-edged cinematography for which Kubrick has become known. Perhaps the most conspicuous aspect of his films is the consistency of the world they portray. Of the somberness of this spectacle Kubrick has said, "We're never going to get down to doing anything about the things that are really bad in the world until there is recognition within us of the darker side of our natures, the shadow side."

Having made his home in England since 1963 and begun his career creating animations for the popular British TV comedy series *Monty Python,* **Terry Gilliam** has absorbed much of the British sensibility. Although he has worked on both sides of the Atlantic, his taste for distopic fantasy and mordant social satire are reminiscent of the work of Irish writer Jonathan Swift. *Brazil* (1985), *The Adventures of Baron Munchausen* (1988), and *Twelve Monkeys* (1995) are Gilliam's most highly regarded productions to date, the first two cartoonish portraits of fantasmagoric worlds, the last a more subdued reworking of French director Chris Marker's short science-fiction film about time travel.

In 2004 *Vera Drake,* a new film from British director Mike Leigh, was released to widespread acclaim. Here, in a single film, many of the motifs associated with the tradition of British cinema were in evidence. Its credentials as a piece of social criticism were evident in its plot, which told the tale of a warmhearted charwoman in 1940s London who performed illegal abortions. British acting, too, was placed center stage when Imelda Staunton, who played Vera, received kudos from a number of international festival juries for her performance; Staunton's role required her to alter her demeanor from the bustling energy and cheer Vera radiates during the early scenes to the terror-stricken catatonia she sinks into after she is arrested. Shot in a working-class neighborhood of London, *Vera Drake* has the documentary feel one associates with the legacy of John Grierson. Moreover, though the overall tone of the film is somber, scenes centered on its secondary characters, such as one in which Vera's son sells a gullible customer a suit, or another when her shy daughter is courted by their neighbor, highlight the comic spirit for which British film has long been known. Productions such as *Vera Drake* attest to the continued vitality and distinctive virtues that make British films the first choice of American art-house patrons. Though the verbal language is the same in both countries, the cultural language is Britain's own.

Films of the Period

1963
Billy Liar (John Schlesinger)
This Sporting Life (Lindsay Anderson)

1964
Dr. Strangelove (Stanley Kubrick)
A Hard Day's Night (Richard Lester)
King and Country (Joseph Losey)

1965
Darling (John Schlesinger)
Help! (Richard Lester)
The Knack (Richard Lester)
The War Game (Peter Watkins)

1966
Blow-Up (Michelangelo Antonioni)

1967
Accident (Joseph Losey)
How I Won the War (Richard Lester)

1968
Petulia (Richard Lester)
2001: A Space Odyssey (Stanley Kubrick)

1969
If . . . (Lindsay Anderson)
Kes (Ken Loach)
Women in Love (Ken Russell)

1970
The Music Lovers (Ken Russell)
Performance (Nicolas Roeg)

1971
A Clockwork Orange (Stanley Kubrick)
The Devils (Ken Russell)
The Go-Between (Joseph Losey)
Sunday Bloody Sunday (John Schlesinger)
Walkabout (Nicolas Roeg)

1972
Family Life (Ken Loach)

1973
Don't Look Now (Nicolas Roeg)
O Lucky Man! (Lindsay Anderson)

1975
Barry Lyndon (Stanley Kubrick)

1976
The Man Who Fell to Earth (Nicolas Roeg)

1977
Providence (Alain Resnais)

1979
That Sinking Feeling (Bill Forsyth)
Thriller (Sally Potter)

1980
Bad Timing (Nicolas Roeg)
The Shining (Stanley Kubrick)

1981
Chariots of Fire (Hugh Hudson)
Gregory's Girl (Bill Forsyth)

1982
The Draughtsman's Contract (Peter Greenaway)

1983
Local Hero (Bill Forsyth)

1984
Comfort and Joy (Bill Forsyth)

1985
Brazil (Terry Gilliam)
My Beautiful Laundrette (Stephen Frears)

1986
Carravagio (Derek Jarman)
Mona Lisa (Neil Jordan)

1987
Hope and Glory (John Boorman)
Sammy and Rosie Get Laid (Stephen Frears)

1988
Distant Voices, Still Lives (Terence Davies)
A Fish Called Wanda (Charles Crichton)
High Hopes (Mike Leigh)

1989
The Cook, the Thief, His Wife, and Her Lover (Peter Greenaway)
Henry V (Kenneth Branaugh)

1991
Edward II (Derek Jarman)
Howard's End (James Ivory)
Life Is Sweet (Mike Leigh)
Prospero's Books (Peter Greenaway)
Young Soul Rebels (Isaac Julien)

1992
The Crying Game (Neil Jordan)
Orlando (Sally Potter)

1993
Bhaji on the Beach (Gurinder Chadha)
Naked (Mike Leigh)
The Remains of the Day (James Ivory)

1994
Four Weddings and a Funeral (Mike Newell)
Ladybird, Ladybird (Ken Loach)

1995
Land and Freedom (Ken Loach)
The Pillow Book (Peter Greenaway)

1996
Carla's Song (Ken Loach)
Frantz Fanon: Black Skin, White Mask (Isaac Julien)
Hamlet (Kenneth Branaugh)
Secrets and Lies (Mike Leigh)
Trainspotting (Danny Boyle)

1997
The Tango Lesson (Sally Potter)

1998
Elizabeth (Shakhar Kapur)

1999
The End of the Affair (Neil Jordan)
Lock, Stock and Two Smoking Barrels (Guy Ritchie)
Ratcatcher (Lynn Ramsay)
Shakespeare in Love (John Madden)
Topsy Turvy (Mike Leigh)

2000
Bread and Roses (Ken Loach)
The Man Who Cried (Sally Potter)

2001
Sexy Beast (Jonathan Glazer)

2002
Bend It Like Beckham (Gurinder Chadha)
Bloody Sunday (Paul Greengrass)
Dirty Pretty Things (Stephen Frears)
In This World (Michael Winterbottom)
Morvern Callar (Lynn Ramsay)

Sweet Sixteen (Ken Loach)
24 Hour Party People (Michael Winterbottom)

2004
Bride and Prejudice (Gurinder Chadha)
Ae Fond Kiss (Ken Loach)
9 Songs (Michael Winterbottom)
Vera Drake (Mike Leigh)
Yes (Sally Potter)

Books on the Period

Barton, Ruth. *Irish National Cinema.* New York: Routledge, 2004.

Chibnall, Steve, and Robert Murphy. *British Crime Cinema.* New York: Routledge, 1999.

Gillett, Philip. *The British Working Class in Postwar Film.* London: Palgrave, 2003.

Hewing, Wendy. *British Cinema in the 1960s: An Educational Resource.* London: BFI Publishing, 2003.

Higson, Andrew. *English Heritage, English Cinema.* New York: Oxford University Press, 2003.

Hill, John. *British Cinema in the 1980s: Issues and Themes.* New York: Oxford University Press, 1999.

Hogenkamp, Bert. *Film, Television, and the Left in Britain: 1950 to 1970.* London: Laurence and Wishart, 2000.

Hunter, I. Q., ed. *British Science Fiction Cinema.* New York: Routledge, 1999.

McIlroy, Brian. *Shooting to Kill: Filmmaking and the "Troubles" in Northern Ireland.* Richmond, BC: Steveston Press, 2001.

McLoone, Martin. *Irish Film: The Emergence of a Contemporary Cinema.* London: BFI Publishing, 2001.

Murphy, Robert, ed. *British Cinema of the '90s.* London: British Film Institute, 2000.

Petrie, Duncan. *Screening Scotland.* London: BFI Publishing, 2000.

Rowbotham, Shelia, and Huw Beynon, eds. *Looking at Class: Film, Television, and the Working Class in Britain.* New York: New York University Press, 2001.

Street, Sarah. *Transatlantic Crossings: British Feature Films in the USA.* New York: Continuum, 2002.

19

New Theories, New Films: France

★ ★ ★ ★

1968–

May 1968 was a watershed moment in French history. Galvanized by the escalation of the war in Vietnam and other political events, student radicals joined striking workers to stage violent protests in Paris and around the country, hoping to bring down the government. Although the movement failed to meet its immediate goals, these disturbances and the sentiments leading up to them had a lasting effect on the outlook of many young people. The cinema world was additionally galvanized by the attempted removal of Henri Langlois, longtime champion of film preservation, from his post as director of the French Cinémathèque. Reacting to these occurrences, a new generation of *Cahiers* critics turned away from a romantic, idealist conception of film *auteurs* to a more political approach to cinema informed by the theories of the Marxist German playwright Bertolt Brecht and others. Brecht had espoused a political art that actively engaged audiences by foregrounding its formal structures. In the words of one *Cahiers* critic, "What is needed is an attempt to understand the work not at the level of the 'humanistic' intentions of its *auteur* but at the level of its meanings—the work understood as a *mediation*." The idea was that auteurs—and, indeed, all artists who created works with the goal of expressing their inner feelings—were furthering the goals of a corrupt capitalist system that fostered competition and the hero worship of individuals divorced from culture in place of cooperation and group activity. The critic's job as now defined was to understand the way in which films related to the larger society that produced and consumed them, not to the transcendent vision of an isolated individual. The most immediate consequence of this more politicized understanding of art was a renunciation of the concept of individual authorship altogether, not only by the *Cahiers* critics but also by some radical film makers as well, most notably Godard and Marker.

A Radicalized Godard

As was noted in Chapter 12, **Jean-Luc Godard** had been interested in a politicized, Brechtian cinema from the beginning of his career. Following Brechtian precepts to their logical, antiauteurist conclusion, his work in the late 1960s and early 1970s was carried out either in partnership with Anne-Marie Miéville or with a collective that called itself "the Dziga Vertov Group" in honor of the visionary Soviet film maker of the 1920s. (The Dziga Vertov Group was actually composed of Godard and Marxist intellectual Jean-Pierre Gorin.) The move to a model of anonymous group authorship by Godard and other French film makers was echoed in the policies of *Cahiers* itself, as the editors began to sign their articles as a collective rather than as individual writers. However, these attempts to deny individuality were destined to be short-lived. By the mid-1970s both Godard and the *Cahiers* writers were again signing their works as individual authors.

Godard's films made just before and after the May 1968 uprising were extraordinarily daring in their push to dismantle realist illusionism and narrative, which Godard denounced as bourgeois. Intended as spurs to discussion for committed Marxist groups, they presented too daunting a viewing experience for most general audiences. Films such as *Made in USA* (1966), *La Chinoise* (1967), and *Weekend* (1967) were defiantly expository and didactic. In *Le Gai Savoir* (1969), Godard's first film after the uprising, he abolished narrative altogether in an effort to find a revolutionary form suitable to revolutionary content.

Produced immediately before the events of May and released immediately afterward, *Weekend* begins with a caption that identifies it as "a film found on a scrap heap" and ends with another that reads "The end of cinema." Its minimal plot concerns a young bourgeois couple who set out on an automobile trip to borrow money from the woman's parents. En route they are waylaid first by a traffic jam, then by an encounter with a group of cannibalistic revolutionaries. Filled with digressions, the action meanders from incident to incident. A series of unconnected set pieces includes three 360-degree tracking shots around a farmyard to the accompaniment of a lecture on a Mozart sonata and a long closeup of an Algerian garbage collector, who glares silently into the camera as the voice of another garbage collector delivers an offscreen monologue. The film abounds in shock tactics, from the four-minute tracking shot of the devastation wreaked by the monumental traffic tie-up to the on-screen slaughter of a pig. In part, *Weekend* is constructed as an assault on its audience. Watching it is a frustrating but unforgettable experience.

Godard's absorption with politics and formal rarefactions meant that with the exception of *Tout va bien* (1972) and *Numéro deux* (1975)—both of which received limited commercial distribution—his work disappeared from public view after 1968. Later, however, *Sauve qui peut (la vie) (Every Man for Himself,* 1980) seemed to connect back to *Weekend* (1967) and the films that preceded it. The narrative structure and character psychology offer difficulty to be sure—like Resnais's *Mon Oncle d'Amérique* it is built around three characters whose lives become intertwined—but there is a story and there are characters. Formal experimentation is present—video techniques and stop motion, for example—along with Godard's abiding concern for "the politics of the image," and there is much visual beauty.

If *Sauve qui peut* might be thought of as being about the nature of cinema, as was said at the time, *Passion* (1982) most certainly can be. At its center are two east European film makers making a film called *Passion*. However, their film-within-the-film, and therefore Godard's film, is full of famous paintings (by Rembrandt, Goya, Delacroix, El Greco) brought to life in *tableaux vivant* accompanied by famous music (extracts from Mozart, Fauré, Ravel). Although art and politics are linked in *Passion*, as they are in Godard's thinking, the political problems don't receive as much attention as the aesthetic ones. It is then a familiar Godardian jumble of elements treated with philosophical engagement and emotional detachment—a truly "modern" film, we might say.

Following a series of marginally more conventional productions, such as *Détective* in 1984, a star-studded *King Lear* in 1987, and *Nouvelle Vague* in 1990, Godard turned to investigating the past of his chosen art form in a video series entitled *Histoire(s) du cinéma,* completed in 1994. Regarded by some critics as one of the cinematic highlights of the 1990s, *Histoire(s) du cinéma* is made up of film clips and commentary rendered in Godard's customary elliptical style.

Ever inventive, Godard continued to test the limits of cinematic expression in the new millennium with productions such as *In Praise of Love* in 2001 and *Our Music* in 2004. Like all of Godard's late work, *In Praise of Love* is partly a narrative and partly an essay, a collage of references to history, politics, art, love, and philosophy, with a smidgen of a story tucked in here and there. The story itself remains enigmatic: Edgar, a film maker (or playwright, one is never sure which), is attempting to put together a production about four stages of love (meeting, passion, loss, and recovery), using three couples of differing ages. In a coda, Edgar is shown two years earlier. He is interviewing a couple who were active in the French resistance during World War II in connection with a cantata he is then engaged in composing in honor of the French philosopher and resistance heroine Simone Weil.

In Praise of Love lacks the playful audacity of Godard's early work; it is both sadder and angrier. In the background of many scenes, a mournful piano piece accompanies voice-over ruminations that return again and to the subjects of memory and death. Kosovo, Vietnam, and America become at various times the topics of the commentary. America, in particular, does not fare well. "Americans have no past," the voice-over asserts at one point. "They buy the pasts of other people, and sell images." (Godard's film opened in New York on the heels of the September 11 World Trade Center attack, an unfortunate accident of timing that did little to make its anti-American sentiments palatable to the local reviewers.)

Stylistically, *In Praise of Love* provides ample evidence of the director's penchant for peppering his productions with distancing Brechtian allusions. Printed intertitles break the flow of images up into nuggets of sights and sounds. When the plot suddenly shifts into flashback mode, the velvety black-and-white 35 mm images we had been watching give way to vivid digital video. (To make sure the audience understands the artificiality of these colored sequences, Godard begins this final sequence by showing us a red sea and blue sand in the manner of a Fauvist painter.)

Godard's allusions to other works of art repeatedly remind us that his film is not a picture of the world but rather an artifact he himself has made. In one scene two characters converse in front of a poster from the Iranian film *The Apple,* which Godard is known to admire (Figure 19.1a). And we see a poster for yet another of the film maker's favorite movies, Robert Bresson's *Pickpocket.* A scene that takes place on the Seine is accompanied by music taken from the French film classic *L'Atalante,* a movie shot largely on the same river (Figure 19.1b). Less flattering are the movie's references to Hollywood, espe-cially those to Steven Spielberg, whose *Schindler's List* is the object of a few snide asides. All of these touches remind us that we are watching a constructed world—and one that has been put together by a creative presence with definite tastes and opinions.

Edgar, the film's protagonist (insofar as there is one), is and is not a stand-in for the movie's director. True, he is an artist, as is Godard himself. But, unlike the prolific direc-tor, Edgar never seems to complete any project. He is ineffectual. Before he can make up his mind about the casting of his play/movie, his preferred leading lady commits suicide. At more than one point we see his notebook, which is almost empty (Figure 19.1c). One can make many charges against Godard, but a lack of imagination—as an empty notebook would suggest—is not one of them. Nor is dillydallying, for which Edgar—not Godard— pays the price of losing his lead performer.

But where in this scrapbook of failed aspirations and idle thoughts is the love that Godard's title promises to praise? Edgar's financial backer, an aging art collector, treats his paintings with love (Figure 19.1d). "In ancient times they emphasized relationships," he muses while examining two old masters. Later, we observe that the elderly resistance fight-ers Edgar interviews have managed to stay together despite the husband's major betrayal of his wife many years before. Perhaps, then, Godard sees a world in which love is being drained away, still lingering on among those of an older generation, but absent among the young. "The state cannot love," the movie's voice-over announces more than once. Are the young, then, to be seen as the creatures of this soulless state, reduced to thinking about love

FIGURE 19.1a–d *In Praise of Love* ★ France, 2001, Jean-Luc Godard.

and acting out scenarios of love instead of actually experiencing it? Godard's film suggests that they are.

The creativity and freedom with which Godard employs all of the technical and stylistic resources available to the film maker have not been equaled. No matter what his subject matter, he continues to be preoccupied with formal explorations of the possible combinations of moving images and accompanying sounds. The importance of his contributions to an evolving art form and his influence on the work of others is unquestionable.

After the New Wave

Despite the political upheaval that characterized the late 1960s and the subsequent move by the *Cahiers* group as well as film makers such as Godard and Marker to a more politicized and heavily theorized critical approach to cinema that was less preoccupied with its creators than with its effects, the French film public continued to value its auteurs. As the twentieth century drew to a close, new directors continued to appear, supported by the system of state subsidies that continues to be the highest in Europe. The *avance sur recettes* system was further refined by the socialist government that came into power in the early 1980s. Its minister of culture, Jack Lang, added film industry representatives to the group of government bureaucrats who served on judging panels and made awards available directly to directors as well as to production companies. These policies encouraged more adventuresome films as well as more films directed by women, such as Diane Kurys (*Entre Nous*, 1983), Euzhan Palcy (*Sugar Cane Alley*, 1983), and Catherine Breillat (*36 Fillette*, 1988; *Romance*, 1998) [Figure 19.2]).

Throughout the high-pressure negotiations carried on with the United States during the 1980s and 1990s, the strong-willed Lang managed to exclude film from the new free trade agreements. Singling it out in treaties by using the phrase *cultural exception,* he thereby kept in place quotas on the importation of Hollywood films and protected the market for homegrown productions. Lang's proactive strategy has met with limited success. Film production has risen, reaching 212 features by 2003. Despite a brief setback in 2001 when its parent company Vivendi became the object of a bitter takeover battle and its much beloved longtime head Pierre Lescaux was fired, the mammoth French pay-television company Canal-Plus has steadily increased its support of ambitious film-making projects. By 2002 it was providing financing for 80 percent of French film production.

As is true everywhere, it has been difficult for the French to keep Hollywood at bay; nonetheless, the film industry in France has remained far healthier than those of other European nations. After a miserable 2000, which saw domestic films account for less than 30 percent of French box-office revenues while Hollywood fare overwhelmed locally produced offerings, the French industry came roaring back in the new millennium. By 2003 it was reaping almost half of its robust earnings from the global marketplace. To further foster the efforts of French film makers, additional government subsidies were earmarked in 2001 to support distribution. At the same time, to prove that it didn't believe in honoring directors to the exclusion of all others involved in the movie-making process, the government also created a subsidy for script development, which is earmarked for writers.

In this supportive environment, new auteurs appeared, but, as if exhausted from the radical experimentation of the previous decades, the first of the new generation tended to

FIGURE 19.2 *Romance* ⋆ France, 1998, Catherine Breillat; Caroline Ducey and Sagamore Stévenin.

make more conventional films, appealing to audiences around the world through their sensitivity and intelligence. Among these newer figures were Bertrand Tavernier (*A Sunday in the Country*, 1984) (Figure 19.3), Maurice Pialat (*Under the Sun of Satan*, 1987), Claude Sautet (*Un Coeur en Hivre*, 1991), André Téchiné (*My Favorite Season*, 1993, and *Wild Reeds*, 1994), and Jacques Doillon (*Ponette*, 1996).

In the more politicized post-1968 environment, a group of documentary film makers also appeared, producing a series of magisterial works that often took a critical look at the past. Foremost among these documentarians is Marcel Ophüls, whose 1971 *The Sorrow and the Pity* delves into the history of French collaboration with the Nazis during World War II. In 1981 Ophüls produced another meditation on the events of World War II, *The Memory of Justice*, which focuses on the trials of German war criminals. Claude Lanzmann's nine-and-a-half-hour *Shoah* (1985) carries on the project of revisioning the past. Consisting solely of interviews, it examines the impact of the Holocaust on the psyches of some of its victims. The work of French anthropologist Jean Rouch, another documentarian, took a more ethnographic direction, including a number of films shot in West Africa. Rouch coined the phrase *cinéma vérité,* an updating of Dziga Vertov's notion of Kino Pravda (described in Chapter 4) to designate a documentary mode in which the film makers openly acknowledge their presence within the film itself. His most influential documentary, *Chronicle of a Summer* (1961), made in collaboration with the sociologist Edgar Morin, brings ethnographic investigation home; it is made up of the responses of average French people to the question, Are you happy?

FIGURE 19.3   *A Sunday in the Country*   ★   France, 1984, Bertrand Tavernier; Sabine Azema and Louis Ducreux.

Generic Continuities

Popular genres also continued to flourish during this period, especially thrillers, comedies, and heritage films, typically directed by film makers who functioned more like highly professional craftspeople than like idiosyncratic auteurs. The French tradition of ingenious, finely crafted thrillers (***polars***) was kept alive by such international hits as *La Balance* (Bob Swaim, 1982), *Monsieur Hire* (Patrice Leconte, 1989), and *Read My Lips* (Jacques Audiard, 2001). Comedy also flourished—notably *Café au lait* (Matthieu Kassovitz, 1994) (Figure 19.4), *Ma Vie en rose* (Alain Berliner, 1997) (Figure 19.5), and *The Taste of Others* (Agnès Jaoui, 2000). A number of these French comedies, such as *La Cage aux folles* (Edouard Molinero, 1979) and *Three Men and a Cradle* (Coline Serreau, 1985), were subsequently remade in Hollywood (as *The Birdcage* [Mike Nichols, 1998] and *Three Men and a Baby* [Leonard Nimoy, 1987], respectively). The heritage film, which dealt with events in French history and with significant individuals and works from the cultural past, was perhaps the most successful of all French genres during these years, benefiting from the high regard in which such productions were held by culture minister Jack Lang, and the large subsidies they received as a result. Sumptuous productions such as *The Return of Martin Guerre* (Daniel Vigne, 1982), *Cyrano de Bergerac* (Jean-Paul Rappeneau, 1990), and *Indochine* (Régis Warnier, 1992) recuperated France's cultural and political past with taste and style, finding large audiences both at home and abroad.

FIGURE 19.4 *Café au lait* ★ France, 1994, Matthieu Kassovitz; Hubert Koundé, Julie Maude Uech, and Matthieu Kassovitz.

FIGURE 19.5 *Ma Vie en rose* ★ France, 1997, Alain Berliner; Georges du Fresne.

A New Crop of Auteurs

The tradition of auteurism, however, was not forgotten. The 1980s saw the advent of a new group of directors with highly distinctive styles whose films were labeled *cinèma du look*. Featuring glossy, high-tech surfaces that announced their high production values combined with jazzy rhythms inspired by advertising and music videos, films of this sort became cult favorites around the world, but did not always find favor with critics. Most prominent among the films of the *cinèma du look* was Jean-Jacques Beineix's 1981 *Diva*, Luc Besson's 1990 *La Femme Nikita*, and, in a more subdued vein, Leos Carax's 1991 *Lovers on the Bridge*.

In the 1990s a more introspective and ironic group of directors came to the fore. Called "Young French Cinema," their films frequently concern the problems of youthful relationships, especially sexual ones, treated in a style reminiscent of Jean Eustache's post–New Wave production *The Mother and the Whore* (1973). The travails of youth depicted in these films are wittily yet sensitively portrayed by skilled ensemble casts. The actors are encouraged to improvise subtle interactions, supported by the long takes and deep-focus photography favored by the Young French Cinema directors. The paradigmatic examples of the style are Arnaud Desplechin's *My Sex Life (Or, How to Get into an Argument)* and Olivier Assayas's *Irma Vep*, both released in 1996. The former is a gentle satire about an immature young philosophy professor; the latter is a more unforgiving lampoon of French film making, featuring a burned-out director, played by New Wave stalwart Jean-Pierre Léaud, who is attempting to mount a remake of Louis Feuillade's classic 1915 French production *Les Vampires* starring the Hong Kong action star Maggie Cheung.

A politically minded group of film makers also emerged in the 1990s. Concerned with the struggles of working-class and ethnic peoples, these directors produced a series of films that reveal the underside of the economic prosperity of the *fin de siècle*. Foremost among the searing portraits of deprivation and alienation these film makers have produced are Matthieu Kasssovitz's 1995 *La Haine*, a raw portrait of a violent gang of lower-class youths from the Paris suburbs; Claire Denis's 1995 *I Can't Sleep*, a loosely intertwined series of narratives centering on immigrants existing uneasily on the margins of Parisian society; Eric Zonca's 1998 *The Dreamlife of Angels*, about the class barriers faced by two young working-class women who share a flat; and Bruno Dumont's 1999 *L'Humanité*, a controversial Cannes Film Festival winner about a *lumpen* provincial policeman investigating the rape and murder of a young girl. Except for *La Haine*, which is filmed in grainy, high-contrast black and white, these films use muted colors and a drab *mise-en-scène* to create an ambience of bleak hopelessness.

Perhaps the most honored of this last group of directors are the **Dardenne brothers** (Jean-Pierre and Luc), a pair of Belgians working within the French industry. In 1996 they produced *La Promesse*, which told the story about the moral dilemmas faced by the young son of a brutal man who smuggles illegal workers into Belgium from North Africa (Figure 19.6). The Dardennes followed this success in 1999 with the remarkable *Rosetta*, which won top honors at the Cannes Film Festival. Its plot concerns a young girl living in a trailer park whose main ambition is to get a job as a street vendor. For the duration of the action the camera follows Rosetta in relentless, handheld closeups as she battles with the world and especially with her alcoholic mother, trying vainly to achieve a measure of dignity and self-worth. In the brutal hardscrabble environment she inhabits, it is doubly surprising to witness the young girl's encounter with a person who offers her a kind of spiritual salva-

FIGURE 19.6a and b *La Promesse* ★ Belgium–France–Luxemburg, 1996, Luc and Jean-Pierre Dardenne; a. Jérémie Renier; b. Jérémie Renier and Assita Ouédraogo.

tion, even though she is unable to respond to the lifeline he represents. The hyperkinetic style of *Rosetta* is the polar opposite of the contemplative serenity that characterizes the films of Robert Bresson, yet the Dardenne brothers' thematic preoccupations are not far removed from those of the earlier film maker. Although *Rosetta* was made by two directors rather than a single auteur, it conveys a unique and highly personal vision in which the sacred and profane world inextricably echoes the concerns depicted in Robert Bresson's films of forty years before.

At the turn of the millennium a controversial group of French directors came to the fore; their approach was dubbed "the new French extremism." These film makers pushed the envelope on the depiction of sex and violence. Catherine Breillat's explicit explorations of female erotic desire and victimization, such as the 1999 *Romance* and the 2001 *Fat Girl,* were so categorized. So was *Baise-moi,* directed by two former pornography stars, Coralie Trinh Thi and Virginie Despentes, in 2000, along with Michael Haneke's 2001 *The Piano Teacher.* One of the most artistically distinguished of these exercises in unflinching shock tactics was Gaspar Noé's 2002 *Irreversible,* a rape-revenge tale told backward. *Irreversible* begins with a sickeningly realistic head bashing and follows this up with a nine-minute rape scene handled in a single take. Instead of building to a violent climax, the movie starts with a violent climax and proceeds to unravel the events that have led up to it. By the "end" of the film, things have calmed down considerably. Stunningly photographed using mostly handheld camera work and courageously performed, most notably by the husband-and-wife team at the story's center played by Monica Bellucci and Vincent Cassel, *Irreversible* tests the limits on the kind of realism the movies can tackle.

Such iconoclastic fare may not be to everyone's taste, yet it provides further evidence of the vigorous commitment to experimentation that continues to drive French cinema. During the earliest days of film making the Lumière brothers used the new technology to open a window to the world for audiences everywhere while Méliès dazzled spectators with cinematic sleight of hand. By the 1920s, French avant-gardeists were probing the nature of film language. In the 1930s French film makers discovered a poetic idiom that could express inchoate longings. In the 1960s, a new wave of French cineastes pioneered a looser, more kinetic mode of making movies. In the 1970s, a new theoretical matrix determined the way in which many French film makers approached their art and influenced how films were looked at by scholars around the world. Today, politics and provocation are bywords as the French continue to expand the boundaries of what film can do and how it can move us. The Argentine-born Gaspar Noé is only one of many film makers who have flourished in the challenging intellectual and creative climate that France offers. "If I had to choose a place to do movies nowadays I would choose France," he says.

Films of the Period

1968
Les Biches (Claude Chabrol)
One Plus One (Sympathy for the Devil)
   (Jean-Luc Godard)

1969
La Femme infidèle (Claude Chabrol)
My Night at Maud's (Ma Nuit chez Maud)
   (Eric Rohmer)
A Very Curious Girl (La Fiancée du pirate)
   (Nelly Kaplan)
Wind from the East (Le Vent d'est)
   (Dziga Vertov Group [Jean-Luc Godard
   and Jean-Pierre Gorin])
Z (Constantin Costa-Gavras)

1970
Le Boucher (Claude Chabrol)
Claire's Knee (La Genou de Claire) (Eric Rohmer)
The Wild Child (L'Enfant sauvage) (François
   Truffaut)

1971
Coup pour coup (Martin Karmitz)
The Sorrow and the Pity (Le Chagrin et la pitié)
   (Marcel Ophüls)
*Two English Girls (Le Deux Anglasises et le
   continent)* (François Truffaut)

1972
Chloe in the Afternoon (L'Amour l'après-midi)
   (Eric Rohmer)
*The Discreet Charm of the Bourgeoisie (Le Charme
   discret de les bourgeoisie)* (Luis Buñuel)
Letter to Jane (Dziga Vertov Group [Godard and
   Gorin])
Tout va bien (Dziga Vertov Group [Godard and
   Gorin])

1973
Day for Night (La Nuit Americaine) (François
   Truffaut)
Lacombe, Lucien (Louis Malle)
*The Mother and the Whore (La Maman et la
   putain)* (Jean Eustache)

1974
*Celine and Julie Go Boating (Celine et Julie vont
   en batteau)* (Jacques Rivette)
The Clockmaker (L'Horloger de St. Paul) (Bertrand
   Tavernier)
*Get Out Your Handkerchiefs (Préparer vos
   mouchons)* (Bernard Blier)
*Jeanne Dielman, 23 Quai de Commerce, 1080
   Bruxelles* (Chantal Akerman)
Lancelot of the Lake (Lancelot du lac) (Robert
   Bresson)
Stavisky (Alain Resnais)

1975
India Song (Marguerite Duras)
Numéro deux (Jean-Luc Godard and Anne-Marie
   Miéville)
The Story of Adele H. (L'Histoire de Adele H.)
   (François Truffaut)

1976
The Marquise of O . . . (Die Marquise von O . . .)
   (Eric Rohmer)

1977
The Devil, Probably (Le Diable, problement)
   (Robert Bresson)
The Man Who Loved Women (François Truffaut)

1979
La Cage aux folles (Edouard Molinero)

Loulou (Maurice Pialat)
Percival (Percival le Gallois) (Eric Rohmer)

1980
Coup de Torchon (Bertrand Tavernier)
The Last Metro (Le Dernière métro) (François
  Truffaut)
Mon Oncle d'Amerique (Alain Resnais)
Sauve qui peut (la vie) (Every Man for Himself)
  (Jean-Luc Godard and Anne-Marie Miéville)

1981
Diva (Jean-Jacques Beineix)

1982
Passion (Jean-Luc Godard)
*The Return of Martin Guerre (Le Retour
  de Martin Guerre)* (Daniel Vigne)
Sans Soleil (Chris Marker)

1983
L'Argent (Robert Bresson)
City of Pirates (La Ville des pirates) (Raúl Ruiz)
Entre nous (Diane Kurys)
First Name: Carmen (Prenom Carmen)
  (Jean-Luc Godard)
Liberté, la nuit (Philippe Garrel)
Sugar Cane Alley (Rue Casse Nègres)
  (Euzhan Palcy)

1984
Rendezvous d'Anna (Chantal Akerman)
Subway (Luc Besson)
*A Sunday in the Country (Un Dimance à la
  campagne)* (Bertrand Tavernier)

1985
Hail, Mary (Je vous salue Marie) (Jean-Luc Godard)
'Round Midnight (Bertrand Tavernier)
Shoah (Claude Lanzmann)
*Three Men and a Cradle (Trois Hommes
  et un couffin)* (Coline Serreau)
Vagabonde (Sans toît ni loi) (Agnès Varda)

1987
Au revoir, les enfants (Louis Malle)
Under the Sun of Satan (Sous le soleil de satan)
  (Maurice Pialat)

1988
Chocolat (Claire Denis)
Story of Women (Un Affaire de femmes)
  (Claude Chabrol)
36 Fillette (Catherine Breillat)

1989
Monsieur Hire (Patrice Leconte)

1990
Delicatessen (Jean-Pierre Jeunot and Marco Caro)
La Femme Nikita (Luc Besson)

1991
La Belle Noiseuse (Jacques Rivette)
Un Coeur en Hivre (Claude Sautet)
*I Can No Longer Hear the Guitar (J'entends plus
  la guitare)* (Philippe Garrel)
Lovers on the Bridge (Les Amants du Pont-Neuf)
  (Leos Carax)
Treasure Island (L'Isle au tresor) (Raúl Ruiz)
Van Gogh (Maurice Pialat)

1992
Indochine (Régis Warnier)

1993
My Favorite Season (Ma Saison preferée)
  (André Téchiné)

1994
L'Eau froide (Oliver Assayas)
Histoire(s) du cinéma (Jean-Luc Godard)
Queen Margot (La Reine Margot) (Patrice Chéreau)
Wild Reeds (Les Roseaux sauvages)
  (André Téchiné)

1995
City of Lost Children (La Cité des enfants perdus)
  (Jean-Pierre Jeunot and Marco Caro)
Hate (La Haine) (Matthieu Kassovitz)
I Can't Sleep (J'ai pas sommeil) (Claire Denis)
The Ceremony (La Cérémonie) (Claude
  Chabrol)

1996
Irma Vep (Oliver Assayas)
Ponette (Jacques Doillon)

La Promesse (Jean-Pierre Dardenne and Luc
    Dardenne)
*My Sex Life (Or, How to Get into an Argument)
    (Comment je me suis disputé ["ma vie
    sexuelle"])* (Arnaud Desplechin)

1997
The Life of Jesus (La Vie de Jésus) Bruno Dumont
Ma Vie en rose (Alain Berliner)

1998
*The Dreamlife of Angels (La Vie rêvée
    des anges)* (Eric Zonca)
I Stand Alone (Seul contre tous)
    (Gaspar Noé)

1999
L'Humanité (Bruno Dumont)
Pola X (Leos Carax)
Rosetta (The Dardenne brothers)

2000
Baise-moi (Coralie Trinh Thi and Virginie
    Despentes)
Beau Travail (Claire Denis)
L'Anglaise et le duc (Eric Rohmer)
The Taste of Others (Les Goût des autres) (Agnès
    Jaoui)
Under the Sand (Sous le sable) (François Ozon)

2001
Amelie (Le Fabuleux destin d'Amelie poulain)
    (Jean-Pierre Jeunet)

Fat Girl (Á ma soeur) (Catherine Breillat)
In Praise of Love (Éloge de l'amour) (Jean-Luc
    Godard)
The Piano Teacher (Michael Haneke)
Read My Lips (Sur ma lèvres) (Jacques Audiard)
Savage Souls (Les Âmes fortes) (Raúl Ruiz)
Trouble Every Day (Claire Denis)
Who Knows? (Va Savoir!) (Jacques Rivette)
Wild Innocence (Sauvage innocence) (Philippe
    Garrel)

2002
Irreversible (Gaspar Noé)
The Son (Le Fils) (The Dardenne brothers)

2003
Amelie (Amelie de Montmartre) (Jean-Pierre
    Jeunet)
Swimming Pool (François Ozon)
*The Triplets of Belleville (Les Triplettes de
    Belleville)* (Sylvain Chomet)

2004
Anatomy of Hell (Anatomie de l'enfer) (Catherine
    Breillat)
Clean (Olivier Assayas)
Kings and Queen (Rois et reine) (Arnaud
    Desplechin)
Look at Me (Comme une visage) (Agnès Jaoui)
Our Music (Notre musique) (Jean-Luc Godard)
*A Very Long Engagement (un Long dimance de
    fiançailles)* (Jean-Pierre Jeunet)

Books on the Period

Austin, Guy. *Stars in Modern French Film.* New York:
    Oxford University Press, 2003.
Hayward, Susan, and Ginette Vincendeau. *French Film:
    Texts and Contexts.* New York: Routledge, 1999.
Lanzani, Remi Fournier. *French Cinema: From Its Be-
    ginnings to the Present.* New York: Continuum,
    2004.
Mazdon, Lucy. *France on Film: Reflections on Popular
    French Cinema.* London: Wallflower Press, 2001.
Mazdon, Lucy. *Encore Hollywood: Remaking French
    Cinema.* London: BFI Publishing, 2000.

Powrie, Phil. *French Cinema in the 1990s: Continuity
    and Difference.* New York: Oxford University Press,
    2000.
Tarr, Carrie, with Brigitte Rollet. *Cinema and the Sec-
    ond Sex: Women's Filmmaking in France in the
    1980s and 1990s.* New York: Continuum, 2001.
Temple, Michale, and Michael Witt, eds. *The French
    Cinema Book.* London: BFI Publishing, 2003.
Wilson, David, ed. *Cahiers du Cinéma: Volume 4,
    1973–1978: History, Ideology, Cultural Struggle.*
    New York: Routledge, 2000.

20

A Blockbuster Mentality: The United States

★ ★ ★ ★

1975–1993

In the summer of 1975 *Jaws* was released, and a blockbuster mentality was born that continued to shape Hollywood's attitudes toward movie making throughout the remainder of the century. Audiences have responded to the blockbuster strategy; by 1997 American movie admissions had reached 1.38 billion, the highest figure since 1959. But some thought that quality had suffered and costs were out of line. In a piece called "Memo to the Multinationals" *Variety* editor and former studio executive Peter Bart complained that "since taking over the studios a decade or so ago, your corporate leviathans have not contributed a single new idea to the production and distribution of motion pictures. What you've really done is drive up costs. You've achieved this by (a) tilting production slates toward star-driven films geared to the overseas audience, and (b) giving above-the-line performers and film makers whatever they want in the way of money and controls." Fortunately, alternatives emerged during the 1980s to counter this trend in the form of independent films, many of these produced on a shoestring. During the same period Hollywood itself tentatively began to court niche markets in a more concerted manner than it had done in the past with pictures aimed at audiences of women and ethnic minorities.

State of the Industry

During the 1980s the major Hollywood studios—Warner Bros., Universal, Columbia/Tri-Star, Paramount, Disney, M-G-M/UA, and Twentieth Century-Fox—tended to follow the pattern of acquisitions and mergers generally prevalent in American industry. For example, in 1981, United Artists, then owned by Transamerica, was sold to Metro-Goldwyn-Mayer, which had earlier been purchased by Las Vegas real estate magnate Kirk Kerkorian.

Columbia Pictures was obtained by the Coca-Cola Company in 1982. In 1985, an incursion of foreign capital began with the News Corporation (part of the media empire of Australian Rupert Murdoch) purchasing Twentieth Century-Fox. The major thrust of subsequent foreign investment came from Japan, especially from the electronic industry giants. Sony Corporation acquired Columbia in 1989 for $3.4 billion. Matsushita Electric Industrial Company (which includes brand names such as Panasonic, JVC, and Technics) purchased Universal in 1991. These Japanese firms not only had excess capital they wanted to invest; they also could see that being able to provide software (movies) for the hardware they manufactured (home videos) made good business sense. Not to be outdone, two American firms, Time, Inc. and Warner Bros., merged in 1989 to become Time Warner, then the biggest media company in the world. Time Warner owned/controlled newspaper and magazine publishing, a cable television network with more than six million subscribers, the Home Box Office cable channel, the world's largest music company, and the old Warner Bros. studio.

Fewer and bigger was the pattern for the pictures produced as well as for the studios themselves. A major studio that had produced around fifty films a year frequently produced no more than twelve or fifteen, or fewer, by the 1980s, although it distributed independently produced pictures as well. Hollywood executives had discovered that a few movies on which a lot of money is spent can return huge profits: The studios and the independents tried hard to make one of those few. All of Hollywood's top-ten-grossing films of all time have been released since 1975. The extraordinary success of *Jaws* made it a model that has been followed in subsequent films aimed at setting new box-office records.

Increasingly, Hollywood relied on foreign revenues; by the mid-1990s the foreign box office take had overtaken that of the United States. This situation meant that stars whose faces were known around the world were in great demand and could command astronomical salaries. Because foreign audiences frequently do not understand English dialogue, special effects and action are the most reliable gimmicks to sell movies overseas. Thus, superspectacles and science-fiction stories became dominant among box-office winners. *Star Wars* (1977) set the trend. Its record $185 million in income from domestic rentals surpassed even *Jaws*. *Star Wars* also set a trend for sequels—presold properties—with its follow-ups *The Empire Strikes Back* (1980) and *Return of the Jedi* (1983), seemingly completing a trilogy—until the 1998 blockbuster *Star Wars: Episode I—The Phantom Menace* made it a tetralogy.

In 1980 *Heaven's Gate* was a much-publicized financial disaster that led to the sale of United Artists to M-G-M and shook the industry considerably. The lesson learned from this debacle was not that less money should be spent on a given film. Film budgets rose from an average of $8.5 million per picture in 1980 to $75.6 million in 1997. But instead of gambling on the vision of a particular *auteur*/director such as Michael Cimino, the large budgets were allocated to comparatively safe projects. Consistent big moneymakers were (1) the "heavy metal" films of Sylvester Stallone (*Rambo II,* 1984) and Arnold Schwarzenegger (*The Terminator,* 1984); (2) gimmicky comedies *(Ghostbusters,* 1984; *Honey I Shrunk the Kids,* 1989; *Home Alone,* 1990; *The Nutty Professor,* 1996); (3) corporate genre action-adventure pieces (*Die Hard,* 1988; *Indiana Jones and the Last Crusade,* 1989); (4) animations (*The Little Mermaid,* 1989, and *Beauty and the Beast,* 1991); and (5) comic book adaptations (*Batman,* 1989, and *Dick Tracy,* 1990). *Batman,* playing in more than 2,200 North American theaters at its peak, moved into the top-ten-grossing films of all time in a matter of months. Warner Bros. spent $63 million to advertise it, $10 million more than it cost to make. Its sequels were released to similar fanfare.

Technological Advances

The money being spent and returned (or not being returned) is up, and the technology being employed has reached a correspondingly high level. Great advances were made in special effects. For live-action cinematography, **Steadicam** permits the camera to move with a steadiness that formerly would have required a large hydraulic boom or a dolly and tracks. It was first used in 1976 with striking effect in the opening scene of *Bound for Glory* to follow David Carradine from overhead into a crowd of 700 or 800 in a migrant labor camp; then in *Rocky* to run alongside Sylvester Stallone up the steps of the Philadelphia Museum of Art. Since that time its use has become commonplace. Arifflex or Panavision cameras, Nagra tape recorders, and location dollies comprise the standard apparatus. In the new look of films, hand-held technique has come a long way, as has the equipment designed for it: Cameras are lighter and better balanced; cinematographers have learned to operate them with increased skill.

Sound, as well, has evolved during these years. Director Robert Altman's experiments with overlapping dialogue led to the development of an eight-track sound system at the small studio he once owned, Lionsgate, which was based on using tiny radio mikes attached to the actors rather than cumbersome booms. By the turn of the century, digital sound systems were part of many new theater setups, allowing an enhanced audio track that retains its crispness through countless screenings. Warren Beatty's 1990 *Dick Tracy* was the first feature released with digital sound; now all major Hollywood productions have it. Under the leadership of virtuosos such as Walter Mirsch, sound editor for many of Francis Ford Coppola's films, mixing has become a fine art with sound effects, music, and dialogue brilliantly orchestrated to play off one another and add to the drama of the story.

During the 1980s the **colorization** process, employing computer technology, was used to transfer black-and-white film to videotape in approximate color. The motivation for it was admittedly financial—to make profits by re-presenting films from the vaults onto television and video-cassette. The commercial argument is that audiences raised on color tend to skip black-and-white films (and old TV series) as they flip channels. When the colorized *Miracle on 34th Street* (1947) was shown on network television in 1985, it received the highest audience rating of syndicated films for that year. Colorized cassettes of *Yankee Doodle Dandy, The Maltese Falcon, Topper,* and *It's a Wonderful Life* became available soon after. The colorized *Casablanca* premiered in 1988. Along with colorization went a process called **panning and scanning,** which had long been used to reformat movies to fit the requirements of television. The process involves selecting part of the image so that the width of a film frame would be adapted to the more square TV set and increasing the projection speed slightly so that the length would fit into a predetermined time slot. In addition to these distortions, TV film editors often cut whole scenes and narrative linkages in the interests of brevity. Thanks largely to the efforts of the Artists' Rights Foundation, an offshoot of the Directors Guild of America, films that have been subject to such processes now must be labeled "formatted to fit your TV screens." An increasing number of directors now have clauses written into their contracts restricting the liberties TV can take with their productions. But all directors now film with an eye to the "safe zone"—the frame within a frame that signals which parts of the image will appear in TV and video formats.

Scholars, critics, and film makers have been loud in their denunciation of the distortions colorization and panning and scanning cause to the creative intentions of the artists who created the films. Director Fred Zinnemann called such tampering "a cultural crime of the first order." He was joined by others expressing outrage, including Woody Allen, Martin Scorsese, Warren Beatty, John Huston, Steven Spielberg, and Elia Kazan—along with the American Film Institute, the Directors Guild of America, the Writers Guild of America West, the American Society of Cinematographers, and the Society for Cinema and Media Studies.

Emerging Genres

American movie genres that flourished during this era reflected Hollywood's growing attachment to the international marketplace. Social issues and a new cinematic love affair with technology were also major factors that explained the popularity of certain kinds of movies during the period. During these years, a genre labeled "action" consistently dominated Hollywood's thinking. The 1970s and 1980s saw a cycle of Vietnam War films. Science-fiction stories, a staple of genre movie making since the earliest days, also came into their own during this period, fueled by the effects made possible by the cornucopia of technological gadgets available. New technological options also led to a resurgence of animated movies intended for families.

Most conspicuously, the broad category of **action movies** has been at the core of the studios' strategies to win thrill-seeking audiences—especially those powered by "bankable" male stars such as Bruce Willis, Mel Gibson, and Harrison Ford. The formula is simple: A minimal narrative framework on which numerous gory chases and scenes of general mayhem can be hung, preferably launched by a showy set piece that sets the tone. The first of the hugely profitable *Lethal Weapon* series, directed by action pro Richard Donner in 1987, is typical. Starring the racially mixed team of Mel Gibson and Danny Glover (to cast the broadest possible net across the potential audience of racially diverse males), *Lethal Weapon* begins with an episode in which Gibson, in a heart-stopping suicidal gesture, jumps off the top of a building. The film's subsequent string of car chases, explosions, and gunplay is orchestrated in loosely connected episodes that proceed at a relentlessly accelerating pace designed to supply the maximum visceral jolt. During the 1980s, the over-musculatured physiques of action stars such as Arnold Schwarzenegger and Sylvester Stallone hinted at a renewed anxiety about masculinity; by the end of the decade concern over the effects of steroids and other body-enhancing drugs brought an end (or at least a diminution) to this disturbing phenomenon.

Action was combined with substantive social issues in another genre of this period: the **Vietnam War** film, most notoriously in Stallone's bloodfest, *Rambo: First Blood, Part Two,* in 1985 (directed by George Pan Cosmatos, but coscripted by the star). Most films about the Vietnam War did not appear on movie screens in the United States until long after the event. The only exceptions to prove the rule were John Wayne's overstated *Green Berets* (1968) and Ossie Davis's overlooked *Gordon's War* (1973). But in 1978, five years after the last American troops had left Southeast Asia, a number of films dealing with the subject suddenly appeared, including the productions *Go Tell the Spartans, Coming Home, Who'll Stop the Rain?* and *The Deer Hunter.* In 1979, the cycle reached its climax with *Apocalypse Now.* Then, after a hiatus of eight years, a second wave of Vietnam films began with *Platoon,* continued in 1987 with *Gardens of Stone, The Hanoi Hilton, Full Metal Jacket,* and *Hamburger Hill,* followed in 1988 by *Good Morning, Vietnam,* and in 1989 by *Casualties of War* and *Born on the Fourth of July.* Of these, *Platoon* received the widest public response.

It was *The Deer Hunter* (Michael Cimino) that seemed to touch the national nerve most directly. It deals with three buddies from a Pennsylvania steel town who volunteer for Vietnam. They experience dreadful violence and torture, physically and psychologically. One dies in Saigon, one loses his legs, and the remaining survivor has become truncated emotionally. The use of Russian roulette in prison camp and as a game for Saigon gambling created a furor; Cimino acknowledged that it probably didn't happen but insisted on his artist's prerogative to use it as a metaphor for the war. The ending of the film is ambiguous but exalting, even if it might be argued what exactly is being exalted. At a funeral breakfast the returned veterans begin to sing "God Bless America" as a dirge for their dead friend. As they continue the song becomes a hymn to this country and to the values it traditionally holds, for which they and others had fought and died. This scene provides a catharsis of sorts; it is a sad moment but also curiously ennobling. Life goes on, it seems to mean, and we Americans may be, or can again become, the Americans we want to be.

Apocalypse Now (Francis Ford Coppola), with its effort to fuse the mystery and gloom of Joseph Conrad's *Heart of Darkness* with the known and awful actualities of the Vietnam War, was the first film to directly excoriate American involvement. A behemoth of a film, it was years and many millions of dollars in the making. Its production became something like a re-creation of the war it was portraying. Shot in the Philippines, it ran over schedule and over budget; most critics and probably viewers found that it did not conclude satisfactorily. Yet it is a chilling and convincing vision of a kind of madness rampant in the American military command: homicidal, conspiratorial, megalomaniacal. It offers a surreal experience of jungle and battle; colors and sounds overwhelm the senses, and we may feel that this is the way it must have felt to American soldiers, especially if their sensations were heightened by fear and perhaps drugs.

Many people felt that, of any of the films dealing with the subject, *Platoon* came closest to what the combat experience in Vietnam must have been like (Figure 20.1). It centers on the experience of a rookie and was widely assumed to be largely autobiographical. Its writer-director, Oliver Stone, volunteered for the army in 1967 and spent fifteen months in Vietnam. The fragmented structure—a sequence of events rather than a coherent narrative— and number of characters involved—the men of the platoon—add to this sense of actuality. It is a tough film to watch; the violence, the jungle, the heat, and the stench all seem palpable. But there are also mythic elements involved, as in *The Deer Hunter* and *Apocalypse Now*; in this case two sergeants of contrasting temperaments; one has become a hardened killing machine, the other serene and Christ-like. Whatever it was about the combination of its elements—painfully convincing naturalistic detail and mythic confrontation between representatives of good and evil—its reception was extraordinary. Not a film one would expect to be popular or honored, it was a box-office success and won four Academy Awards including best picture and best director.

The new potentials of **special effects** technology led to a renaissance of the **science fiction film,** which was now taken to a whole new level of creative excitement, beginning

FIGURE 20.1 *Platoon* ★ United States, 1986, Oliver Stone; Tom Berenger, Charlie Sheen, and Willem Dafoe.

with *Star Wars* in 1977 and going on to other cult favorites such as the *Star Trek* series. The genre's new vitality also manifested itself in such classic productions as *Alien* (Ridley Scott, 1979), *Blade Runner* (Scott, 1982), *Brazil* (Terry Gilliam, 1985), *Total Recall* (Paul Verhoeven, 1990), and *Terminator II: Judgment Day* (James Cameron, 1991). Many science-fiction films (such as *Tron* [1982] and *Jurassic Park* [1993]) exploited computer-generated special effects or **CGI** to create utopias and distopias of the future. Others (beginning with the George Lucas–Ron Howard fantasy *Willow* in 1988) made use of the new computer-generated technique of **morphing,** by which one thing gradually changes its shape and turns into another, to explore issues around the nature of the body and its relation to technology.

Terminator II: Judgment Day gave rise to especially lively discussion and debate centering on its portrayal of a gutsy mother figure (Linda Hamilton) and its meditations on the nature of fatherhood and its relation to a system of patriarchy. Starring Arnold Schwarzenegger as a good cyborg and Edward Furlong as a bad one, the film features some of the most spectacular morphing effects filmed to date. Though it reportedly cost between $80 million and $100 million to make, it generated a healthy profit, becoming the top-grossing production of 1991.

The other genre resuscitated by special effects technology, animation, takes the idea of comic books more literally by creating wholly manufactured images. New technologies have made this process both cheaper and richer in possibilities. As in earlier days, Disney has been the leader in this realm; kicking off the boom with *The Little Mermaid* (1989), a coproduction with Warner Bros. and Steven Spielberg's Amblin entertainment. Disney followed this success with more projects in the same vein, such as *Beauty and the Beast* (1991) and *Aladdin* (1992). Unlike the daring experiments with the science-fiction genre, these films, created mostly with children in mind, remained fairly traditional, featuring tuneful musical scores that frequently won Academy Awards.

A director who began his career as a Disney animator and continues to use animation and special effects extensively to create fantastical worlds is **Tim Burton.** Burton wrote and produced *The Nightmare Before Christmas* (1993), which is pure animation; other films that he has directed, such as *Pee-Wee's Big Adventure* (1985) and *Batman* (1989) (Figure 20.2), blend animation and live action, creating weird worlds and strange characters. Critic Robin Wood has characterized Burton's highly idiosyncratic *oeuvre* as one focused on freaks—social outsiders who are often physically deformed *(Beetlejuice,* 1988, and *Edward Scissorhands, 1990).*

Another genre that flourished during these years is **comedy,** especially in forms conceived by talented film makers such as the trio of Brookses, who, though not related, appear to share funny bones: Mel Brooks *(Blazing Saddles* and *Young Frankenstein,* both 1974), Albert Brooks *(Real Life,* 1979, and *Modern Romance,* 1981), and James L. Brooks *(Broadcast News,* 1987, and *I'll Do Anything,* 1994). In this often performance-driven mode, brilliant comic actors have also created distinguished bodies of work: Lily Tomlin *(Nine to Five,* 1980; *All of Me,* 1984), Eddie Murphy *(Beverly Hills Cop,* 1985; *The Nutty Professor,* 1996 [Figure 20.3]), Bette Midler *(Down and Out in Beverly Hills,* 1985; *Outrageous Fortune,* 1987), Kevin Kline *(A Fish Called Wanda,* 1988; *Soapdish,* 1991), Bill

FIGURE 20.2 *Batman* ★ United States, 1989, Tim Burton; Kim Basinger and Michael Keaton.

FIGURE 20.3   *The Nutty Professor*   ★   United States, 1996, Tom Shadyac; Eddie Murphy.

Murray *(Ghostbusters,* 1984; *Groundhog Day,* 1993), and Steve Martin *(All of Me,* 1984; *Planes, Trains and Automobiles,* 1987).

Perhaps the most respected maker of film comedies who began his career during the 1970s is **Woody Allen.** In *Annie Hall* (1977), Allen hit full stride with a highly personal brand of humor. Based in New York City, it draws on Jewishness and psychoanalysis, and offers in-jokes about show biz and other films. But most essential to it are the gentle, recognizable, and amusing revelations about certain (male intellectual) sexual insecurities and inadequacies. "Love is the answer," Allen once said. "But while you're waiting for the answer, sex raises some pretty good questions." *Manhattan* (1979) (Figure 20.4), in black-and-white Panavision, is more of the same. Though the humor is darker, it maintains the same high level of exact observation presented in the perfect nuances of Allen's and Diane Keaton's performances. Another Allen film that found particular favor with audiences and critics was *Hannah and Her Sisters* (1986), which recalls Ingmar Bergman's valedictory *Fanny and Alexander.*

During the 1990s Allen's unorthodox personal life hit the media. The scandal involved Mia Farrow, actor in his films and longtime intimate companion, a child custody suit, and allegations of child abuse. Throughout all this Allen's output continued, though his audience dwindled. "Most of the time, I don't have much fun," he has commented. "The rest of the time, I don't have any fun at all." Yet out of this gloomy view of life, Allen has created a body of work that has provided a great deal of fun for his audiences.

FIGURE 20.4 *Manhattan* ★ United States, 1979, Woody Allen; Mariel Hemingway and Allen.

Studio Stalwarts

Within mainstream production a number of film makers who became active during these years were able to maintain sufficient control over their films to make personal statements representing their own ways of seeing and feeling. A list of this sort would include Clint Eastwood, Steven Spielberg, Oliver Stone, and Terrence Malick.

The most senior member of this group, actor **Clint Eastwood,** has directed films in which he appears and films in which he does not. Initially known as a TV cowboy star, he made his name in the movies by starring in the spaghetti westerns of Italian director Sergio Leone (*The Good, the Bad, and the Ugly,* 1966), then in the American-style westerns of Don Siegel (*Two Mules for Sister Sara,* 1969). His *oeuvre* as a director includes westerns (*The Outlaw Josey Wales,* 1976, and *Unforgiven,* 1992) as well as thrillers (his first directorial outing, *Play Misty for Me,* 1971), comedies (*Bronco Billy,* 1980), and a miscellaneous assortment of other genres—including a woman's picture (*The Bridges of Madison County,* 1995). A self-effacing directorial presence, his movies are marked by a relaxed pace, punctuated where appropriate with rousing action sequences, and a recurring interest in the nature of masculinity. Eastwood's master work during this period is surely *Unforgiven* (1992), in which he plays the role of a wandering gunman (Figure 20.5). Dedicated to Sergio Leone and Don Siegel, *Unforgiven* focuses on the pervasiveness of violence in American life and offers meditations on the western as genre and on Eastwood's own dominant persona.

The phenomenal success of *Jaws* (1975), a dark myth about a white shark preying on a seaside community, fixed the direction **Steven Spielberg**'s career would subsequently take. Its popularity was repeated with *Close Encounters of the Third Kind* (1977), about an average fellow who comes in contact with creatures from another planet. He followed this success with the Indiana Jones series, *Raiders of the Lost Ark* (1981), *Indiana Jones and the Temple of Doom* (1984), and *Indiana Jones and the Last Crusade* (1989)—rousing, globe-circling action-adventures full of derring-do. *E.T.—The Extraterrestrial* (1982), with

FIGURE 20.5   *Unforgiven* ★ United States, 1992, Clint Eastwood; Eastwood.

its lovable space creature in the midst of suburbia, achieved some sort of pinnacle in public response. *Jurassic Park* (1993) and its sequel *The Lost World* (1997) are heavy on fear.
Like *Jaws,* these are monster films—in this case genetically engineered dinosaurs. The
themes implicit in many of these films are of a child's fear of growing up and the possibility that an adult can return to a magical childhood state.

After *Indiana Jones and the Temple of Doom* Spielberg began to attempt more serious, adult-oriented fare. Following a few critical failures, such as *The Color Purple* (1985)
and *Empire of the Sun* (1987), Spielberg finally succeeded in this more adult forum with
Schindler's List in 1993 (Figure 20.6), a portrait of a German industrialist who saved thousands of Jews from concentration camps. *Schindler's List* won numerous Academy Awards,
including Oscars for best picture and best director. Spielberg followed up by arranging for
the film to be shown in schools and creating the Shoah Foundation to document the atrocities of the Holocaust.

A more idiosyncratic directorial presence during these years was **Oliver Stone.** His
first successes came as a writer of such films as *Midnight Express* (Alan Parker, 1978), for
which he won an Academy Award. A product of the New York University Film School, he
is a true child of the 1960s: radical and angry. After his great success with *Platoon* in 1986,
he settled into a pattern of bombastic and often controversial revisionist histories, including *JFK* in 1991 (which attempted to expose a conspiracy surrounding the Kennedy assassination) and *Nixon* in 1995 (which provided a version of the Watergate scandal). He

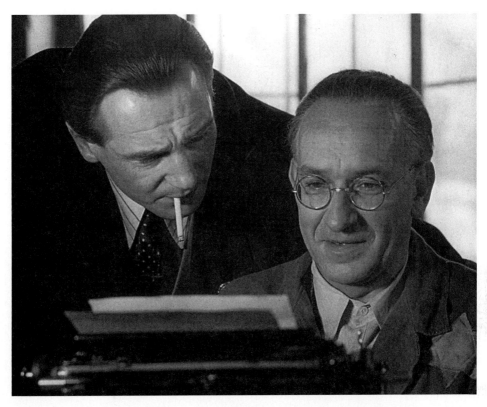

FIGURE 20.6 *Schindler's List* ★ United States, 1993, Steven Spielberg; Liam Neeson and Ben Kingsley.

also returned to the issue of American foreign policy in a series of examinations of people around the world who have been affected by U.S. incursions into their countries in productions such as *Salvador* (1986, about a journalist in Central America who discovers he must take a stand in support of the local population) and *Heaven and Earth* (1993, about Vietnamese refugees). In 1987 he directed what is perhaps his best-known film, *Wall Street,* a satire of American big business in which Michael Douglas speaks a line that has passed into the language, "Greed is good."

Stone's visceral style relies on handheld camera work and heavy editing. *JFK* featured an innovative intermingling of fictional and documentary footage, including the famous Zapruder video of Kennedy's assassination. A Stone movie grabs you by the throat and won't let go. You may not approve of everything he espouses, but his films will never leave you bored.

A somewhat special case is **Terrence Malick,** who, though repeatedly supported by the big studios, has produced work of a consistently delicate and specialized nature. In over twenty years, he has directed only three features: *Badlands* (1973), one of the outlaw-couple-on-the-run subgenre; *Days of Heaven* (1978), about two loners who commit murder in 1930s Texas (Figure 20.7); and *The Thin Red Line* (1998), an adaptation of the James Jones novel about the conflict in the Pacific during World War II. All of Malick's films

FIGURE 20.7   *Days of Heaven* ★ United States, 1978, Terrence Malick

feature voice-over narration, by a woman in *Badlands,* a child in *Days of Heaven,* and several different soldiers in *The Thin Red Line.* All are also filled with magical photography (in the case of *Days of Heaven* all outdoor footage was shot at twilight in order to provide a precise quality of light). In addition, the musical scores Malick uses are uniquely moving and unexpected, from the selection from Saint-Saëns's *Carnival of the Animals* in *Days of Heaven* to the ethereal Hans Zimmer score in *The Thin Red Line.* In total, Malick's cinema is that of an independent sensibility working within a studio context.

Independent Voices

Happily, the mainstream industry's preoccupation with high tech, high finance, and blockbusters didn't completely take over American cinema during the 1980s. In some ways, and inadvertently to be sure, it allowed more space for resolute independent film makers appealing to minority audiences. Worthy independent films are often premiered and may find distributors at the Sundance Festival in Utah. Started as the United States Film Festival in 1981 and absorbed into Robert Redford's Sundance Institute in 1985, the festival has become a hot ticket for aspiring independent film makers and would-be moguls since Steven Soderbergh's *sex, lies, and videotape* was picked up there by upstart independent distributor Miramax in 1989. After being produced on a budget of one million dollars, it went on to win at Cannes and gross seventy million dollars worldwide. Subsequently, every young film maker has seen Sundance as an *entrée* to the big time, and an ever-growing number of industry heavyweights go there searching for the next Soderbergh. Predictable complaints about overcomercialization and declining quality have continued to surface, but Sundance just keeps getting bigger.

Funding for these independent productions often came from completely outside the industry: from Public Television's *American Playhouse* series, the National Endowment for the Arts, and occasionally German television. Mostly the film makers raised their modest (sometimes minuscule) budgets any way they could: borrowing from friends and relatives, huckstering, delaying payment for services. Directorial talents whose careers fit into this model include David Lynch, Jim Jarmusch, the Coen Brothers, David Mamet, and John Sayles.

First into the field, scriptwriter as well as director of his films, was **David Lynch,** who trained as a painter. His *Eraserhead* (1978), an exercise in horror involving notably repugnant images, has gained a considerable cult following. *Blue Velvet* (1986) carries Lynch's attraction to the mysterious and perverse into a picture-postcard American small town (Figure 20.8). Two teenagers discover the underside of this bucolic world and become involved with its moral decay. Featuring a truly creepy performance by Dennis Hopper and

FIGURE 20.8 *Blue Velvet* ⋆ United States, 1986, David Lynch; Kyle MacLachlan and Dennis Hopper.

a bizarre scene in which Dean Stockwell lip-synchs to Roy Orbison's "In Dreams," it represented Lynch's most resounding success until he broke through again in 2001 with the haunting neo-*noir Mulholland Drive.*

Jim Jarmusch's *Stranger Than Paradise* (1984) elevated him into the international spotlight (Figure 20.9). It won the Camera d'or at Cannes (for best new director) and was voted best film of the year by the National Society of Film Critics in the United States. An engaging road comedy, it focuses on an unprepossessing young man, his emigré Hungarian female cousin, and a dull-witted friend who take off on an odyssey that extends from New York's Lower East Side to Cleveland to Florida. *Down by Law* (1986) has some of the same qualities. Jarmusch described it as the story of "a pimp, a disc jockey, and an Italian tourist stuck in a Louisiana prison."

These films share with subsequent Jarmusch efforts the helmer's offbeat sense of narrative structure and visual style. All involve foreigners exploring American culture on the fringes of society—tourists in a sense. Critic James Naremore has suggested that Jarmusch's concerns can be described by the phrase *cognitive estrangement* (a term taken from science-fiction scholar Darko Suvin), which points to the director's preoccupation with juxtaposing disparate cultural types: Japanese teenagers looking for the legacy of Elvis Presley in Memphis (*Mystery Train,* 1989), an Eastern dude thrust into the world of tribal beliefs and customs in *(Dead Man,* 1995), an African American who takes on the role of a samurai warrior

FIGURE 20.9   *Stranger Than Paradise* ★ United States, 1984, Jim Jarmusch; John Lurie, Eszter Balint, and Richard Edson.

(*Ghost Dog,* 1999). These encounters are presented in unusual narrative patterns: three interwoven stories in *Mystery Train,* a series of unrelated episodes in *Night on Earth* (1992). Jarmusch's camera style is also related to cognitive estrangement. He likes to contemplate elements of the landscape after his characters have left the frame; in *Mystery Train,* for example, as the Japanese tourists pass through a rundown part of Memphis, the camera lets them walk on ahead as it lingers to gaze at the unprepossessing cityscape.

Brothers **Joel and Ethan Coen** also had their first big hit, *Blood Simple,* in 1984. Like Jarmusch, Joel is from New York University; the undergraduate film program in his case. He directed, Ethan produced, and they wrote the script together. It is a clever, slick, highly stylized suspense-thriller in the manner of Hitchcock. Action-horror is the Coens's label for it, and, to be sure, it has considerable shock value. Set in Texas, the beginning of its intricate plotting occurs when a cuckholded husband hires an unsavory character to kill his wife and her boyfriend. Deception and double-cross, a body thought to be dead buried alive, rekilled with a shovel, and the like occupy the remainder. *Raising Arizona* (1987) is a wacky farce about an ex-con husband and police officer wife. When they discover they cannot have a child they kidnap one of the newborn Arizona quintuplets, sons of Nathan Arizona, an unfinished-furniture tycoon. The Coens brought their unique brand of black humor and over-the-top style to numerous other productions during the 1990s, most notably *Miller's Crossing* (1990, another gangster story) and *Barton Fink* (1991, loosely based on the Hollywood experiences of Broadway playwright Clifford Odets) (Figure 20.10).

FIGURE 20.10   *Barton Fink*   ★   United States, 1991, Joel Coen; John Goodman and John Turturro.

David Mamet is also an astute and knowledgeable craftsman, but his craft so far has been more closely related to theater than to movies or novels. He was an established playwright *(American Buffalo, Sexual Perversity in Chicago,* and *Glengarry Glen Ross)* before he became a screenwriter *(The Verdict,* 1981; *The Untouchables,* 1987; and *Wag the Dog,* 1997). He became a writer-director of his own film, *House of Games,* in 1987 (Figure 20.11), and went on to write and direct a series of tense thrillers and deadpan comedies, including *Things Change* (1988) and *Homicide* (1991). As one might expect, Mamet's strength is in his scriptwriting ability. His thrillers are intricately plotted and his dialogue is unmistakable, relying on laconic phrases, repetition, and a heavy use of profanity to create a kind of superrealist effect. In the Hitchcockian tradition, his visual style favors carefully composed point of view shots and precise editing.

Another director who first achieved fame as a writer is **John Sayles.** Working from a reformist agenda, Sayles has written and directed a series of films about social issues such as lesbian lifestyles *(Lianna,* 1982), labor unrest among West Virginia miners *(Matewan,* 1987), corruption in big-time sports *(Eight Men Out,* 1988) (Figure 20.12), interracial friendship *(Passion Fish,* 1992), and small-town life *(Lone Star,* 1996). Always beautifully observed, Sayles's films avoid generic forms and conspicuous stylistic flourishes, focusing instead on characterization. "If storytelling has a positive function," he has said, "it's to put us in touch with other people's lives, to help us connect or draw strength or knowledge from people we'll never meet, to help us see beyond our own experience."

FIGURE 20.11   *House of Games*   ★   United States, 1987, David Mamet; Joe Mantegna and Lindsay Crouse.

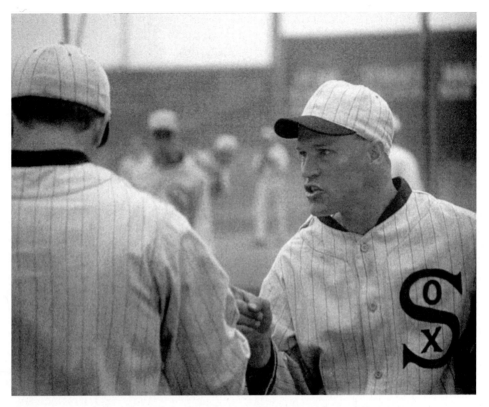

FIGURE 20.12 *Eight Men Out* ★ United States, 1988, John Sayles; Michael Rooker.

Representing Diversity

At a certain point Hollywood executives figured out that their audience was made up of more than just white males like themselves. They had earlier learned this lesson with the woman's film of the 1930s, 1940s, and 1950s, then forgot it during the 1960s. For a brief period in the 1970s, the lesson was again applied when blaxploitation films targeted African American audiences. But it was during the 1980s that attempts to understand that female, gay, and minority audiences might be interested in seeing something other than Sylvester Stallone shoot-'em-ups really got under way. Of course, one way to attract these audiences is to give jobs to female, gay, and minority film makers and performers. Gradually, this turnaround has been happening, with many of these new talents increasingly demonstrating crossover appeal as well.

In Hollywood, sexism has long been notorious, from the storied casting couch to the demonstrable absence of women in key administrative and creative positions. During the 1980s, however, women began making gains, particularly as executives. For example, in an unprecedented appointment, Sherry Lansing became president in charge of film production at Twentieth Century-Fox in 1980. Other women soon followed her into top leadership positions: Dawn Steel at Columbia in 1987 and during the 1990s, Lucy Fisher at Fox, Stacey Snider at Universal, and Amy Pascal at Columbia. In addition, female directorial talents such as Amy Heckerling and Susan Seidelman began to be entrusted with major film projects.

Among directors, **Amy Heckerling** had a solid hit with *Fast Times at Ridgemont High* in 1982, about teenage growing pains in southern California, one of the best of the genre and a big boost in the career of imminent star Sean Penn. Marked by a relaxed but fast-paced style and a sly sense of humor, the film became a model for subsequent productions such as *The Breakfast Club,* which chronicles the adventures of a group of high school students. Heckerling again hit the box-office jackpot with *Look Who's Talking* (1989) and *Clueless* (1995).

Susan Seidelman's first feature, following graduate film school at New York University, was *Smithereens* (1982). It is a tough-minded, painfully believable film about a near-psychotic young female hustler on the fringe of the punk-rock scene. Seidelman's next effort, *Desperately Seeking Susan* (1985), tells the tale of a bored New Jersey housewife (Rosanna Arquette) who becomes infatuated with a woman she knows only through a personal ad (Figure 20.13). The film was a smash hit, in part because it focused on the funky lifestyles of denizens of New York's Greenwich Village—including, most prominently, the "Susan" of the movie's title, played with captivating nonchalance by pop star Madonna.

FIGURE 20.13   *Desperately Seeking Susan* ★ United States, 1985, Susan Seidelman; Rosanna Arquette.

Other American-born female directors came to the fore in the 1980s as well, including Kathryn Bigelow (*Blue Steel,* 1989) (Figure 20.14), Martha Coolidge (*Rambling Rose,* 1991), and Allison Anders (*Gas Food Lodging,* 1992). Moreover, during the 1980s and 1990s important female stars such as Barbra Streisand and Jodie Foster also established themselves as directors, Streisand with *Yentl* in 1983 and Foster with *Little Man Tate* in 1991.

If it was easier for women to become directors during the 1980s than it had been in earlier years, it remained a difficult road to hoe. Female directors asserted that they continued to be denied access to the "boys' club," that is the predominantly male group of executives who have the power to "greenlight" projects. Moreover, they still fell prey to male stereotyping that holds that women can't direct action pictures, can't direct commercial movies, can't control crews, and so on. Male prejudices within the industry are still a formidable barrier, it seems.

The **woman's film** was also revived during these years, renamed "chick flicks" or "mom movies." Many of these were notable commercial and critical hits. Some focused on mother–daughter bonds (*Terms of Endearment,* James L. Brooks, 1983; *Steel Magnolias,* Herbert Ross, 1989; and *Postcards from the Edge,* Mike Nichols, 1990) or the bonds between sisters or woman friends (*The Turning Point,* Herbert Ross, 1977, and *Beaches,*

FIGURE 20.14   *Blue Steel*   ✶   United States, 1990, Kathryn Bigelow; Jamie Lee Curtis.

Garry Marshall, 1988); others featured the trials and rewards of romance (*When Harry Met Sally,* Rob Reiner, 1989; *Pretty Woman,* Garry Marshall, 1990; and *Sleepless in Seattle,* Nora Ephron, 1993); still others stressed the power and justifications of female rage (*The Accused,* Jonathan Kaplan, 1988, and *Thelma and Louise,* Ridley Scott, 1991 [Figure 20.15]).

Shirley MacLaine established herself as the reigning diva of the genre during these years with a series of remarkable performances in films such as *Terms of Endearment, Steel Magnolias,* and *Postcards from the Edge* that comment on the glamorous image female stars usually maintain. In *Terms of Endearment* and *Postcards from the Edge* MacLaine plays vain, spoiled women, but she appears without makeup in certain scenes to show how deeply affected her characters are by what is happening to them. In *Steel Magnolias* she portrays a woman who is unconcerned with her appearance, and MacLaine's own appearance reflects this quality of character. In all of these roles, MacLaine showed that she was willing to throw off the glamorous façade female stars ordinarily flaunt in the service of revealing the realities of women's lives. She won a well-deserved Academy Award for her role in *Terms of Endearment.*

Gender politics were taken to another level in the **gay and lesbian cinema** of the 1980s and early 1990s. Though gay characters had always played a part in Hollywood productions, from the mannish behavior of the maiden aunt in Griffith's *Way Down East* (1919) to the fussy *shtick* Edward Everett Horton perfected in the Astaire-Rogers musicals of the 1930s to the demonized gay men featured in *film noir.* (To be sure, these characters' sexual orientation was rarely explicitly stated, but many audience members could read them eas-

FIGURE 20.15   *Thelma and Louise*   ★   United States, 1991, Ridley Scott; Susan Sarandon and Geena Davis.

ily enough.) There have also been a number of mainstream films about cross-dressing and gender confusion over the years, from *Sylvia Scarlett* (George Cukor, 1935) to *Some Like It Hot* (Billy Wilder, 1959) to *Victor/Victoria* (Blake Edwards, 1982). In 1982 the first mainstream film built around a gay issue (in this instance, AIDS) appeared: *Philadelphia* (Jonathan Demme), though it was notably ginger in presenting gay lifestyles.

At the end of the 1980s a movement known as New Queer Cinema took root, first among foreign film makers, then in America, following a trajectory feminist critic Ruby Rich has described as a "short, sweet climb from radical impulse to niche market." The godfather of the movement was British director Derek Jarman, whose 1986 *Caravaggio,* with its unabashed representation of gay sexuality, became a model others followed. In African American director Marlon T. Riggs's expressionistic documentary *Tongues Untied* (1989), a disparate group of unidentified black gay men relate their personal experiences. Gus Van Sant's *My Own Private Idaho* (1991) was the breakthrough production (Figure 20.16). Loosely based on Shakespeare's *Henry IV, Part I,* the plot focused on a narcoleptic male hustler played by River Phoenix slumming on the Seattle streets. It was widely shown and reviewed.

Another group that came a long way in relation to American cinema during the 1980s were black film makers. The new visibility of African American films began with a radical group of black directors who came together at the UCLA film school in the 1970s and later came to be known as the L.A. Underground. The most famous members of the group are Charles Burnett (*Killer of Sheep,* 1977, and *To Sleep with Anger,* 1990), Ethiopan-born

FIGURE 20.16 *My Own Private Idaho* ★ United States, 1991, Gus Van Sant; River Phoenix and William Reichart.

Haile Gerima (*Bush Mama,* 1974), Billy Woodbury (*Bless Their Little Hearts,* 1984), and Julie Dash (*Daughters of the Dust,* 1991). Mentored by UCLA faculty such as Teshome Gabriel and Basil Wright, the British documentarian, the group formed a third-world film club that sponsored screenings and discussions with leading third-world film makers, especially those from Latin America, during the late 1970s.

Probably the most important film made by a member of this group is *To Sleep with Anger* 1990, directed by **Charles Burnett.** Starring Danny Glover as a mysterious devil-figure that intrudes on the lives of a prosperous black family in Los Angeles, the film explores the uneasy position blacks occupy in American society, in which they must accommodate themselves to the mainstream while acknowledging the divergent African traditions they have inherited. The film's style gives expression to each of these poles, veering from realism to magic realism as the characters find themselves confronted with both quotidian and supernatural dilemmas. The movie's gospel and blues musical score celebrates the vitality of African American culture while evoking the struggles and suffering African Americans have undergone.

The breakthrough of black film making into the mainstream was *She's Gotta Have It* (1986). Its director, Spike Lee, has become a sort of bellwether for black film making. He writes, directs, edits, and acts in his films and has built up a company of black collaborators, including his father as composer and his sister as writer and performer, who have worked with him.

With *Do the Right Thing* (1989) Lee created a highly controversial, markedly successful direct attack on the problems of interethnic relations in the urban ghetto, in this instance the Bedford Stuyvesant section of Brooklyn. This was the most talked about film of the year, with critics and viewers alike taking sides. The plot centers around a pizzeria owned by Sal (Danny Aiello), an Italian who struggles to do business and live amicably in a neighborhood of indigent and angry African Americans. Sal's own anger eventually leads to murder. This, in turn triggers Mookie, Sal's delivery man, to initiate a race riot (Figure 20.17a), which culminates in the conflagration of the pizza parlor (Figure 20.17b). The film ends on a note of tentative reconciliation, which leaves the essential problems of racial discord unresolved. The final frames display contradictory quotes from Martin Luther King, Jr., urging nonviolent protest, and Malcolm X, approving violence that is carried out in self-defense.

Lee's helter-skelter principle of storytelling demonstrates its sympathy with the disenfranchised characters it portrays, who live unstructured moment-to-moment lives. The plot of *Do the Right Thing* is accordingly multifocused, episodic, and frequently unmotivated by cause–effect logic. The movie has many characters and cuts freely back and forth among them. Some change (two characters, "Da Mayor" and mother-sister [Ossie Davis and Ruby Dee], develop a romantic relationship [Figure 20.17c]), while others remain stagnant (a group of older black men who spend their days sitting in an alley and commenting on the events happening around them never tire of going over the same issues again and again [Figure 20.17d]).

Do the Right Thing asks audiences to think about the issues it raises rather than to immerse themselves in a make-believe world. The characters are one-dimensional, not realistically rounded. Often they appear in closeups taken with a wide-angle lens that makes them appear as caricatures rather than ordinary people. At some points, they address the audience directly, most conspicuously in the middle of the film, when a brief montage features various personages hurling racial epithets directly at the camera (Figure 20.17e).

FIGURE 20.17a–h *Do the Right Thing* ★ United States, 1989, Spike Lee; a. Lee; c. Ossie Davis and Ruby Dee; d. Frankie Faison, Robin Harris, and Paul Benjamin; e. Frank Vincent; f. photographs of Joe Dimaggio and Frank Sinatra; g. Bill Nunn and Giancarlo Esposito; h. Lee and Danny Aiello.

The cacophony of clashing colors and grating noises that characterizes urban life in multicultural America is made palpable in Lee's film, and the virulent enmity between competing social groups that these clashes often reflect is made explicit in the plot. Early on, a quarrel erupts over whether the pictures on the pizzeria's walls should be those of African Americans or Italian Americans, foregrounding competing claims to visual space (Figure 20.17f). Later, the "ghetto-blaster" of neighborhood denizen Radio Raheem (Bill Nunn) is pitted against the radio of a group of young Puerto Ricans to see whose music can drown out the other's. Raheem later tries to blast his radio in Sal's pizzeria, filling the room with strains of the theme of the film, Public Enemy's "Fight the Powers that Be," and thereby asserting his right to ownership of the audial space of the establishment (Figure 20.17g).

The main character in *Do the Right Thing* is played by the film's director, inviting a double reading of this figure as both Mookie and Lee. Thus, when Mookie ultimately asks Sal for his back pay after having started the fire that has destroyed his boss's pizza parlor, the scene evokes the image of an African American director who makes a film in which violence against the white establishment is presented as a legitimate option and then expects his white Hollywood producers to pay for it (Figure 20.17h). Like Mookie, Lee seems to feel caught between serving those in power and rebelling against them—and both Mookie and Lee end up doing a little of each.

The financial success of *She's Gotta Have It* (it grossed $8 million against a budget of $175,000) and *Do the Right Thing* ($28 million against $6.5 million) enabled Lee to continue making roughly a film a year and led to a veritable explosion of black films in 1990–1991—some nineteen features of this type were released. *Boyz N the Hood* (1991, John Singleton) was most widely seen and discussed of the black films, apart from Spike Lee's. It's about four young black male high school students with different aims, ambitions, and family situations trying to survive amidst Los Angeles gangs and bigotry.

If black film makers are still struggling to gain parity in Hollywood, Latino film makers have had an even harder time. The year 1987 saw a breakthrough of sorts with the success of Luis Valdez's *La Bamba,* which chronicled the life of Latino pop star Richie Valens; and "Cheech" Marin's *Born in East L.A.,* a clever comedy about a non-Spanish-speaking Chicano who finds himself trapped south of the border (Figure 20.18). A moving force in the development of this tradition has been actor Edward James Olmos, who has been a loyal supporter of such films from his appearance in Robert Young's *The Ballad of Gregorio Cortez* in 1983. A beautifully poetic rendering of an actual court case in Texas at the end of the nineteenth century, *The Ballad of Gregorio Cortez* raises difficult questions about the relation of language to culture. Olmos also starred in *Zoot Suit* (1981) and *Stand and Deliver* (1989), as well as in his own directorial effort *American Me* (1992).

Finally, these years saw the rise of Asian American themed films as well. The cycle got a well-publicized start with Wayne Wang's small gem *Chan Is Missing* in 1982. Wang followed up in 1985 with *Dim Sum: A Little Bit of Heart.* Both movies were set in San Francisco's Chinatown. Having made his mark with these well-received portraits of Chinese American life, Wang went on to direct a variety of mainstream fare. In a more experimental mode Trinh T. Minh-Ha's *Surname Viet: Given Name Nam* (1989) showcased the experiences of Vietnamese women who had suffered hardships during the war there. A similarly avant-garde approach characterizes Rea Tajiri's *History and Memory: For Akiko and*

FIGURE 20.18 *Born in East L.A.* ★ United States, 1987, "Cheech" Marin.

Takashige (1992), in which the film maker attempted to capture the personal meaning of the Japanese American internment during World War II. In 1991, the New York–based Indian film maker Mira Nair produced a more mainstream look at the lives of Asian Americans with *Mississippi Masala,* a warm, widely seen study of the East Indian community in the American South.

Multinationalism

Hollywood's blockbuster mentality led to a profound change that made itself felt during the 1980s: the increasing internationalization of the industry. Gradually, it became less and less possible to draw distinctions among films of different nations with assurance; film money, film makers, and film production increasingly moved indiscriminately across national boundaries in search of megaprofits. Since the 1980s, some of the most important films have been multinational mixes, not only of finance, crew, and cast but also of subjects, themes, and styles—"Euro-puddings," "transatlantic" productions, or U.S.-Asian "fusion" cinema.

If the United States remained at the center of the film universe, controlling an estimated 56 percent of the world film market, it is not coterminous with that universe.

Among major Academy Award–winning films of this period, *The Last Emperor* (1987) may be the most conspicuous example. A British–Italian–Hong Kong coproduction, its source was the autobiography of Pu Yi, *From Emperor to Citizen,* published in China in 1964. The screenplay was by Mark Peploe (English) and Bernardo Bertolucci (Italian). It had to be approved by the Chinese authorities before production could proceed. The budget of $25 million was raised by British independent producer Jeremy Thomas from five British and European banks. Principal crew members were Italian: director Bertolucci, set designer Ferdinando Scarfiotta, and cinematographer Vittorio Storaro. The musical score was composed by a Japanese, Ryuichi Sakamoto; an American, David Byrne; and a Chinese, Cong Su. The cast was comprised of a substantial number of Chinese Americans from California, plus Chinese nationals, plus Irish Peter O'Toole. The leading role was played by Hong Kong–born John Lone. Shooting was divided between sixteen weeks in China and five weeks of interiors in the studio in Rome. It was distributed by Shoiku-Fugi, a Japanese entertainment conglomerate. Commenting on the production's subsequent success, its producer said that "it was presold virtually everywhere in the world."

The metaphor pursued throughout this book of a country stepping into the international spotlight with a particularly innovative national contribution to the evolution of film art becomes increasingly hard to sustain as one approaches the present. Instead of more or less separable national developments, we are increasingly confronted with multinational blockbuster productions reaching out to audiences in places near and far—if not always easily, certainly more readily than ever before. This development—coupled with the profound changes brought about by the new digital technology—have irrevocably altered the movie landscape. We will explore the implication of these innovations when we return to the American film scene in Chapter 23.

Films of the Period

1975
Alice Doesn't Live Here Anymore
   (Martin Scorsese)
Grey Gardens (Albert and David Maysles)
Jaws (Steven Spielberg)
Nashville (Robert Altman)
One Flew Over the Cuckoo's Nest (Miloš Forman)

1976
All the President's Men (Alan J. Pakula)
Carrie (Brian De Palma)
Harlan County, USA (Barbara Kopple)
Heaven's Gate (Michael Cimino)

The Life and Times of Rosie the Riveter
   (Connie Field)
Network (Sidney Lumet)
The Outlaw Josey Wales (Clint Eastwood)
Rocky (John G. Avildsen)
Taxi Driver (Martin Scorsese)

1977
Annie Hall (Woody Allen)
Killer of Sheep (Charles Burnett)
New York, New York (Martin Scorsese)
Saturday Night Fever (John Badham)
Star Wars (George Lucas)

3 Women (Robert Altman)

1978
Days of Heaven (Terrence Malik)
The Deer Hunter (Michael Cimino)
Gates of Heaven (Errol Morris)

1979
Alien (Ridley Scott)
American Gigolo (Paul Schrader)
Apocalypse Now (Francis Ford Coppola)
Manhattan (Woody Allen)
The Return of the Secaucus Seven (John Sayles)

1980
Bronco Billy (Clint Eastwood)
Dressed to Kill (Brian De Palma)
Gloria (John Cassavetes)
Heaven's Gate (Michael Cimino)
Love Streams (John Cassavetes)
Raging Bull (Martin Scorsese)

1981
Body Heat (Lawrence Kasden)
Raiders of the Lost Ark (Steven Spielberg)
Reds (Warren Beatty)

1982
The Ballad of Gregorio Cortez (Robert M. Young)
Blade Runner (Ridley Scott)
Chan Is Missing (Wayne Wang)
E.T.—The Extra Terrestrial (Steven Spielberg)
Fast Times at Ridgemont High (Amy Heckerling)
Lianna (John Sayles)
Tootsie (Sydney J. Pollack)
Victor/Victoria (Blake Edwards)

1983
The King of Comedy (Martin Scorsese)
The Right Stuff (Philip Kaufman)
Terms of Endearment (James L. Brooks)
Zelig (Woody Allen)

1984
Amadeus (Miloš Forman)

Blood Simple (Joel Coen)
Choose Me (Alan Rudolph)
The Cotton Club (Francis Ford Coppola)
El Norte (Gregory Nava)
Once Upon a Time in America (Sergio Leone)
Pretty Woman (Garry Marshall)
Stranger Than Paradise (Jim Jarmusch)
This Is Spinal Tap (Rob Reiner)

1985
Brazil (Terry Gilliam)
The Color Purple (Steven Spielberg)
Dim Sum: A Little Bit of Heart (Wayne Wang)
Desperately Seeking Susan (Susan Seidelman)
Out of Africa (Sydney J. Pollack)
Prizzi's Honor (John Huston)
Witness (Peter Weir)

1986
Blue Velvet (David Lynch)
Down by Law (Jim Jarmusch)
The Fly (David Cronenberg)
Hannah and Her Sisters (Woody Allen)
Platoon (Oliver Stone)
A Room with a View (James Ivory)
Sherman's March (Ross McElwee)
She's Gotta Have It (Spike Lee)
Something Wild (Jonathan Demme)

1987
Broadcast News (James L. Brooks)
The Dead (John Huston)
House of Games (David Mamet)
The Last Emperor (Bernardo Bertolucci)
Radio Days (Woody Allen)
Raising Arizona (Joel Coen)
The Unbearable Lightness of Being (Philip Kaufman)
The Untouchables (Brian De Palma)
Wall Street (Oliver Stone)

1988
Bird (Clint Eastwood)
Eight Men Out (John Sayles)
The Thin Blue Line (Errol Morris)
Tucker: The Man and His Dream (Francis Ford Coppola)

Who Framed Roger Rabbit? (Robert Zemeckis
and Richard Williams)

1989
Batman (Tim Burton)
Do the Right Thing (Spike Lee)
Drugstore Cowboy (Gus Van Sant)
The Little Mermaid (John Musker and Ron
Clements)
Mystery Train (Jim Jarmusch)
Roger and Me (Michael Moore)
sex, lies, and videotape (Stephen
Soderbergh)
Surname Viet, Given Name Nam (Trinh T. Minh-Ha)
When Harry Met Sally (Rob Reiner)

1990
All the Vermeers in New York (Jon Jost)
Dances with Wolves (Kevin Costner)
Edward Scissorhands (Tim Burton)
Godfather III (Francis Ford Coppola)
Goodfellas (Martin Scorsese)
The Grifters (Stephen Frears)
Home Alone (John Hughes)
Miller's Crossing (Joel Coen)
Privilege (Yvonne Rainer)
The Sheltering Sky (Bernardo Bertolucci)
To Sleep with Anger (Charles Burnett)
Tongues Untied (Marlon Riggs)
White Hunter, Black Heart (Clint Eastwood)
Wild at Heart (David Lynch)

1991
Barton Fink (Joel Coen)
Beauty and the Beast (Gary Trousdale and
Kirk Wise)

Boyz N the Hood (John Singleton)
Daughters of the Dust (Julie Dash)
JFK (Oliver Stone)
Mississippi Masala (Mira Nair)
My Own Private Idaho (Gus Van Sant)
One False Move (Carl Franklin)
Paris Is Burning (Jennie Livingston)
Rambling Rose (Martha Coolidge)
The Silence of the Lambs (John Demme)
Terminator II: Judgment Day (James
Cameron)
Thelma and Louise (Ridley Scott)

1992
Aladdin (John Musker)
American Me (Edward James Olmos)
The Bad Lieutenant (Abel Ferera)
Bram Stoker's Dracula (Francis Ford
Coppola)
Deep Cover (Bill Duke)
Gas Food Lodging (Allison Anders)
Howard's End (James Ivory)
My Own Private Idaho (Gus Van Sant)
The Player (Robert Altman)
Reservoir Dogs (Quentin Tarantino)
Unforgiven (Clint Eastwood)

1993
Jurassic Park (Steven Spielberg)
Philadelphia (Jonathan Demme)
Schindler's List (Steven Spielberg)
Short Cuts (Robert Altman)

Books on the Period

Acland, Charles. *Screen Traffic: Movies, Multiplexes,
and Global Culture.* Durham, NC: Duke University
Press, 2003.
Biskind, Peter. *Down and Dirty Pictures: Miramax,
Sundance and the Rise of Independent Films.* New
York: Simon and Schuster, 2004.
Devine, Jeremy. *Vietnam at 24 Frames a Second.*
Austin: University of Texas Press, 1999.

Feng, Peter X., ed. *Screening Asian Americans.* New
Brunswick, NJ: Rutgers University Press, 2002.
Grant, William R. *Post–Soul Cinema: Discontinuities,
Innovations, and Breakpoints, 1970–1995.* New
York: Routledge, 2004.
Hamamoto, Darrell Y., and Sandra Liu. *Countervisions:
Asian American Film Criticism.* Philadelphia: Tem-
ple University Press, 2000.

Hillier, Jim, ed. *American Independent Cinema: A Sight and Sound Reader.* London: British Film Institute, 1999.

Jordon, Chris. *Movies and the Reagan Presidency: Success and Ethics.* Westport, CT: Praeger, 2003.

Levy, Emanuel. *Cinema of Outsiders: The Rise of American Independent Film.* New York: New York University Press, 1999.

Lewis, Jon, ed. *The End of Cinema As We Know It: American Film in the Nineties.* New York: New York University Press, 2003.

LoBrutto, Vincent. *The Encyclopedia of American Independent Filmmaking.* Westport, CT: Greenwood Press, 2002.

Mendik, Xavier, and Steven Jay Schneider, eds. *Underground USA: Filmmaking beyond the Hollywood Canon.* London: Wallflower Press, 2002.

Merritt, Greg. *Celluloid Mavericks: History of American Independent Film.* New York: Thunder's Mouth Press, 1999.

Noriega, Chon A. *Shot in America: Television, the State and the Rise of Chicano Cinema.* Minneapolis: University of Minnesota Press, 2000.

Prince, Stephen. *A New Pot of Gold: Hollywood Under the Electronic Rainbow, 1980–1989* (Vol. 10 of *History of American Cinema*). Berkeley: University of California Press,

Sandler, Kevin S., and Gaylyn Studlar, eds. *Titanic: Anatomy of a Blockbuster.* New Brunswick, NJ: Rutgers University Press, 1999.

Singer, Beverly R. *Wiping the War Paint off the Lens: Native American Film and Video.* Minneapolis: University of Minnesota Press, 2001.

Thompson, Kristin. *Storytelling in the New Hollywood: Understanding Classical Narrative Technique.* Cambridge, MA: Harvard University Press, 1999.

Turan, Kenneth. *Sundance to Sarajevo: Film Festivals and the World They Made.* Berkeley: University of California Press, 2002.

21

China: Three Cinemas

1984–

Because of its unique history, China has three cinemas, each associated with a different location: mainland China, Hong Kong, and Taiwan. Separated geographically and politically, they share a common heritage but little else. Until the 1980s, mainland China had largely been closed off to the rest of the world and its films unavailable. In 1984, however, Chen Kaige's breakthrough production *Yellow Earth* caught the attention of cinephiles around the world and directed attention to the diverse cinema traditions of mainland China and her neighbors. It quickly became clear that vast caches of cinema riches were waiting to be discovered in this ancient land. Hong Kong, the world's largest and most widely known producer of Chinese entertainment films, is a tiny area perched on China's southern coast and until 1997 was a British crown colony. In Taiwan, an island off the country's southeast coast, many of the most artistically distinguished films reflect a nativist value system not readily accessible to Western audiences. Although quite a number of Hong Kong films have been shot in China, and coproduction deals among the three film centers have increased, their diverse aesthetic approaches continue to set them apart from one another.

Mainland China

Until 1949, China's film industry, based in Shanghai, was overwhelmed by American and British imports. The People's Republic of China (PRC), established in that year, first produced so-called worker–peasant–soldier films mainly for revolutionary indoctrination and education, much as had its communist mentor, the Soviet Union. In 1956, however, Communist leader Mao Zedong announced a new policy: "Let a hundred flowers bloom and a hundred schools of thoughts contend." As a result, censorship temporarily loosened. An exceptional fiction feature made during this period was *Two Stage Sisters* (1964), directed by Xie Jin, China's most highly regarded veteran director (Figure 21.1). It chronicles the parallel lives of two actresses during the political turmoil of 1935 to 1950, intermingling melodramatic and dialectic treatment, bravura camera style, and fine performances. Following the precepts of the revolutionary realist style dominant during this era, the plot turns on the desirability of valuing one's loyalty to the group over aspiring to an individualized form of stardom—a message encapsulated in a striking mirror shot in which the heroine recognizes that all Chinese women are her sisters.

During the so-called Cultural Revolution (1966–1976), very few films were made and those were mostly confined to the themes of the "revolutionary operas" approved by communist authorities. Studios were closed; writers, directors, actors, producers, technicians (and millions of others) were sent off to the countryside to be "re-educated." In 1978, however, a second "hundred flowers" policy was announced, and constraints on the studios were again loosened. Since then, Chinese film production has resumed on a larger scale with a more sophisticated approach to the needs of the nation and its vast population. Now fully financially accountable, the studios began to create movies for entertainment rather than indoctrination. By the end of the 1990s, between 130 and 140 films a year were

FIGURE 21.1 *Two Stage Sisters* ✶ China, 1964, Xie Jim; Cao Tindi and Xie Fang, left rear.

being produced. In 1982 the People's Republic was represented for the first time in the official competition at Cannes with *The True Story of Ah Q*. Though the Tiananmen Square massacre of student protesters by the government in 1989 led to yet another temporary censorship crackdown, the momentum that had been established has continued to drive film production in new creative directions.

Outside the major cities, exhibition practices are primitive. Until recently, exhibitors traveling on foot carried films and equipment to remote villages where viewers saw educational and entertainment productions on crudely improvised screens set up outdoors. In the past, these screenings were supported by the government; now the villagers must pay. Often special screenings are arranged for weddings and other community celebrations.

For the past twenty years some of the films attracting most attention at the Hong Kong International Film Festival—and more recently in Cannes, Venice, and Berlin—have come from the People's Republic of China. These have been directed by graduates of the Beijing Film Academy—especially by members of the class of 1982, the so-called Fifth Generation. Although these films vary widely from director to director, they have in common stories set in the past and a brilliant pictorial sense (greatly enhanced by the Technicolor laboratory still extant in China, which can produce images of incomparably rich hues). Often critical of Chinese society and history, Fifth Generation films have been subjected to harsh treatment at home, often looked on with disfavor by a government with a limited tolerance for dissent; in fact, some of the films have been banned in China. The *oeuvres* of the Fifth Generation directors fall into two periods: first, a cluster of exploratory films featuring elliptical narratives and extended poetic passages, and second, a more widely appealing series of productions with more conventional plot lines and fully developed characters. The first group includes *One and Eight* (1984) and *The Horse Thief* (1987). In the second group are most of the Chinese films that received international distribution during the 1990s, especially those directed by the best-known practitioners of the Fifth Generation style: Chen Kaige and Zhang Yimou.

Chen Kaige's *Yellow Earth* (1984), the first of the Fifth Generation films sent out to international festivals, is widely known abroad and was also influential at home (Figure 21.2). It tells the story of an encounter in the late 1930s between a soldier of the Communist Eighth Route Army and peasants in Shaanxi Province in northwestern China. Anthropological notations on the feudal culture and the superstitions of the tradition-bound peasant community are contrasted with observations on the ways in which some of the characters become "liberated" and react positively toward revolution. The film is distinguished by the inclusion of traditional Chinese folk songs and by Zhang Yimou's ravishing cinematography, which features extreme long shots of the stark, mountainous countryside in pictorial compositions with high horizon lines reminiscent of traditional Chinese landscape painting.

Chen's second feature, *The Big Parade* (1986), is about a group of military cadets who train and rehearse for the huge celebration in 1984 of the Chinese Revolution's thirty-fifth anniversary. *Life on a String* (1991), Chen's first film made with foreign backing, is a folkloristic tale of the lifelong quests of a master musician and his pupil. Its narrative is abstract, even metaphysical. Again, cinematographer Zhang Yimou's choreographed views of breathtaking scenery are stunning. *Farewell My Concubine* (1992), starring the exquisite Gong Li, was made with Taiwanese money by a producer based in Hong Kong. It concerns a Beijing Opera star's fifty-year unrequited passion for his costar. Both characters are male. A reformed prostitute is the wife of the loved one, romantic rival of the lover. In

FIGURE 21.2   *Yellow Earth* ★ China, 1984, Chen Kaige; Xue Bai and Wang Xueqi.

1999 Chen made his most conventional film to date, *The Emperor and the Assassin,* again starring Gong Li. Featuring lavish costumes and sets, it tells the story of palace intrigue during China's struggle for unification in ancient times.

Chen's relationship to his homeland is equivocal. While dealing resolutely with Chinese subjects and themes, his films veer from political correctness. Alhough his background includes passionate commitment to Maoist policies in the 1960s (he was, in fact, a Red Guard), he has subsequently spent much time in New York, living there for more than three years. Chinese film scholar Rey Chow has argued that Chen's 1988 *King of the Children* constitutes a patriarchal affirmation of traditional Chinese national identity, which positions him as a conservative presence among the Fifth Generation directors.

Zhang Yimou, the cinematographer for two of Chen's early films, directed his own first feature, *Red Sorghum,* in 1988. Injecting a powerful erotic element into the Fifth Generation style, it won the Golden Bear at the Berlin Film Festival, thus becoming the first PRC film to achieve the highest honor at one of the leading international festivals. The film was also selected as the closing-night film of the New York festival and was subsequently released in the United States. Its look was characteristic of Zhang's early cinematographic technique, with low lighting, radiant Technicolor images, and studied, asymmetrical compositions. It typified Zhang's outlook in its ardent championing of individualism over group values.

Throughout his career Zhang has been concerned with the experiences of women. The story of *Red Sorghum,* which is set in the 1930s, is based on a northern Chinese legend of a young woman sold into wifehood by her unfeeling father. His second feature, *Ju*

Dou (1990), wholly Japanese financed, is an earthy sexual melodrama of an old and vicious owner of a textile factory who buys a lovely bride and mistreats her. His nephew and she become lovers, and violence and revenge ensue. Studded with shimmering images of freshly dyed swathes of silk drying on the rafters of the factory, the film met with considerable success abroad. *Raise the Red Lantern* (1991), set in northern China in the 1920s, concerns a beautiful young woman from an impoverished family who becomes the fourth wife of an elderly potentate. *The Story of Qiu Ju* (1992) features a contemporary setting; the central figure is again a young woman of fierce will. In 1994 the epic-scale *To Live* was about a couple living through the seismic upheavals of twentieth-century China (Figure 21.3). Zhang's rendition of a gangster tale, *Shanghai Triad* (1995), tells its saga of corruption and social upheaval through the eyes of a young boy; here again, however, the focus is on a woman, the doomed mistress of an underworld chieftain.

Gong Li, featured in Chen's *Farewell My Concubine* and *The Emperor and the Assassin,* starred in all of Zhang's films in the late 1980s and early to mid-1990s; as a result, she became China's best-known performer internationally and was labeled the most beautiful woman in the world by one Western critic. "Almost all her parts were bigger-than-life women," the director later recalled, "symbols living under the oppression of feudalism and patriarchy."

When the professional and personal relationship between director and star broke up in the late 1990s, Zhang turned to other performers and cultivated a more subdued style of cinematography and *mise-en-scène.* His 1999 production, *Not One Less,* about a young girl who teaches school in a small Chinese village, uses nonprofessional actors and is shot in

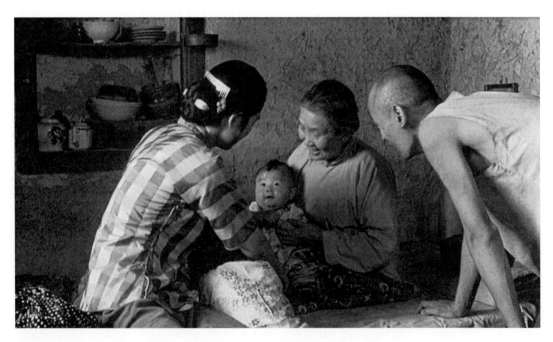

FIGURE 21.3   *To Live* ★ China, 1994, Zhang Yimou; Gong Li and Ge You.

the documentary style he had experimented with in *The Story of Qiu Ju,* sometimes using a hidden camera. The film won him a Golden Lion at the Venice Film Festival.

Following this experiment, Zhang found a replacement for Gong Li in the young Zhang Ziyi, who starred in his subsequent productions. First appearing as a country school-marm in the 1999 *Not One Less,* the director's new Galatea figure went on to appear in the immensely popular and critically acclaimed Hong Kong style martial arts epics her mentor turned to in the twenty-first century, including *Hero* in 2002 and *The House of Flying Daggers* in 2004.

As the century drew to a close, a new group of film makers came to the fore. Called the Sixth Generation because they graduated from the Bejing Film Academy a few years after their more famous colleagues, they rejected the elegant pictorialism and historical revisionism that characterized the work of Chen, Zhang, and other Fifth Generation figures. Members of the younger group began by examining the realities of Chinese life in a downbeat *cinema vérité* manner. But they were soon captivated by the postmodern posturings of Hong Kong *auteur* Wong Kar-Wai (whose work will be explored in the next section). Following Wong's lead, they began to produce fragmented studies of social anomie that are often thought to represent the psychic dislocations brought about by China's slow slide from communism to capitalism. Prominent among the Sixth Generation group are Lou Ye (*Suzhou River,* 2000*), Zhang Ke Jia (*Platform,* 2000), Jiang Wen (*Devils on the Doorstep,* 2000), Zhang Yang (*Quitting,* 2001), and Wang Xiaoshuai (*Beijing Bicycle,* 2001).

As the new millennium got under way, China's admission to the World Trade Organization and the gradual loosening of government restrictions regarding film imports found Hollywood moguls salivating at the potential market that exists in a country with 1.3 billion people and only 5,000 movie screens. Because the Chinese enjoy easy access to pirated movie videos, they have, in the past, had little incentive to spend money to go to theaters. But Hollywood industry honchos hope to change this situation. "It's just too tempting a pasture not to attempt to break in there," says Gareth Wigand, vice chairman of the Columbia TriStar Motion Picture Group. Accordingly, in 2002 Warner Bros., in partnership with a Shanghai theater company and a Hong Kong real estate firm, opened a nine-screen multiplex in Shanghai. "I believe that China will become, before long, the single most important foreign market for Hollywood movies," says Han Samping, vice chairman of the China Film Group. What this development—if it comes about—will mean for China's homegrown movie industry is anyone's guess.

Hong Kong

The antithesis of the tightly controlled film making of mainland China is the free-wheeling capitalist film industry of Hong Kong. Productions there typically proceed at breakneck speed on tight schedules, often with fragmentary scripts. At its peak in the early 1990s the industry released two hundred thirty films a year. Movie making suffered a temporary setback in the mid-1990s due to uncertainty about the Chinese takeover of the former British colony in 1997, but fears were quickly allayed when it became clear that the mainland government would maintain a hands-off policy. Thus, by 2002 the industry had rebounded; one hundred thirty-three new films were released that year. The staples of Hong Kong production are the popular genres of **martial arts,** crazy comedies, gangster films,

and soft-core pornography. To serve a population divided between Mandarin- and Can-
tonese-speaking audiences, virtually all Hong Kong movies are subtitled in Chinese.

Hong Kong films are distributed mostly within Asia, but in the 1970s and 1980s the
style achieved international renown through the global appeal of two of its major stars:
Bruce Lee and Jackie Chan. Both were masters of martial arts technique, engaging in sequences of violence and mayhem that made liberal use of filmic techniques such as fast-
motion photography and flash editing to create visually flamboyant set pieces of surpassing
grace and energy. The sinewy Lee starred in a series of riveting action pictures, culminating in the 1973 Hollywood-sponsored blockbuster *Enter the Dragon,* made just before he
died. Chan combines martial arts with comedy; extended reaction shots allow him to showcase his rubber-faced grimaces and to create mischievous yet sympathetic comic characters with whom the audience can identify in productions such as the 1978 *Drunken Master*
(Woo-ping Yuen).

At Cannes in 1975 Hong Kong's *A Touch of Zen* won the Grand Prix (Figure 21.4).
Directed by King Hu, it was large in scale, three hours in length, and added Buddhism to
martial arts. Hu's *Legend of the Mountain* and *Raining in the Mountains,* shown at Edinburgh in 1979, also evoke the legends of ancient China and contain much visual elegance
and a philosophical dimension along with their balletic fight scenes. More recently, Tsui
Hark, a major player in the Hong Kong industry, has made a name for himself through a series of fast-paced "chop-socky" productions with incomprehensible plots, such as the 1986
Peking Opera Blues. Hong Kong film scholar Steven Jao has labeled Tsui's style "nationalism on speed."

The virtuoso of Hong Kong action movies is **John Woo,** who deploys formulaic martial arts elements and gunplay in hyperstylized action sequences of overpowering visual
energy, replete with special effects–aided acrobatics and shock cutting. In films such as *A*

FIGURE 21.4   *A Touch of Zen* ★ Hong Kong, 1975, King Hu.

FIGURE 21.5 *The Killer* ⭐ Hong Kong, 1989, John Woo; Chow Yun Fat and Danny Lee.

Better Tomorrow (1986), *The Killer* (1989) (Figure 21.5), and *Hard-Boiled* (1992). Woo embellishes conventional Hollywood crime story elements with flashy visual flourishes, frequently relying on the kaleidescopic patterns of light and reflections created by shattering glass. *The Killer,* for example, begins with a scene in which Woo's frequent leading man Chow Yun-Fat, playing a reluctant mob hit man, enters a church illuminated by thousands of candles. The next scene finds him engaged in a ferocious gun battle in which a seemingly endless barrage of windows and mirrors are smashed, creating meteoric showers of light over the proceedings. At one point the weary hit man confides in a friend that he seeks the solace of a church to find peace and quiet, a quality conspicuously lacking in the world Woo creates.

Unlike Woo, who specializes in action movies, **Ann Hui** has worked in a variety of genres. Her first film, *The Secret* (1979), was a thriller; her next, *The Spooky Bunch* (1980), was a comedy. She followed these commercially successful productions in 1982 with *Boat People,* a searing portrait of South Vietnamese refugees, which was shot on location in China and premiered at Cannes. In 1990 Hui made *Song of the Exile,* a semiautobiographical exploration of the emotional and cultural gap between a British-educated Hong Kong girl and her Japanese mother. *My American Grandson* (1991), a Taiwanese production, focuses on a Chinese American child visiting his grandfather in Shanghai for the summer. In 1996 Hui made another award-winning drama, *Summer Snow,* about a middle-aged woman who must care for a father-in-law with Alzheimer's disease.

The career of Hui's protegé, **Stanley Kwan,** has also been characterized by versatility. He first drew international attention with his 1987 *Rouge,* a wry ghost story. Then, in 1991 he made *Center Stage,* a biopic about the legendary Chinese film star Ruan Ling-yu. *Center Stage,* his most acclaimed film, is crafted as a Brechtian collage of old movie clips, interviews, and fictional footage. Maggie Cheung, who won the best actress award at the Berlin Festival for her portrayal, plays the lead.

Center Stage marked the advent of a more postmodern mode of Hong Kong film making that came to the fore in the 1990s, most prominently in the work of **Wong Kar-Wai.** Thanks to the efforts of the American film maker Quentin Tarantino, who arranged for Wong's 1994 comedy *Chungking Express* to be commercially distributed in the United States, this unconventional Hong Kong director has achieved considerable international renown, with a number of commentators labeling him as one of the most significant presences on the contemporary movie-making scene. His influence on a younger generation of film makers has been profound. *Chungking Express* tells two stories about a pair of young police detectives getting over failed romances. One falls for a mysterious female drug smuggler, played by Brigitte Lin (known as "the Asian Garbo"), a character putatively inspired by the Gena Rowlands character in the American independent film *Gloria,* directed by John Cassavetes. The other police detective is pursued by a pixie-ish fast-food worker, played by Hong Kong pop singer Faye Wong. Like other Wong productions *Chungking Express* focuses on characters reminiscent of those in American "B" pictures. Adding to their sleazy Hollywood feel, Wong's movies are littered with American pop culture references. His edgy style comes across as a kind of updated *film noir* look, featuring grainy, darkly lit images of a nighttime urban world sometimes accompanied by *noir*-ish voice-over narration. Jumpy, handheld camera work, slow motion and stop motion photography, strobe-effect editing, frequently shifting points of view, sudden time shifts, and a dearth of establishing shots complete the look, keeping the viewer off balance but wide awake.

Wong followed *Chungking Express* with *Fallen Angels* in 1995 and, in 1997, *Happy Together,* which won the best director prize at Cannes (Figure 21.6). A tale of two gay Chinese men caught in a destructive sadomasochistic relationship, *Happy Together* is set against the backdrop of modern Buenos Aires, reflecting the director's affection for Latin American novelists, such as Manuel Puig and Julio Cortázar.

In 2000 Wong turned to a more traditional love story with *In the Mood for Love,* a nostalgic vision of romantic longing for which he toned down his style to achieve an aura of elegance and restraint. "Too many other directors are doing Wong Kar-Wai these days," he commented as he was making it, "so I have to do something different."

Set among a group of displaced Shanghai residents in Hong Kong during the 1960s, *In the Mood for Love* tells the tale of two neighbors, Mrs. Chan (Maggie Cheung) and Mr. Chow (Tony Leung), who discover that their respective spouses are having an affair. Refusing to come to terms with their own growing attraction to one another, they obsessively playact the roles of the adulterous partners as a way of probing their feelings about the deception that is being practiced on them. Ultimately their dedication to the tenets of respectability—another kind of role-playing—leads them to an emotional stalemate, and they part. Some time later, Mr. Chow finds himself in Cambodia's Angkor Wat and whispers the secret of his love into a hole in the ancient ruins there.

The stifling conventions that keep the lovers apart are visually echoed in the film's constricted spaces and narrow doorways (Figure 21.7a). As the roles Mrs. Chan and Mr. Chow play become increasingly strained, Wong includes a long, slow panning shot (one of many in the film) that focuses on the multiple reflections of each character that appear in a three-way mirror (Figure 21.7b). Their strategy of circuitousness and indirection, it appears, is fragmenting their identities; they have lost their ability to please themselves instead of others, and they are unable to act on their desires. So love passes them by.

Wong's film is bathed in allusions to its setting in the 1960s, from the then-stylish high-necked *cheongsam* dresses worn by Maggie Cheung (Figure 21.7c) to the popular

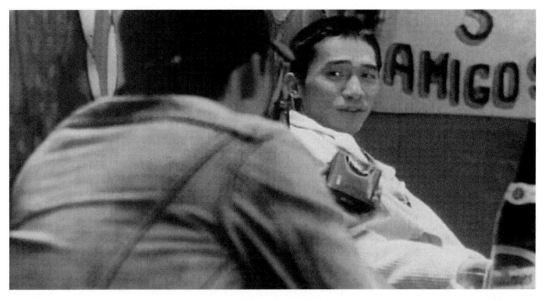

FIGURE 21.6   *Happy Together* ★ Hong Kong, 1997, Wong Kar-Wai; Tony Leung and Leslie Cheung.

FIGURE 21.7a–d   *In the Mood for Love* ★ Hong Kong, 2000, Wong Kar-Wai; a. Maggie Cheung and Rebecca Pan; b. Tony Leung; c. Maggie Cheung; d. Angkor Wat.

music we hear played on the radio and on the sound track. Like Hong Kong culture itself, the film's music is a pastiche of East and West, drawing from Chinese, Japanese, Western classical, and American pop sources (the lovers' stifled desire for one another is repeatedly evoked by the strains of Nat King Cole singing in Spanish on the soundtrack). Like the lovers, Hong Kong itself is here seen suspended in a moment in time. For these Shanghai expatriates who were escaping the culture of mainland China it becomes a liminal space both inside and outside of their homeland.

In the deepest sense *In the Mood for Love* is a study of nostalgia. The film's final scene in Angkor Wat suggests that all civilizations, like all individuals, exist in a perpetual state of mourning for a past that can never be possessed (Figure 21.7d). At the beginning of the sequence, before Mr. Chow performs his private ritual of longing and regret, we see newsreel footage of Charles de Gaulle, whose farewell visit to Cambodia in 1966 heralded the country's conversion from a colony to a free nation—a change, but also a loss. The ruins represent a loss of a more tragic and irrecoverable kind; their beauty resides largely in the absences they imply. Wong's film is finally about all of the losses that time inevitably brings about: the loss of love, the loss of home, and the loss of culture.

Taiwan

In Taiwan, martial law was lifted in 1987 and it became possible to show previously taboo aspects of the island's history and to undertake coproductions with mainland China (though officially forbidden). Taiwanese films have been honored at international film festivals but not shown widely in the United States. Influenced by the reigning aesthetic philosophy of nativism, they often emphasize Taiwanese history and traditional Chinese formal techniques, making many of them somewhat daunting for Western audiences.

A City of Sadness (1988), directed by **Hou Hsiao-hsien,** was Taiwan's first international artistic success (awarded the Golden Lion at the Venice Film Festival), while also doing very well commercially at home. Hou went on to make a series of nativist-oriented cinematic meditations on Taiwanese and Chinese history, including *The Puppetmaster* (1993), *Good Men, Good Women* (1995) (Figure 21.8), *Goodbye, South, Goodbye* (1996), and *Flowers of Shanghai* (1998). Hou favors contemplative long shots in which the camera remains at a distance from his actors; thus his films lack the dramatic intensity American filmgoers are accustomed to. "I always tell my cameraman, 'Pull back! More detached!'" Hou says. Often there is more than one center of dramatic interest—or perhaps none at all. Nonetheless, the results can be deeply affecting. The three-hour *City of Sadness* tells the traumatic tale of the massacre of thousands of native Taiwanese by the incoming Chinese Nationalist government in 1947. Although Hou claims to have been influenced by *The Godfather* in his conception of this film, it takes a far more stoic and externalized perspective on the action than its American predecessor. *Flowers of Shanghai,* which a number of critics have labeled Hou's most accomplished work, is set in a Shanghai brothel at the end of the nineteenth century. Softly lit rooms photographed with long, flowing camera movements reveal the intrigues that seal the fate of the female inhabitants of the house, who are at the mercy of their powerful male patrons. The film's first shot, lasting ten minutes, introduces us to a number of the major characters, then surveys the

FIGURE 21.8   *Good Men, Good Women* ★ Taiwan, 1995, Hou Hsiao-hsien.

room, lingering on objects and views that, although void of immediate dramatic interest, create a richly textured vision of a surrounding world against which the action unfolds.

Besides directing, Hou has also acted. Among other roles, he starred in the 1985 *Taipei Story,* the breakthrough production of fellow Taiwanese film maker **Edward Yang.** Yang was born and raised in Taiwan but received his graduate education in America (Florida State University and University of Southern California). Like Hou, Yang has followed the nativist line, turning out a series of emotionally detached studies of Taiwanese culture. "The future of Western civilization lies right here," one of the characters in *Taipei Story* remarks. Unlike Hou, however, Yang usually sets his films in the present rather than in the past. Although he has been compared to Antonioni, his films lack the psychologically complex central characters that mark the work of the Italian director. Instead, he favors multiple plot lines made up of intricately woven narrative strands involving many characters, who may act in seemingly unmotivated ways. Among his most notable films, *The Terrorizor* (1986) follows the activities of three modern Taiwanese couples and their interactions with a police detective. The four-hour *A Brighter Summer Day* (1991), set in Taiwan in the early 1960s, concerns teenagers who have no memory of life on the Chinese mainland and who gravitate toward gangs as they reject the ideals of their parents (Figure 21.9). With a cast made up of mostly nonprofessionals, the film was inspired by a true incident in which a fourteen-year-old girl was murdered by a male high school student. In 2000 Yang made *Yi yi (A One and a Two),* a tangled family drama that won him a best director award at Cannes.

If Hou Hsiao-hsien and Edward Yang represent a movie-making style that relies on cultural specificity, a younger Taiwanese directorial talent, **Tsai Ming-liang,** works in a more personal, even private mode. Born in Malaysia, Tsai is now based in Taipei. His spare, elliptical productions are mostly shot in his own apartment using a stock company of actors who reappear again and again. The visual style of these films is minimalist: long takes with a stationary camera dominate. Not much happens, and there is little dialogue. The overall mood mixes anomie with subtle humor—rather as if a Michelangelo Antonioni movie had been crossed with one by Jacques Tati. In most cases the main character is Hsiao Kang, played by Lee Kang-Sheng, who is usually seen as a stand-in for the director himself. Tsai's most well-known film, *What Time Is It There?,* follows the daily routine of Hsiao Kang, a watch salesman in Taipei who sells a timepiece to a young woman headed for Paris. We intermittently follow the woman's experiences in Paris while we witness Hsaio turn all the clocks he can find in Taipei to Paris time. Is he in love with her? Probably. Meanwhile, his newly widowed mother performs increasingly bizarre rituals before the household shrine. Like all of Tsai's films, *What Time Is It There?* is finally enigmatic, but for those attuned to its slow rhythms and eccentric preoccupations, it can weave a hypnotic spell.

A more Westernized and accessible Taiwanese sensibility is represented by **Ang Lee,** whose interests have shifted from Chinese to Western subjects and back again. Lee is particularly adept at depicting self-deluded characters with gentle humor, revealing their

FIGURE 21.9   *A Brighter Summer Day* ★ Taiwan, 1991, Edward Yang.

quirks and foibles without causing the audience to lose sympathy for them. His second film, *The Wedding Banquet* (1993), portrays the travails of a gay Taiwanese man living in New York City who must conceal his relationship with his lover from his traditional parents. In a plot device that recalls the popular French farce *The Birdcage,* the Taiwanese parents arrange a marriage for their son, and the three young people must engage in an elaborate charade to prevent the truth from coming out. Lee followed up this success in 1994 with an equally engaging comedy, this time set in Taiwan rather than New York. Entitled *Eat, Drink, Man, Woman,* it concerns an eminent Taiwanese chef and his relationship with his three marriageable daughters. More recently, Lee has worked on large-scale Hollywood productions such as the 1995 *Sense and Sensibility* with Emma Thompson and Kate Winslet, and the 1997 *Ice Storm* with Sigourney Weaver and Kevin Kline. In 2000 he returned to mainland China to make *Crouching Tiger, Hidden Dragon* (Figure 21.10), a lighthearted martial arts film with a feminist slant. It went on to win a number of Academy Awards and became the most widely seen foreign film in the United States.

If the experience of Ang Lee is any guide, globalization will operate to bring the three Chinese cinemas closer together in future years. As a Taiwanese film maker who has worked in his home country, in America, and in mainland China, he is a truly international figure. Yet, if we are to judge from developments thus far, increased globalization need not operate to create a homogeneous film culture that will obliterate the venerable traditions of Asian art. Rather, what we often observe in Chinese film is an aesthetic of hybridization: allusions to American-style pop culture, Hollywood storytelling techniques, and a Latin American–inspired postmodernism combined with traditional Chinese subjects and techniques. So as the three Chinas come together, they are bonding with the rest of the world as well.

FIGURE 21.10 *Crouching Tiger, Hidden Dragon* ⋆ Taiwan, 2000, Ang Lee; Zhang Ziyi.

Films of the Period

MAINLAND CHINA

1964
Two Stage Sisters (Wutai jiemei) (Xie Jin)

1984
One and Eight (Yi ge he ba ge) (Zhang Junzhao)
Yellow Earth (Huang tudi) (Chen Kaige)

1986
The Big Parade (Da yue bing) (Chen Kaige)
The Black Cannon Incident (Hei pao shijian)
  (Huang Jianxin)

1987
The Horse Thief (Dao ma zei) (Tian Zhuangzhuang)

1988
King of the Children (Haizi wang) (Chen Kaige)
Red Sorghum (Hong gaoliang) (Zhang Yimou)

1990
Ju Dou (Zhang Yimou)

1991
Life on a String (Bian zou bian chang) (Chen Kaige)
*Raise the Red Lantern (Da hong denglong gao gao
  gua)* (Zhang Yimou)

1992
Farewell My Concubine (Ba wang bie ji) (Chen
  Kaige)
The Story of Qiu Ju (Qiu Ju da guansi) (Zhang
  Yimou)

1995
Shanghai Triad (Zhang Yimou)

1999
Not One Less (Yi ge dou bung neng shao) (Zhang
  Yimou)
The Road Home (Wo de fuqin muchin) (Zhang
  Yimou)
Shower (Xizao) (Zhang Yang)

2000
Devils on the Doorstep (Guizi lai le) (Jiang Wen)

Platform (Zhangtai) (Zhang ke Jia)
Suzhou River (Suzhou He) (Lou Ye)

2001
Beijing Bicycle (Shiqi sui de dan che) (Wang
  Xiaoshuai)
Quitting (Zuotain) (Zhang Yang)

2002
Hero (Yingxiong) (Zhang Yimou)
Springtime in a Small Town (Xiao xheng zhi chun)
  (Tian Zhuangzhuang)
Unknown Pleasures (Ren xiao yao) (Zhang ke Jia)

2003
Purple Butterfly (Zi hudie) (Lou Ye)

2004
House of Flying Daggers (Shi mian mai fu)
  (Zhang Yimou)
Shijie (Zhang Ke Jia)

HONG KONG

1975
A Touch of Zen (Hsia nu) (King Hu)

1982
Boat People (Tou bun no hoi) (Ann Hui)

1986
A Better Tomorrow (Ying huang boon sik)
  (John Woo)

1987
Rouge (Yin ji Kau) (Stanley Kwan)

1989
The Killer (Die xue shuang xiong) (John Woo)

1990
Song of the Exile (Ketu qiuhen) (Ann Hui)

1991
Center Stage (Yuen Ling-Yuk) (Stanley Kwan)
Days of Being Wild (A Fei jing juen) (Wong Kar-Wai)

1992
Hard-Boiled (Lashou shentan) (John Woo)

1994
Ashes of Time (Dung che sai duk) (Wong Kar-Wai)
Chungking Express (Chonqing Samlam) (Wong Kar-Wai)

1995
The Blade (Dao) (Tsui Hark)
Fallen Angels (Duo Puo tian shi) (Wong Kar-Wai)

1997
Happy Together (Cheun guong tsa sit) (Wong Kar-Wai)

2000
In the Mood for Love (Fa yeung nin wa) (Wong Kar-Wei)

2001
Lan Yu (Stanley Kwan)

2004
2046 (Wong Kar-Wai)

TAIWAN
1985
Taipei Story (Qingmei Zhuma) (Edward Yang)
A Time to Live and a Time to Die (Tong nien wang shi) (Hou Hsiao-hsien)

1986
The Terrorizer (Kongbu fenzi) (Edward Yang)

1988
A City of Sadness (Beiqing chengshi) (Hou Hsiao-hsien)

1991
A Brighter Summer Day (Guling jie shaonian sha ren shijian) (Edward Yang)

1993
The Puppet Master (Hsimeng jensheng) (Hou Hsiao-hsien)
The Wedding Banquet (Hsi yen) (Ang Lee)

1994
Eat, Drink, Man, Woman (Yin shi nan nu) (Ang Lee)

1996
Goodbye, South, Goodbye (Nanguo zaijan, nanguo) (Hou Hsiao-hsien)
Vive L'Amour (Aiqing Wansui) (Tsai Ming-liang)

1997
River (He liu) (Tsai Ming-liang)

1998
Flowers of Shanghai (Hai shang hua) (Hou Hsaio-hsien)
The Hole (Dong) (Tsai Ming-liang)

2000
Crouching Tiger, Hidden Dragon (Wo hu cang long) (Ang Lee)
Yi yi (Edward Yang)

2001
Millennium Mambo (Qianxi manbo) (Hou Hsaio-hsien)
What Time Is It There? (Ni neibian jidian) (Tsai Ming-liang)

2003
Good Bye, Dragon Inn (Bu san) (Tsai Ming-liang)

Books on the Period

Berry, Chris. *Chinese Films in Focus: Twenty-five New Takes.* London: British Film Institute, 2004.

Bordwell, David. *Planet Hong Kong: Popular Cinema and the Art of Entertainment.* Cambridge, MA: Harvard University Press, 2000.

Cornelius, Shelia. *New Chinese Cinema: Challenging Representations.* London: Wallflower Press, 2001.

Cui, Shuqin. *Women through the lens: Gender and nation in a century of Chinese cinema.* Honolulu: University of Hawaii Press, 2003.

Ehrlich, Linda C., and David Desser. *Cinematic Landscapes: Observations on the Visual Arts and Cinema of China and Japan.* Austin: University of Texas Press, 2000.

Fonoroff, Paul. *At the Hong Kong Movies: 600 Reviews from 1988 till the Handover.* London: Odyssey Publications, 1999.

Fu, Poshek, and David Desser, eds. *The Cinema of Hong Kong: History, Arts, Identity.* New York: Cambridge University Press, 2000.

Hoover, Michael, and Lisa Stokes. *City on Fire: Hong Kong Cinema.* New York: Verso, 1999.

Hu, Jubin. *Projecting a Nation: Chinese National Cinema before 1949.* Hong Kong: Hong Kong University Press, 2003.

Hunt, Leon. *Kung Fu Cult Masters: From Bruce Lee to "Crouching Tiger."* London: Wallflower Press, 2003.

Lau, Jenny Kwok Wah, ed. *Multiple modernities: Cinema and popular media in transcultural East Asia.* Philadelphia: Temple University Press, 2003.

Lu Sheldon Hsiao-peng, ed. *Transnational Chinese cinemas: Identity, nationhood, gender.* Honolulu, HI: University of Hawaii Press, 1997.

Lu, Tonglin. *Confronting modernity in the cinemas of Taiwan and Mainland China.* New York: Cambridge University Press, 2002.

Martin, Fran. *Situating Sexualities: Queer Representation in Taiwanese Fiction, Film, and Public Culture.* Hong Kong: Hong Kong University Press, 2003.

Ni Zhen. *Memoirs from the Beijing film academy: The genesis of China's fifth generation.* Trans. Chris Berry. Durham, NC: Duke University Press, 2002.

Palmer, Bill, Karen Palmer, and Ric Meyer. *The Encyclopedia of Martial Arts Movies.* New York: Scarecrow, 2003.

Pang, Laikwan. *Building a new China in cinema: The Chinese left-wing cinema movement, 1932–1937.* New York: Romman & Littlefield, 2002.

Silbergeld, Jerome. *China into Film: Frames of Reference in Contemporary Chinese Cinema.* Reaktion Books, 2000.

Stokes, Lisa Oldham, and Michael Hoover. *City on Fire: Hong Kong Cinema.* New York: Verso, 1999.

Tam, Kwok-Kan, and Wimal Dissanayake. *New Chinese Cinema (Images of Asia).* New York: Oxford University Press, 1998.

Teo, Stephen. *Hong Kong Cinema: The Extra Dimensions.* London: British Film Institute, 1998.

Yau Ching. *Filming Margins: Tang Shu Shuen, A Forgotten Hong Kong Woman Director.* Hong Kong: Hong Kong University Press, 2004.

Yau, Esther C. M., ed. *At Full Speed: Hong Kong Cinema in a Borderless World.* Minneapolis: University of Minnesota Press, 2001.

Zhang, Yingjin, ed. *Cinema and Urban Culture in Shanghai, 1922–1943.* Stanford: Stanford University Press, 1999.

Zhang, Yingjin, and Zhiwei Xiao. *Encyclopedia of Chinese Film.* New York: Routledge, 1999.

Zhu, Ying. *Chinese Cinema during the Era of Reform: The Ingenuity of the System.* Westport, CT: Praeger, 2003.

22

Recent National Movements

1959–

The last half of the twentieth century saw important cinema movements develop in countries beyond the orbit of Europe, the United States, and the major Asian nations. Post-colonial cultures in Latin America and Africa have nurtured distinctive movie-making traditions, as have the commonwealth nations of Australia, New Zealand, and Canada. Most recently, films from Middle Eastern countries, especially Iran, have appeared on the global stage. Early films from developing nations, which attracted international attention, generally expressed a strong sense of nationalism, frequently accompanied by anti-imperialism and sometimes a call to revolution. Film making in some of the Latin American countries, as well as in Africa, especially, conformed to these generalizations. Other places, such as Mexico and the British Commonwealth countries, have developed nationalist cinematic agendas in less politically stressed climates. The Middle East has its own political issues; in Iran, these are closely tied to questions of religious propriety, and its films reflect this concern.

Latin America

Although each Latin American country has given birth to its own, particularized cinematic culture, a common heritage, along with abundant opportunities for cross-fertilization, has led to a common set of principles and values. All of the Latin American film movements have built on a shared aesthetic in the other arts. The surrealist strain so prominent in Spanish painting and sculpture found its way into the New World as well. These nations, in turn, added their own brand of what has come to be called *magic realism* to the mix. Out of these ingredients Latin Americans have crafted a literary tradition that has proved to be a major

423

wellspring for postmodernist narrative explorations—the writings of José Luis Borges, Carlos Fuentes, Gabriel García Márquez, and others. Filled with hallucinatory fantasies, labyrinthine mysteries, and unexpected shifts in character, style, and structure, these works have become the very definition of the postmodern aesthetic.

To this rich artistic heritage, most Latin American film makers have added strong political commitments, reacting against the military and fascist ruling elites and oppressive colonialist policies that have long governed the affairs of most of these countries. Unlike other third-world directors, such as Satyajit Ray of India, the Latin Americans historically made their films for local audiences, not international festivals. Although most of these movie makers come from upper-class backgrounds, their goal is to connect with the peasantry and the urban poor of their countries in order to raise social awareness and ultimately improve conditions. "By testifying, critically to [the reality of] misery, cinema refuses it," Argentinean director Fernando Birri, a leader of the movement, once wrote, "because it shows matters as they irrefutably are and not as we would like them to be."

Principles derived from the Italian neorealists were a major inspiration to many Latin American movie makers—particularly because several had been trained at Italy's documentary film school, the Centro Sperimentale, in Rome. Other Latin American directors attended the documentary school in Santa Fé, Argentina—La Escuela Documental de Santa Fé—set up in the 1950s by Birri, a graduate of Italy's Centro Sperimentale. To the neorealist principles of shooting on location, using nonprofessional actors, and focusing on lower-class lifestyles, accents, and dialects, the Latin Americans have added their own carnival-esque flavor, a style called *tropicalism,* consisting of surrealism, allegory, vivid color, flashy images, and powerful music. Their preferred subjects include contemporary social and political issues (for example, Bolivian Jorge Sanjinés's 1969 *Blood of the Condor,* which deals with the attempts by the American Peace Corps to sterilize Bolivian Indian women) (Figure 22.1) as well as historical stories, especially those dealing with slavery (such as Brazilian Carlos Diegues's 1964 *Ganga Zumba* and Cuban Sergio Gilal's 1973 *The Other Francisco*). After many Latin American film makers were driven out of their countries by political crackdowns, exile films (Chilean Miguel Littin's 1975 *Letters from Marusia* and Argentinean Fernando Solanas's 1985 *Tangos: The Exile of Gardel*) became another favored genre.

In 1954 a film festival was set up in Montevideo, Argentina, providing the region's directors with both a venue for showing their work and a forum for exchanging ideas. In 1958 the festival honored British documentary pioneer John Grierson. The occasion drew film makers from all over South America, including Birri, who screened his collectively produced documentary, *Throw Me a Dime,* and the Brazilian Nelson Pereira dos Santos, who showed his neorealist fiction film, *Rio, North Zone.* In 1967 another meeting of directors from an array of Latin American nations was held in Viña del Mar, Chile. Out of this came the label *Nuevo Cinema Latinamericano* to designate the new movement that was afoot.

Among Latin American cinematic traditions, **Cuba**'s has been preeminent. Movies have always been popular there. Moreover, with its socialist revolution achieved in 1959, Cuba was able to offer inspiration, encouragement, and actual assistance to the independent leftist film makers in the neighboring countries of South America. The Cubans had rebelled against foreign (i.e., American) domination as well as the Fulgencio Batista government.

FIGURE 22.1 *Blood of the Condor* ★ Bolivia, 1969, Jorge Sanjinés.

Following from this anti-American sentiment, the revolution's triumph brought sweeping changes in the Cuban motion-picture industry that sought to sever its relationship to Hollywood. Like Russia following its revolution in 1917, or the Eastern Republics after 1945, Cuba established a government agency to organize and regulate all production, distribution, and exhibition. Called *Instituto Cubano del Arte y Industria Cinematográficos (ICAIC),* it created first-rate production facilities and invited Czechoslovakian film makers in to train Cuban personnel.

Consistent with Lenin's advice to the earlier Soviet film makers, the Cubans used newsreels and documentaries to meet the needs of the people as seen by the new state. The leading figure of this nonnarrative short-film output was Santiago Alvarez, who made documentaries such as *L.B.J.* (1968) and *79 Springtimes* (1969, about Vietnamese leader Ho Chi Minh). The ironic and experimental forms of attack on the violence of the United States in these films, and their lyrical portrayal of "the struggle of the underdeveloped and small peoples for their human dignity," as Alvarez has put it, place him among the leading innovators in art used for political persuasion.

The best-known Cuban director is **Tomás Gutiérrez Alea,** whose *Memories of Underdevelopment* (1968) was the first Cuban feature to achieve international recognition. Far from serving any obvious agitprop function, it chronicles the spiritual displacement of a bourgeois intellectual within postrevolutionary Cuban culture with a kind of cinematic sophistication and emotional detachment that place it within the mainstream of modern world cinema. Alea's *Up to a Point* (1983) deals with the problems raised by a long tradition of

Latin American *machismo*. The title comes from one of the brief interviews with real workers interspersed throughout this fictional narrative. A young black male questioned about *machismo* laughingly replies, "Oh, they've managed to change my attitudes on that score: I've certainly changed up to a certain point."

The topic of *machismo* has also been taken up in the many Cuban films that focus on issues facing women, including Humberto Solás's *Lucía* (1968) and Pastor Vega's *Portrait of Teresa* (1979). *One Way or Another* (1977), a fiction-documentary mix, is an especially memorable example of Cuban feminist discourse. Directed by Sara Gómez, who died before editing was completed, its plot concerns a young, idealistic social worker who, while trying to teach ghetto kids, falls in love with a local man struggling to break out of the neighborhood's deprived existence.

Alea's own *Strawberry and Chocolate* in 1994 carries the gender issue into the realm of gay sexuality, which poses a further challenge to Latin *machismo*. Critical of the prejudice against homosexuals that prevails in Castro's Cuba, Alea's film also mourns the country's loss of a proud artistic tradition. As the story's main character David, a politically idealistic student, comes under the influence of Diego, an older gay mentor figure (Figure 22.2a), Diego begins to educate his young friend about Cuban art and literature. At one point, Diego takes David on a tour of historic Havana, drawing his attention to crumbling ruins that had once been magnificent edifices (Figure 22.2b). *Strawberry and Chocolate,* Alea's cinematic elegy to Cuba's past artistic glory, marked the diminution of the nation's preeminent film culture as well as the decline of the arts in general in this once culturally rich country; after its release few local productions attracted much international interest.

In **Brazil,** an upsurge of nationalism occurred at about the same time as the Cuban Revolution. In response, a cooperative formed by Glauber Rocha, Nelson Pereira dos Santos (*Barren Lives,* 1963), and Ruy Guerra *(The Guns,* 1964) produced what they called *Cinema Nôvo*. Ironically, the group got their start through support from Embrafilme, a state funding agency set up in the 1960s by the reigning military government to promote Brazil abroad through films praising the existing regime. Needless to say the productions of the Cinema Nôvo directors were of quite a different order. But they got funding all the same. The abolition of Embrafilme in 1990 caused a major setback for the country's production activities, but in 1994 the institution of another system of government grants revitalized the industry once again.

The Cinema Nôvo group offered a more applicable model than did Cuba for other Latin American film makers on the left working independently within entrenched capitalist regimes. Dedicated to a principle of "miserabilism," which pledged them to focus on the poor and needy, these directors quickly moved away from the documentary-type approach of neorealism to develop a cinema in which dark political allegories were rendered in an exuberantly tropicalist style. Rocha was the Cinema Nôvo's leader and spokesman, labeling the movement's approach an "aesthetics of hunger." Another member of the group, Joaquin Pedro de Andrade, took this allusion to starvation to its logical conclusion in his 1969 production, *Macunaima,* a carnival-esque tale of cannibalism. "Cannibalism is an exemplary mode of consumerism adopted by underdeveloped peoples," he later commented by way of explanation.

Glauber Rocha's own films, including *Black God, White Devil* (1964) (Figure 22.3) and *Antônio das Mortes* (1969), are set in the barren northeastern region of the country and explore the mythic folk roots of banditry and mystical religion that extreme poverty had

FIGURE 22.2a and b *Strawberry and Chocolate* ★ Cuba, 1994, Tomás Guitiérrez Alea;
a. Vladimir Cruz and Jorge Perugorría.

bred. Strange and haunting in their combination of severe naturalism and stylized ritual,
they portray a world of violence and madness. Following the release of *Antônio das
Mortes,* Rocha left Brazil and worked abroad. He made films in Europe and Africa that attempted to deal with the problems of the third world—underdevelopment and neocolonialist
exploitation—and to explore the possibilities for political action to bring about radical social change. In 1976 he returned to Brazil, but completed little of significance before his
death in 1981.

FIGURE 22.3   *Black God, White Devil* ⋆ Brazil, 1964, Glauber Rocha.

Post–Cinema Nôvo production has become prolific. A line of leftist criticism has been maintained but added to it is a diversity of popular films. Pereira dos Santos continued the political line in, for instance, *How Tasty Was My Little Frenchman* (1971), *Amulet of Orgum* (1974), *Tent of Miracles* (1977), and *Prison Memories* (1984); as did Carlos Diegues in *Xica de Silva* (1976) and *Bye Bye Brazil* (1979); and Argentine emigré Hector Babenco in *Pixote* (1981). For the most part, however, revolutionary Brazilian film makers have blended into the commercial film industry, which became more visible following the wide showing of Bruno Barreto's *Dona Flor and Her Two Husbands* in 1978. The international popularity of Brazilian cinema reached its peak in 1985 with Babenco's first English-language film, *Kiss of the Spider Woman,* a U.S.-Brazilian coproduction that centers on the relationship of two very different prison cell mates: a sensitive, imaginative, homosexual "queen" (William Hurt) and a tough-minded Marxist militant (Raul Julia).

In 1999 Brazilian cinema again stepped into the international cinema spotlight with Walter Salles's *Central Station,* a socially progressive, if sentimentalized, tale about the relationship between a single woman and a destitute child; it garnered an Oscar nomination for its star Fernanda Montenegro. This success coincided with a rise in the local box-office support for homegrown releases—from $12 million in 1999 to $17.5 million in 2000.

The new prominence of Brazilian movie production at the turn of the century was bolstered by generous government tax incentives to lure global investment. This policy paid off handsomely in 2002, when *City of God,* a U.S.–U.K.–German–Brazilian coproduction, garnered four Oscar nominations and numerous international awards (Figure

FIGURE 22.4   *City of God*   ★   Brazil, 2002, Fernando Meirelles and Katiá Lund.

22.4). As codirected by Fernando Meirelles and Katiá Lund, *City of God*'s episodic narrative focuses on a young slum dweller who longs to become a professional photographer. The cast is made up of nonprofessionals who were at the time ghetto dwellers themselves. Though the movie's kinetic style and extreme violence owe much to the influence of Quentin Tarantino, it has national roots as well, reviving the traditions of miserablism and tropicalism that Brazil's Cinema Nôvo movement had put in place many years earlier. Though made with foreign money and tailored to foreign audiences, *City of God* is finally a Brazilian film.

In **Argentina** in the 1960s another group of political film makers set up an independent cooperative, in their case called *Grupo Cine Liberación (GCL)*. Its manifesto, "Toward a Third Cinema," advocated film making that was "independent in production, militant in politics, and experimental in language." The group's program also called for collective film authorship and audience involvement in political discussion as part of the film experience. (The manifesto defines the first two cinemas as the Hollywood studio system and *auteur* films; films made according to Grupo Cine Liberación principles was the third.) The GCL's principal organizer was Fernando Solanas and its major work was his *The Hour of the Furnaces* (1968, codirected with Octavio Getino) (Figure 22.5). This huge documentary (nearly four-and-a-half hours long) is in three separate parts: "Neo-Colonialism and Violence," "An Act for Liberation," and "Violence and Liberation." The first part presents a historical, geographical, economic, and social analysis of Argentina. The content of the second and third parts was developed out of points raised during audience discussion following the necessarily clandestine screenings of the first. Because of the time at which it appeared, its ambitious scope, its formal eclecticism, and the circumstances surrounding its production and distribution, *The Hour of the Furnaces* has been regarded as the single most influential

FIGURE 22.5   *The Hour of the Furnaces* ⋆ Argentina, 1968, Fernando Solanas and Octavio Getino.

documentary to have come out of the entire Cinema Latinamericano movement. With the resumption of military rule in Argentina in 1976, not only were the films of the GCL no longer smuggled abroad but they also were also not shown in Argentina itself, even clandestinely, because of the severe penalties attached to any activities critical of the government.

With the defeat of Argentina in the Falklands War of 1982, the military was weak enough to be opposed. Following the election of a civilian government in 1983, *The Official Story* was produced. The plot deals with the disappearance of roughly thirty thousand Argentinians—the *desaparecidos*—between 1976 and 1983. The first feature of Luis Puenzo, a director of television commercials, it won the 1985 Academy Award for Best Foreign Film. Other Argentinean directors who came to the fore at the century's end have also adopted a tough line of political and social criticism, including Eliseo Subiola (*Man Facing Southeast,* 1986) (Figure 22.6) and María Luisa Bemberg, who crafted a distinguished series of searching feminist cinematic studies before her death in 1995, including *Camila* (1984), *Miss Mary* (1986), *I, the Worst of All* (1990), and *We Don't Want to Talk About It* (1993).

By the late 1990s, Argentinean movie making had begun a steep decline. Massive foreign debt forced the government to cut film funding, and a devastating recession at the end of 2001 made the financial climate even worse. But by 2004 movie-making activities were back on track, and President Nestor Kirchner announced a new government program of subsidies and credits to encourage local production. At the time of this writing the results of this more hospitable economic climate remain to be seen, but for Argentineans, often called the Parisians of Latin America, intelligent film making occupies a privileged position on the cultural agenda.

FIGURE 22.6 *Man Facing Southeast* ★ Argentina, 1986, Eliseo Subiola; Hugo Soto.

As a country with a less turbulent political history throughout most of the twentieth century than most other Latin American nations, **Mexico** has not witnessed the genesis of the kind of radical film movement that came to the fore in other parts of the Hispanic New World. Its cinema has historically been most consistently notable for the broad distribution of its formulaic genre productions, called *churros,* throughout the region. Most of these films focused on the rural peasantry and had a folkloric flavor, with loosely organized plots and plenty of music. Described by one critic as "big skies, big sombreros," the genre was inspired in part by the example of Soviet director Sergei Eisenstein, whose unfinished *Que Viva Mexico* (1932) brought the richness of Mexican folk culture to the fore. The folk-oriented muralist movement championed by prominent artists such as Diego Rivera was another influence. Such productions presented Latin American audiences with an alternative to Hollywood fare. The *churros* formula "unearthed what Latin American audiences seemed to have been looking for in the Mexican cinema," Latin American film scholar Ana Lopez has commented, "the presentation of a 'Mexican' vision of Mexico that coincided with their expectations of the nature of national 'local color.'"

Mexico's film culture has produced works of enduring value as well as mass appeal. The 1940s and 1950s are thought of as a Golden Age, crowned by the films made by Spanish director Luis Buñuel from 1945 to 1960. During this period Mexico produced more than one hundred movies a year. Among the most highly esteemed of Buñuel's films made during this time are *Los Olvidados,* a searing exploration of the lives of young slum dwellers in Mexico City; *A Mexican Bus Ride* (1951), an unusually gentle Buñuelian comedy featuring a warm description of Mexican peasant life; *Él* (1953), a study of sexual obsession; and *Nazarín* (1958), a dark satire of the Catholic Church. Many of these featured striking visuals executed by world-class Mexican cinematographer Gabriel Figueroa. Figueroa also worked extensively with Emilio Fernández, another star director of the period, most notably on the classic cinematic ode to Mexico's Indian culture, *María Candelaria* (1945) (Figure 22.7).

Following World War II a group of Mexico City–based directors began to create challenging, surrealist-tinted films for the international art cinema market; this group included Paul Leduc (*Reed: Insurgent Mexico,* 1973, and *Frida,* 1986) and Arturo Ripstein (*The Castle of Purity,* 1973, and *The Beginning and the End,* 1993). In 1992 Mexican film achieved an unprecedented international visibility with the runaway success of Alfonzo Arau's erotic, magic realist fantasy, *Like Water for Chocolate,* adapted from a novel by his wife, Laura Esquivel. By the beginning of the twenty-first century, talk of a revival of Mexico's Golden Age was in the air in the wake of critical and commerical hits such as the moving melodrama *Midaq Alley* (Jorge Fons, 1995), the daring political satire *Herod's Law* (Luis Estrada, 1999), and most of all, the riveting *Amores Perros* (Alejandro González Iñárritu, 2001), with its brutal images and complex, interwoven narrative.

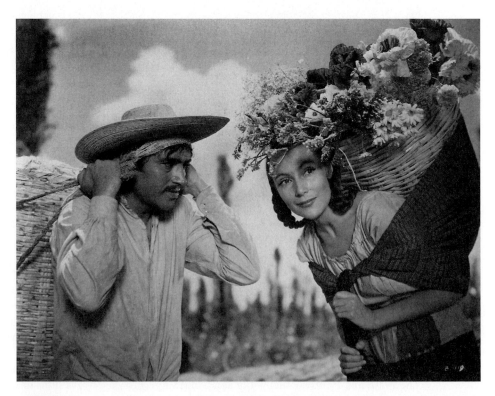

FIGURE 22.7 *Mariá Candelaria* ★ Mexico, 1945, Emilio Fernández; Pedro Armendáriz and Delores del Rio.

Iñárritu followed the success of *Amores Perros* with an American-based production, *21 Grams* (2003), following the path taken by many other Mexican talents before him, including Salma Hayak, Dolores Del Rio, Anthony Quinn, Ricardo Montalban, and Katy Jurado. The money and exposure offered by Hollywood has tempted many Mexicans to head north of the border, but in 2001 an artistically ambitious Mexican film maker traveled in the other direction. Alfonzo Cuarón, who had made his reputation in Hollywood with movies such as *A Little Princess* (1995), returned to his homeland to make the daring road film *Y tu mamá también*. It was a huge hit in the United States as well as Mexico and was nominated for an Oscar for best screenplay that year.

The climax of South American political film making, reached at the end of the 1960s, receded into an unpromising denouement. In the 1970s many of the principal film makers were working in exile abroad, without benefit of the strengths they had derived from their native cultures and the national political goals that had infused their work with revolutionary energy. Those at home were forced to remain silent or work within the noncommitted commercial film industries. In the 1980s and 1990s Cuba continued steadily on a modest scale, attracting little attention abroad. Among the other Latin American nations, both Brazil and Argentina achieved sporadic successes without eschewing altogether earlier political commitments. Many films from Latin America that found international success at the end of the century were directed by women, including Venezuelan Fina Torres's 1985 *Oriane* and Helena Solberg's postmodern documentary about Brazilian star Carmen Miranda, *Bananas Is My Business* in 1995. Mexico's Jaime Humberto Hermosillo has brought a gay sensibility to bear on an array of issues in films such as *Appearances Deceive* (1977) and *Dona Herlinda and Her Two Sons* (1984), providing further evidence to support the contention that in Latin America, as elsewhere, the meaning of politics has expanded to include gender politics.

Africa

In Africa—except Algeria and other Arab countries of the North, where a certain amount of noteworthy production is evident—the development of national film industries has been limited. The region is among the poorest in the world; at the millennium, 42 percent of Africa's population was living on less than $1 per day. In such a climate of economic scarcity, it is hardly surprising that sub-Saharan cinema of the late 1950s and early 1960s was little more than the work of a few isolated creators. Although white South African Jaime Uys's 1980 hit comedy, *The Gods Must Be Crazy,* drew world attention to the African continent, it took longer for the films of black African movie makers to find audiences abroad. As in Latin America, African films, when they finally appeared, were socially and politically inspired, post- (and anti-) colonialist, part of what was then called "third-world Euphoria."

Most of the important black African film makers to emerge since the 1970s are from countries that had been colonies of France or Belgium, with French their common language. (Over 80 percent of African films are made in French.) In large part this situation stemmed from the hands-on colonialist policies of the French, who, unlike the less involved British, have been ready to supply money and know-how to aspiring film makers in Francophone countries. Many African directors have been trained in France or Moscow. Under such a paternalistic system, however, censorship, in all of its forms, has played a major role.

The process of making films in Africa has been characterized as *mégotage*—like making cigarettes from discarded butts, an allusion to the difficulty of finding usable film stock. The Africans have also encountered major barriers when attempting to break into an entrenched distribution system dominated by Americans, Europeans, and East Indians. In such a context, international cooperation has been essential; the Africans have achieved this goal through the *Fédération Pan-Africane des Cinéastes (FEPACI),* an entity that established film centers around the continent, which in turn set up production and distribution facilities. The FEPACI also instituted the region's first film festival in Ouagadougou. In the 1990s, funding for African films from France was cut back and production slowed. At the turn of the century, however, the European economic community stepped in, beginning a funding program to compensate for the loss. But because the procedure requires submission by local governments rather than by individual film makers, censorship remains a factor. In addition, obstacles to adequate distribution remain.

The film-making style that has emerged in the region has sometimes been described as *folkloric.* Many African films build on the tradition of the *griot,* or oral storyteller. Political criticism is frequently softened in these works by their beguiling look; bathed in the clear light of the tropics, they typically feature lambent pastel hues and sun-drenched settings that overlay their forceful political messages with a fairy tale-ish patina. Senegal assumed early leadership in the development of the favored approach, especially in the work of Ousmane Sembène.

Novelist as well as film maker, **Ousmane Sembène,** more than any other figure, has come to represent the values and style of black African cinema. With painful irony, his first film, *Black Girl* (1966), attacked the exploitation and racism to which blacks were subjected by the French colonists. In *Xala* (1974), using satire and bawdy humor, he shows how the leaders of the new black state mimic the ways of their former colonial masters to the continued detriment of the people. With *Ceddo* (1977), Sembène continues his attempts to develop a truly African film language, making use of the griot as the center of the narrative. "There is no longer a traditional storyteller in our day," the director has said, "and I think the cinema can replace him." His next feature after *Ceddo, Camp de Thiaroye* (1987), made with Thierno Faty Sow, deals with an event of World War II in which a group of West African infantrymen awaiting demobilization after active service in Europe were suspected of mutiny and fired on by the French. Sembène maintained his preeminence as the father of black African film throughout the 1990s with productions such as *Guelwaar* (1995), a droll comedy about a misplaced corpse, *Faat Kine* in 2001, and *Moolaade* in 2004.

Following Sembène were a group of younger film makers whose films have been inspired by the oral tradition of African narrative and deal with indigenous subjects close to the people. Angolan film maker Sarah Maldorer's visually ravishing 1972 *Sambizanga,*for example, focuses on the political awakening of its female protagonist. Med Hondo's *Sarraounia* (Mauritania, 1986) recounts the story of the successful resistance against the French in the 1890s. Led by the queen of the Aznas, the rebellion united pagan and Moslem Africans to defeat a powerful and well-armed invading force. (African film scholar Nwachu Frank Ukadike has called *Sarraounia* the most ambitious African production ever in terms of its inventiveness and professionalism.) Souleymane Cissé's *Yeelen (Brightness,* Mali, 1987), set in a remote desert area in the sixteenth century, is concerned with superstitions and the supernatural invoked in a conflict between son and father, and the impact of these forces on the people (Figure 22.8). Shot in mellow tones of beiges, tans, and chocolate browns, it is a work of arresting dignity and visual power. Idressa Ouedraogo's *Yaaba (The*

FIGURE 22.8 *Yeelen* ★ Senegal, 1987, Souleymane Cissé; Issiaka Kane.

Grandmother, Burkina Faso, 1989) takes place in a village near the film maker's home and performances are by the villagers and some of his relatives. It is built around an African tale of the oral tradition, as is *Yeelen.* Both films won the Jury Prize at Cannes. The 1990s brought other admirable examples of African folkloric cinema, most notably Malian director Cheik Oumar Sissoko's historical allegory *Guimba* (*The Tyrant,* 1995), which the director has called "a fable about power—its atrocities and its absurdities."

Meanwhile, by the turn of the century Africa was also making a name for itself as a producer of popular cinema. In Nigeria, dubbed "Nollywood" in homage to the Indian center of popular Hindi film, Bollywood, low-budget productions (averaging $15,000) were becoming hits all over Africa. Typically shot in digital video with a single camera, many of these movies feature African motifs such as witchcraft and ritual killings. By 2004 Nollywood had become a $45-million-a-year industry, employing thousands. As one Nollywood actor commented, "It's like a dream come true."

Australia and New Zealand

The antipodal lands of Australia and New Zealand remained largely invisible on the global cinema stage until the 1970s. Thousands of miles away from the major international festivals in Europe and the United States, these countries nonetheless provided fertile soil for film-making initiatives. Apart from the United States, more people go to the movies more often in Australia and New Zealand than in any other country, and there are more movie theaters in these countries than anywhere else save the United States and Sweden. As a haven for Hollywood runaway productions, these faraway places also hold major attractions: lower production costs; striking, unspoiled locations; and willing workforces that speak English. The ingredients for movie-making success have thus long been in place.

In 1970 the government of Australia established an experimental fund for neophyte film makers, a film and television school, and a national development corporation to provide starting money for film productions. Although a distribution network dominated by Hollywood continued to pose a formidable barrier, the Australian movie industry began to show signs of life. Before that time Australia had been known on the screen chiefly in a few films made by Britons and Americans. (During the entire decade of the 1960s, Australia itself produced only eight features.) Once Australians were able to make their own films, they tended to feature the history and topography of their subcontinent, with its vast, wild outback and pioneer heritage. Australia's indigenous people, the Aborigines, also figure in many of these films. In addition, after an initial period in which male values were celebrated, Australia has nurtured a vigorous tradition of women's cinema.

The first evidence of the newly revitalized Australian film industry came in the form of reliable genre pictures. The popular "Ocker" comedies featured a (male) protagonist presented as being "typically" Australian: naive, vulgar, not too bright, good hearted, and down to earth. An early version was *The Adventures of Barry McKenzie* (1972), the first feature directed by Bruce Beresford. The pinnacle of the Ocker comedies was *"Crocodile" Dundee* (1986), the biggest box-office hit ever in Australia. In addition, George Miller's privately financed "Mad Max" road warrior movies (1979, 1981, 1985) created a genre of their own and made an international star of Mel Gibson (Figure 22.9). Miller went on to establish yet another viable franchise in 1982 with *The Man From Snowy River,* which married an Australian outback set-

FIGURE 22.9 *Road Warrior* ★ Australia, 1981, George Miller.

ting to an American western plot and an American star (Kirk Douglas); it was followed by a sequel in 1988.

In 1975 an *auteur*-oriented art cinema emerged when Ken Hannam's *Sunday Too Far Away,* an engaging film about the lives of itinerant Australian sheepshearers, was shown at the Cannes Film Festival. It was followed the next year by **Peter Weir**'s *Picnic at Hanging Rock* (1975), the first Australian art film to achieve significant commercial success both in Australia and abroad (Figure 22.10). Weir's film was also the first of what would prove to be an enduring genre of Australian heritage productions set at the end of the nineteenth century when the country had declared nominal independence from Britain. A haunting story of a girls' boarding-school outing on which a number of the students disappear mysteriously, it evokes turn-of-the-century dress and manners and makes stunning use of its country's scenery.

Weir went on to become one of the leaders in the new Australian cinema with productions such as *The Last Wave* (1977), about a lawyer who becomes engulfed by the tribal mysteries of his aboriginal clients; *Gallipoli* (1981), a big-budget spectacular about Australians fighting under English command in Turkey during World War I; and *The Year of Living Dangerously* (1982), partly financed by M-G-M, about an Australian journalist in Indonesia in the mid-1960s, around the time of Sukarno's fall from power. At this point Weir moved on to Hollywood, directing a string of critically acclaimed, star-driven projects, including *Witness* (1985), *The Mosquito Coast* (1986) (both with Harrison Ford), *Dead Poets' Society* (1989, Robin Williams), *Green Card* (1990, Gerard Depardieu and Andie MacDowell), and *The Truman Show* (1998, Jim Carrey).

Possessed of a mystical, poetic sensibility, Weir has a penchant for enigmatic, unresolved narratives, most prominently on display in *Picnic at Hanging Rock, The Last Wave,*

FIGURE 22.10   *Picnic at Hanging Rock*   ★   Australia, 1975, Peter Weir.

and *The Truman Show.* He is frequently drawn to stories about charismatic individuals such as the scientist in *The Mosquito Coast* and the teacher in *Dead Poets' Society.* Weir's sensitivity to mood and nuance has enabled him to create scenes of tremendous erotic power, such as Mel Gibson and Sigourney Weaver's kiss in the rain in *The Year of Living Dangerously* and Harrison Ford's impromptu dance with Kelly McGillis in *Witness.* He has said that his initial image for each of his films has been a musical one. Given this approach, it is not surprising that a number of his productions feature stunning set pieces in which music takes center stage: the long tracking shot over a group of heartbreaking photographs backed by one of Richard Strauss's four last songs in *The Year of Living Dangerously,* and the barn-raising scene in *Witness,* which is brought alive by the addition of Maurice Jarré's stately fugue.

Films by other Australian film makers have achieved considerable international success as well. *Newsfront* (1978), directed by Phillip Noyce, weaves actual newsreel footage into its fictional plot about Australian newsreel companies after World War II. Aboriginal culture is the subject of Fred Schepisi's *The Chant of Jimmie Blacksmith* (1978), about a young half-caste who turns to violence and revenge after being exploited by whites. Gillian Armstrong's *My Brilliant Career* (1979) chronicles the progress of a spirited young woman from a poor farming family who persists in her resolution to become a writer; it became a feminist rallying cry at the time of its release. *Breaker Morant* (1980), directed by Bruce Beresford, dramatizes the politically motivated court-martial of Australian soldiers fighting under the English in the Boer War in South Africa. Joselyn Moorhouse also garnered accolades for her 1991 production of *Proof,* which took as its subject the unlikely character of a blind photographer.

During the 1980s and 1990s most directors of the important Australian films of the 1970s followed Weir's example and began making films abroad. By 1984 those with international reputations—Fred Schepisi, Phillip Noyce, Bruce Beresford, and Gillian Armstrong—were all working in the United States. Armstrong found success in Hollywood with films such as *Mrs. Soffel* (1984) and *Little Women* (1994). But, like Campion, she returned home to helm other projects, including *The Last Days of Chez Nous* (1990), *Oscar and Lucinda* (1998), and *Charlotte Gray* (2001). The protean Mel Gibson also succumbed to Hollywood. His roles included several in the American films of Australian directors.

Australian films are not noticeably to the left politically; their contemplation of their own culture and past is mainly nostalgic (with a few swipes at the former British Empire, to be sure). The problem for Australian films seems to be the familiar one of hanging on to "Australianness" and international success at the same time within a global industry dominated by the United States. Gillian Armstrong's 1998 heritage production, *Oscar and Lucinda,* is a good example of this dilemma (Figure 22.11). A period melodrama set at the turn of the twentieth century with a long concluding section centering on a journey into the Australian bush, it features a strong female leading role played by Aussie actor Cate Blanchett and an interest in Aboriginal culture; at the same time, however, this Australian core is somewhat compromised by the presence of a "bankable" British star, Ralph Fiennes, and a genteel Eurofilm ambience.

New Zealand's spectacular scenery has long marked it as a place where visually stunning natural backdrops can enhance a variety of filmic narratives. This unique advantage, combined with low production costs (30 percent lower than in Canada) and the appeal of the country's inimitable southern light, has resulted in a bounty of New Zealand films made and funded both locally and globally. Many of these productions also feature portraits of the little-known culture of New Zealand's indigenous people, the Maori.

FIGURE 22.11 *Oscar and Lucinda* ★ Australia, 1998, Gillian Armstrong; Ralph Fiennes on wagon.

The industry was slow in developing. Only one film was made in New Zealand in the 1940s, one in the 1950s, and two in the 1960s. In 1977, New Zealand caught the attention of international festival programmers with Roger Donaldson's *Sleeping Dogs,* the first starring role of New Zealand actor Sam Neill. Shortly afterward, in 1978, the New Zealand Film Commission was formed to provide investment finance for local film makers. There followed a series of international successes, including Donaldson's *Smash Palace* (1982), Lee Tamahori's *Once Were Warriors* (1994), Peter Jackson's *Heavenly Creatures* (1994), and Niki Caro's *Whale Rider* (2002) (Figure 22.12).

Among New Zealand film makers **Jane Campion** is one of the most prominent. Campion's recurring concerns center on women's issues, especially female sexuality, which she often examines using an unlikely blend of surrealistic fantasy and tacky realism. Her first widely distributed film was *Sweetie* (1989), a tragicomedy made in Australia, about a pair of bizarre and mismatched sisters. A controversial entry in the Cannes film festival, it was subsequently released to great acclaim. Campion followed up with *An Angel at My Table* (1989), an adaptation of the autobiography of New Zealand writer/poet Janet Frame, which originated as a television miniseries. Campion's most resounding success came with her next film, *The Piano,* in 1993, a French–Australian–New Zealand co-production that shared the top prize at Cannes and won several Academy Awards besides. Like *An Angel at My Table,* it features magnificent New Zealand landscapes. Its story concerns Ada (Holly Hunter), a nineteenth-century mail-order bride who refuses to speak. She falls in love with her husband's neighbor Baines (Harvey Keitel), to whom she is giving piano lessons. This gothic tale was based on an original script by Campion herself, who claimed that it was inspired by Emily Brontë's *Wuthering Heights.*

As film scholar Dana Polan has shown in his book on the director, in *The Piano* Campion contrives to endow the film's central image with an aura of erotic longing. Substituting for the voice of the story's mute heroine, the piano represents all of Ada's repressed desires. In an early scene, her husband forces her to leave this precious object on the wild New Zealand beach (Figure 22.13a), and she looks after it sadly (Figure 22.13b). Later,

FIGURE 22.12   *Whale Rider* ★ New Zealand, 2003, Niki Caro; Keisha Castle-Hughes.

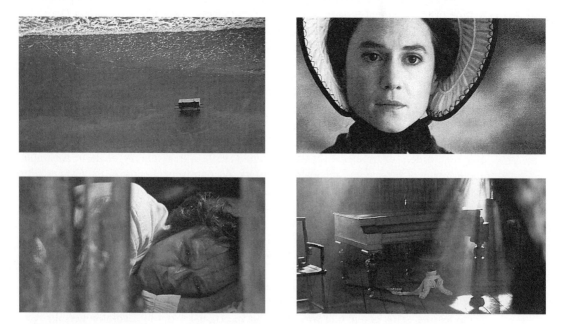

FIGURE 22.13a–d   *The Piano* ★ France–Australia–New Zealand, 1993, Jane Campion;
b. Holly Hunter; c. Harvey Keitel.

FIGURE 22.14   *The Lord of the Rings: The Fellowship of the Ring* ★ New Zealand, 2001, Peter Jackson; Dominic Monaghan, Sean Astin, and Elijah Wood.

Baines, too, becomes obsessed with the piano, gazing at it longingly from his bed (Figure 22.13c and d). The piano and its music thus comes to represent the emotional bond that ties the lovers together.

At the turn of the century New Zealand reached a pinnacle of international success with the release of Peter Jackson's *The Lord of the Rings* trilogy in 2001, 2002, and 2003 (Figure 22.14). This mammoth undertaking, financed by Hollywood money, showcased not only New Zealand's magnificent locales but also its special effects wizardry. Kiwi company Weta seamlessly integrated the story's scenic splendors with dazzling apparitions that gilded Jackson's ambitious conception with an otherworldly patina. Prominent among its achievements was the creation of Gollum, a winsome yet sinister gnome that was part actor Andy Serkis and part Weta fantasy. Gollum's success provided strong evidence to disprove the claim that special effects enhancements of an actor's performance would deprive the character he or she plays of emotional resonance, because many people who saw *The Lord of the Rings* became more engaged with the internal struggles of Gollum than with those undergone by Frodo, the movie's putative hero.

Canada

If antipodal Australia and New Zealand had problems overcoming the domination of the U.S. film industry, Canada, just across the border, has been affected far more profoundly. The country's situation vis-á-vis its powerful neighbor was once described by its longtime Prime Minister Pierre Trudeau as "like sleeping next to an elephant." Talented Canadian actors and directors have repeatedly been lured across the border by the promise of money and fame, including Mary Pickford, Walter Pigeon, Norma Shearer, Donald Sutherland, Norman Jewison, Michael J. Fox, James Cameron, and Mike Meyers. In addition, Canada has long served as a favorite location for "runaway" Hollywood productions attempting to escape high union costs and take advantage of unspoiled scenery and favorable exchange rates. And, of course, Hollywood productions continue to flood Canadian screens.

Canada's quest to develop a strong national cinematic identity has also been hampered by its history—or lack of it. Unlike the United States, which has endured the Revolutionary War in the eighteenth century and the Civil War in the nineteenth century, Canada has known only peace since the European settlement. The nation's most contentious political issue has arisen in the present, as its large French-speaking population, concentrated mostly in Quebec, debates the wisdom of seceding from the rest of the country, a movement called the *révolution tranquille.*

Insofar as Canadian cinema can be said to have achieved a distinctive character, it is the National Film Board of Canada (NFB) that deserves the credit. Set up in 1939 under the direction of legendary British documentarian John Grierson, the NFB was shrewdly designed to establish a cinematic culture that would not attempt to compete with Hollywood but would establish an alternative tradition (Figure 22.15). The result was an unqualified success. By 1945 the NFB was producing three hundred movies a year, the great majority of which were short documentaries and newsreels targeted for nontheatrical distribution rather than for the theaters. The board dealt with a variety of subjects, including intimate regional studies (for example, on the life of a Quebec priest), the building of the Alaska Highway, and the workings of credit unions. An animation unit was also set up; it sup-

FIGURE 22.15 John Grierson at the National Film Board of Canada, looking over a recently released poster that art director Harry Mayerovitch has just produced, January 1944.

ported, among others, Norman McLaren, who created a noteworthy series of classic animated films, winning an Oscar in 1952 for *Neighbors*. In 1962 a separate unit was established to sponsor the work of Québécois directors. The Francophone film makers focused their energies on producing documentaries that employed variants on the direct cinema approach, including Gilles Groulx's *Les Raquetteurs* in 1958 and Pierre Perrault's *Pour la suite du monde* in 1963.

To bring NFB productions to audiences around the nation, a comprehensive system of nontheatrical distribution and exhibition was developed, including rural circuits, national trade union circuits, and industrial circuits. Showings were also sponsored by women's clubs, libraries, YMCAs, and schools. As a result of these efforts, the annual audience for NFB productions during the 1940s was larger than the national population. Audience response was a key term, uniquely important in the growth of the movement.

The work of the NFB has shaped all subsequent developments in Canadian cinema, either directly or indirectly, both by training production personnel and by creating a model of non-Hollywood film-making practice. In later years the Canadian Council opened up another avenue of funding, providing support for an internationally honored group of avant-garde film makers, including Michael Snow and Joyce Wieland, whose work was discussed in Chapter 17. Avant-garde and related nontheatrical traditions have also influenced many Canadian feature film directors, notably Patricia Rozema (*I've Heard the Mermaids Singing,* 1986) and Canada's most internationally celebrated movie makers, David Cronenberg, Atom Egoyan, and Guy Maddin.

David Cronenberg's early avant-garde films, including *Stereo* (1969) and *Crimes of the Future* (1970), were funded by the Canadian Film Development Corporation, but he caught the wave of horror-film fever that hit during the 1970s to establish a career in commercial cinema. Today, many of his films are funded by Hollywood, although he maintains a home base in Toronto, where he also shoots most of his productions. Actor James Woods has observed that Cronenberg "works from his dreams." Obsessed with the interplay of technology and the human body, he has produced a highly idiosyncratic *oeuvre* consisting of a series of bizarre, ghoulish studies of physicality in the modern world, most notably *Videodrome* (1982), *Dead Ringers* (1986) (Figure 22.16), and *The Fly* (1986). His most honored production, *Dead Ringers,* features a virtuoso performance by Jeremy Irons as a pair of twin gynecologists, one of whom is going insane. In the 1990s Cronenberg moved on to other, less horror-bound projects, including an adaptation of William S. Burroughs's novel, *Naked Lunch,* in 1992 and a version of David Henry Hwang's play, *M. Butterfly,* in 1993. He created an international scandal in 1996 with the release of *Crash,* starring Holly Hunter and James Spader. Based on a novel by science-fiction writer J. G. Ballard, it tells a tale in which sexual desire, physical mutilation, and automobile crashes are combined in a phantasmagoric stew that borders on the pornographic. Cronenberg returned to the project of filming his dreams in 1999 with *eXistenZ,* a thriller about a video game designer that he wrote himself.

A less controversial figure is Armenian-born **Atom Egoyan,** who, like Cronenberg, began his career with an avant-garde orientation. Influenced by avant-gardist Michael Snow as well as by mainstream and art cinema directors such as Martin Scorsese and Ingmar Bergman, Egoyan makes films that are noticeably self-reflexive. "In my films," he has said, "you're always encouraged to remember that you're watching a collection of designed images." His 1993 *Calendar* cunningly blends documentary and fiction in a tale about a photographer who embarks on a project to film a dozen Armenian churches for a

FIGURE 22.16   *Dead Ringers*   ★   Canada, 1986, David Cronenberg; Jeremy Irons.

calendar but gets sidetracked by his growing jealousy over his wife's attraction to their Armenian guide. In 1997 Egoyan won the grand prize at Cannes with a more conventional production, *The Sweet Hereafter,* about a lawyer working with a group of families in rural British Columbia whose children have been killed in a bus crash (Figure 22.17).

The wildest of all these wild Canadians is probably **Guy Maddin.** Inspired in large part by the wacky style of early silent film (and who knows what else), Maddin has created a gallery of cinematic oddities that defy comparison with anything else ever put on celluloid. Think the Marx Brothers in *The Twilight Zone.* Maddin first came to the attention of the international film community with his 1988 short film *Tales from the Gimli Hospital,* a surreal fantasy about the past of a small Manitoba town. In 2001, the Toronto International Film Festival commissioned him to make an even shorter film, the six-minute *In the Heart of the World.* In this frenetic parody of Soviet science-fiction films of the silent era, two brothers, Nikolai, a mortician, and Osip, an actor playing Christ in the Passion play, vie for the love of Anna, a scientist (Figure 22.18a). Anna has invented a device that enables her to see into the earth's core (Figure 22.18b). She discovers that the earth is having a heart attack; she must go into the core in order to save humanity from destruction. Much more happens in this whirlwind of a plot, all of it rendered in low-resolution images

FIGURE 22.17   *The Sweet Hereafter* ★ Canada, 1997, Atom Egoyan; Ian Holm and Sarah Polley.

that have the look of old silent footage. The Soviet montage editing style is given the full treatment in this brief exercise: Each image stays on the screen for only a few seconds before being crowded out by another. A pounding musical score completes the effect of breathless zaniness.

Maddin's most widely shown production, *The Saddest Music in the World* (2003), boasts an actual Hollywood star at its center, Isabella Rossellini, who wears a fake blond wig and fake legs made of glass for her role. In this getup, Rossellini enacts the part of a rich widow who creates a contest to find—yes—the saddest music in the world. Of course, this being a Guy Maddin movie, the music is scarcely sad at all: Eskimos dancing to "California, Here I Come" and endless renditions of Jerome Kern's rhapsodic ode to romance, "The Song Is You." Though putatively set in 1930s Winnipeg, the *mise-en-scène* of Maddin's movie looks like nothing on earth. Shot with grainy black-and-white film stock and photographed through a lens slathered with Vaseline to create halos around every image, the film casts an eerie spell and entertains with the blackest of black humor.

In the meantime, Québécois cinema has continued to thrive, spurred by the success of Claude Jutra's 1971 hit, *My Uncle Antoine,* about a young boy growing up in rural Quebec at the turn of the century. The most notable Québécois film maker to emerge since then has been Denys Arcand, who, like so many other Canadian directors, began his career at the National Film Board. Arcand has helmed such widely screened features as the Oscar-nominated *The Decline and Fall of the American Empire* (1986), about the decadent sexual mores of modern middle-class culture, and *Jesus of Montreal* (1989), a tale about an actor who begins to live his on-stage role as the Messiah.

FIGURE 22.18a and b   *In the Heart of the World* ★ Canada, 2001, Guy Maddin.

Given Canada's diverse cinematic traditions of documentary, avant-garde, and gothic genre pictures, as well as its two languages, how is it possible to discern a common thread? What does *My Uncle Antoine* have to do with *Crash?* In other words, is there any quality that can be said to constitute "Canadianness"? Director Atom Egoyan has described the Canadian experience as one shaped by its location at the edge of a vast northern wilderness. "You can't but be aware of the idea of space and what it means to live on the fringe of this unexplored territory and of possibility," he has said. "We're sort of overwhelmed by it." The idea that the Canadian character is defined by the country's proximity to the Arctic tundra is rendered with emphatic self-consciousness in a 1980 film called *Why Shoot the Teacher?* directed by Silvio Narrizanno. In it, a young schoolteacher from the urban center of Toronto finds work in Bleke, Saskatchewan, educating the children of the local farm families. His classroom is a drafty schoolhouse in the middle of a vast, featureless tract of northern prairie. In such a setting, he finds that the concept of geographical difference means nothing to his students. Despairing of success, he comes to sympathize with a local woman whose husband has driven her to the point of madness with the complacent phrase, "Winter never killed anyone."

Iran

If Canada has had difficulties establishing a recognizable national cinematic identity, the same cannot be said for the most recent country to emerge as a potent international film presence: Iran. In its early days, the Iranian film industry consisted of documentaries commissioned by and shown to the upper classes. As popular cinema developed, India and Hollywood models were drawn upon. Iran, however, has always nurtured a cinema of directors rather than actors, which laid a groundwork for the international preeminence of its current *auteurs*.

An oil-rich society, Iran has long harbored a tradition of Islamic fundamentalism, which came to the fore following the revolution against the Shah in 1979. Since that time, the Iranians have followed a policy of international isolationism. A war with Iraq in the mid-1980s brought with it an economic slowdown, but this setback proved to be only temporary.

Immediately after the 1979 revolution, Islamic fundamentalists, who had long opposed cinema in principle, destroyed 180 of Iran's movie theaters, leaving a shortage of screens, which has remained a problem today. But the revolutionary regime soon realized the worth of a cinematic tradition that could satisfy the desires of a local population that had always loved moviegoing and could also introduce international audiences to the values it held dear. Government supports for the film industry were accordingly strengthened and expanded, and Iran began actively to pursue a policy of entering its productions into international festivals. The pace of production accelerated: In 1983, twenty-two films were released; by 1986, the number had reached fifty-seven. As Iranian film scholar Hamid Naficy has observed, Iran has rethought the place of film in its culture. "Cinema, rejected in the past as a frivolous *superstructure*," he has written, "has been adopted as part of the necessary *infrastructure* of Islamic culture."

Under the new regime, censorship, long a major factor in the cultural life of the country, became even tighter. Women could not be shown unveiled, even within their homes (although, in fact, few Iranian women actually wear veils when at home); moreover, men and women could not be shown touching one another on screen. Even the nature of glances between men and women were proscribed, as the rules called for an "averted look" instead of a direct gaze. Given such a context, it is hardly surprising that many of Iran's movie makers have focused on films about children, some of which were supported by the well-funded Institute for the Intellectual Development of Children and Young Adults (IIDCYA).

The so-called Iranian New Wave was inspired in part by the example of Italian neorealism. The movement was initiated in 1969 with the release of Mas'ud Kimia'i's *Qaisar* and Dariush Mehrju'i's *The Cow*. Both films celebrated Iranian lifestyles and mores. In addition, *The Cow*, with its focus on the day-to-day existence of the peasantry, was readily traceable to a neorealist aesthetic. Many subsequent Iranian films have continued to follow this socially progressive neorealist mode by depicting the daily lives of the downtrodden (for example, *Bashu, the Little Stranger* [Bahram Baiza'i, 1985] and *The Runner* [Amir Naderi, 1985]). As the New Wave developed, however, more films took formal experimentation and self-reflexivity as their touchstone. The movement culminated in the widespread international critical and popular acclaim that greeted the release of a film cast in this more formalistic mode: Jafar Panahi's *The White Balloon,* released in 1996, a simple but formally innovative tale about a little girl trying to buy a goldfish.

The White Balloon was scripted and edited by **Abbas Kiarostami,** who is generally regarded as the country's première director. Employed for many years by the IIDCYA, he frequently puts children at the center of his stories. Although his films use neorealist techniques such as nonprofessional actors, location photography, and real-time narratives, the ultimate impression they convey is one of studied formalism. This latter concern is especially evident in the endings of his stories, which, in films such as *The White Balloon* and *A Taste of Cherry* (1997), veer off course to take in the activities of the director and crew (Figure 22.19a). Other films—for instance, *Close-Up* (1989) and *Through the Olive Trees* (1994)—are self-reflexive throughout. Many of Kiarostami's movies are about journeys, and he has a penchant for dwelling for inordinate amounts of time on shots of characters traversing long roads or pathways, a process that encourages viewers to read their journeys as allegories of life itself (for example, in *Where Is the Friend's Home?* [1987] and *A Taste of Cherry* [Figure 22.19b]). In a sense, one could think of Kiarostami's technique as metaphysical, an exercise in questioning the nature of the world we live in and even the act of viewing film itself. "We are never able to reconstruct truth as it is in the reality of our daily lives, and we are always witnessing things from far away while we are trying to depict them as close as we can to reality," he has said. "So if we distance the audience from the film and even the film from itself, it helps to understand the subject matter better."

Mohsen Makhmalbaf is the other Iranian director who has become an internationally recognized *auteur.* A former Islamic activist, he was imprisoned for four years before the revolution; subsequently, he turned to film making. In contrast to Kiarostami's contemplative long takes, however, Makhmalbaf has fashioned a more mercurial style that favors quick cuts, often among differing views of the same action, a technique that Chicago critic Jonathan Rosenbaum has labeled "the Makhmalbaf twitch." Following honored neorealist principles, his films often feature the poor; *The Cyclist* (1987), for example, is about a penniless Afghani immigrant who undertakes a week-long bicycle marathon to make money for his sick wife; similarly, the first episode of the three-part *The Peddler* (1987) concerns an impoverished family who try to give away one of their children. During the 1990s Makhmalbaf turned away from his earlier neorealist agenda to make movies in the less politicized, self-reflexive mode favored by Kiarostami. His *Once Upon a Time, Cinema* (1992) takes movie making as its subject, whereas *Salaam Cinema* (1995) focuses on the process of auditioning for film roles. His award-winning 1996 production, *Gabbeh,* is cast in the form of a folktale (Figure 22.20). Deeply indebted to the films of Russian director Sergei Paradjanov, *Gabbeh* has been described as "a symphony of color," especially in relation to the garb of its female characters (who appear in the vivid costumes of nomadic tribespeople in contrast to the all-black clothing prescribed for most other Iranian women). "Life is color," a character says at one point. Makhmalbaf is also the father of Samira Makhmalbaf, herself a director; her first feature, *The Apple,* released in 1998, drew international praise.

FIGURE 22.19a and b   *A Taste of Cherry* ☆ Iran, 1998, Abbas Kiarostami.

Samira Makhmalbaf is just one of a number of female film makers who have come to the fore in Iran. Marzieh Meshkini, Mohsen Makhmalbaf's wife and the director of *The Day I Became a Woman* (2000), is another. Yet another Iranian woman, Tamineh Milani, made two outspoken films, *Two Women* (1999) and *The Hidden Half* (2001), about the plight of intelligent, educated females living in a country ruled by the tenets of religious fundamentalism. Milani's cinematic statements made a deep impression on audiences worldwide and caused her some political trouble at home.

FIGURE 22.20   *Gabbeh* ★ Iran, 1996, Mohsen Makhmalbaf.

The female movie maker in Iran who has created the most substantial body of work is **Rakhshan Bani-Etemad,** director of such films as *Nargess* (1992) and *Under the Skin of the City* (2001). *May Lady* (1998), Bani-Etemad's masterwork, paints a self-reflexive portrait of a woman documentary film maker named Forough, who is very similar to the director herself. Clips from Forough's films shown in *May Lady* are actually scenes from Bani-Etemad's films.

Bani-Etemad's works make good case studies for an investigation into the unique conventions of postrevolutionary Iranian films. Media scholar Hamid Naficy has commented on the characteristic manner in which the New Iranian Cinema directors handle gazes between characters. Naficy explains that Iranian culture values the inner self of private thoughts and feelings; modesty codes (or *hejab,* as they are called) shield this inner self from public scrutiny. Women, in particular, are subject to such codes. Foremost among the strategies aimed at preserving hejab is what Naficy calls the neutralized look, which is often interpreted in films as a dictum to avoid closeups of women, but may also involve depicting certain kinds of gazes: "the unfocused look, the averted look, the fleeting glance [and] the desexualized look." Bani-Etemad's *May Lady* offers a compendium of female gazes that comment on the conventions of *hejab.* When Forough arranges for her friend Tuba to visit the latter's son Abbas in prison, for example, Abbas, humiliated by the shame he has brought on his family, refuses to meet his mother's eyes while Tuba entreats him to "raise your head and let me see" and tells him, "I am a devotee of one look of yours" (Figure 22.21a). Forough, meanwhile, looks on through a window from a protected space outside of the room (Figure 22.21b). Later Forough examines videotapes she has made of various women discussing their roles as mothers for a documentary she is making. Con-

FIGURE 22.21a–d *May Lady* ★ Iran, 1998, Rakhshan Bani-Etemad.

forming to the codes of *hejab,* the women's faces are shrouded in darkness. Forough herself, as she appears in a formal self-portrait hung in her living room, gazes downward in similar deference to the conventions of modesty (Figure 22.21c). But as she examines the women in her videos while in the privacy of her own home, Forough feels free to look at them intently, trying to understand what they are saying and how it relates to her own conflicted situation (Figure 22.21d). Thus, though attention to the ways in which looks operate in the lives of both Tuba and Forough, Bani-Etemad comments on the need these women feel to engage with the world through full and free gazes—and the frustration of this desire brought about by the codes of *hejab.*

The critical praise garnered by the films of the Iranian New Wave speaks for the success of the government's investment in cinema. Certainly, part of the interest generated by these films lies in the novel sensibilities at work in them—they are radically unlike anything that has come before. Rather than following the more common path of creating a movie-making tradition that declares its singularity by straining accepted boundaries of decorum, the Iranians have worked within a much narrower set of restrictions than any that would be tolerated in the West; yet they have produced a magisterial cinematic canon that has commanded the admiration of critics and audiences worldwide.

In an increasingly globalized environment, non-American films made in almost any other country face formidable obstacles, especially films from poor nations in Africa and Latin America. The dominant U.S. industry has always faced the same problem, of course; it has solved it with sufficient success so that what comes from the United States is popular around the world. The growing prevalence of video, however, is creating new options for film makers from other parts of the globe. The greater accessibility of video cameras and editing facilities and the greater ease with which these new technologies can be utilized, along with the proliferation of television channels, VCRs, and DVD players in all parts of the world, are providing new avenues for the production and distribution of moving images, enabling the development of more localized film cultures. In the words of African film maker Jean-Marie Teno, "The new digital video technologies can liberate us, allowing us to create our own work, accessible to our own populations."

Films of the Period

ARGENTINA

1958
Throw Me a Dime (Tire die) (Fernando Birri et al.)

1961
Hand in the Trap (La Mano en la trampa) (Leopoldo Torre Nilsson)

1965
Chronicle of a Lonely Child (Crónica de un niño solo) (Leonardo Favio)

1968
The Hour of the Furnaces (La Hora de los hornos) (Fernando Solanas and Octavio Getino)

1974
Nazareno Cruz and the Wolf (Nazareno Cruz y el lobo) (Leonardo Favio)

1983
The Offical Story (La historia official) (Luis Puenzo)

1984
Camila (María Luisa Bemberg)
A Funny, Dirty Little War (No habrá más penas ni olvido) (Héctor Olivera)

1985
Tangos: The Exile of Gardel (Tangos: el exilio do Gardel) (Fernando Solanas)

1986
Man Facing Southeast (Hombre mirando al sudeste) (Eliseo Subiola)
Miss Mary (María Luisa Bemberg)

1988
The South (Sur) (Fernando Solanas)

1990
I, the Worst of All (Yo, la pior de todas) (María Luisa Bemberg)

1991
The Voyage (Fernando Solanas)

1992
The Dark Side of the Heart (El Lado oscuro del corazón) (Eliseo Subiola)

2001
The Swamp (La Cíenaga) (Lucrecia Martel)

2002
Minimal Stories (Historias mínimas) (Carlos Sorin)

2004
The Holy Girl (La Niña Santa) (Lucrecia Martel)
Lost Embrace (El Abrazo partido) (Daniel Burman)
The Motorcycle Diaries (Diarios de motocicleta) (Walter Salles)

BRAZIL

1957
Rio, North Zone (Rio, zona norte) (Nelson Pereira dos Santos)

1963
Barren Lives (Vidas Secas) (Nelson Pereira dos Santos)

1964
Black God, White Devil (Deus e o diablo na terra do sol) (Glauber Rocha)
Ganga Zumba (Carlos Diegues)

1969
Antônio das Mortes (Glauber Rocha)
Macunaima (Joachin Pedro de Andrade)

1971
How Tasty Was My Little Frenchman (Como era gostoso o meu frances) (Nelson Pereira dos Santos)

1976
Xica de Silva (Carlos Diegues)

1977
Hour of the Star (A hora da estrela) (Suzana Amaral)
Tent of Miracles (Tenda dos milagres) (Nelson Pereira dos Santos)

1978
Dona Flor and Her Two Husbands (Dona Flor e seus dois maridos) (Bruno Barreto)

1979
Bye, Bye Brazil (Bye bye Brasil) (Carlos Diegues)

1981
Lucia (Bruno Barreto)
Pixote (Hector Babenco)

1984
Prison Memories (Memorias do carcere) (Nelson Pereira dos Santos)
Quilombo (Carlos Diegues)

1985
Kiss of the Spider Woman (Hector Babenco)

1998
Central Station (Central do Brasil) (Walter Salles)

2001
Madame Satã (Karim Ainowz)

2002
City of God (Fernando Meirelles and Katiá Lund)

CUBA
1966
Death of a Bureaucrat (La muerte de ub burocrata) (Tomás Guitiérrez Alea)

1967
The Adventures of Juan Quin Quin (Las aventuras de Juan Quin Quin) (Julio García Espinoza)

1968
Lucía (Humberto Solás)
Memories of Underdevelopment (Memorias del subdesarrollo) (Tomás Guitiérrez Alea)

1973
The Other Francisco (El otro Francisco) (Sergio Gilal)

1976
The Last Supper (La Última cena) (Tomás Guitiérrez Alea)

1977
One Way or Another (De cierta manera) (Sara Gomez)

1983
Up to a Point (Hasta cierto puoto) (Tomás Guitiérrez Alea)

1994
Strawberry and Chocolate (Fresa y chocolate) (Tomás Guitiérrez Alea)

MEXICO
1943
María Candelaria (Emilio Fernández)

1945
The Pearl (La Perla) (Emilio Fernández)

1948
Maclovia (Emilio Fernández)

1950
Los Olvidados (The Young and the Damned) (Luis Buñuel)

1951
A Mexican Bus Ride (Subida al cielo) (Luis Buñuel)

1953
Él (Luis Buñuel)

1955
The Criminal Life of Archibaldo de la Cruz (Essayo de un crimen) (Luis Buñuel)

1958
Nazarín (Luis Buñuel)

1973
The Castle of Purity (El Castillo de la pureza)
   (Arturo Ripstein)
Reed: Insurgent Mexico (Reed: Mexico insurgente)
   (Paul Leduc)

1984
*Dona Herlinda and Her Two Sons (Doña Herlinda
   y su hijo)* (Jaime Humberto Hermosillo)

1986
Frida (Paul Leduc)

1992
*Like Water for Chocolate (Como ague para
   chocolate)* (Alfonzo Arau)

1993
The Beginning and the End (Principio y fin)
   (Arturo Ripstein)

1995
Midaq Alley (El callegon de los Milagros)
   (Jorge Fons)

1999
Herod's Law (La Ley de Herodes) (Luis Estrada)

2001
Amores Perros (Alejandro González Iñárritu)
The Devil's Backbone (El Espinazo del Diablo)
   (Guillermo del Toro)
Y tu mamá tambíen (Alfonzo Cuarón)

2002
*The Crime of Father Amero (El Crimen de Padre
   Amero)* (Carlos Carrera)

AFRICA
1966
Black Girl (La Noire de . . .) (Senegal,
   Ousmane Sembène)

1972
Sambizanga (Angola, Sarah Maldorer)

1973
Touki Bouki (Senegal, Djibril Diop Mambéty)

1974
Xala (Senegal, Ousmane Sembène)

1976
Ajani Ogun (Nigeria, Ola Balogun)

1977
Ceddo (The People) (Senegal, Ousmane
   Sembène)

1980
The Gods Must Be Crazy (South Africa,
   Jaime Uys)

1982
The Gift of God (Wend Kuuni) (Burkina Faso,
   Gaston Kaboré)

1986
Garbage Boys (Nyamanton) (Mali, Cheik Oumar
   Sissoko)
Sarraounia (Mauritania, Med Hondo)

1987
Camp de Thiaroye (Senegal, Ousmane Sembène
   and Thierno Faty Sow)
Life Is Rosy (La Vie est belle) (Congo, Mweze
   Ngangura)
Yeelen (Brightness) (Mali, Souleymane Cissé)

1988
Dancing in the Dust (Bal Poussière) (Ivory Coast,
   Henri Duparc)
Harvest: 3,000 Years (Ethiopia, Haile Gerima)
Heritage . . . Africa (Ghana, Kwaw Ansah)
Whom Death Refused (Montu Nega) (Guinea
   Bissou, Flora Gomez)
Zan Boko (Homeland) (Burkina Faso, Gaston
   Kaboré)

1989
Finzan (Mali, Cheik Oumar Sissoko)
Yaaba (The Grandmother) (Burkina Faso, Idressa
   Ouedraogo)

1990
Tilai (Burkina Faso, Idressa Ouedraogo)

1991
Sango Malo (Cameroon, Bassek Ba Kobhio)

1992
Guelwaar (Senegal, Ousmane Sembène)
Quartier Mozart (Cameroon, Jean-Pierre
  Bekolo)

1993
Sankofa (Ethiopia, Haile Gerima)

1994
Black Light (Mauritania, Med Hondo)
Le Cri du Cour (Burkina Faso, Idressa
  Ouedraogo)

1995
Guimba (The Tyrant) (Mali, Cheik Oumar
  Sissoko)
Waati (Mali, Souleymane Cissé)

1996
Aristotle's Plot (Le Complot d'Aristote)
  (Zimbabwe, Jean-Pierre Bekolo)

1998
*Napumocento's Will (O Testamento do Senhor
  Napumocento)* (Cape Verde, Francisco Manso,
  1998)
Pièces d'identités (Congo, Mweze Ngangura)

1999
Genesis (La Genèse) (Mali, Cheik Oumar Sissoko)
*La Petite Vendeuse de Soleil (The Little Girl Who
  Sold the Sun)* (Senegal, Djibril Diop Mambéty)

2000
Battu (Mali, Cheik Oumar Sissoko)

2001
Faat Kine (Senegal, Ousmane Sembène)

2004
Moolaade (Senegal, Ousmane Sembène)

AUSTRALIA
1975
Picnic at Hanging Rock (Peter Weir)

1977
The Last Wave (Peter Weir)

1978
The Chant of Jimmie Blacksmith (Fred Schepisi)

1979
Mad Max (George Miller)
My Brilliant Career (Gillian Armstrong)

1980
Breaker Morant (Bruce Beresford)

1981
Gallipoli (Peter Weir)

1982
The Man From Snowy River (George Miller)
The Year of Living Dangerously (Peter Weir)

1986
"Crocodile" Dundee (Peter Faiman)

1989
Sweetie (Jane Campion)

1990
The Last Days of Chez Nous (Gillian Armstrong)

1991
Proof (Joselyn Moorhouse)

1992
Strictly Ballroom (Baz Luhrmann)

2000
Chopper (Andre Domineck)

2001
Charlotte Gray (Gillian Armstrong)
Lantana (Ray Lawrence)

NEW ZEALAND
1977
Sleeping Dogs (Roger Donaldson)

1982
Smash Palace (Roger Donaldson)

1989
An Angel at My Table (Jane Campion)

1993
The Piano (Jane Campion)

1994
Heavenly Creatures (Peter Jackson)
Once Were Warriors (Lee Tamahori)

2001
The Lord of the Rings: The Fellowship of the Ring
   (Peter Jackson)

2002
The Lord of the Rings: The Two Towers (Peter
   Jackson)
Whale Rider (Niki Caro)

2003
The Lord of the Rings: The Return of the King
   (Peter Jackson)

CANADA
1971
My Uncle Antoine (Mon Oncle Antoine)
   (Claude Jutra)

1979
Scanners (David Cronenberg)

1982
Videodrome (David Cronenberg)

1986
Dead Ringers (David Cronenberg)
The Decline of the American Empire
   (Le Déclin de l'empire Americaine)
   (Denys Arcand)
I've Heard the Mermaids Singing
   (Patricia Rozema)

1988
Tales from the Gimli Hospital (Guy Maddin)

1989
Jesus of Montreal (Jesus de Montréal) (Denys
   Arcand)

1993
Calendar (Atom Egoyan)
Love and Human Remains (Amour et restes
   humains) (Denys Arcand)

1994
Exotica (Atom Egoyan)

1996
Crash (David Cronenberg)

1997
The Sweet Hereafter (Atom Egoyan)

1999
eXistenZ (David Cronenberg)
Felicia's Journey (Atom Egoyan)

2000
Stardom (Denys Arcand)

2001
Atanarjuat, the Fast Runner (Zacharius Kunuk)
Maelstrom (Denis Villeneuve)

2002
Ararat (Atom Egoyan)
The Fast Runner (Zacharias Kunuk)

2003
The Barbarian Invasions (Denys Arcand)
The Saddest Music in the World (Guy Maddin)
Spider (David Cronenberg)

IRAN
1969
The Cow (Gav) (Dariush Mehrju'i)
Qaisar (Mas'ud Kimia'i)

1985
Bashu, the Little Stranger (Bashu, gharibeh-ye
   kuchak) (Bahram Baiza'i)
The Runner (Davandeh) (Amir Naderi)

1987
The Peddler (Daskforoush) (Mohsen Makhmalbaf)
Where Is the Friend's Home? (Khane-ye Doush
   Kodjast?) (Abbas Kiarostami)

1989
Close-Up (Nema-ye nazdik) (Abbas Kiarostami)
The Cyclist (Bicycleran) (Mohsen Makhmalbaf)

1992
Life and Nothing More (Zendegi va digar hich)
  (Abbas Kiarostami)
Nargess (Rakhshan Bani-Etemad)

1994
Through the Olive Trees (Zire darakhatan zeyton)
  (Abbas Kiarostami)

1995
The Blue Veiled (Rusari abi) (Rakhshan Bani-
  Etemad)
Salaam Cinema (Mohsen Makhmalbaf)

1996
Gabbeh (Mohsen Makhmalbaf)
The White Balloon (Badkonake sefid) (Jafar Panahi)

1998
The Apple (Sib) (Samira Makhmalbaf)
May Lady (Banoo-ye ordibehesht) (Rakhshan Bani-
  Etemad)
The Silence (Sokhout) (Mohsen Makhmalbaf)
A Taste of Cherry (Ta'm e guilass) (Abbas
  Kiarostami)

1999
Two Women (Do zan) (Tamineh Milani)

2000
Blackboards (Takhté siah) (Samira Makhmalbaf)
The Circle (Dayereh) (Jafar Panahi)
*The Day I Became a Woman (Roozi khe zan
  shodam)* (Marzieh Meshkini)
Kandahar (Safar e ghandehar) (Mohsen
  Makhmalbaf)

2001
Baran (Majid Majidi)
The Hidden Half (Nimeh-ye penhan) (Tamineh
  Milani)
Secret Ballot (Raye makhfi) (Babak Payami)
*A Time for Drunken Horses (Zamani barayé masti
  asbha)* (Bahman Ghobadi)
Under the Skin of the City (Zir-e post-e shahr)
  (Rakhshan Bani-Etemad)

2002
Marooned in Iraq (Gomgashtei dar Aragh)
  (Bahman Ghobadi)
Ten (Abbas Kiarostami)

2003
Crimson Gold (Talaye sorkh) (Jafar Panahi)

2004
*Turtles Can Fly (Lakposhtha hâm parvaz
  mikonand)* (Bahman Ghobadi)

Books on the Period

Gamm, Kate. *Teaching World Cinema.* London: BFI
  Publishing, 2004.
Guneratne, Anthony, and Wimal Dissanayake, eds.
  Rethinking Third Cinema. London: Routledge,
  2003.
Hjort, Mette, and Scott Mackenzie. *Cinema and Nation.*
  New York: Routledge, 2000.
Murphy, Patrick D., and Marwan Kraidy. *Global Media
  Studies: Ethnographic Perspectives.* New York:
  Routledge, 2003.
Shohat, Ella, and Robert Stam. *Multiculturalism, Post-
  coloniality and Transnational Media.* New Bruns-
  wick, NJ: Rutgers University Press, 2003.

Williams, Alan. *Film and Nationalism.* New Brunswick,
  NJ: Rutgers University Press, 2002.

LATIN AMERICA

Acevedo-Munoz, Ernesto R. *Bunuel and Mexico: The
  Crisis of National Cinema.* Berkeley: University of
  California Press, 2003.
Chanan, Michael. *Cuban Cinema.* Minneapolis: Min-
  nesota University Press, 2004.
Foster, David William. *Gender and Society in Contem-
  porary Brazilian Cinema.* Austin: University of
  Texas Press, 1999.

Fregoso, Linda Rosa. *Mexicana Encounters: The Making of Social Indentities on the Borderland.* Berkeley: University of California Press, 2003.

Johnson, Randal, and Robert Stam, eds. *Brazilian Cinema,* ex. ed. New York: Columbia University Press, 1995.

King, John. *A History of Cinema in Latin America,* new ed. New York: Verso, 2000.

Maciel, David R., and Joanne Hershfield, eds. *Mexico's Cinema: A Century of Film and Filmmakers.* Wilmington, DE: Scholarly Resources, 1999.

Nagib, Lucia, ed. *The New Brazilian Cinema.* London: Palgrave, 2003.

Noriega, Chon A., ed. *Visible Nations: Latin American Cinema and Video.* Minneapolis: University of Minnesota Press, 2000.

Pilcher, Jeffrey M. *Cantinflas and the Chaos of Mexican Modernity.* Wilmington, DE: Scholarly Resources, 2000.

Rashkin, Elissa. *Women Filmmakers in Mexico: The Country of Which We Dream.* Austin: University of Texas Press, 2001.

Sanchez-H., José. *The Art and Politics of Bolivian Cinema.* Lanham, MD: Scarecrow Press, 1999.

Shaw, Deborah. *Contemporary Cinema of Latin America: Ten Key Films.* New York: Continuum, 2003.

Stam, Robert. *Tropical Multiculturalism: A Comparative History of Race in Brazilian Cinema and Culture.* Durham, NC: Duke University Press, 1997.

AFRICA

Armes, Roy. *Postcolonia Images: Studies in North African Film.* Bloomington: Indiana University Press, 2004.

Balseiro, Isabel, and Ntongela Masilela, eds. *To Change Reels: Film and Film Culture in South Africa.* Detroit: Wayne State University Press, 2003.

Barlet, Olivier. *African Cinemas: Decolonizing the Gaze.* Translated by Chris Turner. London: Zed Books, 2000.

Givanni, June, ed. *Symbolic Narrative/African Cinema: Audiences, Theory and the Moving Image.* London: British Film Institute, 1999.

Gugler, Josef. African Film: *Reimagining a Continent.* Bloomington: Indiana University Press, 2003.

Mirzoeff, Nicholas, ed. *Diaspora and Visual Culture Representing Africans and Jews.* New York: Routledge, 1999.

Pfaff, François, ed. *Focus on African Films.* Bloomington: Indiana University Press, 2004.

Thackway, Melissa. *Africa Shoots Back: Alternative Perspectives in Sub-Saharan Francophone African Film.* Bloomington: Indiana University Press, 2003.

Ukadike, Nwachukwu Frank. *Questioning African Cinema: Conversations with Filmmakers.* Minneapolis: University of Minnesota Press, 2002.

AUSTRALIA AND NEW ZEALAND

Haynes, Roslynn D. *Seeking the Centre: The Australian Desert in Literature, Art and Film.* New York: Cambridge University Press, 1999.

Martin, Helen, and Sam Edward. *New Zealand Film: 1912–1996.* New York: Oxford University Press, 1998.

McFarlane, Brian, Geoff Mayer, and Ina Bertrand, eds. *The Oxford Companion to Australian Film.* New York: Oxford University Press, 2000.

CANADA

Alemany-Galway, Mary. *A Postmodern Cinema: The Voice of the Other in Canadian Film.* Lanham, MD: Scarecrow Press, 2002.

Armatage, Kay, and Kak Armatage, eds. *Gendering the Nation: Canadian Women's Cinema.* Toronto: University of Toronto Press, 1999.

Beard, William, and Jerry White, eds. *North of Everything: English–Canadian Cinema.* Edmonton, Canada: University of Alberta Press, 2002.

IRAN

Dabashi, Hamid. *Close Up: Iranian Cinema, Past, Present, and Future.* New York: Verso, 2001.

Tapper, Richard, ed. *The New Iranian Cinema: Politics, Representation and Identity.* New York: I. B. Tauris, 2002.

23

The Digital Future:
The United States

★ ★ ★ ★

1994–

In 1994 the movie *Forrest Gump* was released. In this film, computer graphics artists pixilated the lips of Presidents John Kennedy and Lyndon Johnson so that these prominent historical figures appeared to carry on conversations with Tom Hanks, who played the movie's hero (Figure 23.1). Other scenes showed Gary Sinise, a well-known actor who played an amputee, as legless. The special effects wizardry that made such visions possible had been a long time in the making, but the use made of the new technology in this hit film was nonetheless startling. At this moment, the virtual world of the movies came unstuck from the real one; *Forrest Gump* was not a high-flying science-fiction or action movie but an "ordinary" story centered on the doings of well-developed characters in quotidian settings. Witnessing this new direction the film medium was taking, audiences began increasingly to wonder about the veracity of moving images. Was seeing truly believing? Or could Hollywood's capacity for visual trickery fool the most sophisticated spectator? How far could special effects be taken? Could dead actors be resurrected? Could live actors be replaced entirely by fake people masquerading as real ones? Such questions as these called into question the very nature of the photographic image as it had been understood in the past; its essential verisimilitude could no longer be assumed.

Technology on Fast Forward

The American public eagerly embraced the virtual worlds that were replacing actual ones on their movie screens. From 1994 forward, the films nominated for special effects Oscars, on average, outgrossed those nominated for best picture. Effects houses such as Digital Domain, George Lucas's Industrial Light and Magic, and Sony's Imageworks became ever more central to Hollywood's production agenda. Each new advance in computer generated

FIGURE 23.1   *Forrest Gump* ★ United States, 1994, Robert Zemeckis; Tom Hanks "with" President Kennedy.

imagery (or **CGI**) was accompanied by the release of a megaproduction designed to show off its capacities: wind effects in *Twister* (1996, Jan de Bont); **subsurface scattering** (to make the skin of animated creatures appear to glow from within) in *The Lord of the Rings: The Fellowship of the Ring* (2001, Peter Jackson); water effects in *The Perfect Storm* (2000, Wolfgang Peterson); digital doubles in *Spider-Man* (2002, Sam Raimi); virtual settings in *Sky Captain and the World of Tomorrow* (2004, Kerry Conran); and **performance capture** (in which electrodes attached to actors' bodies are used to graft their actions and expressions onto animated characters) in *The Polar Express* (2004, Robert Zemeckis). The aim in each case is to replicate people and nature in a believable fashion. The process of crafting the huge, octopus-like appendages Alfred Molina wore in *Spider-Man 2* (2004), for example, involved far more than simply rendering the movements of these creepy add-ons in a mechanically sound way. As effects supervisor John Dystra stated, "We all worked on creating the personality of the tentacles."

The Matrix, released in 1999 and directed by former comic book creators Larry and Andy Wachowski, borrowed techniques from Hong Kong action movies to create a gripping story set in a virtual world that featured sensational fight sequences, with characters flying through the air to attack one another (Figure 23.2). Like so many of the best science-fiction offerings, it focused on the nature of identity, this time playing off the unreality of its fake environment to suggest that in the technology-driven world of the future, it will become less and less possible for human beings to retain a grip on what is actually "real" and what is only "virtual" reality.

Excitement and uncertainty surround the new **digital filmmaking** processes. Electronic cameras and editing machines are steadily replacing the photochemical system of the traditional motion picture. Electronic transmission and playback possibilities already include—in addition to broadcast television—satellite, cable, videocassette, DVD re-

FIGURE 23.2 *The Matrix* ⋆ United States, 1998, Larry and Andy Wachowski.

corders, and computers. In 1999 *Star Wars: Episode I—The Phantom Menace* was the first film to be shown digitally in images bounced off a satellite in a few theaters.

Widespread availability of feature films for home video began about 1981; by the turn of the century, DVD players began to proliferate, and by 2004 they had found a place in 70 percent of American households, making DVD the fastest-growing technology in history. Americans in 2004 spent $24.5 billion buying and renting DVDs and videos—nearly three times as much money on DVDs as in movie theaters. As one industry observer remarked, "Basically, the movies are commercials for the DVDs."

High-definition-television (HDTV), also introduced in 1981, is gradually being phased in. Standard HDTV systems more than double the number of lines currently available on a video screen (525), giving sharpness and detail of image comparable at least to 16 mm projection. With the use being made of fiber optics and the advances toward high-definition-television, in a comparatively short while the motion picture as art form, replete with computer graphics no doubt, will be part of the audiovisual material filling the walls of our living rooms with crisp wide-screen images accompanied by stereophonic digital sound. Once this transformation occurs, will we still go out to see movies in theaters?

As computer technologies are increasingly with us, a computer-inspired aesthetic of interactivity was bound to leak into movie making. DVDs fed the appetite computer games had created by providing extras such as deleted scenes and alternate versions, which allowed purchasers to sample various renderings of their favorite movies. Danny Boyle's *28 Days Later* (2002), for example, offered two alternative endings; viewers could choose the one they preferred. In theaters, Mike Figgis's 1999 production *Time Code* used real-time video technology to present the audience with four simultaneous interrelated stories and asked us to choose among them (Figure 23.3). By adjusting the sound tracks, our attention is directed to one or another of the four screens at any given moment, but the choice about where to focus is ultimately ours. *Time Code* may be only the first of many more attempts to create a new aesthetic experience by integrating the values of traditional art forms with those of games in which the outcome is uncertain and the audience exercises a certain degree of control. DVDs, with all their extra material, are accelerating the process whereby viewers can become quasi–film makers. "It's no longer 'I saw that movie,' " observed Jim

FIGURE 23.3   *Time Code* ★ United States, 1999, Mike Figgis.

Gianopolos, co-chair of Twentieth Century Fox. "It's 'I saw that movie, now I'm going to see multiple dimensions of that movie on DVD.' "

The rise of digital film making changed things for producers as well as consumers. New digital video techniques meant that good-looking films were cheaper to make than ever, so experimentation was encouraged, even by Hollywood veterans. Digital video was the technology of choice for Wayne Wang's sexually daring *The Center of the World* (2001) and for Jennifer Jason Leigh's directorial debut *The Anniversary Party* (2001, cohelmed by Alan Cumming). The gleaming night-time views of downtown L.A. in Michael Mann's 2004 thriller *Collateral* were created with digital video as well. Digital processes have eased the jobs of movie editors as well, freeing them from the necessity of organizing hundreds of film strips; instead, they can now join shots together with the touch of a button.

State of the Industry

Special effects, along with other facets of movie making, have been driving up the cost of production at an astonishing rate. So film makers need more money. And they can get it from big corporations. For this and other reasons, the process of media consolidation that began in the 1970s continued into the new century. The Canadian-based liquor company Seagrams purchased MCA/Universal in 1995, and a few years later sold it to the French bottled water company Vivendi, which soon unloaded its prize onto General Electric after a highly publicized bidding war. In 1996 a consortium backed by Kirk Kerkorian bought the troubled M-G-M/UA from the French bank Crédit Lyonnaise for $1.3 billion—the same Kirk Kerkorian who had bought and sold the studio in the 1970s. Kerkorian sold it again in 2004, this time to Sony, and again pocketed a tidy profit. Also in 1996, Time Warner bought Turner Broadcasting Company to become the world's largest media company. By the end of the century film studios were also joining with television networks (Disney and ABC, Paramount and CBS, Universal and NBC). Movie companies also became integrated with the new electronic environments of computers when the Internet provider America OnLine acquired Time Warner at the end of the decade. Synergy was the name of the game, with movies made from books owned by the parent companies, advertised on network shows owned by the parent companies, and later screened on cable stations also owned by the parent companies. Movies, it seemed, had become a kind of software that could be plugged on and plugged into any number of media outlets.

The most important media conglomerate that was formed during the 1990s, however, declined to play the synergy game. DreamWorks SKG, launched in 1994, was the brainchild of three Hollywood heavyweights: music mogul David Geffen; director Steven Spielberg; and production executive Jeffrey Katzenberg, who had earlier left Disney in a highly publicized falling out with his boss Michael Eisner. After an uncertain start with some embarrassing failures, the new company achieved its first big hit in the business the triumvirate knew best—movies—with Spielberg's *Saving Private Ryan* in 1998. In the late 1990s too, Katzenberg, who had been responsible for the animation revival at Disney when he served as head of production there, set up an animation studio at DreamWorks, offering traditionally undervalued animators better terms of employment, including profit sharing. DreamWorks' animated features, including *Antz* (1988), *Chicken Run* (2000), and *Shrek* (2001), aimed at a higher level of sophistication than the Disney movies and opened up the genre to new audiences in the process.

By 2000 DreamWorks had climbed to second place among all the studios in overall box-office take, with a 12.8 percent share of the market, and had far outstripped all others in terms of revenues for each film released, with three out of its seven productions grossing over $100 million by mid-September (*Gladiator*, $185 million; *Chicken Run*, $104.9 million; *What Lies Beneath*, $148.5 million). And in 2004 the studio saw its *Shrek 2* revenues soar into the stratosphere, making it the third highest-grossing domestic film of all time. Despite an eye-catching track record, which could easily tempt a corporate mega-suitor, DreamWorks protested that it has no merger plans. "We started DreamWorks because it allows us to do what we do in an atmosphere where we are in charge of it," Geffen has been quoted as saying. "We're not frustrated by having to deal with other people and their agendas and their priorities and their tastes. We're dealing with our own." Those who deal with the studio agree. "If there is a big difference at DreamWorks it is that the people you're having your discussion with, on the studio level, are all passionate about movies and all come from movie backgrounds," says Tom Pollock, cohead of Montecito Picture Co. "You're not arguing with accountants."

In the 1990s many formerly independent production houses were bought out by the majors including independent powerhouse Miramax, which Disney acquired in 1993. Run by brothers Bob and Harvey Weinstein, Miramax was seen as the leading independent studio of the day and a potent force in the popularization of independent film. The company made its name by acquiring art house projects and marketing them energetically, focusing especially on mounting aggressive Oscar campaigns. *The Crying Game* (Neil Jordan, 1992), *The English Patient* (1996, Anthony Minghella), and *Shakespeare in Love* (1998, John Madden) were a few of its greatest successes. Miramax pursued an activist approach not only to marketing but also to handling properties it acquired, often insisting on participating in the editing process. (Such practices eventually earned cochief Harvey Weinstein the nickname "Harvey Scissorshands.") By the first years of the twenty-first century the Weinsteins's golden touch with art-house fare had faded. The company backed increasingly expensive productions such as *The Shipping News* (2001, Lasse Hallstrom) and *Cold Mountain* (2003, Anthony Minghella), which proved to be both critical and commercial disappointments. The brothers also dumped millions into an ill-fated magazine venture. By the beginning of 2005, Disney had had enough, and the Weinsteins were cut loose.

Sitting across the bargaining table from the studio chieftains are the workers. During the 1990s and into the new century Hollywood's labor unions grew increasingly alarmed about so-called "runaway" productions, movies filmed outside of the United States that reaped the financial benefits of cheaper workforces in other countries. In addition, the major talent guilds (actors, writers, and directors) became louder in their demands for a greater share of the profits from DVDs.

Yet another labor issue involved just the writers and directors and concerned cultural capital more than actual capital. For years the two guilds had squabbled over the so-called "possessory credit," a notation above the title of a movie that identifies it as belonging to its director ("A Film by . . ."). This kind of credit, which appears in addition to the "Directed by . . ." credit at the end of the front role, is anathema to writers. The issue, which has almost erupted into strikes on several occasions, came to a head again in 2001, when the writers became vehement about the lavish way in which studios were bestowing possessory credits on virtually all directors.

More is at stake in assigning possessory credit than bruised egos. For writers, the practice calls into question the essentially collaborative nature of the movie medium, in which many people work together cooperatively to turn out the final product. To writers, "a film by . . ." denies the contributions they and others make to film art. In 2004 the Directors' Guild tried to quiet the storm around this issue by issuing a statement that defined a set of good practices for producers to refer to when assigning possessory credits. These guidelines specified that such credits should not be given to first-time directors unless they had also written the script on which the movie was based. The writers accepted the statement as a good-faith effort but remained dissatisfied. Writer-director Steve Martin lampooned the practice of granting possessory credits in a short piece he contributed to the screenwriters' online newsletter during the fray. In it, he assumed the persona of a fictional director. "'Directed by . . .' says I'm the guy who directs the actors, approves the sets and costumes, approves the script, and that's all," Martin wrote in part. "'A film by . . .' says much, much, more. I'm more of a . . . how can I say it? A film personality, I guess. I'm a guy who makes films. I supply the aura. What if someone watching in Oklahoma sees the film and there's no 'A film by . . .' credit? He sees the 'Directed by . . .' credit and wonders, 'Yes, but who made the film? Whose film is it in the existential sense?'"

During this period one screenwriter who became a hot property in Hollywood produced such an idiosyncratic body of work that the movies he wrote could never be thought of as the sole creations of their directors. This was **Charlie Kaufman,** who penned such distinctive films as *Being John Malkovich* (1999, directed by Spike Jonze) and *Eternal Sunshine of the Spotless Mind* (2004, directed by Michael Gondry). No matter that he was a screenwriter rather than a director; Kaufman was a genuine *auteur.*

In *Adaptation* (2002, directed by Spike Jonze) Kaufman foregrounded the struggle writers face to fashion films, both internally with their creative demons and externally with an unsympathetic industry. The film's main character is a screenwriter named Charlie Kaufman (Nicholas Cage). On two occasions Kaufman is shown visiting the set of *Being John Malkovich* (Figure 23.4a). On the set the star is top dog and the director, next in the pecking order, feels free to snub the writer who supplied the movie's script. Undeterred by this evidence of his low status on the Hollywood totem pole, Kaufman embarks on another movie project. While he battles writer's block, his identical twin Donald (also played by Cage) comes to visit (Figure 23.4b). Donald, an aspiring screenwriter himself, is planning to take a screenplay seminar from Robert McKee, a well-known teacher. "Those teachers are dangerous if your goal is to try to do something new," Charlie counsels his brother. "And a writer should always have that goal. Writing is a journey into the unknown." Charlie's screenplay is to be based on a *New Yorker* article called "The Orchid Thief" by Susan Orlean. "There's never been a movie about flowers," he tells Donald. Charlie fantasizes about the process Orlean went through to write her piece as she interacted with the eccentric John La Roche (Chris Cooper) (Figure 23.4c), who is at the center of her essay. But in the end Charlie must face the fact that he is not writing an essay for the *New Yorker* like Orlean but a mainstream movie—a fictional narrative aimed at a mass audience. So he attends McKee's seminar (Figure 23.4d) and finishes his screenplay off with a Hollywood ending.

FIGURE 23.4a–d   *Adaptation* ★ United States, 2002, Spike Jonze (script: Charlie Kaufman);
a. Nicholas Cage; b. Nicholas Cage and Nicholas Cage; c. Chris Cooper; d. Brian Cox.

Using the conceit of writer-twins, Kaufman's screenplay for *Adaptation* ingeniously explores both the private and public aspect of writing: Although writers want to express their inner selves, they must also address the needs and expectations of an audience. The creative journey chronicled in this film is thus that of its scenarist, not its director. Though Spike Jonze helmed the production with panache, *Adaptation* is unmistakably "A Film by Charlie Kaufman."

Bigger Blockbusters

The increased use of television and other national (and international) forums for advertising, coupled with fears about movie piracy, means that the older pattern of stepped releases, which would play first in a few major cities then trickle down to second- and third-run houses in neighborhoods and small towns, is no longer viable. The new pattern calls for a blanket release accompanied by a media blitz designed to create a "must see" attitude on the part of potential viewers who want to be among the first to experience the latest hit. The business generated on a film's first weekend determines what happens next. By 1997, the average cost of this marketing strategy had risen to $22.2 million per film, an increase of 166 percent from what it had been a decade before. Costs continued to accelerate in the new millennium. Not only is the new marketing strategy costly in itself; it means that many more 35 mm prints must be struck for simultaneous distribution nationwide—another added expense. The cost of marketing also includes, in most cases, one or more test screenings and sessions with focus groups at $15,000 each. In 1996 the special effects–driven blockbuster *Independence Day* took in a record $104.3 million worldwide in its first week after a saturation publicity blitz, becoming the fastest-grossing film to date. In 2000 *Blair Witch 2: The Book of Shadows* carried this process one step further by staging a globally coordinated release pattern in which the movie opened on the same day at 3,600 theaters around the world. The tremendous distribution networks of the big studios, with hundreds of offices in cities everywhere selling their product, have enabled this global strategy. No matter that in past years many films that went on to become big moneymakers (such as *Dances with Wolves, Driving Miss Daisy,* and *Fatal Attraction*) built audiences slowly; studios are now locked into the opening weekend syndrome. As one studio executive complained, "There's no breathing room for good pictures that may have had mediocre openings."

A few microdistributors such as New Yorker and First Look are still out there, willing to release films that eke out only one million dollars following a platform release schedule designed to build on good reviews and word of mouth. But for the big studios, the opening week is all, even for independent fare; they roll the dice and wait for a big winner to emerge. "It's the studio mentality," says Sony Classics copresident Tom Bernard. "Buy ten and have the tenth one pay for the other losses."

Along with marketing goes merchandising: *Wedding Singer* nightshirts, *Mulan* Happy Meals at McDonald's, *Goldeneye* Matchbox Aston Martins, *Austin Powers* talking key chains. The *Star Wars* franchise alone is estimated to have taken in over $2 billion in tie-ins over the years. The synergy works the other way as well: Manufacturers pay to have their products featured in the movies themselves. In 1997 Reebok sued TriStar, the producer of *Jerry Maguire,* for cutting out a final scene in which Reeboks would appear after the athletic shoe company had provided the production with more than $1.5 million in merchandise, advertising, and promotional support in exchange. The so-called "product placement" phenomenon grew to such a degree that a new term, *branding,* came to signify the way in which some companies were able to make movies into two-hour commercials for their products by underwriting much of the financing. The 2000 hit *Cast Away,* for example, involved two years of cooperative script development work between star Tom Hanks's production company and Federal Express, which is heavily featured in the film.

Yet despite Hollywood's growing marketing sophistication, theater attendance in the United States is becoming flat—just under 1.5 billion in 2000, down 1 percent from the year before. Nonetheless, by the turn of the century, ever-greater competition among theaters for this gradually shrinking audience had fueled an unprecedented overbuilding of multiplexes and luxurious megaplexes. The 27,805 screens that existed in 1985 had swollen to 37,185 in 1995. By 2000 New York's Times Square had 38 screens on a single block. Many exhibition chains were close to bankruptcy. Some began to show ads to increase revenue, thereby canceling out some of their perceived superiority to television.

In the face of declining business at American theaters, so-called "back-end" revenue from television, cable, video and DVD sales has come to play a major role in the studios' profit pictures. In addition, competition from cable and the need for high-profile "event" programming during crucial "sweeps" weeks, when advertising rates are set, has made television an ever-more-eager customer for high-profile films: In 2000 the twenty-one biggest-grossing summer movie hits raked in $385 million from TV sales (about 16 percent of domestic box-office revenue, up from 13 percent in the mid-1990s). Foreign television sales are also soaring; *The Matrix,* for example, was sold to Japanese television for $8 million.

In 1997, the aptly titled *Titanic,* featuring teen idol Leonardo Di Caprio, cost an astronomical $200 million, but took in over $1 billion at the box office worldwide. "So does this prove, once and for all, that size does matter?" asked its director, James Cameron.

An Auteur *for the* Fin de Siècle

The hottest directorial talent to emerge in the 1990s has been **Quentin Tarantino.** A former video store clerk and self-taught movie buff, Tarantino borrowed his slam-bang technique from Hong Kong action movies. His first production, *Reservoir Dogs,* in 1991, brought him instant fame with its ultraviolence, hyperkinetic style, and offbeat conversations. His next effort, *Pulp Fiction,* in 1994, won the top prize at Cannes and an Oscar for Tarantino's screenplay (Figure 23.5). He followed up with *Jackie Brown* in 1997, featuring former blaxploitation star Pam Grier; and in 2003 and 2004 turned to the Hong Kong martial arts formula for *Kill Bill, Volumes 1* and *2.*

Tarantino's major strength is as a scriptwriter, a talent that reached its zenith in the intricately plotted *Pulp Fiction,* in which three different stories are followed as they gradually intertwine. He also has a pronounced flair for dialogue, showcased in scenes such as the one in *Pulp Fiction* when John Travolta explains to fellow hood Samuel L. Jackson what a hamburger is called at McDonald's restaurants in Paris. Tarantino also excels in finding has-been or "B" movie performers and revitalizing their careers, as he did for Travolta in *Pulp Fiction* and Pam Grier in *Jackie Brown.* He favors settings in sleazy, rundown parts of L.A., where his characters, most of whom are low-level criminals, seem right at home.

FIGURE 23.5   *Pulp Fiction*   ★   United States, 1994, Quentin Tarantino; Uma Thurman and
John Travolta

Following the lead of other important film makers such as Francis Ford Coppola and
Martin Scorsese, Tarantino has arranged American distribution deals for a number of foreign films. The most successful of these efforts was his sponsorship of *Chungking Express,*
by the postmodernist Hong Kong director Wong Kar-Wai, in 1994. By century's end,
movie buff Tarantino was trying to drum up support for another of his discoveries, William
Witney, the director of numerous Roy Rogers programs during the 1950s. "His camera
movements, when they happen, are so cool," he explained.

Other independent film makers of note who have been active since the mid-1990s
include Todd Solondz (*Welcome to the Dollhouse,* 1995, and *Happiness,* 1998), Richard
Linklater (*Before Sunrise,* 1995, and *Before Sunset,* 2004), and Sophia Coppola (*Lost in
Translation,* 2003). Earlier independent presences such as Stephen Soderbergh *(sex, lies,
and videotape,* 1989), David O. Russell *(Flirting with Disaster,* 1996), and Neil LaBute (*In
the Company of Men,* 1997) have moved into the mainstream with productions such as *Out
of Sight* (Soderbergh, 1998), *Three Kings* (Russell, 1999), and *Nurse Betty* (LaBute, 2000).

Representing Diversity, Part 2

By century's end gay themes and characters had been integrated into mainstream film with
productions such as *I Shot Andy Warhol* (Mary Harron, 1996), *Gods and Monsters* (Bill
Condon, 1998), *Being John Malkovich* (Spike Jonze, 1999), *The Talented Mr. Ripley* (Anthony Minghella, 1999), *Boys Don't Cry* (Kimberly Pierce, 1999), *Far From Heaven* (Todd
Haynes, 2002), *Monster* (Patty Jenkins, 2003), and *Kinsey* (Bill Condon, 2004). Perhaps

more significantly, gay-identified stars such as Anne Heche and Rupert Everett began to be seen as viable romantic leads. Heterosexual stars also began to appear as gay characters, including Cher, Sharon Stone, Tom Hanks, Antonio Banderas, Allie Sheedy, Cameron Diaz, and Hilary Swank. Swank's Oscar for *Boys Don't Cry* represented a breakthrough for queer cinema, because director Kimberly Pierce had made a film that was quite a radical statement. Employing many of the techniques of avant-garde film making, it tells the tale of Teena Brandon, a young woman who lives as a man, and the emotional and physical costs of her decision. Based on a true story, the film is unsparing in its depiction of the bigotry Brandon's behavior gives rise to in the midwestern town in which she lives. The images are dark, reflecting the mood of the story.

Independent lesbian films and film makers also came to the fore in the 1990s with productions such as *Flat Is Beautiful* (Sadie Benning, 1998), *Go Fish* (Rose Troche, 1994), *Watermelon Woman* (Cheryl Dunye, 1997), and *High Art* (Lisa Cholodenko, 1998). *High Art,* about a talented lesbian photographer, is especially memorable for the way it captures the ambience of the New York art scene and its unique brand of downbeat chic (Figure 23.6).

FIGURE 23.6 *High Art* ☆ United States, 1998, Lisa Cholodenko; Ally Sheedy and Radha Mitchell.

One of the most welcome developments that occurred during the 1990s was the effort put forth by major black performers who had achieved crossover status to enable the production of ambitiously conceived black-made films. *Eve's Bayou* (Kazi Lemmons, 1997) was made possible by the support of star Samuel L. Jackson, who gets a meaty role as a beloved, but philandering husband and father in 1950s Louisiana. The financing for both *Set It Off* (Gary Gray, 1996) and *Get on the Bus* (Spike Lee, 1996) was wholly supplied by blacks, including Will Smith and Danny Glover. Former basketball star Magic Johnson dedicated himself to building theaters in black neighborhoods to serve a previously neglected audience. Yet by the turn of the century there was still much to be achieved. In an article published in *The New York Times* in 1999, Spike Lee wrote, "There is no high-ranking African American who can greenlight a picture." Lee went on to observe that at least part of what stands in the way of the production of a broad array of black films is the audience. "Black people complain about black films," he wrote, "but nobody shows up to support a different type of film. Where was the black audience for *Daughters of the Dust, Rosewood, Eve's Bayou,* and *Beloved?* Where? Packing theaters to see *Set It Off* and *Booty Call.*"

A New Life for Documentaries

As if to disprove the thesis that the twenty-first century cinema was all about virtual realities, movies about real realities—documentaries—came back into favor, fueled by new approaches and new audiences. Beginning in the 1980s, young documentarians began countering the *cinema verité* style of the previous decades by putting themselves into their films, taking their cue from the examples set by earlier self-reflexive documentary stylists such as the Soviet Dziga Vertov and the French Chris Marker. Among the new American talents were Ross McElwee (*Sherman's March,* 1986, and *Bright Leaves,* 2003) and Errol Morris (*The Thin Blue Line,* 1988, and *The Fog of War: Eleven Lessons from the Life of Robert S. McNamara,* 2003). By putting themselves front and center (as McElwee did) or foregrounding obvious fake re-creations of actual events (as Morris did), these film makers made documentaries into personal essays, often leavening the effect with quirky humor. Documentaries were also given a new lease on life in the new millennium by the political ferment that accompanied the 2004 presidential election, which stimulated interest in muckraking films such as *The Corporation* (Jennifer Abbott and Mark Achbar, 2003) and *The Control Room* (Jehane Noijaim, 2004).

A documentarian who capitalized on both of these trends is **Michael Moore,** whose politically incendiary *Fahrenheit 9/11* created a media sensation when it was released in the midst of the 2004 presidential campaign (Figure 23.7). Using an approach he had pioneered in his earlier productions *Roger and Me* (1989) and *Bowling for Columbine* (2002), Moore combined archival footage with aggressively conducted interviews in which he badgered assorted powerbrokers about their putative wrongdoings. The belligerent tone thus created was leavened with humorous asides and sympathetic portraits of social victims. Assertive editing that juxtaposed disparate images to create cause-and-effect chains gave rhetorical force to the movie's argument about the shortcomings of President George W. Bush and the wrongheadedness of his war in Iraq. Though some observers on the right side of the political spectrum saw Moore's cinematic statement as yet another exercise in vir-

FIGURE 23.7 *Fahrenheit 9/11* ★ United States, 2004, Michael Moore; Moore (on right).

tual reality, enough people went to see the film to make it the highest-grossing documentary of all time and a top moneymaker of that year. Moore's razzle-dazzle techniques were especially appreciated at the Cannes Film Festival, where *Fahrenheit 9/11* took the top prize that year.

Like all movies, Moore's *Fahrenheit 9/11* speaks unmistakably about the time and place in which it was made, and, like many, it came during a rich period of film production in its country of origin. The eloquence of modern film has been built on the foundation of numerous similar moments of national creative flowering. This history has surveyed some of these moments. To go back and review the old by visiting film archives and museums, participating in film history courses, taking in retrospective series, and now renting and purchasing videocassettes and DVDs enriches our understanding of what is new in cinematic art.

Cinema has historically been an awesomely difficult medium in which to create. The very characteristics that distinguish it from the older arts have frequently impeded artists: the massive and complex technology, the demands of high finance, the necessity for a huge and diverse audience. But now, with cheap digital video technology readily available, more people than ever before can make "films." And, as films made for theaters have yielded their place as mass entertainment to television and now the Internet, and as the rigid production-distribution-exhibition systems have been shaken and cracked in many places, film art of a new seriousness and difficulty, greater originality and individuality, has begun to appear. As Abbas Kiarostami once declared, "The best form of cinema is one which poses questions for the audience."

It's said that speculation about the future reveals more about the present than about what's in store. Nonetheless, the urge to anticipate things to come is inevitable as the dawn of the second millennium has brought what promise to be radical innovations in the ways people entertain themselves. The advent of digital technology has coincided with other innovations to create a world in which the movies are being reborn, a world of virtual reality, convergence, synergy, open-endedness, and interactivity. The virtual worlds cinema has made have become less and less dependent on the real one. Additionally, cinema, once a distinctive art, now bleeds into TV via movie-themed cable channels and pay per view. Films are also available on computers in the form of streaming video. Moreover, received wisdom about the passive cinema spectator caught in a dream-like state in front of a huge screen in a darkened auditorium is now challenged by the reality of viewers who watch videos and DVDs in their living rooms, starting and stopping them at their pleasure, jumping to their favorite scenes, and dismantling their suspension of disbelief by accessing behind-the-scenes footage. Through all of these changes, however, the manipulation of moving images has remained a powerful means by which storytelling, arguing a point, or creating a mood can be achieved. The movies as we have known them may be dying, but other kinds of movies—even more enjoyable and more exciting—are taking their place.

The cinema is dead. Long live cinema!

Films of the Period

1994
Clerks (Kevin Smith)
Ed Wood (Tim Burton)
Forrest Gump (Robert Zemeckis)
Hoop Dreams (Steve James)
The Lion King (Roger Allers and Rob Minkoff)
Pulp Fiction (Quentin Tarantino)

1995
Babe (Chris Noonan)
Before Sunrise (Richard Linklater)
Clueless (Amy Heckerling)
Crumb (Terry Zwigoff)
Dead Man (Jim Jarmusch)
Devil in a Blue Dress (Carl Franklin)
From the Journals of Jean Seberg (Mark Rappaport)
Leaving Las Vegas (Mike Figgis)
A Little Princess (Alfonzo Cuarón)
My Family/Mia Familia (Gregory Nava)
Sense and Sensibility (Ang Lee)
Toy Story (John Lassiter)

The Usual Suspects (Brian Singer)
Waiting to Exhale (Forest Whitaker)
Welcome to the Dollhouse (Todd Solondz)

1996
Fargo (Joel Coen)
The First Wives Club (Hugh Wilson)
I Shot Andy Warhol (Mary Harron)
Independence Day (Roland Emmerich)
Jerry Maguire (Cameron Crowe)
Lone Star (John Sayles)
Natural Born Killers (Oliver Stone)
The Nutty Professor (Tom Shadyac)
William Shakespeare's Romeo and Juliet (Baz Luhrmann)

1997
Boogie Nights (Paul Thomas Anderson)
Chasing Amy (Kevin Smith)
Henry Fool (Hal Hartley)
In the Company of Men (Neal LaBute)
L.A. Confidential (Curtis Hanson)

Titanic (James Cameron)

1998
Affliction (Paul Shrader)
Gods and Monsters (Bill Condon)
Happiness (Todd Solondz)
High Art (Lisa Cholodenko)
Out of Sight (Stephen Soderbergh)
The Prince of Egypt (Brenda Chapman)
Saving Private Ryan (Steven Spielberg)
A Simple Plan (Billy Bob Thornton)
The Thin Red Line (Terrence Malick)

1999
Being John Malkovich (Spike Jonze)
The Blair Witch Project (Daniel Myrick and
    Eduardo Sánchez)
Boys Don't Cry (Kimberly Pierce)
Dogma (Kevin Smith)
Ghost Dog (Jim Jarmusch)
Magnolia (Paul Thomas Anderson)
The Matrix (Andy and Larry Wachowski)
The Sixth Sense (M. Night Shamalyan)
Three Kings (David O. Russell)
Toy Story II (John Lassiter)

2000
Almost Famous (Cameron Crowe)
American Psycho (Mary Harron)
Cast Away (Robert Zemeckis)
Erin Brockovich (Stephen Soderbergh)
O Brother, Where Art Thou? (Joel Coen)
Traffic (Stephen Soderbergh)

2001
AI: Artificial Intelligence (Steven Spielberg)
The Man Who Wasn't There (Joel Coen)
Moulin Rouge (Baz Luhrman)

Mulholland Drive (David Lynch)
Ocean's Eleven (Stephen Soderbergh)
Shrek (Andrew Adamson and Vicky Jensen)

2002
About Schmidt (Alexander Payne)
Adaptation (Spike Jonze)
Bowling for Columbine (Michael Moore)
Far From Heaven (Todd Haynes)
Gangs of New York (Martin Scorsese)
Minority Report (Steven Spielberg)

2003
American Splendor (Shari Springer Bergman and
    Robert Pulcini)
Capturing the Friedmans (Andrew Jarecki)
Elephant (Gus Van Sant)
Finding Nemo (Andrew Stanton and Lee Unkrich)
The Fog of War (Errol Morris)
Kill Bill, Vol. 1 (Quentin Tarantino)
Lost in Translation (Sophia Coppola)
Mystic River (Clint Eastwood)
School of Rock (Richard LInklater)
21 Grams (Alejandro González Iñárritu)

2004
The Aviator (Martin Scorsese)
Before Sunset (Richard Linklater)
Eternal Sunshine of the Spotless Mind (Michael
    Gondry)
Fahrenheit 9/11 (Michael Moore)
I ♥ Huckabees (David O. Russell)
Kill Bill, Vol. 2 (Quentin Tarantino)
The Life Aquatic with Steve Zissou (Wes Anderson)
Sideways (Alexander Payne)
Spanglish (James L. Brooks)
Super Size Me (Morgan Spurlock)

Books on the Period

Acland, Charles. *Screen Traffic: Movies, Multiplexes, and Global Culture.* Durham, NC: Duke University Press, 2003.

Biskind, Peter. *Down and Dirty Pictures: Miramax, Sundance and the Rise of Independent Film.* New York: Simon and Schuster, 2004.

Dixon, Wheeler Winston, ed. *Film and Television after 9/11.* Carbondale: Southern Illinois University Press, 2004.

Hillier, Jim, ed. *American Independent Cinema: A Sight and Sound Reader.* London: British Film Institute, 1999.

Hoberman, J. *The Magic Hour: Film at Fin De Siècle.* Philadelphia: Temple University Press, 2003.

Le Grice, Malcolm. *Experimental Cinema in the Digital Age.* London: BFI Publishing, 2002.

Levy, Emanuel. *Cinema of Outsiders: The Rise of American Independent Film.* New York: New York University Press, 1999.

Lewis, Jon, ed. *The End of Cinema as We Know It: American Film in the Nineties.* New York: New York University Press, 2003.

Mendik, Xavier, and Steven Jay Schneider, eds. *Underground USA: Filmmaking beyond the Hollywood Canon.* London: Wallflower Press, 2002.

Merritt, Greg. *Celluloid Mavericks: History of American Independent Film.* New York: Thunder's Mouth Press, 1999.

Natoli, Joseph. *Postmodern Journeys: Film and Culture 1996–1998.* Albany, NY: SUNY Press, 2000.

Thompson, Kristin. *Storytelling in the New Hollywood: Understanding Classical Narrative Technique.* Cambridge, MA: Harvard University Press, 1999.

Usai, Paolo Cherchi. *The Death of Cinema: History, Cultural Memory, and the Digital Dark Age.* London: BFI Publishing, 2001.

Glossary

Academic films Films that treat significant subjects in a self-effacing style.

Action and adventure films A genre of movies featuring motifs of chase and pursuit, set in exotic locales.

Adaptations Filmed versions of works originally produced in other media, typically literary or theatrical.

Animated cartoons Short, comic *animated films,* generally featuring chases and mayhem.

Auteur theory A way of looking at films as the personal expressions of their directors.

Avant-garde film See *experimental films.*

Animated film Still images are drawn or photographed on single frames and then joined in such a way as to suggest movement.

Animé Japanese *animated films.*

Aspect ratio The width of a movie's image in relation to its height. Most of today's films have a rectangular shape (usually a 1.85:1 aspect ratio) but some, especially epic and spectacular productions, are shown in widescreen (a 2.35:1 aspect ratio).

Benshi Commentators who narrated the action and spoke the dialogue during film screenings in Japan during the silent era.

Blaxploitation A cycle of violent crime films released in the early to mid-1970s in which African American heroes triumphed over the White establishment.

Blind buying A Hollywood business strategy common during the first part of the century whereby exhibitors were forced to book films unseen in order to guarantee an advance market for the studios.

Block booking A Hollywood business strategy common during the first part of the century whereby exhibitors were forced to rent films in packages that included "dogs" as well as hits.

"B" movies Low-budget productions intended to occupy the second half of a double bill.

CGI Computer generated imagery. Identifies special effects and images composed with computers.

Chamber play films See *Kammerspielfilm.*

Churros Mexican genre films featuring singing and dancing in a rural setting, with prominent folkloric elements.

Ciné club A movement launched in France during the 1920s by Louis Delluc in which honored films were screened and critiqued.

Cinema of attractions Movies that appeal through spectacle and imagery rather than narrative. Associated especially with the short films produced in the early days of cinema.

Cinéma pur (or "pure cinema") A style featuring films without plots advocated in French avant-garde circles during the late 1920s.

CinemaScope A wide-screen process popular during the 1950s with an *aspect ratio* of 2.55:1 (later changed to 2.35:1).

Cinématographie A quality prized by the French *Impressionist* avant-garde movement of the 1920s in which a film strives to render internal states of mind.

Cinéma vérité A term coined by documentary film maker Jean Rouch to describe a mode of unscripted

475

recordings of actual events carried out using lightweight synchronous sound equipment.

Cinerama   A wraparound film experience in which images appear on a deeply curved screen. The *aspect ratio* is 2:85:1.

Clearance   A Hollywood business strategy whereby an exhibitor is assured that a film booked will not be shown in any other theater nearby until after a certain time has elapsed.

Closeup   The camera observes an actor's face or other object at close range. If the shot is of an actor's face, usually only the head and shoulders are visible in the frame. Usually conveys dramatic intensity.

Colorization   A computer process that turns old black-and-white films into color films.

Comedy   A genre of films emphasizing laughter and happy endings.

Commedia dell'arte   An ancient style of comic performance that relies on improvisation and broad stereotypes.

Continuity editing   The editing style associated with classical Hollywood film making in which the editing techniques are designed to be inconspicuous and to help advance the story.

Crane shot   The camera is mounted on a crane to move through the air both up and down and laterally.

Cross-cutting   Cutting back and forth between two different locales. Often employed to create suspense during rescue or chase sequences.

Cut   One shot is replaced by another. Used for ordering and pacing the action.

Digital film making   A computer-based system that has enabled a host of new film making practices in the production, distribution, and exhibition spheres.

Dissolve   One image is gradually superimposed over, and then replaces, the other. Ordinarily employed as a transition between scenes.

Documentary   Captures the real world with the intention of revealing it more fully.

Dolly shot   The camera moves laterally on a track. (See also *tracking shot*.)

Domestic melodrama   A subtype of the *woman's film* that focuses on issues related to family life.

Ealing comedy   One of the cycle of comic films produced by Britain's Eling Studios in the years after the Second World War.

Editing   The process by which two different shots are joined together.

Experimental films   Poetic, nonnarrative works, often short, that exploit the formal potential of the medium.

Frequently evoke the mood of dreams and the unconscious. Sometimes referred to as avant-garde film.

Eyeline match   A principle of the *continuity editing* system whereby a shot of a character's gaze is followed by a shot of what he or she is looking at taken from the point of view of the character.

Fade out/fade in   One image gradually goes dark, then another slowly appears. Usually signals a large break in the dramatic action, moving it to a different place and/or time. Conventionally used to mark off *sequences.*

Film d'art   A genre of films that flourished during the 1910s in which famous plays were recorded exactly as performed by theatrical stars and intertitles were abridged substitutions for the unheard dialogue the actors mouthed.

Film noir   A genre of crime films that flourished in Hollywood during the 1940s featuring *low-key lighting* and urban settings.

Fitas cantinas   A genre of films popular in Brazil during the silent era in which filmed stage musicals were lip-synched in theaters.

Formalism   See *Russian formalism.*

Gangster films   A movie genre focused on the rise and fall of a notorious head of a criminal gang.

Gay and lesbian cinema   Movies that feature plots and issues focused on gay lifestyles and problems, usually written and directed by gay filmmakers.

Gendai-geki   Japanese films with contemporary settings.

Giallos   A cycle of Italian horror films built around elaborate set pieces featuring extreme gore and striking visual design.

Gothic fantasy films   A genre that focuses on fantastic and horrific events that take place in a historical setting.

Halation   A halo effect is created by illumination around the image.

Heritage films   A genre popular in European cinema wherein works and subjects from a nation's cultural store are filmed in a sumptuous, but conventional manner.

High angle shot   The camera is placed above the actors and looks down on them.

Horror films   A genre of films that emphasizes sinister (usually supernatural) forces that terrorize the hero and/or society in general.

Impressionism   A French avant-garde film movement of the 1920s that emphasized the rhythmic and lyrical possibilities of the medium.

Iris   A popular method of beginning a scene during the silent era. A black screen containing only a small circle (or other shape) of the total image appears. Then the iris opens up to reveal the whole action and setting. Can also be used in reverse to end a scene: A contracting circle (or other shape) isolates a portion of the image.

Jidai-geki   Japanese historical films.

Kammerspielfilm   A type of German film popular in the 1920s marked by unity of time, place, and action, with few or no intertitles; few characters (usually lower middle class); sparse décor, with objects given extraordinary importance; and intimate psychological content. Also called chamber play film.

Key light   The brightest light on a set, usually appearing to come from a source within the scene.

Kino-Eye Group   See *Kino-Pravda.*

Kino-Pravda (literally "film truth")   A series of newsreels of unstaged activities produced by Dziga Vertov and the Kino-Eye Group during the 1920s.

Lenses   A combination of transparent pieces, usually made of glass, mounted on a camera that receives and refracts light rays. The lens controls the way in which images are recorded in the camera and can usually be adjusted to achieve a range of effects.

Lighting   The illumination of various elements within the image.

Location shooting   Shooting that occurs out of the studio, usually in the setting specified in the story being filmed.

Long shot   The camera is placed at a distance from the subject, showing actors' entire bodies and their placement in the surroundings. Usually begins a *scene,* establishing the action and the setting.

Low camera angle   The camera is placed close to the ground and looks up at actors and/or objects.

Low-key lighting   The image is underlit, creating large areas of darkness and shadows.

Martial arts films   A popular genre associated especially with the Hong Kong cinema of the last part of the twentieth century, featuring many fight sequences in which techniques such as karate, kung fu, and the like are used.

Masking   Part of the image is blacked out to provide a distinctive frame for a particular shot.

Master shot   A long shot that takes in all the action occurring in a given *scene.* It is customarily used to begin a scene and is returned to from time to time to reestablish spatial orientation.

Match on action   A cut to a different view of a moving object.

Medium shot   Shows people from the knees up. The standard framing from which the director departs for special purposes. Also known as an American shot.

Mise-en-scène   Literally, "what is placed in the scene." Includes everything visible within the frame, including the actors and setting, as well as the way these elements are composed.

Montage   An editing style associated with Soviet film makers of the silent era in which short shots were *cut* together to achieve new meanings.

Montage of attractions   A theory developed by Sergei Eisenstein in which a rapid and rhythmic *cutting* together of shots, startling in their visual contrasts, physical in their impact, involves the spectators and carries them along a predetermined path of emotional response.

Morphing   A *CGI* technique in which one object gradually melts into another in a fluid manner.

Motion Picture Production Code   A system of self-censorship adopted by the Hollywood studios in 1922 spelling out restrictions on what could be dealt with on the screen and how it could be shown.

MPAA   Motion Picture Association of America. The lobbying arm of the Hollywood industry. Among other functions, it administers the *ratings* system, helps to negotiate movie trade agreements with other countries, and sponsors legislation to combat film piracy.

Moving camera   The camera changes position in a way that makes the image appear to shift or change perspective.

Musical   A movie genre that emphasizes scenes of singing and dancing.

Narrative fiction film   Tells a story not based on actual events.

Neue Sachlichkeit   A term employed in describing some of the German *street films* of the 1920s, which were considered to embody a new spirit of realism and objectivity.

Overbuying   In the days of block booking and blind buying, exhibitors sometimes were forced to book more films than could actually be shown in order to get those that would attract large audiences.

Panavision   The most commonly used wide-screen process, with an *aspect ratio* of 2.35:1.

Panning   The camera moves laterally on its axis, usually to follow a moving character or survey a scene.

Panning and scanning   Films are rephotographed for television showings in a way that captures the major centers of action within each frame in a reduced *aspect ratio.*

Peep shows   A mode of film viewing popular in the early days whereby individual spectators looked into machines designed to display moving images.

Performance capture   A *CGI* effect in which electrodes attached to an actor's body are used to graft actions and epxressions onto animated characters.

Performance style   The techniques and principles an actor draws on to create a given role.

Photogenie   A quality of film celebrated by the French *impressionist* film movement of the 1920s in which the camera focused on the physical world and transformed it through lighting, framing, and movement.

Pink films   A genre of Japanese soft core pornography.

Poetic realism   A film style associated with France during the 1930s in which working-class protagonists trapped in a dark universe were portrayed with *low-key lighting* and fatalistic themes.

Polars   A genre of French thrillers distinguished by elegant visuals and plots of extreme ingenuity.

Polyvision   A triple-screen process similar to Cinerama famously employed by Abel Gance for the battle sequences in *Napoléon.*

Problem pictures   A genre that treats social and moral concerns. Such films appeared in the early days of the medium and have remained popular since then.

Pure cinema   See *cinéma pur.*

Race movies   Films made before the Second World War intended for African American audiences.

Ratings   A system put in place by the MPAA in 1966 by which films are classified in terms of the age group for which they are deemed appropriate.

Russian formalism   A style of film making associated with Soviet directors of the 1920s in which scenes were highly *edited* and conspicuous *shot* juxtapositions were featured.

Scene   Group of shots joined together to present action occurring in a single time and place.

Science fiction films   A movie genre that focuses on the ways in which technological changes could affect life in the future.

Script   The written blueprint that guides the production of a film.

Sequence   Groups of *scenes* joined by dramatic unity.

Serial film   Features continuing story lines continued over many individual episodes or installments.

Series film   A continuing set of characters engage in various adventures featured in several different films. The *Star Wars* series is an example.

Set design   The process of creating an environment in which the action of a film occurs.

Seventh art   A term applied to film in French avant-garde circles during the 1920s.

Shot   A single camera operation.

Shot/reverse shot   Cuts back and forth between two points of view in a *scene,* normally between two characters speaking.

Socialist realism   A style of film making defined in the Soviet bloc during the 1930s involving simple plots, group solidarity, and politically sanctioned themes. *Formalist* techniques were explicitly outlawed.

Spaghetti western   An Italian variation on the *western.*

Special effects   An image or part of an image created by technical means in the studio or on computers.

Spectacle   A genre of films that features mammoth sets and legions of extras.

Split screen   Multiple images appear simultaneously on different parts of the screen.

Steadicam   A camera and harness device that allows cinematographers to move the camera without *dollies, tracks,* or *cranes* while avoiding the erratic, agitated movements associated with conventional hand-held camera shots.

Street films   A genre popular in Germany during the 1920s in which the protagonist is drawn away from home by the lure of the city.

Subjective camera   The camera takes on a character's point of view or state of mind.

Subsurface scattering   A *CGI* effect that makes the skin of an animated character appear to glow from within.

Superimposition   One image appears over another.

Surrealism   An avant-garde movement that flourished in France and Spain during the 1920 and has continued to exert a strong influence on Hispanic culture. Films of this type seek to reproduce the working of the unconscious mind through shocking images and illogical juxtapositions.

Synchronous sound   Sound recorded as the image is being filmed.

Tableau   An image held in suspension that invites contemplation as an expressive composition.

Technicolor   A cumbersome and expensive process that produces glowing images of unequaled richness and depth. Used widely in Hollywood film making during the 1950s, it fell out of favor in the 1960s.

Tilting   The camera moves up and down on its axis, for example, to slowly survey a character from the feet on up.

Tinting and toning   Processes used in the silent film era in which strips of film were dyed in order to convey particular moods (e.g., blue for night, yellow for day).

3-D films   A process briefly popular during the 1950s in which audiences donned Polaroid lenses to watch films in which objects appeared to jump out of the screen toward them.

Tracking shot The camera moves laterally along a track, usually to follow action or to survey a scene.

Trucking shot See *tracking shot.*

Typage A strategy popular among Soviet film makers of the 1920s in which actors were cast according to their appearance rather than their performance skills.

Undercranking A technique popular in the early days of slapstick comedy in which the film was pushed through the camera more slowly than normal during the shooting of a particular scene in order to produce the effect of fast motion when the movie was later projected in theaters.

Vertical control Describes a mode of production whereby the Hollywood studios, which made movies, also owned the theaters, which exhibited them. In 1948 the U.S. Supreme Court declared this business practice a violation of antitrust legislation and ordered the studios to sell their theaters.

Vietnam war films A genre of films set during the Vietnam conflict.

War dramas A film genre set in wartime, typically emphasizing the senseless carnage of battle and/or the heroism of soldiers.

Westerns A genre made up of movies set in the Western states during the last part of the nineteenth century, typically concerned with issues of land rights, law, and race relations.

Woman's film A genre of films intended for female audiences featuring themes of romantic love and domestic conflict.

Yakuza films Japanese *gangster films.*

Youth films A genre popular in Hollywood during the 1960s that focused on the radical lifestyles that had been adopted by the young people of the era.

Zoning See *clearance.*

Index

Note: Bold numbers indicate pages on which topics are discussed as key terms.